JUSTICE
Alternative
Political Perspectives

JUSTICE
Alternative Political Perspectives

Third Edition

James P. Sterba
University of Notre Dame

Wadsworth Publishing Company

I(T)P® An International Thomson Publishing Company

Belmont, CA • Albany, NY • Boston • Cincinnati • Johannesburg • London • Madrid • Melbourne
Mexico City • New York • Pacific Grove, CA • Scottsdale, AZ • Singapore • Tokyo • Toronto

Philosophy Editor: Peter Adams
Assistant Editor: Kerri Abdinoor
Editorial Assistant: Kelly Bush
Marketing Manager: Dave Garrison
Print Buyer: Stacey Weinberger
Permissions Editor: Susan Walters
Production: Matrix Productions Inc.
Copy Editor: Judy Winthrop
Cover Design: Bill Stanton
Cover Image: PhotoDisc
Compositor: Eisner/Martin Typographics
Printer: Transcontinental Printing, Louiseville

Printed in Canada
2 3 4 5 6 7 8 9 10

For more information, contact Wadsworth Publishing Company, 10 Davis Drive, Belmont, CA 94002, or electronically at http://www.wadsworth.com

International Thomson Publishing Europe
Berkshire House
168-173 High Holborn
London, WC1V7AA, United Kingdom

Nelson ITP, Australia
102 Dodds Street
South Melbourne
Victoria 3205 Australia

Nelson Canada
1120 Birchmount Road
Scarborough, Ontario
Canada M1K 5G4

International Thomson Publishing Southern Africa
Building 18, Constantia Square
138 Sixteenth Road, P.O. Box 2459
Halfway House, 1685 South Africa

International Thomson Editores
Seneca, 53
Colonia Polanco
11560 México D.F. México

International Thomson Publishing Asia
60 Albert Street #15-01
Albert Complex
Singapore 189969

International Thomson Publishing Japan
Hirakawa-cho Kyowa Building, 3F
2-2-1 Hirakawa-cho, Chiyoda-ku
Tokyo 102, Japan

Library of Congress Cataloging-in-Publication Data

Justice : alternative political perspectives / [edited by] James P.
Sterba. — 3rd ed.
        p.   cm.
     Includes bibliographical references.
     ISBN 0-534-52749-3
     1. Justice.   I. Sterba, James P.
JC578.J87   1998
320.5—dc21

98-23038

 This book is printed on acid-free recycled paper.

To Janet
As always
A philosopher's philosopher

Contents

Preface to the Third Edition

THIS THIRD EDITION of *Justice: Alternative Political Perspectives* has been revised and expanded to keep abreast of current discussions of conceptions of justice. New readings have been added to each of the sections on Libertarian Justice, Liberal Democratic Justice, Communitarian Justice, and Feminist Justice. In addition, the anthology has been expanded to include two new sections of readings on Discourse Ethics and Postmodern Justice. In all there is a total of fifteen new readings. *Justice: Alternative Political Perspectives* still remains the only anthology of its kind. It contains classic and contemporary defenses and critiques of six major conceptions of justice, and the introduction provides background and critique for each of the selections. All of the selections have been class tested and edited for accessibility.

For help in putting this third edition together, I would like to thank Heidi M. Hurd, University of Pennsylvania; Joseph Raz, Oxford University; my colleagues, David Solomon and Paul Weithman; and especially John Davenport, Fordham University. I would also like to thank the following reviewers: Kenneth Aman, Montclair State University; Mitchell Avila, California State University, Fresno; Marilyn Fischer, University of Dayton; Heidi M. Hurd, University of Pennsylvania Law School; as well as Peter Adams, Philosophy Editor at Wadsworth Publishing Co. for putting up with my delays; and Merrill Peterson of Matrix Productions Inc. for supervising the production of the book.

James P. Sterba

Part I

Introduction

Introduction

JAMES STERBA

Virtually all of us become involved at one time or another in disputes about justice. Sometimes our involvement in such disputes is rooted in the fact that we believe ourselves to be victims of some form of injustice; sometimes our involvement is rooted in the fact that others believe us to be the perpetrators or at least the beneficiaries of some form of injustice affecting them. Sometimes the injustice at issue seems to require eliminating a drastic reform, or even a revolutionary change in the political system—such as has taken place in Eastern Europe. Sometimes elimination only seems to require some electoral pressure or administrative decision—what might be required, say, in ending a war. But whatever the origin and whatever the practical effect, such disputes about justice are difficult to avoid, especially when dealing with issues (such as the distribution of income, the control and use of natural resources, and the distribution of educational and employment opportunities) that have widespread social effects.

How can we resolve such disputes in a reasonable way? Reasonable resolution of such disputes requires careful consideration of whatever reasons have been, or might be, advanced in favor of the alternative conceptions of justice that are available to us. Hopefully, through such a process of critical evaluation, one of these conceptions will begin to emerge as the most defensible—maybe it will even be the conception we initially endorsed.

This anthology has been designed to help you carry out this process of critical evaluation. The readings in it defend and critique six contemporary conceptions of justice. All of these conceptions of justice regard their requirements as belonging to the domain of obligation rather than to the domain of charity; they simply disagree about where to draw the line between these two domains. Each is concerned with giving people what they deserve or should rightfully possess; they simply tend to disagree about what it is that people deserve or rightfully possess.

Turning from common ground to disputed territory, each of these conceptions of justice appeals to a different political ideal. First is a Libertarian Conception of Justice. In recent years, libertarian party candidates have not done very well. But Ronald Reagan, George Bush, and Margaret Thatcher, whose views on economic issues are close to a Libertarian Conception of Justice, were successful politically and succeeded in refashioning the economies of their respective nations. According to this conception of justice, liberty is the ultimate political ideal. Thus all assignments of rights and duties are ultimately to be justified in terms of an ideal of liberty.

Second is a Socialist Conception of Justice. In the United States there has never been a viable socialist presidential candidate, but elsewhere there have been many successful socialist candidates. For example, the late Olof Palme led the Social Demo-crats back to power in Sweden and the late François Mitterand, a socialist, was the longest serving president in France, holding office for 14 years until May of 1995. According to a Socialist Conception of Justice, equality is the ultimate political ideal. Thus all assignments of rights and duties are ultimately to be justified in terms of an ideal of equality.

Third is a Liberal Democratic Conception of Justice. This is the conception of jus-tice endorsed, for example, by the left wing of the Democratic Party in the United States, whose leaders have been George McGovern, Ted Kennedy, and Jesse Jackson. According to this conception of justice, the ultimate political ideal is a blend of lib-erty and equality, and this blend can be characterized as contractual fairness, maximal utility, or discourse ethics. Thus all assignments of rights and duties are ultimately to be justified in terms of these ideals.

Fourth is a Communitarian Conception of Justice. This conception is somewhat difficult to associate with any particular political group, but it does seem to be re-flected in a wide range of Supreme Court decisions in the United States today, and has its roots in the republicanism of Madison and Jefferson. According to this Communitarian Conception of Justice, the common good is proclaimed to be the ul-timate political ideal, and this ideal is said to support a virtue-based conception of human flourishing.

Fifth is a Feminist Conception of Justice. This is the conception endorsed by the National Organization for Women (NOW) and by numerous other women's organi-zations in the United States and elsewhere. According to a Feminist Conception of Justice, the ultimate political ideal can be seen to be androgyny. Thus all assignments of rights and duties can ultimately be justified in terms of an ideal of androgyny.

Last is a Postmodern Conception of Justice. This conception is also somewhat dif-ficult to associate with any particular political group, but it has many adherents in literary and academic circles. According to a Postmodern Conception of Justice, we should reject all metanarratives or grand theories, which would seem to include our other five conceptions of justice. According to this conception, the justification for rights and duties is local and limited. It applies only with respect to individuals in a given setting and is not universalizable.

What we need to do, therefore, is examine each of these conceptions of justice, along with their historical roots where appropriate, in order to determine which is most defensible. Happily the readings in this anthology have been designed to help you do just that by providing classical and contemporary defenses and critiques of each of the six conceptions of justice. Working through the readings in this anthol-ogy will not always be an easy task. Some articles will be clear on the first reading, whereas others will require closer scrutiny. You should also make sure you give each selection a fair hearing, for while some will accord with your current views, others will not. It is important that you evaluate the latter with an open mind, allowing for the possibility that after sufficient reflection you may come to view them as the most de-fensible. Indeed, to approach the selections of this anthology in any other way would surely undermine your ability to reasonably resolve those disputes about justice in which you are inescapably involved.

Libertarian Justice

In 1972, John Hospers was nominated as the first U.S. Presidential candidate of the Libertarian Party. In the first selection, Hospers takes liberty to be the ultimate moral and political ideal, and he defines *liberty* as "the state of being unconstrained by other persons from doing what one wants." This definition limits the scope of liberty in two ways. First, not all constraints, whatever the source, count as a restriction on liberty; the constraints must come from other persons. For example, people who are constrained by natural forces from getting to the top of Mount Everest do not lack liberty in this regard. Second, the constraints must run counter to people's wants. Thus, people who do not want to hear Beethoven's Fifth Symphony do not feel their liberty is restricted when other people forbid its performance, even though the proscription does in fact constrain what they are able to do.

Of course, libertarians may argue that these constraints do restrict a person's liberty because people normally want to be unconstrained by others. But other philosophers have claimed that such constraints point to a serious defect in the libertarian's definition of liberty, which can only be remedied by defining *liberty* more broadly as "the state of being unconstrained by other persons from doing what one is able to do." If we apply this revised definition to the previous example, we find that people's liberty to hear Beethoven's Fifth Symphony would be restricted even if they did not want to hear it (and even if, perchance, they did not want to be unconstrained by others) because other people would still be constraining them from doing what they are able to do.

Confident that problems of defining liberty can be overcome in some satisfactory manner, libertarians go on to characterize their moral and political ideal as requiring that each person should have the greatest amount of liberty commensurate with the same liberty for all. From this ideal, libertarians claim that a number of more specific requirements,—in particular a right to life, a right to freedom of speech, press, and assembly, and a right to property—can be derived.

It is important to note that the libertarian's right to life is not a right to receive from others the goods and resources necessary for preserving one's life; it is simply a right not to be killed. So understood, the right to life is not a right to receive welfare. In fact, libertarians are concerned to show that there are no welfare rights in their view. Accordingly, the libertarian's understanding of the right to property is not a right to receive from others the goods and resources necessary for one's welfare, but rather a right to acquire goods and resources either by initial acquisition or by voluntary agreement.

Obviously, by defending rights such as these, libertarians can only support a limited role for government. That role is simply to prevent and punish initial acts of coercion—the only wrongful actions for libertarians.

Libertarians do not deny that it is a good thing for people to have sufficient goods and resources to meet at least their basic nutritional needs, but libertarians do deny that government has a duty to provide for such needs. Some good things, such as the provision of welfare to the needy, are requirements of charity rather than justice, libertarians claim. Accordingly, failure to make such provisions is neither blame-worthy nor punishable.

In selection 2, I argue that a libertarian ideal of liberty, which appears to reject the rights of a welfare state, can be seen to support such rights through an application of the "ought" implies "can" principle to conflicts between the rich and the poor. In one interpretation, the principle supports such rights by favoring the liberty of the poor over the liberty of the rich. In another interpretation, the principle supports such rights by favoring a conditional right to property over an unconditional right to property. In either interpretation, what is crucial in the derivation of these rights is the claim that it would be unreasonable to ask the poor to deny their basic needs and accept anything less than these rights as the condition for their willing cooperation.

In selection 3, Tibor Machan attacks my view that a libertarian ideal of liberty leads to what I call "action welfare rights." An action welfare right is the right of the poor, under certain conditions, not to be interfered with when taking from the rich what is required to satisfy their basic needs. An action welfare right differs from what are usually called "welfare rights" because it is a negative right rather than a positive right. However, I further argue that when libertarians are brought to see the legiti-macy of action welfare rights they will want to institutionalize positive welfare rights in order to avoid the possibly arbitrary exercise by the poor of their action welfare rights. In this way, I claim, a liberal democratic state would come to have a ground-ing in a libertarian ideal of (negative) liberty.

In criticizing my argument that a libertarian ideal of liberty leads to action welfare rights and thence to positive welfare rights, Machan accepts the theoretical thrust of my argument, but rejects its practical significance. In the revised version of the argu-ment, which is reprinted as selection 2, I have responded to this criticism. In selec-tion 3, however, Machan, seeking to further undercut the practical force of my argument, has contended that when we compare economic systems to determine which produce more poverty

No one can seriously dispute that the near-libertarian systems have fared much better than those going in the opposite direction, including the welfare state.[1]

Here one would think that Machan has the United States in mind as a "near-liber-tarian system" because earlier in the same paragraph he claims

America is still the freest of societies, with many of its legal principles giving expression to classical liberal, near-libertarian ideas.[2]

Yet apparently this is not what Machan thinks since in a footnote to the same text he says,

It is notable that the statistics that Sterba cites [in my above response to Machan's cri-tique] are drawn from societies, including the United States of America, which are far from libertarian in their legal construction and are far closer to the welfare state, if not to outright socialism.[3]

Obviously, then, Machan is surprisingly unclear as to whether he wants to call the United States a near-libertarian state, a welfare state, or a socialist state. Yet, whichever of these designations is most appropriate, what is clear is that the poor do less well in the United States than they do in the liberal democratic or socialist states of Western Europe such as Germany, Sweden, and Switzerland.[4] For example, 22.4 percent of children live below the poverty line in the United States as compared to 4.9 percent in Germany, 5 percent in Sweden, and 7.8 percent in Switzerland, and the United States shares with Italy the highest infant mortality rate of the major industrialized nations. The United States also ranks 67 among all nations in the percentage of national income received by the poorest 20 percent of its population, ranking the absolute lowest among industrialized nations.[5] Accordingly, the success that liberal democratic and socialist states have had, especially in Western Europe, in coming close to truly meeting the basic needs of their deserving poor should give us good reason to doubt what Machan proclaims is the superior practical effectiveness of "near-libertarian states" in dealing with poverty.

In selection 4, Jan Narveson argues for libertarianism by trying to give it a contractarian foundation in what people want. Narveson argues that if we consider the choice between

1. knowing that I will be forced to help others whom I wouldn't choose to help if I had my choice, with all others, in turn, being similarly forced to help me; and
2. knowing that our right to use our resources as we judge best, without interference by others, will always be respected, even though we also know that we won't *necessarily* be helped by others when the chips are down, (i.e., nobody will *force* them to help)

not everyone will favor (1) over (2). But since Narveson also acknowledges that most people want a social minimum (see p. 63), which is equivalent to favoring (2), he should presumably abandon his contractarian defense and claim instead that, despite what most people want, the best reasons really do favor libertarianism. But do the best reasons favor libertarianism? Narveson argues that if there are enough votes to legislate the welfare state, then there must be enough charitable people out there to easily meet welfare needs without requiring anyone to help. Yet is this really the case? Historically, haven't tax-supported welfare systems come into existence because voluntary giving turned out to be insufficient?[6] If so, then tax-supported welfare institutions are needed to take care of the poor who are not provided for by the available private charity just as tax-supported educational institutions are needed to take care of the educational needs of those who are not provided for by existing private educational institutions.

Narveson in his response to my article argues that the constraints that a welfare system would impose on the rich would be unreasonable for them to accept. Yet in my article I argued that the constraints of a property system without welfare would be even more unreasonable for the poor to accept. Moreover, even if Narveson were right that the (European) poor in the United States did not starve in the early days when the United States was nearly a libertarian society, that would not show that the poor today, as I argued above, are not be better off in the liberal democratic or socialist countries of Western Europe. Nor should we neglect to note that the well-being of early European settlers was frequently secured by decimating and exterminating American Indian tribes, precisely those who should, on libertarian principles, have been regarded as the rightful owners of the land.

Socialist Justice

In contrast with libertarians, socialists take equality to be the ultimate political ideal. In the first part of selection 5, which is taken from the *Communist Manifesto*, Karl Marx and Friedrich Engels maintain that the abolition of bourgeois property and bourgeois family structure is a necessary first requirement for building a society that accords with the political ideal of equality. In the second part of selection 5 Marx provides a much more positive account of what is required to build a society based upon the political ideal of equality. In such a society, Marx claims that the distribution of social goods must conform, at least initially, to the principle "from each according to his ability, to each according to his contribution." But when the highest stage of communist society has been reached, Marx adds, distribution will conform to the principle "from each according to his ability, to each according to his need."

This final principle of socialist justice is discussed and defended by Edward Nell and Onora O'Neill in selection 6. They argue that any incentive problems associated with the principle will be resolved when, quoting Marx, "labor is no longer a means of life but has become life's principal need." They further contend that when it is at last appropriate to apply this principle of socialist justice there will exist a system for distributing the burdens of nonfulfilling but socially necessary tasks as well as a system for equitably distributing the benefits of goods not required for anyone's needs. What this means is that because some jobs, such as collecting garbage or changing bedpans, probably can't be made intrinsically rewarding, socialists propose to divide them up in some equitable manner. Some people might, for example, collect garbage one day a week and then work at intrinsically rewarding jobs for the rest of the week. Others would change bedpans or do some other slop job one day a week and then work at an intrinsically rewarding job the other days of the week. By making jobs as intrinsically rewarding as possible, in part through democratic control of the workplace and an equitable assignment of unrewarding tasks, socialists believe people will contribute according to their ability even when distribution proceeds according to need.

Finally, it is important to note that the socialist ideal of equality does not accord with what existed in countries like the Soviet Union or Albania. Judging the acceptability of the socialist ideal of equality by what took place in those countries would be as unfair as judging the acceptability of the libertarian ideal of liberty by what took place in countries such as Chile or South Korea, where citizens are arrested and imprisoned without cause. By analogy, it would be like judging the merits of college football by the way Vanderbilt or Rutgers plays rather than by the way Michigan or Notre Dame plays. Actually, a fairer comparison would be to judge the socialist ideal of equality by what takes place in countries like Norway or Sweden and to judge the libertarian ideal of liberty by what takes place in the United States. Even these comparisons, however, are not wholly appropriate because none of these countries fully conform to those ideals.

To justify the ideal of equality, Kai Nielson (selection 7) argues that it is required by *liberty* or at least by a fair distribution of liberty. By *liberty* Nielson means both "positive liberty to receive certain goods" and "negative liberty not to be interfered with," so his argument from liberty will not have much weight with libertarians, who only value negative liberty. Rather, his argument is directed primarily at liberal democrats, who value both positive and negative liberty as well as a fair distribution of liberty.

Another basic difficulty with Nielson's socialist conception of justice concerns the proclaimed necessity of abolishing private property and socializing the means of production. It seems perfectly possible to give workers more control over their workplace while at the same time the means of production remain privately owned. Of course, private ownership would have a somewhat different character in a society with democratic control of the workplace, but it need not cease to be private ownership. After all, private ownership would also have a somewhat different character in a society where private holdings, and hence bargaining power, were distributed more equally than is found in most capitalist societies, yet it would not cease to be private ownership. Accordingly, we could imagine a society where the means of production are privately owned but where—because ownership is so widely dispersed throughout the society (e.g., nearly everyone owns 10 shares of major industrial stock and no one more than 20 shares) and because of the degree of democratic control of the workplace—many of the valid criticisms socialists make of existing capitalist societies would no longer apply.

In selection 8, Robert Nozick illustrates another argument often used against a socialist conception of justice—that it is opposed to liberty. Nozick asks us to imagine that we are in a society that has just distributed income according to some ideal pattern, possibly a pattern of equality. We are to further imagine that in such a society Wilt Chamberlain (or Michael Jordan, if we wish to update the example) offers to play basketball for us provided that he receives a quarter for every home game ticket that is sold. Suppose we agree to these terms and a million people attend the home games to see Wilt Chamberlain (or Michael Jordan) play, thereby securing him an income of $250,000. Since such an income would surely upset the initial pattern of income distribution, whatever that happened to be, Nozick contends that this illustrates how an ideal of liberty upsets the patterns required by other political ideals and hence calls for their rejection.

Nozick's critique, however, seems to apply only to political ideals that require an absolute equality of income. Yet for many political ideals, the inequalities of income generated in Nozick's example would be objectionable only if they deprived people of something to which they had a right, such as equal opportunity. And whether people were so deprived would depend on to what uses the Wilt Chamberlains or Michael Jordans of the world put their greater income. However, there is no necessity for those who have legitimately acquired greater income to use it in ways that violate the rights of others.

Liberal Democratic Justice:
The Contractarian Perspective

Finding merit in both the libertarian's ideal of liberty and the socialist's ideal of equality, liberal democrats attempt to combine both liberty and equality into one political ideal that can be characterized as contractual fairness, maximal utility, or discourse ethics.

A classical example of the contractual approach to liberal democratic justice is found in the work of Immanuel Kant, from which selection 9 is taken. In this selection, Kant claims that a civil state ought to be founded on an original contract satisfying the requirements of freedom (the freedom to seek happiness in whatever way one sees fit as long one does not infringe upon the freedom of others to pursue a similar end), equality (the equal right of each person to coerce others to use their freedom in a way that harmonizes with one's own freedom), and independence (that independence of each person that is necessarily presupposed by the free agreement of the original contract).

According to Kant, the original contract, which ought to be the foundation of every civil state, does not have to "actually exist as a fact." It suffices that the laws of a civil state are such that people would agree to them under conditions in which requirements of freedom, equality, and independence obtain. Laws that accord with this original contract would then, Kant claims, give all members of society the right to reach any degree of rank that they could earn through their labor, industry, and good fortune. Thus, the equality demanded by the original contract would not, in Kant's view, exclude a considerable amount of economic liberty.

The Kantian ideal of a hypothetical contract as the moral foundation for a liberal democratic conception of justice has been further developed by John Rawls in *A Theory of Justice*. In selection 10, taken from the book, Rawls, like Kant, argues that principles of justice are those principles that free and rational persons who are concerned to advance their own interests would accept in an initial position of equality. Yet Rawls goes beyond Kant by interpreting the conditions of his "original position" to explicitly require a "veil of ignorance." This veil of ignorance, Rawls claims, has the effect of depriving persons in the original position of the knowledge they would need to advance their own interests in ways that are morally arbitrary.

The justification Rawls offers for the conditions he imposes on the original position takes two forms. First, Rawls claims that the conditions express weak but widely shared moral presumptions. Second, Rawls assures us that the choice of principles in the original position will always conform to our considered moral judgments. In cases of conflict, this will be accomplished either by revising our considered moral judgments or by revising the particular conditions on the original position that gave rise to them.

Rawls presents the principles of justice he believes would be derived in the original position in two successive formulations. The first formulation is as follows:

I. Special conception of justice
   1. Each person is to have an equal right to the most extensive basic liberty compatible with a similar liberty for others.

       2. Social and economic inequalities are to be arranged so that they are
          (a) reasonably expected to be to everyone's advantage and (b) attached to
          positions and offices open to all.

  II. General conception of justice
     All social values—liberty and opportunity, income and wealth, and the bases
     of self-respect—are to be distributed equally unless an unequal distribution of
     any or all of these values is to everyone's advantage.

Later these principles are more accurately formulated as:

   I. Special conception of justice
     1. Each person is to have an equal right to the most extensive total system of
        equal basic liberties compatible with a similar system of liberty for all.
     2. Social and economic inequalities are to be arranged so that they are (a) to
        the greatest benefit of the least advantaged, consistent with the just savings
        principle and (b) attached to offices and positions open to all under condi-
        tions of fair equality of opportunity.

  II. General conception of justice
     All social goods—liberty and opportunity, income and wealth, and the bases
     of self-respect—are to be distributed equally unless an unequal distribution of
     any or all of these goods is to the advantage of the least favored.

Under both formulations, the general conception of justice differs from the special conception of justice by allowing trade-offs between liberty and other social goods. According to Rawls, persons in the original position would want the special concep-tion of justice to be applied in place of the general conception of justice whenever social conditions allowed all representative persons to exercise their basic liberties.

Rawls holds that these principles of justice would be chosen in the original posi-tion because persons so situated would find it reasonable to follow the conservative dictates of a "maximin strategy" and thereby secure for themselves the highest mini-mum payoff.

Rawls's defense of a liberal democratic conception of justice has been challenged in a variety of ways. Some critics have endorsed Rawls's contractual approach while disagreeing with Rawls over what principles of justice would be derived thereby. These critics usually attempt to undermine the use of a maximin strategy in the orig-inal position. Other critics, however, have found fault with the contractual approach itself. The criticism that Ronald Dworkin directs at Rawls's theory of justice in selec-tion 11 is of this latter sort.

Dworkin argues that hypothetical agreements do not (unlike actual agreements) provide independent arguments for the fairness of those agreements. For example, suppose because I did not know the value of a painting I owned, if you had offered me $100 for it yesterday, I would have accepted your offer. Such hypothetical accep-tance, Dworkin argues, in no way shows that it would be fair to force me to sell the painting to you today for $100 now that I have discovered it to be more valuable. Accordingly, Dworkin holds that the fact that a person would agree to do something in the original position does not provide an independent argument for abiding by that agreement in everyday life.

But while it seems correct to argue that hypothetical agreement in the painting case does not support a demand that I presently sell you the painting for $100, it is not clear how this undermines the normal relevance of the hypothetical agreement that emerges from the original position. For surely a defender of the original position is not committed to the view that all hypothetical agreements are morally binding. Nor could Dworkin reasonably argue that his example supports the conclusion that no hypothetical agreements are morally binding. For by parity of reasoning from the fact that some actual agreements are not binding (such as an agreement to commit murder), it would follow that *no* actual agreements are morally binding, which is absurd. Consequently, further argument is required to show that the specific agreement that would result from the original position is not morally binding.

Dworkin goes on to argue that the true warrant for accepting the principles that Rawls derives from his original position is that these principles give expression to an underlying natural right. This underlying right is not a right to liberty, nor even, presumably, a right to fair treatment, but rather a right to equal concern and respect; and the original position, Dworkin maintains, is simply designed to accord with that right. Dworkin thus concludes that the original position is unnecessary and dispensable, for he assumes that it is always possible to argue directly from each person's equal right to concern and respect.

In more recent work, Dworkin has argued that this equal right to concern and respect does not require equality of welfare but rather equality of resources.[7] In attempting to set out more precisely the type of equality of resources that is demanded, Dworkin introduces the idea of a hypothetical insurance market in which people ignorant of the economic rent their talents would attract choose to insure themselves against faring poorly through lack of social and economic opportunities. Payments that would have gone to this hypothetical insurance fund are said to determine the compensation that is due to the less talented members of a society.

Dworkin appeals to a similar hypothetical insurance market to determine the compensation required for the handicapped. In this hypothetical insurance market, the participants are to suppose that they have the same risk of developing physical or mental handicaps in the future (which assumes that no one has developed these yet) but where the total number of handicaps remains whatever it happens to be in the society.

Unfortunately, Dworkin does not work out these two applications of his hypothetical insurance market in parallel fashion. In the talent case, to distinguish his hypothetical choice situation from the original position, Dworkin allows the participants to *know* what the talents happen to be. But with such knowledge the more talented, even when ignorant of their social and economic opportunities, would still have reason to purchase less insurance than those less favored in the natural lottery. Dworkin fails to detect this consequence because he thinks that even with the knowledge provided in his hypothetical choice situation each participant would still suppose that she "has the same chance as anyone else of occupying any particular level of income in the economy." But there is no reason why the more talented should be this pessimistic about their chances of faring well in their society. Of course, this objection could be answered just by removing the knowledge of talents from Dworkin's hypothetical choice situation, but then his choice situation would be virtually equivalent to the original position. So interpreted, Dworkin would be simply disagreeing with Rawls over what principles of justice would be chosen in that choice situation.

In his more recent work from which selection 12 is taken, Rawls explains how his theory of justice is intended to be a political conception that is supported by an overlapping consensus. If his theory is successful, then, it will function as the common ground for a diverse set of comprehensive doctrines. According to Rawls, comprehensive doctrines should be judged not as true or false, but only as reasonable or unreasonable insofar as they accord with a political conception that is supported by an overlapping consensus. Similarly, a political conception of justice should be itself judged not as true or false, but only as reasonable or unreasonable insofar as it is supported by an overlapping consensus of comprehensive doctrines.

In selection 13, Joseph Raz rejects Rawls's way of characterizing a political conception of justice. According to Raz, to claim that a political theory of justice is reasonable is to claim that it is true. He holds that there is no justice without truth. But even assuming that this is a valid objection to Rawls's theory, it is one that Rawls could easily accept without making any fundamental change in his theory.

Liberal Democratic Justice: The Utilitarian Perspective

One way to avoid the challenges that have been directed at a contractarian defense of liberal democratic justice is to find some alternative way of defending liberal democratic justice. Historically, utilitarianism has been thought to provide such an alternative defense. What has been claimed is that the requirements of a liberal democratic conception of justice can be derived from considerations of utility in such a way that following these requirements will result in the maximization of total happiness or satisfaction in society. The best known classical defense of this utilitarian approach is certainly that presented by John Stuart Mill in Chapter 5 of *Utilitarianism,* from which selection 14 is drawn.

In this selection, Mill surveys various types of actions and situations that are ordinarily described as just or unjust and concludes that justice (by which he understands a liberal democratic conception of justice) simply denotes a certain class of fundamental rules, the adherence to which is essential for maximizing social utility. Thus Mill rejects the ideal that justice and social utility are ultimately distinct ideals, maintaining instead that (liberal democratic) justice is in fact derivable from the moral ideal of social utility.

Nevertheless, various problems remain for the utilitarian defense of liberal democratic justice. Consider, for example, a society in which the members are equally divided between the Privileged Rich and the Alienated Poor, and suppose that the incomes for two alternative social arrangements for this society are the following:

	Social Arrangement A	*Social Arrangement B*
Privileged Rich	$100,000	$60,000
Alienated Poor	$5,000	$15,000

Given these alternatives, considerations of maximizing utility would appear to favor Social Arrangement A over Social Arrangement B. But suppose that liberal justice required a high minimum for each person in society. Then it would seem that liberal democratic justice would favor Social Arrangement B over Social Arrangement A, in apparent conflict with the requirements of utility. Obviously, the possibility of such a conflict places the utilitarian defense of liberal democratic justice in some doubt. In selection 15, R. M. Hare attempts to remove the grounds for that doubt.

Hare argues that in fashioning a theory of justice we must proceed in accordance with the formal constraints of the concept of justice; that is, our judgments must be universalizable and impartial. But in addition, Hare argues, we must take relevant empirical considerations into account, such as the fact that people experience a declining marginal utility for money and other social goods. For example, considerations of declining marginal utility of money and other social goods, Hare believes, would render a utilitarian approach to a theory of justice moderately egalitarian in its requirements. Applied to our example, considerations of declining marginal utility of money and other social goods would seem to render Social Arrangement B preferable to Social Arrangement A from a utilitarian point of view, thus removing the grounds for thinking that liberal justice and social utility conflict in this case.

Of course, when considerations of declining marginal utility of money and other social goods are taken into account, the utility values for the two alternatives given above might end up to be something like:

	Social Arrangement A	*Social Arrangement B*
Privileged Rich	55	40
Alienated Poor	10	20

And if they did, then there would still remain a conflict between liberal democratic justice and utility, with liberal democratic justice favoring Social Arrangement B, and utility favoring Social Arrangement A . . . unless, of course, additional empirical considerations could be advanced to show that this is not the case.

Still another objection to a utilitarian defense of liberal justice is developed by John Rawls in selection 16. In this selection Rawls criticizes utilitarianism, particularly classical utilitarianism, for applying to society as a whole the principle of rational choice for one person, and thereby treating the desires and satisfactions of separate persons as if they were the desires and satisfactions of just one person. In this way, Rawls claims, utilitarianism fails to preserve the distinction between persons.

What Rawls must be claiming is that even after considerations of declining marginal utility of money and other social goods are taken into account, utilitarianism will still fail to adequately preserve the distinction between persons. But is Rawls right? It may well be that a proper assessment of the relative merits of the contractual and utilitarian approaches to liberal democratic justice will turn on this very issue.

Liberal Democratic Justice: The Discourse Ethics Perspective

The Kantian ideal of a hypothetical contract as the moral foundation for a liberal democratic conception of justice has been developed in a somewhat different direction by Jürgen Habermas. A significant part of Habermas's work has been to show that the basic requirements of a political conception of justice can be derived from the common presuppositions of argumentation to which we all are committed. In selection 17, however, Habermas tries to show how the most defensible political conception of justice also strikes a balance between popular sovereignty and human rights or between "the freedom of the ancients" and "the freedom of the moderns." What Habermas wants to avoid is conceiving of humans rights either as simply external constraints imposed on legislators or as simply means to legislative goals. Accordingly, he maintains that human rights are what makes the exercise of popular sovereignty possible. For him, they are not constraints but rather enabling conditions for the proper exercise of popular sovereignty. Habermas then goes on to draw out the implications of his analysis for the case of women, arguing that the individual rights necessary to guarantee women the autonomy to pursue their lives in the private sphere cannot be formulated adequately unless women and their male supporters first articulate and justify in public debate those aspects of women's lives that are relevant to equal or unequal treatment in typical cases.

In selection 18, Charles Larmore challenges two aspects of Habermas's defense of a liberal democratic conception of justice. First, Larmore challenges Habermas's tendency to reject metaphysics and religion as obsolete. While allowing that a political conception of justice cannot be based on metaphysical or religious views that reasonable people can reject, Larmore holds that reasonable people can and still do disagree about the validity of particular metaphysical or religious views, so that reason does not require that we all reject such views. Nevertheless, Habermas's view here may be closer to Larmore's than Larmore allows. Thus, Habermas may not be rejecting metaphysics and religion as a private doctrine but only as a public foundation for a political conception of justice, and that is exactly what Larmore does as well.

Second, Larmore questions whether Habermas succeeds in striking a proper balance between popular sovereignty and human rights. As Larmore sees it, Habermas favors the former over the latter since he maintains that human rights are what makes democratic self-rule possible; for example, a right to freedom of speech recommends itself simply as a means to the formation of a common political will. Larmore thinks that a further sign that Habermas is privileging popular sovereignty is the way he conceives of both popular sovereignty and human rights in terms of autonomy, public autonomy in the one case and private autonomy in the other. According to Larmore, however, there is a better way to interpret Habermas's view. Given that Habermas thinks that a political conception of justice ought be rationally acceptable to all those who are bound by it, Larmore thinks that this implies an underlying requirement that each person be treated as an end and thus be shown respect. So interpreted, Larmore contends, popular sovereignty would itself rest on a fundamental individual right to equal respect.

In selection 19, Seyla Benhabib provides an even more expansive discussion of the discourse ethics perspective. She begins by discussing the presuppositions of argumentation on which a discourse ethics is grounded and then goes on to consider two criticisms of a strong model of deliberative democracy. The first is that this model leads to the corrosion of individual liberties. The second is by feminist theorists who are skeptical about the model because they see it as privileging a certain mode of discourse at the cost of silencing others that are more utilized by women and minorities.

Benhabib responds to the first criticism by noting that in her version of discourse ethics, which she shares with Habermas, all the participants in a deliberative democracy are entitled to mutual respect and egalitarian reciprocity. Since these fundamental rights both require and guide deliberative democracy, she contends that there is no sense in which the model can lead to the corrosion of individual rights.

In response to the second criticism, Benhabib argues that her model of deliberative democracy will not silence women and minorities, but, in fact, will take into account their different perspectives. She also criticizes Iris Young for requiring the participants in deliberative democracy to transcend and transform their initial situated knowledge at the same time that she denies them the standards of fairness and impartiality to do so properly.

Communitarian Justice

Another prominent political ideal defended by contemporary philosophers is the communitarian ideal of the common good. As one might expect, many contemporary defenders of a communitarian conception of justice regard their conception as rooted in Aristotelian moral theory. In selection 20, Aristotle distinguishes between different varieties of justice. He first distinguishes between justice as the whole of virtue and justice as a particular part of virtue. In the former sense, justice is understood as what is lawful and the just person is equivalent to the moral person. In the latter sense, justice is understood as what is fair or equal and the just person is the person who takes only a proper share. Aristotle focuses his discussion on justice in the latter sense, which further divides into distributive justice, corrective justice, and justice in exchange. Each of these varieties of justice can be understood to be concerned with achieving equality. For distributive justice it is equality between equals; for corrective justice it is equality between punishment and the crime; and for justice in exchange it is equality between whatever goods are exchanged. Aristotle also claims that justice has both its natural and conventional aspects: This twofold character of justice seems to be behind Aristotle's discussion of equity, in which equality is described as a corrective to legal or conventional justice.

Note that few of the distinctions Aristotle makes here seem tied to the acceptance of any particular conception of justice. One could, for example, accept the view that justice requires formal equality but then specify the equality that is required in different ways. Even the ideal of justice as giving people what they deserve, which has its roots in Aristotle's account of distributive justice, is also subject to various interpretations. For a correct analysis of the concept of desert would show that there is no conceptual difficulty with claiming, for example, that everyone deserves to have his or her needs satisfied or that everyone deserves an equal share of the goods distributed by his or her society.[8] Consequently, Aristotle's account is primarily helpful for getting clear about the distinctions belonging to the concept of justice that can be made without committing oneself to any particular conceptions of justice.

Yet rather than drawn out the particular requirements of their own conception of justice, contemporary communitarians have frequently chosen to defend their conception by attacking other conceptions of justice, and, by and large, they have focused their attacks on the liberal democratic conception of justice.

One of the best-known attacks of this sort has been put forth by Michael J. Sandel (selection 21). According to Sandel, our current political philosophy is that of a procedural republic. We hold to the priority of fair procedures over particular ends. We emphasize toleration and respect for individual rights. We respect people's freedom to choose. This political philosophy, Sandel claims, comes in both utilitarian and Kantian varieties. While allowing that Rawls rightly criticizes utilitarianism for failing to take into account the separateness of persons, Sandel claims that Rawls's conception of the self as prior to the ends or purposes that are affirmed by it has a problem of its own. This is because it leads to the view that the obligations we have are either universally owed or voluntarily incurred. The problem with this, Sandel argues, is that we have obligations of membership and solidarity that are neither universally owed nor voluntarily incurred. Sandel cites here the example of Robert E. Lee's obligations to his relations and to Virginia at the outbreak of the Civil War.

Sandel also questions the view held by Rawls and other liberals that we should set aside moral and religious views about which there is reasonable disagreement when fashioning a political conception of justice. Here Sandel discusses two examples, the current abortion debate and the Lincoln–Douglas debate of 1858. Sandel claims that in both cases whether we should set aside our moral and religious views to achieve agreement depends upon whether or not we think those moral and religious views are true. According to Sandel, if we think that the Catholic Church's official doctrine on abortion is true, then it isn't clear why we should set aside this belief when fashioning a political conception of justice. But surely, we could believe something to be true while granting that other people in our society who lack our particular background or experience will not come to see it as true. Knowing this, we can see how they can reasonably disagree with us, and, for that reason, we might not think it right to coercively require them to live in accord with our (true) belief. Generally, it would seem that beliefs that are true but not accessible should not be the basis for coercive policies by the state.

In addition, the fact that there is disagreement as there was at the time of the Lincoln–Douglas debate does not show that those who disagreed were all reasonable. One could even argue that by 1858 there were sufficient reasons generally accessible to everyone to show that slavery was morally wrong, and that those who failed to believe this at the time were simply being unreasonable and could, therefore, be coercively required to oppose slavery.

In selection 22, MacIntyre argues that virtually all forms of liberalism attempt to separate rules defining right action from conceptions of the human good. Or, as

John Rawls has put it, in all these forms of liberalism "the right is prior to the good." MacIntyre contends that these forms of liberalism not only fail but have to fail because the rules defining right action cannot be adequately grounded apart from a conception of the good. For this reason, MacIntyre claims, only some version of an Aristotelian theory that grounds rules supporting right action in a complete conception of the good can ever hope to be adequate.

But why can't we view most forms of liberalism as attempting to ground moral rules on part of a conception of the good—specifically, the part of a conception of the good that is more easily recognized, and needs to be publicly recognized, as good? For Rawls, for example, this partial conception of the good is a conception of fairness, according to which no one deserves his or her native abilities nor his or her initial starting place in society. For Ronald Dworkin (and similarly for other liberals), it is a conception of equal concern and respect for each and every person. If this way of interpreting forms of liberalism is correct, then in order to properly evaluate liberal and Aristotelian political theories we would need to do a comparative analysis of their conceptions of the good and their practical requirements.

In selection 23, Jean Hampton defends liberalism against the communitarian critique. She argues that both liberals and communitarians acknowledge the sociality of human nature while differing in their views of state power. Communitarians want the state to use its power to protect and encourage the development of communities and community values while liberals want the state to stay out of community life. She argues that liberalism has implicit within it a kind of critical facility for judging cultures that communitarianism appears to lack. At the same time, she allows that liberalism has trouble appreciating the moral wisdom implicit in community practices.

Feminist Justice

Defenders of a feminist conception of justice present a distinctively challenging critique to defenders of other conceptions of justice. John Stuart Mill, one of the earliest male defenders of women's liberation argues in selection 24 that the subjection of women was never justified but was imposed upon them because they were physically weaker than men and that later this subjection was confirmed by law. Mill argues that society must remove the legal restrictions that deny women the same opportunities that are enjoyed by men in society. However, Mill does not consider whether because of past discrimination against women it may be necessary to do more than simply removing legal restrictions to provide women with the same opportunities that men now enjoy. He doesn't consider whether positive assistance may also be required.

But usually it is not enough simply to remove unequal restrictions to make a competition fair among those who have been participating. Positive assistance to those who have been disadvantaged in the past may also be required, as would be the case if one were running a race in which one was unfairly impeded by having to carry a 10-pound weight. Similarly, positive assistance, such as affirmative action programs, may be necessary if women who have been disadvantaged in the past are now for the first time to enjoy equal opportunity with men.

In selection 25, Susan Okin points out that in the face of the radical inequality that exists between women and men in our society there is still a widespread failure of political philosophers to address gender issues in their political theories. Ironically this is true even among those philosophers who have seen the need to adopt gender neutral language. Okin argues that no theory of justice can be adequate until it address these issues.

In selection 26, I set out and defend an ideal of androgyny that I identify with feminist justice. This ideal requires that traits that are truly desirable in society be equally available to both women and men, or in the case of virtues, equally inculcated in both women and men. I consider attempts to derive the ideal of androgyny either from a right to equal opportunity that is a central requirement of a liberal democratic conception of justice or from an equal right of self-development that is a central requirement of a socialist conception of justice. I argue that although the ideal of androgyny is compatible with the requirements of these two conceptions of justice, it also transcends them by requiring that all virtue be equally inculcated in both women and men.

I further argue that the ideal of androgyny would require 1) that all children irrespective of their sex must be given the same type of upbringing consistent with their native capabilities and 2) that mothers and fathers must also have the same opportunities for education and employment consistent with their native capabilities. I go on to consider how achieving equal opportunity for women and men requires vastly improved day care facilities and flexible (usually part-time) work schedules for both women and men.

In Selection 27, Christina Sommers criticizes the attack by feminist philosophers, such as Okin and myself, on the traditional family structures. She distinguishes liberal feminists from radical feminists. She contends that liberal feminists, like herself, want equal opportunity in the workplace and politics, but would leave marriage and motherhood "untouched and unimpugned." By contrast, Sommers contends that radical feminists are committed to an assimilationist or androgynous ideal that would destroy the (traditional) family and deny most women what they want. Sommers, however, never explains how it is possible to secure for women equal opportunity in the workplace and politics while rejecting androgyny in favor of traditional gender roles. For example, how could women be passive, submissive, dependent, indecisive, and weak and still enjoy the same opportunities in the workplace and politics that are enjoyed by men who are aggressive, dominant, independent, decisive, and strong?

Marilyn Friedman (selection 28) does not challenge Sommers's contention that radical feminists are committed to an assimilationist or androgynous ideal. There is, however, an important distinction between these two ideals. According to an assimilationist ideal, "one's sex should be no more noticeable than one's eye color," but according to an androgynous ideal, this need not be the case, as long as all desirable traits are equally open to both women and men, and all virtues equally expected of both women and men.

Friedman does, however, question whether what Sommers supports is really what most women want. She quotes a 1983 survey which indicated that 63 percent of women preferred nontraditional family relationships, and points out that in 1977 only 16 percent of American households were traditional families in the sense of families consisting of a legally married heterosexual couple and their children, in which the man is the sole breadwinner and "head" of the household, and the woman does the domestic work and childcare. In responding to Friedman, Sommers explains that what she means by a traditional family is one that consists of two heterosexual parents and one or more children in which the mother plays a distinctive gender role in caring for the children.[9] This definition obviously broadens the class of families to which Sommers is referring. But in her response, Sommers goes on to renounce any attempt at promoting even the traditional family as she defines it. What she claims to be promoting is simply "the right and liberty to live under the arrangement of one's choice." According to Sommers, if people want to live in nontraditional families, they should be free to do so.

Friedman further disagrees with Sommers, contending that no woman should "swoon at the sight of Rhett Butler carrying Scarlett O'Hara up the stairs to a fate undreamt of in feminist philosophy." According to Friedman, what Rhett Butler is doing in *Gone With the Wind* is raping Scarlett O'Hara. In a subsequent response to Sommers, Friedman, noting that Scarlett O'Hara, although initially unwilling, later appears to be a willing sexual partner, defines "rape" as "any very intimate sexual contact which is *initiated* forcefully or against the will of the recipient.[10] Friedman allows that others might want to define such activity as sexual domination rather than rape, but under either definition, Friedman condemns it, whereas Sommers does not. In her response, Sommers cites approvingly the following passage from *Scarlett's Women: Gone With the Wind and Its Female Fans*.

> [T]he majority of my correspondents (and I agree) recognize the ambiguous nature of the encounter and interpret it as a scene of mutually pleasurable rough sex . . . By far the majority of women who responded to me saw the episode as erotically exciting, emotionally stirring and profoundly memorable. Few of them referred to it as "rape."[11]

Postmodern Justice

Jean-Francois Lyotard is usually given credit for first introducing the term "postmodern" into the current discussions of philosophy, politics, and social theory with his book *The Postmodern Condition* from which selection 29 is taken. Lyotard defines postmodernism as incredulity toward metanarratives or grand theories. By metanarratives, Lyotard is primarily referring to Marxism and Hegelianism, but the term also refers to any univeralistic theory including our other five conceptions of justice. In its place, Lyotard wants justification to proceed by way of a multitude of localized mini-narratives, because he takes this to be the only form of justification possible.

According to Jeffrey Reiman in selection 30, modernism is the Enlightenment belief in a single unified rational perspective. By contrast, postmodernism, Reiman claims, rejects the idea of a given and claims that any interpretation can be shown to have been purchased only by the exclusion of other possible ones. Accordingly, postmodernists regard libertarians who interpret liberty to be our ultimate political ideal to be arbitrarily excluding other possible interpretations, but the same could be said of liberal democrats, socialists, communitarians, or feminists as well. Reiman's response to the postmodern challenge is to maintain that all arguments must proceed from beliefs that people already hold, which is to say they must be ad hominem. While Reiman thinks that an argument for liberalism can be derived from beliefs that everybody shares, that may not be necessary. For instance, if we could show that the libertarian ideal of liberty requires a right to welfare and further that implementing this right around the world and into the future would lead to the equality that socialists favor, that should serve to bring libertarians, liberal democrats and socialists together at a practical level despite their differing starting points.[12]

In selection 31, Nancy Fraser and Linda Nicholson try to combine the best elements of both postmodernism and feminism into a postmodern feminism. According to Fraser and Nicholson, feminists should learn from postmodernists to attend to the cultural specificity of different societies and historical periods and beware of oversimplistic explanations or false generalizations as they seek to uncover the cause or causes of the domination of women. Nevertheless, Frazer and Nicholson claim that this can be done without abandoning the large scale historical narratives and analyses that is needed for a wide-ranging critical theory or theory of justice. All postmodern feminism has to do is be concerned with the subordination of women in both its "endless variety and monotonous similarity." In addition, if people could be led to see that feminist justice is compatible with or required by the ideals of libertarian justice, liberal democratic justice, socialist justice, and communitarian justice that they hold dear, then the case for feminist justice would be strengthened immeasurably. It could make the practical requirements of feminist justice virtually inescapable.

What this suggests is that our overall task of critically evaluating alternative conceptions of justice in order to reasonably resolve disputes about justice may not be as difficult as it initially appeared. If libertarian justice, liberal democratic justice, socialist justice, communitarian justice, feminist justice, and postmodern justice, when correctly interpreted, can all be seen to have virtually the same practical requirements, then there is really no need to choose between them. To reasonably resolve our disputes about justice, all we would have to do is get clear about what are the shared practical requirements of these conceptions of justice and then simply act upon them.[13]

NOTES

1. Selection 3.

2. *Ibid.*

3. *Ibid.*

4. Richard Rose and Rei Shiratori, eds. *The Welfare State East and West* (Oxford: Oxford University Press, 1986). In fact, the living standards of poor children in Switzerland, Sweden, Finland, Denmark, Belgium, Norway, Luxembourg, Germany, the Netherlands, Austria, Canada, France, Italy, the United Kingdom, and Australia are all better than they are in the United States. See James Carville, *We're Right They're Wrong* (New York: Random House, 1996), pp. 31–32.

5. Michael Wolff, *Where We Stand* (New York: Bantam Books, 1992) pp. 23 and 115; George Kurian, *The New Book of Work Rankings,* 3rd ed. (New York: Facts on File, 1990), p. 73; *New York Times,* April 17, 1995.

6. Joel Handler, *Poverty of Welfare Reform* (New Haven: Yale University Press, 1995); Herbert Gans, *The War Against the Poor* (New York: Basic Books, 1995).

7. Ronald Dworkin, "Liberalism," in Stuart Hamphire, ed., *Public and Private Morality* (Cambridge University Press, 1978), pp. 113–143; "What is Equality? Part I and II," *Philosophy and Public Affairs* (1981), pp. 185–246, 283–345; "Why Liberals Should Believe in Equality," *The New York Review of Books* (1983), pp. 32–34.

8. For further argument, see my article "Justice and the Concept of Desert," *The Personalist* (1976), pp. 118–197.

9. Christina Sommers, "Do These Feminists Like Women?" *The Journal of Social Philosophy* (1991), pp. 66–74.

10. Marilyn Friedman, "Does Sommers Like Women?" *The Journal of Social Philosophy* (1991), pp. 75–90.

11. *Ibid.*, p. 72.

12. For further argument for this practical reconciliation thesis, see my book *How To Make People Just* (Rowman and Littlefield, 1988) and *Justice for Here and Now* (Cambridge University Press, 1998).

13. For further argument for this practical reconciliation thesis, see *How To Make People Just* and *Justice for Here and Now.*

Part II

Libertarian Justice

1 The Libertarian Manifesto

JOHN HOSPERS

THE POLITICAL PHILOSOPHY that is called libertarianism (from the Latin *libertas,* liberty) is the doctrine that every person is the owner of his own life, and that no one is the owner of anyone else's life: and that consequently every human being has the right to act in accordance with his own choices, unless those actions infringe on the equal liberty of other human beings to act in accordance with their choices.

There are several other ways of stating the same libertarian thesis:

1. *No one is anyone else's master, and no one is anyone else's slave.* Since I am the one to decide how my life is to be conducted just as you decide about yours, I have no right (even if I had the power) to make you my slave and be your master, nor have you the right to become the master by enslaving me. Slavery is *forced* servitude, and since no one owns the life of anyone else, no one has the right to enslave another. Political theories past and present have traditionally been concerned with who should be the master (usually the king, the dictator, or government bureaucracy) and who should be the slaves, and what the extent of the slavery should be. Libertarianism holds that no one has the right to. use force to enslave the life of another, or any portion or aspect of that life.

2. *Other men's lives are not yours to dispose of.* I enjoy seeing operas; but operas are expensive to produce. Opera-lovers often say, "The state (or the city, etc.) should subsidize opera, so that we can all see it. Also it would be for people's betterment, cultural benefit, etc." But what they are advocating is nothing more or less than legalized plunder. They can't pay for the productions themselves, and yet they want to see opera, which involves a large number of people and their labor; so what they are saying in effect is, "Get the money through legalized force. Take a little bit more out of every worker's pay-check every week to pay for the operas we want to see." But I have no right to take by force from the workers' pockets to pay for what I want.

Perhaps it would be better if he *did* go to see opera—then I should try to convince him to go voluntarily. But to take the money from him forcibly, because in my opinion it would be good for *him,* is still seizure of his earnings, which is plunder.

Besides, if I have the right to force him to help pay for my pet projects, hasn't he equally the right to force me to help pay for his? Perhaps he in turn wants the government to subsidize rock-and-roll,

From *"What Libertarianism Is,"* in The Libertarian Alternative, *edited by Tibor Machan (1974). Reprinted by permission of Nelson–Hall, Inc.*

or his new car, or a house in the country? If I have the right to milk him, why hasn't he the right to milk me? If I can be a moral cannibal, why can't he too?

We should beware of the inventors of utopias. They would remake the world according to their vision—with the lives and fruits of the labor of *other* human beings. Is it someone's utopian vision that others should build pyramids to beautify the landscape? Very well, then other men should provide the labor; and if he is in a position of political power, and he can't get men to do it voluntarily, then he must *compel* them to "cooperate"—i.e. he must enslave them.

A hundred men might gain great pleasure from beating up or killing just one insignificant human being; but other men's lives are not theirs to dispose of. "In order to achieve the worthy goals of the next five-year-plan, we must forcibly collectivize the peasants . . ."; but other men's lives are not theirs to dispose of. Do you want to occupy, rent-free, the mansion that another man has worked for twenty years to buy? But other men's lives are not yours to dispose of. Do you want operas so badly that everyone is forced to work harder to pay for their subsidization through taxes? But other men's lives are not yours to dispose of. Do you want to have free medical care at the expense of other people, whether they wish to provide it or not? But this would require them to work longer for you whether they want to or not, and other men's lives are not yours to dispose of. . . .

3. *No human being should be a nonvoluntary mortgage on the life of another.* I cannot claim your life, your work, or the products of your effort as mine. The fruit of one man's labor should not be fair game for every freeloader who comes along and demands it as his own. The orchard that has been carefully grown, nurtured, and harvested by its owner should not be ripe for the plucking for any bypasser who has a yen for the ripe fruit. The wealth that some men have produced should not be fair game for looting by government, to be used for whatever purposes its representatives determine, no matter what their motives in so doing may be. The theft of your money by a robber is not justified by the fact that he used it to help his injured mother.

It will already be evident that libertarian doctrine is embedded in a view of the rights of man. Each human being has the right to live his life as he chooses, compatibly with the equal right of all other human beings to live their lives as they choose.

All man's rights are implicit in the above statement. Each man has the right to life: any attempt by others to take it away from him, or even to injure him, violates this right, through the use of coercion against him. Each man has the right to liberty: to conduct his life in accordance with the alternatives open to him without coercive action by others. And every man has the right to property: to work to sustain his life (and the lives of whichever others he chooses to sustain, such as his family) and to retain the fruits of his labor.

People often defend the rights of life and liberty but denigrate property rights, and yet the right to property is as basic as the other two: indeed, without property rights no other rights are possible. Depriving you of property is depriving you of the means by which you live. . . .

I have no right to decide how *you* should spend your time or your money. I can make that decision for myself, but not for you, my neighbor. I may deplore your choice of life-style, and I may talk with you about it provided you are willing to listen to me. But I have no right to use force to change it. Nor have I the right to decide how you should spend the money you have earned. I may appeal to you to give it to the Red Cross, and you may prefer to go to prize-fights. But that is your decision, and however much I may chafe about it I do not have the right to interfere forcibly with it, for example by robbing you in order to use the money in accordance with *my* choices. (If I have the right to rob you, have you also the right to rob me?)

When I claim a right, I carve out a niche, as it were, in my life, saying in effect, "This activity I must be able to perform without interference from others. For you and everyone else, this is off limits." And so I put up a "no trespassing" sign, which marks off the area of my right. Each individual's right is his "no trespassing" sign in relation to me and others. I may not encroach upon his domain any more than he upon mine, without my consent. Every right entails a duty, true—but the duty is only that of *forbearance*— that is, of *refraining* from violating the other person's right. If you have a right to life, I have no right to take your life; if you have a right to the products of your labor (property), I have no right to take it from you without your consent. The nonviolation of these rights will not guarantee you protection against natural catastrophes such as floods and earthquakes, but it will protect you against the aggressive activities *of other men*. And rights, after all, have to do with one's relations to other human beings, not with one's relations to physical nature.

Nor were these rights created by government; governments—some governments, obviously not all—*recognize* and *protect* the rights that individuals already have. Governments regularly forbid homicide and theft; and, at a more advanced stage, protect individuals against such things as libel and breach of contract. . . .

The *right to property* is the most misunderstood and unappreciated of human rights, and it is one most constantly violated by governments. "Property" of course does not mean only real estate; it includes anything you can call your own—your clothing, your car, your jewelry, your books and papers.

The right of property is not the right to just *take* it from others, for this would interfere with *their* property rights. It is rather the right to work for it, to obtain non-coercively, the money or services which you can present in voluntary exchange.

The right to property is consistently underplayed by intellectuals today, sometimes even frowned upon, as if we should feel guilty for upholding such a right in view of all the poverty in the world. But the right to property is absolutely basic. It is your hedge against the future. It is your assurance that what you have worked to earn will still be there and be yours, when you wish or need to use it, especially when you are too old to work any longer.

Government has always been the chief enemy of the right to property. The officials of government, wishing to increase their power, and finding an increase of wealth an effective way to bring this about, seize some or all of what a person has earned—and since government has a monopoly of physical force within the geographical area of the nation, it has the power (but not the right) to do this. When this happens, of course, every citizen of that country is insecure: he knows that no matter how hard he works the government can swoop down on him at any time and confiscate his earnings and possessions. A person sees his life savings wiped out in a moment when the tax-collectors descend to deprive him of the fruits of his work; or, an industry which has been fifty years in the making and cost millions of dollars and millions of hours of time and planning, is nationalized overnight. Or the government, via inflation, cheapens the currency, so that hard-won dollars aren't worth anything any more. The effect of such actions, of course, is that people lose hope and incentive: if no matter how hard they work the government agents can take it all away, why bother to work at all, for more than today's needs? Depriving people of property is *depriving them of the means by which they live*—the freedom of the individual citizen to do what he wishes with his own life and to plan for the future. Indeed only if property rights are respected is there any point to planning for the future and working to achieve one's goals. *Property rights are what makes long-range planning possible*—the kind of planning which is a distinctively human endeavor, as opposed to the day-to-day activity of the lion who hunts, who depends on the supply of game tomorrow but has no real insurance against starvation in a day or a week. Without the right to property, the right to life itself amounts to little: how can you sustain your life if you cannot plan ahead? and how can you plan ahead if the fruits of your labor can at any moment by confiscated by government? . . .

Indeed, the right to property may well be considered second only to the right to life. Even the freedom of speech is limited by considerations of property. If a person visiting in your home behaves in a way undesired by you, you have every right to evict him; he can scream or agitate elsewhere if he wishes, but not in your home without your consent. Does a person have a right to shout obscenities in a cathedral? No, for the owners of the cathedral (presumably the Church) have not allowed others on their property for that purpose; one may go there to worship or to visit, but not just for any purpose one wishes. Their property right is prior to your or my wish to scream or expectorate or write graffiti on their building. Or, to take the stock example, does a person have a right to shout "Fire!" falsely in a crowded theater? No, for the theater owner has permitted others to enter and use his property only for a specific purpose, that of seeing a film or watching a stage show. If a person heckles or otherwise disturbs other members of the audience, he can be thrown out. (In fact, he can be removed for any reason the owner chooses, provided his admission money is returned.) And if he shouts "Fire!" when there is no fire, he may be endangering other lives by causing a panic or a stampede. The right to free speech doesn't give one the right to say anything anywhere; it is circumscribed by property rights.

Again, some people seem to assume that the right of free speech (including written speech) means that they can go to a newspaper publisher and demand that he print in his newspaper some propaganda or policy statement for their political party (or other group). But of course they have no right to the use of his newspaper. Ownership of the newspaper is the product of his labor, and he has a right to put into his newspaper whatever he wants, for whatever reason. If he excludes material which many readers would like to have in, perhaps they can find it in another newspaper or persuade him to print it himself (if there are enough of them, they will usually do just that). Perhaps they can even cause his newspaper to fail. But as long as he owns it, he has the right to put in it what he wishes; what would a property right be if he could not do this? They have no right to place their material in his newspaper without his consent—not for free, nor even for a fee. Perhaps other newspapers will include it, or perhaps they can start their own newspaper (in which case they have a right to put in it what they like). If not, an option open to them would be to mimeograph and distribute some handbills.

In exactly the same way, no one has a right to "free television time" unless the owner of the television station consents to give it; it is his station, he has the property rights over it, and it is for him to decide how to dispose of his time. He may not decide wisely, but it is his right to decide as he wishes. If he makes enough unwise decisions, and courts enough unpopularity with the viewing public or the sponsors, he may have to go out of business; but as he is free to make his own decisions, so is he free to face their consequences. (If the government owns the television station, then government officials will make the decisions, and there is no guarantee of *their* superior wisdom. The difference is that when "the government" owns the station, you are forced to help pay for its upkeep through your taxes, whether the bureaucrat in charge decides to give you television time or not.)

"But why have *individual* property rights? Why not have lands and houses owned by everybody together?" Yes, this involves no violation of individual rights, as long as everybody consents to this arrangement and no one is forced to join it. The parties to it may enjoy the communal living enough (at least for a time) to overcome certain inevitable problems: that some will work and some not, that some will achieve more in an hour than others can do in a day, and still they will all get the same income. The few who do the most will in the end consider themselves "workhorses" who do the work of two or three or twelve, while the others will be "freeloaders" on the efforts of these few. But as long as they can get out of the arrangement if they no longer like it, no violation of rights is involved. They got in voluntarily, and they can get out voluntarily; no one had used force.

"But why not say that everybody owns everything? That we *all* own everything there is?"

To some this may have a pleasant ring—but let us try to analyze what it means. If everybody owns everything, then everyone has an equal right to go everywhere, do what he pleases, take what he likes, destroy if he wishes, grow crops or burn them, trample them under, and so on. Consider what it would be like in practice. Suppose you have saved money to buy a house for yourself and your family. Now suppose that the principle, "everybody owns everything," becomes adopted. Well then, why shouldn't every itinerant hippie just come in and take over, sleeping in your beds and eating in your kitchen and not bothering to replace the food supply or clean up the mess? After all, it belongs to all of us, doesn't it? So we have just as much right to it as you, the buyer, have. What happens if we *all* want to sleep in the bedroom and there's not room for all of us? Is it the strongest who wins?

What would be the result? Since no one would be responsible for anything, the property would soon be destroyed, the food used up, the

facilities nonfunctional. Beginning as a house that *one* family could use, it would end up as a house that *no one* could use. And if the principle continued to be adopted, no one would build houses any more—or anything else. What for? They would only be occupied and used by others, without remuneration.

Suppose two men are cast ashore on an island, and they agree that each will cultivate half of it. The first man is industrious and grows crops and builds a shelter, making the most of the situation with which he is confronted. The second man, perhaps thinking that the warm days will last forever, lies in the sun, picks coconuts while they last, and does a minimum of work to sustain himself. At the time of harvest, the second man has nothing to harvest, nor does he assist the first man in his labors. But later when there is a dearth of food on the island, the second man comes to the first man and demands half of the harvest as his right. But of course he has no right to the product of the first man's labors. The first man may freely choose to give part of his harvest to the second out of charity rather than see him starve; but that is just what it is—charity, not the second man's right.

How can any of man's rights be violated? Ultimately, only by the use of force. I can make suggestions to you, I can reason with you, entreat you (if you are willing to listen), but I cannot *force* you without violating your rights; only by forcing you do I cut the cord between your free decisions and your actions. Voluntary relations between individuals involve no deprivation of rights, but murder, assault, and rape do, because in doing these things I make you the unwilling victim of my actions A man's beating his wife involves no violation of rights if she *wanted* to be beaten. *Force is behavior that requires the unwilling involvement of other persons.*

Thus the use of force need not involve the use of physical violence. If I trespass on your property or dump garbage on it, I am violating your property rights, as indeed I am when I steal your watch; although this is not force in the sense of violence, it *is* a case of your being an unwilling victim of my action. Similarly, if you shout at me so that I cannot be heard when I try to speak, or blow a siren in my ear, or start a factory next door which pollutes my land, you are again violating my rights (to free speech, to property); I am, again, an unwilling victim of your actions. Similarly, if you steal a manuscript of mine and publish it as your own, you are confiscating a piece if my property and thus violating my right to keep what is the product of my labor. Of course, if I give you the manuscript with permission to sign your name to it and keep the proceeds, no violation of rights is involved—any more than if I give you permission to dump garbage on my yard.

According to libertarianism, the role of government should be limited to the retaliatory use of force against those who have initiated its use. It should not enter into any other areas such as religion, social organization, and economics.

Government

Government is the most dangerous institution known to man. Throughout history it has violated the rights of men more than any individual or groups of individuals could do: it has killed people, enslaved them, sent them to forced labor and concentration camps, and regularly robbed and pillaged them of the fruits of their expended labor. Unlike individual criminals, government has the power to arrest and try; unlike individual criminals, it can surround and encompass a person totally, dominating every aspect of one's life, so that one has no recourse from it but to leave the country (and in totalitarian nations even that is prohibited). Government throughout history has a much sorrier record than any individual, even that of a ruthless mass murderer. The signs we see on bumper stickers are chillingly accurate: "Beware: the Government Is Armed and Dangerous."

The only proper role of government, according to libertarians, is that of the protector of the citizen against aggression by other individuals. The government, of course, should never initiate aggression; its proper role is as the embodiment of the *retaliatory* use of force against anyone who initiates its use.

If each individual had constantly to defend himself against possible aggressors, he would have to spend a considerable portion of his life in target practice, karate exercises, and other means of self-defense, and even so he would probably be helpless against groups of individuals who might try to kill, maim, or rob him. He would have little time for cultivating those qualities which are essential to civilized life, nor would improvements in science, medicine, and the arts be likely to occur. The function of government is to take this responsibility off his shoulders: the government undertakes to defend him against aggressors and to punish them if they attack him. When the government is effective in doing this, it enables the citizen to go about his business unmolested and without constant fear for his life. To do this, of course, government must have physical power—the police, to protect the citizen from aggression within its borders, and the armed forces, to protect him from aggressors outside. Beyond that, the government should not intrude upon his life, either to run his business, or adjust his daily activities, or prescribe his personal moral code.

Government, then, undertakes to be the individual's protector; but historically governments have gone far beyond this function. Since they already have the physical power, they have not hesitated to use it for purposes far beyond that which was entrusted to them in the first place. Undertaking initially to protect its citizens against aggression, it has often itself become an aggressor—a far greater aggressor, indeed, than the criminals against whom it was supposed to protect its citizens. Governments have done what no private citizen can do: arrest and imprison individuals without a trial and send them to slave labor camps. Government must have power in order to be effective—and yet the very means by which alone it can be effective make it vulnerable to the abuse of power, leading to managing the lives of individuals and even inflicting terror upon them.

What then should be the function of government? In a word, the *protection of human rights*.

1. *The right to life:* libertarians support all such legislation as will protect human beings against the use of force by others, for example, laws against killing, attempting killing, maiming, beating, and all kinds of physical violence.
2. *The right to liberty:* there should be no laws compromising in any way freedom of speech, of the press, and peaceable assembly. There should be no censorship of ideas, books, films, or of anything else by government.
3. *The right to property:* libertarians support legislation that protects the property rights of individuals against confiscation, nationalization, eminent domain, robbery, trespass, fraud and misrepresentation, patent and copyright, libel and slander.

Someone has violently assaulted you. Should he be legally liable? Of course. He has violated one of your rights. He has knowingly injured you and since he has initiated aggression against you he should be made to expiate.

Someone has negligently left his bicycle on the sidewalk where you trip over it in the dark and injure yourself. He didn't do it intentionally; he didn't mean you any harm. Should he be legally liable? Of course; he has, however unwittingly, injured you, and since the injury is caused by him and you are the victim, he should pay.

Someone across the street is unemployed. Should you be taxed extra to pay for his expenses? Not at all. You have not injured him, you are not responsible for the fact that he is unemployed (unless you are a senator or bureaucrat who agitated for further curtailing of business, which legislation passed, with the result that your neighbor was laid off by the curtailed busi-

ness). You may voluntarily wish to help him out, or better still, try to get him a job to put him on his feet again; but since you have initiated no aggressive act against him, and neither purposely nor accidentally injured him in any way, you should not be legally penalized for the fact of his unemployment. (Actually, it is just such penalties that increase unemployment.)

One man, A, works hard for years and finally earns a high salary as a professional man. A second man, B, prefers not to work at all, and to spend wastefully what money he has (through inheritance), so that after a year or two he has nothing left. At the end of this time he has a long siege of illness and lots of medical bills to pay. He demands that the bills be paid by the government—that is, by the taxpayers of the land, including Mr. A.

But of course B has no such right. He chose to lead his life in a certain way—that was his voluntary decision. One consequence of that choice is that he must depend on charity in case of later need. Mr. A chose not to live that way. (And if everyone lived like Mr. B, on whom would he depend in case of later need?) Each has a right to live in the way he pleases, but each must live with the consequences of his own decision (which, as always, fall primarily on himself). He cannot, in time of need, claim A's beneficence as his right.

If a house-guest of yours starts to carve his initials in your walls and break up your furniture, you have a right to evict him, and call the police if he makes trouble. If someone starts to destroy the machinery in a factory, the factory-owner is also entitled to evict him and call the police. In both cases, persons other than the owner are permitted on the property only under certain conditions, at the pleasure of the owner. If those conditions are violated, the owner is entitled to use force to set things straight. The case is exactly the same on a college or university campus: if a campus demonstrator starts breaking windows, occupying the president's office, and setting fire to a dean, the college authorities

But do both ppl. really have the same opportunity?

are certainly within their rights to evict him forcibly; one is permitted on the college grounds only under specific conditions, set by the administration: study, peaceful student activity, even political activity if those in charge choose to permit it. If they do not choose to permit peaceful political activity on campus, they may be unwise, since a campus is after all a place where all sides of every issue should get discussed, and the college that doesn't permit this may soon lose its reputation and its students. All the same, the college official who does not permit it is quite within his rights; the students do not own the campus, nor do the hired troublemakers imported from elsewhere. In the case of a privately owned college, the owners, or whoever they have delegated to administer it, have the right to make the decisions as to who shall be permitted on the campus and under what conditions. In the case of a state university or college, the ownership problem is more complex: one could say that the "government" owns the campus or that "the people" do since they are the taxpayers who support it; but in either case, the university administration has the delegated task of keeping order, and until they are removed by the state administration or the taxpayers, it is theirs to decide who shall be permitted on campus, and what nonacademic activities will be permitted to their students on the premises.

Property rights can be violated by physical trespass, of course, or by anyone entering on your property for any reason without your consent. (If you *do* consent to having your neighbor dump garbage on your yard, there is no violation of your rights.) But the physical trespass of a person is only a special case of violation of property rights. Property rights can be violated by sound-waves, in the form of a loud noise, or the sounds of your neighbor's hi-fi set while you are trying to sleep. Such violations of property rights are of course the subject of action in the courts.

But there is another violation of property rights that has not thus far been honored by the courts; this has to do with the effects of *pollution* of the atmosphere.

From the beginnings of modern air pollution, the courts made a conscious decision not to protect, for example, the orchards of farmers from the smoke of nearby factories or locomotives. They said, in effect, to the farmers: yes, your private property is being invaded by this smoke, but we hold that "public policy" is more important than private property, and public policy holds factories and locomotives to be good things. These goods were allowed to override the defense of property rights—with our consequent headlong rush into pollution disaster. The remedy is both "radical" and crystal clear, and it has nothing to do with multibillion dollar palliative programs at the expense of the taxpayers which do not even meet the real issue. The remedy is simply to enjoin anyone from injecting pollutants into the air, and thereby invading the rights of persons and property. Period. The argument that such an injunction prohibition would add to the costs of industrial production is as reprehensible as the pre-Civil War argument that the abolition of slavery would add to the costs of growing cotton, and therefore should not take place. For this means that the polluters are able to impose the high costs of pollution upon those whose property rights they are allowed to invade with impunity.[1]

What about automobiles, the chief polluters of the air? One can hardly sue every automobile owner. But one can sue the manufacturers of automobiles who do not install anti-smog devices on the cars which they distribute—and later (though this is more difficult), owners of individual automobiles if they discard the equipment or do not keep it functional.

The violation of rights does not apply only to air-pollution. If someone with a factory upstream on a river pollutes the river, anyone living downstream from him, finding his water polluted, should be able to sue the owner of the factory. In this way the price of adding the anti-pollutant devices will be the owner's responsibility, and will probably be added to the cost of the products which the factory produces and thus spread around among all consumers, rather than the entire cost being borne by the users of the river in the form of polluted water, with the consequent impossibility of fishing, swimming, and so on. In each case, pollution would be stopped at the source rather than having its ill effects spread around to numerous members of the population.

What about property which you do not work to earn, but which you *inherit* from someone else? Do you have a right to that? You have no right to it until someone decides to give it to you. Consider the man who willed it to you; it was his, he had the right to use and dispose of it as *he* saw fit; and if he decided to give it to you, this is a windfall for you, but it was only the exercise of *his* right. Had the property been seized by the government at the man's death, or distributed among numerous other people designated by the government, it *would* have been a violation of his rights: for he, who worked to earn and sustain it, would not have been able to dispose of it according to his own judgment. If he doesn't have the right to determine who shall have it, who does?

What about the property status of your intellectual activity, such as inventions you may devise and books you write? These, of course, are your property also; they are the products of your mind; you worked at them, you created them. Prior to that, they did not exist. If you worked five years to write a book, and someone stole it and published it as his own, receiving royalties from its sales, he would have stolen your property just as surely as if he had robbed your home. The same is true if someone used and sold without your permission an invention which was the product of your labor and ingenuity.

The role of government with respect to this issue, at least most governments of the Western world, is a proper one: government protects the products of your labor from the moment they materialize. Copyright law protects your writings from piracy. In the United States, one's writings are protected for a period of twenty-seven years, and another twenty-seven if one applies for renewal of the copyright. In most other countries, they are protected for a period of fifty years after the author's death, permitting both himself and his surviving heirs to reap the fruits of his labor. After that they enter the "public domain"—that is, anyone may reprint them without your or your heir's permission. Patent law protects your inventions for a limited period, which varies according to the type of invention. In no case are you forced to avail yourself of this protection; you need not apply for patent or copyright coverage if you do not wish to do so. But the protection of your intellectual property is there, in case you wish to use it.

What about the property status of the airwaves? Here the government's position is far more questionable. The government now claims ownership of the airwaves, leasing them to individuals and corporations. The government renews leases or refuses them depending on whether the programs satisfy authorities in the Federal Communications Commission. The official position is that "we all own the airwaves"; but since only one party can broadcast on a certain frequency at a certain time without causing chaos, it is simply a fact of reality that "everyone" cannot use it. In fact the government decides who shall use the airwaves and one courts its displeasure only at the price of a revoked license. One can write without government approval, but one cannot use the airwaves without the approval of government.

What policy should have been observed with regard to the airwaves? Much the same as the policy that was followed in the case of the Homestead Act, when the lands of the American West were opening up for settlement. There was a policy of "first come, first served," with the government parcelling out a certain acreage for each individual who wanted to claim the land as his own. There was no charge for the land, but if a man had not used it and built a dwelling during the first two-year period, it was assumed that he was not homesteading and the land was given to the next man in line. The airwaves too could have been given out on a "first come, first served" basis. The first man who used a given frequency would be its owner, and the government would protect him in the use of it against trespassers. If others wanted to use the same frequency, they would have to buy it from the first man, if he was willing to sell, or try to buy another, just as one now does with the land.

Laws may be classified into three types: (1) laws protecting individuals against themselves, such as laws against fornication and other sexual behavior, alcohol, and drugs; (2) laws protecting individuals against aggressions by other individuals, such as laws against murder, robbery, and fraud; (3) laws requiring people to help one another; for example, all laws which rob Peter to pay Paul, such as welfare.

Libertarians reject the first class of laws totally. Behavior which harms no one else is strictly the individual's own affair. Thus, there should be no laws against becoming intoxicated, since whether or not to become intoxicated is the individual's own decision: but there should be laws against driving while intoxicated, since the drunken driver is a threat to every other motorist on the highway (drunken driving falls into type 2). Similarly, there should be no laws against drugs (except the prohibition of sale of drugs to minors) as long as the taking of these drugs poses no threat to anyone else. Drug addiction is a psychological problem to which no present solution exists. Most of the social harm caused by addicts, other than to themselves, is the result of thefts which they perform in order to continue their habit—and then the *legal* crime is the theft, not the addiction. The actual cost of heroin is about ten cents a shot; if it were legalized, the enormous traffic in illegal sale and purchase of it would stop, as well as the accompanying proselytization to get new addicts (to make more money for the pusher) and the thefts performed by addicts who often require eighty dollars a day just to keep up the habit. Addiction would not

stop, but the crimes would: it is estimated that 75 percent of the burglaries in New York City today are performed by addicts, and all these crimes could be wiped out at one stroke though the legalization of drugs. (Only when the taking of drugs could be shown to constitute a threat to *others*, should it be prohibited by law. It is only laws protecting people against *themselves* that libertarians oppose.)

Laws should be limited to the second class only: aggression by individuals against other individuals. These are laws whose function is to protect human beings against encroachment by others; and this, as we have seen, is (according to libertarianism) the sole function of government.

Libertarians also reject the third class of laws totally: no one should be forced by law to help others, not even to tell them the time of day if requested, and certainly not to give them a portion of one's weekly paycheck. Governments, in the guise of humanitarianism, have given to some by taking from others (charging a "handling fee" in the process, which, because of the government's waste and inefficiency, sometimes is several hundred percent). And in so doing they have decreased incentive, violated the rights of individuals and lowered the standard of living of almost everyone.

All such laws constitute what libertarians call *moral cannibalism.* A cannibal in the physical sense is a person who lives off the flesh of other human beings. A *moral* cannibal is one who believes he has a right to live off the "spirit" of other human beings—who believes that he has a moral claim on the productive capacity, time, and effort expended by others.

It has become fashionable to claim virtually everything that one needs or desires as one's *right.* Thus, many people claim that they have a right to a job, the right to free medical care, to free food and clothing, to a decent home, and so on. Now if one asks, apart from any specific context, whether it would be desirable if everyone had these things, one might well say yes. But there is a gimmick attached to each of them: *At whose expense?* Jobs, medical care, education, and so on, don't grow on trees. These are goods and services *produced only by men*. Who then is to provide them, and under what conditions?

If you have a right to a job, who is to supply it? Must an employer supply it even if he doesn't want to hire you? What if you are unemployable, or incurably lazy? (If you say "the government must supply it," does that mean that a job must be created for you which no employer needs done, and that you must be kept in it regardless of how much or little you work?) If the employer is forced to supply it at his expense even if he doesn't need you, then isn't *he* being enslaved to that extent? What ever happened to *his* right to conduct his life and his affairs in accordance with his choices?

If you have a right to free medical care, then, since medical care doesn't exist in nature as wild apples do, some people will have to supply it to you for free: that is, they will have to spend their time and money and energy taking care of you whether they want to or not. What ever happened to *their* right to conduct their lives as they see fit? Or do you have a right to violate theirs? Can there be a right to violate rights?

All those who demand this or that as a "free service" are consciously or unconsciously evading the fact that there is in reality no such thing as free services. All man-made goods and services are the result of human expenditure of time and effort. There is no such thing as "something for nothing" in this world. If you demand something free, you are demanding that other men give their time and effort to you without compensation. If they voluntarily choose to do this, there is no problem; but if you demand that they be *forced* to do it, you are interfering with their right not to do it if they so choose. "Swimming in this pool ought to be free!" says the indignant passerby. What he means is that others should

build a pool, others should provide the material and still others should run it and keep it in functioning order, so that *he* can use it without fee. But what right has he to the expenditure of *their* time and effort? To expect something "for free" is to expect it *to be paid for by others* whether they choose to or not.

Many questions, particularly about economic matters, will be generated by the libertarian account of human rights and the role of government. Should government have a role in assisting the needy, in providing social security, in legislating minimum wages, in fixing prices and putting a ceiling on rents, in curbing monopolies, in erecting tariffs, in guaranteeing jobs, in managing the money supply? To these and all similar questions the libertarian answers with an equivocal no.

"But then you'd let people go hungry!" comes the rejoinder. This, the libertarian insists, is precisely what would not happen; with the restrictions removed, the economy would flourish as never before. With the controls taken off business, existing enterprises would expand and new ones would spring into existence satisfying more and more consumer needs; millions more people would be gainfully employed instead of subsisting on welfare, and all kinds of research and production, released from the stranglehold of government, would proliferate, fulfilling man's needs and desires as never before. It has always been so whenever government has permitted men to be free traders on a free market. But *why* this is so, and how the free market is the best solution to all problems relating to the material aspect of man's life, is another and far longer story.

NOTE

1. Murray Rothbard, "The Great Ecology Issue," *The Individualist*, 2, no. 2 (Feb. 1970), p. 5.

2   From Liberty to Welfare

JAMES P. STERBA

LIBERTARIANS TODAY are deeply divided over whether a night watchman state can be morally justified. Some, like Robert Nozick, hold that a night watchman state would tend to arise by an invisible-hand process if people generally respected each other's Lockean rights.[1] Others, like Murray Rothbard, hold that even the free and informed consent of all the members of a society would not justify such a state.[2] Despite this disagreement, libertarians are strongly united in opposition to welfare rights and the welfare state. According to Nozick, "the state may not use its coercive apparatus for the purpose of getting some citizens to aid others."[3] For Rothbard, "the libertarian position calls for the complete abolition of governmental welfare and reliance on private charitable aid."[4] Here I argue that this libertarian opposition to welfare rights and a welfare state is ill-founded. Welfare rights can be given a libertarian justification, and once this is recognized, a libertarian argument for a welfare state, unlike libertarian arguments for the night watchman state, is both straightforward and compelling. . . .

Libertarians have defended their view in basically two different ways. Some libertarians, following Herbert Spencer, have 1) defined liberty as the absence of constraints, 2) taken a right to liberty to be the ultimate political ideal, and 3) derived all other rights from this right to liberty. Other libertarians, following John Locke, have 1) taken a set of rights, including, typically, a right to life or self-ownership and a right to property, to be the ultimate political ideal, 2) defined liberty as the absence of constraints in the exercise of these fundamental rights, and 3) derived all other rights including a right to liberty, from these fundamental rights.

Each of these approaches has its difficulties. The principal difficulty with the first approach is that unless one arbitrarily restricts what is to count as an interference, conflicting liberties will abound, particularly in all areas of social life.[5] The principal difficulty with the second approach is that as long as a person's rights have not been violated, her liberty would not have been restricted either, even if she were kept in prison for the rest of her days.[6] I don't propose to try to decide between these two approaches. What I do want to show, however, is that on either approach welfare rights and a welfare state are morally required.

Spencerian Libertarianism

Thus suppose we were to adopt the view of those libertarians who take a right to liberty to be the ultimate political ideal. According to this view, liberty is usually defined as follows:

The Want Conception of Liberty: Liberty is being unconstrained by other persons from doing what one wants.

This conception limits the scope of liberty in two ways. First, not all constraints whatever their

From Social Theory and Practice, *vol. 11, no. 3 (fall 1985), pp. 285–305, with revisions.*

source count as a restriction of liberty; the constraints must come from other persons. For example, people who are constrained by natural forces from getting to the top of Mount Everest do not lack liberty in this regard. Second, constraints that have their source in other persons, but that do not run counter to an individual's wants, constrain without restricting that individual's liberty. Thus, for people who do not want to hear Beethoven's Fifth Symphony, the fact that others have effectively proscribed its performance does not restrict their liberty, even though it does constrain what they are able to do.

Of course, libertarians may wish to argue that even such constraints can be seen to restrict a person's liberty once we take into account the fact that people normally want, or have a general desire, to be unconstrained by others. But other philosophers have thought that the possibility of such constraints points to a serious defect in this conception of liberty, which can only be remedied by adopting the following broader conception of liberty:

> The Ability Conception of Liberty: Liberty is being unconstrained by other persons from doing what one is able to do.

Applying this conception to the above example, we find that people's liberty to hear Beethoven's Fifth Symphony would be restricted even if they did not want to hear it (and even if, perchance, they did not want to be unconstrained by others) since other people would still be constraining them from doing what they are able to do. . . .

Of course, there will be numerous liberties determined by the Ability Conception that are not liberties according to the Want Conception. For example, there will be highly talented students who do not want to pursue careers in philosophy, even though no one constrains them from doing so. Accordingly, the Ability Conception but not the Want Conception would view them as possessing a liberty. And even though such liberties are generally not as valuable as those liberties that are common to both conceptions, they still

are of some value, even when the manipulation of people's wants is not at issue.

Yet even if we accept all the liberties specified by the Ability Conception, problems of interpretation still remain. The major problem in this regard concerns what is to count as a constraint. On the one hand, libertarians would like to limit constraints to positive acts (that is, acts of commission) that prevent people from doing what they are otherwise able to do. On the other hand, . . . liberal [democrats] and socialists interpret constraints to include, in addition, negative acts (that is, of omission) that prevent people from doing what they are otherwise able to do. In fact, this is one way to understand the debate between defenders of "negative liberty" and defenders of "positive liberty." For defenders of negative liberty would seem to interpret constraints to include only positive acts of others that prevent people from doing what they otherwise are able to do, while defenders of positive liberty would seem to interpret constraints to include both positive and negative acts of others that prevent people from doing what they are otherwise able to do.[8]

Suppose we interpret constraints in the manner favored by libertarians to include only positive acts by others that prevent people from doing what they are otherwise able to do, and let us consider a typical conflict situation between the rich and the poor.

In this conflict situation, the rich, of course, have more than enough resources to satisfy their basic needs. By contrast, the poor lack the resources to meet their most basic nutritional needs even though they have tried all the means available to them that libertarians regard as legitimate for acquiring such resources. Under circumstances like these, libertarians usually maintain that the rich should have the liberty to use their resources to satisfy their luxury needs if they so wish. Libertarians recognize that this liberty might well be enjoyed at the expense of the satisfaction of the most basic nutritional needs of the poor. Libertarians just think that a right to liberty

(The right to equal opportunity)

always has priority over other political ideals, and since they assume that the liberty of the poor is not at stake in such conflict situations, it is easy for them to conclude that the rich should not be required to sacrifice their liberty so that the basic nutritional needs of the poor may be met.

From a consideration of the liberties involved, libertarians claim to derive a number of more specific requirements, in particular, a right to life, a right to freedom of speech, press and assembly, and a right to property.

Here it is important to observe that the libertarian's right to life is not a right to receive from others the goods and resources necessary for preserving one's life; it is simply a right not to be killed unjustly. Correspondingly, the libertarian's right to property is not a right to receive from others the goods and resources necessary for one's welfare, but rather a right to acquire goods and resources either by initial acquisition or by voluntary agreement.

Rights such as these, libertarians claim, can at best support only a limited role for government. That role is simply to prevent and punish initial acts of coercion—the only wrongful actions for libertarians. And, as we noted before, libertarians are deeply divided over whether a government with even such a limited role, that is, a night watchman state, can be morally justified.

Of course, libertarians would allow that it would be nice of the rich to share their surplus resources with the poor. Nevertheless, according to libertarians, such acts of charity should not be coercively required, because the liberty of the poor is not thought to be at stake in such conflict situations.

In fact, however, the liberty of the poor is at stake in such conflict situations. What is at stake is the liberty of the poor to take from the surplus possessions of the rich what is necessary to satisfy their basic nutritional needs. When libertarians are brought to see that this is the case, they are often genuinely surprised, for they had not previously seen the conflict between the rich and the poor as a conflict of liberties.[9]

When the conflict between the rich and the poor is viewed as a conflict of liberties, we can either say that the rich should have the liberty to use their surplus resources for luxury purposes, or we can say that the poor should have the liberty to take from the rich what they require to meet their basic nutritional needs. If we choose one liberty, we must reject the other. What needs to be determined, therefore, is which liberty is morally preferable: the liberty of the rich or the liberty of the poor.

I submit that the liberty of the poor, which is the liberty to take from the surplus resources of others what is required to meet one's basic nutritional needs, is morally preferable to the liberty of the rich, which is the liberty to use one's surplus resources for luxury purposes. To see that this is the case we need only appeal to one of the most fundamental principles of morality, one that is common to all political perspectives, namely, the "ought" implies "can" principle. According to this principle, people are not morally required to do what they lack the power to do or what would involve so great a sacrifice that it would be unreasonable to ask them to perform such an action.[10] For example, suppose I promised to attend a meeting on Friday, but on Thursday I am involved in a serious car accident which puts me into a coma. Surely it is no longer the case that I ought to attend the meeting now that I lack the power to do so. Or suppose instead that on Thursday I develop a severe case of pneumonia for which I am hospitalized. Surely I could legitimately claim that I no longer ought to attend the meeting on the grounds that the risk to my health involved in attending is a sacrifice that it would be unreasonable to ask me to bear.

Now applying the "ought" implies "can" principle to the case at hand, it seems clear that the poor have it within their power to willingly relinquish such an important liberty as the liberty to take from the rich what they require to meet their basic nutritional needs. Nevertheless, it would be unreasonable to require them to make so great a sacrifice. In the extreme case, it would involve requiring the poor to sit back and starve to death. Of course, the poor may have no real alternative to relinquishing this liberty. To do anything else may involve worse consequences for themselves and their loved ones and may invite a painful death. Accordingly, we may expect that the poor would acquiesce, albeit unwillingly, to a political system that denied them the welfare rights supported by such a liberty, at the same time that we recognize that such a system imposed an unreasonable sacrifice upon the poor—a sacrifice that we could not morally blame the poor for trying to evade.[11] Analogously, we might expect that a woman whose life was threatened would submit to a rapist's demands, at the same time that we recognize the utter unreasonableness of those demands.

By contrast, it would not be unreasonable to require the rich to sacrifice the liberty to meet some of their luxury needs so that the poor can have the liberty to meet their basic nutritional needs. Naturally, we might expect that the rich for reasons of self-interest and past contribution might be disinclined to make such a sacrifice. We might even suppose that the past contribution of the rich provides a good reason for not sacrificing their liberty to use their surplus for luxury purposes. Yet, unlike the poor, the rich could not claim that relinquishing such a liberty involved so great a sacrifice that it would be unreasonable to require them to make it; unlike the poor, the rich could be morally blameworthy for failing to make such a sacrifice.

Consequently, if we assume that however else we specify the requirements of morality, they cannot violate the "ought" implies "can" principle, it follows that, despite what libertarians claim, the right to liberty endorsed by libertarians actually favors the liberty of the poor over the liberty of the rich.

Yet couldn't libertarians object to this conclusion, claiming that it would be unreasonable to require the rich to sacrifice the liberty to meet some of their luxury needs so that the poor could have the liberty to meet their basic nutritional needs? As I have pointed out, libertarians don't usually see the situation as a conflict of liberties, but suppose they did. How plausible would such an objection be? Not very plausible at all, I think.

Consider this: what are libertarians going to say about the poor? Isn't it clearly unreasonable to require the poor to sacrifice the liberty to meet their basic nutritional needs so that the rich can have the liberty to meet their luxury needs? Isn't it clearly unreasonable to require the poor to sit back and starve to death? If it is, then there is no resolution of this conflict that would be reasonable to require both the rich and the poor to accept. But that would mean that the libertarian ideal of liberty cannot be a moral ideal that resolves conflicts of interest in ways that it would be reasonable to require everyone affected to accept. Therefore, as long as libertarians think of themselves as putting forth such a moral ideal, they cannot allow that it would be unreasonable both to require the rich to sacrifice the liberty to meet some of their luxury needs in order to benefit the poor and to require the poor to sacrifice the liberty to meet their basic nutritional needs in order to benefit the rich. But I submit that if one of these requests is to be judged reasonable, then, by any neutral assessment, it must be the requirement that the rich sacrifice the liberty to meet some of their luxury needs so that the poor can have the liberty to meet their basic nutritional needs; there is no other plausible resolution, if libertarians intend to be putting forth a moral ideal that reasonably resolves conflicts of interest.

But might not libertarians hold that putting forth a moral ideal means no more than being willing to universalize one's fundamental commitments? Surely we have no difficulty imagining the rich willing to universalize their commitments to relatively strong property rights. Yet, at the same time, we have no difficulty imagining the poor and their advocates willing to universalize their commitments to relatively weak property rights. Consequently, if the libertarian's moral ideal is interpreted in this fashion, it would not be able to provide a basis for reasonably resolving conflicts of interest between the rich and the poor. But without such a basis for conflict resolution, how could societies flourish, as libertarians claim they would, under a minimal state or with no state at all?[12] Surely, in order for societies to flourish in this fashion, the libertarian ideal must resolve conflicts of interest in ways that it would be reasonable to require everyone affected to accept. But, as we have seen, that requirement can only be satisfied if the rich sacrifice the liberty to meet some of their luxury needs so that the poor can have the liberty to meet their basic nutritional needs.

It should also be noted that this case for restricting the liberty of the rich depends upon the willingness of the poor to take advantage of whatever opportunities are available to them for satisfying their basic needs by engaging in mutually beneficial work, so that failure of the poor to take advantage of such opportunities would normally either cancel or at least significantly reduce the obligation of the rich to restrict their own liberty for the benefit of the poor.[13] In addition, the poor would be required to return the equivalent of any surplus possessions they have taken from the rich once they are able to do so and still satisfy their basic needs. Nor would the poor be required to keep the liberty to which they are entitled. They could give up part of it, or all of it, or risk losing it on the chance of gaining a greater share of liberties or other social goods.[14] Consequently, the case for restricting the liberty of the rich for the benefit of the poor is neither unconditional nor inalienable.

Even so, libertarians would have to be disconcerted about what turns out to be the practical upshot of taking a right to liberty to be the ultimate political ideal. For libertarians contend that their political ideal would support welfare rights only when constraints are "illegitimately" interpreted to induce both positive and negative acts by others that prevent people from doing what they are otherwise able to do. By contrast, when constraints are interpreted to include only positive acts, libertarians contend, no such welfare rights can be justified.

Nevertheless, what the foregoing argument demonstrates is that this view is mistaken. For even when the interpretation of constraints favored by libertarians is employed, a moral assessment of the competing liberties still requires an allocation of liberties to the poor that will be generally sufficient to provide them with the goods and resources necessary for satisfying their basic nutritional needs.

One might think that once the rich realize that the poor should have the liberty not to be interfered with when taking from the surplus possessions of the rich what they require to satisfy their basic needs, it would be in the interest of the rich to stop producing any surplus whatsoever. Yet that would only be the case if first, the recognition of the rightful claims of the poor would exhaust the surplus of the rich and second, the poor would never be in a position to be obligated to repay what they appropriated from the rich. Fortunately for the poor both of these conditions are unlikely to obtain.

Of course, there will be cases where the poor fail to satisfy their basic nutritional needs, not because of any direct restriction of liberty on the part of the rich, but because the poor are in such dire need that they are unable even to attempt to take from the rich what they require to meet their basic nutritional needs. Accordingly, in such cases, the rich would not be performing any act of commission that prevents the poor from taking what they require. Yet, even in such cases, the rich would normally be performing acts of commission that prevent other persons from aiding the poor by taking from the surplus possessions of the rich. And when assessed from a moral point of view, restricting the liberty of these other persons would not be morally justified for the very same reason that restricting the liberty of the poor to meet their own basic nutritional needs would not be morally justified: it would not be reasonable to ask all of those affected to accept such a restriction of liberty. . . .

In brief, what this shows is that if a right to liberty is taken to be the ultimate political ideal, then, contrary to what libertarians claim, not only would a system of welfare rights be morally required, but also such a system would clearly benefit the poor.

Lockean Libertarianism

Yet suppose we were to adopt the view of those libertarians who do not take a right to liberty to be the ultimate political ideal. According to this view, liberty is defined as follows:

> *The Rights Conception of Liberty.* Liberty is being unconstrained by other persons from doing what one has a right to do.

The most important ultimate rights in terms of which liberty is specified are, according to this view, a right to life understood as a right not to be killed unjustly and a right to property understood as a right to acquire goods and resources either by initial acquisition or voluntary agreement. In order to evaluate this view, we must determine what are the practical implications of these rights.

Presumably, a right to life understood as a right not to be killed unjustly would not be violated by defensive measures designed to protect one's person from life-threatening attacks. Yet would this right be violated when the rich prevent the poor from taking what they require to satisfy their basic nutritional needs? Obviously, as a consequence of such preventive actions poor people sometimes do starve to death. Have the rich, then, in contributing to this result, killed the poor, or simply let them die; and, if they have killed the poor, have they done so unjustly?

Sometimes the rich, in preventing the poor from taking what they require to meet their basic nutritional needs, would not in fact be killing the poor, but only causing them to be physically or mentally debilitated. Yet since such preventive acts involve resisting the life-preserving activities of the poor, when the poor do die as a

consequence of such acts, it seems clear that the rich would be killing the poor, whether intentionally or unintentionally.

Of course, libertarians would want to argue that such killing is simply a consequence of the legitimate exercise of property rights, and hence, not unjust. But to understand why libertarians are mistaken in this regard, let us appeal again to that fundamental principle of morality, the "ought" implies "can" principle. In this context, the principle can be used to assess two opposing accounts of property rights. According to the first account, a right to property is not conditional upon whether other persons have sufficient opportunities and resources to satisfy their basic needs. This view holds that the initial acquisition and voluntary agreement of some can leave others, through no fault of their own, dependent upon charity for the satisfaction of their most basic needs. By contrast, according to the second account, initial acquisition and voluntary agreement can confer title of property on all goods and resources except those surplus goods and resources of the rich that are required to satisfy the basic needs of those poor who through no fault of their own lack opportunities and resources to satisfy their own basic needs.

Clearly, only the first of these two accounts of property rights would generally justify the killing of the poor as a legitimate exercise of the property rights of the rich. Yet it would be unreasonable to require the poor to accept anything other than some version of the second account of property rights. Moreover, according to the second account, it does not matter whether the poor would actually die or are only physically or mentally debilitated as a result of such acts of prevention. Either result would preclude property rights from arising. Of course, the poor may have no real alternative to acquiescing to a political system modeled after the first account of property rights, even though such a system imposes an unreasonable sacrifice upon them—a sacrifice that we could not blame them for trying to evade. At the same time, although the rich would be disinclined to do so, it would not be unreasonable to require them to accept a political system modeled after the second account of property rights—the account favored by the poor.

Consequently, if we assume that however else we specify the requirements of morality, they cannot violate the "ought" implies "can" principle, it follows that, despite what libertarians claim, the right to life and the right to property endorsed by libertarians actually support a system of welfare rights. . . .

Nevertheless, it might be objected that the welfare rights that have been established against the libertarian are not the same as the welfare rights endorsed by . . . liberal [democrats]. We could mark this difference by referring to the welfare rights that have been established against the libertarian as "action welfare rights" and referring to the welfare rights endorsed by liberal [democrats] as both "action and recipient welfare rights." The significance of this difference is that a person's action welfare right can be violated only when other people through acts of commission interfere with a person's exercise of that right, whereas a person's action and recipient welfare right can be violated by such acts of commission and by acts of omission as well. However, this difference will have little practical import. For once libertarians come to recognize the legitimacy of action welfare rights, then in order not to be subject to the poor person's discretion in choosing when and how to exercise her action welfare right, libertarians will tend to favor two morally legitimate ways of preventing the exercise of such rights. First, libertarians can provide the poor with mutually beneficial job opportunities. Second, libertarians can institute adequate recipient welfare rights that would take precedence over the poor's action welfare rights. Accordingly, if libertarians adopt either or both of these ways of legitimately preventing the poor from exercising their action welfare rights, libertarians will end up endorsing the same sort of welfare institutions favored by . . . liberal [democrats].

Finally, once a system of welfare rights is seen to follow irrespective of whether one takes a right to liberty or rights to life and property as the ultimate political ideal, the justification for a welfare state becomes straightforward and compelling. For while it is at least conceivable that rights other than welfare rights could be adequately secured in a society without the enforcement agencies of a state, it is inconceivable that welfare rights themselves could be adequately secured without such enforcement agencies. Only a welfare state would be able to effectively solve the large-scale coordination problem necessitated by the provision of welfare. Consequently, once a system of welfare rights can be seen to have a libertarian justification, the argument for a welfare state hardly seems to need stating.[15]

Libertarian Objections

In his book, *Individuals and their Rights,* Tibor Machan criticizes the preceding argument that a libertarian ideal of liberty leads to a right to welfare, accepting its theoretical thrust but denying its practical significance.[16] He appreciates the force of the argument enough to grant that if the type of conflict cases that we have described between the rich and the poor actually obtained, the poor would have a right to welfare. But he denies that such cases—in which the poor have done all that they legitimately can to satisfy their basic needs in a libertarian society—actually obtain. "Normally," he writes, "persons do not lack the opportunities and resources to satisfy their basic needs."[17]

But this response virtually concedes everything that the preceding argument intended to establish, for the poor's right to welfare is not claimed to be unconditional. Rather, it is said to be conditional principally upon the poor doing all that they legitimately can to meet their own basic needs. So it follows that only when the poor lack sufficient opportunity to satisfy their own basic needs would their right to welfare have any practical moral force. Accordingly, on libertarian grounds, Machan has conceded the legitimacy of just the kind of right to welfare that the preceding argument hoped to establish.

The only difference that remains is a practical one. Machan thinks that virtually all of the poor have sufficient opportunities and resources to satisfy their basic needs and that, therefore, a right to welfare has no practical moral force. In contrast, I think that many of the poor do not have sufficient opportunities and resources to satisfy their basic needs and that, therefore, a right to welfare has considerable practical moral force.

But isn't this practical disagreement resolvable? Who could deny that most of the 1.2 billion people who are currently living in conditions of absolute poverty "lack the opportunities and resources to satisfy their basic needs?"[18] And even within our own country, it is estimated that some 32 million Americans live below the official poverty index, and that one-fifth of American children are growing up in poverty.[19] Surely, it is impossible to deny that many of these Americans also "lack the opportunities and resources to satisfy their basic needs." Given the impossibility of reasonably denying these factual claims, Machan would have to concede that the right to welfare, which he grants can be theoretically established on libertarian premises, also has practical moral force.[20]

Douglas Rasmussen has developed another libertarian challenge to the previous argument that begins by conceding what Machan denied—that the poor lack the opportunity to satisfy their basic needs.[21] Rasmussen distinguishes two ways that this can occur. In one case, only a few of the poor lack the opportunity to satisfy their basic needs. Here, Rasmussen contends that libertarian property rights still apply even though the poor who are in need morally ought to take from the surplus property of the rich what they need for survival. Because libertarian property rights still apply, Rasmussen contends that the poor who do take from the legal property of the rich can be arrested and tried for their actions, but

what their punishment should be, Rasmussen contends, should simply be left up to judges to decide.[22] Rasmussen also rejects the suggestion that the law should make an exception for the poor in such cases on the grounds that one can never have perfect symmetry between what is moral and what the law requires.[23]

But why should the question of punishment be simply left up to judges to decide? If the judicial proceedings determine what is assumed in this case—that the poor morally ought to take from the legal property of the rich what they need for survival—then it is difficult to see on what grounds a judge could inflict punishment. Surely, if it would be unreasonable to require the poor to do anything contrary to meeting their basic needs at minimal cost to the rich, it would be equally unreasonable to punish the poor for actually doing just that—meeting their basic needs at minimal cost to the rich.

Nor will it do to claim that we cannot expect symmetry between what morality requires and what the law requires in this case. Of course, there is no denying that sometimes the law can justifiably require us to do what is morally wrong. In such cases opposing the law, even when what it requires is immoral, would do more harm than good. This can occur when there is a bona fide disagreement over whether what the law requires is morally wrong (for example, the *Roe* v. *Wade* decision), with those in favor of the law justifiably thinking that it is morally right and those against the law justifiably thinking that it is morally wrong. When this occurs, failing to obey the law, even when what it requires is immoral, could, by undermining the legal system, do more harm than good. However, in our case of severe conflict of interest between the rich and the poor, nothing of the sort obtains. In our case, it is judged that the poor morally ought to take from the legal property of the rich and that no other moral imperative favoring the rich overrides this moral imperative favoring the poor. So it is clear in this case that there are no grounds for upholding any asymmetry between what morality and the law require. Accordingly, the law in this case should be changed to favor the poor.

However, Rasmussen distinguishes another case in which many of the poor lack the opportunity to satisfy their basic needs.[24] In this case, so many of the poor lack the opportunity to satisfy their basic needs that Rasmussen claims that libertarian property rights no longer apply. Here Rasmussen contends that morality requires that the poor should take what they need for survival from the legal property of the rich and that the rich should not refuse assistance. Still Rasmussen contends that the poor have no right to assistance in this case, nor the rich presumably any corresponding obligation to help the poor because "the situation cannot be judged in social and political terms."[25] ✱✱✱✱

But why cannot the situation be judged in social and political terms? If we know what the moral directives of the rich and the poor are in the case, as Rasmussen admits that we do, why would we not be justified in setting up a legal system or altering an existing legal system so that the poor would have a guaranteed right to welfare? Now it may be that Rasmussen is imagining a situation where it is not possible for the basic needs of everyone to be met. Such situations are truly lifeboat cases. But while such cases are difficult to resolve (maybe only a chance mechanism would offer a reasonable resolution) they surely do not represent the typical conflict situation between the rich and the poor. For in such situations, it is recognized that it is possible to meet everyone's basic needs, and what is at issue is whether (some of) the nonbasic or luxury needs of the rich should be sacrificed so that everyone's basic needs can be met. So when dealing with typical conflict situations between the rich and the poor, there is no justification for not securing a legal system that reflects the moral directives in these cases.

In sum, both Machan's and Rasmussen's objections to grounding a right to welfare on libertarian premises have been answered. Machan's

attempt to grant the theoretical validity of a libertarian right to welfare, but then deny its practical validity, fails once we recognize that there are many poor who lack the opportunity to satisfy their basic needs. Rasmussen's attempt to grant that there are poor who lack the opportunity to meet their basic needs, but then deny that the poor have any right to welfare, fails once we recognize that the moral directives that Rasmussen grants apply to the rich and the poor in severe conflict of interest cases provide ample justification for a right to welfare.

NOTES

1. Robert Nozick, *Anarchy, State and Utopia* (New York: Basic Books, 1974), Part I.

2. Murray Rothbard, *The Ethics of Liberty* (Atlantic Highlands: Humanities Press, 1982), p. 230.

3. Nozick, *Anarchy, State and Utopia*, p. ix.

4. Murray Rothbard, *For a New Liberty* (New York: Collier Books, 1978), p. 148.

5. See, for example, James P. Sterba, "Neo-Libertarianism," *American Philosophical Quarterly* 15 (1978): 17–19; Ernest Loevinsohn, "Liberty and the Redistribution of Property," *Philosophy and Public Affairs* 6 (1977): 226–39; David Zimmerman, "Coercive Wage Offers," *Philosophy and Public Affairs* 10 (1981): 121–45. To limit what is to count as coercive, Zimmerman claims that in order for P's offer to be coercive

(I)t must be the case that P does more than merely prevent Q *from taking from* P resources necessary for securing Q's strongly preferred preproposal situation; P must prevent Q *from acting on his own* (or with the help of others) *to produce or procure* the strongly preferred proposal situation.

But this restriction seems arbitrary, and Zimmerman provides little justification for it. See David Zimmerman, "More on Coercive Wage Offers," *Philosophy and Public Affairs* 12 (1983): 67–68.

6. It might seem that this second approach could avoid this difficulty if a restriction of liberty is understood as the curtailment of one's prima facie rights. But in order to avoid the problem of a multitude of conflicting liberties, which plagues the first approach, the specification of prima facie rights must be such that they only can be overridden when one or more of them is violated. And this may involve too much precision for our notion of prima facie rights.

7. Isaiah Berlin, *Four Essays on Liberty* (New York: Oxford University Press, 1969), pp. XXXVIII–XL.

8. On this point, see Maurice Cranston, *Freedom* (New York: Basic Books, 1953), pp. 52–53; C. B. Macpherson, *Democratic Theory* (Oxford: Oxford University Press, 1973), p. 95; Joel Feinberg, *Rights, Justice and the Bounds of Liberty* (Princeton, N.J.: Princeton University Press, 1980). Chapter 1.

9. See John Hospers, *Libertarianism* (Los Angeles: Nash Publishing Co., 1971), Chapter 7.

10. Alvin Goldman, *A Theory of Human Action* (Englewood Cliffs, N.J.: Prentice-Hall, 1970), pp. 208–15; William Frankena, "Obligation and Ability," in *Philosophical Analysis,* edited by Max Black (Ithaca, N.Y.: Cornell University Press, 1950), pp. 157–75.

Judging from some recent discussions of moral dilemmas by Bernard Williams and Ruth Marcus, one might think that the "ought" implies "can" principle would only be useful for illustrating moral conflicts rather than resolving them. (See Bernard Williams, *Problems of the Self* (Cambridge: Cambridge University Press, 1977), Chapters 11 and 12; Ruth Marcus, "Moral Dilemmas and Consistency," *The Journal of Philosophy* 80 (1980): 121–36. See also Terrance C. McConnell, "Moral Dilemmas and Consistency in Ethics," *Canadian Journal of Philosophy* 18 (1978): 269–87. But this is only true if one interprets that "can" in the principle to exclude only "what a person lacks the power to do." If one interprets the "can" to exclude in addition "what would involve so great a sacrifice that it would be unreasonable to ask the person to do it" then the principle can be used to resolve moral conflicts as well as state them. Nor would libertarians object to this broader interpretation of the "ought" implies "can" principle since they do not ground their claim to liberty on the existence of irresolvable moral conflicts.

11. See James P. Sterba, "Is there a Rationale for Punishment?", *The American Journal of Jurisprudence* 29 (1984): 29–44.

12. As further evidence, notice that those libertarians who justify a minimal state do so on the grounds that such a state would arise from reasonable disagreements concerning the application of libertarian rights. They do not justify the minimal state on the grounds that it would be needed to keep in submission large numbers of people who could not come to see the reasonableness of libertarian rights.

13. Obviously, the employment opportunities offered to the poor must be honorable and supportive of self-respect. To do otherwise would be to offer the poor the opportunity to meet some of their basic needs at the cost of denying some of their other basic needs.

14. The poor cannot, however, give up the liberty to which their children are entitled.

15. Of course, someone might still want to object to welfare states on the grounds that they "force workers to sell their labor" (see G. A. Cohen, "The Structure of Proletarian Unfreedom," *Philosophy and Public Affairs* 12 (1982): 3–33) and subject workers to "coercive wage offers." (See Zimmerman, "Coercive Wage Offers.") But for a defense of at least one form of welfare state against such an objection, see James P. Sterba, "A Marxist Dilemma for Social Contract Theory," *American Philosophical Quarterly* 21 (1981): 51–59.

16. Tibor Machan, *Individuals and their Rights* (La Salle: Open Court, 1989), pp. 100–111.

17. *Ibid.*, p. 107.

18. Alan Durning, "Life on the Brink," *World Watch,* Vol. 3 (1990), p. 24.

19. *Ibid.*, p. 29.

20. Machan also sketches another line of argument which unfortunately proceeds from premises that contradict his line of argument that I have discussed here. The line of argument that I have discussed here turns on Machan's claim that "normally, persons do not lack the opportunities and resources to satisfy their basic needs." Machan's second line of argument, by contrast, concedes that many of the poor lack the opportunities and resources to satisfy their basic needs but then contends that this lack is the result of political oppression in the absence of libertarian institutions. See Machan, *Individuals and their Rights,* p. 109. See also Machan's contribution to James P. Sterba, Tibor Machan, et. al., *Morality and Social Justice: Point and Counterpoint* (Lanham: Rowman and Littlefield, 1994), pp. 59–106, where Machan develops this second line of argument in more detail. For my response to this line of argument, see "Comments by James P. Sterba," in *Morality and Social Justice: Point and Counterpoint,* pp. 110–113.

21. Douglas Rasmussen, "Individual Rights and Human Flourishing," *Public Affairs Quarterly,* Vol. 3 (1989), pp. 89–103. See also Douglas Rasmussen and Douglas Den Uyl, *Liberty and Nature* (La Salle: Open Court, 1991), Chapters 2–4.

22. Rasmussen, "Individual Rights and Human Flourishing," p. 98.

23. *Ibid.*, p. 99.

24. *Ibid.*, p. 100.

25. *Ibid.*, p. 101.

3 The Nonexistence of Basic Welfare Rights

TIBOR R. MACHAN

JAMES STERBA AND OTHERS maintain that we all have the right to "receive the goods and resources necessary for preserving" ourselves. This is not what I have argued human beings have a right to. They have the right, rather, not to be killed, attacked, and deprived of their property—by persons in or outside of government. As Abraham Lincoln put it, "no man is good enough to govern another man, without that other's consent."[1]

Sterba claims that various political outlooks would have to endorse these "rights." He sets out to show, in particular, that welfare rights follow from libertarian theory itself.[2] Sterba wishes to show that *if* Lockean libertarianism is correct, then we all have rights to welfare and equal (economic) opportunity. What I wish to show is that since Lockean libertarianism—as developed in this work—is true, and since the rights to welfare and equal opportunity require their violation, no one has these latter rights. The reason some people, including Sterba, believe otherwise is that they have found some very rare instances in which some citizens could find themselves in circumstances that would require disregarding rights altogether. This would be in situations that cannot be characterized to be "where peace is possible."[3] And every major libertarian thinker from Locke to the present has treated these kinds of cases.[4]

Let us be clear about what Sterba sets out to show. It is that libertarians are philosophically unable to escape the welfare-statist implications of their commitment to negative liberty. This means that despite their belief that they are only supporting the enforceable right of every person not to be coerced by other persons, libertarians must accept, by the logic of their own position, that individuals also possess basic enforceable rights to being provided with various services from others. He holds, then, that basic negative rights imply basic positive rights.

To Lockean libertarians the ideal of liberty means that we all, individually, have the right not to be constrained against our consent within our realm of authority—ourselves and our belongings. Sterba states that for such libertarians "Liberty is being constrained by persons from doing what one has a right to do."[5] Sterba adds, somewhat misleadingly, that for Lockean libertarians "a right to life [is] a right not to be killed unjustly and a right to property [is] a right to acquire goods and resources either by initial acquisition or voluntary agreement."[6] Sterba does realize that these rights do not entitle one to receive from others the goods and resources necessary for preserving one's life.

A problem with this foundation of the Lockean libertarian view is that political justice—not the justice of Plato, which is best designated in our time as "perfect virtue"—for natural-rights theorists presupposes individual rights. One cannot then explain rights in terms of justice but must explain justice in terms of rights.

Reprinted from Individuals and Their Rights *by Tibor Machan by permission of The Open Court Publishing Company, La Salle, Illinois.*

For a Lockean libertarian, to possess any basic right to receive the goods and resources necessary for preserving one's life conflicts with possessing the right not to be killed, assaulted, or stolen from. The latter are rights Lockean libertarians consider to be held by all individual human beings. Regularly to protect and maintain—that is, enforce—the former right would often require the violation of the latter. A's right to the food she has is incompatible with B's right to take this same food. Both the rights could not be fundamental in an integrated legal system. The situation of one's having rights to welfare, and so forth, and another's having rights to life, liberty, and property is thus theoretically intolerable and practically unfeasible. The point of a system of rights is the securing of mutually peaceful and consistent moral conduct on the part of human beings. As Rand observes,

> "Rights" are . . . the link between the moral code of a man and the legal code of a society, between ethics and politics. *Individual rights are the means of subordinating society to moral law.*[7]

Sterba asks us—in another discussion of his views—to consider what he calls "a *typical* conflict situation between the rich and the poor." He says that in his situation "the rich, of course, have more than enough resources to satisfy their basic needs. By contrast, the poor lack the resources to meet their most basic needs even though *they have tried all the means available to them that libertarians regard as legitimate for acquiring such resources*"[8] (my emphasis).

The goal of a theory of rights would be defeated if rights were typically in conflict. Some bureaucratic group would have to keep applying its moral intuitions on numerous occasions when rights claims would *typically* conflict. A constitution is workable if it helps remove at least the largest proportion of such decisions from the realm of arbitrary (intuitive) choice and avail a society of men and women of objective guidelines that are reasonably integrated, not in relentless discord.

Most critics of libertarianism assume some doctrine of basic needs that they invoke to show that whatever basic needs are not satisfied for some people, while others have "resources" that are not basic needs for them, the former have just claims against the latter. (The language of resources of course loads the argument in the critic's favor since it suggests that these goods simply come into being and happen to be in the possession of some people, quite without rhyme or reason, arbitrarily [as John Rawls claims].)[9]

This doctrine is full of difficulties. It lacks any foundation for why the needs of some persons must be claims upon the lives of others. And why are there such needs anyway—to what end are they needs, and whose ends are these and why are not the persons whose needs they are held responsible for supplying the needs? (Needs, as I have already observed, lack any force in moral argument without the prior justification of the purposes they serve, or the goals they help to fulfill. A thief has a basic need of skills and powers that are clearly not justified if theft is morally unjustified. If, however, the justification of basic needs, such as food and other resources, presupposes the value of human life, and if the value of human life justifies, as I have argued earlier, the principle of the natural rights to life, liberty and property, then the attainment or fulfillment of the basic need for food may not involve the violation of these rights.)

Sterba claims that without guaranteeing welfare and equal-opportunity rights, Lockean libertarianism violates the most basic tenets of any morality, namely, that "ought" implies "can." The thrust of "'ought' implies 'can'" is that one ought to do that which one is free to do, that one is morally responsible only for those acts that one had the power either to choose to engage in or not to engage in. (There is debate on just how this point must be phrased—in terms of the will being free or the person being free to will something. For our purposes, however, all that counts is that the person must have [had] a genuine option to do X or not to do X before it can be true that he or she ought to do X or ought to have done X.) If an innocent person is forced by the actions of another to forgo significant moral choices, then that innocent person is not free to act morally and thus his or her human dignity is violated.

This is not so different from the common-sense legal precept that if one is not sound of mind one cannot be criminally culpable. Only free agents, capable of choosing between right and wrong, are open to moral evaluation. This indeed is the reason that many so-called moral theories fail to be anything more than value theories. They omit from consideration the issue of self-determination. If either hard or soft determinism is true, morality is impossible, although values need not disappear.[10]

If Sterba were correct about Lockean libertarianism typically contradicting "'ought' implies 'can,'" his argument would be decisive. (There are few arguments against this principle that I know of and they have not convinced me. They trade on rare circumstances when persons feel guilt for taking actions that had bad consequences even though they could not have avoided them.)[11] It is because Karl Marx's and Herbert Spencer's systems typically, normally, indeed in every case, violate this principle that they are not bona fide moral systems. And quite a few others may be open to a similar charge.[12]

Sterba offers his strongest argument when he observes that "'ought' implies 'can'" is violated "when the rich prevent the poor from taking what they require to satisfy their basic needs even though they have tried all the means available to them that libertarians regard as legitimate for acquiring such resources."[13]

Is Sterba right that such are—indeed, must be—typical conflict cases in a libertarian society? Are the rich and poor, even admitting that there is some simple division of people into such economic groups, in such hopeless conflict all the time? Even in the case of homeless people, many find help without having to resort to theft. The political factors contributing to the presence of

helpless people in the United States and other Western liberal democracies are a hotly debated issue, even among utilitarians and welfare-state supporters. Sterba cannot make his argument for the typicality of such cases by reference to history alone. (Arguably, there are fewer helpless poor in near-libertarian, capitalist systems than anywhere else—why else would virtually everyone wish to live in these societies rather than those where welfare is guaranteed, indeed enforced? Not, at least originally, for their welfare-statist features. Arguably, too, the disturbing numbers of such people in these societies could be due, in part, to the lack of consistent protection of all the libertarian natural rights.)

Nonetheless, in a system that legally protects and preserves property rights there will be cases where a rich person prevents a poor person from taking what belongs to her (the rich person)—for example, a chicken that the poor person might use to feed herself. Since after such prevention the poor person might starve, Sterba asks the rhetorical question, "Have the rich, then, in contributing to this result, killed the poor, or simply let them die; and if they have killed the poor, have they done so unjustly?"[14] His answer is that they have. Sterba holds that a system that accords with the Lockean libertarian's idea that the rich person's preventive action is just "imposes an unreasonable sacrifice upon" the poor, one "that we could not blame them for trying to evade." Not permitting the poor to act to satisfy their basic needs is to undermine the precept that "'ought' implies 'can,'" since, as Sterba claims, that precept means, for the poor, that they ought to satisfy their basic needs. This they must have the option to do if they ought to do it.

When people defend their property, what are they doing? They are protecting themselves against the intrusive acts of some other person, acts that would normally deprive them of something to which they have a right, and the other has no right. As such, these acts of protectiveness make it possible for men and women in society to retain their own sphere of jurisdiction intact, protect their own "moral space."[15] They refuse to have their human dignity violated. They want to be sovereigns and govern their own lives, including their own productive decisions and actions. Those who mount the attack, in turn, fail or refuse to refrain from encroaching upon the moral space of their victims. They are treating the victim's life and its productive results as though these were unowned resources for them to do with as they choose.

Now the argument that cuts against the above account is that on some occasions there can be people who, with no responsibility for their situation, are highly unlikely to survive without disregarding the rights of others and taking from them what they need. This is indeed possible. It is no less possible that there be cases in which someone is highly unlikely to survive without obtaining the services of a doctor who is at that moment spending time healing someone else, or in which there is a person who is highly unlikely to survive without obtaining one of the lungs of another person, who wants to keep both lungs so as to be able to run the New York City marathon effectively. And such cases could be multiplied indefinitely.

But are such cases typical? The argument that starts with this assumption about a society is already not comparable to the libertarianism that has emerged in the footsteps of Lockean natural-rights doctrine, including the version advanced in this book. That system is developed for a human community in which "peace is possible." Libertarian individual rights, which guide men and women in such an adequately hospitable environment to act without thwarting the flourishing of others, are thus suitable bases for the legal foundations of a human society. It is possible for people in the world to pursue their proper goals without thwarting a similar pursuit by others.

The underlying notion of society in such a theory rejects the description of human communities implicit in Sterba's picture. Sterba sees conflict as typically arising from some people producing and owning goods, while others

having no alternative but to take these goods from the former in order to survive. But these are not the typical conflict situations even in what we today consider reasonably free human communities—most thieves and robbers are not destitute, nor are they incapable of doing something aside from taking other people's property in order to obtain their livelihood.

The typical conflict situation in society involves people who wish to take shortcuts to earning their living (and a lot more) by attacking others, not those who lack any other alternative to attacking others so as to reach that same goal. This may not be evident from all societies that teem with human conflict—in the Middle East, or Central and South America, for example. But it must be remembered that these societies are far from being even near-libertarian. Even if the typical conflicts there involved the kind Sterba describes, that would not suffice to make his point. Only if it were true that in comparatively free countries the typical conflict involved the utterly destitute and helpless arrayed against the well-to-do, could his argument carry any conviction.

The Lockean libertarian has confidence in the willingness and capacity of *virtually all persons* to make headway in life in a free society. The very small minority of exceptional cases must be taken care of by voluntary social institutions, not by the government, which guards self-consistent individual rights.

The integrity of law would be seriously endangered if the government entered areas that required it to make very particular judgments and depart from serving the interest of the public as such. We have already noted that the idea of "satisfying basic needs" can involve the difficulty of distinguishing those whose actions are properly to be so characterized. Rich persons are indeed satisfying their basic needs as they protect and preserve their property rights. . . . Private property rights are necessary for a morally decent society.

The Lockean libertarian argues that private property rights are morally justified in part because they are concrete requirements for delineating the sphere of jurisdiction of each person's moral authority, where her own judgment is decisive.[16] This is a crucial basis for the right to property. And so is the contention that we live in a metaphysically hospitable universe wherein people normally need not suffer innocent misery and deprivation—so that such a condition is usually the result of negligence or the violation of Lockean rights, a violation that has made self-development and commerce impossible. If exceptional emergencies set the agenda for the law, the law itself will disintegrate. (A just legal system makes provision for coping with emergencies that are brought to the attention of the authorities, for example, by way of judicial discretion, without allowing such cases to determine the direction of the system. If legislators and judges don't uphold the integrity of the system, disintegration ensues. This can itself encourage the emergence of strong leaders, demagogues, who promise to do what the law has not been permitted to do, namely, satisfy people's sense of justice. Experience with them bodes ill for such a prospect.)

Normally persons do not "lack the opportunities and resources to satisfy their own basic needs." Even if we grant that some helpless, crippled, retarded, or destitute persons could offer nothing to anyone that would merit wages enabling them to carry on their lives and perhaps even flourish, there is still the other possibility for most actual, known hard cases, namely seeking help. I am not speaking here of the cases we know: people who drop out of school, get an unskilled job, marry and have kids, only to find that their personal choice of inadequate preparation for life leaves them relatively poorly off. "'Ought' implies 'can'" must not be treated ahistorically—some people's lack of current options results from their failure to exercise previous options prudently. I refer here to the "truly needy," to use a shop-worn but still useful phrase—those who have never been able to help themselves and are not now helpless from their own neglect. Are such people being treated

unjustly, rather than at most uncharitably, ungenerously, indecently, pitilessly, or in some other respect immorally—by those who, knowing of the plight of such persons, resist forcibly efforts to take from them enough to provide the ill-fated with what they truly need? Actually, if we tried to pry the needed goods or money from the well-to-do, we would not even learn if they would act generously. Charity, generosity, kindness, and acts of compassion presuppose that those well enough off are not coerced to provide help. These virtues cannot flourish, nor can the corresponding vices, of course, without a clearly identified and well-protected right to private property for all.

If we consider the situation as we are more likely to find it, namely, that desperate cases not caused by previous injustices (in the libertarian sense) are rare, then, contrary to what Sterba suggests, there is much that unfortunate persons can and should do in those plausible, non-emergency situations that can be considered typical. They need not resort to violating the private-property rights of those who are better off. The destitute can appeal for assistance both from the rich and from the many voluntary social service agencies that emerge from the widespread compassion of people who know about the mishaps that can at times strike perfectly decent people.

Consider, as a prototype of this situation on which we might model what concerns Sterba, that if one's car breaks down on a remote road, it would be unreasonable to expect one not to seek a phone or some other way of escaping one's unfortunate situation. So one ought to at least try to obtain the use of a phone.

But should one break into the home of a perfect stranger living nearby? Or ought one instead to request the use of the phone as a favor? "'Ought' implies 'can'" is surely fully satisfied here. Actual practice makes this quite evident. When someone is suffering from misfortune and there are plenty of others who are not, and the unfortunate person has no other avenue for obtaining help than to obtain it from others, it would not be unreasonable to expect, morally, that the poor seek such help as surely might be forthcoming. We have no justification for assuming that the rich are all callous, though this caricature is regularly painted by communists and in folklore. Supporting and gaining advantage from the institution of private property by no means implies that one lacks the virtue of generosity. The rich are no more immune to virtue than the poor are to vice. The contrary view is probably a legacy of the idea that only those concerned with spiritual or intellectual matters can be trusted to know virtue—those concerned with seeking material prosperity are too base.

The destitute typically have options other than to violate the rights of the well-off. "'Ought' implies 'can'" is satisfiable by the moral imperative that the poor ought to seek help, not loot. There is then no injustice in the rich preventing the poor from seeking such loot by violating the right to private property. "'Ought' implies 'can'" is fully satisfied if the poor can take the kind of action that could gain them the satisfaction of their basic needs, and this action could well be asking for help.

All along here I have been considering only the helplessly poor, who through no fault of their own, nor again through any rights violation by others, are destitute. I am taking the hard cases seriously, where violation of "'ought' implies 'can'" would appear to be most probable. But such cases are by no means typical. They are extremely rare. And even rarer are those cases in which all avenues regarded as legitimate from the libertarian point of view have been exhausted, including appealing for help.

The bulk of poverty in the world is not the result of natural disaster or disease. Rather it is political oppression, whereby people throughout many of the world's countries are not legally permitted to look out for themselves in production and trade. The famines in Africa and India, the poverty in the same countries and in Central and Latin America, as well as in China, the Soviet Union, Poland, Rumania, and so forth, are not the result of lack of charity but of oppression. It

is the kind that those who have the protection of even a seriously compromised document and system protecting individual negative human rights, such as the U.S. Constitution, do not experience. The first requirement for men and women to ameliorate their hardship is to be free of other people's oppression, not to be free to take others people's belongings.

Of course, it would be immoral if people failed to help out when this was clearly no sacrifice for them. But charity or generosity is not a categorical imperative, even for the rich. There are more basic moral principles that might require the rich to refuse to be charitable—for example, if they are using most of their wealth for the protection of freedom or a just society. Courage can be more important than charity or benevolence or compassion. But a discussion of the ranking of moral virtues would take us far afield. One reason that many critics of libertarians find their own cases persuasive is that they think the libertarian can only subscribe to *political* principles or values. But this is mistaken.[17]

There can be emergency cases in which there is no alternative available to disregarding the rights of others. But these are extremely rare, and not at all the sort invoked by critics such as Sterba. I have in mind the desert-island case found in ethics books where instantaneous action, with only one violent alternative, faces persons—the sort we know from the law books in which the issue is one of immediate life and death. These are not cases, to repeat the phrase quoted from Locke by H. L. A. Hart, "where peace is possible." They are discussed in the libertarian literature and considerable progress has been made in integrating them with the concerns of law and politics. Since we are here discussing law and politics, which are general systematic approaches to how we normally ought to live with one another in human communities, these emergency situations do not help us except as limiting cases. And not surprisingly many famous court cases illustrate just this point as they now and then confront these kinds of instances after they have come to light within the framework of civilized society.

———————

Since the time of the original publication of the above discussion—as part of my book *Individuals and Their Rights*—James Sterba has made several attempts to counter the arguments advanced here. The central claim on which he attempts to rest the argument that within a libertarian system many people would have no chance for self-directed flourishing goes as follows:

> [W]ho could deny that most of 1.2 billion people who are currently living in conditions of absolute poverty "lack the opportunities and necessities to satisfy their basic needs"? And even within our country [USA], it is estimated that some 32 million Americans live below the official poverty index [$14,000 per annum for a family, $7,000 per annum for an individual], and that one fifth of American children are growing up in poverty. Surely, it is impossible to deny that many of these Americans also "lack the opportunities and resources to satisfy their basic needs."[18]

There is little discussion in Sterba's work of why people are poor or otherwise experience circumstances that afford them little or no opportunity for flourishing. Among libertarians, however, there is considerable agreement on the position that many who face such circumstances make significant contribution to their own plight. Many others suffer such circumstances because their negative rights to liberty (to produce and to keep what they produce) are violated.

Certainly, libertarians draw a sharp distinction between those who are in dire straits because they are unfortunate, through no fault of their own, and those who fail to act in ways that would probably extricate them from their adverse living conditions. In the philosophical literature that draws on the legacy of Marx, Engels, and their followers, this distinction is not easy to make, since in this tradition human behavior is taken to be determined by a person's economic circumstances, so one is bound by one's situation and cannot make choices that would overcome them. More generally, in modern political philosophy there has been a strong tendency to view human beings as passive, unable to initiate their own conduct and moved by innate drives or environmental stimuli. Thus, those who are well-off could not have achieved this through their own initiative, nor could those who are badly off have failed in significant ways. Accordingly, all the poor or badly off, be they victims of others' oppression, casualties of misfortune, or products of their own misconduct are regarded alike. It is not clear how much Sterba's reasoning may be influenced by these considerations. In the absence of significant discussion of the matter, it is understandable why Sterba appears to view life as largely a zero sum game.[19]

Sterba claims, then, that poverty is typical, including, we must assume, of libertarian societies. Without that assumption, the story about poverty would have no bearing on libertarian politics. Sterba, therefore, needs to argue, as he does, that in a fully libertarian system, which respects and protects only negative individual rights (to life, liberty, and property), massive poverty would ensue—it would be the typical situation for there to be great masses of poor people.

Libertarians, as suggested above, seriously dispute this point. Indeed, they are not pure deontologists regarding negative individual liberty or the right to it, for they believe that respect for and protection of it would produce a better life for most people, in all relevant respects (moral, economic, intellectual, psychological, and cultural), provided they make an effort to improve themselves. They argue, in the main, that the most prosperous and otherwise beneficial societies are also those that give greatest respect and protection to negative individual rights. In turn, they hold, that where poverty is widespread, negative individual liberty is, in the main, left unrespected and unprotected.

This part of their argument is, for most libertarians, a fairly reasonable analytical and historical stance. They would argue, analytically, that it is the protection of negative individual liberty—the right to free association, freedom of trade, freedom of wealth accumulation, freedom of contract, freedom of entrepreneurship, freedom of speech, freedom of thought—that provides the most hospitable social climate for the creation of wealth. While no libertarian claims that this guarantees that no one will be destitute, those who are poor would either have failed of their own accord or would have been the few unfortunate people who are innocently incapacitated and do not enjoy the benefit of others' generosity, charity, compassion, and similar support. According to libertarians, there is no reason to think that there would be many such persons, at least compared to the numbers one can expect in societies lacking respect and protection for negative individual rights. Thus, even the most well known opponent of capitalism (the economic system of libertarianism), Karl Marx, was aware that unless human nature itself changes and the "new man" develops, socialism can do no more than to socialize poverty, i.e., make everyone poor.

As to the historical evidence, it is hard to argue that other than substantially capitalist economic systems, which tend in the direction of libertarianism (at least as far as the legal respect for and protection of private property or the right to it are concerned) have fared much better in reducing poverty than have others, without also causing massive political and other social failures (such as abolition of civil liberties, institution for forced labor and involuntary servitude, regimentation of the bulk of social relations, arresting scientific and technological progress, or censorship of the arts and other intellectual endeavors). Thus, America is still the freest of societies, with many of its legal principles giving expression to classical liberal, near-libertarian ideas, and it is, at the same time, the most generally productive (creative and culturally rich) of all societies, with its wealth aiding in the support of hundreds of other societies across the globe. Barring the impossible-to-conduct controlled sociopolitical-economic experiment, such historical evidence is all we can adduce to examine which political economic system produces more poverty. No one can seriously dispute that the near-libertarian systems have fared much better than those going in the opposite direction, including the welfare state. Even though some people wish for more in the way of empirical backing, it is difficult to know what they could wish for apart from the relatively plain fact of history that societies in which negative liberty flourishes produce far more (tangible) wealth than do ones in which such freedom is systematically denied. It is no secret that the Western liberal nations in general and the United States of America in particular contribute the most to the rescue of casualties of famines and other natural disasters across the globe. The US supports the United Nations' treasury far more than do other nations. While factors other than the political-economic conditions of a country contribute to these circumstances, barring some kind of controlled experiment in which those factors can be isolated, this will have to do for present purposes.

There is another point to be stressed, though, that Sterba has not taken into consideration. This is that there can be people in a libertarian society—indeed, in any society—for whom a lack of wealth, even extreme poverty relative to the mean, may not be a great liability. Not everyone wants to, or even ought to, live prosperously. For some individuals a life of ostensible poverty could be of substantial benefit. Contenders would be monks, hobos, starving artists, and the like who, despite the protection of their negative liberty or the right to it, do not elect to seek economic prosperity, at least in preference to other important objectives. Among the citizens of a libertarian society, then, we could find some who are poor but who are not, therefore, worse off than the rich, provided we do not confine ourselves to counting economic prosperity as the prime source of well-being.

At one point, Sterba suggests that libertarians, because they do not see the need to affirm as a principle of justice the right to welfare, may not care sufficiently for the poor. As he puts it:

> Machan seems reluctant to take the steps required to secure the basic needs of the poor. Why then does he balk at taking any further steps? Could it be that he does not see the oppression of the poor as truly oppressive after all?[20]

There is perhaps something to this, although not in the way Sterba's rhetorical question suggests, namely, that libertarians are callous or uncaring where the cultivation of care is warranted. But it is true enough that just being poor does not necessarily warrant being cared for, just as simply being sick does not place upon another the obligation to help, if the sickness is the result of self-abuse or gross negligence, or affects a thoroughly evil person.

Furthermore, some artists who are poor are happier than some merchants who are rich. There is no justification for feeling compassion for such artists, despite their poverty. In short, being poor in and of itself does not justify special consideration.[21] Being in need of what it takes to attain one's well-being warrants, if the need is a matter of natural misfortune or injury from others, feelings and conduct amounting to care, generosity, and charity. Poverty does not always constitute such neediness.

Nevertheless, Sterba may also underestimate what Marxists might call the objective generosity or charity of libertarians. One must consider just how much greater the long range prospects for economic well-being are for everyone within a libertarian political economy, and how benevolent it is for people not to be cuddled and treated as if they were inept in attaining prosperity; this system fosters institutional conditions within which they will probably be much better off than they would be in any welfare state (which seems clearly to encourage long-range economic ineptitude and dependence) the libertarian could

well be regarded as the political theory with the greatest concern for the poor.[22]

It seems, therefore, that Sterba hasn't supported his main contention: that libertarianism implies the welfare state. The reason is that he has failed to appreciate the analytical and historical context within which libertarianism is argued. But there is more.

Sterba has also failed to appreciate that, although in some cases a person might not be required to respect the negative individual rights all citizens have—e.g., in some rare case of helpless destitution—nothing follows from this regarding the rights that everyone in society has by virtue of being a human individual living in a community of other human individuals. As Rasmussen and Den Uyl so carefully argue, the system of negative individual rights is a metanormative system or, in other words, a political framework within which human beings normally would and should pursue their highly varied flourishing. Focusing on exceptional, rare cases, wherein "peace is not possible," and, thus, it is justified to disregard consideration of basic (political) rights, does not justify the abrogation of the system of justice based on such rights that does, in fact, best befit human beings in their communities. On rare occasions, for particular persons, exceptions might be made, just as courts in extraordinary circumstances make such exceptions in the criminal law by pardoning someone who has violated a law but could not be expected to abide by it; these pardons do not abolish the law in question.

The point is, one ought not to abandon political principles to accommodate what can only be deemed extraordinary circumstances, Sterba's advice to the contrary notwithstanding.

NOTES

1. Quoted in Harry V. Jaffa, *How to Think About the American Revolution* (Durham, NC: Carolina Academic Press, 1978), p. 41 (from *The Collected Works of Abraham Lincoln* [R. Basler (ed.), 1953], 108–15).

2. See, in particular, James Sterba, "A Libertarian Justification for a Welfare State," *Social Theory and*

Practice, 11 (Fall 1985), 285–306. I will be referring to this essay as well as a more developed version, titled "The U.S. Constitution: A Fundamentally Flawed Document" in *Philosophy Reflections on the United States Constitution,* edited by Christopher Gray (1989).

3. H. L. A. Hart, "Are There Any Natural Rights?" *Philosophical Review* 64 (1955), 175.

4. See, for my own discussions, Tibor R. Machan, *Human Rights and Human Liberties* (Chicago: Nelson-Hall, 1975), 213–22; "Prima Facie versus Natural (Human) Rights," *Journal of Value Inquiry* 10 (1976), 119–31; "Human Rights: Some Points of Clarification," *Journal of Critical Analysis* 5 (1973), 30–39.

5. Sterba, op. cit, "A Libertarian Justification," 295.

6. Ibid.

7. Ayn Rand, "Value and Rights," in J. Hospers, (ed.), *Readings in Introductory Philosophical Analysis* (Englewood Cliffs, NJ: Prentice-Hall, 1968), 382.

8. Sterba, "The U.S. Constitution: A Fundamentally Flawed Document."

9. John Rawls, *A Theory of Justice* (Cambridge, MA: Harvard University Press, 1971), 101–02. For a discussion of the complexities in the differential attainments of members of various ethnic groups— often invoked as evidence for the injustice of a capitalist system, see Thomas Sowell, *Ethnic America: A History* (New York: Basic Books, 1981). There is pervasive prejudice in welfare-state proponents' writings against crediting people with the ability to extricate themselves from poverty without special political assistance. The idea behind the right to negative liberty is to set people free from others so as to pursue their progressive goals. This is the ultimate teleological justification of Lockean libertarian natural rights. See Tibor R. Machan, *Human Rights and Human Liberties: A Radical Reconsideration of the American Political Tradition* (Chicago: Nelson-Hall, 1975). Consider also this thought from Herbert Spencer:

> The feeling which vents itself in "poor fellow!" on seeing one in agony, excludes the thought of "bad fellow," which might at another time arise. Naturally, then, if the wretched are unknown or but vaguely known, all the demerits they may have are ignored: and thus it happens that when the miseries of the poor are dilated upon, they are thought of as the miseries of the deserving poor, instead of being thought of as the miseries of undeserving poor, which in large measure they should be. Those whose hardships are set forth in pamphlets and proclaimed in sermons and speeches which echo throughout society, are assumed to be all worthy souls, grievously wronged; and none of them are thought of as bearing the penalties of their own misdeeds.

(*Man versus the State* [Caldwell, ID: Caxton Printers, 1940], 22)

10. Tibor R. Machan, "Ethics vs. Coercion: Morality of Just Values?" in L. H. Rockwell, Jr. et al., (ed.), *Man, Economy and Liberty: Essays in Honor of Murray N. Rothbard* (Auburn, AL: Ludwig von Mises Institute, 1988), 236–46.

11. John Kekes, "'Ought Implies Can' and Two Kinds of Morality," *The Philosophical Quarterly* 34 (1984), 459–67.

12. Tibor R. Machan, "Ethics vs. Coercion." In a vegetable garden or even in a forest, there can be good things and bad, but no morally good things and morally evil things (apart from people who might be there).

13. Sterba, "The U.S. Constitution: A Fundamentally Flawed Document."

14. Sterba, "A Libertarian Justification," 295–96.

15. Robert Nozick, *Anarchy, State, and Utopia* (New York: Basic Books, 1974), 57. See, also, Tibor R. Machan, "Conditions for Rights, Sphere of Authority," *Journal of Human Relations* 19 (1971), 184–87, where I argue that "within the context of a legal system where the *sphere of authority* of individuals and groups of individuals cannot be delineated independently of the sphere of authority of the public as a whole, there is an inescapable conflict of rights specified by the same legal system." (186). See, also, Tibor R. Machan, "The Virtue of Freedom in Capitalism," *Journal of Applied Philosophy* 3 (1986), 49–58, and Douglas J. Den Uyl, "Freedom and Virtue," in Tibor R. Machan (ed.), *The Main Debate: Communism versus Capitalism* (New York: Random House, 1987), 200–16. This last essay is especially pertinent to the understanding of the ethical or moral merits of coercion and coerced conduct. Thus it is argued here that "coercive charity" amounts to an oxymoron.

16. See, Machan, op. cit., "The Virtue of Freedom in Capitalism" and "Private Property and the Decent Society" in J. K. Roth and R. C. Whittemore (eds.), *Ideology and American Experience* (Washington, DC: Washington Institute Press, 1986).

17. E.g., James Fishkin, *Tyranny and Legitimacy* (Baltimore, MD: Johns Hopkins University Press, 1979). Cf., Tibor R. Machan, "Fishkin on Nozick's Absolute Rights," *Journal of Libertarian Studies* 6 (1982), 317–20.

Sterba has gone on to raise further objections, for example, in his "From Liberty to Welfare," *Ethics* 105 (October 1994), 64–98. All these rest on Sterba's refusal to examine the ethical foundations of natural rights. Thus Sterba can claim that "Machan seems reluctant to take the steps required to secure the basic needs of the poor." This, simply because I will not sanction theft as a means to "secure" those needs. What about generosity, charity, philanthropy, kindness, compassion, help, assistance, etc.? All these appear not to interest Sterba, since they do not involve the force of law or coercion, whereby Machan and others can be compelled, one may assume by Sterba & Co., "to secure the basic needs of the poor." But there is more to coping with life's problems than foisting political "solutions" on people.

If history is any indication, what the oppressed poor need is not giving them permission to steal but a polity of liberty where they can put their own initiative to productive use, where what they create or obtain by trade may be kept by them, invested and built into nest eggs or substantial wealth. The poor, as the saying goes, need to become rich, not be placed into a polity wherein no one is allowed to get too rich and all those who have unsatisfied basic needs can legally raid the wealth of others.

18. James P. Sterba, *Morality and Social Justice* (Lanham, MD: Rowman & Littlefield, 1995), 15.

19. In so far as Sterba is a reasonably close follower of John Rawls' thinking in politics, and since Rawls denies the efficacy of individual initiative in the formation of personal assets such as one's character, it is quite possible that Sterba follows suit. (See John Rawls, *A Theory of Justice* [Cambridge: Harvard University Press, 1971], 104.) Since, however, Sterba also endorses the Kantian notion of "ought implies can" and advances numerous claims as to what people ought to do, there is evidence that he is also committed to a theory of free will. Which view dominates is unclear since there is no explicit discussion of this matter in Sterba's work with which I am familiar.

In contrast, most libertarians would invoke views drawn from philosophers of human nature, action theory, or motivational psychology, and embrace the position that when human beings are not kept in subjugation, they will tend or have good reasons to work toward their improvement, regardless of where they are on the continuum between destitution and abundance. Libertarians differ on the details, of course, with some subscribing to a neo-Hobbesian idea about what leads people to act and others to an agency view drawing from Ayn Rand and others. Some embrace the Hayekian notion of natural evolution. None

accept what seems to underlie many statist positions, namely, that most people are congenitally passive, even when they are not actively kept in subjugation. On this view, of course, neither the poor (and some among them who are lazy) nor the rich (and some among them who are greedy) are personally responsible for their economic position in life. Nor, of course, can those who resist Sterba's analysis be blamed for possible moral blindness (a charge implicit in some of what Sterba has said about libertarians), since they, too, presumably are the way they are because of circumstances beyond their control.

It is notable that the statistics Sterba cites are drawn from societies, including the United States of America, which are far from libertarian in their legal construction and are far closer to the welfare state, if not to outright socialism. It is surprising why Sterba does not consider that perhaps what accounts for those statistics is the absence of libertarianism, given that there is ample historical evidence for the impact of socialism on the economic conditions of the members of various societies around the globe. Seeing, then, that socialism does not improve the general welfare and the welfare state leaves a great many people badly off, a not unreasonable alternative would be that greater stress on the protection of negative individual liberty would promise the results Sterba desires. In contrast to Sterba's empirical assertions about poverty *vis-a-vis* capitalism (the economic system of libertarianism), see Nathan Rosenberg, *How the West Grew Rich: The economic transformation of the industrial world* (New York: Basic Books, 1986), and Nathan Rosenberg, Ralph Landau, and David C. Mowery, *Technology and the Wealth of Nations* (Stanford, CA: Stanford University Press, 1992). Both works go a long way toward demonstrating the superior wealth-creating record of economies that rest, more so than alternative systems, on the principles of the right to private property, free competition and the pursuit of private profit.

20. James P. Sterba, "Liberty and Welfare," note 34. In this paper Sterba repeats the claims about the alleged connection between libertarianism and significantly widespread poverty, with no attempt to establish them except by reference to unanalyzed statistics. (An attempt by the present author to challenge his analysis was rejected by the editors on grounds that the challenge was based on no more than "confident empirical speculations." See note 19, above, however, for references to works containing historical evidence supportive of the claim against Sterba's unanalyzed statistics.)

21. This may account, in part, for the indignation felt by some poor when they are offered help. Their

dignity has been offended, for they know that their poverty follows from their conscious or implicit choices, ones they find and which may indeed be fully justified. For a general argument against the enforceable duty to serve others, see Lester H. Hunt, "An Argument Against a Legal Duty to Rescue," *Journal of Social Philosophy* 36 (1994), 22.

22. Let me spend a few paragraphs on the difference between meaning and doing good, for Sterba's implied charge gains its moral force from what seems to me a misunderstanding of morality along certain Kantian lines. (See, for a comment along lines similar to what follows, Shelby Steele, "How Liberals Lost Their Virtue Over Race," *Newsweek,* January 1995, 41–42.)

There is, among many moral theorists as well as politicians and pundits, much concern with who is mean spirited, who lacks compassion, who is kinder and gentler among those vying to be political leaders. For too many people what appears to count most for having moral character is the quality of the feelings that motivate one's conduct. If you *mean or intend* well, if what you feel in your heart is good, decent, caring and such, what follows is supposed to be morally upstanding, commendable. It doesn't even matter much what actually results from the conduct motivated by such good feelings. "It's the thought that counts," as the saying goes.

Yet there is clearly something wrong with this idea. People may feel good for having done one thing or another from certain generous, charitable, kind or compassionate sensibilities or motives but it doesn't follow at all that this assures that the consequences are actually going to produce much benefit. Indeed, it is often quite likely that by focusing on how one feels about what one does, one loses sight of whether the action actually achieves any good at all. Furthermore, by focusing on these evaluating feelings, one can run the very real risk of trying to please others instead of actually helping them.

Very often, indeed, helpful conduct does not square with conduct that pleases. One knows this well enough in personal relations: some friends or relatives want us to do for them things that are definitely not very helpful. Such conduct more often simply satisfies some desire, never mind whether it is actually worthy of being satisfied. Consider young friends who want to have, say, cigarettes or alcohol purchased for them,

never mind what these actually produce. Consider the deadbeat who would so much like another loan, or the lazy person who would like to escape all hardship and just sit around. Or consider the moments when you, too, are tempted to plead merely to be satisfied, hoping that no one will critically examine the merits of your desires. Those who comply with such calls for unwise generosity may often fool themselves and feel moral righteousness about what they do. And they are certainly often liked for this by the people whom they have "helped."

In contrast, bona fide help is much more risky. And it is demanding. One needs to learn what actually is good for the person who seeks it. One needs to do some research. And one often upsets those whom one helps, just as doctors often displease patients with treatments or prescriptions that are unpleasant, as coaches do with the training they demand from athletes.

The more remote one is from those in need of help, the less likely it is going to be that such research is going to be undertaken. Instead some standard formulas will be invoked and the gauge to success will be how much gratitude is forthcoming, never mind whether such gratitude means serious thanks for useful help or mere pleasure in response to compliance.

In the current political climate there is a lot of talk about how some people are mean-spirited, who lack compassion, versus others who care and feel for those in need. It will pay handsomely, especially for those who are to be benefited from various public policies, to take a very close look at what actually is at issue. Are those derided for callousness perhaps thinking harder than their critics about what will be most helpful to the targeted beneficiaries? Are their proposals perhaps more fruitful in the long run, than those motivated by kinder and gentler feelings, regarding the actual task of securing for people a better life? And are these so called mean spirited policy architects perhaps the ones who ought to obtain real moral credit for generosity and compassion, rather than those who are flooded with feelings of compassion and kindness and thus are filled with moral pride and righteousness?

If one considers, also, that the generosity and compassion of those full of good feelings for others tend to come at other people's expense, the answer might be quite easy to discover.

4   Contracting for Liberty

JAN NARVESON

Politics and Reason

MANY HAVE FOUND THE POLITICAL outlook now generally known as "libertarianism" attractive, but most of them have held it in much the same way as most who adhere strongly to any other political outlook: they regard it as *obviously* true—scarcely in need of argument. They might even hold that no argument at this level is possible—just what people often say about religious beliefs. And in both cases, there is the same result: they are virtually barred from convincing anyone who doesn't already incline toward their outlook. Only nonrational methods are possible—not rational discourse, but maneuvering for power, if not by naked force of arms, then by conspiring to wield the arm of the law against all rivals.

It would be nice if we could do better than that. It may even be of genuine practical importance that the basic tenets of a political society should be amenable to reasoned discussion instead of war, soap-box rhetoric, or back-room machinations. The present essay is a brief defense of the proposal that there are actually good reasons for adopting the libertarian program above any other, and that these reasons can be explicated in a plausible way. I am proposing, then, that there actually are reasonable "foundations" for this political theory. . . .

The Other Views

Political and moral theories have been argued for on such bases as ideals of virtue, the will of God, self-evidence, and, in one way or another, nature. Why reject all these? Actually, as we will see, we needn't reject them all, quite: the contractarian view may be aligned with one kind of "natural law."

Meanwhile, we can say something about the inadequacy of such theories. *Virtue theories* fail because their ideas of virtue are never shared by *all*, and are unprovable to those who disagree. Appeals to *authority* are useless because they are circular. What the Authority says is right, we are told. And why? Well, because he knows what is right. His commands are a fifth wheel. And if we appeal to "self-evidence," what do we do about those who, alas, do not "see" the self-evident? The usual answer—kick'em!—lacks cogency.

Morals are for people: if a theory is to work, it must be shown that it appeals to people. Those who propose that politics are based on "natural law" or "nature" may be obscurely appreciating this point. But the claim that some view is "based on the nature of things" or on "human nature" is unclear. Talk of "conforming to nature" makes no literal sense; nature simply *is*. It sets limits to what is possible, but can prescribe nothing.

From Liberty for the Twenty-First Century: Contemporary Libertarian Thought, *edited by Tibor R. Machan and Douglas B. Rasmussen, pp. 19–39, 217–221. Reprinted by permission of Rowman & Littlefield Publishers, Inc.*

Can the idea of natural law be given a useful interpretation? I suggest this: a natural law theory should say, in the end, that in view of the way things and people are, subscribing to *this* set of rules or virtues is our *best* means of accommodating them.

So, what *makes* it best, then? People make choices. To say that nature *determines* which choice to make is pointless: *we* must choose. But given that I *want* this or that, then with good information I can see that *this* is the thing to do. And so we might adapt the terminology of natural law for this purpose and suggest that a rule or a value is "natural" when it is one's rationally best response to one's circumstances. In just that spirit, Hobbes proposed his Laws of Nature. And he got them right: modern decision-theoretic arguments confirm Hobbes' basic moral ideas, even as they fail to support his argument for the State.

The Contractarian Idea

John Stuart Mill declared that "society is not founded on a contract, and . . . no good purpose is answered by inventing a contract in order to deduce social obligations from it"—yet he adds the remarkably contract-like suggestion that "everyone who receives the protection of society owes a return for the benefit, and the fact of living in society renders it indispensable that each should be bound to observe a certain line of conduct toward the rest."[1] To any who envisage a need to justify the ways of their fellows to themselves or vice versa, that line of argument is inevitable. There is no alternative. . . .

Contract

Why "contract"? And especially, why the "social" contract? Does the idea of a "contract" at the universal level we contemplate here make any sense? We need a characterization sufficiently general to capture what is in common both to the many explicit arrangements normally so-called in ordinary life, and to that pattern or

principle of interactions, *not* the result of explicit negotiations, that the social-contract theorist proposes as the basis of morals and politics.

The answer has been identified plausibly by Hobbes and Hume, and latterly, in a more precise and general form, by David Gauthier.[2] In contracts, people make their behavior *conditional on each other's performance*. In so doing, at least one of them typically makes himself vulnerable to the other's decision not to carry through on it.[3] An inward impetus of the will is required to make it work. That is morality. Now and again, one of the parties concerned may lack the necessary inner commitment. We may then have to resort to external imposition, sometimes to force.

A contract in the relevant sense is *social* when it is a conditional arrangement of *each with all*. The building block of such a contract is an arrangement between oneself and whomever comes to treat them thus-and-so *provided* they do likewise. "Social contract" does not refer to anything not analyzable into the plans of action of particular individuals. And if, as is likely, we fall short of unanimity, near-unanimity contract will somehow have to serve. That problem will be carefully considered below. Meanwhile, though, the prospect of mutual benefit is what underwrites social reinforcement of contracts generally, and in particular the commitment to refrain from force in the pursuit of one's goals. We rationally expect all to adhere to that rule: it is a rational commitment.

Commitment is rational only where one can expect reciprocity—which in turn can only be expected if the other party can expect it from you. Can either really expect it, though? Here we must make an obvious and familiar distinction, between two senses of "expect": (1) to *predict*, and (2) to *insist*, that is, to feel entitled to performance. As to (1), whether we can expect others to perform depends on their characters, and we sometimes know enough of that to form reliable predictions, and sometimes not. But (2) we can always *insist* on others' keeping the terms of any particular promise, provided that we do our share and provided that it was made in a suitably well-informed and uncoerced fashion. In so insisting, we invoke the support of anyone and everyone in the social environment—not just that of our interactee. This social element is a substantial reinforcer, if applied consistently and carefully. Being the general object of disapprobation, with accompanying withdrawal of assorted amenities of civilized exchange, is a heavy price to pay for displaying a tendency to renege, and those who are motivated to avoid getting caught at their reneging pay a price in having to devote effort to covering their tracks and avoiding detection. They can and sometimes do succeed, more or less, and just what that shows is debatable—certainly that morality is imperfect, but not that it is irrational nor even that it is less than fully rational. Any doctrine that made immorality incomprehensible would be convicted of unreality on that account. My claim is only that rational people will give weight to morality as here explained, in the form of a disposition to abide by agreements and to refrain from trying to get one's way be sheer force.

The "social contract" has in common with all contracts that (1) it is the reciprocal conditionalizing of behavior and (2) it involves commitment from those concerned. But it is, of course, an unspoken understanding, a *non*-negotiated agreement—an agreement in action, not in words nor preceded by words. Each party adopts a disposition to respond in ways that make the resulting interaction mutually preferable to its alternatives. Such dispositions are moral virtues: dispositions we do well to have. But the contractarian view differs from theories claiming to found morals on a prior discernment of what is virtuous, independently of interaction. On the view defended here, we can *show* that this disposition is a virtue. It isn't a matter of what's "in the eye of the beholder."

The Libertarian Idea[4]

It cannot be too strongly emphasized that libertarianism is not a view about the same thing as contractarianism. The latter is a *metatheory* of morals and politics. It holds that the principles of morals, whatever they may turn out to be, are those we all do have reason to agree on provided all others accept them as well. The reason for agreeing is simple: we do better in the condition where all comply with the proposed principles. But only if others agree too; absent agreement, we revert to the unsatisfactory condition in which no one can trust anyone else. Libertarianism is a view about the substance of that agreement.

That substance is the principle that force—the stick, as I call it—ought to be restricted, in human affairs, to countering those who would or do employ force without that restriction: namely, to the initiators of violence, those who propose to make their way by removing the human obstacles to it by brute force or threat of same. The libertarian strategy, then, is *to resort to force only to counter the aggression of others*. And the libertarian theory is contractually *grounded* only if (1) libertarianism is the best rule for everybody in the way of general restrictions on behavior, and (2) no other way of arriving at the virtue in question is plausible. Our argument is that the Universal Social Contract, the agreement of all with all, calls for nothing more nor less than to refrain from the use of force to attain one's goals. In Hobbes' words, it is to "seek peace, and follow it," which, together with its famous corollary, that when peace is unattainable, one may then use "all the helps and advantages of war"[5] constitute his First Law of Nature, and really the only one, if he is right in holding that all the others flow from it. The job is to show that it is indeed the only reasonable candidate for the role of fundamental principle of morality, and showing that is not a purely a priori matter. The argument may not only be difficult, but varyingly plausible under different conditions.

Why is this "libertarian"? To be at liberty, in general, is to have no obstacles impeding one's efforts. To be at *social* liberty, liberty in relation to one's fellows, is for them to refrain from impeding one's efforts. For people in general to have social liberty is for all to refrain from impeding each other's efforts—that each person, A, has no obstacles to A's efforts imposed by the voluntary actions of A's fellow persons. Of course the expectation of liberty at the hands of others is unreasonable if it is not reciprocal: A won't impede B, but only on condition that B in turn will not impede A. The social contract is necessary for liberty. But is it sufficient? That is the big question.

Liberty cannot sensibly be regarded as an *intrinsic* value. One values liberty because there are things that one values, and liberty is necessary for getting them by one's own efforts. But what if we can get it by somebody else's efforts? Terrific—if we can. But how can we? Perhaps by happenstance appeal to the goodness of their hearts—which, no doubt, will sometimes work and sometimes not. But if not, then what? The answer, as we have already seen, is by force or fraud—means that the person against whom they are used has the strongest reason for objecting to. Universal agreement precludes use of those methods.

Others will talk of "positive" liberty, perhaps. Of what use to a paraplegic is the liberty to walk, it will be asked? The answer to that is easy: none, until he becomes equipped with devices to move him around; and then it's plenty of use, just as it is for the rest of us. But those who propose to equip him at our expense, involuntarily incurred, need to tell *us* why *we* should accept that imposition. To look myopically at the paraplegic alone is absurd, and it is dishonest. "We" do *not* prefer supposed positive liberty, which must always be at the expense of others, to negative liberty, which can be had by all. Only *some* prefer that.

Liberty and Property

Liberty is the absence of impediments, and thus of impositions. What constitutes an "impediment" must, then, be one of the first questions on our conceptual agenda. The libertarian has a specific view about this. He proposes that in general nonimpediment entails respecting *property,* broadly speaking. Explicating this idea carefully and plausibly is our first conceptual task. If we don't know what constitutes impediment, then we don't know what constitutes liberty, and if we don't know that, we don't know what we are advocating under the banner of libertarianism. If we do know what it is, however, then we can also understand how to formulate a workable notion of property.

The libertarian holds, in effect, that *liberty = property*. To own something is to have the right to do with it as one pleases: the disposition of that thing is up to you, not someone else. Take the special case in which the "something" is the person himself, and it follows immediately that liberty consists in self-ownership. Locke's confidence that a man owns himself was, therefore, correct. To act is to make use of one's own capacities, one's own equipment and abilities—limbs, memory, pianistic talents, the works. Too many talk as though property were not only entirely distinct from but perhaps antithetical to liberty. That is nonsense. If one's tongue is not one's own, what means freedom of speech? If one's mind isn't, what sense is there in freedom of thought?

The large question about this must concern external property: land, amplifiers, hotels, metal-working machines. Many writers seem to think that there is a terrible problem about extending a right of personal freedom to the use of items in the external world. While too large an issue for this essay to deal with completely,[6] the basic idea is simple: just as we can do what we wish with the natural parts of our own person, bodily and psychological, so we may do what we wish with bits of external nature, so long only as we do not thereby damage or impede the uses by others of such objects. In particular, it is not an impediment that if A acquires x, B is thereby unable to do so. The implication of an argument along those lines is that nobody may use anything— a strange doctrine of *liberty*! The correct view is that you can use *whatever* you find if nobody else already has it. Once you begin to use it, then anyone else who comes along will interfere with your already-commenced train of action if he renders it impossible for you to continue. To own x is to have control over the further disposition of x. Once we acquire hitherto unowned nature, all further acquisition of property must be via agreement: that is, by voluntary exchange, of things for things, things for services, or services for services. Liberty = property. If we have no property rights, we have no rights. Period. . . .

The "State of Nature"

The classic political philosophers of the modern era thought to derive the principles of politics from hypotheses about how things would be for people in a "state of nature," this being the situation where people interact in the absence of *any* authoritatively exercised general controls. They then hoped to justify proposals by demonstrating the superiority of the situations envisaged by them over the original condition. This raises two questions. First, can this be a useful conception, seeing that such states do not seem to occur in human affairs? Second, does the utility of contractarianism depend on the real possibility of such states? We briefly consider these central issues here.

First, let us note three distinctions. One is the familiar distinction between hypothetical and actual states of nature. Even if they are never actual, the idea may be useful. If (1) such a condition is at least possible, and if (2) from the point of view of any individual it would be terrible if it did occur, and if (3) certain behavior patterns in humans do head us toward such a condition unless certain social arrangements are made, then there need not ever actually be any such to show that we have reason to avoid those patterns.

The second distinction is between *political* and *moral* versions of the idea. A political state of nature is a social condition without political institutions. A moral state of nature is a social condition without morals: no one has any moral inhibitions about doing *anything*. The moral version is the more general and profound.

A third distinction is between *partial* and *complete* states of nature. A social condition is a partial

state of nature if it has aspects of apoliticality or amorality, even though in other respects there are laws or moral inhibitions. A more abstract and useful characterization of the "state of nature" is that it displays certain game-theoretic structures, in particular what is called a prisoner's dilemma. State of nature is then identified with the default option. This again is relevant to our two questions: there are plenty of such dilemmas at hand; we needn't go to the ultimate one envisaged by Hobbes in order to make the argument for morality. (Or maybe the state? Note that I do *not* assume that the argument can work to justify a state, but do not pursue the question here.)

We can now make progress on the question before us. A state of nature that couldn't even approximately obtain under *any* circumstances is indeed pointless. But if the condition in question is clearly possible, and it can be established that we really would tend toward that condition unless we do x, while x produces a condition clearly superior to it, then we have an argument for doing x. So, for example, it is *logically* impossible that we should actually be behind Rawls' "veil of ignorance." But it is not obviously impossible at all to be in a situation where no body of people has effective political power—where there is a "breakdown of law and order." And we know cases of immoral behavior; generalizing from them doesn't seem impossible either. And so there is no problem about the reality of states of nature. At any given time, there are many matters that are not subject to specific controls of either the legal or the moral type, and where arguably all concerned would be better off if they were. That's all we need.

Starting Where We Are

The fundamental question in life is: what do I do *now*? Speculation on what we should have done yesterday might help answer that question, or it might not; the past is, after all, past. Speculation on what we should do if some or another condition should obtain is useful if the condition is probable. But deliberation about what to do right now isn't speculation—it's life. In my daily doings, I will encounter various people and innumerable features of my environment that are substantially different from what they would have been had previous human activity been different, and that are decidedly subject to change at the hands of further human activity in the foreseeable future. Having helpful dispositions at hand for dealing with various of these is likely to be useful. The contractarian proposal is that among these handy dispositions are recognizably moral ones, whose utility has a lot to do with the network of expectations we can or do generate by encountering and reflecting on the behavior of others with whom we interact. It is a useful idea if, and only if, features of our social situations answer to the contractarian descriptions and call for their sort of solutions.

The status quo itself may be taken as our point of departure for many purposes of theory, as it must for all purposes of practice. If my proposed action and your proposed response would produce alterations for the better from both our points of view, as compared with any obvious alternatives, and by reference to the status quo, then agreement between us about that particular interaction is, *prima facie*, rational. If a proposed rule would make for improvement over the current situation for all concerned, then we have a plausible argument for adopting such a rule. These are options that obviously can and often do obtain—thus showing that the contractarian idea is at least partially practical and cannot be rejected out of hand.

That the status quo itself may be affected by injustice, stupidity, or other defects is clearly possible. But we show this by looking at aspects of *preceding* states of affairs and showing how certain departures from those states were contrary to the contractual criterion. If we learn, for example, that the reason why A has $100 to offer and B has nothing is that A got it from B by threatening to beat him to a pulp if he didn't hand it over, that makes quite a difference. No *general* agreement could have led to that development. Of course the status quo is not sacred. But we detect defects by looking back as far as necessary to see where the alleged defects came from and whether those involved agreed or could have agreed to what produced them. . . .

Nonunanimity?

Any contract view must address the question of what to do about those who will agree to nothing. My answer is Hobbes's: everyone else's behavior is, obviously, utterly unrestricted in relation to them. If in the process they end up on the gallows or in the tar-pit, that's tough for them—but it is not unjust. And the same for us, of course: if he does us in, that's too bad for us. All we can say is that in an all-out war, victory goes to the strong. However, our bet is that there are a great many more of us than of them—especially after they have finished doing each other in! . . .

Sorting Interests

For purposes of morals, what matters about an interest in others is whether that interest is positive or negative: would its satisfaction be a pro or a con to those others? If positive, then we have, prima facie, a situation of harmony, and there should be no problem, nuances apart; but if satisfying A's interest in B requires dissatisfying B, we have problems. What would we do about public controls on the pursuit of interests of these types? No one will allow others routinely to block his pursuit of his own interest. Where interests conflict, agreement requires a rationale for allowing one to be subject to overturning at the hands of some other. This agreement is not going to be forthcoming from the one who loses out. It must be shown that there's something in it *for him*—that he stands to gain from the rule even if it is imposed on him by force. Inherently, conflictual interests cannot be accommodated by a public charter.

There simply is no basis for agreement to actions on interests that from their very nature can only be satisfied at the expense of someone else. These necessarily set people against each other.

We may now define a class of what we may call *liberal* interests. These are interests that do not take as their object the dissatisfaction of anyone else. There are no inherent obstacles to acceptance of interests that have no bearing on others' interests. They may be pursued unrestrictedly. On the other hand, interests that do affect the interest of others must be cleared with those others before we proceed.

To take an extremely important example, the pursuit of private wealth—contrary to the doctrines of socialists—is, if pursued by consensual means, inherently nonconflictual. One person's having more than he had before does not entail that any other persons have less than they had before. And if we make our way by exchange, then both of us must, barring accident or mistake, do better in each instance. This furthers the case for private property; such relations are inherently nonconflictual.

Of course, A's having more than B implies that B has less than A. But the interest in having more, or less, or the same as B has no status in the public charter. For example, egalitarianism, the passion for equality, has exactly the same inherently conflict structure as any other relational motive. Society may not adopt as a goal that persons in class X have more, or less, *or the same,* as persons in class Y. By contrast, endeavoring to increase one's own wealth has no logical relation to other persons' levels of wealth. Each may do the best he or she can do; in principle, we can *all* win, improving our wealth with no adverse affects on any others. But we should also note that when we improve it by commerce—free exchange with others—then we benefit others even as we benefit ourselves. For this reason, it is plausible to propose that free exchange benefits the community maximally. Thus, the familiar policy of "soaking the rich" is absurd in all cases where the rich get rich by buying and selling. To

have gotten rich by that means is to have improved the lot of many others. Reducing the incentive to acquire by such means reduces the real incomes of those other people, as well as of the immediate victim. Theft is counterproductive from the public point of view. It improves the lot of the thief (if it does) only by worsening the lot of someone else.

Charity, on the other hand, has a place of honor. The charitable person enjoys helping others; when they are helped, so is he. It should be noted, though, that charity has to be the exception, not the rule. If we *all* tried to live by charity, that would be the end of all wealth. Someone must actually produce in order for there to be anything to give away. . . .

Welfare

Would contractarianism confirm the libertarian's refusal to allow coercively extracted support of the so-called safety net for the poor, public schooling, socialized medicine, and so on? I shall argue that it would indeed.

Nobody can deny that people enjoying a higher rather than a lower level of welfare is, generally speaking, a good thing. Even those who profess not to care about the well-being of their fellows will, in the first place, sign up for a general duty of nonaggression: they too will "seek peace and follow it," using violence only when necessary to counter the violence of aggressors.

It has to be pointed out that if this duty is perfectly general, it extends also to the case where the supposedly caring A steals from B in order to feed needy C. But it's not enough to point that out, as if it were a proof. What must be shown is that rational people will not modify or qualify the general duty of nonimposition, and opt instead for the idea that we do all owe each other something: for instance, a social minimum, funds for which we may extract from everyone, by force if need be. Unfortunately, most people we know do think that a social minimum is owed. They think there is a difference between my putting a gun in your ribs and extracting a transfer of cash from you to me, on the one hand, and representatives of "the public" doing the same thing, with the difference that the transfer is only partly from you to them—some of the extracted cash really does end up in the pockets of the supposed poor or provides schooling "free" to all who can benefit from it; or pays for the appendectomies of those who might not otherwise be able to afford them. Are they right to make such a distinction? No—or so I will argue.

First, let's attend to what most defenders of the welfare state overlook. The world we live in has around five billion inhabitants at present, of whom perhaps one billion enjoy "first world" status. But if the alleged duty to provide a safety net for the poor had the status of a general duty to poor humans, no state welfare program would make any sense. All such programs would have to become universal-scope foreign aid programs. Yet virtually no supporter of the Welfare State accepts this obligation. Why not?

The short answer is that politics and the self-interest of some few play the major role in the equation, high principle having little to do with it. In fact, the supposed "high" principle is considered by most people to be *too* high. They do not believe that all well-off people have an enforceable duty to provide for all badly-off ones. Yet they don't actually have a *reason* for confining welfare programs to their own nations or their own communities.

The libertarian principle says that force is to be confined to dealing with aggression, and may not be used for any other end, however noble it may seem. That includes the welfare of others such as the poor. Why, it may be asked, should we insist on sticking only with the Scrooge-like principle advocated by us libertarians at the most fundamental level? There is a ready answer. If person A does not in fact care about person B, why would he accept an enforceable duty to help care for B? Perhaps A anticipates the possibility that one day he might be in bad shape and would like B to help him. This is solid reasoning.

We should all be disposed to help those in need. But should we be so disposed to the point where we agree that if we don't help those people, we'll go to jail? Or the point where we allow others to garnish our wages forever after? Surely not! The scope of the familiar idea of aid is much more restricted than that. If we can be very helpful without much cost to us, we should do so—yet we will not consent to being *forced* to do so.

On the other hand, there is good reason to consider arrangements whereby many people agree each to pay for the operations of the others, should need arise, for example, by paying a certain set sum each month. That is precisely what insurance systems do, and they make perfect sense. But they in no way involve the involuntary duties considered in the foregoing. The fact of their availability in principle, however, makes a huge difference to arguments about welfare. It is not rational to sign up for an "insurance" pact from which you are certain to lose. Agreement to pay for operations by fellow "members" who didn't pay, didn't even have to join, and will never be any use to the ones who do pay makes no sense. Hardly fit material for a rational agreement!

Now consider the choice between (1) knowing that I will be forced to help others whom I wouldn't choose to help if I had my choice, with all others, in turn, being similarly forced to help me; and (2) knowing that our right to use our resources as we judge best, without interference by others, will always be respected, even though we also know that we won't *necessarily* be helped by others when the chips are down (i.e., nobody will *force* them to help). Is it obvious that everyone would take (1) rather than (2)? Certainly not. But that is not all. For to (2) let us add the knowledge that people are generally well-disposed toward their fellows and inclined to help when they can, and, of course, that no one may prevent them from helping when they are so inclined; add the fact that one has the right to refuse unwanted help, and you have a package that dominates the alternatives. Any supposed advantage that anyone might derive from being a beneficiary is utterly negated by his also being a forced contributor, whatever he might have preferred to do with his life.

How do we know, though, that this argument really holds? There are two points. First, it has to be noted that if most people were not at least disposed to be charitable, they also would not choose the welfare state in a social contract. But if there are enough votes to legislate the welfare state, then there must be so many charitable people out there that they can easily fulfill welfare needs without forcing their neighbors to help: most will help in any case.

Most have conceived the social contract as being concerned only with enforceable duties, that is, with strict justice. But that is a mistake. There are such things as public attitudes as well. In opting for the carrot rather than the stick in matters relating to welfare, what we are opting for is a public resolution that all will prefer that others be well-off to their being badly off, apart from any personal relation they may have to those others. That is to say, the way we should regard each other *qua* fellow persons, rather than in more local capacities such as fellow inhabitant of this part of town or fellow believer in the same religion, is not as indifferent pieces of furniture but as fellow humans trying to live good lives, and we are more likely to do so if people are well-disposed than if they are ill-disposed. This kind of disposition costs us little, after all. We do not take on a great burden when we agree that, all else being at least roughly equal, it is a better thing that Jones or Smith do well than badly, and to be disposed—but not conscripted—to lend an occasional hand or an occasional dollar if need be.

If by contrast we take the welfare-state option, it would mean that others over whom you have no control would be authorized to decide that a sizable fraction of your money will be spent on "the poor," whatever you may have wanted to do with it if you had your own way. Empirical considerations add to the case. Welfare expenditures tend to be counterproductive,

discouraging or even effectively preventing the recipient from working, and thus from acquiring useful skills. And those who do not work when they might leave us as well as themselves with a lesser array of goods and services than we would otherwise enjoy. . . .

According to James Sterba, libertarians, far from being committed to the free market and the absence of welfare legislation as I have suggested, "must endorse a welfare system." He arrives at this conclusion in the following way. Consider, he says, "a typical conflict situation between the rich and the poor. In this situation, the rich have more than enough goods and resources to satisfy their basic needs."

In such a situation, he thinks, "What is at stake is the liberty of the poor not to be interfered with in taking from the surplus possessions of the rich what is necessary to satisfy their basic needs." The rich, he says, have "more than enough," while the poor do not. So if we stop the latter from taking from the former, we deny them liberty. There is, he thinks, a "conflict of liberties" here, those of the rich vs. those of the poor.

Whether you are at liberty is a question of whether people restrict you from doing as you would like to do. But some restrictions may be made in the interests of liberty, and others not— that is the whole point of talking of a right to liberty, since rights, as such, restrict. Now, the "rich" in his argument, we are assuming, got where they are by fair means: they always acquired only by finding what was previously unowned, or by making things out of what they found, or by trading things got by one of those ways, or by other liberty-respecting trades, with others on mutually agreed terms. Whenever anyone has done so, he has satisfied the condition that his activities do not, as such, interfere with the activities of anyone else. They are harmonious. Now along come the poor with their proposal to take from the rich, and to do so without an agreement by the latter to have them do so. What the rich have is acquired in the ways noted; thus the poor do not have a right to take anything from them, so far as the right to liberty only is concerned. Whether they have such a right has nothing to do with how much they need the things in question. But it has everything to do with the fundamental moral agreement among us all: do we let each other live in peace, or don't we? The rich whom we are considering in this argument do not make war on anyone, poor or otherwise, in the process of getting rich. How, then, can Sterba imagine that what we have here is a "conflict of liberties" which cannot be decided on libertarian grounds? If his specifications are strictly observed, then the rich in question have the right to refuse to allow the poor to take what they need, and the poor, presumably, will starve.

Sterba thinks, of course, that it would be "unreasonable" to ask the poor to accept a principle such as I have been advocating. It is not clear whether he thinks this to be a distinct issue from the issue of what a liberty principle, of the type I have been supporting, as such implies. If we stick to the latter question, it is plain that the liberty principle does not imply that the poor have a right, *qua* right of liberty, to do what he describes. They do, of course, have a right to ask, and the rich a right to give as well as refuse.

Now, Aquinas supposed that the poor taking from the rich in such cases wouldn't even be theft; perhaps Sterba is following in his footsteps here. But that is surely just special pleading on Aquinas' part; it seems clearly to be a question of whether the theft in question is somehow excusable, and not whether it is theft at all.

That it is "unreasonable" to ask people to accept that principle is plainly a discussable claim. Is it unreasonable? I think not. On the contrary, welfarism, which makes everyone in principle a slave to anyone in need, is unreasonable. Welfarism taken to the extreme of socialism is an invitation to the productive to cease producing, since they are not allowed to enjoy the fruits of their labor, except in the special case where they are Mother Theresa. But the principles of morals are not made for Mother Theresa: They are made for us all.

On the very different, but certainly important, question of whether the poor would do better in a libertarian society where people have rights to their property, or in a welfare liberal society where, in effect, they do not, it is not clear what our terms of reference are. But insofar as we can point to real-world cases, certainly the evidence is overwhelmingly on the side of the libertarians. In Mao's China, as we now know, tens of millions of people starved to death; in America, cases of actual starvation, even during the days when it was pretty nearly a "libertarian" country, were extremely rare. If we are permitted to equip the information base of the poor with facts like that, the appearance of unreason will surely diminish drastically. Giving people the right to get rich if they can assures us that the social world will be well equipped with people who can feed the hungry should they need feeding; and people being what they are, it is extremely unlikely that persons in need will go long without, with all those wealthy persons' doors to knock on.

The welfare liberal "guarantee" is a delusion. All you can guarantee is that the people who are done down will indeed be done down. But as to a guarantee that people who would otherwise starve will not starve—which is what the socialist claims to be offering us—it is hollow. Absence of starvation is a function of ample supply and some generous hearts. Only libertarianism actually gets us the former, and the latter is the only real refuge for those genuinely in need. The efficacy of both depends on security of property and freedom of exchange. Systems biased toward the incapable are systems that perpetuate poverty, with no compensating advantages.

Concluding Note

The position here advocated takes on, I suppose, the heaviest burden of proof in the field. On the one hand, it disavows any appeal to transcendental considerations in its defense of liberty—including a priori impositions on what the people who are party to the social contract may believe.

On the other hand, it refuses to assume that we *must* sign some social contract or other. Everything needs to be supported, nothing simply assumed. Yet this is a burden of proof that can be borne. The appeal of social life for everyone is so enormous that our motivation to accept the terms proposed here greatly exceeds any interest in remaining outside. What we would sign for, I have argued, is, purely and simply, liberty—not, for instance, a package of handouts from our hapless fellows. Your private club or religion, and certainly your marriage or your job, may indeed involve much more. The advantage of liberty in that respect is precisely that it leaves the widest possible array of such further involvements open to all who, together with willing others, are ready to take them on. Precisely what makes that possible is the exclusion of arrangements that press unwilling participants into the act.

My argument, then, does not *presuppose* the libertarian scheme of rights. Instead it argues for those rights, by showing that that scheme of rights can be expected to work out better for every reasonable person, if applied uniformly to all, than any alternative scheme. That is why we should support strong rights of individual liberty rather than schemes imposing involuntary duties for the alleged benefit of the public, on shaky or confused grounds. The best politics, in short, is no politics.

NOTES

1. Mill, *On Liberty,* Ch. IV, 3rd paragraph.

2. The central source is David Gauthier, *Morals by Agreement* (New York: Oxford University Press, 1986).

3. Anthony De Jasay, *Social Contract, Free Ride* (New York: Oxford University Press, 1989) distinguishes three sorts of contract: the "spot" contract, where performance is essentially immediate for both parties, the "half-forward" contract where one acts significantly before the other, and the "fully forward" contract where both act in the medium to far future. Of these, only the second poses a major problem; it is my standard model, though he is right to point out that the others are at least as frequent. See 22–25 for starters.

4. See Jan Narveson, *The Libertarian Idea* (Philadelphia: Temple University Press, 1988).

5. Hobbes, *Leviathan,* Ch. XIV.

6. The author's unpublished study, "Property Rights, Original Acquisition, and Lockean Provisos," read at the meetings of the Canadian Philosophical Association. Calgary, Alberta, June 1994, goes into this at length. See also the exposition in *The Libertarian Idea*, Chs. 6–8.

Part III

Socialist Justice

5 The Socialist Ideal

KARL MARX AND FRIEDRICH ENGELS

A SPECTRE IS HAUNTING EUROPE—the spectre of Communism. All the Powers of old Europe have entered into a holy alliance to exorcise this spectre: Pope and Czar, Metternich and Guizot, French Radicals and German police-spies.

Where is the party in opposition that has not been decried as Communistic by its opponents in power? Where the Opposition that has not hurled back the branding reproach of Communism, against the more advanced opposition parties, as well as against its reactionary adversaries?

Two things result from this fact.

I. Communism is already acknowledged by all European Powers to be itself a Power.

II. It is high time that Communists should openly, in the face of the whole world, publish their views, their aims, their tendencies, and meet this nursery tale of the Spectre of Communism with a Manifesto of the party itself . . .

The Communist Program

The Communists do not form a separate party opposed to other working-class parties.

They have no interests separate and apart from those of the proletariat as a whole.

They do not set up any sectarian principles of their own, by which to shape and mould the proletarian movement.

The Communists are distinguished from the other working-class parties by this only: (1) In the national struggles of the proletarians of the different countries, they point out and bring to the front the common interests of the entire proletariat, independently of all nationality. (2) In the various stages of development which the struggle of the working class against the bourgeoisie has to pass through they always and everywhere represent the interests of the movement as a whole.

The Communists, therefore, are on the one hand, practically, the most advanced and resolute section of the working-class parties of every country, that section which pushes forward all others; on the other hand, theoretically, they have over the great mass of the proletariat the advantage of clearly understanding the line of march, the conditions and the ultimate general results of the proletarian movement.

The immediate aim of the Communists is the same as that of all the other proletarian parties: formation of the proletariat into a class, overthrow of the bourgeois supremacy, conquest of political power by the proletariat.

The theoretical conclusions of the Communists are in no way based on ideas or principles that have been invented, or discovered, by this or that would-be universal reformer.

They merely express, in general terms, actual relations springing from an existing class struggle, from a historical movement going on under our very eyes. The abolition of existing property

From the Communist Manifesto, *first published in English by Friedrich Engels in 1888, and the* Critique of the Gotha Program, *edited by C. P. Dutt (1966), pp. 5–11. Reprinted by permission of International Publishers.*

relations is not at all a distinctive feature of Communism.

All property relations in the past have continually been subject to historical change consequent upon the change in historical conditions.

The French Revolution, for example, abolished feudal property in favour of bourgeois property.

The distinguishing feature of Communism is not the abolition of property generally, but the abolition of bourgeois property. But modern bourgeois private property is the final and most complete expression of the system of producing and appropriating products, that is based on class antagonisms, on the exploitation of the many by the few.

In this sense, the theory of the Communists may be summed up in the single sentence: Abolition of private property.

We Communists have been reproached with the desire of abolishing the right of personally acquiring property as the fruit of man's own labour, which property is alleged to be the groundwork of all personal freedom, activity and independence.

Hard-won, self-acquired, self-earned property! Do you mean the property of the petty artisan and of the small peasant, a form of property that preceded the bourgeois form? There is no need to abolish that; the development of industry has to a great extent already destroyed it, and is still destroying it daily.

Or do you mean modern bourgeois private property?

But does wage-labour create any property for the labourer? Not a bit. It creates capital, *i.e.*, that kind of property which exploits wage-labour, and which cannot increase except upon condition of begetting a new supply of wage-labour for fresh exploitation. Property, in its present form, is based on the antagonism of capital and wage-labour, Let us examine both sides of this antagonism.

To be capitalist, is to have not only a purely personal, but a social *status* in production. Cap-

ital is a collective product, and only by the united action of many members, nay, in the last resort, only by the united action of all members of society, can it be set in motion.

Capital is, therefore, not a personal, it is a social power.

When, therefore, capital is converted into common property, into the property of all members of society, personal property is not thereby transformed into social property. It is only the social character of the property that is changed. It loses its class-character.

Let us now take wage-labour.

The average price of wage-labour is the minimum wage, *i.e.*, that quantum of the means of subsistence, which is absolutely requisite to keep the labourer in bare existence as a labourer. What, therefore, the wage-labourer appropriates by means of his labour, merely suffices to prolong and reproduce a bare existence. We by no means intend to abolish this personal appropriation of the products of labour, an appropriation that is made for the maintenance and reproduction of human life, and that leaves no surplus wherewith to command the labour of others. All that we want to do away with, is the miserable character of this appropriation, under which the labourer lives merely to increase capital, and is allowed to live only in so far as the interest of the ruling class requires it.

In bourgeois society, living labour is but a means to increase accumulated labour. In Communist society, accumulated labour is but a means to widen, to enrich, to promote the existence of the labourer.

In bourgeois society, therefore, the past dominates the present; in Communist society, the present dominates the past. In bourgeois society capital is independent and has individuality, while the living person is dependent and has no individuality.

And the abolition of this state of things is called by the bourgeois, abolition of individuality and freedom! And rightly so. The abolition of bourgeois individuality, bourgeois independence, and bourgeois freedom is undoubtedly aimed at.

By freedom is meant, under the present bourgeois conditions of production, free trade, free selling and buying.

But if selling and buying disappears, free selling and buying disappears also. This talk about free selling and buying, and all the other "brave words" of our bourgeoisie about freedom in general, have a meaning, if any, only in contrast with restricted selling and buying, with the fettered traders of the Middle Ages, but have no meaning when opposed to the Communistic abolition of buying and selling, of the bourgeois conditions of production, and of the bourgeoisie itself.

You are horrified at our intending to do away with private property. But in your existing society, private property is already done away with for nine-tenths of the population; its existence for the few is solely due to its non-existence in the hands of those nine-tenths. You reproach us, therefore, with intending to do away with a form of property, the necessary condition for whose existence is the non-existence of any property for the immense majority of society.

In one word, you reproach us with intending to do away with your property. Precisely so; that is just what we intend.

From the moment when labour can no longer be converted into capital, money, or rent, into a social power capable of being monopolised, *i.e.*, from the moment when individual property can no longer be transformed into bourgeois property, into capital, from that moment, you say, individuality vanishes.

You must, therefore, confess that by "individual" you mean no other person than the bourgeois, than the middle-class owner of property. This person must, indeed, be swept out of the way, and made impossible.

Communism deprives no man of the power to appropriate the products of society; all that it does is to deprive him of the power to subjugate the labour of others by means of such appropriation.

It has been objected that upon the abolition of private property all work will cease, and universal laziness will overtake us.

According to this, bourgeois society ought long ago to have gone to the dogs through sheer idleness; for those of its members who work, acquire nothing, and those who acquire anything, do not work. The whole of this objection is but another expression of the tautology: that there can no longer be any wage-labour when there is no longer any capital.

All objections urged against the Communistic mode of producing and appropriating material products, have, in the same way, been urged against the Communistic modes of producing and appropriating intellectual products. Just as, to the bourgeois, the disappearance of class property is the disappearance of production itself, so the disappearance of class culture is to him identical with the disappearance of all culture.

That culture, the loss of which he laments, is, for the enormous majority, a mere training to act as a machine.

But don't wrangle with us so long as you apply, to our intended abolition of bourgeois property, the standard of your bourgeois notions of freedom, culture, law, [and so on]. Your very ideas are but the outgrowth of the conditions of your bourgeois production and bourgeois property, just as your jurisprudence is but the will of your class made into a law for all, a will, whose essential character and direction are determined by the economical conditions of existence of your class.

The selfish misconception that induces you to transform into eternal laws of nature and reason, the social forms springing from your present mode of production and form of property—historical relations that rise and disappear in the progress of production—this misconception you share with every ruling class that has preceded you. What you see clearly in the case of ancient property, what you admit in the case of feudal property, you are of course forbidden to admit in the case of your own bourgeois form of property.

Abolition of the family! Even the most radical flare up at this infamous proposal of the Communists.

On what foundation is the present family, the bourgeois family, based? On capital, on private gain. In its completely developed form this family exists only among the bourgeoisie. But this state of things finds its complement in the practical absence of the family among the proletarians, and in public prostitution.

The bourgeois family will vanish as a matter of course when its complement vanishes, and both will vanish with the vanishing of capital.

Do you charge us with wanting to stop the exploitation of children by their parents? To this crime we plead guilty.

But, you will say, we destroy the most hallowed of relations, when we replace home education by social.

And your education! Is not that also social, and determined by the social conditions under which you educate, by the intervention, direct or indirect, of society, by means of schools, [and so on]? The Communists have not invented the intervention of society in education; they do but seek to alter the character of that intervention, and to rescue education from the influence of the ruling class.

The bourgeois clap-trap about the family and education, about the hallowed co-relation of parent and child, becomes all the more disgusting, the more, by the action of Modern Industry, all family ties among the proletarians are torn asunder, and their children transformed into simple articles of commerce and instruments of labour.

But you Communists would introduce community of women, screams the whole bourgeoisie in chorus.

The bourgeois sees in his wife a mere instrument of production. He hears that the instruments of production are to be exploited in common, and, naturally, can come to no other conclusion than that the lot of being common to all will likewise fall to the women.

He has not even a suspicion that the real point aimed at is to do away with the status of women as mere instruments of production.

For the rest, nothing is more ridiculous than the virtuous indignation of our bourgeois at the community of women which, they pretend, is to be openly and officially established by the Communists. The Communists have no need to introduce community of women; it has existed almost from time immemorial.

Our bourgeois, not content with having the wives and daughters of their proletarians at their disposal, not to speak of common prostitutes, take the greatest pleasure in seducing each other's wives.

Bourgeois marriage is in reality a system of wives in common and thus, at the most, what the Communists might possibly be reproached with, is that they desire to introduce, in substitution for a hypocritically concealed, an openly legalised community of women. For the rest, it is self-evident that the abolition of the present system of production must bring with it the abolition of the community of women springing from that system, *i.e.*, of prostitution both public and private.

The Communists are further reproached with desiring to abolish countries and nationality.

The working men have no country. We cannot take from them what they have not got. Since the proletariat must first of all acquire political supremacy, must rise to be the leading class of the nation, must constitute itself *the* nation, it is, so far, itself national, though not in the bourgeois sense of the word.

National differences and antagonisms between peoples are daily more and more vanishing, owing to the development of the bourgeoisie, to freedom of commerce, to the world-market, to uniformity in the mode of production and in the conditions of life corresponding thereto.

The supremacy of the proletariat will cause them to vanish still faster. United action, of the leading civilised countries at least, is one of the first conditions for the emancipation of the proletariat.

In proportion as the exploitation of one individual by another is put an end to, the exploitation of one nation by another will also be put an end to. In proportion as the antagonism between classes within the nation vanished, the hostility of one nation to another will come to an end.

Unification

The charges against Communism made from a religious, a philosophical, and, generally, from an ideological standpoint, are not deserving of serious examination.

Does it require deep intuition to comprehend that man's ideas, views and conceptions, in one word, man's consciousness, changes with every change in the conditions of his material existence, in his social relations and in his social life?

What else does the history of ideas prove, than that intellectual production changes its character in proportion as material production is changed? The ruling ideas of each age have ever been the ideas of its ruling class.

When people speak of ideas that revolutionise society, they do but express the fact, that within the old society, the elements of a new one have been created, and that the dissolution of the old ideas keeps even pace with the dissolution of the old conditions of existence.

When the ancient world was in its last throes, the ancient religions were overcome by Christianity. When Christian ideas succumbed in the 18th century to rationalist ideas, feudal society fought its death battle with the then revolutionary bourgeoisie. The ideas of religious liberty and freedom of conscience merely gave expression to the sway of free competition within the domain of knowledge.

"Undoubtedly," it will be said, "religious, moral, philosophical and juridical ideas have been modified in the course of historical development. But religion, morality, philosophy, political science, and law, constantly survived this change."

"There are, besides, eternal truths, such as Freedom, Justice, etc., that are common to all states of society. But Communism abolishes eternal truths, it abolishes all religion, and all morality, instead of constituting them on a new basis; it therefore acts in contradiction to all past historical experience."

What does this accusation reduce itself to? The history of all past society has consisted in the development of class antagonisms, antagonisms that assumed different forms at different epochs.

But whatever form they may have taken, one fact is common to all past ages, *viz.*, the exploitation of one part of society by the other. No wonder, then, that the social consciousness of past ages, despite all the multiplicity and variety it displays, moves within certain common forms, or general ideas, which cannot completely vanish except with the total disappearance of class antagonisms.

The Communist revolution is the most radical rupture with traditional property relations; no wonder that its development involves the most radical rupture with traditional ideas.

But let us have done with the bourgeois objections to Communism.

We have seen above, that the first step in the revolution by the working class, is to raise the proletariat to the position of ruling class, to win the battle of democracy.

The proletariat will use its political supremacy to wrest, by degrees, all capital from the bourgeoisie, to centralise all instruments of production in the hands of the State, *i.e.*, of the proletariat organised as the ruling class; and to increase the total of productive forces as rapidly as possible.

Of course, in the beginning, this cannot be effected except by means of despotic inroads on the rights of property, and on the conditions of bourgeois production; by means of measures, therefore, which appear economically insufficient and untenable, but which, in the course of the movement, outstrip themselves, necessitate further inroads upon the old social order, and are unavoidable as a means of entirely revolutionising the mode of production.

These measures will of course be different in different countries.

Nevertheless in the most advanced countries, the following will be pretty generally applicable.

1. Abolition of property in land and application of all rents of land to public purposes.
2. A heavy progressive or graduated income tax.
3. Abolition of all right of inheritance.
4. Confiscation of the property of all emigrants and rebels.
5. Centralisation of credit in the hands of the State, by means of a national bank with State capital and an exclusive monopoly.
6. Centralisation of the means of communication and transport in the hands of the State.
7. Extension of factories and instruments of production owned by the State; the bringing into cultivation of waste-lands, and the improvement of the soil generally in accordance with a common plan.
8. Equal liability of all to labour. Establishment of industrial armies, especially for agriculture.
9. Combination of agriculture with manufacturing industries; gradual abolition of the distinction between town and country, by a more equable distribution of the population over the country.
10. Free education for all children in public schools. Abolition of children's factory labour in its present form. Combination of education with industrial production [and so on].

When, in the course of development, class distinctions have disappeared, and all production has been concentrated in the hands of a vast association of the whole nation, the public power will lose its political character. Political power, properly so called, is merely the organized power of one class for oppressing another. If the proletariat during its contest with the bourgeoisie is compelled, by the force of circumstances, to organise itself as a class, if, by means of a revolution, it makes itself the ruling class, and, as such, sweeps away by force the old conditions of production, then it will, along with these conditions, have swept away the conditions for the existence of class antagonisms and of class generally, and will thereby have abolished its own supremacy as a class.

In place of the old bourgeois society, with its classes and class antagonisms, we shall have an association, in which the free development of each is the condition for the free development of all. . . .

Critique of Social Democracy

In present-day society, the instruments of labour are the monopoly of the capitalist class; the resulting dependence of the working class is the cause of misery and servitude in all its forms.

This sentence, borrowed from the Statutes of the International, is incorrect in this "improved" edition.

In present-day society the instruments of labour are the monopoly of the landowners (the monopoly of property in land is even the basis of the monopoly of capital) *and* the capitalists. In the passage in question, the Statutes of the International do not mention by name either the one or the other class of monopolists. They speak of the "*monopoly of the means of labour, that is the sources of life.*" The addition, "*sources of life*" makes it sufficiently clear that land is included in the instruments of labour.

The correction was introduced because Lassalle, for reasons now generally known, attacked *only* the capitalist class and not the landowners.

In England, the capitalist is usually not even the owner of the land on which his factory stands.

The emancipation of labour demands the promotion of the instruments of labour to the common property of society, and the co-operative regulation of the total labour with equitable distribution of the proceeds of labour.

"Promotion of the instruments of labour to the common property" ought obviously to read, their "conversion into the common property," but this only in passing.

What are the "proceeds of labour"? The product of labour or its value? And in the latter case, is it the total value of the product or only that part of the value which labour has newly added to the value of the means of production consumed?

The "proceeds of labour" is a loose notion which Lassalle has put in the place of definite economic conceptions.

What is "equitable distribution"?

Do not the bourgeois assert that the present-day distribution is "equitable"? And is it not, in fact, the only "equitable" distribution on the basis of the present-day mode of production? Are economic relations regulated by legal conceptions or do not, on the contrary, legal relations arise from economic ones? Have not also the socialist sectarians the most varied notions about "equitable" distribution?

To understand what idea is meant in this connection by the phrase "equitable distribution," we must take the first paragraph and this one together. The latter implies a society wherein "the instruments of labour are common property, and the total labour is co-operatively regulated," and from the first paragraph we learn that "the proceeds of labour belong undiminished with equal right to all members of society."

"To all members of society"? To those who do not work as well? What remains then of the "undiminished proceeds of labour"? Only to those members of society who work? What remains then of the "equal right" of all members of society?

But "all members of society" and "equal right" are obviously mere phrases. The kernel consists in this, that in this communist society every worker must receive the "undiminished" Lassallean "proceeds of labour."

Let us take first of all the words "proceeds of labour" in the sense of the product of labour, then the co-operative proceeds of labour are the *total social product*.

From this is then to be deducted:

First, cover for replacement of the means of production used up.

Secondly, additional portion for expansion of production.

Thirdly, reserve or insurance fund to provide against mis-adventures, disturbances through natural events, etc.

These deductions from the "undiminished proceeds of labour" are an economic necessity and their magnitude is to be determined by available means and forces, and partly by calculation of probabilities, but they are in no way calculable by equity.

There remains the other part of the total product, destined to serve as means of consumption.

Before this is divided among the individuals, there has to be deducted from it:

First, the general costs of administration not belonging to production.

This part will, from the outset, be very considerably restricted in comparison with present-day society and it diminishes in proportion as the new society develops.

Secondly, that which is destined for the communal satisfaction of needs, such as schools, health services, etc.

From the outset this part is considerably increased in comparison with present-day society and it increases in proportion as the new society develops.

Thirdly, funds for those unable to work, etc., in short, what is included under so-called official poor relief today.

Only now do we come to the "distribution" which the programme, under Lassallean influence, alone has in view in its narrow fashion, namely that part of the means of consumption which is divided among the individual producers of the co-operative society.

The "undiminished proceeds of labour" have already quietly become converted into the "diminished" proceeds, although what the producer is deprived of in his capacity as a private individual benefits him directly or indirectly in his capacity as a member of society.

Just as the phrase "undiminished proceeds of labour" has disappeared, so now does the phrase "proceeds of labour" disappear altogether.

Within the co-operative society based on common ownership of the means of production, the producers do not exchange their products; just as little does the labour employed on the products appear here *as the value* of these products, as a material quality possessed by them, since now, in contrast to capitalist society, individual labour no longer exists in an indirect fashion but directly as a component part of the total labour. The phrase "proceeds of labour," objectionable even today on account of its ambiguity, thus loses all meaning.

What we have to deal with here is a communist society, not as it has *developed* on its own foundations, but, on the contrary, as it *emerges* from capitalist society; which is thus in every respect, economically, morally and intellectually, still stamped with the birthmarks of the old society from whose womb it emerges. Accordingly the individual producer receives back from society—after the deductions have been made— exactly what he gives to it. What he has given to it is his individual amount of labour. For example, the social working day consists of the sum of the individual labour hours; the individual labour time of the individual producer is the part of the social labour day contributed by him, his share in it. He receives a certificate from society that he has furnished such and such an amount of labour (after deducting his labour for the common fund), and with this certificate he draws from the social stock of means of consumption as much as the same amount of labour costs. The same amount of labour which he has given to society in one form, he receives back in another.

Here obviously the same principle prevails as that which regulates the exchange of commodities, as far as this is exchange of equal values. Content and form are changed, because under the altered circumstances no one can give anything except his labour, and because, on the other hand, nothing can pass into the ownership of individuals except individual means of consumption. But, as far as the distribution of the latter among the individual producers is concerned, the same principle prevails as in the exchange of commodity-equivalents, so much labour in one form is exchanged for an equal amount of labour in another form.

Hence, *equal right* here is still in principle— *bourgeois right*, although principle and practice are no longer in conflict, while the exchange of equivalents in commodity exchange only exists on the *average* and not in the individual case.

In spite of this advance, this *equal right* is still stigmatised by a bourgeois limitation. The right of the producers is *proportional* to the labour they supply; the equality consists in the fact that measurement is made with an *equal standard*, labour.

But one man is superior to another physically or mentally and so supplies more labour in the same time, or can labour for a longer time; and labour, to serve as a measure, must be defined by its duration or intensity, otherwise it ceases to be a standard of measurement. This *equal* right is an unequal right for unequal labour. It recognises no class differences, because everyone is only a worker like everyone else; but it tacitly recognises unequal individual endowment and thus productive capacity as natural privileges. *It is therefore a right of inequality in its content, like every right.* Right by its very nature can only consist in the application of an equal standard; but unequal individuals (and they would not be different individuals if they were not unequal) are only measurable by an equal standard in so far as they are brought under an equal point of view, are taken from one *definite* side only, *e.g.,* in the present case are regarded *only as workers,* and nothing more seen in them, everything else being ignored. Further, one worker is married, another not; one has more children than another and so on and so forth. Thus with an equal output, and hence an equal share in the social consumption fund, one will in fact receive more than another, one will be richer than another, and so on. To avoid all these defects, right, instead of being equal, would have to be unequal.

But these defects are inevitable in the first phase of communist society as it is when it has just emerged after prolonged birth pangs from capitalist society. Right can never be higher than the economic structure of society and the cultural development thereby determined.

In a higher phase of communist society, after the enslaving subordination of individuals under division of labour, and therewith also the antithesis between mental and physical labour, has vanished; after labour, from a mere means of life, has itself become the prime necessity of life; after the productive forces have also increased with the all-round development of the individual, and all the springs of co-operative wealth flow more abundantly—only then can the narrow horizon of bourgeois right be fully left behind and society inscribe on its banners: from each according to his ability, to each according to his needs!

I have dealt more at length with the "undiminished proceeds of labour" on the one hand, and with "equal right" and "equitable distri-

bution" on the other, in order to show what a crime it is to attempt, on the one hand, to force on our party again, as dogmas, ideas which in a certain period had some meaning but have now become obsolete rubbishy phrases, while on the other, perverting the realistic outlook, which has cost so much effort to instill into the party, but which has now taken root in it, by means of ideological nonsense about "right" and other trash common among the democrats and French Socialists.

Quite apart from the analysis so far given, it was in general incorrect to make a fuss about so-called "*distribution*" and put the principal stress on it.

The distribution of the means of consumption at any time is only a consequence of the distribution of the conditions of production themselves. The latter distribution, however, is a feature of the mode of production itself. The capitalist mode of production, for example, rests on the fact that the material conditions of production are in the hands of non-workers in the form of property in capital and land, while the masses are only owners of the personal condition of production, *viz.,* labour power. Once the elements of production are so distributed, then the present-day distribution of the means of consumption results automatically. If the material conditions of production are the co-operative property of the workers themselves, then this likewise results in a different distribution of the means of consumption from the present one. Vulgar socialism (and from it in turn a section of democracy) has taken over from the bourgeois economists the consideration and treatment of distribution as independent of the mode of production and hence the presentation of socialism as turning principally on distribution. After the real position has long been made clear, why go back again?

6 Justice Under Socialism

EDWARD NELL AND ONORA O'NEILL

"From each according to his ability, to each according to his need."

THE STIRRING SLOGAN THAT ENDS *The Critique of the Gotha Program* is generally taken as a capsule summary of the socialist approach to distributing the burdens and benefits of life. It can be seen as the statement of a noble ideal and yet be found wanting on three separate scores. First, there is no guarantee that, even if all contribute according to their abilities, all needs can be met: the principle gives us no guidance for distributing goods when some needs must go unmet. Second, if all contribute according to their abilities, there may be a material surplus after all needs are met: again, the principle gives us no guidance for distributing such a surplus. Third, the principle incorporates no suggestion as to why each man would contribute according to his ability: no incentive structure is evident.

These apparent shortcomings can be compared with those of other principles a society might follow in distributing burdens and benefits. Let us call

1. "From each according to his ability, to each according to his need," the *Socialist Principle of Justice.*

Its Capitalist counterpart would be

2. From each according to his choice, given his assets, to each according to his contribution. We shall call this the *Laissez-Faire Principle.*

These two principles will require a good deal of interpretation, but at the outset we can say that in the Socialist Principle of Justice "abilities" and "needs" refer to persons, whereas the "choices" and "contributions" in the Laissez-Faire Principle refer also to the management of impersonal property, the given assets. It goes without saying that some of the "choices," particularly those of the propertyless, are normally made under considerable duress. As "choice" is the ideologically favored term, we shall retain it.

In a society where the Socialist Principle of Justice regulates distribution, the requirement is that everyone use such talents as have been developed in him (though this need not entail any allocation of workers to jobs), and the payment of workers is contingent not upon their contributions but upon their needs. In a laissez-faire society, where individuals may be endowed with more or less capital or with bare labor power, they choose in the light of these assets how and how much to work (they may be dropouts or moonlighters), and/or how to invest their capital, and they are paid in proportion.

None of the three objections raised against the Socialist Principle of Justice holds for the

From "Justice Under Socialism," Dissent, *Vol 18 (1972), pp. 483–491. Reprinted by permission of the authors and Dissent Publishing Corporation.*

Laissez-Faire Principle. Whatever the level of contribution individuals choose, their aggregate product can be distributed in proportion to the contribution—whether of capital or of labor—each individual chooses to make. The Laissez-Faire Principle is applicable under situations both of scarcity and of abundance, and it incorporates a theory of incentives: people choose their level of contribution in order to get a given level of material reward.

Principles 1 and 2 can be crossfertilized, yielding two further principles:

3. From each according to his ability, to each according to his contribution.
4. From each according to his choice, to each according to his need.

Principle 3 could be called an *Incentive Socialist Principle* of distribution. Like the Socialist Principle of Justice, it pictures a society in which all are required to work in proportion to the talents that have been developed in them. Since unearned income is not available and rewards are hinged to contribution rather than need, all work is easily enforced in an economy based on the Incentive Socialist Principle. This principle, however, covers a considerable range of systems. It holds for a Stalinist economy with an authoritarian job allocation. It also holds for a more liberal, market socialist economy in which there is a more or less free labor market, though without an option to drop out or live on unearned income, or the freedom to choose the level and type of qualification one is prepared to acquire. The Incentive Socialist Principle rewards workers according to their contribution: it is a principle of distribution in which an incentive system—reliance on material rewards—is explicit. Marx believed this principle would have to be followed in the early stages of socialism, in a society "still stamped with the birthmarks of the old society."

Under the Incentive Socialist Principle, each worker receives back the value of the amount of work he contributes to society in one form or another. According to Marx, this is a form of bourgeois right that "tacitly recognizes unequal individual endowments, and thus natural privileges in respect of productive capacity." So this principle holds for a still deficient society where the needs of particular workers, which depend on many things other than their productive capacity, may not be met. Although it may be less desirable than the Socialist Principle of Justice, the Incentive Socialist Principle clearly meets certain criteria the Socialist Principle of Justice cannot meet. It provides a principle of allocation that can be applied equally well to the various situations of scarcity, sufficiency, and abundance. Its material incentive structure explains how under market socialism, given a capital structure and a skill structure, workers will choose jobs and work hard at them—and also why under a Stalinist economy workers will work hard at jobs to which they have been allocated.

Under the Incentive Socialist Principle, workers—whether assigned to menial work or to specific jobs—respond to incentives of the same sort as do workers under the Laissez-Faire Principle. The difference is that, while the Laissez-Faire Principle leaves the measurement of the contribution of a worker to be determined by the level of wage he is offered, the Incentive Socialist Principle relies on a bureaucratically determined weighting that takes into account such factors as the difficulty, duration, qualification level, and risk involved in a given job.

There is another difference between societies living under the Laissez-Faire Principle and those following the Incentive Socialist Principle. Under the Laissez-Faire Principle, there is no central coordination of decisions, for assets are managed according to the choices of their owners. This gives rise to the well-known problems of instability and unemployment. Under the Incentive Socialist Principle, assets are managed by the central government; hence one would expect instability to be eliminated and full employment guaranteed. However, we do not regard this difference as a matter of principle on the same level with others we are discussing.

Moreover, in practice some recognizable capitalist societies have managed to control fluctuations without undermining the Laissez-Faire Principle as the principle of distribution.

Let us call Principle 4 the *Utopian Principle of Justice*. It postulates a society without any requirement of contribution or material incentives, but with guaranteed minimal consumption. This principle suffers from the same defect as the Socialist Principle of Justice: it does not determine distributions of benefits under conditions either of scarcity or of abundance, and it suggests no incentive structure to explain why enough should be contributed to its economy to make it possible to satisfy needs. Whether labor is contributed according to choice or according to ability, it is conceivable that the aggregate social product should be such that either some needs cannot be met or that, when all needs are met, a surplus remains that cannot be divided on the basis of needs.

On the surface, this Utopian Principle of Justice exudes the aroma of laissez-faire: though needs will not go unmet in utopia, contributions will be made for no more basic reason than individual whim. They are tied neither to the reliable effects of the incentive of material reward for oneself, nor to those of the noble ideal of filling the needs of others, nor to a conception of duty or self-sacrifice. Instead, contributions will come forth, if they do, according to the free and unconstrained choices of individual economic agents, on the basis of their given preferences. Preferences, however, are not "given"; they develop and change, are learned and unlearned, and follow fashions and fads. Whim, fancy, pleasure, desire, wish are all words suggesting this aspect of consumer choice. By tying the demand for products to needs and the supply of work to choice, the Utopian Principle of Justice ensures stability in the former but does not legislate against fluctuations and unpredictable variability in the latter.

So the Socialist Principle of Justice and the Utopian Principle of Justice suffer from a common defect. There is no reason to suppose these

systems will operate at precisely the level at which aggregate output is sufficient to meet all the needs without surplus. And since people do not need an income in money terms but rather an actual and quite precisely defined list of food, clothing, housing, etc. (bearing in mind the various alternatives that might be substituted), the *aggregate* measured in value terms could be right, yet the *composition* might still be unable to meet all the people's needs. People might choose or have the ability to do the right amount of work, but on the wrong projects. One could even imagine the economy growing from a situation of scarcity to one of abundance without ever passing through any point at which its aggregate output could be distributed to meet precisely the needs of its population.

So far, we have been considering not the justification or desirability of alternative principles of distribution, but their practicality. It appears that, in this respect, principles hinging reward on contribution rather than on need have a great advantage. They can both provide a general principle of distribution and indicate the pattern of incentives to which workers will respond.

It might be held that these advantages are restricted to the Incentive Socialist Principle in its various versions, since under the Laissez-Faire Principle there is some income—property income—which is not being paid in virtue of any contribution. This problem can be dealt with either, as we indicated above, by interpreting the notion of contribution to cover the contribution of one's assets to the capital market, or by restricting the scope of the Laissez-Faire Principle to cover workers only, or by interpreting the notion of property income so as to regard wages as a return to property, i.e., property in one's labor power. One can say that under capitalism part of the aggregate product is set aside for the owners of capital (and another part, as under market socialism, for government expenditure) and the remainder is distributed according to the Laissez-Faire Principle. Or one may say that property income is paid in virtue of

[margin handwriting:] What about ppl. who can't get jobs? No opp.?

past contributions, whose reward was not consumed at the time it was earned but was stored. Apologists tend to favor interpretations that make the worker a sort of capitalist or the capitalist a sort of slow-consuming worker. Whichever line is taken, it is clear that the Laissez-Faire Principle—however undesirable we may find it—is a principle of distribution that can be of general use in two senses. Appropriately interpreted, it covers the distribution of earned and of unearned income, and it applies in situations both of scarcity and of abundance.

So we seem to have reached the paradoxical conclusion that the principle of distribution requiring that workers' needs be met is of no use in situations of need, since it does not assign priorities among needs, and that the principle demanding that each contribute according to his ability is unable to explain what incentives will lead him to do so. In this view, the Socialist Principle of Justice would have to be regarded as possibly noble but certainly unworkable.

The Socialist Principle Defended

But this view should not be accepted. Marx formulated the Socialist Principle of Justice on the basis of a conception of human abilities and needs that will yield some guidance to its interpretation. We shall now try to see whether the difficulties discussed above can be alleviated when we consider this principle in the light of Marxian theory.

Marx clearly thought that the Socialist Principle of Justice was peculiarly relevant to situations of abundance. In the last section we argued that, on the contrary, it was an adequate principle of distribution only when aggregate output exactly covered total needs. The source of this discrepancy lies in differing analyses of human needs.

By fulfillment of needs we understand at least a subsistence income. Needs are not met when a person lacks sufficient food, clothing, shelter, medical care, or socially necessary training/education. But beyond this biological and social minimum

we can point to another set of needs, which men do not have qua men but acquire qua producers. Workers need not merely a biological and social minimum, but whatever other goods—be they holidays or contacts with others whose work bears on theirs or guaranteed leisure, which they need to perform their jobs as well as possible. So a principle of distribution according to needs will not be of use only to a subsistence-level economy. Very considerable goods over and above those necessary for biological subsistence can be distributed according to a principle of need.

But despite this extension of the concept of need the Socialist Principle of Justice still seems to face the three problems listed [earlier]:

1. What guarantees are there that even under abundance the *composition* of the output with all contributing according to their abilities, will suffice to fill all needs? (There may still be scarcities of goods needed to fill either biological or job-related needs.)
2. What principle can serve to distribute goods that are surplus both to biological and to job-related needs?
3. What system of incentives explains why each will contribute to the full measure of his abilities, though he is not materially rewarded for increments of effort? Whether or not there is authoritative job allocation, job performance cannot be guaranteed.

Marx's solution to these problems does not seem too explicit. But much is suggested by the passage at the end of the *Critique of the Gotha Program* where he describes the higher phase of communist society as one in which "labor is no longer merely a means of life but has become life's principal need."

To most people it sounds almost comic to claim that labor could become life's principal need: it suggests a society of compulsive workers. Labor in the common view is intrinsically undesirable, but undertaken as a means to some further, typically material, end. For Marx this popular view would have been confirmation of his own view of the degree to which most labor under capitalism is alienating. He thought that under capitalism laborers experienced a three-fold alienation: alienation from the *product* of their labor, which is for them merely a means to material reward; alienation from the *process* of labor, which is experienced as forced labor rather than as desirable activity; and alienation from *others,* since activities undertaken with others are undertaken as a means to achieving further ends, which are normally scarce and allocated competitively. Laborers cooperate in production but, under capitalism, compete for job and income, and the competition overrides the co-operation. Hence Marx claims (in the *Economic and Philosophical Manuscripts*) that "life itself appears only as a means to life." Though the horror of that situation is apparent in the very words, many people accept that labor should be only a means to life—whose real ends lie elsewhere; whether in religion, consumption, personal relations, or leisure.

Marx, on the other hand, held that labor could be more than a means; it could also be an end of life, for labor in itself—*the activity*—can, like other activities, be something for whose sake one does other things. We would be loath to think that activity itself should appear only as a means to life—on the contrary, life's worth for most people lies in the activities undertaken. Those we call labor do not differ intrinsically from the rest, only in relation to the system of production. In Marx's view a system was possible in which all activities undertaken would be nonalienating. Nobody would have to compete to engage in an activity he found unpleasant for the sake of a material reward. Instead, workers would cooperate in creative and fulfilling activities that provide occasions for the experience of talents, for taking responsibilities, and that result in useful or beautiful products. In such a situation one can see why labor would be regarded as life's greatest need, rather than as its scourge. Nonalienated labor is humanly fulfilling activity.

In the course of switching from the conception of alienating labor to that of nonalienating labor, it might seem that we have moved into a realm for which principles of distribution may be irrelevant. What can the Socialist Principle of Justice tell us about the distribution of burdens and benefits in "the higher phase of Communist society?"

In such a society each is to contribute according to his abilities. In the light of the discussion of nonalienated labor, it is clear that there is no problem of incentives. Each man works at what he wants to work at. He works because that is his need. (This is not a situation in which "moral incentives" have replaced material ones, for both moral and material incentives are based on alienating labor. The situation Marx envisages is one for which incentives of *all* sorts are irrelevant.)

Though this disposes of the problem of incentives under the Socialist Principle of Justice, it is much less clear whether this principle can work for a reasonable range of situations. Can it cope with both the situation of abundance and that of scarcity?

In the case of abundance, a surplus of goods over and above those needed is provided. But if all activities are need-fulfilling, then no work is done that does not fulfill some need. In a sense there is no surplus to be distributed, for nothing needless is being done. Nevertheless, there may be a surplus of material goods that are the by-product of need-fulfilling activity. In a society where everybody fulfills himself by painting pictures, there may be a vast surplus of pictures. If so, the Socialist Principle of Justice gives no indication of the right method for their distribution; they are not the goal for which the task was undertaken. Since they do not fulfill an objective need, the method for their distribution is not important. In this the higher phase of communist society is, as one might expect, the very antithesis of consumerism; rather than fabricate reasons for desiring and so acquiring what is not needed, it disregards anything that is not needed in decisions of distribution.

There, nevertheless, is a problem of distribution the Socialist Principle of Justice does not attempt to solve. Some of the products of need-fulfilling activity may be things other people either desire or detest. When need-fulfilling activity yields works of art or noisy block parties, its distribution cannot be disregarded. Not all planning problems can be solved by the Socialist Principle of Justice. We shall not discuss the merits of various principles that could serve to handle these cases, but shall only try to delimit the scope of the Socialist Principle of Justice.

This brings us to the problem of scarcity. Can the Socialist Principle of Justice explain why, when all contribute to the extent of their abilities, all needs can be met? Isn't it conceivable that everyone should find fulfillment in painting, but nobody find fulfillment in producing either biological necessities or the canvases, brushes, and paints everybody wants to use? Might not incentive payments be needed, even in this higher phase of communist society, to guarantee the production of subsistence goods and job-related necessities? In short, will not any viable system involve some alienating labor?

Marx at any rate guarantees that communism need not involve much alienating labor. He insists that the Socialist Principle of Justice is applicable only in a context of abundance. For only when man's needs can be met is it relevant to insist that they ought to be met. The Socialist Principle of Justice comes into its own only with the development of the forces of production. But, of course, higher productivity does not by itself guarantee the right composition of output. Subsistence goods and job-related services and products might not be provided as the population fulfills itself in painting, poetry, and sculpture. Man cannot live by works of art alone.

This socialist version of the story of Midas should not alarm us too much. The possibility of starvation amidst abundant art works seemed plausible only because we abstracted it from other features of an abundant socialist society. Such a society is a planned society, and part of its planning concerns the ability structure of the population. Such a society would include people able to perform all tasks necessary to maintain a high level of material well-being.

Nevertheless, there may be certain essential tasks in such a society whose performance is not need-fulfilling for anybody. Their allocation presents another planning problem for which the Socialist Principle of Justice, by hypothesis, is not a solution. But the degree of coercion need not be very great. In a highly productive society the amount of labor expended on nonfulfilling tasks is a diminishing proportion of total labor time. Hence, given equitable allocation of this burden (and it is here that the planning decisions are really made), nobody would be prevented from engaging principally in need-fulfilling activities. In the limiting case of abundance, where automation of the production of material needs is complete, nobody would have to do any task he did not find intrinsically worthwhile. To the extent that this abundance is not reached, the Socialist Principle of Justice cannot be fully implemented.

However, the degree of coercion experienced by those who are allocated to necessary but nonfulfilling chores may be reducible if the planning procedure is of a certain sort. To the extent that people participate in planning and that they realize the necessity of the nonfulfilling chores in order for everyone to be able to do also what he finds need-fulfilling, they may find the performance of these chores less burdensome. As they want to achieve the ends, so—once they are informed—they cannot rationally resent the means, provided they perceive the distribution of chores as just.

The point can be taken a step further. Under the Socialist Principle of Justice, households do not put forth productive effort to be rewarded with an aliquot portion of time and means for self-fulfillment. It is precisely this market mentality from which we wish to escape. The miserable toil of society should be

> performed gratis for the benefit of society . . . performed not as a definite duty, not for the purpose of obtaining a right to certain products, not according to previously established and

legally fixed quotas, but voluntary labor . . . performed because it has become a habit to work for the common good, and because of a conscious realization (that has become a habit) of the necessity of working for the common good.[1]

Creative work should be done for its own sake, not for any reward. Drudgery should be done for the common good, not to be rewarded with opportunity and means for creative work. Of course, the better and more efficient the performance of drudgery, the more will be the opportunities for creative work. To realize this, however, is to understand the necessity of working for the common good, not to be animated by private material incentives. For the possibilities of creative work are opened by the simultaneous and parallel development of large numbers of people. To take the arts, poets need a public, authors readers, performers audiences, and all need (though few want) critics. One cannot sensibly wish, under the Socialist Principle of Justice, to be rewarded *privately* with opportunities and means for nonalienated work.

There is a question regarding the distribution of educational opportunities. Before men can contribute according to their abilities, their abilities must be developed. But in whom should society develop which abilities? If we regard education as consumption, then according to the Socialist Principle of Justice, each should receive it according to his need.

It is clear that all men require some early training to make them viable social beings; further, all men require certain general skills necessary for performing work. But we could hardly claim that some men need to be doctors or economists or lawyers, or need to receive any other specialized or expensive training. If, on the other hand, we regard education as production of those skills necessary for maintaining society and providing the possibility of fulfillment, then the Socialist Principle of Justice can determine a lower bound to the production of certain skills: so-and-so many farmers/doctors/mechanics must be produced to satisfy future subsistence and job-related needs. But the Socialist Principle of

Justice cannot determine who shall get which of these educational opportunities. One traditional answer might be that each person should specialize at whatever he is relatively best suited to do. Yet this only makes sense in terms of tasks done as onerous means to desirable ends. Specialization on the basis of comparative advantage minimizes the effort in achieving given ends; but if work is itself fulfilling, it is not an "effort" that must be minimized.

In conditions of abundance, it is unlikely that anyone will be denied training they want and can absorb, though they may have to acquire skills they do not particularly want, since some onerous tasks may still have to be done. For even in conditions of abundance, it may be necessary to compel some or all to undertake certain unwanted training in the interests of the whole. But it is not necessary to supplement the Socialist Principle of Justice with an incentive scheme, whether material or moral. The principle already contains the Kantian maxim: develop your talents to the utmost, for only in this way can a person contribute to the limits of his ability. And if a society wills the end of self-fulfillment, it must will sufficient means. If the members of society take part in planning to maintain and expand the opportunities for everyone's nonalienated activity, they must understand the necessity of allocating the onerous tasks, and so the training for them.

Perhaps we can make our point clearer by looking briefly at Marx's schematic conception of the stages of modern history—feudalism, capitalism, socialism, communism—where each stage is characterized by a higher productivity of labor than the preceding stage. In feudalism, the principle of distribution would be:

5. From each according to his status, to each according to his status—the *Feudal Principles of Justice.*

There is no connection between work and reward. There are no market incentives in the "ideal" feudal system. Peasants grow the stuff for their own subsistence and perform traditional labor services for their lord on domain land. He in turn provides protection and government in traditional fashion. Yet, though labor is not performed as a means to a distant or abstract end, as when it is done for money, it still is done for survival, not for its own sake, and those who do it are powerless to control their conditions of work or their own destinies. Man lives on the edge of famine and is subject to the vagaries of the weather and the dominion of tradition. Only a massive increase in productive powers frees him. But to engender this increase men must come to connect work directly with reward. This provides the incentive to labor, both to take those jobs most needed (moving from the farm to the factory) and to work sufficiently hard once on the job.

But more than work is needed; the surplus of output over that needed to maintain the work force (including materials) and replace and repair the means of production (machines, raw materials) must be put to productive use; it must be reinvested, not consumed. In capitalism, station at birth determines whether one works or owns capital; workers are rewarded for their contribution of work, capitalists for theirs of reinvestment. There is a stick as well as a carrot. Those workers who do not work, starve; those capitalists who fail to reinvest, fail to grow and will eventually be crushed by their larger rivals. Socialism rationalizes this by eliminating the two-class dichotomy and by making reinvestment a function of the institutions of the state, so that the capital structure of the society is the collective property of the citizenry, all of whom must work for reward. In this system the connection between work and reward reaches its fullest development, and labor in one sense is most fully alienated. The transition to communism then breaks this link altogether.

The link between work and rewards serves a historical purpose; namely, to encourage the development of the productive forces. But as the productive forces continue to develop, the demand for additional rewards will tend to decline, while the difficulty of stimulating still further growth in productivity may increase. This at least, seems to be implied by the principles of conventional economics—diminishing marginal utility and diminishing marginal productivity. Even if one rejects most of the conventional wisdom of economics, a good case can be made for the diminishing efficacy of material incentives as prosperity increases. For as labor productivity rises, private consumption needs will be met, and the most urgent needs remaining will be those requiring *collective* consumption—and, indeed, some of these needs will be generated by the process of growth and technical progress. These last needs, if left unmet, may hinder further attempts to raise the productive power of labor. So the system of material incentives could in principle come to a point where the weakened encouragements to extra productivity offered as private reward for contribution might be offset by the accumulated hindrances generated by the failures to meet collective needs and by the wastes involved in competition. At this point, it becomes appropriate to break the link between work and reward. Breaking the link, however, is not enough. Both the Socialist Principle of Justice and the Utopian Principle of Justice break the link between work and reward. But the Utopian Principle of Justice leaves the distinction between them. Work is a means, the products of work are the ends. Given a high productivity of labor, workers would in principle choose their occupations and work-leisure patterns, yet still producing enough to satisfy everyone's needs. This would be a society devoted to minimizing effort, a sort of high-technology Polynesia. Since it neither makes consumption dependent upon work nor regards work as other than a regrettable means to consumption, it fails to explain why sufficient work to supply basic needs should ever be done. The alienation of labor cannot be overcome by eliminating labor rather than alienation.

Breaking the link, between work and reward, while leaving the distinction itself intact, may also lead to the loss of the productive powers of labor. For without reward, and when the object is to work as little as possible, why expend the effort to acquire highly complex skills? What is the motive to education, self-improvement, self-development? A high-technology Polynesia contains an inner contradiction.

By contrast, the Socialist Principle of Justice not only does not make reward depend upon work but denies that there is a distinction between the two. Because man needs fulfilling activity—work that he chooses and wants—men who get it contribute according to their ability.

Yet there still may remain routine and menial, unfulfilling jobs. But who wills the end wills the means. The society must plan to have such jobs done. No doubt many will be mechanized or automated, but the remaining ones will form a burden that must be allocated.

The Socialist Principle of Justice cannot solve this problem of allocation. But everyone has some interest in getting uncoveted but essential work done. Hence it should not be difficult to find an acceptable supplementary principle of distribution for allocating these chores. For instance, the Principle of Comparative Advantage might be introduced to assign each the

drudgery at which he is relatively best. There can be no quarrel with this so long as such alienating work is only a small fraction of a man's total activity, conferring no special status. It is only when alienating work takes up the bulk of one's waking hours, and determines status, that specialization inevitably entails some form of class structure.

The Socialist Principle of Justice cannot solve all allocation problems. But once one understands that it is based on a denial of a distinction between work, need, and reward, it is clear that it can solve an enormous range of such problems. In a highly productive society the only allocation problems the Socialist Principle of Justice cannot solve are the distribution of unmechanized and uncoveted chores and of the material by-products of creative endeavor.

NOTE

1. V. I. Lenin, "From the Destruction of the Old Social System to the Creation of the New," April 11, 1920. From *Collected Works*, English trans., 40 vols. (London: Lawrence & Wishart, 1965), vol. 30, p. 517.

7 Radical Egalitarianism

KAI NIELSON

I

I HAVE TALKED OF EQUALITY as a right and of equality as a goal. And I have taken, as the principal thing, to be able to state what goal we are seeking when we say equality is a goal. When we are in a position actually to achieve that goal, then that same equality becomes a right. The goal we are seeking is an equality of basic condition for everyone. Let me say a bit what this is: everyone, as far as possible, should have equal life prospects, short of genetic engineering and the like and the rooting out of any form of the family and the undermining of our basic freedoms. There should, where this is possible, be an equality of access to equal resources over each person's life as a whole, though this should be qualified by people's varying needs. Where psychiatrists are in short supply only people who are in need of psychiatric help should have equal access to such help. This equal access to resources should be such that it stands as a barrier to there being the sort of differences between people that allow some to be in a position to control and to exploit others; such equal access to resources should also stand as a barrier to one person having power over other adult persons that does not rest on the revokable consent on the part of the persons over whom he comes to have power. Where, because of some remaining scarcity in a society of considerable productive abundance, we cannot reasonably distribute resources equally, we should first,

where considerations of desert are not at issue, distribute according to stringency of need, second according to the strength of unmanipulated preferences and third, and finally, by lottery. We should, in trying to attain equality of condition, aim at a condition of autonomy (the fuller and the more rational the better) for everyone and at a condition where everyone alike, to the fullest extent possible, has his or her needs and wants satisfied. The limitations on the satisfaction of people's wants should be only where the satisfaction is incompatible with everyone getting the same treatment. Where we have conflicting wants, such as where two persons want to marry the same person, the fair thing to do will vary with the circumstances. In the marriage case, freedom of choice is obviously the fair thing. But generally, what should be aimed at is having everyone have their wants satisfied as far as possible. To achieve equality of condition would be, as well, to achieve a condition where the necessary burdens of the society are equally shared, where to do so is reasonable, and where each person has an equal voice in deciding what these burdens shall be. Moreover, everyone, as much as possible, should be in a position—and should be equally in that position—to control his own life. The goals of egalitarianism are to achieve such equalities.

Minimally, classlessness is something we should all aim at if we are egalitarians. It is necessary for

Abridged from Equality and Liberty *(1985), pp. 283–292, 302–306, 309. Reprinted by permission of* Rowman & Littlefield, Publishers. Notes renumbered.

the stable achievement of equalities of the type discussed in the previous paragraph. Beyond that, we should also aim at a statusless society, though not at an undifferentiated society or a society which does not recognize merit. . . . It is only in such a classless, statusless society that the ideals of equality (the conception of equality as a very general goal to be achieved) can be realized. In aiming for a statusless society, we are aiming for a society which, while remaining a society of material abundance, is a society in which there are to be no extensive differences in life prospects between people because some have far greater income, power, authority or prestige than others. This is the *via negativa* of the egalitarian way. The *via positiva* is to produce social conditions, where there is generally material abundance, where well-being and satisfaction are not only maximized (the utilitarian thing) but, as well, a society where this condition, as far as it is achievable, is sought equally for all (the egalitarian thing). This is the underlying conception of the egalitarian commitment to equality of condition.

II

Robert Nozick asks, "How do we decide how much equality is enough?"[1] In the preceding section we gestured in the direction of an answer. I should now like to be somewhat more explicit. Too much equality, as we have been at pains to point out, would be to treat everyone identically, completely ignoring their differing needs. Various forms of "barracks equality" approximating that would also be too much. Too little equality would be to limit equality of condition, as did the old egalitarianism, to achieving equal legal and political rights, equal civil liberties, to equality of opportunity and to a redistribution of gross disparities in wealth sufficient to keep social peace, the rationale for the latter being that such gross inequalities if allowed to stand would threaten social stability. This Hobbesist stance indicates that the old egalitarianism proceeds in a

very pragmatic manner. Against the old egalitarianism I would argue that we must at least aim at an equality of whole life prospects, where that is not ready simply as the right to compete for scarce positions of advantage, but where there is to be brought into being the kind of equality of condition that would provide everyone equally, as far as possible, with the resources and the social conditions to satisfy their needs as fully as possible compatible with everyone else doing likewise. (Note that between people these needs will be partly the same but will still often be importantly different as well.) Ideally, as a kind of ideal limit for a society of wondrous abundance, a radical egalitarianism would go beyond that to a similar thing for wants. We should, that is, provide all people equally, as far as possible, with the resources and social conditions to satisfy their wants, as fully as possible compatible with everyone else doing likewise. (I recognize that there is a slide between wants and needs. As the wealth of a society increases and its structure changes, things that started out as wants tend to become needs, e.g. someone in the Falkland Islands might merely reasonably want an auto while someone in Los Angeles might not only want it but need it as well. But this does not collapse the distinction between wants and needs. There are things in any society people need, if they are to survive at all in anything like a commodious condition, whether they want them or not, e.g., they need food, shelter, security, companionship and the like. An egalitarian starts with basic needs, or at least with what are taken in the cultural environment in which a given person lives to be basic needs, and moves out to other needs and finally to wants as the productive power of the society increases.)

I qualified my above formulations with "as far as possible" and with "as fully as possible compatible with everyone else doing likewise." These are essential qualifications. Where, as in societies that we know, there are scarcities, even rather minimal scarcities, not everyone can have the resources or at least all the resources necessary to have their needs satisfied. Here we must first ensure that, again as far as possible, their basic needs are all satisfied and then we move on to other needs and finally to wants. But sometimes, to understate it, even in very affluent societies, everyone's needs cannot be met, or at least they cannot be equally met. In such circumstances we have to make some hard choices. I am thinking of a situation where there are not enough dialysis machines to go around so that everyone who needs one can have one. What then should we do? The thing to aim at, to try as far as possible to approximate, if only as a heuristic ideal, is the full and equal meeting of needs and wants of everyone. It is when we have that much equality that we have enough equality. But, of course, "ought implies can," and where we can't achieve it we can't achieve it. But where we reasonably can, we ought to do it. It is something that fairness requires.

The "reasonably can" is also an essential modification: we need situations of sufficient abundance so that we do not, in going for such an equality of condition, simply spread the misery around or spread very Spartan conditions around. Before we can rightly aim for the equality of condition I mentioned, we must first have the productive capacity and resource conditions to support the institutional means that would make possible the equal satisfaction of basic needs and the equal satisfaction of other needs and wants as well.

Such achievements will often not be possible; perhaps they will never be fully possible, for, no doubt, the physically handicapped will always be with us. Consider, for example, situations where our scarcities are such that we cannot, without causing considerable misery, create the institutions and mechanisms that would work to satisfy all needs, even all basic needs. Suppose we have the technology in place to develop all sorts of complicated life-sustaining machines all of which would predictably provide people with a quality of life that they, viewing the matter clearly, would rationally choose if they were simply choosing for themselves. But suppose, if we put such technologies in place, we will then not have the wherewithal to provide basic health care in outlying regions in the country or adequate educational services in such places. We should not, under those circumstances, put those technologies in place. But we should also recognize that where it becomes possible to put these technologies in place without sacrificing other more pressing needs, we should do so. The underlying egalitarian rationale is evident enough: produce the conditions for the most extensive satisfaction of needs for everyone. Where A's need and B's need are equally important (equally stringent) but cannot both be satisfied, satisfy A's need rather than B's if the satisfaction of A's need would be more fecund for the satisfaction of the needs of others than B's, or less undermining of the satisfaction of the needs of others than B's. (I do not mean to say that this is our only criterion of choice but it is the criterion most relevant for us here.) We should seek the satisfaction of the greatest compossible set of needs where the conditions for compossibility are (a) that everyone's needs be considered, (b) that everyone's needs be *equally* considered and where two sets of needs cannot both be satisfied, the more stringent set of needs shall first be satisfied. (Do not say we have no working criteria for what they are. If you need food to keep you from starvation or debilitating malnutrition and I need a vacation to relax after a spate of hard work, your need is plainly more stringent than mine. There would, of course, be all sorts of disputable cases, but there are also a host of perfectly determinate cases indicating that we have working criteria.) The underlying rationale is to seek compossible sets of needs so that we approach as far as possible as great a satisfaction of needs as possible for everyone.

This might, it could be said, produce a situation in which very few people got those things that they needed the most, or at least wanted the most. Remember Nozick with his need for the resources of Widener Library in an annex to his house. People, some might argue, with expensive tastes and extravagant needs, say a need for really good wine, would never, with a stress on such compossibilia, get things they are really keen about.[2] Is that the kind of world we would reflectively want? Well, *if* their not getting them is the price we have to pay for everyone having their basic needs met, then it is a price we ought to pay. I am very fond of very good wines as well as fresh ripe mangoes, but if the price of my having them is that people starve or suffer malnutrition in the Sahel, or indeed anywhere else, then plainly fairness, if not just plain human decency, requires that I forgo them.

In talking about how much equality is enough, I have so far talked of the benefits that equality is meant to provide. But egalitarians also speak of an equal sharing of the necessary burdens of the society as well. Fairness requires a sharing of the burdens, and for a radical egalitarian this comes to an equal sharing of the burdens where people are equally capable of sharing them. Translated into the concrete this does *not* mean that a child or an old man or a pregnant woman are to be required to work in the mines or that they be required to collect garbage, but it would involve something like requiring every able bodied person, say from nineteen to twenty, to take his or her turn at a fair portion of the necessary unpleasant jobs in the world. In that way all, where we are able to do it, would share equally in these burdens—in doing the things that none of us want to do but that we, if we are at all reasonable, recognize the necessity of having done. (There are all kinds of variations and complications concerning this—what do we do with the youthful wonder at the violin? But, that notwithstanding, the general idea is clear enough.) And, where we think this is reasonably feasible, it squares with our considered judgments about fairness.

I have given you, in effect appealing to my considered judgments but considered judgments I do not think are at all eccentric, a picture of what I would take to be enough equality, too little equality and not enough equality. But how

can we know that my proportions are right? I do not think we can avoid or should indeed try to avoid an appeal to considered judgments here. But working with them there are some arguments we can appeal to get them in wide reflective equilibrium. Suppose we go back to the formal principle of justice, namely that we must treat like cases alike. Because it does not tell us *what* are like cases, we cannot derive substantive criteria from it. But it may, indirectly, be of some help here. We all, if we are not utterly zany, want a life in which our needs are satisfied and in which we can live as we wish and do what we want to do. Though we differ in many ways, in our abilities, capacities for pleasure, determination to keep on with a job, we do not differ about wanting our needs satisfied or being able to live as we wish. Thus, *ceterus paribus,* where questions of desert, entitlement and the like do not enter, it is only fair that all of us should have our needs equally considered and that we should, again *ceterus paribus,* all be able to do as we wish in a way that is compatible with others doing likewise. From the formal principle of justice and a few key facts about us, we can get to the claim that *ceterus paribus* we should go for this much equality. But this is the core content of a radical egalitarianism.

However, how do we know that *ceterus* is *paribus* here? What about our entitlements and deserts? Suppose I have built my house with my own hands, from materials I have purchased and on land that I have purchased and that I have lived in it for years and have carefully cared for it. The house is mine and I am entitled to keep it even if by dividing the house into two apartments greater and more equal satisfaction of need would obtain for everyone. Justice requires that such an entitlement be respected here. (Again, there is an implicit *ceterus paribus* clause. In extreme situations, say after a war with housing in extremely short supply, that entitlement could be rightly overridden.)

There is a response on the egalitarian's part similar to a response utilitarianism made to criticisms of a similar logical type made of utilitarians by pluralistic deontologists. One of the things that people in fact need, or at least reflectively firmly want, is to have such entitlements respected. Where they are routinely overridden to satisfy other needs or wants, we would *not* in fact have a society in which the needs of everyone are being maximally met. To the reply, but what if more needs for everyone were met by ignoring or overriding such entitlements, the radical egalitarian should respond that that is, given the way we are, a thoroughly hypothetical situation and that theories of morality cannot be expected to give guidance for all logically possible worlds but only for worlds which are reasonably like what our actual world is or plausibly could come to be. Setting this argument aside for the moment, even if it did turn out that the need satisfaction linked with having other things—things that involved the overriding of those entitlements—was sufficient to make it the case that more need satisfaction all around for *everyone* would be achieved by overriding those entitlements, then, for reasonable people who clearly saw that, these entitlements would not have the weight presently given to them. They either would not have the importance presently attached to them or the need for the additional living space would be so great that their being overridden would seem, everything considered, the lesser of two evils (as in the example of the postwar housing situation).

There are without doubt genuine entitlements and a theory of justice must take them seriously, but they are not absolute. If the need is great enough we can see the merit in overriding them, just as in law as well as morality the right of eminent domain is recognized. Finally, while I have talked of entitlements here, parallel arguments will go through for desert.

III

I want now to relate this articulation of what equality comes to to my radically egalitarian principles of justice. My articulation of justice is a certain spelling out of the slogan proclaimed by Marx "From each according to his ability, to each according to his needs." The egalitarian conception of society argues for the desirability of bringing into existence a world, once the springs of social wealth flow freely, in which everyone's needs are as fully satisfied as possible and in which everyone gives according to his ability. Which means, among other things, that everyone, according to his ability, shares the burdens of society. There is an equal giving and equal responsibility here according to ability. It is here, with respect to giving according to ability and with respect to receiving according to need, that a complex equality of result, i.e., equality of condition, is being advocated by the radical egalitarian. What it comes to is this: each of us, where each is to count for one and none to count for more than one, is to give according to ability and receive according to need.

My radical egalitarian principles of justice read as follows:

1. Each person is to have an equal right to the most extensive total system of equal basic liberties and opportunities (including equal opportunities for meaningful work, for self-determination and political and economic participation) compatible with a similar treatment of all. (This principle gives expression to a commitment to attain and/or sustain equal moral autonomy and equal self-respect.)

2. After provisions are made for common social (community) values, for capital overhead to preserve the society's productive capacity, allowances made for differing unmanipulated needs and preferences, and due weight is given to the just entitlements of individuals, the income and wealth (the common stock of means) is to be so divided that each person will have a right to an equal share. The necessary burdens requisite to enhance human well-being are also to be equally shared, subject, of course, to limitations by differing abilities and

differing situations. (Here I refer to different natural environments and the like and not to class position and the like.)

Here we are talking about equality as a right rather than about equality as a goal as has previously been the subject matter of equality in this chapter. These principles of egalitarianism spell out rights people have and duties they have under *conditions of very considerable productive abundance*. We have a right to certain basic liberties and opportunities and we have, subject to certain limitations spelled out in the second principle, a right to an equal share of the income and wealth in the world. We also have a duty, again subject to the qualifications mentioned in the principle, to do our equal share in shouldering the burdens necessary to protect us from ills and to enhance our well-being.

What is the relation between these rights and the ideal of equality of condition discussed earlier? That is a goal for which we can struggle now to bring about conditions which will some day make its achievement possible, while these rights only become rights when the goal is actually achievable. We have no such rights in slave, feudal or capitalist societies or such duties in those societies. In that important way they are not natural rights for they depend on certain social conditions and certain social structures (socialist ones) to be realizable. What we can say is that it is always desirable that socio-economic conditions come into being which would make it possible to achieve the goal of equality of condition so that these rights and duties I speak of could obtain. But that is a far cry from saying we have such rights and duties now.

It is a corollary of this, if these radical egalitarian principles of justice are correct, that capitalist societies (even capitalist welfare state societies such as Sweden) and statist societies such as the Soviet Union or the People's Republic of China cannot be just societies or at least they must be societies, structured as they are, which are defective in justice. (This is not to say that some of these societies are not juster than others. Sweden is juster than South Africa, Canada than the United States and Cuba and Nicaragua than Honduras and Guatemala.) But none of these statist or capitalist societies can satisfy these radical egalitarian principles of justice, for equal liberty, equal opportunity, equal wealth or equal sharing of burdens are not at all possible in societies having their social structure. So we do not have such rights now but we can take it as a goal that we bring such a society into being with a commitment to an equality of condition in which we would have these rights and duties. Here we require first the massive development of productive power.

The connection between equality as a goal and equality as a right spelled out in these principles of justice is this. This equality of condition appealed to in equality as a goal would, if it were actually to obtain, have to contain the rights and duties enunciated in those principles. There could be no equal life prospects between all people or anything approximating an equal satisfaction of needs if there were not in place something like the system of equal basic liberties referred to in the first principle. Furthermore, without the rough equality of wealth referred to in the second principle, there would be disparities in power and self-direction in society which would render impossible an equality of life prospects or the social conditions required for an equal satisfaction of needs. And plainly, without a roughly equal sharing of burdens, there cannot be a situation where everyone has equal life prospects or has the chance equally to satisfy his needs. The principles of radical egalitarian justice are implicated in its conception of an ideally adequate equality of condition.

IV

The principles of radical egalitarian justice I have articulated are meant to apply globally and not just to particular societies. But it is certainly fair to say that not a few would worry that such principles of radical egalitarian justice, if applied globally, would force the people in wealthier sections of the world to a kind of financial hari-kari. There are millions of desperately impover-ished people. Indeed millions are starving or malnourished and things are not getting any better. People in the affluent societies cannot but worry about whether they face a bottomless pit. Many believe that meeting, even in the most minimal way, the needs of the impoverished is going to put an incredible burden on people—people of all classes—in the affluent societies. Indeed it will, if acted on non-evasively, bring about their impoverishment, and this is just too much to ask. Radical egalitarianism is forgetting Rawls' admonitions about "the strains of com-mitment"—the recognition that in any rational account of what is required of us, we must at least give a minimal healthy self-interest its due. We must construct our moral philosophy for human beings and not for saints. Human nature is less fixed than conservatives are wont to assume, but it is not so elastic that we can rea-sonably expect people to impoverish themselves to make the massive transfers between North and South—the industrialized world and the Third World—required to begin to approach a situation where even Rawls' principles would be in place on a global level, to say nothing of my radical egalitarian principles of justice.[3]

The first thing to say in response to this is that my radical egalitarian principles are meant actually to guide practice, to directly determine what we are to do, only in a world of extensive abundance where, as Marx put it, the springs of social wealth flow freely. If such a world cannot be attained with the underminings of capitalism and the full putting into place, stabilizing, and developing of socialist relations of production, then such radical egalitarian principles can only remain as heuristic ideals against which to mea-sure the distance of our travel in the direction of what would be a perfectly just society.

Aside from a small capitalist class, along with those elites most directly and profitably be-holden to it (together a group constituting not

more than 5 percent of the world's population), there would, in taking my radical egalitarian principles as heuristic guides, be no impoverish-ment of people in the affluent societies, if we moved in a radically more egalitarian way to start to achieve a global fairness. There would be massive transfers of wealth between North and South, but this could be done in stages so that, for the people in the affluent societies (cap-italist elites apart), there need be no undermin-ing of the quality of their lives. Even what were once capitalist elites would not be impoverished or reduced to some kind of bleak life though they would, the incidental Spartan types aside, find their life styles altered. But their health and general well being, including their opportunities to do significant and innovative work, would, if anything, be enhanced. And while some of the sources of their enjoyment would be a thing of the past, there would still be a considerable range of enjoyments available to them sufficient to afford anyone a rich life that could be lived with verve and zest.

A fraction of what the United States spends on defense spending would take care of imme-diate problems of starvation and malnutrition for most of the world. For longer range prob-lems such as bringing conditions of life in the Third World more in line with conditions of life in Sweden and Switzerland, what is necessary is the dismantling of the capitalist system and the creation of a socio-economic system with an un-derlying rationale directing it toward producing for needs—everyone's needs. With this altered productive mode, the irrationalities and waste of capitalist production would be cut. There would be no more built-in obsolescence, no more merely cosmetic changes in consumer durables, no more fashion roulette, no more useless prod-ucts and the like. Moreover, the enormous ex-penditures that go into the war industry would be a thing of the past. There would be great transfers from North to South, but it would be from the North's capitalist fat and not from things people in the North really need. (There would, in other words, be no self-pauperization of people in the capitalist world.) . . .

V

It has been repeatedly argued that equality undermines liberty. Some would say that a society in which principles like my radical egalitarian principles were adopted, or even the liberal egalitarian principles of Rawls or Dworkin were adopted, would not be a free society. My arguments have been just the reverse. I have argued that it is only in an egalitarian society that full and extensive liberty is possible.

Perhaps the egalitarian and the anti-egalitarian are arguing at cross purposes? What we need to recognize, it has been argued, is that we have two kinds of rights both of which are important to freedom but to rather different freedoms and which are freedoms which not infrequently conflict.[4] We have rights to *fair terms of cooperation* but we also have rights to non-interference. If a right of either kind is overridden our freedom is diminished. The reason why it might be thought that the egalitarian and the anti-egalitarian may be arguing at cross purposes is that the egalitarian is pointing to the fact that rights to fair terms of cooperation and their associated liberties require equality while the anti-egalitarian is pointing to the fact that rights to noninterference and their associated liberties conflict with equality. They focus on different liberties.

What I have said above may not be crystal clear, so let me explain. People have a right to fair terms of cooperation. In political terms this comes to the equal right of all to effective participation in government and, in more broadly social terms, and for a society of economic wealth, it means people having a right to a roughly equal distribution of the benefits and burdens of the basic social arrangements that affect their lives and for them to stand in such relations to each other such that no one has the power to dominate the life of another. By contrast, rights to non-interference come to the equal right of all to be left alone by the government and more broadly to live in a society in which people have a right peacefully to pursue their interests without interference.

The conflict between equality and liberty comes down to, very essentially, the conflicts we get in modern societies between rights to fair terms of cooperation and rights to noninterference. As Joseph Schumpeter saw and J. S. Mill before him, one could have a thoroughly democratic society (at least in conventional terms) in which rights to noninterference might still be extensively violated. A central anti-egalitarian claim is that we cannot have an egalitarian society in which the very precious liberties that go with the rights to non-interference would not be violated.

Socialism and egalitarianism plainly protect rights to fair terms of cooperation. Without the social (collective) ownership and control of the means of production, involving with this, in the initial stages of socialism at least, a workers' state, economic power will be concentrated in the hands of a few who will in turn, as a result, dominate effective participation in government. Some right-wing libertarians blind themselves to that reality, but it is about as evident as can be. Only an utter turning away from the facts of social life could lead to any doubts about this at all. But then this means that in a workers' state, if some people have capitalistic impulses, that they would have their rights peacefully to pursue their own interests interfered with. They might wish to invest, retain and bequeath in economic domains. In a workers' state these capitalist acts in many circumstances would have to be forbidden, but that would be a violation of an individual's right to non-interference and the fact, if it was a fact, that we by democratic vote, even with vast majorities, had made such capitalist acts illegal would still not make any difference because individuals' rights to noninterference would still be violated.

We are indeed driven, by egalitarian impulses, of a perfectly understandable sort, to accept interference with laissez-faire capitalism to protect non-subordination and non-domination of people by protecting the egalitarian right to fair terms of cooperation and the enhanced liberty that that brings. Still, as things stand, this leads inevitably to violations of the right to non-interference and this brings with it a diminution of liberty. There will be people with capitalist impulses and they will be interfered with. It is no good denying, it will be said, that egalitarianism and particularly socialism will not lead to interference with very precious individual liberties, namely with our right peacefully to pursue our interests without interference.[5]

The proper response to this, as should be apparent from what I have argued throughout, is that to live in any society at all, capitalist, socialist or whatever, is to live in a world in which there will be some restriction or other on our rights peacefully to pursue our interests without interference. I can't lecture in Albanian or even in French in a standard philosophy class at the University of Calgary, I can't jog naked on most beaches, borrow a book from your library without your permission, fish in your trout pond without your permission, take your dog for a walk without your say so and the like. At least some of these things have been thought to be things which I might peacefully pursue in my own interests. Stopping me from doing them is plainly interfering with my peaceful pursuit of my own interests. And indeed it is an infringement on liberty, an interference with my doing what I may want to do.

However, for at least many of these activities, and particularly the ones having to do with property, even right-wing libertarians think that such interference is perfectly justified. But, justified or not, they still plainly constitute a restriction on our individual freedom. However, what we must also recognize is that there will always be some such restrictions on freedom in any society whatsoever, just in virtue of the fact that a normless society, without the restrictions that having norms implies, is a contradiction in terms.[6] Many restrictions are hardly felt as restrictions, as in the attitudes of many people toward seat-belt legislation, but they are, all the same, plainly

restriction on our liberty. It is just that they are thought to be unproblematically justified.

To the question would a socialism with a radical egalitarianism restrict some liberties, including some liberties rooted in rights to non-interference, the answer is that it indeed would; but so would laissez-faire capitalism, aristocratic conceptions of justice, liberal conceptions or any social formations at all, with their associated conceptions of justice. The relevant question is which of these restrictions are justified.

The restrictions on liberty preferred by radical egalitarianism and socialism, I have argued, are justified for they, of the various alternatives, give us both the most extensive and the most abundant system of liberty possible in modern conditions with their thorough protection of the right to fair terms of cooperation. Radical egalitarianism will also, and this is central for us, protect our civil liberties and these liberties are, of course, our most basic liberties. These are the liberties which are the most vital for us to protect. What it will not do is to protect our unrestricted liberties to invest, retain and bequeath in the economic realm and it will not protect our unrestricted freedom to buy and sell. There is, however, no good reason to think that these restrictions are restrictions of anything like a basic liberty. Moreover, we are justified in restricting our freedom to buy and sell if such restrictions strengthen, rather than weaken, our total system of liberty. This is in this way justified, for only by such market restrictions can the rights of the vast majority of people to effective participation in government and an equal role in the control of their social lives be protected. I say this because if we let the market run free in this way, power will pass into the hands of a few who will control the lives of the many and determine the fundamental design of the society. The actual liberties that are curtailed in a radically egalitarian social order are inessential liberties whose restriction in contemporary circumstances enhances human well-being and indeed makes for a firmer entrenchment of basic liberties and for their greater extension globally. That is to say, we here restrict some liberty in order to attain more liberty and a more equally distributed pattern of liberty. More people will be able to do what they want and have a greater control over their own lives than in a capitalist world order with its at least implicit inegalitarian commitments.

However, some might say I still have not faced the most central objection to radical egalitarianism, namely its statism. (I would prefer to say its putative statism.) The picture is this. The egalitarian state must be in the redistribution business. It has to make, or make sure there is made, an equal relative contribution to the welfare of every citizen. But this in effect means that the socialist state or, for that matter, the welfare state, will be deeply interventionist in our personal lives. It will be in the business, as one right-winger emotively put it, of cutting one person down to size in order to bring about that person's equality with another person who was in a previously disadvantageous position.[7] That is said to be morally objectionable and it would indeed be deeply morally objectionable in many circumstances. But it isn't in the circumstances in which the radical egalitarian presses for redistribution. (I am not speaking of what might be mere equalizing upwards.) The circumstances are these: Capitalist A gets his productive property confiscated so that he could no longer dominate and control the lives of proletarians B, C, D, E, F, and G. But what is wrong with it where this "cutting down to size"—in reality the confiscation of productive property or the taxation of the capitalist—involves no violation of A's civil liberties or the harming of his actual well-being (health, ability to work, to cultivate the arts, to have fruitful personal relation, to live in comfort and the like) and where B, C, D, E, F, and G will have their freedom and their well-being thoroughly enhanced if such confiscation or taxation occurs? Far from being morally objectionable, it is precisely the sort of state of affairs that people ought to favor. It certainly protects more liberties and more significant liberties that it undermines.

There is another familiar anti-egalitarian argument designed to establish the liberty-undermining qualities of egalitarianism. It is an argument we have touched upon in discussing meritocracy. It turns on the fact that in any society there will be both talents and handicaps. Where they exist, what do we want to do about maintaining equal distribution? Egalitarians, radical or otherwise, certainly do not want to penalize people for talent. That being so, then surely people should be allowed to retain the benefits of superior talent. But this in some circumstances will lead to significant inequalities in resources and in the meeting of needs. To sustain equality there will have to be an ongoing redistribution in the direction of the less talented and less fortunate. But this redistribution from the more to the less talented does plainly penalize the talented for their talent. That, it will be said, is something which is both unfair and an undermining of liberty.

The following, it has been argued, makes the above evident enough.[8] If people have talents they will tend to want to use them. And if they use them they are very likely to come out ahead. Must not egalitarians say they ought not to be able to come out ahead no matter how well they use their talents and no matter how considerable these talents are? But that is intolerably restrictive and unfair.

The answer to the above anti-egalitarian argument is implicit in a number of things I have already said. But here let me confront this familiar argument directly. Part of the answer comes out in probing some of the ambiguities of "coming out ahead." Note, incidentally, that (1) not all reflective, morally sensitive people will be so concerned with that, and (2) that being very concerned with that is a mentality that capitalism inculcates. Be that as it may, to turn to the ambiguities, note that some take "coming out ahead" principally to mean "being paid well for the use of those talents" where "being paid well" is being paid sufficiently well so that it creates inequalities sufficient to disturb the preferred egalitarian patterns. (Without that, being paid well would give one no relative advantage.) But, as we have seen, "coming out ahead" need not take that form at all. Talents can be recognized and acknowledged in many ways. First, in just the respect and admiration of a fine employment of talents that would naturally come from people seeing them so displayed where these people were not twisted by envy; second, by having, because of these talents, interesting and secure work that their talents fit them for and they merit in virtue of those talents. Moreover, having more money is not going to matter much—for familiar marginal utility reasons—where what in capitalist societies would be called the welfare floors are already very high, this being made feasible by the great productive wealth of the society. Recall that in such a society of abundance everyone will be well off and secure. In such a society people are not going to be very concerned about being a little better off than someone else. The talented are in no way, in such a situation, robbed to help the untalented and handicapped or penalized for their talents. They are only prevented from amassing wealth (most particularly productive wealth), which would enable them to dominate the untalented and the handicapped and to control the social life of the world of which they are both a part. . . .

I think that the moral authority for abstract egalitarianism, for the belief that the interests of everyone matter and matter equally, comes from its being the case that it is *required by the moral point of view*.[9] What I am predicting is that a person who has a good understanding of what morality is, has a good knowledge of the facts, is not ideologically mystified, takes an impartial point of view, and has an attitude of impartial caring, would, if not conceptually confused, come to accept the abstract egalitarian thesis. I see no way of arguing someone into such an egalitarianism who does not in this general way have a love of humankind.[10] A hard-hearted Hobbesist is not reachable here. But given that a person has that love of humankind—that impartial and impersonal caring—together with the other qualities mentioned above, then, I predict, that that person would be an egalitarian at least to the extent of ac-

cepting the abstract egalitarian thesis. What I am claiming is that if these conditions were to obtain (if they ceased to be just counterfactuals), then there would be a consensus among moral agents about accepting the abstract egalitarian thesis. . . .

NOTES

1. See the debate between Robert Nozick, Daniel Bell and James Tobin, "If Inequality Is Inevitable, What Can Be Done About It?", *The New York Times,* January 3, 1982, p. E5. The exchange between Bell and Nozick reveals the differences between the old egalitarianism and right-wing libertarianism. It is not only that the right and left clash but sometimes right clashes with right.

2. Amartya Sen, "Equality of What?", *The Tanner Lectures on Human Values,* vol. 1 (1980), ed. Sterling M. McMurrin (Cambridge, England: Cambridge University Press, 1980), pp. 198–220.

3. Henry Shue, "The Burdens of Justice," *The Journal of Philosophy* 80, no. 10 (October 1983): 600–601; 606–8.

4. Richard W. Miller, "Marx and Morality," in *Marxism,* eds. J. R. Pennock and J. W. Chapman, Nomos 26 (New York: New York University Press, 1983), pp. 9–11.

5. Ibid., p. 10.

6. This has been argued from both the liberal center and the left. Ralf Dahrendorf, *Essays in the Theory of Society* (Stanford, Calif.: Stanford University Press, 1968), pp. 151–78; and G. A. Cohen, "Capitalism, Freedom and the Proletariat," in *The Idea of Freedom: Essays in Honour of Isaiah Berlin,* ed. Alan Ryan (Oxford: Oxford University Press, 1979).

7. The graphic language should be duly noted. Jan Narveson, "On Dworkinian Equality," *Social Philosophy and Policy* 1, no. 1 (autumn 1983): 4.

8. Ibid., pp. 1–24.

9. Some will argue that there is no such thing as a moral point of view. My differences with him about the question of whether the amoralist can be argued into morality not withstanding, I think Kurt Baier, in a series of articles written subsequent to his *The Moral Point of View,* has clearly shown that there is something reasonably determinate that can, without ethnocentrism, be called "the moral point of view."

10. Richard Norman has impressively argued that this is an essential background assumption of the moral point of view. Richard Norman, "Critical Notice of Rodger Beehler's *Moral Life,*" *Canadian Journal of Philosophy* 11, no. 1 (March 1981): 157–83.

8 How Liberty Upsets Patterns

ROBERT NOZICK

IT IS NOT CLEAR HOW those holding alternative conceptions of distributive justice can reject the entitlement conception of justice in holdings. For suppose a distribution favored by one of the nonentitlement conceptions is realized. Let us suppose it is your favorite one and let us call this distribution D_1; perhaps everyone has an equal share, perhaps shares vary in accordance with some dimension you treasure. Now suppose that Wilt Chamberlain is greatly in demand by basketball teams, being a great gate attraction. (Also suppose contracts run only for a year, with players being free agents.) He signs the following sort of contract with a team: In each home game, twenty-five cents from the price of each ticket of admission goes to him. (We ignore the question of whether he is "gouging" the owners, letting them look out for themselves.) The season starts, and people cheerfully attend his team's games; they buy their tickets, each time dropping a separate twenty-five cents of their admission price into a special box with Chamberlain's name on it. They are excited about seeing him play; it is worth the total admission price to them. Let us suppose that in one season one million persons attend his home games, and Wilt Chamberlain winds up with $250,000, a much larger sum than the average income and larger even than anyone else has. Is he entitled to this income? Is this new distribution D_2, unjust? If so, why?

There is *no* question about whether each of the people was entitled to the control over the resources they held in D_1, because that was the distribution (your favorite) that (for the purposes of argument) we assumed was acceptable. Each of these persons *chose* to give twenty-five cents of their money to Chamberlain. They could have spent it on going to the movies, or on candy bars, or on copies of *Dissent* magazine, or of *Monthly Review*. But they all, at least one million of them, converged on giving it to Wilt Chamberlain in exchange for watching him play basketball. If D_1 was a just distribution, and people voluntarily moved from it to D_2 transferring parts of their shares they were given under D_1 (what was it for if not to do something with?), isn't D_2 also just? If people were entitled to dispose of the resources to which they were entitled (under D_1), didn't this include their being entitled to give it to, or exchange it with, Wilt Chamberlain? Can anyone else complain on grounds of justice? Each other person already has his legitimate share under D_1. Under D_1, there is nothing that anyone has that anyone else has a claim of justice against. After someone transfers something to Wilt Chamberlain, third parties *still* have their legitimate shares; *their* shares are not changed. By what process could such a transfer among two persons give rise to a legitimate claim of distributive justice on a portion of what was transferred, by a third party who had no claim of justice on any holding of the others *before* the transfer?[1] To cut off objections irrelevant here, we might imagine the exchanges occurring in a socialist society, after hours: After playing whatever basketball he does in his daily work, or doing whatever other daily work he does, Wilt Chamberlain decides to put in *overtime* to earn additional money. (First his work quota is set; he works time over that.) Or imagine it is a skilled juggler people like to see, who puts on shows after hours.

Why might someone work overtime in a society in which it is assumed their needs are satisfied? Perhaps because they care about things other than needs. I like to write in books that I read, and to have easy access to books for browsing at odd hours. It would be very pleasant and convenient to have the resources of Widener Library in my backyard. No society, I assume, will provide such resources close to each person who would like them as part of his regular allotment (under D_1). Thus, persons either must do without some extra things that they want, or be allowed to do something extra to get some of these things. On what basis could the inequalities that would eventuate be forbidden? Notice also that small factories would spring up in a socialist society, unless forbidden. I melt down some of my personal possessions (under D_1) and build a machine out of the material. I offer you, and others, a philosophy lecture once a week in exchange for your cranking the handle on my machine, whose products I exchange for yet other things, and so on. (The raw materials used by the machine are given to me by others who possess them under D_1, in exchange for hearing lectures.) Each person might participate to gain things over and above their allotment under D_1. Some persons even might want to leave their job in socialist industry and work full time in this private sector. [In any case] I wish merely to note how private property even in means of production would occur in a socialist society that did not forbid people to use as they wished some of the resources they are given under the socialist distribution D_1.[2] The socialist society would have to forbid capitalist acts between consenting adults.

The general point illustrated by the Wilt Chamberlain example and the example of the entrepreneur in a socialist society is that no end-state principle or distributional patterned principle of justice can be continuously realized without continuous interference with people's lives. Any favored pattern would be transformed into one unfavored by the principle, by people choosing to act in various ways; for example, by people exchanging goods and services with other people, or giving things to other people, things the transferrers are entitled to under the favored distribution pattern. To maintain a pattern one must either continually interfere to stop people from transferring resources as they wish to, or continually (or periodically) interfere to take from some persons resources that others for some reason chose to transfer to them. (But if some time limit is to be set on how long people may keep resources others voluntarily transfer to them, why let them keep these resources for *any* period of time? Why not have immediate confiscation?) It might be objected that all persons voluntarily will choose to refrain from actions which would upset the pattern. This presupposes unrealistically (1) that all will most want to maintain the pattern (are those who don't, to be "reeducated" or forced to undergo "self-criticism"?), (2) that each can gather enough information about his own actions and the ongoing activities of others to discover which of his actions will upset the pattern, and (3) that diverse and far-flung persons can coordinate their actions to dovetail into the pattern. Compare the manner in which the market is neutral among persons' desires, as it reflects and transmits widely scattered information via prices, and coordinates persons' activities.

It puts things perhaps a bit too strongly to say that every patterned (or end-state) principle is liable to be thwarted by the voluntary actions of the individual parties transferring some of their shares they receive under the principle. For perhaps some *very* weak patterns are not so thwarted.[3] Any distributional pattern with any egalitarian component is overturnable by the voluntary actions of individual persons over time, as is every patterned condition with sufficient content so as actually to have been proposed as presenting the central core of distributive justice. Still, given the possibility that some weak conditions or patterns may not be unstable in this way, it would be better to formulate an explicit description of the kind of interesting and contentful patterns under discussion, and to prove a theorem about their instability. Since the weaker the patterning, the more likely it is that the entitlement system itself satisfies it, a plausible conjecture is that any patterning either is unstable or is satisfied by the entitlement system. . . .

NOTES

1. Might not a transfer have instrumental effects on a third party, changing his feasible options? (But what if the two parties to the transfer independently had used their holdings in this fashion?) I discuss this question below, but note here that this question concedes the point for distributions of ultimate intrinsic noninstrumental goods (pure utility experiences, so to speak) that are transferable. It also might be objected that the transfer might make a third party more envious because it worsens his position relative to someone else. I find it incomprehensible how this can be thought to involve a claim of justice. . . .

Here and elsewhere in this chapter, a theory which incorporates elements of pure procedural justice might find what I say acceptable, *if* kept in its proper place; that is, if background institutions exist to ensure the satisfaction of certain conditions on distributive shares. But if these institutions are not themselves the sum or invisible-hand result of people's voluntary (nonaggressive) actions, the constraints they impose require justification. At no point does *our* argument assume any background institutions more extensive than those of the minimal nightwatchman state, a state limited to protecting persons against murder, assault, theft, fraud, and so forth.

2. See the selection from John Henry MacKay's novel, *The Anarchists*, reprinted in Leonard Krimmerman and Lewis Perry, eds., *Patterns of Anarchy* (New York: Doubleday Anchor Books, 1966), in which an individualist anarchist presses upon a communist anarchist the following question: "Would you, in the system of society which you call 'free Communism' prevent individuals from exchanging their labor among themselves by means of their own medium of exchange? And further: Would you prevent them from occupying land for the purpose of personal use?" The novel continues: "[the] question was not to be escaped. If he answered 'Yes!' he admitted that society had the right of control over the individual and threw overboard the autonomy of the individual which he had always zealously defended; if, on the other hand, he answered 'No!' he admitted the right of private property which he had just denied so emphatically. . . . Then he answered, 'In Anarchy any number of men must have the right of forming a voluntary association, and so realizing their ideas in practice. Nor can I understand how anyone could justly be driven from the land and house which he uses and occupies . . . every serious man must declare himself: for Socialism, and thereby for force and against liberty, or for Anarchism, and thereby for liberty and against force.'" In contrast, we find Noam Chomsky writing, "Any consistent anarchist must oppose private ownership of the means of production," "the consistent anarchist then . . . will be a socialist . . . of a particular sort." Introduction to Daniel Guerin, *Anarchism: From Theory to Practice* (New York: Monthly Review Press, 1970), pages xiii, xv.

3. Is the patterned principle stable that requires merely that a distribution be Pareto-optimal? One person might give another a gift or bequest that the second could exchange with a third to their mutual benefit. Before the second makes this exchange there is not Pareto-optimality. Is a stable pattern presented by a principle choosing that among the Pareto-optimal positions that satisfies some further condition C? It may seem that there cannot be a counterexample, for won't any voluntary exchange made away from a situation show that the first situation wasn't Pareto-optimal? (Ignore the implausibility of this last claim for the case of bequests.) But principles are to be satisfied over time, during which new possibilities arise. A distribution that at one time satisfies the criterion of Pareto-optimality might not do so when some new possibilities arise (Wilt Chamberlain grows up and starts playing basketball); and though people's activities will tend to move then to a new Pareto-optimal position, *this* new one need not satisfy the contentful condition C. Continual interference will be needed to insure the continual satisfaction of C. (The theoretical possibility of a pattern's being maintained by some invisible-hand process that brings it back to an equilibrium that fits the pattern when deviations occur should be investigated.)

Part IV

Liberal Democratic Justice

9   The Contractual Basis for a Just Society

IMMANUEL KANT

Among all the contracts by which a large group of men unites to form a society, . . . the contract establishing a *civil constitution* . . . is of an exceptional nature. For while, so far as its execution is concerned, it has much in common with all others that are likewise directed toward a chosen end to be pursued by joint effort, it is essentially different from all others in the principle of its constitution. . . . In all social contracts, we find a union of many individuals for some common end which they all *share*. But a union as an end in itself which they all *ought to share* and which is thus an absolute and primary duty in all external relationships whatsoever among human beings (who cannot avoid mutually influencing one another), is only found in a society insofar as it constitutes a civil state, i.e. a commonwealth. . . .

The civil state, regarded purely as a lawful state, is based on the following *a priori* principles:

1. the *freedom* of every member of society as a *human being*
2. the *equality* of each with all the others as a *subject*
3. the *independence* of each member of a commonwealth as a *citizen*

These principles are not so much laws given by an already established state, as laws by which a state can alone be established in accordance with pure rational principles of external human right. Thus:

1. Man's *freedom* as a human being, as a principle for the constitution of a commonwealth, can be expressed in the following formula. No one can compel me to be happy in accordance with his conception of the welfare of others, for each may seek his happiness in whatever way he sees fit, so long as he does not infringe upon the freedom of others to pursue a similar end which can be reconciled with the freedom of everyone else within a workable general law—i.e., he must accord to others the same right as he enjoys himself. A government might be established on the principle of benevolence toward the people, like that of a father toward his children. Under such a *paternal government* . . . the subjects, as immature children who cannot distinguish what is truly useful or harmful to themselves, would be obliged to behave purely passively and to rely upon the judgement of the head of state as to how they *ought* to be happy, and upon his kindness in willing their happiness at all. Such a government is the greatest conceivable *despotism*, i.e., a constitution which suspends the entire freedom of its subjects, who thenceforth have no rights whatsoever. The only conceivable government for men who are capable of possessing rights, even if the ruler is benevolent, is not a *paternal* but a *patriotic* government. . . . A *patriotic* attitude is one where everyone in the state, not excepting its head, regards the commonwealth as a maternal womb, or the land as the paternal ground from

From Kant's Political Writings, *edited by Hans Reiss and translated by H. B. Nisbet (1970), pp. 73–81.*
Reprinted by permission of Cambridge University Press.

which he himself sprang and which he must leave to his descendants as a treasured pledge. Each regards himself as authorized to protect the rights of the commonwealth by laws of the general will, but not to submit it to his personal use at his own absolute pleasure. This right of freedom belongs to each member of the commonwealth as a human being, insofar as each is a being capable of possessing rights.

2. Man's equality as a subject might be formulated as follows. Each member of the commonwealth has rights of coercion in relation to all the others, except in relation to the head of state. For he alone is not a member of the commonwealth, but its creator or preserver, and he alone is authorized to coerce others without being subject to any coercive law himself. But all who are subject to laws are the subjects of a state, and are thus subject to the right of coercion along with all other members of the commonwealth; the only exception is a single person (in either the physical or the moral sense of the word), the head of state, through whom alone the rightful coercion of all others can be exercised. For if he too could be coerced, he would not be the head of state, and the hierarchy of subordination would ascend infinitely. But if there were two persons exempt from coercion, neither would be subject to coercive laws, and neither could do to the other anything contrary to right, which is impossible.

This uniform equality of human beings as subjects of a state is, however, perfectly consistent with the utmost inequality of the mass in the degree of its possessions, whether these take the form of physical or mental superiority over others, or of fortuitous external property and of particular rights (of which there may be many) with respect to others. Thus the welfare of the one depends very much on the will of the other (the poor depending on the rich), the one must obey the other (as the child its parents or the wife her husband), the one serves (the laborer) while the other pays, etc. Nevertheless, they are all equal as subjects *before the law,* which, as the pronouncement of the general will, can only be single in form, and which concerns the form of right and not the material or object in relation to which I possess rights. For no one can coerce anyone else other than through the public law and its executor, the head of state, while everyone else can resist the others in the same way and to the same degree. No one, however, can lose this authority to coerce others and to have rights toward them except through committing a crime. And no one can voluntarily renounce his rights by a contract or legal transaction to the effect that he has no rights but only duties, for such a contract would deprive him of the right to make a contract, and would thus invalidate the one he had already made.

From this idea of the equality of men as subjects in a commonwealth, there emerges this further formula: every member of the commonwealth must be entitled to reach any degree of rank which a subject can earn through his talent, his industry and his good fortune, And his fellow-subjects may not stand in his way by *hereditary* prerogatives or privileges of rank and thereby hold him and his descendants back indefinitely.

All right consists solely in the restriction of the freedom of others, with the qualification that their freedom can co-exist with my freedom within the terms of a general law; and public right in a commonwealth is simply a state of affairs regulated by a real legislation which conforms to this principle and is backed up by power, and under which a whole people live as subjects in a lawful state. . . . This is what we call a civil state, and it is characterized by equality in the effects and countereffects of freely willed actions which limit one another in accordance with the general law of freedom. Thus the *birthright* of each individual in such a state (i.e., before he has performed any acts which can be judged in relation to right) is absolutely *equal* as regards his authority to coerce others to use their freedom in a way which harmonizes with his freedom. Since birth is not an act on the part of the one who is born, it cannot create any inequality in his legal position and cannot make him submit to any coercive laws except insofar as he is subject, along with all the others, of the one supreme legislative power. Thus no member of the commonwealth can have a hereditary privilege as against his fellow-subjects; and no one can hand down to his descendants the privileges attached to the rank he occupies in the commonwealth, nor act as if he were qualified as a ruler by birth and forcibly prevent others from reaching the higher levels of the hierarchy (which are *superior* and *inferior,* but never *imperans* and *subiectus*) through their own merit. He may hand down everything else, so long as it is material and not pertaining to his person, for it may be acquired and disposed of as property and may over a series of generations create considerable inequalities in wealth among the members of the commonwealth (the employee and the employer, the landowner and the agricultural servants, etc.). But he may not prevent his subordinates from raising themselves to his own level if they are able and entitled to do so by their talent, industry and good fortune. If this were not so, he would be allowed to practise coercion without himself being subject to coercive countermeasures from others, and would thus be more than their fellow-subject. No one who lives within the lawful state of a commonwealth can forfeit this equality other than through some crime of his own, but never by contract or through military force. . . . For no legal transaction on his part or on that of anyone else can make him cease to be his own master. He cannot become like a domestic animal to be employed in any chosen capacity and retained therein without consent for any desired period, even with the reservation (which is at times sanctioned by religion, as among the Indians) that he may not be maimed or killed. He can be considered happy in any condition so long as he is aware that, if he does not reach the same level

as others, the fault lies either with himself (i.e., lack of ability or serious endeavour) or with circumstances for which he cannot blame others, and not with the irresistible will of any outside party. For as far as right is concerned, his fellow-subjects have no advantage over him.

3. The *independence* . . . of a member of the commonwealth as a *citizen,* i.e., as a co-legislator, may be defined as follows. In the question of actual legislation, all who are free and equal under existing public laws may be considered equal, but not as regards the right to make these laws. Those who are not entitled to this right are nonetheless obliged, as members of the commonwealth, to comply with these laws, and they thus likewise enjoy their protection (not as *citizens* but as co-beneficiaries of this protection). For all right depends on laws. But a public law which defines for everyone that which is permitted and prohibited by right, is the act of a public will, from which all right proceeds and which must not therefore itself be able to do an injustice to any one. And this requires no less than the will of the entire people (since all men decide for all men and each decides for himself). For only toward oneself can one never act unjustly. But on the other hand, the will of another person cannot decide anything for someone without injustice, so that the law made by this other person would require a further law to limit his legislation. Thus an individual will cannot legislate for a commonwealth. For this requires freedom, equality and *unity* of the will of *all* the members. And the prerequisite for unity, since it necessitates a general vote (if freedom and equality are both present), is independence. The basic law, which can come only from the general, united will of the people, is called the *original contract.*

Anyone who has the right to vote on this legislation is a *citizen* . . . (i.e., citizen of a state). . . . The only qualification required by a citizen (apart, of course, from being an adult male) is that he must be his *own master* . . . , and must have some *property* (which can include any skill, trade, fine art or science) to support himself. In cases where he must earn his living from others, he must earn it only by *selling* that which is his,[1] and not by allowing others to make use of him; for he must in the true sense of the word *serve* no one but the commonwealth. In this respect, artisans and large or small landowners are all equal, and each is entitled to one vote only. As for landowners, we leave aside the questions of how anyone can have rightfully acquired more land than he can cultivate with his own hands (for acquisition by military seizure is not primary acquisition), and how it came about that numerous people who might otherwise have acquired permanent property were thereby reduced to serving someone else in order to live at all. It would certainly conflict with the above principle of equality if a law were to grant them a privileged status so that their descendants would always remain feudal landowners, without their land being sold or divided by inheritance and thus made useful to more people; it would also be unjust if only those belonging to an arbitrarily selected class were allowed to acquire land, should the estates in fact be divided. The owner of a large estate keeps out as many smaller property owners (and their votes) as could otherwise occupy his territories. He does not vote on their behalf, and himself has only *one* vote. It should be left exclusively to the ability, industry and good fortune of each member of the commonwealth to enable each to acquire a part and all to acquire the whole, although this distinction cannot be observed within the general legislation itself. The number of those entitled to vote on matters of legislation must be calculated purely from the number of property owners, not from the size of their properties.

Those who possess this right to vote must agree *unanimously* to the law of public justice, or else a legal contention would arise between those who agree and those who disagree, and it would require yet another higher legal principle to resolve it. An entire people cannot, however, be expected to reach unanimity, but only to show a majority of votes (and not even of direct votes, but simply of the votes of those delegated in a large nation to represent the people). Thus the actual principle of being content with majority decisions must be accepted unanimously and embodied in a contract; and this itself must be the ultimate basis on which a civil constitution is established.

Conclusion

This, then is an *original contract* by means of which a civil and thus completely lawful constitution and commonwealth can alone be established. But we need by no means assume that this contract . . . , based on a coalition of the wills of all private individuals in a nation to form a common, public will for the purposes of rightful legislation, actually exists as a *fact,* for it cannot possibly be so. Such an assumption would mean that we would first have to prove from history that some nation, whose rights and obligations have been passed down to us, did in fact perform such an act, and handed down some authentic record or legal instrument, orally or in writing, before we could regard ourselves as bound by a preexisting civil constitution. It is in fact merely an *idea* of reason, which nonetheless has undoubted practical reality; for it can oblige every legislator to frame his laws in such a way that they could have been produced by the united will of a whole nation, and to regard each subject, insofar as he can claim citizenship, as if he had consented within the general will. This is the test of the rightfulness of every public law. For if the law is such that a whole people could not *possibly* agree to it (for example, if it stated that a certain class of *subjects* must be privileged as a hereditary *ruling class*), it is unjust; but if it is at least *possible* that a people could agree to it, it is our duty to consider the law as just, even if the people is at present in such a position or attitude of mind that it would probably refuse its consent if it were consulted.[2] But this restriction obviously applies only to the judgment of the legislator, not to that of the subject. Thus if a people, under some existing legislation, were asked to make a judgment which in all probability would prejudice its happiness, what should it do? Should the people not oppose the measure? The only possible answer is that they can do nothing but obey. For we are not concerned here with any happiness which the subject might expect to derive from the institutions or administration of the commonwealth, but primarily with the rights which would thereby be secured for everyone. And this is the highest principle from which all maxims relating to the commonwealth must begin, and which cannot be qualified by any other principles. No generally valid principle of legislation can be based on happiness. For both the current circumstances and the highly conflicting and variable illusions as to what happiness is (and no one can prescribe to others how they should attain it) make all fixed principles impossible, so that happiness alone can never be a suitable principle of legislation. The doctrine that *salus publica suprema civitatis lex est*[3] retains its value and authority undiminished; but the public welfare which demands *first* consideration lies precisely in that legal constitution which guarantees everyone his freedom within the law, so that each remains free to seek his happiness in whatever way he thinks best, so long as he does not violate the lawful freedom and rights of his fellow subjects at large. If the supreme power makes laws which are primarily directed toward happiness (the affluence of the citizens, increased population, etc.), this cannot be regarded as the end for which a civil constitution was established, but only as a means of *securing the rightful state,* especially against external enemies of the people. The head of state must be authorized to judge for himself whether such measures are necessary for the commonwealth's prosperity, which is required to maintain its strength and stability both internally and against external enemies. The aim is not, as it were, to make the people happy against its will, but only to ensure its continued existence as a commonwealth.[4] The legislator

may indeed err in judging whether or not the measures he adopts are *prudent,* but not in deciding whether or not the law harmonizes with the principle of right. For he has ready to hand as an infallible *a priori* standard, the idea of an original contract, and he need not wait for experience to show whether the means are suitable, as would be necessary if they were based on the principle of happiness. For so long as it is not self-contradictory to say that an entire people could agree to such a law, however painful it might seem, then the law is in harmony with right. But if a public law is beyond reproach (i.e., *irreprehensible*) with respect to right, it carries with it the authority to coerce those to whom it applies, and conversely, it forbids them to resist the will of the legislator by violent means. In other words, the power of the state to put the law into effect is also *irresistible,* and no rightfully established commonwealth can exist without a force of this kind to suppress all internal resistance. For such resistance would be dictated by a maxim which, if it became general, would destroy the whole civil constitution and put an end to the only state in which men can possess rights.

NOTES

1. He who does a piece of work (*opus*) can sell it to someone else, just as if it were his own property. But guaranteeing one's labor (*praestatio operae*) is not the same as selling a commodity. The domestic servant, the shop assistant, the laborer, or even the barber, are merely laborers (*operarii*), not *artists* (*artifices,* in the wider sense) or members of the state, and are thus unqualified to be citizens. And although the man to whom I give my firewood to chop and the tailor to whom I give material to make into clothes both appear to have a similar relationship toward me, the former differs from the latter in the same way as the barber from the wigmaker (to whom I may in fact have given the requisite hair) or the laborer from the artist or tradesman, who does a piece of work which belongs to him until he is paid for it. For the latter, in pursuing his trade, exchanges his property with someone else (*opus*), while the former allows someone else to make use of him. But I do admit that it is somewhat difficult to define the qualifications

which entitle anyone to claim the status of being his own master.

2. If, for example, a war tax were proportionately imposed on all subjects, they could not claim, simply because it is oppressive, that it is unjust because the war is in their opinion unnecessary. For they are not entitled to judge this issue, since it is at least *possible* that the war is inevitable and the tax indispensable, so that the tax must be deemed rightful in the judgment of the subjects. But if certain estate owners were oppressed with levies for such a war, while others of the same class were exempted, it is easily seen that a whole people could never agree to a law of this kind, and it is entitled at least to make representations against it, since an unequal distribution of burdens can never be considered just.

3. "The public welfare is the supreme law of the state."

4. Measures of this kind might include certain restrictions on imports, so that the means of livelihood may be developed for the benefit of the subjects themselves and not as an advantage to foreigners or an encouragement for their industry. For without the prosperity of the people, the state would not have enough strength to resist external enemies or to preserve itself as a commonwealth.

10 Justice as Rational Choice Behind a Veil of Ignorance

JOHN RAWLS

MY AIM IS TO PRESENT a conception of justice which generalizes and carries to a higher level of abstraction the familiar theory of the social contract as found, say, in Locke, Rousseau, and Kant.[1] In order to do this we are not to think of the original contract as one to enter a particular society or to set up a particular form of government. Rather, the guiding idea is that the principles of justice for the basic structure of society are the object of the original agreement. They are the principles that free and rational persons concerned to further their own interests would accept in an initial position of equality as defining the fundamental terms of their association. These principles are to regulate all further agreements; they specify the kinds of social cooperation that can be entered into and the forms of government that can be established. This way of regarding the principles of justice I shall call justice as fairness.

Thus we are to imagine that those who engage in social cooperation choose together, in one joint act, the principles which are to assign basic rights and duties and to determine the division of social benefits. Men are to decide in advance how they are to regulate their claims against one another and what is to be the foundation charter of their society. Just as each person must decide by rational reflection what constitutes his good—that is, the system of ends which it is rational for him to pursue—so a group of persons must decide once and for all what is to count among them as just and unjust. The choice which rational men would make in this hypothetical situation of equal liberty, assuming for the present that this choice problem has a solution, determines the principles of justice.

In justice as fairness the original position of equality corresponds to the state of nature in the traditional theory of the social contract. This original position is not, of course, thought of as an actual historical state of affairs, much less as a primitive condition of culture. It is understood as a purely hypothetical situation characterized so as to lead to a certain conception of justice.[2] Among the essential features of this situation is that no one knows his place in society, his class position or social status, nor does any one know his fortune in the distribution of natural assets and abilities, his intelligence, strength, and the like. I shall even assume that the parties do not know their conceptions of the good or their special psychological propensities. The principles of justice are chosen behind a veil of ignorance. This ensures that no one is advantaged or disadvantaged in the choice of principles by the outcome of natural chance or the contingency of social circumstances. Since all are similarly situated and no one is able to design principles to favor his particular condition, the principles of

From A Theory of Justice *by John Rawls, Cambridge, Mass.: Harvard University Press, pp. 11–22, 60–65, 150–156, 252–257, 302–303. Copyright © 1971 by the President and Fellows of Harvard College. Reprinted by permission of the publisher. Notes renumbered.*

Original state position — what exists prior to agreeing upon principles of justice

social contract —

justice are the result of a fair agreement or bargain. For given the circumstances of the original position, the symmetry of everyone's relations to each other, this initial situation is fair between individuals as moral persons; that is, as rational beings with their own ends and capable, I shall assume, of a sense of justice. The original position, is, one might say, the appropriate initial status quo, and thus the fundamental agreements reached in it are fair. This explains the propriety of the name "justice as fairness"; it conveys the idea that the principles of justice are agreed to in an initial situation that is fair. The name does not mean that the concepts of justice and fairness are the same, any more than the phrase "poetry as metaphor" means that the concepts of poetry and metaphor are the same.

Justice as fairness begins, as I have said, with one of the most general of all choices which persons might make together, namely, with the choice of the first principles of a conception of justice which is to regulate all subsequent criticism and reform of institutions. Then, having chosen a conception of justice, we can suppose that they are to choose a constitution and a legislature to enact laws, and so on, all in accordance with the principles of justice initially agreed upon. Our social situation is just if it is such that by this sequence of hypothetical agreements we would have contracted into the general system of rules which defines it. Moreover, assuming that the original position does determine a set of principles (that is, that a particular conception of justice would be chosen), it will then be true that whenever social institutions satisfy these principles those engaged in them can say to one another that they are cooperating on terms to which they would agree if they were free and equal persons whose relations with respect to one another were fair. They could all view their arrangements as meeting the stipulations which they would acknowledge in an initial situation that embodies widely accepted and reasonable constraints on the choice of principles. The general recognition of this fact would provide the basis for a public acceptance of the corresponding principles of justice. No society can, of course, be a scheme of cooperation which men enter voluntarily in a literal sense; each person finds himself placed at birth in some particular position in some particular society, and the nature of this position materially affects his life prospects. Yet a society satisfying the principles of justice as fairness comes as close as a society can to being a voluntary scheme, for it meets the principles which free and equal persons would assent to under circumstances that are fair. In this sense its members are autonomous and the obligations they recognize self-imposed.

One feature of justice as fairness is to think of the parties in the initial situation as rational and mutually disinterested. This does not mean that the parties are egoists; that is, individuals with only certain kinds of interests, say in wealth, prestige, and domination. But they are conceived as not taking an interest in one another's interests. They are to presume that even their spiritual aims may be opposed, in the way that the aims of those of different religions may be opposed. Moreover, the concept of rationality must be interpreted as far as possible in the narrow sense, standard in economic theory, of taking the most effective means to given ends. I shall modify this concept to some extent . . . , but one must try to avoid introducing into it any controversial ethical elements. The initial situation must be characterized by stipulations that are widely accepted.

In working out the conception of justice as fairness one main task clearly is to determine which principles of justice would be chosen in the original position. To do this we must describe this situation in some detail and formulate with care the problem of choice which it presents. It may be observed, however, that once the principles of justice are thought of as arising from an original agreement in a situation of equality, it is an open question whether the principle of utility would be acknowledged. Offhand it hardly

People won't be swayed by their personal interest in a particular situation.

seems likely that persons who view themselves as equals, entitled to press their claims upon one another, would agree to a principle which may require lesser life prospects for some simply for the sake of a greater sum of advantages enjoyed by others. Since each desires to protect his interests, his capacity to advance his conception of the good, no one has a reason to acquiesce in an enduring loss for himself in order to bring about a greater net balance of satisfaction. In the absence of strong and lasting benevolent impulses, a rational man would not accept a basic structure merely because it maximized the algebraic sum of advantages irrespective of its permanent effects on his own basic rights and interests. Thus it seems that the principle of utility is incompatible with the conception of social cooperation among equals for mutual advantage. It appears to be inconsistent with the idea of reciprocity implicit in the notion of a well-ordered society. Or, at any rate, so I shall argue.

I shall maintain instead that the persons in the initial situation would choose two rather different principles: the first requires equality in the assignment of basic rights and duties, while the second holds that social and economic inequalities (for example, inequalities of wealth and authority) are just only if they result in compensating benefits for everyone, and in particular for the least advantaged members of society. These principles rule out justifying institutions on the grounds that the hardships of some are offset by a greater good in the aggregate. It may be expedient but it is not just that some should have less in order that others may prosper. But there is no injustice in the greater benefits earned by a few provided that the situation of persons not so fortunate is thereby improved. The intuitive idea is that since everyone's well-being depends upon a scheme of cooperation without which no one could have a satisfactory life, the division of advantages should be such as to draw forth the willing cooperation of everyone taking part in it, including those less well situated. Yet this can be expected only if reasonable terms are proposed. The two principles

mentioned seem to be a fair agreement on the basis of which those better endowed, or more fortunate in their social position, neither of which we can be said to deserve, could expect the willing cooperation of others when some workable scheme is a necessary condition of the welfare of all.[3] Once we decide to look for a conception of justice that nullifies the accidents of natural endowment and the contingencies of social circumstance as counters in a quest for political and economic advantage, we are led to these principles. They express the result of leaving aside those aspects of the social world that seem arbitrary from a moral point of view.

The problem of the choice of principles, however, is extremely difficult. I do not expect the answer I shall suggest to be convincing to everyone. It is, therefore, worth noting from the outset that justice as fairness, like other contract views, consists of two parts: (1) an interpretation of the initial situation and of the problem of choice posed there, and (2) a set of principles which, it is argued, would be agreed to. One may accept the first part of the theory (or some variant thereof), but not the other, and conversely. The concept of the initial contractual situation may seem reasonable although the particular principles proposed are rejected. To be sure, I want to maintain that the most appropriate conception of this situation does lead to principles of justice contrary to utilitarianism and perfectionism, and therefore that the contract doctrine provides an alternative to these views. Still, one may dispute this contention even though one grants that the contractarian method is a useful way of studying ethical theories and of setting forth their underlying assumptions.

Justice as fairness is an example of what I have called a contract theory. Now there may be an objection to the term "contract" and related expressions, but I think it will serve reasonably well. Many words have misleading connotations which at first are likely to confuse. The terms "utility" and "utilitarianism" are surely no exception. They too have unfortunate suggestions which hostile critics have been willing to exploit; yet they are clear enough for those prepared to study utilitarian doctrine. The same should be true of the term "contract" applied to moral theories. As I have mentioned, to understand it one has to keep in mind that it implies a certain level of abstraction. In particular, the content of the relevant agreement is not to enter a given society or to adopt a given form of government, but to accept certain moral principles. Moreover, the undertakings referred to are purely hypothetical: a contract view holds that certain principles would be accepted in a well-defined initial situation.

The merit of the contract terminology is that it conveys the idea that principles of justice may be conceived as principles that would be chosen by rational persons, and that in this way conceptions of justice may be explained and justified. The theory of justice is a part, perhaps the most significant part, of the theory of rational choice. Furthermore, principles of justice deal with conflicting claims upon the advantages won by social cooperation; they apply to the relations among several persons or groups. The word "contract" suggests this plurality as well as the condition that the appropriate division of advantages must be in accordance with principles acceptable to all parties. The condition of publicity for principles of justice is also connoted by the contract phraseology. Thus, if these principles are the outcome of an agreement, citizens have a knowledge of the principles that others follow. It is characteristic of contract theories to stress the public nature of political principles. Finally there is the long tradition of the contract doctrine. Expressing the tie with this line of thought helps to define ideas and accords with natural piety. There are then several advantages in the use of the term "contract." With due precautions taken, it should not be misleading.

A final remark. Justice as fairness is not a complete contract theory. For it is clear that the contractarian idea can be extended to the choice of more or less an entire ethical system; that is, to a system including principles for all the

virtues and not only for justice. Now for the most part I shall consider only principles of justice and others closely related to them; I make no attempt to discuss the virtues in a systematic way. Obviously if justice as fairness succeeds reasonably well, a next step would be to study the more general view suggested by the name "rightness as fairness." But even this wider theory fails to embrace all moral relationships, since it would seem to include only our relations with other persons and to leave out of account how we are to conduct ourselves toward animals and the rest of nature. I do not contend that the contract notion offers a way to approach these questions, which are certainly of the first importance; and I shall have to put them aside. We must recognize the limited scope of justice as fairness and of the general type of view that it exemplifies. How far its conclusions must be revised once these other matters are understood cannot be decided in advance.

The Original Position and Justification

I have said that the original position is the appropriate initial status quo which insures that the fundamental agreements reached in it are fair. This fact yields the name "justice as fairness." It is clear, then, that I want to say that one conception of justice is more reasonable than another, or justifiable with respect to it, if rational persons in the initial situation would choose its principles over those of the other for the role of justice. Conceptions of justice are to be ranked by their acceptability to persons so circumstanced. Understood in this way the question of justification is settled by working out a problem of deliberation: we have to ascertain which principles it would be rational to adopt given the contractual situation. This connects the theory of justice with the theory of rational choice.

If this view of the problem of justification is to succeed, we must, of course, describe in some detail the nature of this choice problem. A problem of rational decision has a definite answer only if we know the beliefs and interests of the parties, their relations with respect to one another, the alternatives between which they are to choose, the procedure whereby they make up their minds, and so on. As the circumstances are presented in different ways, correspondingly different principles are accepted. The concept of the original position, as I shall refer to it, is that of the most philosophically favored interpretation of this initial choice situation for the purposes of a theory of justice.

But how are we to decide what is the most favored interpretation? I assume, for one thing, that there is a broad measure of agreement that principles of justice should be chosen under certain conditions. To justify a particular description of the initial situation one shows that it incorporates these commonly shared presumptions. One argues from widely accepted but weak premises to more specific conclusions. Each of the presumptions should by itself be natural and plausible; some of them may seem innocuous or even trivial. The aim of the contract approach is to establish that taken together they impose significant bounds on acceptable principles of justice. The ideal outcome would be that these conditions determine a unique set of principles; but I shall be satisfied if they suffice to rank the main traditional conceptions of social justice.

One should not be misled, then, by the somewhat unusual conditions which characterize the original position. The idea here is simply to make vivid to ourselves the restrictions that it seems reasonable to impose on arguments for principles of justice, and therefore on these principles themselves. Thus it seems reasonable and generally acceptable that no one should be advantaged or disadvantaged by natural fortune or social circumstances in the choice of principles. It also seems widely agreed that it should be impossible to tailor principles to the circumstances of one's own case. We should ensure further that particular inclinations and aspirations, and persons' conceptions of their good, do not affect the principles adopted. The aim is to rule out those principles that it would be rational to propose for acceptance, however little the chance of success, only if one knew certain things that are irrelevant from the standpoint of justice. For example, if a man knew that he was wealthy, he might find it rational to advance the principle that various taxes for welfare measures be counted unjust; if he knew that he was poor, he would most likely propose the contrary principle. To represent the desired restrictions one imagines a situation in which everyone is deprived of this sort of information. One excludes the knowledge of those contingencies which sets men at odds and allows them to be guided by their prejudices. In this manner the veil of ignorance is arrived at in a natural way. This concept should cause no difficulty if we keep in mind the constraints on arguments that it is meant to express. At any time we can enter the original position, so to speak, simply by following a certain procedure; namely, by arguing for principles of justice in accordance with these restrictions.

It seems reasonable to suppose that the parties in the original position are equal. That is, all have the same rights in the procedure for choosing principles; each can make proposals, submit reasons for their acceptance, and so on. Obviously the purpose of these conditions is to represent equality between human beings as moral persons, as creatures having a conception of their good and capable of a sense of justice. The basis of equality is taken to be similarity in these two respects. Systems of ends are not ranked in value, and each man is presumed to have the requisite ability to understand and to act upon whatever principles are adopted. Together with the veil of ignorance, these conditions define the principles of justice as those which rational persons concerned to advance their interests would consent to as equals when none are known to be advantaged or disadvantaged by social and natural contingencies.

There is, however, another side to justifying a particular description of the original position.

This is to see if the principles which would be chosen match our considered convictions of justice or extend them in an acceptable way. We can note whether applying these principles would lead us to make the same judgments about the basic structure of society which we now make intuitively and in which we have the greatest confidence; or whether, in cases where our present judgments are in doubt and given with hesitation, these principles offer a resolution which we can affirm on reflection. There are questions which we feel sure must be answered in a certain way. For example, we are confident that religious intolerance and racial discrimination are unjust. We think that we have examined these things with care and have reached what we believe is an impartial judgment not likely to be distorted by an excessive attention to our own interests. These convictions are provisional fixed points which we presume any conception of justice must fit. But we have much less assurance as to what is the correct distribution of wealth and authority. Here we may be looking for a way to remove our doubts. We can check an interpretation of the initial situation, then, by the capacity of its principles to accommodate our firmest convictions and to provide guidance where guidance is needed.

In searching for the most favored description of this situation we work from both ends. We begin by describing it so that it represents generally shared and preferably weak conditions. We then see if these conditions are strong enough to yield a significant set of principles. If not, we look for further premises equally reasonable. But if so, and these principles match our considered convictions of justice, then so far well and good. But presumably there will be discrepancies. In this case we have a choice. We can either modify the account of the initial situation or we can revise our existing judgments, for even the judgments we take provisionally as fixed points are liable to revision. By going back and forth, sometimes altering the conditions of the contractual circumstances, at others withdrawing our judgments and conforming them to principle, I assume that eventually we shall find a description of the initial situation that both expresses reasonable conditions and yields principles which match our considered judgments duly pruned and adjusted. This state of affairs I refer to as reflective equilibrium.[4] It is an equilibrium because at last our principles and judgments coincide; and it is reflective since we know to what principles our judgments conform and the premises of their derivation. At the moment everything is in order. But this equilibrium is not necessarily stable. It is liable to be upset by further examination of the conditions which should be imposed on the contractual situation and by particular cases which may lead us to revise our judgments. Yet for the time being we have done what we can to render coherent and to justify our convictions of social justice. We have reached a conception of the original position.

I shall not, of course, actually work through this process. Still, we may think of the interpretation of the original position that I shall present as the result of such a hypothetical course of reflection. It represents the attempt to accommodate within one scheme both reasonable philosophical conditions on principles as well as our considered judgments of justice. In arriving at the favored interpretation of the initial situation there is no point at which an appeal is made to self-evidence in the traditional sense either of general conceptions or particular convictions. I do not claim for the principles of justice proposed that they are necessary truths or derivable from such truths. A conception of justice cannot be deduced from self-evident premises or conditions on principles; instead, its justification is a matter of the mutual support of many considerations, of everything fitting together into one coherent view.

A final comment. We shall want to say that certain principles of justice are justified because they would be agreed to in an initial situation of equality. I have emphasized that this original position is purely hypothetical. It is natural to ask why, if this agreement is never actually entered into, we should take any interest in these principles, moral or otherwise. The answer is that the conditions embodied in the description of the original position are ones that we do in fact accept. Or if we do not, then perhaps we can be persuaded to do so by philosophical reflection. Each aspect of the contractual situation can be given supporting grounds. Thus what we shall do is to collect together into one conception a number of conditions on principles that we are ready upon due consideration to recognize as reasonable. These constraints express what we are prepared to regard as limits on fair terms of social cooperation. One way to look at the idea of the original position, therefore, is to see it as an expository device which sums up the meaning of these conditions and helps us to extract their consequences. On the other hand, this conception is also an intuitive notion that suggests its own elaboration, so that led on by it we are drawn to define more clearly the standpoint from which we can best interpret moral relationships. We need a conception that enables us to envision our objective from afar: the intuitive notion of the original position is to do this for us. . . .

Two Principles of Justice

I shall now state in a provisional form the two principles of justice that I believe would be chosen in the original position. In this section I wish to make only the most general comments, and therefore the first formulation of these principles is tentative. As we go on I shall run through several formulations and approximate step by step the final statement to be given much later. I believe that doing this allows the exposition to proceed in a natural way.

The first statement of the two principles reads as follows:

First: each person is to have an equal right to the most extensive basic liberty compatible with a similar liberty for others.

Second: social and economic inequalities are to be arranged so that they are both (a) reasonably expected to be to everyone's advantage, and (b) attached to positions and offices open to all.

There are two ambiguous phrases in the second principle, namely "everyone's advantage" and "open to all." Determining their sense more exactly will lead to a second formulation of the principle. . . .

By way of general comment, these principles primarily apply, as I have said, to the basic structure of society. They are to govern the assignment of rights and duties and to regulate the distribution of social and economic advantages. As their formulation suggests, these principles presuppose that the social structure can be divided into two more or less distinct parts, the first principle applying to the one, the second to the other. They distinguish between those aspects of the social system that define and secure the equal liberties of citizenship and those that specify and establish social and economic inequalities. The basic liberties of citizens are, roughly speaking, political liberty (the right to vote and to be eligible for public office) together with freedom of speech and assembly; liberty of conscience and freedom of thought; freedom of the person along with the right to hold (personal) property; and freedom from arbitrary arrest and seizure as defined by the concept of the rule of law. These liberties are all required to be equal by the first principle, since citizens of a just society are to have the same basic rights.

The second principle applies, in the first approximation, to the distribution of income and wealth and to the design of organizations that make use of differences in authority and responsibility, or chains of command. While the distribution of wealth and income need not be equal, it must be to everyone's advantage, and at the same time, positions of authority and offices of command must be accessible to all. One applies the second principle by holding positions open, and then, subject to this constraint, arranges social and economic inequalities so that everyone benefits.

These principles are to be arranged in a serial order with the first principle prior to the second. This ordering means that a departure from the institutions of equal liberty required by the first principle cannot be justified by, or compensated for, by greater social and economic advantages. The distribution of wealth and income, and the hierarchies of authority, must be consistent with both the liberties of equal citizenship and equality of opportunity.

It is clear that these principles are rather specific in their content, and their acceptance rests on certain assumptions that I must eventually try to explain and justify. A theory of justice depends upon a theory of society in ways that will become evident as we proceed. For the present, it should be observed that the two principles (and this holds for all formulations) are a special case of a more general conception of justice that can be expressed as follows:

All social values—liberty and opportunity, income and wealth, and the bases of self-respect—are to be distributed equally unless an unequal distribution of any, or all, of these values is to everyone's advantage.

Injustice, then, is simply inequalities that are not to the benefit of all. Of course, this conception is extremely vague and requires interpretation.

As a first step, suppose that the basic structure of society distributes certain primary goods, that is, things that every rational man is presumed to want. These goods normally have a use whatever a person's rational plan of life. For simplicity, assume that the chief primary goods at the disposition of society are rights and liberties, powers and opportunities, income and wealth. (Later on . . . the primary good of self-respect has a central place.) These are the social primary goods. Other primary goods such as health and vigor, intelligence and imagination, are natural

goods; although their possession is influenced by the basic structure, they are not so directly under its control. Imagine, then, a hypothetical initial arrangement in which all the social primary goods are equally distributed: everyone has similar rights and duties, and income and wealth are evenly shared. This state of affairs provides a benchmark for judging improvements. If certain inequalities of wealth and organizational powers would make everyone better off than in this hypothetical starting situation, then they accord with the general conception.

Now it is possible, at least theoretically, that by giving up some of their fundamental liberties men are sufficiently compensated by the resulting social and economic gains. The general conception of justice imposes no restrictions on what sort of inequalities are permissible; it only requires that everyone's position be improved. We need not suppose anything so drastic as consenting to a condition of slavery. Imagine instead that men forgo certain political rights when the economic returns are significant and their capacity to influence the course of policy by the exercise of these rights would be marginal in any case. It is this kind of exchange which the two principles as stated rule out; being arranged in serial order they do not permit exchanges between basic liberties and economic and social gains. The serial ordering of principles expresses an underlying preference among primary social goods. When this preference is rational so likewise is the choice of these principles in this order.

In developing justice as fairness I shall, for the most part, leave aside the general conception of justice and examine instead the special case of the two principles in serial order. The advantage of this procedure is that from the first the matter of priorities is recognized and an effort made to find principles to deal with it. One is led to attend throughout to the conditions under which the acknowledgement of the absolute weight of liberty with respect to social and economic advantages, as defined by the lexical order of the two principles, would be reasonable. Offhand, this ranking appears extreme and too special a case to be of much interest; but there is more justification for it than would appear at first sight. Or at any rate, so I shall maintain. . . . Furthermore, the distinction between fundamental rights and liberties and economic and social benefits marks a difference among primary social goods that one should try to exploit. It suggests an important division in the social system. Of course, the distinctions drawn and the ordering proposed are bound to be at best only approximations. There are surely circumstances in which they fail. But it is essential to depict clearly the main lines of a reasonable conception of justice; and under many conditions, anyway, the two principles in serial order may serve well enough. When necessary we can fall back on the more general conception.

The fact that the two principles apply to institutions has certain consequences. Several points illustrate this. First of all, the rights and liberties referred to by these principles are those that are defined by the public rules of the basic structure. Whether men are free is determined by the rights and duties established by the major institutions of society. Liberty is a certain pattern of social forms. The first principle simply requires that certain sorts of rules, those defining basic liberties, apply to everyone equally and that they allow the most extensive liberty compatible with a like liberty for all. The only reason for circumscribing the rights defining liberty and making men's freedom less extensive than it might otherwise be is that these equal rights as institutionally defined would interfere with one another.

Another thing to bear in mind is that when principles mention persons, or require that everyone gain from an inequality, the reference is to representative persons holding the various social positions, or offices, or whatever, established by the basic structure. Thus in applying the second principle I assume that it is possible to assign an expectation of well-being to representative individuals holding these positions. This expectation indicates their life prospects as

viewed from their social station. In general, the expectations of representative persons depend upon the distribution of rights and duties throughout the basic structure. When this changes, expectations change. I assume, then, that expectations are connected: by raising the prospects of the representative man in one position we presumably increase or decrease the prospects of representative men in other positions. Since it applies to institutional forms, the second principle (or rather the first part of it) refers to the expectations of representative individuals. As I shall discuss below, neither principle applies to distributions of particular goods to particular individuals who may be identified by their proper names. The situation where someone is considering how to allocate certain commodities to needy persons who are known to him is not within the scope of the principles. They are meant to regulate basic institutional arrangements. We must not assume that there is much similarity from the standpoint of justice between an administrative allotment of goods to specific persons and the appropriate design of society. Our common sense intuitions for the former may be a poor guide to the latter.

Now the second principle insists that each person benefit from permissible inequalities in the basic structure. This means that it must be reasonable for each relevant representative man defined by this structure, when he views it as a going concern, to prefer his prospects with the inequality, to his prospects without it. One is not allowed to justify difference in income or organizational powers on the ground that the disadvantages of those in one position are outweighed by the greater advantages of those in another. Much less can infringements of liberty be counter-balanced in this way. Applied to the basic structure, the principle of utility would have us maximize the sum of expectations of representative men (weighted by the number of persons they represent, on the classical view); and this would permit us to compensate for the losses of some by the gains of others. Instead the two principles require that everyone benefit from economic and social inequalities.

The Reasoning Leading to the Two Principles of Justice

It will be recalled that the general conception of justice as fairness requires that all primary social goods be distributed equally unless an unequal distribution would be to everyone's advantage. No restrictions are placed on exchanges of these goods and therefore a lesser liberty can be compensated for by greater social and economic benefits. Now looking at the situation from the standpoint of one person selected arbitrarily, there is no way for him to win special advantages for himself. Nor, on the other hand, are there grounds for his acquiescing in special disadvantages. Since it is not reasonable for him to expect more than an equal share in the division of social goods, and since it is not rational for him to agree to less, the sensible thing for him to do is to acknowledge as the first principle of justice one requiring an equal distribution. Indeed, this principle is so obvious that we would expect it to occur to anyone immediately.

Thus, the parties start with a principle establishing liberty for all, including equality of opportunity, as well as an equal distribution of income and wealth. But there is no reason why this acknowledgment should be final. If there are inequalities in the basic structure that work to make everyone better off in comparison with the benchmark of initial equality, why not permit them? The immediate gain which a greater equality might allow can be regarded as intelligently invested in view of its future return. If, for example, these inequalities set up various incentives which succeed in eliciting more productive efforts, a person in the original position may look upon them as necessary to cover the costs of training and to encourage effective performance. One might think that ideally individuals should want to serve one another. But since the parties are assumed not to take an interest in one another's interests, their acceptance of these inequalities is only the acceptance of the relations in which men stand in the circumstances of justice. They have no grounds for complaining of one another's motives. A person in the original position would, therefore, concede the justice of these inequalities. Indeed, it would be short-sighted of him not to do so. He would hesitate to agree to these regularities only if he would be dejected by the bare knowledge or perception that others were better situated; and I have assumed that the parties decide as if they are not moved by envy. In order to make the principle regulating inequalities determinate, one looks at the system from the standpoint of the least advantaged representative man. Inequalities are permissible when they maximize, or at least all contribute to, the long-term expectations of the least fortunate group in society.

Now this general conception imposes no constraints on what sorts of inequalities are allowed, whereas the special conception, by putting the two principles in serial order (with the necessary adjustments in meaning), forbids exchanges between basic liberties and economic and social benefits. I shall not try to justify this order here. . . . But roughly, the idea underlying this ordering is that if the parties assume that their basic liberties can be effectively exercised, they will not exchange a lesser liberty for an improvement in economic well-being. It is only when social conditions do not allow the effective establishment of these rights that one can concede their limitation; and these restrictions can be granted only to the extent that they are necessary to prepare the way for a free society. The denial of equal liberty can be defended only if it is necessary to raise the level of civilization so that in due course these freedoms can be enjoyed. Thus in adopting a serial order we are in effect making a special assumption in the original position, namely, that the parties know that the conditions of their society, whatever they are, admit the effective realization of the equal liberties. The serial ordering of the two principles of justice eventually comes to be reasonable if the general conception is consistently followed. This lexical ranking is the long-run tendency of the general view. For the most part I shall assume that the requisite circumstances for the serial order obtain.

It seems clear from these remarks that the two principles are at least a plausible conception of justice. The question, though, is how one is to argue for them more systematically. Now there are several things to do. One can work out their consequences for institutions and note their implications for fundamental social policy. In this way they are tested by a comparison with our considered judgments of justice. . . . But one can also try to find arguments in their favor that are decisive from the standpoint of the original position. In order to see how this might be done, it is useful as a heuristic device to think of the two principles as the maximin solution to the problem of social justice. There is an analogy between the two principles and the maximin rule for choice under uncertainty.[5] This is evident from the fact that the two principles are those a person would choose for the design of a society in which his enemy is to assign him his place. The maximin rule tells us to rank alternatives by their worst possible outcomes: we are to adopt the alternative the worst outcome of which is superior to the worst outcomes of the others. The persons in the original position do not, of course, assume that their initial place in society is decided by a malevolent opponent. As I note below, they should not reason from false premises. The veil of ignorance does not violate this idea, since an absence of information is not misinformation. But that the two principles of justice would be chosen if the parties were forced to protect themselves against such a contingency explains the sense in which this conception is the maximin solution. And this analogy suggests that if the original position has been described so that it is rational for the parties to adopt the conservative attitude expressed by this rule, a conclusive argument can

indeed be constructed for these principles. Clearly the maximin rule is not, in general, a suitable guide for choices under uncertainty. But it is attractive in situations marked by certain special features. My aim, then, is to show that a good case can be made for the two principles based on the fact that the original position manifests these features to the fullest possible degree, carrying them to the limit, so to speak.

Consider the gain-and-loss table below. It represents the gains and losses for a situation which is not a game of strategy. There is no one playing against the person making the decision; instead he is faced with several possible circumstances which may or may not obtain. Which circumstances happen to exist does not depend upon what the person choosing decides or whether he announces his moves in advance. The numbers in the table are monetary values (in hundreds of dollars) in comparison with some initial situation. The gain (g) depends upon the individual's decision (d) and the circumstances (c). Thus $g = f(d,c)$. Assuming that there are three possible decisions and three possible circumstances, we might have this gain-and-loss table.

	Circumstances		
Decisions	*C1*	*C2*	*C3*
d1	–7	8	12
d2	–8	7	14
d3	5	6	8

The maximin rule requires that we make the third decision. For in this case the worst that can happen is that one gains five hundred dollars, which is better than the worst for the other actions. If we adopt one of these we may lose either eight or seven hundred dollars. Thus, the choice of d_3 maximizes $f(d,c)$ for that value of c which for a given d, minimizes f. The term "maximin" means the *maximum minimorum;* and the rule directs our attention to the worst that can happen under any proposed course of action, and to decide in the light of that.

(Better to be Safe than sorry)

Now there appear to be three chief features of situations that give plausibility to this unusual rule.[6] First, since the rule takes no account of the likelihoods of the possible circumstances, there must be some reason for sharply discounting estimates of these probabilities. Offhand, the most natural rule of choice would seem to be to compute the expectation of monetary gain for each decision and then to adopt the course of action with the highest prospect. (This expectation is defined as follows: let us suppose that g_{ij} represent the numbers in the gain-and-loss table, where i is the row index and j is the column index; and let p_j, j =1, 2, 3, be the likelihoods of the circumstances, with $\sum p_j = 1$. Then the expectation for the ith decision is equal to $\sum p_j g_{ij}$.) Thus it must be, for example, that the situation is one in which a knowledge of likelihoods is impossible, or at best extremely insecure. In this case it is unreasonable not to be skeptical of probabilistic calculations unless there is no other way out, particularly if the decision is a fundamental one that needs to be justified to others.

The second feature that suggests the maximin rule is the following: the person choosing has a conception of the good such that he cares very little, if anything, for what he might gain above the minimum stipend that he can, in fact, be sure of by following the maximin rule. It is not worthwhile for him to take a chance for the sake of a further advantage, especially when it may turn out that he loses much that is important to him. This last provision brings in the third feature; namely, that the rejected alternatives have outcomes that one can hardly accept. The situation involves grave risks. Of course these features work most effectively in combination. The paradigm situation for following the maximin rule is when all three features are realized to the highest degree. This rule does not, then, generally apply, nor of course is it self-evident. Rather, it is a maxim, a rule of thumb, that comes into its own in special circumstances. Its application depends upon the qualitative structure of the possible gains and losses in relation to one's conception of the good, all this against a background in which it is reasonable to discount conjectural estimates of likelihoods.

It should be noted, as the comments on the gain-and-loss table say, that the entries in the table represent monetary values and not utilities. This difference is significant since for one thing computing expectations on the basis of such objective values is not the same thing as computing expected utility and may lead to different results. The essential point, though, is that in justice as fairness the parties do not know their conception of the good and cannot estimate their utility in the ordinary sense. In any case, we want to go behind de facto preferences generated by given conditions. Therefore expectations are based upon an index of primary goods and the parties make their choice accordingly. The entries in the example are in terms of money and not utility to indicate this aspect of the contract doctrine.

Now, as I have suggested, the original position has been defined so that it is a situation in which the maximin rule applies. In order to see this, let us review briefly the nature of this situation with these three special features in mind. To begin with, the veil of ignorance excludes all but the vaguest knowledge of likelihoods. The parties have no basis for determining the probable nature of their society, or their place in it. Thus they have strong reasons for being wary of probability calculations if any other course is open to them. They must also take into account the fact that their choice of principles should seem reasonable to others, in particular their descendants, whose rights will be deeply affected by it. There are further grounds for discounting that I shall mention as we go along. For the present it suffices to note that these considerations are strengthened by the fact that the parties know very little about the gain-and-loss table. Not only are they unable to conjecture the likelihoods of the various possible circumstances, they cannot say much about what the possible circumstances are, much less enumerate them and foresee the outcome of each alternative available.

Those deciding are much more in the dark than the illustration by a numerical table suggests. It is for this reason that I have spoken of an analogy with the maximin rule.

Several kinds of arguments for the two principles of justice illustrate the second feature. Thus, if we can maintain that these principles provide a workable theory of social justice, and that they are compatible with reasonable demands of efficiency, then this conception guarantees a satisfactory minimum. There may be, on reflection, little reason for trying to do better. Thus much of the argument . . . is to show, by their application to the main questions of social justice, that the two principles are a satisfactory conception. These details have a philosophical purpose. Moreover, this line of thought is practically decisive if we can establish the priority of liberty, the lexical ordering of the two principles. For this priority implies that the persons in the original position have no desire to try for greater gains at the expense of the equal liberties. The minimum assured by the two principles in lexical order is not one that the parties wish to jeopardize for the sake of greater economic and social advantages. . . .

Finally, the third feature holds if we can assume that other conceptions of justice may lead to institutions that the parties would find intolerable. For example, it has sometimes been held that under some conditions the utility principle (in either form) justifies, if not slavery or serfdom, at any rate serious infractions of liberty for the sake of greater social benefits. We need not consider here the truth of this claim, or the likelihood that the requisite conditions obtain. For the moment, this contention is only to illustrate the way in which conceptions of justice may allow for outcomes which the parties may not be able to accept. And having the ready alternative of the two principles of justice which secure a satisfactory minimum, it seems unwise, if not irrational, for them to take a chance that these outcomes are not realized.

So much, then, for a brief sketch of the features of situations in which the maximin rule comes into its own and of the way in which the arguments for the two principles of justice can be subsumed under them. . . .

The Final Formulation of the Principles of Justice

. . . I now wish to give the final statement of the two principles of justice for institutions. For the sake of completeness, I shall give a full statement including earlier formulations.

First Principle
Each person is to have an equal right to the most extensive total system of equal basic liberties compatible with a similar system of liberty for all.

Second Principle
Social and economic inequalities are to be arranged so that they are both:
(a) to the greatest benefit of the least advantaged, consistent with the just savings principle, and
(b) attached to offices and positions open to all under conditions of fair equality of opportunity.

First Priority Rule (The Priority of Liberty)
The principles of justice are to be ranked in lexical order and therefore liberty can be restricted only for the sake of liberty. There are two cases:
(a) a less extensive liberty must strengthen the total system of liberty shared by all;
(b) a less than equal liberty must be acceptable to those with the lesser liberty.

Second Priority Rule (The Priority of Justice over Efficiency and Welfare)
The second principle of justice is lexically prior to the principle of efficiency and to that of maximizing the sum of advantages;

and fair opportunity is prior to the difference principle. There are two cases:

(a) an inequality of opportunity must enhance the opportunities of those with the lesser opportunity;

(b) an excessive rate of saving must on balance mitigate the burden of those bearing this hardship.

General Conception

All social primary goods—liberty and opportunity, income and wealth, and the bases of self-respect—are to be distributed equally unless an unequal distribution of any or all of these goods is to the advantage of the least favored.

By way of comment, these principles and priority rules are no doubt incomplete. Other modifications will surely have to be made, but I shall not further complicate the statement of the principles. It suffices to observe that when we come to nonideal theory, we do not fall back straightway upon the general conception of justice. The lexical ordering of the two principles, and the valuations that this ordering implies, suggest priority rules which seem to be reasonable enough in many cases. By various examples I have tried to illustrate how these rules can be used and to indicate their plausibility. Thus the ranking of the principles of justice in ideal theory reflects back and guides the application of these principles to nonideal situations. It identifies which limitations need to be dealt with first. The drawback of the general conception of justice is that it lacks the definite structure of the two principles in serial order. In more extreme and tangled instances of nonideal theory there may be no alternative to it. At some point the priority of rules for nonideal cases will fail; and indeed we may be able to find no satisfactory answer at all. But we must try to postpone the day of reckoning as long as possible, and try to arrange society so that it never comes. . . .

The Kantian Interpretation

Kant held, I believe, that a person is acting autonomously when the principles of his action are chosen by him as the most adequate possible expression of his nature as a free and equal rational being. The principles he acts upon are not adopted because of his social position or natural endowments, or in view of the particular kind of society in which he lives or the specific things that he happens to want. To act on such principles is to act heteronomously. Now the veil of ignorance deprives the persons in the original position of the knowledge that would enable them to choose heteronomous principles. The parties arrive at their choice together as free and equal rational persons knowing only that those circumstances obtain which give rise to the need for principles of justice.

To be sure, the argument for these principles does add in various ways to Kant's conception. For example, it adds the feature that the principles chosen are to apply to the basic structure of society; and premises characterizing this structure are used in deriving the principles of justice. But I believe that this and other additions are natural enough and remain fairly close to Kant's doctrine, at least when all of his ethical writings are viewed together. Assuming, then, that the reasoning in favor of the principles of justice is correct, we can say that when persons act on these principles they are acting in accordance with principles that they would choose as rational and independent persons in an original position of equality. The principles of their actions do not depend upon social or natural contingencies, nor do they reflect the bias of the particulars of their plan of life or the aspirations that motivate them. By acting from these principles persons express their nature as free and equal rational beings subject to the general conditions of human life. For to express one's nature as a being of a particular kind is to act on the principles that would be chosen if this nature were the decisive determining element. Of course, the choice of the parties in the original position is subject to the restrictions of that situation. But when we knowingly act on the principles of justice in the ordinary course of events, we deliberately assume the limitations of the original position. One reason for doing this, for persons who can do so and want to, is to give expression to one's nature.

The principles of justice are also categorical imperatives in Kant's sense. For by a categorical imperative Kant understands a principle of conduct that applies to a person in virtue of his nature as a free and equal rational being. The validity of the principle does not presuppose that one has a particular desire or aim. Whereas a hypothetical imperative by contrast does assume this: it directs us to take certain steps as effective means to achieve a specific end. Whether the desire is for a particular thing, or whether it is for something more general, such as certain kinds of agreeable feelings or pleasures, the corresponding imperative is hypothetical. Its applicability depends upon one's having an aim which one need not have as a condition of being a rational human individual. The argument for the two principles of justice does not assume that the parties have particular ends, but only that they desire certain primary goods. These are things that it is rational to want whatever else one wants. Thus given human nature, wanting them is part of being rational; and while each is presumed to have some conception of the good, nothing is known about his final ends. The preference for primary goods is derived, then, from only the most general assumptions about rationality and the conditions of human life. To act from the principles of justice is to act from categorical imperatives in the sense that they apply to us whatever in particular our aims are. This simply reflects the fact that no such contingencies appear as premises in their derivation.

We may note also that the motivational assumption of mutual disinterest accords with Kant's notion of autonomy, and gives another reason for this condition. So far this assumption has been used to characterize the circumstances of justice and to provide a clear conception to guide the reasoning of the parties. We have also seen that the concept of benevolence, being a second-order notion, would not work out well. Now we can add that the assumption of mutual disinterest is to allow for freedom in the choice of a system of final ends.[7] Liberty in adopting a conception of the good is limited only by principles that are deduced from a doctrine which imposes no prior constraints on these conceptions. Presuming mutual disinterest in the original position carries out this idea. We postulate that the parties have opposing claims in a suitably general sense. If their ends were restricted in some specific way, this would appear at the outset as an arbitrary restriction on freedom. Moreover, if the parties were conceived as altruists, or as pursuing certain kinds of pleasures, then the principles chosen would apply, as far as the argument would have shown, only to persons whose freedom was restricted to choices compatible with altruism or hedonism. As the argument now runs, the principles of justice cover all persons with rational plans of life, whatever their content, and these principles represent the appropriate restrictions on freedom. Thus it is possible to say that the constraints on conceptions of the good are the result of an interpretation of the contractual situation that puts no prior limitations on what men may desire. There are a variety of reasons, then, for the motivational premise of mutual disinterest. This premise is not only a matter of realism about the circumstances of justice or a way to make the theory manageable. It also connects up with the Kantian idea of autonomy. . . .

The original position may be viewed, then, as a procedural interpretation of Kant's conception of autonomy and the categorical imperative. The principles regulative of the kingdom of ends are those that would be chosen in this position, and the description of this situation enables us to explain the sense in which acting from these principles expresses our nature as free and equal rational persons. No longer are these notions purely transcendent and lacking explicable connections with human conduct, for the procedural conception of the original position allows us to make these ties. . . .

NOTES

1. As the text suggests, I shall regard Locke's *The Second Treatise of Government*, Rousseau's *Social Contract*, and Kant's ethical works beginning with *The Foundations of the Metaphysics of Morals* as definitive of the contract tradition. For all of its greatness, Hobbes's *Leviathan* raises special problems. A general historical survey is provided by J. W. Gough, *The Social Contract*, 2nd ed. (Oxford, The Clarendon Press, 1957), and Otto Gierke, *Natural Law and the Theory of Society*, trans. with an introduction by Ernest Barker (Cambridge, The University Press, 1934). A presentation of the contract view as primarily an ethical theory is to be found in G. R. Grice, *The Grounds of Moral Judgment* (Cambridge, The University Press, 1967). . . .

2. Kant is clear that the original agreement is hypothetical. See *The Metaphysics of Morals*, pt. I (*Rechtslehre*), especially §§ 47, 52; and pt. II of the essay "Concerning the Common Saying: This May Be True in Theory But It Does Not Apply in Practice,"

in *Kant's Political Writings*, ed. Hans Reiss and trans. by H. B. Nisbet (Cambridge, The University Press, 1970), pp. 73–87. [Reprinted above, editor] See Georges Vlachos, *La Pensée politique de Kant* (Paris, Presses Universitaires de France, 1962), pp. 326–335; and J. G. Murphy, *Kant: The Philosophy of Right* (London, Macmillan, 1970), pp. 109–112, 133–136, for a further discussion.

3. For the formulation of this intuitive idea I am indebted to Allan Gibbard.

4. The process of mutual adjustment of principles and considered judgments is not peculiar to moral philosophy. See Nelson Goodman, *Fact, Fiction, and Forecast* (Cambridge, Mass., Harvard University press, 1955), pp. 65–68, for parallel remarks concerning the justification of the principles of deductive and inductive inference.

5. An accessible discussion of this and other rules of choice under uncertainty can be found in W. J. Baumol, *Economic Theory and Operations Analysis*, 2nd ed. (Englewood Cliffs, N.J., Prentice-Hall, 1965), ch. 24. Baumol gives a geometric interpretation of these rules, including the diagram used . . . to illustrate the difference principle. See pp. 558–562. See also R. D. Luce and Howard Raiffa, *Games and Decisions* (New York, John Wiley and Sons, Inc., 1957), ch. XIII. for a fuller account.

6. Here I borrow from William Fellner, *Probability and Profit* (Homewood, Ill., Richard D. Irwin, 1965), pp. 140–142, where these features are noted.

7. For this point I am indebted to Charles Fried.

11   Hypothetical Contracts and Rights

RONALD DWORKIN

I TRUST THAT IT IS NOT NECESSARY to describe John Rawls's famous idea of the original position in any great detail.[1] It imagines a group of men and women who come together to form a social contract. Thus far it resembles the imaginary congresses of the classical social contract theories. The original position differs, however, from these theories in its description of the parties. They are men and women with ordinary tastes, talents, ambitions, and convictions, but each is temporarily ignorant of these features of his own personality, and must agree upon a contract before his self-awareness returns.

Rawls tries to show that if these men and women are rational, and act only in their own self-interest, they will choose his two principles of justice. These provide, roughly, that every person must have the largest political liberty compatible with a like liberty for all, and that inequalities in power, wealth, income, and other resources must not exist except insofar as they work to the absolute benefit of the worst-off members of society. Many of Rawls's critics disagree that men and women in the original position would inevitably choose these two principles. The principles are conservative, and the critics believe they would be chosen only by men who were conservative by temperament, and not by men who were natural gamblers. I do not think this criticism is well taken, but in this essay, at least, I mean to ignore the point. I am interested in a different issue.

Suppose that the critics are wrong, and that men and women in the original position would in fact choose Rawls's two principles as being in their own best interest. Rawls seems to think that that fact would provide an argument in favor of these two principles as a standard of justice against which to test actual political institutions. But it is not immediately plain why this should be so.

If a group contracted in advance that disputes amongst them would be settled in a particular way, the fact of that contract would be a powerful argument that such disputes should be settled in that way when they do arise. The contract would be an argument in itself, independent of the force of the reasons that might have led different people to enter the contract. Ordinarily, for example, each of the parties supposes that a contract he signs is in his own interest; but if someone has made a mistake in calculating his self-interest, the fact that he did contract is a strong reason for the fairness of holding him nevertheless to the bargain.

Rawls does not suppose that any group ever entered into a social contract of the sort he describes. He argues only that if a group of rational men did find themselves in the predicament of the original position, they would contract for the two principles. His contract is hypothetical, and hypothetical contracts do not supply an independent argument for the fairness of enforcing their terms. A hypothetical contract is not simply a

From Taking Rights Seriously (1977), pp. 150–159, 177–183. Reprinted by permission of the author.

pale form of an actual contract; it is no contract at all.

If, for example, I am playing a game, it may be that I would have agreed to any number of ground rules if I had been asked in advance of play. It does not follow that these rules may be enforced against me if I have not, in fact, agreed to them. There must be reasons, of course, why I would have agreed if asked in advance, and these may also be reasons why it is fair to enforce these rules against me even if I have not agreed. But my hypothetical agreement does not count as a reason, independent of these other reasons, for enforcing the rules against me, as my actual agreement would have.

Suppose that you and I are playing poker and we find, in the middle of a hand, that the deck is one card short. You suggest that we throw the hand in, but I refuse because I know I am going to win and I want the money in the pot. You might say that I would certainly have agreed to that procedure had the possibility of the deck being short been raised in advance. But your point is not that I am somehow committed to throwing the hand in by an agreement I never made. Rather you use the device of a hypothetical agreement to make a point that might have been made without that device, which is that the solution recommended is so obviously fair and sensible that only someone with an immediate contrary interest could disagree. Your main argument is that your solution is fair and sensible, and the fact that I would have chosen it myself adds nothing of substance to that argument. If I am able to meet the main argument nothing remains, rising out of your claim that I would have agreed, to be answered or excused.

In some circumstances, moreover, the fact that I would have agreed does not even suggest an independent argument of this character. Everything depends on your reasons for supposing that I would have agreed. Suppose you say that I would have agreed, if you had brought up the point and insisted on your solution, because

I very much wanted to play and would have given in rather than miss my chance. I might concede that I would have agreed for that reason, and then add that I am lucky that you did not raise the point. The fact that I would have agreed if you had insisted neither adds nor suggests any argument why I should agree now. The point is not that it would have been unfair of you to insist on your proposal as a condition of playing; indeed, it would not have been. If you had held out for your proposal, and I had agreed, I could not say that my agreement was in any way nullified or called into question because of duress. But if I had not in fact agreed, the fact that I would have in itself means nothing.

I do not mean that it is never relevant, in deciding whether an act affecting someone is fair, that he would have consented if asked. If a doctor finds a man unconscious and bleeding, for example, it might be important for him to ask whether the man would consent to a transfusion if he were conscious. If there is every reason to think that he would, the fact is important in justifying the transfusion if the patient later, perhaps because he has undergone a religious conversion, condemns the doctor for having proceeded. But this sort of case is beside the present point, because the patient's hypothetical agreement shows that his will was inclined toward the decision at the time and in the circumstances that the decision was taken. He has lost nothing by not being consulted at the appropriate time, because he would have consented if he had been. The original position argument is very different. If we take it to argue for the fairness of applying the two principles we must take it to argue that because a man would have consented to certain principles if asked in advance, it is fair to apply those principles to him later, under different circumstances, when he does not consent.

But that is a bad argument. Suppose I did not know the value of my painting on Monday; if you had offered me $100 for it then I would have accepted. On Tuesday I discovered it was valuable. You cannot argue that it would be fair for the courts to make me sell it to you for $100 on Wednesday. It may be my good fortune that you did not ask me on Monday, but that does not justify coercion against me later.

We must therefore treat the argument from the original position as we treat your argument in the poker game; it must be a device for calling attention to some independent argument for the fairness of the two principles—an argument that does not rest on the false premise that a hypothetical contract has some pale binding force. What other argument is available? One might say that the original position shows that the two principles are in the best interests of every member of any political community, and that it is fair to govern in accordance with them for that reason. It is true that if the two principles could be shown to be in everyone's interest, that would be a sound argument for their fairness, but it is hard to see how the original position can be used to show that they are.

We must be careful to distinguish two senses in which something might be said to be in my interest. It is in my *antecedent* interest to make a bet on a horse that, all things considered, offers the best odds, even if, in the event, the horse loses. It is in my *actual* interest to bet on the horse that wins, even if the bet was, at the time I made it, a silly one. If the original position furnishes an argument that it is in everyone's interest to accept the two principles over other possible bases for a constitution, it must be an argument that uses the idea of antecedent and not actual interest. It is not in the actual best interests of everyone to choose the two principles, because when the veil of ignorance is lifted some will discover that they would have been better off if some other principle, like the principle of average utility, had been chosen.

A judgment of antecedent interest depends upon the circumstances under which the judgment is made, and, in particular, upon the knowledge available to the man making the judgment. It might be in my antecedent interest to bet on a certain horse at given odds before the starting gun, but not, at least at the same odds, after he has stumbled on the first turn. The fact, therefore, that a particular choice is in my interest at a particular time, under conditions of great uncertainty, is not a good argument for the fairness of enforcing that choice against me later under conditions of much greater knowledge. But that is what, on this interpretation, the original position argument suggests because it seeks to justify the contemporary use of the two principles on the supposition that, under conditions very different from present conditions, it would be in the antecedent interest of everyone to agree to them. If I have bought a ticket on a longshot it might be in my antecedent interest, before the race, to sell the ticket to you for twice what I paid; it does not follow that it is fair for you to take it from me for that sum when the longshot is about to win.

Someone might now say that I have misunderstood the point of the special conditions of uncertainty in the original position. The parties are made ignorant of their special resources and talents to prevent them from bargaining for principles that are inherently unfair because they favor some collection of resources and talents over others. If the man in the original position does not know his special interests, he cannot negotiate to favor them. In that case, it might be said, the uncertainty of the original position does not vitiate the argument from antecedent interest as I have suggested, but only limits the range within which self-interest might operate. The argument shows that the two principles are in everyone's interest once obviously unfair principles are removed from consideration by the device of uncertainty. Since the only additional knowledge contemporary men and women have over men and women in the original position is knowledge that they ought not to rely upon in choosing principles of justice, their antecedent interest is, so far as it is relevant, the same, and if that is so the original position argument does offer a good argument for applying the two principles to contemporary politics.

But surely this confuses the argument that Rawls makes with a different argument that he might have made. Suppose his men and women had full knowledge of their own talents and tastes, but had to reach agreement under conditions that ruled out, simply by stipulation, obviously unfair principles like those providing special advantage for named individuals. If Rawls could show that, once such obviously unfair principles had been set aside, it would be in the interest of everyone to settle for his two principles, that would indeed count as an argument for the two principles. My point—that the antecedent self-interest of men in the original position is different from that of contemporary men—would no longer hold because both groups of men would then have the same knowledge about themselves, and be subject to the same moral restrictions against choosing obviously unfair principles.

Rawls's actual argument is quite different, however. The ignorance in which his men must choose affects their calculations of self-interest, and cannot be described merely as setting boundaries within which these calculations must be applied. Rawls supposes, for example, that his men would inevitably choose conservative principles because this would be the only rational choice, in their ignorance, for self-interested men to make. But some actual men, aware of their own talents, might well prefer less conservative principles that would allow them to take advantage of the resources they know they have. Someone who considers the original position an argument for the conservative principles, therefore, is faced with this choice. If less conservative principles, like principles that favor named individuals, are to be ruled out as obviously unfair, then the argument for the conservative principles is complete at the outset, on grounds of obvious fairness alone. In that case neither the original position nor any considerations of self-interest it is meant to demonstrate play any role in the argument. But if less conservative principles cannot be ruled out in advance as obviously unfair, then imposing ignorance on Rawls's men, so that they prefer the more conservative principles, cannot be explained simply as ruling out obviously unfair choices. And since this affects the antecedent self-interest of these men, the argument that the original position demonstrates the antecedent self-interest of actual men must therefore fail. This same dilemma can, of course, be constructed for each feature of the two principles.

I recognize that the argument thus far seems to ignore a distinctive feature of Rawls's methodology, which he describes as the technique of seeking a "reflective equilibrium" between our ordinary, unreflective moral beliefs and some theoretical structure that might unify and justify these ordinary beliefs.[2] It might now be said that the idea of an original position plays a part in this reflective equilibrium, which we will miss if we insist, as I have, on trying to find a more direct, one-way argument from the original position to the two principles of justice.

The technique of equilibrium does play an important role in Rawls's argument, and it is worth describing that technique briefly here. The technique assumes that Rawls's readers have a sense, which we draw upon in our daily life, that certain particular political arrangements or decisions, like conventional trials, are just and others, like slavery, are unjust. It assumes, moreover, that we are each able to arrange these immediate intuitions or convictions in an order that designates some of them as more certain than others. Most people, for example, think that it is more plainly unjust for the state to execute innocent citizens of its own than to kill innocent foreign civilians in war. They might be prepared to abandon their position on foreign civilians in war, on the basis of some argument, but would be much more reluctant to abandon their view on executing innocent countrymen.

It is the task of moral philosophy, according to the technique of equilibrium, to provide a structure of principles that supports these immediate convictions about which we are more or less secure, with two goals in mind. First, this structure of principles must explain the convictions by showing the underlying assumptions they reflect; second, it must provide guidance in those cases about which we have either no convictions or weak or contradictory convictions. If we are unsure, for example, whether economic institutions that allow great disparity of wealth are unjust, we may turn to the principles that explain our confident convictions, and then apply these principles to that difficult issue.

But the process is not simply one of finding principles that accommodate our more or less settled judgments. These principles must support, and not merely account for, our judgments, and this means that the principles must have independent appeal to our moral sense. It might be, for example, that a cluster of familiar moral convictions could be shown to serve an undeserving policy—perhaps that the standard judgments we make without reflection serve the purpose of maintaining one particular class in political power. But this discovery would not vouch for the principle of class egoism; on the contrary, it would discredit our ordinary judgments, unless some other principle of a more respectable sort could be found that also fits our intuitions, in which case it would be this principle and not the class-interest principle that our intuitions would recommend.

It might be that no coherent set of principles could be found that has independent appeal and that supports the full set of our immediate convictions; indeed it would be surprising if this were not often the case. If that does happen, we must compromise, giving way on both sides. We might relax, though we could not abandon, our initial sense of what might be an acceptable principle. We might come to accept, for example, after further reflection, some principle that seemed to us initially unattractive, perhaps the principle that men should sometimes be made to be free. We might accept this principle if we were satisfied that no less harsh principle could support the set of political convictions we were especially reluctant to abandon. On the other hand, we must also be ready to modify or adjust,

or even to give up entirely immediate convictions that cannot be accommodated by any principle that meets our relaxed standards; in adjusting these immediate convictions we will use our initial sense of which seem to us more and which less certain, though in principle no immediate conviction can be taken as immune from reinspection or abandonment if that should prove necessary. We can expect to proceed back and forth between our immediate judgments and the structure of explanatory principles in this way, tinkering first with one side and then the other, until we arrived at what Rawls calls the state of reflective equilibrium in which we are satisfied, or as much satisfied as we can reasonably expect.

It may well be that, at least for most of us, our ordinary political judgments stand in this relation of reflective equilibrium with Rawls's two principles of justice, or, at least, that they could be made to do so through the process of adjustment just described. It is nevertheless unclear how the idea of the original position fits into this structure or, indeed, why it has any role to play at all. The original position is not among the ordinary political convictions that we find we have, and that we turn to reflective equilibrium to justify. If it has any role, it must be in the process of justification, because it takes its place in the body of theory we construct to bring our convictions into balance. But if the two principles of justice are themselves in reflective equilibrium with our convictions, it is unclear why we need the original position to supplement the two principles on the theoretical side of the balance. What can the idea contribute to a harmony already established?

We should consider the following answer. It is one of the conditions we impose on a theoretical principle, before we allow it to figure as a justification of our convictions, that the people the principle would govern would have accepted that principle, at least under certain conditions, if they had been asked, or at least that the principle can be shown to be in the antecedent interest of every such person. If this is so, then the original position plays an essential part in the process of justification through equilibrium. It is used to show that the two principles conform to this established standard of acceptability for political principles. At the same time, the fact that the two principles, which do conform to that standard, justify our ordinary convictions in reflective equilibrium reinforces our faith in the standard and encourages us to apply it to other issues of political or moral philosophy.

This answer does not advance the case that the original position furnishes an argument for the two principles, however; it merely restates the ideas we have already considered and rejected. It is certainly not part of our established political traditions or ordinary moral understanding that principles are acceptable only if they would be chosen by men in the particular predicament of the original position. It is, of course, part of these traditions that principles are fair if they have in fact been chosen by those whom they govern, or if they can at least be shown to be in their antecedent common interest. But we have already seen that the original position device cannot be used to support either of these arguments in favor of applying the two principles to contemporary politics. If the original position is to play any role in a structure of principles and convictions in reflective equilibrium, it must be by virtue of assumptions we have not yet identified.

It is time to reconsider an earlier assumption. So far I have been treating the original position construction as if it were either the foundation of Rawls's argument or an ingredient in a reflective equilibrium established between our political intuitions and his two principles of justice. But, in fact, Rawls does not treat the original position that way. He describes the construction in these words:

> I have emphasized that this original position is purely hypothetical. It is natural to ask why, if this agreement is never actually entered into, we should take any interest in these principles, moral or otherwise. The answer is that the conditions embodied in the description of the original position are ones that we do in fact accept. Or if we do not, then perhaps we can be persuaded to do so by philosophical reflection. Each aspect of the contractual situation can be given supporting grounds. . . . On the other hand, this conception is also an intuitive notion that suggests its own elaboration, so that led on by it we are drawn to define more clearly the standpoint from which we can best interpret moral relationships. We need a conception that enables us to envision our objective from afar: the intuitive notion of the original position is to do this for us.[3]

This description is taken from Rawls's first statement of the original position. It is recalled and repeated in the very last paragraph of [his] book.[4] It is plainly of capital importance, and it suggests that the original position, far from being the foundation of his argument, or an expository device for the technique of equilibrium, is one of the major substantive products of the theory as a whole. Its importance is reflected in another crucial passage. Rawls describes his moral theory as a type of psychology. He wants to characterize the structure of our (or, at least, one person's) capacity to make moral judgments of a certain sort; that is, judgments about justice. He thinks that the conditions embodied in the original position are the fundamental "principles governing our moral powers, or more specifically, our sense of justice."[5] The original position is therefore a schematic representation of a particular mental process of at least some, and perhaps most, human beings, just as depth grammar, he suggests, is a schematic presentation of a different mental capacity.

All this suggests that the original position is an intermediate conclusion, a halfway point in a deeper theory that provides philosophical arguments for its conditions. In the next part of this essay I shall try to describe at least the main outlines of this deeper theory. I shall distinguish three features of the surface argument of the book—the technique of equilibrium, the social contract, and the original position itself—and try to discern which of various familiar philosophical principles or positions these represent.

First, however, I must say a further word about Rawls's exciting, if imprecise, idea that the principles of this deeper theory are constitutive of our moral capacity. That idea can be understood on different levels of profundity. It may mean, at its least profound, that the principles that support the original position as a device for reasoning about justice are so widely shared and so little questioned within a particular community, for whom the book is meant, that the community could not abandon these principles without fundamentally changing its patterns of reasoning and arguing about political morality. It may mean, at its most profound, that these principles are innate categories of morality common to all men, imprinted in their neural structure, so that man could not deny these principles short of abandoning the power to reason about morality at all.

I shall be guided, in what follows, by the less profound interpretation, though what I shall say, I think, is consistent with the more profound. I shall assume, then, that there is a group of men and women who find, on reading Rawls, that the original position does strike them as a proper "intuitive notion" from which to think about problems of justice, and who would find it persuasive, if it could be demonstrated that the parties to the original position would in fact contract for the two principles he describes. I suppose, on the basis of experience and the literature, that this group contains a very large number of those who think about justice at all, and I find that I am a member myself. I want to discover the hidden assumptions that bend the inclinations of this group that way, and I shall do so by repeating the question with which I began. Why does Rawls's argument support his claim that his two principles are principles of justice? My answer is complex and it will take us, at times, far from his text, but not, I think, from its spirit. . . .

The Original Position

I said that the use of a social contract, in the way that Rawls uses it, presupposes a deep theory that assumes natural rights. I want now to describe, in somewhat more detail, how the device of a contract applies that assumption. It capitalizes on the idea, mentioned earlier, that some political arrangements might be said to be in the antecedent interest of every individual even though they are not, in the event, in his actual interest.

Everyone whose consent is necessary to a contract has a veto over the terms of that contract, but the worth of that veto, to him, is limited by the fact that his judgment must be one of antecedent rather than actual self-interest. He must commit himself, and so abandon his veto, at a time when his knowledge is sufficient only to allow him to estimate the best odds, not to be certain of his bet. So the contract situation is in one way structurally like the situation in which an individual with specific political rights confronts political decisions that may disadvantage him. He had a limited, political right to veto these, a veto limited by the scope of the rights he has. The contract can be used as a model for the political situation by shaping the degree or character of a party's ignorance in the contractual situation so that this ignorance has the same force on his decision as the limited nature of his rights would have in the political situation.

This shaping of ignorance to suit the limited character of political rights is most efficiently done simply by narrowing the individual goals that the parties to the contract know they wish to pursue. If we take Hobbes's deep theory, for example, to propose that men have a fundamental natural right to life, so that it is wrong to take their lives, even for social goals otherwise proper, we should expect a contract situation of the sort he describes. Hobbes's men and women, in Rawls's phrase, have lexically ordered security of life over all other individual goals; the same situation would result if they were simply ignorant of any other goals they might have and unable to speculate about the chances that they have any particular one or set of these.

The ignorance of the parties in the original position might thus be seen as a kind of limiting case of the ignorance that can be found, in the form of a distorted or eccentric ranking of interests, in classical contract theories and that is natural to the contract device. The original position is a limiting case because Rawls's men are not simply ignorant of interests beyond a chosen few; they are ignorant of all the interests they have. It would be wrong to suppose that this makes them incapable of any judgments of self-interest. But the judgments they make must nevertheless be very abstract; they must allow for any combination of interests, without the benefit of any supposition that some of these are more likely than others.

The basic right of Rawls's deep theory, therefore, cannot be a right to any particular individual goal, like a right to security of life, or a right to lead a life according to a particular conception of the good. Such rights to individual goals may be produced by the deep theory, as rights that men in the original position would stipulate as being in their best interest. But the original position cannot itself be justified on the assumption of such a right, because the parties to the contract do not know that they have any such interest or rank it lexically ahead of others.

So the basic right of Rawls's deep theory must be an abstract right, that is, not a right to any particular individual goal. There are two candidates, within the familiar concepts of political theory, for this role. The first is the right to liberty, and it may strike many readers as both plausible and comforting to assume that Rawls's entire structure is based on the assumption of a fundamental natural right to liberty—plausible because the two principles that compose his theory of justice give liberty an important and dominant place, and comforting because the argument attempting to justify that place seems uncharacteristically incomplete.[6]

Nevertheless, the right to liberty cannot be taken as the fundamental right in Rawls's deep theory. Suppose we define general liberty as the overall minimum possible constraints, imposed by government or by other men, on what a man might want to do.[7] We must then distinguish this general liberty from particular liberties, that is, freedom from such constraints on particular acts thought specially important, like participation in politics. The parties to the original position certainly have, and know that they have, an interest in general liberty, because general liberty will, *pro tanto,* improve their power to achieve any particular goals they later discover themselves to have. But the qualification is important, because they have no way of knowing that general liberty will in fact improve this power overall, and every reason to suspect that it will not. They know that they might have other interests, beyond general liberty, that can be protected only by political constraints on acts of others.

So if Rawlsian men must be supposed to have a right to liberty of some sort, which the contract situation is shaped to embody, it must be a right to particular liberties. Rawls does name a list of basic liberties, and it is these that his men do choose to protect through their lexically ordered first principle of justice.[8] But Rawls plainly casts this principle as the product of the contract rather than as a condition of it. He argues that the parties to the original position would select these basic liberties to protect the basic goods they decide to value, like self-respect, rather than taking these liberties as goals in themselves. Of course they might, in fact, value the activities protected as basic liberties for their own sake, rather than as means to some other goal or interest. But they certainly do not know that they do.

The second familiar concept of political theory is even more abstract than liberty. This is equality, and in one way Rawlsian men and women cannot choose other than to protect it. The state of ignorance in the original position is so shaped that the antecedent interest of everyone must lie, as I said, in the same solution. The right of each man to be treated equally without regard to his person or character or tastes is enforced by the fact that no one else can secure a better position by virtue of being different in any such respect. In other contract situations, when ignorance is less complete, individuals who share the same goal may nevertheless have different antecedent interests. Even if two men value life above everything else, for example, the antecedent interest of the weaker might call for a state monopoly of force rather than some provision for private vengeance, but the antecedent interest of the stronger might not. Even if two men value political participation above all else, the knowledge that one's views are likely to be more unorthodox or unpopular than those of the other will suggest that his antecedent interest calls for different arrangements. In the original position no such discrimination of antecedent interests can be made.

It is true that, in two respects, the principles of justice that Rawls thinks men and women would choose in the original position may be said to fall short of an egalitarian ideal. First, they subordinate equality in material resources, when this is necessary, to liberty of political activity, by making the demands of the first principle prior to those of the second. Second, they do not take account of relative deprivation, because they justify any inequality when those worse off are better off than they would be, in absolute terms, without that inequality.

Rawls makes plain that these inequalities are required, not by some competing notion of liberty or some overriding goal, but by a more basic sense of equality itself. He accepts a distinction between what he calls two conceptions of equality:

> Some writers have distinguished between equality as it is invoked in connection with the distribution of certain goods, some of which will almost certainly give higher status or prestige to those who are more favored, and equality as it applies to the respect which is owed to persons irrespective of their social position. Equality of the first kind is defined by the second principle of justice. . . . But equality of the second kind is fundamental.[9]

We may describe a right to equality of the second kind, which Rawls says is fundamental, in this way. We might say that individuals have a right to equal concern and respect in the design and administration of the political institutions that govern them. This is a highly abstract right. Someone might argue, for example, that it is satisfied by political arrangements that provide equal opportunity for office and position on the basis of merit. Someone else might argue, to the contrary, that it is satisfied only by a system that guarantees absolute equality of income and status, without regard to merit. A third man might argue that equal concern and respect is provided by that system, whatever it is, that improves the average welfare of all citizens counting the welfare of each on the same scale. A fourth might argue, in the name of this fundamental equality, for the priority of liberty, and for the other apparent inequalities of Rawls's two principles.

The right to equal concern and respect, then, is more abstract than the standard conceptions of equality that distinguish different political theories. It permits arguments that this more basic right requires one or another of these conceptions as a derivative right or goal.

The original position may now be seen as a device for testing these competing arguments. It supposes, reasonably, that political arrangements that do not display equal concern and respect are those that are established and administered by powerful men and women who, whether they recognize it or not, have more concern and respect for members of a particular class, or people with particular talents or ideals, than they have for others. It relies on this supposition in shaping the ignorance of the parties to the contract. Men who do not know to which class they belong cannot design institutions, consciously or unconsciously, to favor their own class. Men who have no idea of their own conception of the good cannot act to favor those who hold one ideal over those who hold another. The original position is well designed to enforce the abstract right to equal concern and respect, which must be understood to be the fundamental concept of Rawls's deep theory.

If this is right, then Rawls must not use the original position to argue for this right in the same way that he uses it, for example, to argue for the rights to basic liberties embodied in the first principle. The text confirms that he does not. It is true that he once says that equality of respect is "defined" by the first principle of justice.[10] But he does not mean, and in any case he does not argue, that the parties choose to be respected equally in order to advance some more basic right or goal. On the contrary, the right to equal respect is not, on his account, a product of the contract, but a condition of admission to the original position. This right, he says, is "owed to human beings as moral persons," and follows from the moral personality that distinguishes humans from animals. It is possessed by all men who can give justice, and only such men can contract.[11] This is one right, therefore, that does not emerge from the contract, but is assumed, as the fundamental right must be, in its design.

Rawls is well aware that his argument for equality stands on a different footing from his argument for the other rights within his theory:

> Now of course none of this is literally argument. I have not set out the premises from which this conclusion follows, as I have tried to do, albeit not very rigorously, with the choice of conceptions of justice in the original position. Nor have I tried to prove that the characterization of the parties must be used as the basis of equality. Rather this interpretation seems to be the natural completion of justice as fairness.[12]

It is the "natural completion," that is to say, of the theory as a whole. It completes the theory by providing the fundamental assumption that charges the original position, and makes it an "intuitive notion" for developing and testing theories of justice.

We may therefore say that justice as fairness rests on the assumption of a natural right of all men and women to equality of concern and respect, a right they possess not by virtue of birth or characteristic or merit or excellence but simply as human beings with the capacity to make plans and give justice. Many readers will not be surprised by this conclusion, and it is, as I have said, reasonably clear from the text. It is an important conclusion, nevertheless, because some forms of criticism of the theory, already standard, ignore it. I shall close this long essay with one example.

One form of criticism has been expressed to me by many colleagues and students, particularly lawyers. They point out that the particular political institutions and arrangements that Rawls says men in the original position would choose are merely idealized forms of those now in force in the United States. They are the institutions, that is, of liberal constitutional democracy. The critics conclude that the fundamental assumptions of Rawls's theory must, therefore, be the assumptions of classical liberalism, however they define these, and that the original position, which appears to animate the theory, must somehow be an embodiment of these assumptions. Justice as fairness therefore seems to them, in its entirety, as particularly subtle rationalization of the political status quo, which may safely be disregarded by those who want to offer a more radical critique of the liberal tradition.

If I am right, this point of view is foolish, and those who take it lose an opportunity, rare for them, to submit their own political views to some form of philosophical examination. Rawls's most basic assumption is not that men have a right to certain liberties that Locke or Mill thought important, but that they have a right to equal respect and concern in the design of political institutions. This assumption may be contested in many ways. It will be denied by those who believe that some goal, like utility or the triumph of a class or the flowering of some conception of how men should live, is more fundamental than any individual right, including the right to equality. But it cannot be denied in the name of any more radical concept of equality, because none exists.

Rawls does argue that this fundamental right to equality requires a liberal constitution, and supports an idealized form of present economic and social structures. He argues, for example, that men in the original position would protect the basic liberties in the interest of their right to equality, once a certain level of material comfort has been reached, because they would understand that a threat to self-respect, which the basic liberties protect, is then the most serious threat to equal respect. He also argues that these men would accept the second principle in preference to material equality because they would understand that sacrifice out of envy for another

is a form of subordination to him. These arguments may, of course, be wrong. I have certainly said nothing in their defense here. But the critics of liberalism now have the responsibility to show that they are wrong. They cannot say that Rawls's basic assumptions and attitudes are too far from their own to allow a confrontation.

NOTES

1. John Rawls, *A Theory of Justice* (Cambridge, Mass.: Harvard University Press, 1971).

2. pp. 48 ff.

3. pp. 21–2.

4. p. 587.

5. p. 51.

6. See Hart, 'Rawls on Liberty and Its Priority,' 40 *U. Chi. L. Rev.* 534 (1973).

7. Cf. Rawls's definition of liberty at p. 202.

8. p. 61.

9. p. 511.

10. Id.

11. Chapter 77.

12. p. 509.

12 The Domain of the Political and Overlapping Consensus

JOHN RAWLS

[handwritten annotation: You cannot both make abortion legal and illegal @ the same time.]

Introduction

IN THIS ARTICLE, I SHALL examine the idea of an overlapping consensus[1] and its role in a political conception of justice for a constitutional regime. A political conception, I shall suppose, views the political as a special domain with distinctive features that call for the articulation within the conception of the characteristic values that apply to that domain. Justice as fairness, the conception presented in my book *A Theory of Justice* [*Theory*][2] is an example of a political conception and I refer to it to fix ideas. By going over these matters I hope to allay misgivings about the idea of an overlapping consensus, especially the misgiving that it makes political philosophy political in the wrong way.[3] That is, this idea may suggest to some the view that consensus politics is to be taken as regulative and that the content of first principles of justice should be adjusted to the claims of the dominant political and social interests.

This misgiving may have resulted from my having used the idea of an overlapping consensus without distinguishing between two stages in the exposition of justice as fairness and without stressing that the idea of an overlapping consensus is used only in the second. To explain: in the first stage justice as fairness should be presented as a free-standing political conception that articulates the very great values applicable to the special domain of the political, as marked out by the basic structure of society. The second stage consists of an account of the stability of justice as fairness, that is, its capacity to generate its own support,[4] in view of the content of its principles and ideals as formulated in the first stage. In this second stage the idea of an overlapping consensus is introduced to explain how, given the plurality of conflicting comprehensive religious, philosophical, and moral doctrines always found in a democratic society—the kind of society that justice as fairness itself enjoins—free institutions may gain the allegiance needed to endure over time.

I Four General Facts

I begin with some background. Any political conception of justice presupposes a view of the political and social world, and recognizes certain general facts of political sociology and human psychology. Four general facts are especially important.

The first fact is that the diversity of comprehensive religious, philosophical, and moral doctrines found in modern democratic societies is not a mere historical condition that may soon pass away; it is a permanent feature of the public culture of democracy. *[handwritten: FACT ONE]* Under the political and social conditions that the basic rights and liberties of free institutions secure, a diversity of conflicting and irreconcilable comprehensive doctrines will emerge, if such diversity does not

From John Rawls, The Domain of the Political and Overlapping Consensus, 64 N. Y. U. L. Rev. 233, 233–51 (1989). Reprinted by permission of the New York University Law Review.

[handwritten notes:]
1) Different views, (pluralism)
2) oppressive state power is necessary to maintain one ideology
3) Citizens must willingly + freely support the society (most citizens)
4) A dem. society must contain certain fundamental ideas

already exist. Moreover, it will persist and may increase. The fact about free institutions is the fact of pluralism.

A second and related general fact is that only the oppressive use of state power can maintain a continuing common affirmation of one comprehensive religious, philosophical, or moral doctrine. If we think of political society as a community when it is united in affirming one and the same comprehensive doctrine, then the oppressive use of state power is necessary to maintain a political community. In the society of the Middle Ages, more or less united in affirming the Catholic faith, the Inquisition was not an accident; preservation of a shared religious belief demanded the suppression of heresy. The same holds, I believe, for any comprehensive philosophical and moral doctrine, even for secular ones. A society united on a form of utilitarianism, or on the liberalism of Kant or Mill, would likewise require the sanctions of state power to remain so.

A third general fact is that an enduring and secure democratic regime, one not divided into contending doctrinal confessions and hostile social classes, must be willingly and freely supported by at least a substantial majority of its politically active citizens. Together with the first general fact, this means that for a conception of justice to serve as the public basis of justification for a constitutional regime, it must be one that widely different and even irreconcilable comprehensive doctrines can endorse. Otherwise the regime will not be enduring and secure. As we shall see later, this suggests the need for what I have referred to as a political conception of justice.[5]

A fourth fact is that the political culture of a reasonably stable democratic society normally contains, at least implicitly, certain fundamental intuitive ideas from which it is possible to work up a political conception of justice suitable for a constitutional regime. This fact is important when we come to specify the general features of a political conception of justice and to elaborate justice as fairness as such a view.

II The Burdens of Reason

These facts, especially the first two—namely, the fact that a diversity of comprehensive doctrines is a permanent feature of a society with free institutions, and that this diversity can be overcome only by the oppressive use of state power—call for explanation. For why should free institutions with their basic rights and liberties lead to diversity, and why should state power be required to suppress it? Why does our sincere and conscientious attempt to reason with one another fail to lead us to agreement? It seems to lead to agreement in science, or if disagreement in social theory and economics often seems intractable, at least—in the long run—in natural science.

There are, of course, several possible explanations. We might suppose that most people hold views that advance their own more narrow interests; and since their interests are different, so are their views. Or perhaps people are often irrational and not very bright, and this mixed with logical errors leads to conflicting opinions.

But such explanations are too easy, and not the kind we want. We want to know how reasonable disagreement is possible, for we always work at first within ideal theory. Thus we ask: how might reasonable disagreement come about?

One explanation is this. We say that reasonable disagreement is disagreement between reasonable persons, that is, between persons who have realized their two moral powers[6] to a degree sufficient to be free and equal citizens in a democratic regime, and who have an enduring desire to be fully cooperating members of society over a complete life. We assume such persons share a common human reason, similar powers of thought and judgment, a capacity to draw inferences and to weigh evidence and to balance competing considerations, and the like.

Now the idea of reasonable disagreement involves an account of the sources, or causes, of disagreement between reasonable persons. These sources I shall refer to as the "burdens of reason." The account of these burdens must be such that it is fully compatible with, and so does not impugn, the reasonableness of those who disagree among themselves.

What, then, goes wrong? If we say it is the presence of prejudice and bias, of self- and group-interest, of blindness and willfulness—not to mention irrationality and stupidity (often main causes of the decline and fall of nations)—we impugn the reasonableness of at least some of those who disagree. We must discover another explanation.

An explanation of the right kind is that the burdens of reason, the sources of reasonable disagreement among reasonable persons, are the many hazards involved in the correct (and conscientious) exercise of our powers of reason and judgment in the ordinary course of political life. Except for the last two sources below, the ones I mention now are not peculiar to reasoning about values; nor is the list I give complete. It covers only the more obvious sources of reasonable disagreement:

(a) The evidence—empirical and scientific—bearing on the case may be conflicting and complex, and hence hard to assess and evaluate.

(b) Even where we agree fully about the kinds of considerations that are relevant, we may disagree about their weight, and so arrive at different judgments.

(c) To some extent all of our concepts, not only our moral and political concepts, are vague and subject to hard cases; this indeterminacy means that we must rely on judgment and interpretation (and on judgments about interpretations) within some range (not itself sharply specifiable) wherein reasonable persons may differ.

(d) To some unknown extent, our total experience, our whole course of life up to now, shapes the way we assess evidence and weight moral and political values, and our total experiences surely differ. Thus, in a modern society with its numerous offices and positions, its various divisions of labor, its many social groups and often their ethnic variety, the total experiences of citizens are disparate enough for their judgments to diverge, at least to some degree, on many if not most cases of any significant complexity.

(e) Often there are different kinds of normative considerations of different force on both sides of a question and it is difficult to make an overall assessment.[7]

(f) Finally, since any system of social institutions can admit only a limited range of values, some selection must be made from the full range of moral and political values that might be realized. This is because any system of institutions has, as it were, but a limited social space, In being forced to select among cherished values, we face great difficulties in setting priorities, and other hard decisions that may seem to have no clear answer.[8]

These are some sources of the difficulties in arriving at agreement in judgment, sources that are compatible with the full reasonableness of those judging. In noting these sources—these burdens of reason—we do not, of course, deny that prejudice and bias, self- and group-interest, blindness and willfulness, play an all-too-familiar part in political life. But these sources of unreasonable disagreement stand in marked contrast to sources of disagreement compatible with everyone's being fully reasonable.

I conclude by stating a fifth general fact: we make many of our most important judgments subject to conditions which render it extremely unlikely that conscientious and fully reasonable persons, even after free discussion, can exercise their powers of reason so that all arrive at the same conclusion.

III Precepts of Reasonable Discussion

Next I consider how, if we are reasonable, we should conduct ourselves in view of the plain facts about the burdens of reason. I suppose that, as reasonable persons, we are fully aware of these burdens, and try to take them into account. On this basis we recognize certain precepts to govern deliberation and discussion. A few of these follow.

First, the political discussion aims to reach reasonable agreement, and hence so far as possible it should be conducted to serve that aim. We should not readily accuse one another of self- or group-interest, prejudice or bias, and of such deeply entrenched errors as ideological blindness and delusion. Such accusations arouse resentment and hostility, and block the way to reasonable agreement. The disposition to make such accusations without compelling grounds is plainly unreasonable, and often a declaration of intellectual war.

Second, when we are reasonable we are prepared to find substantive and even intractable disagreements on basic questions. The first general fact means that the basic institutions and public culture of a democratic society specify a social world within which opposing general beliefs and conflicting comprehensive doctrines are likely to flourish and may increase in number. It is unreasonable, then, not to recognize the likelihood—indeed the practical certainty—of irreconcilable reasonable disagreements on matters of the first significance. Even when it seems that agreement should in principle be possible, it may be unattainable in the present case, at least in the foreseeable future.[9]

Third, when we are reasonable, we are ready to enter discussion crediting others with a certain good faith. We expect deep differences of opinion, and accept this diversity as the normal state of the public culture of a democratic society. To hate that fact is to hate human nature, for it is to hate the many not unreasonable expressions of human nature that develop under free institutions.[10]

I have suggested that the burdens of reason sufficiently explain the first two general facts—the facts of pluralism, given free institutions, and the necessity of the oppressive use of state power to maintain a political community (a political society united on a comprehensive doctrine)—whatever further causes those facts might have. Those facts are not, then, mere historical contingencies. Rather, they are rooted in the difficulties of exercising our reason under the normal conditions of human life.

IV Features of a Political Conception of Justice

Recall that the third general fact was that an enduring and stable democratic regime is one that at least a substantial majority of its politically active citizens freely support. Given this fact, what are the more general features of a political doctrine underlying a regime able to gain such allegiance? Plainly, it must be a doctrine that a diversity of comprehensive religious, philosophical, and moral doctrines can endorse, each from its own point of view.[11] This follows not only from the third general fact but also from the first, the fact of pluralism: for a democratic regime will eventually, if not from the outset, lead to a pluralism of comprehensive doctrines.

Let us say that a political conception of justice (in contrast to a political regime) is stable if it meets the following condition: those who grow up in a society well-ordered by it—a society whose institutions are publicly recognized to be just, as specified by that conception itself—develop a sufficient allegiance to those institutions, that is, a sufficiently strong sense of justice guided by appropriate principles and ideals, so that they normally act as justice requires, provided they are assured that others will act likewise.[12]

Now what more general features of a political conception of justice does this definition of stability suggest? The idea of a political conception of justice includes three such features:[13]

First, while a political conception of justice is, of course, a moral conception, it is worked out for a specific subject, namely, the basic structure of a constitutional democratic regime. This structure consists in society's main political, social, and economic institutions, and how they fit together into one unified system of social cooperation.

Second, accepting a political conception of justice does not presuppose accepting any particular comprehensive doctrine. The conception presents itself as a reasonable conception for the basic structure alone.[14]

Third, a political conception of justice is formulated so far as possible solely in terms of certain fundamental intuitive ideas viewed as implicit in the public political culture of a democratic society. Two examples are the idea of society as a fair system of social cooperation over time from one generation to the next, and the idea of citizens as free and equal persons fully capable of engaging in social cooperation over a complete life. (That there are such ideas is the fourth general fact.) Such ideas of society and citizen are normative and political ideas; they belong to a normative political conception, and not to metaphysics or psychology.[15]

Thus the distinction between political conceptions of justice and other moral conceptions is a matter of scope, that is, of the range of subjects to which a conception applies, and of the wider content which a wider range requires. A conception is said to be general when it applies to a wide range of subjects (in the limit to all subjects); it is comprehensive when it includes conceptions of what is of value in human life, ideals of personal virtue and character, and the like, that inform much of our nonpolitical conduct (in the limit, our life as a whole).

Religious and philosophical conceptions tend to be general and fully comprehensive; indeed, their being so is sometimes regarded as a philosophical ideal to be attained. A doctrine is fully comprehensive when it covers all recognized values and virtues within one rather precisely articulated scheme of thought; whereas a doctrine is partially comprehensive when it comprises certain but not all, nonpolitical values and virtues and is rather loosely articulated. By definition, then, for a conception to be even partially comprehensive it must extend beyond the political and include nonpolitical values and virtues.

Keeping these points in mind, political liberalism tries to articulate a workable political conception of justice. The conception consists in a view of politics and of the kind of political institutions which would be most just and appropriate when we take into account the five general facts. From these facts rises the need to found social unity on a political conception that can gain the support of a diversity of comprehensive doctrines. Political liberalism is not, then, a view of the whole of life: it is not a (fully or partially) comprehensive doctrine.

Of course, as a liberalism, it has the kind of content we historically associate with liberalism. It affirms certain basic political and civil rights and liberties, assigns them a certain priority, and so on. Justice as fairness begins with the fundamental intuitive idea of a well-ordered society as a fair system of cooperation between citizens regarded as free and equal. This idea together with the five general facts shows the need for a political conception of justice, and such a conception in turn leads to the idea of "constitutional essentials," as we may refer to them.

A specification of the basic rights and liberties of citizens—rights and liberties they are to have in their status as free and equal—falls under those essentials. For such rights and liberties concern the fundamental principles that determine the structure of the political process—the powers of the legislative, executive and the judiciary, the limits and scope of majority rule, as well as the basic political and civil rights and liberties legislative majorities must respect, such as the right to vote and to participate in politics, freedom of thought and liberty of conscience, and also the protections of the rule of law.

These matters are a long story; I merely mention them here. The point is that a political understanding of the constitutional essentials is of utmost urgency in securing a workable basis of fair political and social cooperation between citizens viewed as free and equal. If a political conception of justice provides a reasonable framework of principles and values for resolving questions concerning these essentials—and this must be its minimum objective—then a diversity of comprehensive doctrines may endorse it. In this case a political conception of justice is already of great significance, even though it may have little specific to say about innumerable economic and social issues that legislative bodies must regularly consider.

V   The Special Domain of the Political

The three features of a political conception[16] make clear that justice as fairness is not applied moral philosophy. That is, its content—its principles, standards, and values—is not presented as an application of an already elaborated moral doctrine, comprehensive in scope and general in range. Rather, it is a formulation of a family of highly significant (moral) values that properly apply to basic political institutions; it gives a specification of those values which takes account of certain special features of the political relationship, as distinct from other relationships.

The political relationship has at least two significant features:

First, it is a relationship of persons within the basic structure of society, a structure of basic institutions we enter only by birth and exit only by death (or so, we may appropriately assume[17]). Political society is closed, as it were; and we do not, and indeed cannot, enter or leave it voluntarily.

Second, the political power exercised within the political relationship is always coercive power backed by the state's machinery for enforcing its laws. In a constitutional regime political power is also the power of equal citizens as a collective body. It is regularly imposed on citizens as individuals, some of whom may not accept the reasons widely thought to justify the general structure of political authority (the constitution), some of whom accept that structure, but do not regard as well grounded many of the statutes and other laws to which they are subject.

Political liberalism holds, then, that there is a special domain of the political identified by at least these features. So understood, the political is distinct from the associational, which is voluntary in ways that the political is not; it is also distinct from the personal and the familial, which are affectional domains, again in ways the political is not.[18]

Taking the political as a special domain, let us say that a political conception formulating its basic values is a "free-standing" view. It is a view for the basic structure that formulates its values independent of non-political values and of any specific relationship to them. Thus a political conception does not deny that there are other values that apply to the associational, the personal, and the familial; nor does it say that the political is entirely separate from those values. But our aim is to specify the special domain of the political in such a way that its main institutions can gain the support of an overlapping consensus.

As a form of political liberalism, then, justice as fairness holds that, with regard to the constitutional essentials, and given the existence of a reasonably well-ordered constitutional regime, the family of very great political values expressed by its principles and ideals normally will have sufficient weight to override all other values that may come into conflict with them. Justice as fairness also holds, again with respect to constitutional essentials, that so far as possible, questions about those essentials should be settled by appeal to those *political values alone*. For it is on those questions that agreement among citizens who affirm opposing comprehensive doctrines is most urgent.

Now, in holding these convictions we clearly imply some relation between political and non-political values. Thus, if it is said that outside the church there is no salvation,[19] and that hence a constitutional regime, with its guarantees of freedom of religion, cannot be accepted unless it is unavoidable, we must make some reply. From the point of view of political liberalism, the appropriate reply is to say that the conclusion is unreasonable:[20] it proposes to use the public's political power—a power in which citizens have an equal share—to enforce a view affecting constitutional essentials about which citizens as reasonable persons, given the burdens of reason, are bound to differ uncompromisingly in judgment.

It is important to stress that this reply does not say that a doctrine *Extra ecclesiam nulla salus* is not true. Rather, it says that it is unreasonable to use the public's political power to enforce it. A reply from within an alternative comprehensive view—the kind of reply we should like to avoid in political discussion—would say that the doctrine in question is incorrect and rests on a misapprehension of the divine nature. If we do reject the enforcement by the state of a doctrine as unreasonable we may of course also regard that doctrine itself as untrue. And there may be no way entirely to avoid implying its lack of truth, even when considering constitutional essentials.[21]

Note, however, that in saying it is unreasonable to enforce a doctrine, we do not necessarily reject it as incorrect, though we may do so. Indeed, it is vital to the ideal of political liberalism that we may with perfect consistency hold that it would be unreasonable to use political power to enforce our own comprehensive religious, philosophical or moral views—views which we must, of course, affirm as true or reasonable (or at least as not unreasonable).

VI How is Political Liberalism Possible?

The question now arises, how, as I have characterized it, is political liberalism possible? That is, how can the values of the special domain of the political—the values of a sub-domain of the realm of all values—normally outweigh any values that may conflict with them? Or put another way: how can we affirm our comprehensive doctrines as true or reasonable and yet hold that it would not be reasonable to use the state's power to gain the allegiance of others to them?[22]

The answer to this question has two complementary parts. The first part says that values of the political are very great values indeed and hence not easily overridden. These values govern the basic framework of social life, "the very groundwork of our existence,"[23] and specify the fundamental terms of political and social cooperation. In justice as fairness some of these great values are expressed by the principles of justice for the basic structure: the values of equal political and civil liberty, of fair equality of opportunity, of economic reciprocity, the social bases of mutual respect among citizens, and so on.

Other great values fall under the idea of free public reason, and are expressed in the guidelines for public inquiry and in the steps taken to secure that such inquiry is free and public, as well as informed and reasonable. These values include not only the appropriate use of the fundamental concepts of judgment, inference, and evidence, but also the virtues of reasonableness and fair-mindedness as shown in the adherence to the criteria and procedures of common sense knowledge, and to the methods and conclusion of science when not controversial, as well as respect for the precepts governing reasonable political discussion.[24]

Together these values give expression to the liberal political ideal that since political power is the coercive power of free and equal citizens as a corporate body, this power should be exercised, when constitutional essentials are at stake, only in ways that all citizens can reasonably be expected to endorse publicly in the light of their own common, human reason.[25]

So far as possible, political liberalism tries to present a free-standing account of these values as those of a special domain—the political. It is left to citizens individually, as part of their liberty of conscience, to settle how they think the great values of the political domain relate to other values within their comprehensive doctrine. We hope that by doing this we can, in working political practice, firmly ground the constitutional essentials in those political values alone, and that these values will provide a satisfactory shared basis of public justification.

The second part of the answer as to how political liberalism is possible complements the first. This part says that the history of religion and philosophy shows that there are many reasonable ways in which the wider realm of values can be understood so as to be either congruent with, or supportive of, or else not in conflict with, the values appropriate to the special domain of the political as specified by a political conception of justice for a democratic regime. History tells of a plurality of not unreasonable comprehensive doctrines. That these comprehensive doctrines are divergent makes an overlapping consensus necessary. That they are not unreasonable makes it possible. A model case of an overlapping consensus of the kind I have considered elsewhere shows how this is so.[26] Many other such cases could make the same point.

VII   The Question of Stability

Justice as fairness, as I have said, is best presented in two stages.[27] In the first stage it is worked out as a free-standing political (but of course moral) conception for the basic structure of society. Only when this is done and its content—its principles of justice and ideals—is provisionally on hand do we take up, in the second stage, the problem of stability and introduce the idea of an overlapping consensus: a consensus in which a diversity of conflicting comprehensive doctrines endorse the same political conception, in this case, justice as fairness.

In describing the second stage, let us agree that a political conception must be practicable, that is, must fall under the art of the possible. This contrasts with a moral conception that is not political; a moral conception may condemn the world and human nature as too corrupt to be moved by its precepts and ideals.

There are, however, two ways in which a political conception may be concerned with stability.[28] In one way, we suppose that stability is a purely practical matter: if a conception fails to be stable, it is futile to try to base a political structure upon it. Perhaps we think there are two separate tasks: one is to work out a political conception that seems sound, or reasonable, at least to us; the other is to find ways to bring others who reject the conception to share it in due course, or failing that, to act in accordance with it, prompted if need be by penalties enforced by state power. As long as the means of persuasion or enforcement can be found, the conception is viewed as stable; it is not utopian in the pejorative sense.

But as a liberal conception, justice as fairness is concerned with stability in a second, very different way. Finding a stable conception is not simply a matter of avoiding futility. Rather, what counts is the kind of stability and the nature of the forces that secure it. The idea is that, given certain assumptions specifying a reasonable human psychology[29] and the normal conditions of human life, those who grow up under basic institutions that are just—institutions that justice as fairness itself enjoins—acquire a reasoned and informed allegiance to those institutions sufficient to render the institutions stable. Put another way, the sense of justice of citizens, in view of their traits of character and interests as formed by living under a just basic structure, is strong enough to resist the normal tendencies to injustice. Citizens act willingly so as to give one another justice over time. Stability is secured by sufficient motivation of the appropriate kind acquired under just institutions.[30]

The kind of stability required of justice as fairness is based, then, on its being a liberal political view, one that aims at being acceptable to citizens as reasonable and rational, as well as free and equal, and so addressed to their free public reason. Earlier we saw how this feature of liberalism connects with the feature of political power in a constitutional regime, namely, that it is the power of equal citizens as a collective body. It follows that if justice as fairness were not expressly designed to gain the reasoned support of citizens who affirm reasonable although conflicting comprehensive doctrines—the existence of such conflicting doctrines being a feature of the kind of public culture which that conception itself encourages—it would not be liberal.[31]

The point, then, is that, as a liberal conception, justice as fairness must not merely avoid futility; the explanation of why it is practicable must be of a special kind. The problem of stability is not the problem of bringing others who reject a conception to share it, or to act in accordance with it, by workable sanctions if necessary—as if the task were to find ways to impose that conception on others once we are ourselves convinced it is sound. Rather, as a liberal political conception, justice as fairness relies for its reasonableness in the first place upon generating its own support in a suitable way by addressing each citizen's reason, as explained within its own framework.[32]

Only in this manner is justice as fairness an account of political legitimacy. Only so does it escape being a mere account of how those who hold political power can satisfy themselves, in the light of their own convictions, whether political or fully comprehensive, that they are acting properly—satisfy themselves, that is, and not citizens generally.[33] A conception of political legitimacy aims for a public basis of justification and appeals to free public reason, and hence to all citizens viewed as reasonable and rational.

VIII Comparison with A Theory of Justice

It may seem that the idea of an overlapping consensus and related topics are a significant departure from *Theory*. They are some departure certainly; but how much? *Theory* never discusses whether justice as fairness is meant as a comprehensive moral doctrine or as a political conception of justice. In one place it says that if justice as fairness succeeds reasonably well, a next step would be to study the more general view suggested by the name "rightness as fairness."[34]

But *Theory* holds that even this view would not be fully comprehensive: it would not cover, for example, our relations to other living things and to the natural order itself.[35] *Theory* emphasizes the limited scope of justice as fairness, and the limited scope of the kind of view it exemplifies; the book leaves open the question of how

far its conclusions might need revision once these other matters are taken into account. There is, however, no mention of the distinction between a political conception of justice and a comprehensive doctrine. The reader might reasonably conclude, then, that justice as fairness is set out as part of a comprehensive view that may be developed later were success to invite.

This conclusion is supported by the discussion of the well-ordered society of justice as fairness in Part III of *Theory*.[36] There it is assumed that the members of any well-ordered society, whether it be a society of justice as fairness or of some other view, accept the same conception of justice and also, it seems, the same comprehensive doctrine of which that conception is a part, or from which it can be derived. Thus, for example, all the members of a well-ordered society associated with utilitarianism (classical or average), are assumed to affirm the utilitarian view, which is by its nature (unless expressly restricted) a comprehensive doctrine.

Although the term was introduced in another context,[37] the idea of an overlapping consensus was first introduced to think of the well-ordered society of justice as fairness in a different and more realistic way.[38] Given the free institutions which that conception itself enjoins, we can no longer assume that citizens generally, even if they accept justice as fairness, also accept the particular comprehensive view in which it might seem to be embedded in *Theory*. We now assume citizens hold two distinct views; or perhaps better, we assume their overall view has two parts. One part can be seen to be, or to coincide with, a political conception of justice; the other part is a (fully or partially) comprehensive doctrine to which the political conception is in some manner related.[39]

The political conception may be simply a part of, or an adjunct to, a partially comprehensive view; or it may be endorsed because it can be derived within a fully articulated comprehensive doctrine. It is left to citizens individually to decide for themselves in what way their shared political conception is related to their wider and more comprehensive views. A society is well-ordered by justice as fairness so long as, first, citizens who affirm reasonable comprehensive doctrines generally endorse justice as fairness as giving the content of their political judgments; and second, unreasonable comprehensive doctrines do not gain enough currency to compromise the essential justice of basic institutions.

This is a better and no longer utopian way of thinking of the well-ordered society of justice as fairness. It corrects the view in *Theory*, which fails to take into account the condition of pluralism to which its own principles lead.

Moreover, because justice as fairness is now seen as a free-standing political conception that articulates fundamental political and constitutional values, endorsing it involves far less than is contained in a comprehensive doctrine. Taking such a well-ordered society as the aim of reform and change does not seem altogether impracticable; under the reasonably favorable conditions that make a constitutional regime possible, that aim is a reasonable guide and may be in good part realized. By contrast, a free democratic society well-ordered by any comprehensive doctrine, religious or secular, is surely utopian in a pejorative sense. Achieving it would, in any case, require the oppressive use of state power. This is as true of the liberalism of rightness as fairness, as it is of the Christianity of Aquinas or Luther.

IX *In What Sense Political?*

To trace our steps, I put before you this brief summary.[40] I have suggested that once we recognize the five general facts[41] and the inevitable burdens of reason even under favorable conditions,[42] and once we reject the oppressive use of state power to impose a single comprehensive doctrine as the way to achieve social unity, then we are led to democratic principles and must accept the fact of pluralism as a permanent feature of political life. Hence, to achieve social unity for a well-ordered democratic regime, what I have called political liberalism introduces the idea of an overlapping consensus and along

with it the further idea of the political as a special domain. Political liberalism does this not only because its content includes the basic rights and liberties the securing of which leads to pluralism, but also because of the liberal ideal of political legitimacy, namely, that social cooperation, at least as it concerns the constitutional essentials, is to be conducted so far as possible on terms both intelligible and acceptable to all citizens as reasonable and rational. Those terms are best stated by reference to the fundamental political and constitutional values (expressed by a political conception of justice) that, given the diversity of comprehensive doctrines, all citizens may still be reasonably expected to endorse.

We must, however, be careful that a political conception is not political in the wrong way. It should aim to formulate a coherent view of the very great (moral) values applying to the political relationship and to set out a public basis of justification for free institutions in a manner accessible to free public reason. It must not be political in the sense of merely specifying a workable compromise between known and existing interests, nor political in looking to the particular comprehensive doctrines known to exist in society and in then being tailored to gain their allegiance.

In this connection let us ensure that the assumptions about pluralism do not make justice as fairness political in the wrong way. Consider first the five general facts reviewed in Parts I and II. These we suppose are accepted from the point of view of you and me as we try to develop justice as fairness. When the original position is viewed as a device of representation, these facts are made available to the parties in that position as they decide which principles of justice to select. So if principles that require free democratic institutions are accepted in the first stage, then the account of the stability in the second stage must show how justice as fairness can be endorsed by an overlapping consensus. As we have seen, this follows because free institutions themselves lead to pluralism.

The crucial question, then, is whether the five general facts, along with other premises allowed by the constraints of the original position in the first stage, suffice to lead the parties to select the two principles of justice,[43] or whether certain further assumptions related to pluralism are also needed, assumptions that make justice as fairness political in the wrong way. I cannot settle this matter here; it would require a survey of the argument from the original position.

I believe we need only suppose in the first stage that the parties assume the fact of pluralism to obtain, that is, that a plurality of comprehensive doctrines exists in society.[44] The parties must then protect against the possibility that the person each party represents may be a member of a religious, ethnic, or other minority. This suffices for the argument for the equal basic liberties to get going. In the second stage, when stability is considered, the parties again assume that pluralism obtains. They confirm principles leading to a social world that allows free play to human nature and thus, we hope, encourages a diversity of reasonable rather than unreasonable comprehensive doctrines, given the burdens of reason.[45] This makes stability possible.

Now it is often said that the politician looks to the next election, the statesman to the next generation. To this we add that the student of philosophy looks to the standing conditions of human life, and how these affect the burdens of reason. Political philosophy must take into account the five general facts we noted, among them the fact that free institutions encourage a diversity of comprehensive doctrines. But in doing this we abstract from the particular content of these doctrines, whatever it may be, and from the many contingencies under which the doctrines exist. A political conception so arrived at is not political in the wrong way but suitably adapted to the public political culture that its own principles shape and sustain. And although such a conception may not apply to all societies at all times and places, this does not make it historicist, or relativist; rather, it is universal in virtue of its extending appropriately to specify a reasonable conception of justice among all nations.[46]

NOTES

1. An overlapping consensus exists in a society when the political conception of justice that regulates its basic institutions is endorsed by each of the main religious, philosophical, and moral doctrines likely to endure in that society from one generation to the next. I have used this idea mainly in Rawls, Justice as Fairness: Political not Metaphysical, 14 Phil. & Pub. Aff. 223 (1985) [hereafter Justice as Fairness] and Rawls, The Idea of an Overlapping Consensus, 7 Oxford J. Legal Stud. 1 (1987) [hereinafter Overlapping Consensus]. The idea is introduced in J. Rawls, A Theory of Justice 387–88 (1971) [hereinafter Theory].

2. Theory, supra note 1.

3. For an awareness of these misgivings I am indebted to the comments of G. A. Cohen and Paul Seabright (soon after the lecture "Overlapping Consensus" was given at Oxford in May 1986), see Overlapping Consensus, supra note 1, and to discussions with Jürgen Habermas (at Harvard the following October). For a better understanding of and suggestions for how to deal with the misgivings, I am greatly indebted to Ronald Dworkin, Thomas Nagel, and T. M. Scanlon. I also have gained much from Wilfried Hinsch, to whom I owe the important idea of a reasonable comprehensive doctrine, which I have simply elaborated a bit. This idea, when joined with suitable companion ideas such as the burdens of reason, see Part II infra, and the precepts of reasonable discussion, see Part III infra, imposes an appropriate limit on the comprehensive doctrines we may reasonably expect to be included in an overlapping consensus.

4. See Part VIII infra.

5. See Part VII infra.

6. These powers are those of a capacity for a sense of justice and a capacity for a conception of the good. Theory, supra note 1, at 505; Justice as Fairness, supra note 1, at 232–34.

7. This source of disagreement I have expressed in a somewhat flat way. It could be put more strongly by saying, as Thomas Nagel does, that there are basic conflicts of value in which there seem to be decisive and sufficient (normative) reasons for two or more incompatible courses of action; and yet some decision must be made. See T. Nagel, Mortal Questions 128–41 (1979). Moreover, these normative reasons are not evenly balanced, and so it matters greatly what decision is made. The lack of even balance holds because in such cases the values are incomparable. They are each specified by one of the several irreducibly different perspectives within which values arise, in particular, the perspectives that specify obligations, rights, utility, perfectionist ends, and personal commitments. Put another way, these values have different bases

which their different formal features reflect. These basic conflicts reveal what Nagel thinks of as the fragmentation of value. See id. I find much in Nagel's discussion very plausible, and I might endorse it were I stating my own (partially) comprehensive moral doctrine; since I am not doing that, but rather trying so far as possible to avoid controversial philosophical theses and to give an account of the difficulties of reason that rest on the plain facts open to all, I refrain from any statement stronger than (e).

8. This point has often been stressed by Sir Isaiah Berlin, most recently in his article, On the Pursuit of the Ideal, N.Y. Rev. Books, Mar 17, 1988, at 11.

9. For instance, consider the questions of the causes of unemployment and the more effective ways to reduce it.

10. I have adapted this idea from Pliny the Younger's remark, "He who hates vice, hates mankind," quoted in J. Shklar, Ordinary Vices 192 (1984).

11. Here I assume that any substantial majority will include citizens who hold conflicting comprehensive doctrines.

12. Note that this is a definition of stability for a political conception of justice. It is not to be mistaken for a definition of stability, or of what I call the security, of a political regime (as a system of institutions).

13. The features of a political conception of justice are discussed in more detail in Justice as Fairness, supra note 1, at 224–34.

14. A political conception for the basic structure must also generalize to, or else fit in with, a political conception for an international society of constitutionally democratic states; but here I put this important matter aside. See note 46 infra.

15. See Justice as Fairness, supra note 1, at 239–40 & n.22 (discussing a "political conception of the person").

16. See Part IV supra.

17. The appropriateness of this assumption rests in part on a point I shall only mention here, namely, that the right of emigration does not make the acceptance of political authority voluntary in the way that freedom of thought and liberty of conscience make the acceptance of ecclesiastical authority voluntary. This brings out a further feature of the domain of the political, one that distinguishes it from the associational.

18. The associational, the personal, and the familiar are only three examples of the nonpolitical; there are others.

19. The common medieval maxim *Extra ecclesian nullas salus* ("Outside the church there is no salvation") was used, for example, in the famous bull "Unam sanctam" of Nov. 18, 1302, by Pope Boniface VIII, reprinted in Enchiridion symbolorum defini-

tionum et declarationum de rebus fidei et morum 870 at 279 (33d ed. H. Denzinger & A. Schönmetzer eds. 1965).

20. For clarity on this point I owe thanks to Wilfried Hinsch and Peter de Marneffe.

21. See Rawls, Overlapping Consensus, supra note 1, at 14.

22. Recall here the formulation of political liberalism a few lines back, namely, given the existence of a well-ordered constitutional democratic regime, the family of great values expressed by its principles and ideals, and realized in its basic institutions, normally has sufficient weight to override whatever other values may come into conflict with them. See Part IV supra.

23. J. S. Mill, Utilitarianism, ch. 5, ¶ 25 (3rd ed. 1867), reprinted in John Stuart Mill: A Selection of His Works 216 (J. Robson ed. 1982).

24. See Part III supra.

25. On this point see the instructive discussion by Jeremy Waldron, Theoretical Foundations of Liberalism, 37 Phil. Q. 127 (1987).

26. See Justice as Fairness, supra note 1, at 250. The model case of an overlapping consensus is one in which the political conception is endorsed by three comprehensive doctrines: the first endorses justice as fairness, say, because its religious beliefs and understanding of faith lead to the principle of toleration and support the basic equal liberties; the second doctrine affirms justice as fairness as a consequence of a comprehensive liberal conception such as that of Kant or Mill; while the third affirms justice as fairness as a political conception, that is, not as a consequence of a wider doctrine but as in itself sufficient to express very great values that normally outweigh whatever other values might oppose them, at least under reasonably favorable conditions. Id. See also Overlapping Consensus, supra note 1, § III, at 9–12 (more fully discussing this model case).

27. These two stages correspond to the two parts of the argument from the original position for the two principles of justice contained in Theory, supra note 1. In the first part the parties select principles without taking the effects of the special psychologies into account. Id. at 118–93. In the second part they ask whether a society well-ordered by the principles selected in the first part would be stable, that is, would generate in its members a sufficiently strong sense of justice to counteract tendencies to injustice. Id. at 395–587. The argument for the principles of justice is not complete until the principles selected in the first part are shown in the second part to be sufficiently stable. So in *Theory* the argument is not complete until the next to last section, section 86. Id. at 567–77. For these two parts, see id. at 144, 530–31.

28. In this and the next several paragraphs I am indebted to a very helpful discussion with T. M. Scanlon.

29. The assumptions of such a psychology are noted briefly in Overlapping Consensus, supra note 1, at 22–23. In Section VI of the same essay I also consider the way in which a political conception can gain an allegiance to itself that may to some degree shape comprehensive doctrines to conform to its requirements. Id. at 18–22. This is plainly an important aspect of stability and strengthens the second part of the answer as to how political liberalism is possible. See Part VI supra.

I wish to thank Francis Kamm for pointing out to me several significant complications in the relation between a political conception and the comprehensive doctrines it shapes to accord with it, and how far as a result the viability of political liberalism depends on the support of such doctrines. It seems best not to pursue these matters here but to postpone them until a more complete account of stability can be given.

30. As stated in *Theory*, the question is whether the just and the good are congruent. Theory, supra note 1, at 395, 567–77. In section 86 of *Theory*, it is argued that a person who grows up in a society well-ordered by justice as fairness, and who has a rational plan of life, and who also knows, or reasonably believes, that everyone else has an effective sense of justice, has sufficient reason, founded on that person's good (and not on justice) to comply with just institutions. Id. at 567–77. These institutions are stable because the just and the good are congruent. That is, no reasonable and rational person in the well-ordered society of justice as fairness is moved by rational considerations of the good not to honor what justice requires.

31. Recall that reasonable comprehensive doctrines are ones that recognize the burdens of reason and accept the fact of pluralism as a condition of human life under free democratic institutions, and hence accept freedom of thought and liberty of conscience. See Parts II and III supra.

32. The force of the phrase "within its own framework" as used in the text emerges in the two parts of the argument from the original position in Theory, supra note 1. Both parts are carried out within the same framework and subject to the same conditions embedded in the original position as a device of representation.

33. For this distinction, see Nagel, What Makes Political Theory Utopian? 5 (unpublished paper, dated Apr. 1988, on file at New York University Law Review).

34. *Theory*, supra note 1, at 17.

35. Id. at 512.

36. Id. at 453–62.

37. Id. at 387–88.

38. Justice as Fairness, supra note 1, at 248–51.

39. For example, in the well-ordered society of justice as fairness, some may hold a form of utilitarianism as their comprehensive doctrine, provided they understand that doctrine, as I believe J. S. Mill did, so as to coincide in its requirements with justice as fairness, at least for the most part. See J. S. Mill, supra note 23, ch. 3, ¶ 10.

40. I am grateful to Erin Kelley for valuable discussion about how to put this summary.

41. See Parts I & II supra.

42. See Part II supra.

43. These two principles are:

1. Each person has an equal right to a fully adequate scheme of equal basic rights and liberties, which scheme is compatible with a similar scheme for all.

2. Social and economic inequalities are to satisfy two conditions: first, they must be attached to offices and positions open to all under conditions of fair equality of opportunity; and second, they must be to the greatest benefit of the least advantaged members of society.

Justice as Fairness, supra note 1, at 227.

44. I should like to thank David Chow for very helpful comments on this point.

45. The reasons for thinking reasonable rather than unreasonable doctrines are encouraged are sketched briefly in Overlapping Consensus, supra note 1, at 18–23.

46. Perhaps I should explain briefly that the political conception so arrived at may not apply to some societies because the general facts we have assumed may not appropriately obtain in their case. Nevertheless, those facts do obtain widely in the modern world, and hence the political conception applies. Its not applying in some cases, however, does not make that conception relativist or historicist so long as it provides grounds for judging the basic institutions of different societies and their social policies.

13   Justice and Truth

JOSEPH RAZ

BOTH FRIENDS AND FOES often emphasize the way liberal thought is concerned primarily with individuals. The pursuit of freedom is often pictured as the protection of the individual from the tyranny of the majority. All too often this concern with individuals is taken to show liberalism's neglect of the importance of communities. Whatever truth this accusation may have when leveled at the way some writers have understood the liberal ideal, it is misguided when aimed at the ideal of individual freedom itself. People's individuality expresses itself in ways fashioned by social practices, and through their ability and inclination to engage in socially formed relations and pursuits. Concern for individual freedom requires recognition that an important aspect of that ideal is the freedom of people to belong to distinctive groups, with their own beliefs and practices, and the ability of such groups to prosper.

In recent years several liberal writers have made the response to pluralism—the response to the fact that our societies consist of groups and communities with diverse practices and beliefs, including groups whose beliefs are inconsistent with each other—central to their concern. In their work the connection between individual freedom and group prosperity becomes particularly evident. . . .

[According to John Rawls,] "The aim of justice as fairness as a political conception is practical. . . . it presents itself not as a conception of justice that is true, but one that can serve as a basis of informed and willing political agreement."[1] A society that has achieved consensual unity and stability by endorsing a common doctrine of justice is called by Rawls "a well-ordered society":

> To say a society is well ordered by a conception of justice means three things: (1) that it is a society in which all citizens accept, and acknowledge before one another that they accept, the same principles of justice; (2) that its basic structure—its main political and social institutions and the way they hang together as one system of cooperation—is publicly known or with good reason believed, to satisfy those principles, and (3) that citizens have a normally effective sense of justice, that is, one that enables them to understand and to apply the principles of justice, and for the most part to act from them as their circumstances require. *I believe that social unity so understood is the most desirable conception of unity available to us; it is the limit of the practical best.*[2]

This is of course the stuff of all democratic politics. It is concerned with give and take, with exploring a common ground for agreement on common policies and principles. When politics is concerned with fashioning a constitution, it requires near unanimity, and, of course, it deals with principles which will provide the framework within which all other political issues will

From "Facing Diversity" Philosophy and Public Affairs *(1990) pp. 9–14. Copyright © 1990. Reprinted by permission of Princeton University Press.*

be resolved. It sounds as if Rawls's practical aim is to engage in practical constitutional politics, with one difference: whereas politicians, at least sometimes, try to secure agreement by convincing people that the principles underlying their proposals are true, Rawls abjures this argument, and seeks to secure agreement simply by pointing out that certain principles are already implicitly agreed to, or nearly so.[3]

There is nothing wrong with engaging in politics, though some may doubt whether this is really what political philosophy is about. The suggestion that political philosophy should be no more than the sort of politics where the only thing that counts is success in commanding general agreement, the kind of politics where any principle, whatever its content, will be accepted provided it commands general assent, and where every principle will be compromised or rejected if it fails to gain universal approval, is objectionable. But is this really what Rawls has in mind?

Rawls assures us that "political philosophy is not mere politics." But he simply points out that it takes a longer view.[4] It is essentially constitutional politics. It would be wrong, however (though, given much of what he says, entirely understandable), to regard the politics Rawls advocates as an unprincipled search for consensus at all costs. Two crucial elements in his thought rebut this misinterpretation. First, his aim is to reach "a consensus that includes all the opposing philosophical and religious doctrines likely to persist and to gain adherents in a more or less just constitutional democratic society."[5] In other words, only because our societies are nearly just societies can it be right for political philosophy to regard the pursuit of consensus as its overriding goal, and the consensus need not encompass every passing fashion, but only those comprehensive outlooks which are likely to persist in nearly just societies.

There is a problem here. The doctrine of justice itself reflects the consensus of our societies. Is it not inevitable that they will live up to their own standards? Rawls unflinchingly recognizes the self-referential nature of the condition. The consensus to be sought, he says, is one between the opposing doctrines likely to thrive "over generations in a more or less just constitutional democracy *where the criterion of justice is that political conception itself.*"[6] Of course, a society may avow principles which it does not live up to. There is no reason to refuse to pursue consensus in such a society. The consensus sought is among the competing moral, religious, or philosophical theories. The fact that the practice of that society does not conform to them is not reflected in the consensus view of justice which emerges, and does nothing to discredit it. So perhaps the condition of near justice imposed by Rawls is vacuous, and does little to qualify the unqualified pursuit of consensus at any price.[7] Though I do not know what non-self-fulfilling condition Rawls may have in mind, it is clear that he means this condition, or something like it, to have substantial bite and to place the pursuit of consensus in a context which makes it an appropriate aim.

That consensus is the goal only in nearly just societies is an external condition on Rawls's methodological conception. It limits its applicability. The second corrective to the "consensus at any price" understanding of Rawls is the internal condition built into the special meaning he gives the expression "an overlapping consensus." He discusses this as part of his explanation of why an overlapping consensus is to be distinguished from a mere *modus vivendi*. Of the various marks of that distinction two are relevant here.[8]

First, and this factor explains all the others, a *modus vivendi* is a compromise based on self- or group interests; it reflects no principles other than the fact that it is an acceptable compromise.[9] A theory like Rawls's is genuinely a theory of justice. Not every consensus can be presented as a theory of justice. To be that, it must be a moral conception (though of course neither a comprehensive nor a deep one). It must possess internal coherence in expressing "conceptions of person and society, and concepts of right and fairness, as well as principles of justice with their complement of the virtues."[10] Second, the theory of justice is one which each of the many incompatible comprehensive moral, religious, and philosophical views can accept from its own standpoint. It is not, or not merely, based on a consensus among members of a society; it is primarily a consensus among the different conceptions of the good in that society: "We hope to make it possible for all to accept the political conception as true, or as reasonable, from the standpoint of their own comprehensive view, whatever it may be."[11]

These internal conditions on a doctrine of justice make it much harder to achieve. A prudential give and take among relatively rational individuals may well lead to a compromise, but it is likely to lack the complexity and the structure of internal justification required by Rawls. Rawls's aim is a genuinely philosophical conception of justice, not merely a political expediency. It is not surprising that he is not particularly optimistic about the chances of actually achieving consensus on a theory which meets these conditions. "All this is highly speculative and raises questions which are little understood." All we can do is hope that a basis for such a consensus may be found, and that a consensus may emerge on that basis.[12]

Can There Be Justice without Truth?

These comments help to explain in what sense Rawls's theory is both philosophical and practical. It is philosophical in that it calls for a complex moral doctrine of justice. Yet it is practical, for the one and only reason Rawls mentions for the desirability of setting political philosophy this task is that it is necessary to ensure consensus-based social stability and unity. These practical goals explain the desirability of a doctrine of justice based on overlapping consensus, and one which is internally coherent and complex, that is, which constitutes a moral doctrine.[13] The fact that political philosophy can only assure us of the possibility of consensus and that its actuality is merely speculative does not make the philosophical enterprise any less practical.[14] The only reason for philosophy to establish the possibility of stability is, presumably, that that is the only way philosophy can contribute towards achieving noncoerced social unity and stability.

But why should philosophy contribute to these goals rather than to others? Presumably because they are worthwhile goals. So it would appear that while the goal of political philosophy is purely practical—while it is not concerned to establish any evaluative truths—it accepts some such truths as the presuppositions which make its enterprise intelligible. It recognizes that social unity and stability based on a consensus—that is, achieved without excessive resort to force—are valuable goals of sufficient importance to make them and them alone the foundations of a theory of justice for our societies. Without this assumption it would be unwarranted to regard the theory as a theory of *justice,* rather than a theory of social stability. In an uplifting conclusion Rawls declares that political philosophy aims at "the defence of reasonable faith in the real possibility of a just constitutional regime"[15]—by which he surely means that the real possibility, which he has argued for, of achieving consensus and securing stability is reason for faith in the possibility of a truly just regime, not merely the possibility of a regime which is called just by its members.

My argument is simple. A theory of justice can deserve that name simply because it deals with these matters, that is, matters that a true theory of justice deals with. In this sense there are many theories of justice, and they are all acceptable to the same degree as theories of justice. To recommend one as a theory of justice for our societies is to recommend it as a just theory of justice, that is, as a true, or reasonable, or valid theory of justice. If it is argued that what makes it *the* theory of justice for us is that it is built on an overlapping consensus and therefore secures stability and unity, then consensus-based stability and unity are the values that a theory of justice, for our society, is assumed to depend on. Their achievement—that is, the fact that endorsing the theory leads to their achievement—makes the theory true, sound, valid, and so forth. This at least is what such a theory is committed to. There can be no justice without truth.[16]

NOTES

1. Rawls, "Political not Metaphysical," p. 230.

2. John Rawls, "The Priority of Right and Ideas of the Good." *Philosophy & Public Affairs* 17, no. 4 (Fall 1988): 269, italics added (hereafter referred to as "The Priority of Right"). The language and emphasis of this article, seen here in the use of the expression "the practical best," while not explicitly withdrawing from epistemic abstinence, is inconsistent with it. I will return to this point below.

3. Rawls is aware that there may not be enough common ground in a society actually to reach an overlapping consensus on a doctrine of justice. Narrowing down apparent differences is all that can be aspired to. Alternatively, the desire to reach agreement may lead people to modify those of their views which stand in the way of a consensus, thus making it possible after all. See "Political not Metaphysical," p. 228, and "Overlapping Consensus," pp. 7, 16, 19.

4. Rawls, "Overlapping Consensus," p. 24.

5. Rawls, "Political not Metaphysical." pp. 225–26; see also pp. 246–47, 249, and "Overlapping Consensus," pp. 1, 9.

6. Rawls, "Overlapping Consensus," p. 1.

7. A similar problem applies to a second, related condition imposed by Rawls. The consensus is between conceptions of the good which are "each compatible with the full rationality of human persons" ("Political not Metaphysical," p. 248). But Rawls suggests that the concept of the person he is employing is itself simply the one current in our culture. I will return to this text, and discuss the related statement on p. 9 of "Overlapping Consensus," below.

8. It is worth remembering that the distinction is introduced for a different purpose—that is, to show that the doctrine of justice is not advocated on purely prudential grounds. See Rawls, "Political not Metaphysical," p. 247.

9. See, for example, Rawls, "Overlapping Consensus," pp. 1, 2, 10, 11.

10. Rawls, "Political not Metaphysical," p. 247.

11. Rawls, "Overlapping Consensus," p. 13.

12. Rawls, "Political not Metaphysical," p. 250; "Overlapping Consensus," p. 25.

13. Rawls, "Political not Metaphysical," pp. 250–51; "Overlapping Consensus, pp. 1, 11–12.

14. Naturally, the theory, if successful, establishes the truth of instrumental judgments to the effect that certain policies make stability and unity possible, or likely. Every practical inquiry does that. I take Rawls's point to be merely that the theory need not go into moral issues.

15. Rawls, "Overlapping Consensus," p. 25.

16. I have been equating 'true', 'sound', 'valid', and so on. Could it be that Rawls merely refuses to endorse truth, while being willing to apply one of the other adjectives? I think that the text suggests otherwise. The important point, however, is that he is committed to applying to the theory of justice whichever adjective is appropriately applied to moral propositions. There is no room for epistemic distance.

Noncognitivists and some others will find the reference to the possible truth of a theory of justice unintelligible. Theories of justice, in their view, are not the sort of things which can be either true or false. I am not taking sides in this debate here. My argument is purely an *ad hominem* one. Rawls is happy to contemplate the possibility that theories of justice are bearers of truth values, and that at least one is true. His argument is that the truth or falsity of a theory of justice does not matter to its acceptability. His is the theory of justice for us even if it is false. Therefore, his epistemic abstinence gives no support to noncognitivists or others who find the application of "truth" to theories of justice objectionable. He cannot and does not wish to rely on arguments from that source. Neither does he claim that it is unknowable whether a theory of justice is true or false. He is willing to contemplate the possibility that there are some who know what the true theory of justice is, and that it is incompatible with his. He is, in effect, arguing that such persons should nevertheless support his theory rather than the incompatible true theory, for his theory is the theory for us.

My argument above is not so much that such a claim is not morally justified as that it is incoherent, for in claiming that this is the theory of justice for us for such-and-such reasons, one is claiming that those reasons show (or make) this the true theory of justice (if truth applies to theories of justice).

14 On the Connection Between Justice and Utility

JOHN STUART MILL

IN ALL AGES OF SPECULATION one of the strongest obstacles to the reception of the doctrine that utility or happiness is the criterion of right and wrong has been drawn from the idea of justice. The powerful sentiment and apparently clear perception which that word recalls with a rapidity and certainty resembling an instinct have seemed to the majority of thinkers to point to an inherent quality in things; to show that the just must have an existence in nature as something absolute, generically distinct from every variety of the expedient and, in idea, opposed to it, though (as is commonly acknowledged) never, in the long run, disjoined from it in fact.

In the case of this, as of our other moral sentiments, there is no necessary connection between the question of its origin and that of its binding force. That a feeling is bestowed on us by nature does not necessarily legitimate all its promptings. The feeling of justice might be a peculiar instinct, and might yet require, like our other instincts, to be controlled and enlightened by a higher reason. If we have intellectual instincts leading us to judge in a particular way, as well as animal instincts that prompt us to act in a particular way, there is no necessity that the former should be more infallible in their sphere than the latter in theirs; it may as well happen that wrong judgments are occasionally suggested by those, as wrong actions by these. But though it is one thing to believe that we have natural feelings of justice, and another to acknowledge them as an ultimate criterion of conduct, these two opinions are very closely connected in point of fact. Mankind is always predisposed to believe that any subjective feeling not otherwise accounted for, is a revelation of some objective reality. Our present object is to determine whether the reality to which the feeling of justice corresponds is one which needs any such special revelation, whether the justice or injustice of an action is a thing intrinsically peculiar and distinct from all its other qualities or only a combination of certain of those qualities presented under a peculiar aspect. For the purpose of this inquiry it is practically important to consider whether the feeling itself, of justice and injustice, is *sui generis* like our sensations of color and taste or a derivative feeling formed by a combination of others. And this it is the more essential to examine, as people are in general willing enough to allow that objectively the dictates of justice coincide with a part of the field of general expediency; but inasmuch as the subjective mental feeling of justice is different from that which commonly attaches to simple expediency, and, except in the extreme cases of the latter, is far more imperative in its demands, people find it difficult to see in justice only a particular kind or branch of general utility, and think that its superior binding force requires a totally different origin.

From Utilitarianism, *Chapter V. First published 1863.*

To throw light upon this question, it is necessary to attempt to ascertain what is the distinguishing character of justice, or of injustice; what is the quality, or whether there is any quality, attributed in common to all modes of conduct designated as unjust (for justice, like many other moral attributes, is best defined by its opposite), and distinguishing them from such modes of conduct as are disapproved, but without having that particular epithet of disapprobation applied to them. If in everything which men are accustomed to characterize as just or unjust some one common attribute or collection of attributes is always present, we may judge whether this particular attribute or combination of attributes would be capable of gathering round it a sentiment of that peculiar character and intensity by virtue of the general laws of our emotional constitution, or whether the sentiment is inexplicable and requires to be regarded as a special provision of nature. If we find the former to be the case, we shall, in resolving this question, have resolved also the main problem; if the latter, we shall have to seek for some other mode of investigating it.

To find the common attributes of a variety of objects, it is necessary to begin by surveying the objects themselves in the concrete. Let us therefore advert successively to the various modes of action and arrangements of human affairs which are classed by universal or widely spread opinion, as just or as unjust. The things well known to excite the sentiments associated with those names are of a very multifarious character. I shall pass them rapidly in review, without studying any particular arrangement.

In the first place, it is mostly considered unjust to deprive anyone of his personal liberty, his property, or any other thing which belongs to him by law. Here, therefore, is one instance of the application of the terms "just" and "unjust" in a perfectly definite sense, namely, that it is just to respect, unjust to violate, the *legal rights* of anyone. But this judgment admits of several

exceptions, arising from the other forms in which the notions of justice and injustice present themselves. For example, the person who suffers the deprivation may (as the phrase is) have *forfeited* the rights which he is so deprived of—a case to which we shall return presently But also—

Secondly, the legal rights of which he is deprived may be rights which *ought* not to have belonged to him; in other words, the law which confers on him these rights may be a bad law. When it is or when (which is the same thing for our purpose) it is supposed to be so, opinions will differ as to the justice or injustice of infringing it. Some maintain that no law, however, bad, ought to be disobeyed by an individual citizen; that his opposition to it, if shown at all, should only be shown in endeavoring to get it altered by competent authority. This opinion (which condemns many of the most illustrious benefactors of mankind, and would often protect pernicious institutions against the only weapons which, in the state of things existing at the time, have any chance of succeeding against them) is defended by those who hold it on grounds of expediency, principally on that of the importance to the common interest of mankind, of maintaining inviolate the sentiment of submission to law. Other persons, again, hold the directly contrary opinion that any law, judged to be bad, may blamelessly be disobeyed, even though it be not judged to be unjust but only inexpedient, while others would confine the license of disobedience to the case of unjust laws; but, again, some say that all laws which are inexpedient are unjust, since every law imposes some restriction on the natural liberty of mankind, which restriction is an injustice unless legitimated by tending to their good. Among these diversities of opinion it seems to be universally admitted that there may be unjust laws, and that law, consequently, is not the ultimate criterion of justice, but may give to one person a benefit, or impose on another an evil, which justice condemns. When, however, a law is thought to be unjust, it seems always to be regarded as being so in the same way in which a breach of law is unjust; namely, by infringing somebody's right, which, as it cannot in this case be a legal right, receives a different appellation and is called a moral right. We may say, therefore, that a second case of injustice consists in taking or withholding from any person that to which he has a *moral right.*

Thirdly, it is universally considered just that each person should obtain that (whether good or evil) which he *deserves,* and unjust that he should obtain a good or be made to undergo an evil which he does not deserve. This is, perhaps, the clearest and most emphatic form in which the idea of justice is conceived by the general mind. As it involves the notion of desert, the question arises, what constitutes desert? Speaking in a general way, a person is understood to deserve good if he does right, evil if he does wrong; and in a more particular sense, to deserve good from those to whom he does or has done good, and evil from those to whom he does or has done evil. The precept of returning good for evil has never been regarded as a case of the fulfillment of justice, but as one in which the claims of justice are waived, in obedience to other considerations.

Fourthly, it is confessedly unjust to *break faith* with anyone: to violate an engagement, either express or implied, or disappoint expectations raised by our own conduct, at least if we have raised those expectations knowingly and voluntarily. Like the other obligations of justice already spoken of, this one is not regarded as absolute, but as capable of being overruled by a stronger obligation of justice on the other side, or by such conduct on the part of the person concerned as is deemed to absolve us from our obligation to him and to constitute a *forfeiture* of the benefit which he has been led to expect.

Fifthly, it is, by universal admission, inconsistent with justice to be *partial*—to show favor or preference to one person over another in matters to which favor and preference do not properly apply. Impartiality, however, does not seem to be regarded as a duty in itself, but rather as instrumental to some other duty; for it is admitted that favor and preference are not always censurable, and, indeed, the cases in which they are condemned are rather the exception than the rule. A person would be more likely to be blamed than applauded for giving his family or friends no superiority in good offices over strangers when he could do so without violating any other duty; and no one thinks it unjust to seek one person in preference to another as a friend, connection, or companion. Impartiality where rights are concerned is of course obligatory, but this is involved in the more general obligations of giving to everyone his right. A tribunal, for example, must be impartial because it is bound to award, without regard to any other consideration, a disputed object to the one of two parties who has the right to it. There are other cases in which impartiality means being solely influenced by desert, as with those who, in the capacity of judges, preceptors, or parents, administer reward and punishment as such. There are cases, again, in which it means being solely influenced by considerations for the public interest, as in making a selection among candidates for a government employment. Impartiality, in short, as an obligation of justice, may be said to mean being exclusively influenced by the considerations which it is supposed ought to influence the particular case in hand, and resisting solicitation of any motives which prompt to conduct different from what those considerations would dictate.

Nearly allied to the idea of impartiality is that of *equality,* which often enters as a component part of both into the conception of justice and into the practice of it, and, in the eyes of many persons, constitutes its essence. But in this, still more than in any other case, the notion of justice varies in different persons, and always conforms in its variations to their notion of utility. Each person maintains that equality is the dictate of justice, except where he thinks that expediency requires inequality. The justice of giving equal protection to the rights of all is maintained by those who support the most outrageous inequality in the rights themselves. Even in slave countries it is theoretically admitted that the rights of the slave, such as they are, ought to be as sacred as those of the master, and that a tribunal which fails to enforce them with equal strictness is wanting injustice; while, at the same time, institutions which leave to the slave scarcely any rights to enforce are not deemed unjust because they are not deemed inexpedient. Those who think that utility requires distinctions of rank do not consider it unjust that riches and social privileges should be unequally dispensed; but those who think this inequality inexpedient think it unjust also. Whoever thinks that government is necessary sees no injustice in as much inequality as is constituted by giving to the magistrate powers not granted to other people. Even among those who hold leveling doctrines, there are differences of opinion about expediency. Some communists consider it unjust that the produce of the labor of the community should be shared on any other principle than that of exact equality; others think it just that those should receive most whose wants are greatest; while others hold that those who work harder, or who produce more, or whose services are more valuable to the community, may justly claim a larger quota in the division of the produce. And the sense of natural justice may be plausibly appealed to in behalf of every one of these opinions.

Among so many diverse applications of the term "justice," which yet is not regarded as ambiguous, it is a matter of some difficulty to seize the mental link which holds them together, and on which the moral sentiment adhering to the term essentially depends. Perhaps, in this embarrassment, some help may be derived from the history of the word, as indicated by its etymology.

In most if not all languages, the etymology of the word which corresponds to "just" points distinctly to an origin connected with the ordinances of law. *Justum* is a form of *jussum,* that which has been ordered. *Dikaion* comes directly from *dike,* a suit at law. *Recht,* from which came *right* and *righteous,* is synonymous with law. The courts of justice, the administration of justice, are the courts and the administration of law. *La justice,* in French, is the established term for judicature. I am not committing the fallacy, imputed with some show of truth to Horne Tooke, of assuming that a word must still continue to mean what it originally meant. Etymology is slight evidence of what the idea now signified is, but the very best evidence of how it sprang up. There can, I think, be no doubt that the *idée mère,* the primitive element, in the formation of the notion of justice was conformity to law. It constituted the entire idea among the Hebrews, up to the birth of Christianity; as might be expected in the case of a people whose laws attempted to embrace all subjects on which precepts were required, and who believed those laws to be a direct emanation from the Supreme Being. But other nations, and in particular the Greeks and Romans, who knew that their laws had been made originally, and still continued to be made, by men, were not afraid to admit that those men might make bad laws; might do, by law, the same things, and from the same motives, which if done by individuals without the sanction of law would be called unjust. And hence the sentiment of injustice came to be attached, not to all violations of law, but only to violations of such laws as *ought* to exist, including such as ought to exist but do not, and to laws themselves if supposed to be contrary to what ought to be law. In this manner the idea of law and of its injunctions was still predominant in the notion of justice, even when the laws actually in force ceased to be accepted as the standard of it.

It is true that mankind consider the idea of justice and its obligations as applicable to many things which neither are, nor is it desired that they should be, regulated by law. Nobody desires that laws should interfere with the whole detail of private life; yet everyone allows that in all daily conduct a person may and does show himself to be either just or unjust. But even here, the idea of the breach of what ought to be law still lingers in a modified shape. It would always give us pleasure, and chime in with our feelings of fitness, that acts which we deem unjust should be punished, though we do not always think it expedient that this should be done by the tribunals. We forego that gratification on account of incidental inconveniences. We should be glad to see just conduct enforced and injustice repressed, even in the minutest details, if we were not, with reason, afraid of trusting the magistrate with so unlimited an amount of power over individuals. When we think that a person is bound in justice to do a thing, it is an ordinary form of language to say that he ought to be compelled to do it. We should be gratified to see the obligation enforced by anybody who had the power. If we see that its enforcement by law would be inexpedient, we lament the impossibility, we consider the impunity given to injustice as an evil and strive to make amends for it by bringing a strong expression of our own and the public disapprobation to bear upon the offender. Thus the idea of legal constraint is still the generating idea of the notion of justice, though undergoing several transformations before that notion as it exists in an advanced state of society becomes complete.

The above is, I think, a true account, as far as it goes, of the origin and progressive growth of the idea of justice. But we must observe that it contains as yet nothing to distinguish that obligation from moral obligation in general. For the truth is that the idea of penal sanction, which is the essence of law, enters not only into the conception of injustice, but into that of any kind of wrong. We do not call anything wrong unless we mean to imply that a person ought to be punished in some way or other for doing it— if not by law, by the opinion of his fellow creatures; if not by opinion, by the reproaches of his own conscience. This seems the real turning point of the distinction between morality and simple expediency. It is a part of the notion of duty in every one of its forms that a person may rightfully be compelled to fulfill it. Duty is a thing which may be *exacted* from a person, as one exacts a debt. Unless we think that it may be exacted from him, we do not call it his duty. Reasons of prudence, or the interest of other people, may militate against actually exacting it, but the person himself, it is clearly understood, would not be entitled to complain. There are other things, on the contrary, which we wish that people should do, which we like or admire them for doing, perhaps dislike or despise them for not doing, but yet admit they are not bound to do; it is not a case of moral obligation; we do not blame them; that is, we do not think that they are proper objects of punishment. How we come by these ideas of deserving and not deserving punishment will appear, perhaps, in the sequel; but I think there is no doubt that this distinction lies at the bottom of the notions of right and wrong; that we call any conduct wrong, or employ, instead, some other term of dislike or disparagement, according as we think that the person ought, or ought not, to be punished for it; and we say it would be right to do so and so, or merely that it would be desirable or laudable, according as we would wish to see the person whom it concerns compelled, or only persuaded and exhorted, to act in that manner.

Justice Correlated with Certain Rights

This, therefore, being the characteristic difference which marks off, not justice, but morality in general from the remaining provinces of expediency and worthiness, the character is still to be sought which distinguishes justice from other branches of morality. Now it is known that ethical writers divide moral duties into two classes, denoted by the ill-chosen expressions, duties of perfect and of imperfect obligation; the latter being those in which, though the act is obligatory, the particular occasions of performing it are left to our choice, as in the case of charity or beneficence, which we are indeed bound to practice but not toward any definite person, nor at any prescribed time. In the more precise language of philosophic jurists, duties of perfect obligation are those duties in virtue of which a correlative *right* resides in some person or persons; duties of imperfect obligation are those moral obligations which do not give birth to any right. I think it will be found that this distinction exactly coincides with that which exists between justice and the other obligations of morality. In our survey of the various popular acceptations of justice, the term appeared generally to involve the idea of a personal right—a claim on the part of one or more individuals, like that which the law gives when it confers a proprietary or other legal right. Whether the injustice consists in depriving a person of a possession, or in breaking faith with him, or in treating him worse than he deserves, or worse than other people who have no greater claims—in each case the supposition implies two things: a wrong done, and some assignable person who is wronged. Injustice may also be done by treating a person better than others; but the wrong in this case is to his competitors, who are also assignable persons. It seems to me that this feature in the case—a right in some person, correlative to the moral obligation—constitutes a specific difference between justice and generosity or beneficence. Justice implies something which it is not only right to do, and wrong not to do, but which some individual person can claim from us as his moral right. No one has a moral right to our generosity or beneficence because we are not morally bound to practice those virtues toward any given individual. And it will be found with respect to this as to every correct definition that the instances which seem to conflict with it are those which most confirm it. For if a moralist attempts, as some have done, to make out that mankind generally, though not any given individual, have a right to all the good we can do them, he at once, by that thesis, includes generosity and beneficence within the category of justice. He is obliged to say that our utmost exertions are *due* to our fellow creatures, thus assimilating them to a debt; or that nothing less can be a sufficient *return* for what society does for us, thus classing

the case as one of gratitude; both of which are acknowledged cases of justice, and not of the virtue of beneficence; and whoever does not place the distinction between justice and morality in general, where we have now placed it, will be found to make no distinction between them at all, but to merge all morality in justice. . . . When we call anything a person's right, we mean that he has a valid claim on society to protect him in the possession of it, either by the force of law or by that of education and opinion. If he has what we consider a sufficient claim, on whatever account, to have something guaranteed to him by society, we say that he has a right to it. If we desire to prove that anything does not belong to him by right, we think this done as soon as it is admitted that society ought not to take measures for securing it to him, but should leave him to chance or to his own exertions. Thus a person is said to have a right to what he can earn in fair professional competition, because society ought not to allow any other person to hinder him from endeavoring to earn in that manner as much as he can. But he has not a right to three hundred a year, though he may happen to be earning it; because society is not called on to provide that he shall earn that sum. On the contrary, if he owns ten thousand pounds three-percent stock, he *has* a right to three hundred a year because society has come under an obligation to provide him with an income of that amount.

To have a right, then, is I conceive, to have something which society ought to defend me in the possession of. If the objector goes on to ask why it ought, I can give him no other reason than general utility. If that expression does not seem to convey a sufficient feeling of the strength of the obligation, nor to account for the peculiar energy of the feeling, it is because there goes to the composition of the sentiment, not a rational only but also an animal element— the thirst for retaliation; and this thirst derives its intensity, as well as its moral justification, from the extraordinarily important and impressive kind of utility which is concerned. The interest involved is that of security, to everyone's feelings the most vital of all interests. All other earthly benefits are needed by one person, not needed by another; and many of them can, if necessary be cheerfully foregone or replaced by something else; but security no human being can possibly do without; on it we depend for all our immunity from evil and for the whole value of all and every good, beyond the passing moment, since nothing but the gratification of the instant could be of any worth to us if we could be deprived of everything the next instant by whoever was momentarily stronger than ourselves. Now this most indispensable of all necessaries, after physical nutriment, cannot be had unless the machinery for providing it is kept unintermittedly in active play. Our notion, therefore, of the claim we have on our fellow creatures to join in making safe for us the very groundwork of our existence gathers feelings around it so much more intense than those concerned in any of the more common cases of utility that the difference in degree (as is often the case in psychology) becomes a real difference in kind. The claim assumes that character of absoluteness, that apparent infinity and incommensurability with all other considerations which constitute the distinction between the feeling of right and wrong and that of ordinary expediency and inexpediency. The feelings concerned are so powerful, and we count so positively on finding a responsive feeling in others (all being alike interested) that *ought* and *should* grow into *must,* and recognized indispensability becomes a moral necessity, analogous to physical, and often not inferior to it in binding force.

Justice and Utility

If the preceding analysis, or something resembling it, be not the correct account of the notion of justice—if justice be totally independent of utility, and be a standard *per se,* which the mind can recognize by simple retrospection of itself—it is hard to understand why that internal oracle is so ambiguous, and why so many things appear either just or unjust, according to the light in which they are regarded.

We are continually informed that utility is an uncertain standard, which every different person interprets differently, and that there is no safety but in the immutable, ineffaceable, and unmistakable dictates of justice, which carry their evidence in themselves and are independent of the fluctuations of opinion. One would suppose from this that on questions of justice there could be no controversy; that, if we take that for our rule, its application to any given case could leave us in as little doubt as a mathematical demonstration. So far is this from being the fact that there is as much difference of opinion, and as much discussion, about what is just as about what is useful to society. Not only have different nations and individuals different notions of justice, but in the mind of one and the same individual, justice is not some one rule, principle, or maxim, but many which do not always coincide in their dictates, and, in choosing between which, he is guided either by some extraneous standard or by his own personal predilections. . . . [to take an] example from a subject already once referred to. In cooperative industrial association, is it just or not that talent or skill should give a title to superior remuneration? On the negative side of the question it is argued that whoever does the best he can deserves equally well, and ought not in justice to be put in a position of inferiority for no fault of his own; that superior abilities have already advantages more than enough, in the admiration they excite, the personal influence they command, and the internal sources of satisfaction attending them, without adding to these a superior share of the world's goods; and that society is bound in justice rather to make compensation to the less favored for this unmerited inequality of advantages than to aggravate it. On the contrary side it is contended that society receives more from the more efficient laborer; that, his services being more useful, society owes him a larger return for them; that a greater share of the joint result is actually his work, and not to allow his claim to it is a kind of robbery; that, if he is only to receive as much as others, he can only be justly required to produce as much, and to give a smaller amount of time and exertion, proportioned to his superior efficiency. Who shall decide between these appeals to conflicting principles of justice? Justice has in this case two sides to it, which it is impossible to bring into harmony, and the two disputants have chosen opposite sides; the one looks to what it is just that the individual should receive, the other to what it is just that the community should give. Each, from his own point of view, is unanswerable; and any choice between them, on the grounds of justice, must be perfectly arbitrary. Social utility alone can decide the preference.

How many, again, and how irreconcilable are the standards of justice to which reference is made in discussing the repartition of taxation. One opinion is that the payment to the state should be in numerical proportion to pecuniary means. Others think that justice dictates what they term graduated taxation—taking a higher percentage from those who have more to spare. In point of natural justice a strong case might be made for disregarding means altogether, and taking the same absolute sum (whenever it could be got) from everyone; as the subscribers to a mess or to a club all pay the same sum for the same privileges, whether they can all equally afford it or not. Since the protection (it might be said) of law and government is afforded to and is equally required by all, there is no injustice in making all buy it at the same price. It is reckoned justice, not injustice, that a dealer should charge to all customers the same price for the same article, not a price varying according to their means of payment. This doctrine, as applied to taxation, finds no advocates because it conflicts so strongly with man's feelings of humanity and of social expediency; but the principle of justice which it invokes is as true and as binding as those which can be appealed to against it. Accordingly it exerts a tacit influence on the line of defense employed for other modes of assessing taxation.

People feel obliged to argue that the state does more for the rich man than for the poor, as a justification for its taking more from them, though this is in reality not true, for the rich would be far better able to protect themselves, in the absence of law or government, than the poor, and indeed would probably be successful in converting the poor into their slaves. Others, again, so far defer to the same conception of justice as to maintain that all should pay an equal capitation tax for the protection of their persons (these being of equal value to all), and an unequal tax for the protection of their property, which is unequal. To this others reply that the all of one man is as valuable to him as the all of another. From these confusions there is no other mode of extrication than the utilitarian.

Is, then, the difference between the just and the expedient a merely imaginary distinction? Have mankind been under a delusion in thinking that justice is a more sacred thing than policy, and that the latter ought only to be listened to after the former has been satisfied? By no means. The exposition we have given of the nature and origin of the sentiment recognizes a real distinction; and no one of those who profess the most sublime contempt for the consequences of actions as an element in their morality attaches more importance to the distinction than I do. While I dispute the pretensions of any theory which sets up an imaginary standard of justice not grounded on utility, I account the justice which is grounded on utility to be the chief part and incomparably the most sacred and binding part, of all morality. Justice is a name for certain classes of moral rules which concern the essentials of human well-being more nearly, and are therefore of more absolute obligation, than any other rules of the guidance of life; and the notion which we have found to be of the essence of the idea of justice—that of a right residing in an individual—implies and testifies to this more binding obligation.

The moral rules which forbid mankind to hurt one another (in which we must never forget to include wrongful interference with each other's freedom) are more vital to human well-being than any maxims, however important, which only point out the best mode of managing some department of human affairs. They have also the peculiarity that they are the main element in determining the whole of the social feelings of mankind. It is their observance which alone preserves peace among human beings; if obedience to them were not the rule, and disobedience the exception, everyone would see in everyone else an enemy against whom he must be perpetually guarding himself. What is hardly less important, these are the precepts which mankind have the strongest and the most direct inducements for impressing upon one another. By merely giving to each other prudential instruction or exhortation, they may gain, or think they gain, nothing; in inculcating on each other the duty of positive beneficence, they have an unmistakable interest, but far less in degree; a person may possibly not need the benefits of others, but he always needs that they should not do him hurt. Thus the moralities which protect every individual from being harmed by others, either directly or by being hindered in his freedom of pursuing his own good, are at once those which he himself has most at heart and those which he has the strongest interest in publishing and enforcing by word and deed. It is by a person's observance of these that his fitness to exist as one of the fellowship of human beings is tested and decided; for on that depends his being a nuisance or not to those with whom he is in contact. Now it is these moralities primarily which compose the obligations of justice. The most marked cases of injustice, and those which give the tone to the feeling of repugnance which characterizes the sentiment, are acts of wrongful aggression or wrongful exercise of power over someone; the next are those which consist in wrongfully withholding from him something which is his due—in both cases inflicting on him a positive hurt, either in the form of direct suffering or of the privation of some good which he had reasonable ground, either of a physical or of a social kind, for counting upon.

The same powerful motives which command the observance of these primary moralities enjoin the punishment of those who violate them; and as the impulses of self-defense, of defense of others, and of vengeance are all called forth against such persons, retribution, or evil for evil, becomes closely connected with the sentiment of justice, and is universally included in the idea. Good for good is also one of the dictates of justice; and this, though its social utility is evident, and though it carries with it a natural human feeling, has not at first sight that obvious connection with hurt or injury which, existing in the most elementary cases of just and unjust, is the source of the characteristic intensity of the sentiment. But the connection, though less obvious, is not less real. He who accepts benefits and denies a return of them when needed inflicts a real hurt by disappointing one of the most natural and reasonable of expectations, and one which he must at least tacitly have encouraged, otherwise the benefits would seldom have been conferred. The important rank, among human evils and wrongs, of the disappointment of expectation is shown in the fact that it constitutes the principal criminality of two such highly immoral acts as a breach of friendship and a breach of promise. Few hurts which human beings can sustain are greater, and none wound more, than when that on which they habitually and with full assurance relied fails them in the hour of need; and few wrongs are greater than this mere withholding of good; none excite more resentment, either in the person suffering or in a sympathizing spectator. The principle, therefore, of giving to each what they deserve, that is, good for good as well as evil for evil, is not only included within the idea of justice as we have defined it, but is a proper object of that intensity of sentiment which places the just in human estimation above the simply expedient.

Most of the maxims of justice current in the world, and commonly appealed to in its transactions, are simply instrumental to carrying into effect the principles of justice which we have now spoken of. That a person is only responsible for what he has done voluntarily, or could voluntarily have avoided; that it is unjust to condemn any person unheard; that the punishment ought to be proportioned to the offense; and the like, are maxims intended to prevent the just principle of evil for evil from being perverted to the infliction of evil without that justification. The greater part of these common maxims have come into use from the practice of courts of justice, which have been naturally led to a more complete recognition and elaboration than was likely to suggest itself to others, of the rules necessary to enable them to fulfill their double function—of inflicting punishment when due, and of awarding to each person his right.

That first of judicial virtues, impartiality, is an obligation of justice, partly for the reason last mentioned, as being a necessary condition of the fulfillment of other obligations of justice. But this is not the only source of the exalted rank, among human obligations, of those maxims of equality and impartiality which, both in popular estimation and in that of the most enlightened, are included among the precepts of justice. In one point of view, they may be considered as corollaries from the principles already laid down. If it is a duty to do to each according to his deserts, returning good for good, as well as repressing evil by evil, it necessarily follows that we should treat all equally well (when no higher duty forbids) who have deserved equally well of *us,* and that society should treat all equally well who have deserved equally well of *it,* that is, who have deserved equally well absolutely. This is the highest abstract standard of social and distributive justice, toward which all institutions and the efforts of all virtuous citizens should be made in the utmost possible degree to converge. But this great moral duty rests upon a still deeper foundation, being a direct emanation from the first principle of morals, and not a mere logical corollary from secondary or derivative doctrines. It is involved in the very meaning of utility, or the greatest happiness principle. That principle is a mere form of words without rational signification unless one person's happiness, supposed equal in degree (with the proper allowance made for kind), is counted for exactly as much as another's. Those conditions being supplied, Bentham's dictum, "everybody to count for one, nobody for more than one," might be written under the principle of utility as an explanatory commentary.[1] The equal claim of everybody to happiness, in the estimation of the moralist and of the legislator, involves an equal claim to all the means of happiness except insofar as the inevitable conditions of human life and the general interest in which that of every individual is included set limits to the maxim; and those limits ought to be strictly construed. As every other maxim of justice, so this is by no means applied or held applicable universally; on the contrary, as I have already remarked, it bends to every person's ideas of social expediency. But in whatever case it is deemed applicable at all, it is held to be the dictate of justice. All persons are deemed to have a *right* to equality of treatment, except when some recognized social expediency requires the reverse. And hence all social inequalities which have ceased to be considered expedient assume the character, not of simple inexpediency, but of injustice, and appear so tyrannical that people are apt to wonder how they ever could have been tolerated—forgetful that they themselves, perhaps, tolerate other inequalities under an equally mistaken notion of expediency, the correction of which would make that which they approve seem quite as monstrous as what they have at last learned to condemn. The entire history of social improvement has been a series of transitions by which one custom or institution after another, from being a supposed primary necessity of social existence, has passed into the rank of a universally stigmatized injustice and tyranny. So it has been with the distinction of slaves and freemen, nobles and serfs, patricians and plebeians; and so it will be, and in part already is, with the aristocracies of color, race, and sex.

It appears from what has been said that justice is a name for certain moral requirements which, regarded collectively, stand higher in the scale of social utility, and are therefore of more paramount obligation, than any others, though particular cases may occur in which some other social duty is so important as to overrule any one of the general maxims of justice. Thus, to save a life, it may not only be allowable, but a duty, to steal or take by force the necessary food or medicine, or to kidnap and compel to officiate the only qualified medical practitioner. In such cases, as we do not call anything justice which is not a virtue, we usually say, not that justice must give way to some other moral principle, but that what is just in ordinary cases is, by reason of that other principle, not just in the particular case. By this useful accommodation of language, the character of indefeasibility attributed to justice is kept up, and we are saved from the necessity of maintaining that there can be laudable injustice.

The considerations which have now been adduced resolve, I conceive, the only real difficulty in the utilitarian theory of morals. It has always been evident that all cases of justice are also cases of expediency; the difference is in the peculiar sentiment which attaches to the former, as contradistinguished from the latter. If this characteristic sentiment has been sufficiently accounted for; if there is no necessity to assume for it any peculiarity of origin; if it is simply the natural feeling of resentment, moralized by being made co-extensive with the demands of social good; and if this feeling not only does but ought to exist in all the classes of cases to which the idea of justice corresponds—that idea no longer presents itself as a stumbling block to the utilitarian ethics. Justice remains the appropriate name for certain social utilities which are vastly more important, and therefore more absolute and imperative, than any others are as a class (though not more so than others may be in particular cases); and which, therefore, ought to be, as well as naturally are, guarded by a sentiment, not only different in degree, but also in kind; distinguished from the milder feeling which attaches to the mere idea of promoting human pleasure or convenience at once by the more

definite nature of its commands and by the sterner character of its sanctions.

NOTE

1. This implication, in the first principle of the utilitarian scheme, of perfect impartiality between persons is regarded by Mr. Herbert Spencer (in his *Social Statics*) as a disproof of the pretensions of utility to be a sufficient guide to right; since (he says) the principle of utility presupposes the anterior principle that everybody has an equal right to happiness. It may be more correctly described as supposing that equal amounts of happiness are equally desirable, whether felt by the same or different persons. This, however, is not a *pre*supposition, not a premise needful to support the principle of utility, but the very principle itself; for what is the principle of utility if it be not that "happiness" and "desirable" are synonymous terms? If there is any anterior principle implied, it can be no other than this, that the truths of arithmetic are applicable to the valuation of happiness, as of all other measurable quantities.

(Mr. Herbert Spencer, in a private communication on the subject of the preceding note, objects to being considered an opponent of utilitarianism and states that he regards happiness as the ultimate end of morality; but deems that end only partially attainable by empirical generalizations from the observed results of conduct, and completely attainable only by deducing, from the laws of life and the conditions of existence, what kinds of action necessarily tend to produce happiness, and what kinds to produce unhappiness. With the exception of the word "necessarily," I have no dissent to express from this doctrine; and (omitting that word) I am not aware that any modern advocate of utilitarianism is of a different opinion. Bentham, certainly, to whom in the *Social Statics* Mr. Spencer particularly referred, is, least of all writers, chargeable with unwillingness to deduce the effect of actions on happiness from the laws of human nature and the universal conditions of human life. The common charge against him is of relying too exclusively upon such deductions and declining altogether to be bound by the generalizations from specific experience which Mr. Spencer thinks that utilitarians generally confine themselves to. My own opinion (and, as I collect, Mr. Spencer's) is that in ethics, as in all other branches of scientific study, the concilience of the results of both these processes, each corroborating and verifying the other, is requisite to give to any general proposition the kind and degree of evidence which constitutes scientific proof.)

15 Justice and Equality

R. M. HARE

THERE ARE SEVERAL REASONS why a philosopher of my persuasion should wish to write about justice. The first is the general one that ethical theory ought to be applied to practical issues, both for the sake of improving the theory and for any light it may shed on the practical issues, of which many of the most important involve questions of justice. This is shown by the frequency with which appeals are made to justice and fairness and related ideals when people are arguing about political or economic questions (about wages for example, or about schools policy or about relations between races or sexes). If we do not know what "just" and "fair" mean (and it looks as if we do not) and therefore do not know what would settle questions involving these concepts, then we are unlikely to be able to sort out these very difficult moral problems. I have also a particular interest in the topic: I hold a view about moral reasoning which has at least strong affinities with utilitarianism;[1] and there is commonly thought to be some kind of antagonism between justice and utility or, as it is sometimes called, expediency. I have therefore a special need to sort these questions out.

We must start by distinguishing between different kinds of justice, or between different senses or uses of the word "just" (the distinction between these different ways of putting the matter need not now concern us). In distinguishing between different kinds of justice we

shall have to make crucial use of a distinction between different levels of moral thinking which I have explained at length in other places.[2] It is perhaps simplest to distinguish three levels of thought, one ethical or meta-ethical and two moral or normative-ethical. At the meta-ethical level we try to establish the meanings of the moral words, and thus the formal properties of the moral concepts, including their logical properties. Without knowing these a theory of normative moral reasoning cannot begin. Then there are two levels of (normative) moral thinking which have often been in various ways distinguished. I have myself in the past called them "level 2" and "level 1"; but for ease of remembering I now think it best to give them names, and propose to call level 2 the *critical* level and level 1 the *intuitive* level. At the intuitive level we make use of *prima facie* moral principles of a fairly simple general sort, and do not question them but merely apply them to cases which we encounter. This level of thinking cannot be (as intuitionists commonly suppose) self-sustaining; there is a need for a critical level of thinking by which we select the *prima facie* principles for use at the intuitive level, settle conflict between them, and give to the whole system of them a justification which intuition by itself can never provide. It will be one of the objects of this paper to distinguish those kinds of justice whose place is at the intuitive level and which are

From "Justice and Equality," Justice and Economic Distribution, *edited by John Arthur and William Shaw (1978), pp. 116–131. Reprinted by permission of the author.*

embodied in *prima facie* principles from those kinds which have a role in critical and indeed in meta-ethical thinking.

The principal result of meta-ethical enquiry in this field is to isolate a sense or kind of justice which has come to be known as "formal justice." Formal justice is a property of all moral principles (which is why Professor Rawls heads his chapter on this subject not "Formal constraints of the concept of *just*" but "Formal constraints of the concept of *right*,"[3] and why his disciple David Richards is able to make a good attempt to found the whole of morality, and not merely a theory of justice, on a similar hypothetical-contrast basis).[4] Formal justice is simply another name for the formal requirement of universality in moral principles on which, as I have explained in detail elsewhere,[5] golden-rule arguments are based. From the formal, logical properties of the moral words, and in particular from the logical prohibition of individual references in moral principles, it is possible to derive formal canons of moral argument, such as the rule that we are not allowed to discriminate morally between individuals unless there is some qualitative difference between them which is the ground for the discrimination; and the rule that the equal interests of different individuals have equal moral weight. Formal justice consists simply in the observance of these canons in our moral arguments; it is widely thought that this observance by itself is not enough to secure justice in some more substantial sense. As we shall see, one is not offending against the first rule if one says that extra privileges should be given to people just because they have white skins; and one is not offending against either rule if one says that one should take a cent from everybody and give it to the man with the biggest nose, provided that he benefits as much in total as they lose. The question is, How do we get from formal to substantial justice?

This question arises because there are various kinds of material or substantial justice whose content cannot be established directly by appeal to the uses of moral words or the formal properties of moral concepts (we shall see later how much can be done indirectly by appeal to these formal properties *in conjunction with* other premises or postulates or presuppositions). There is a number of different kinds of substantial justice, and we can hardly do better than begin with Aristotle's classification of them,[6] since it is largely responsible for the different senses which the word "just" still has in common use. This is a case where it is impossible to appeal to common use, at any rate of the word "just" (the word "fair" is better) in order to settle philosophical disputes, because the common use is itself the product of past philosophical theories. The expressions "distributive" and "retributive" justice go back to Aristotle,[7] and the word "just" itself occupies the place (or places) that it does in our language largely because of its place in earlier philosophical discussions.

Aristotle first separated off a generic sense of the Greek word commonly translated "just," a sense which had been used a lot by Plato: the sense in which justice is the whole of virtue in so far as it concerns our relations with other people.[8] The last qualification reminds us that this is not the most generic sense possible. Theognis had already used it to include the whole of virtue, full stop.[9] These very generic senses of the word, as applied to men and acts, have survived into modern English to confuse philosophers. One of the sources of confusion is that, in the less generic sense of "just" to be discussed in most of this paper, the judgment that an act would be unjust is sometimes fairly easily overridden by other moral considerations ("unjust," we may say, "but right as an act of mercy"; or "unjust, but right because necessary in order to avert an appalling calamity"). It is much more difficult for judgments that an act is required by justice in the generic sense, in which "unjust" is almost equivalent to "not right," to be overridden this way.

Adherents of the "*fiat justitia ruat caelum*"[10] school seldom make clear whether, when they say "Let justice be done though the heavens fall," they are using a more or less generic sense of "justice"; and they thus take advantage of its non-overridability in the more generic sense in order to claim unchallengeable sanctity for judgments made using one of the less generic senses. It must be right to do the just thing (whatever that may be) in the sense (if there still is one in English) in which "just" *means* "right." In this sense, if it were right to cause the heavens to fall, and therefore just in the most generic sense, it would of course be right. But we might have to take into account, in deciding whether it would be right, the fact that the heavens would fall (that causing the heavens to fall would be one of the things we were doing if we did the action in question). On the other hand, if it were merely the just act in one of the less generic senses, we might hold that, though just, it was not right, because it would not be right to cause the heavens to fall merely in order to secure justice in this more limited sense; perhaps some concession to mercy, or even to common sense, would be in order.

This is an application of the "split-level" structure of moral thinking sketched above. One of the theses I wish to maintain is that principles of justice in these less generic senses are all *prima facie* principles and therefore overridable. I shall later be giving a utilitarian account of justice which finds a place, at the intuitive level, for these *prima facie* principles of justice. At this level they have great importance and utility, but it is in accordance with utilitarianism, as indeed with common sense, to claim that they can on unusual occasions be overridden. Having said this, however, it is most important to stress that this does *not* involve conceding the overridability of either the generic kind of justice, which has its place at the critical level, or of formal justice, which operates at the meta-ethical level. These are preserved intact, and therefore defenders of the sanctity of justice ought to be content, since these are the core of justice as of morality. We may call to mind here Aristotle's[11] remarks about the "better justice" or "equity" which is required in order to rectify the crudities, giving rise to

unacceptable results in particular cases, of a justice whose principles are, as they have to be, couched in general (i.e. simple) terms. The lawgiver who, according to Aristotle, "would have" given a special prescription if he had been present at this particular case, and to whose prescription we must try to conform if we can, corresponds to the critical moral thinker, who operates under the constraints of formal justice and whose principles are not limited to simple general rules but can be specific enough to cover the peculiarities of unusual cases.

Retributive and Distributive Justice

After speaking briefly of generic justice, Aristotle goes on[12] to distinguish two main kinds of justice in the narrow or more particular sense in which it means "fairness." He calls these retributive and distributive justice. They have their place, respectively, in the fixing of penalties and rewards for bad and good actions, and in the distribution of goods and the opposite between the possible recipients. One of the most important questions is whether these two sorts of justice are reducible to a single sort. Rawls, for example, thinks that they are, and so do I. By using the expression "justice as fairness," he implies that all justice can be reduced to kinds of distributive justice, which itself is founded on procedural justice (i.e. on the adoption of fair procedures) in distribution.[13]

We may (without attempting complete accuracy in exposition) explain how Rawls might effect this reduction as follows. The parties in his 'original position' are prevented by his "veil of ignorance" from knowing what their own positions are in the world in which they are to live; so they are unable when adopting principles of justice to tailor them to suit their own individual interests. Impartiality (a very important constituent, at least, of justice) is thus secured. Therefore the principles which govern *both* the distribution of wealth and power and other good things *and* the assignment of rewards and penalties (and indeed all other matters which have to be regulated by principles of justice) will be impartial as between individuals, and in this sense just. In this way Rawls in effect reduces the justice of acts of retribution to justice in distributing between the affected parties the good and bad effects of a system of retributions, and reduces this distributive justice in turn to the adoption of a just procedure for selecting the system of retributions to be used.

This can be illustrated by considering the case of a criminal facing a judge (a case which has been thought to give trouble to me too, though I dealt with it adequately, on the lines which I am about to repeat here, in my book *Freedom and Reason*).[14] A Rawlsian judge, when sentencing the criminal, could defend himself against the charge of injustice or unfairness by saying that he was faithfully observing the principles of justice which would be adopted in the original position, whose conditions are procedurally fair. What these principles would be requires, no doubt, a great deal of discussion, in the course of which I might find myself in disagreement with Rawls. But my own view on how the judge should justify his action is, in its formal properties, very like his. On my view likewise, the judge can say that, when he asks himself what universal principles he is prepared to adopt for situations exactly like the one he is in, and considers examples of such logically possible situations in which *he* occupies, successively, the positions of judge, and of criminal, and of all those who are affected by the administration and enforcement of the law under which he is sentencing the criminal, including, of course, potential victims of possible future crimes—he can say that when he asks himself this, he has no hesitation in accepting the principle which bids him impose such and such a sentence in accordance with the law.

I am assuming that the judge is justifying himself at the critical level. If he were content with justifying himself at the intuitive level, his task would be easier, because, we hope, he, like most of us, has intuitions about the proper

administration of justice in the courts, embodying *prima facie* principles of a sort whose inculcation in judges and in the rest of us has a high social utility. I say this while recognizing that *some* judges have intuitions about these matters which have a high social *dis*utility. The question of what intuitions judges ought to have about retributive justice is a matter for *critical* moral thinking.

On both Rawls' view and mine retributive justice has thus been reduced to distributive; on Rawls' view the principles of justice adopted are those which *distribute* fairly between those affected the good and the evil consequences of having or not having certain enforced criminal laws; on my own view likewise it is the impartiality secured by the requirement to universalize one's prescription which makes the judge say what he says, and here too it is an impartiality in distributing good and evil consequences between the affected parties. For the judge to let off the rapist would not be *fair* to all those who would be raped if the law were not enforced. I conclude that retributive justice can be reduced to distributive, and that therefore we shall have done what is required of us if we can give an adequate account of the latter.

What is common to Rawls' method and my own is the recognition that to get solutions to particular questions about what is just or unjust, we have to have a way of selecting principles of justice to answer such questions, and that to ask them in default of such principles is senseless. And we both recognize that the method for selecting the principles has to be founded on what he calls "the formal constraints of the concept of right." This measure of agreement can extend to the method of selecting principles of distributive justice as well as retributive. Neither Rawls nor I need be put off our stride by an objector who says that we have not addressed ourselves to the question of what acts are just, but have divagated on to the quite different question of how to select principles of justice. The point is that the first question cannot be answered without answering the second. Most of the apparently intractable conflicts about justice and rights that plague the world have been generated by taking certain answers to the first question as obvious and requiring no argument. We shall resolve these conflicts only by asking what arguments are available for the principles by which questions about the justice of individual acts are to be answered. In short, we need to ascend from intuitive to critical thinking; as I have argued in my review of his book, Rawls is to be reproached with not *completing* the ascent.[15]

Nozick, however, seems hardly to have begun it.[16] Neither Rawls nor I have anything to fear from him, so long as we stick to the formal part of our systems which we in effect share. When it comes to the application of this formal method to produce substantial principles of justice, I might find myself in disagreement with Rawls, because he relies much too much on his own intuitions which are open to question. Nozick's intuitions differ from Rawls', and sometimes differ from, sometimes agree with mine. This sort of question is simply not to be settled by appeal to intuitions, and it is time that the whole controversy ascended to a more serious, critical level. At this level, the answer which both Rawls and I should give to Nozick is that whatever sort of principles of justice we are after, whether structural principles, as Rawls thinks, or historical principles, as Nozick maintains, they have to be supported by critical thinking, of which Nozick seems hardly to see the necessity. This point is quite independent of the structural-historical disagreement.

For example, if Nozick thinks that it is just for people to retain whatever property they have acquired by voluntary exchange which benefited all parties, starting from a position of equality but perhaps ending up with a position of gross inequality, and if Rawls, by contrast, thinks that such inequality should be rectified in order to make the position of the least advantaged in society as good as possible, how are we to decide between them? Not by intuition, because there

seems to be a deadlock between their intuitions. Rawls has a procedure, which *need* not appeal to intuition, for justifying distributions; this would give him the game, if he were to base the procedure on firm logical grounds, and if he followed it correctly. Actually he does not so base it, and mixes up so many intuitions in the argument that the conclusions he reaches are not such as the procedure really justifies. But Nozick has no procedure at all: only a variety of considerations of different sorts, all in the end based on intuition. Sometimes he seems to be telling us what arrangements in society would be arrived at if bargaining took place in accordance with games-theory between mutually disinterested parties; sometimes what arrangements would maximize the welfare of members of society; and sometimes what arrangements would strike them as fair. He does not often warn us when he is switching from one of these grounds to another; and he does little to convince us by argument that the arrangements so selected would be in accordance with justice. He hopes that we will think what he thinks; but Rawls at least thinks otherwise.

Formal Justice and Substantial Equality

How then do we get from formal to substantial justice? We have had an example of how this is done in the sphere of retributive justice; but how is this method to be extended to cover distributive justice as a whole, and its relation, if any, to equality in distribution? The difficulty of using formal justice in order to establish principles of substantial justice can indeed be illustrated very well by asking whether, and in what sense, justice demands equality in distribution. The complaint is often made that a certain distribution is unfair or unjust because unequal; so it looks, at least, as if the substantial principle that goods ought to be distributed equally in default of reasons to the contrary forms part of some people's conception of justice. Yet, it is argued, this substantial principle cannot be established simply on the basis of the formal notions we have mentioned. The following kind of schematic example is often adduced: consider two possible distributions of a given finite stock of goods, in one of which the goods are distributed equally, and in the other of which a few of the recipients have nearly all the goods, and the rest have what little remains. It is claimed with some plausibility that the second distribution is unfair, and the first fair. But it might also be claimed that impartiality and formal justice alone will not establish that we ought to distribute the goods equally.

There are two reasons which might be given for this second claim, the first of them a bad one, the other more cogent. The bad reason rests on an underestimate of the powers of golden-rule arguments. It is objected, for example, that people with white skins, if they claimed privileges in distributing purely on the ground of skin-colour, would not be offending against the formal principle of impartiality or universalizability, because no individual reference need enter into the principle to which they are appealing. Thus the principle that blacks ought to be subservient to whites is impartial as between *individuals;* any individual whatever who has the bad luck to find himself with a black skin or the good luck to find himself with a white skin is impartially placed by the principle in the appropriate social rank. This move receives a brief answer in my *Freedom and Reason,*[17] and a much fuller one in a forthcoming paper.[18] If the whites are faced with the decision, not merely of whether to frame this principle, but of whether to prescribe its adoption universally in all cases, including hypothetical ones in which their own skins turn black, they will at once reject it.

The other, more cogent-sounding argument is often used as an argument against utilitarians by those who think that justice has a lot to do with equality. It could also, at first sight, be used as an argument against the adequacy of formal justice or impartiality as a basis for distributive justice. That the argument could be leveled against both these methods is no accident; as I have tried to

show elsewhere,[19] utilitarianism of a certain sort is the embodiment of—the method of moral reasoning which fulfills in practice—the requirement of universalizability or formal justice. Having shown that neither of these methods can produce a direct justification for equal distribution, I shall then show that both can produce indirect justifications, which depend, not on a priori reasoning alone, but on likely assumptions about what the world and the people in it are like.

The argument is this. Formal impartiality only requires us to treat everybody's interest as of equal weight. Imagine, then, a situation in which utilities are equally distributed. (There is a complication here which we can for the moment avoid by choosing a suitable example. Shortly I shall be mentioning the so-called principle of diminishing marginal utility, and shall indeed be making important use of it. But for now let us take a case in which it does not operate, so that we can, for ease of illustration, treat money as a linear measure of utility.) Suppose that we can vary the equal distribution that we started with by taking a dollar each away from everybody in the town, and that the loss of purchasing power is so small that they hardly notice it, and therefore the utility enjoyed by each is not much diminished. However, when we give the resulting large sum to one man, he is able to buy himself a holiday in Acapulco, which gives him so much pleasure that his access of utility is equal to the sum of the small losses suffered by all the others. Many would say that this redistribution was unfair. But we were, in the required sense, being impartial between the equal interests of all the parties; we were treating an equal access or loss of utility to any part as of equal value or disvalue. For, on our suppositions, the taking away of a dollar from one of the unfortunate parties deprived him of just as much utility as the addition of that dollar gave to the fortunate one. But if we are completely impartial, we have to regard *who has* that dollar or that access of utility as irrelevant. So there will be nothing to choose, from an impartial point of view, between our original equal distribution and our later highly unequal one, in which everybody else is deprived of a dollar in order to give one person a holiday in Acapulco. And that is why people say that formal impartiality alone is not enough to secure social justice, nor even to secure impartiality itself in some more substantial sense.

What is needed, in the opinion of these people, is some principle which says that it is unjust to give a person more when he already has more than the others—some sort of egalitarian principle. Egalitarian principles are only one possible kind of principles of distributive justice; and it is so far an open question whether they are to be preferred to alternative inegalitarian principles. It is fairly clear as a matter of history that different principles of justice have been accepted in different societies. As Aristotle says, "everybody agrees that the just distribution is one in accordance with desert of some kind; but they do not call desert the same thing, but the democrats say it is being a free citizen, the oligarchs being rich, others good lineage, and the aristocrats virtue."[20] It is not difficult to think of some societies in which it would be thought unjust for one man to have privileges not possessed by all men, and of others in which it would be thought unjust for a slave to have privileges which a free man would take for granted, or for a commoner to have sort of house which a nobleman could aspire to. Even Aristotle's democrats did not think that slaves, but only citizens, had equal rights; and Plato complains of democracy that it "bestows equality of a sort on equals and unequals alike."[21] We have to ask, therefore, whether there are any reasons for preferring one of these attitudes to another.

At this point some philosophers will be ready to step in with their intuitions, and tell us that some distributions or ways of achieving distributions are *obviously* more just than others, or that *everyone will agree on reflection* that they are. These philosophers appeal to our intuitions or prejudices in support of the most widely divergent methods or patterns of distribution. But this is a way of arguing which should be abjured by anybody who wishes to have rational grounds for his moral judgments. Intuitions prove nothing; general consensus proves nothing; both have been used to support conclusions which *our* intuitions and our consensus may well find outrageous. We want arguments, and in this field seldom get them.

However, it is too early to despair of finding some. The utilitarian, and the formalist like me, still have some moves to make. I am supposing that we have already made the major move suggested above, and have ruled out discrimination on grounds of skin colour and the like, in so far as such discrimination could not be accepted by all for cases where they were the ones discriminated against. I am supposing that our society has absorbed this move, and contains no racists, sexists or in general discriminators, but does still contain economic men who do not think it wrong, in pursuit of Nozickian economic liberty, to get what they can, even if the resulting distribution is grotesquely unequal. Has the egalitarian any moves to make against them, and are they moves which can be supported by appeal to formal justice, in conjunction with the empirical facts?

Two Arguments for Equal Distribution

He has two. The first is based on that good old prop of egalitarian policies, the diminishing marginal utility, within the ranges that matter, of money and of nearly all goods. Almost always, if money or goods are taken away from someone who has a lot of them already, and given to someone who has little, total utility is increased, other things being equal. As we shall see, they hardly ever are equal; but the principle is all right. Its ground is that the poor man will get more utility out of what he is given than the rich man from whom it is taken would have got. A millionaire minds less about the gain or loss of a dollar than I do, and I than a pauper.

It must be noted that this is not an *a priori* principle. It is an empirical fact (if it is) that people are so disposed. The most important thing I have to say in this paper is that when we are, as we now are, trying to establish *prima facie* principles of distributive justice, it is enough if they can be justified in the world as it actually is, among people as they actually are. It is a wholly illegitimate argument against formalists or utilitarians that states of society or of the people in it could be *conceived of* in which gross inequalities could be justified by formal or utilitarian arguments. We are seeking principles for practical use in the world as it is. The same applies when we ask what qualifications are required to the principles.

Diminishing marginal utility is the firmest support for policies of progressive taxation of the rich and other egalitarian measures. However, as I said above, other things are seldom equal, and there are severe empirical, practical restraints on the equality that can sensibly be imposed by governments. To mention just a few of these hackneyed other things: the removal of incentives to effort may diminish the total stock of goods to be divided up; abrupt confiscation or even very steep progressive taxation may antagonize the victims so much that a whole class turns from a useful element in society to a hostile and dangerous one; or, even if that does not happen, it may merely become demoralized and either lose all enterprise and readiness to take business risks, or else just emigrate if it can. Perhaps one main cause of what is called the English sickness is the alienation of the middle class. It is an empirical question, just when egalitarian measures get to the stage of having these effects; and serious political argument on this subject should concentrate on such empirical questions, instead of indulging in the rhetoric of equal (or for that matter of unequal) rights. Rights are the offspring of *prima facie*, intuitive principles, and I have nothing against them; but the question is, What *prima facie* principles ought we to adopt? What intuitions ought we to have? On these questions the rhetoric of rights sheds no light

whatever, any more than do appeals to intuition (i.e. to prejudice, i.e. to the *prima facie* principles, good or bad, which our upbringings happen to have implanted in us). The worth of intuitions is to be known by their fruits; as in the case of the principles to be followed by judges in administering the law, the best principles are those with the highest acceptance-utility, i.e. those whose general acceptance maximizes the furtherance of the interests, in sum, of all the affected parties, treating all those interests as of equal weight, i.e. impartially, i.e. with formal justice.

We have seen that, given the empirical assumption of diminishing marginal utility, such a method provides a justification for moderately egalitarian policies. The justification is strengthened by a second move that the egalitarian can make. This is to point out that inequality itself has a tendency to produce envy, which is a disagreeable state of mind and leads people to do disagreeable things. It makes no difference to the argument whether the envy is a good or a bad quality, nor whether it is justified or unjustified— any more than it makes a difference whether the alienation of the middle class which I mentioned above is to be condemned or excused. These states of minds are facts, and moral judgments have to be made in the light of the facts as they are. We have to take account of the actual state of the world and of the people in it. We can very easily think of societies which are highly unequal, but in which the more fortunate members have contrived to find some real or metaphorical opium of some Platonic noble lie[22] to keep the people quiet, so that the people feel no envy of privileges which we should consider outrageous. Imagine, for example, a society consisting of happy slave-owners and of happy slaves, all of whom know their places and do not have ideas above their station. Since there is *ex hypothesi* no envy, this source of disutility does not exist, and the whole argument from envy collapses.

It is salutary to remember this. It may make us stop looking for purely formal, *a priori* reasons for demanding equality, and look instead at the actual conditions which obtain in particular societies. To make the investigation more concrete, albeit oversimplified, let us ask what would have to be the case before we ought to be ready to push this happy slaveowning society into a revolution—peaceful or violent—which would turn the slaves into free and moderately equal wage-earners. I shall be able only to sketch my answer to this question, without doing nearly enough to justify it.

Arguments For and Against Egalitarian Revolutions

First of all, as with all moral questions, we should have to ask what would be the actual consequences of what we were doing—which is the same as to ask what we should be *doing*, so that accusations of "consequentialism"[23] need not be taken very seriously. Suppose, to simplify matters outrageously, that we can actually predict the consequences of the revolution and what will happen during its course. We can then consider two societies (one actual and one possible) and a possible process of transition from one to the other. And we have to ask whether the transition from one to the other will, all in all, promote the interest of all those affected more than to stay as they are, or rather, to develop as they would develop if the revolution did not occur. The question can be divided into questions about the process of transition and questions about the relative merits of the actual society (including its probably subsequent "natural" development) and the possible society which would be produced by the revolution.

We have supposed that the slaves in the existing society feel no envy, and that therefore the disutility of envy cannot be used as an argument for change. If there *were* envy, as in actual cases is probable, this argument *could* be employed; but let us see what can be done without it. We have the fact that there is gross inequality in the actual society and much greater equality in the possible one. The principle of diminishing marginal utility

will therefore support the change, provided that its effects are not outweighed by a reduction in total utility resulting from the change and the way it comes about. But we have to be sure that this condition is fulfilled. Suppose, for example, that the actual society is a happy bucolic one and is likely to remain so, but that the transition to the possible society initiates the growth of an industrial economy in which everybody has to engage in a rat-race and is far less happy. We might in that case pronounce the actual society better. In general it is not self-evident that the access of what is called wealth makes people happier, although they nearly always think that it will.

Let us suppose, however, that we are satisfied that the people in the possible society will be better off all round than in the actual. There is also the point that there will be more generations to enjoy the new regime than suffer in the transition from the old. At least, this is what revolutionaries often say; and we have set them at liberty to say it by assuming contrary to what is likely to be the case, that the future state of society is predictable. In actual fact, revolutions usually produce states of society very different from, and in most cases worse than, what their authors expected—which does not always stop them being better than what went before, once things have settled down. However, let us waive these difficulties and suppose that the future state of society can be predicted, and that it is markedly better than the existing state, because a greater equality of distribution has, owing to diminishing marginal utility, resulted in greater total utility.

Let us also suppose that the more enterprising economic structure which results leads to increased production without causing a rat-race. There will then be more wealth to go round and the revolution will have additional justification. Other benefits of the same general kind may also be adduced; and what is perhaps the greatest benefit of all, namely liberty itself. That people like having this is an empirical fact; it may not be a fact universally, but it is at least *likely* that by freeing slaves we shall *pro tanto* promote their interests. Philosophers who ask for *a priori* arguments for liberty or equality often talk as if empirical facts like this were totally irrelevant to the question. Genuine egalitarians and liberals ought to abjure the aid of these philosophers, because they have taken away the main ground for such views, namely the fact that people are as they are.

The arguments so far adduced support the call for a revolution. They will have to be balanced against the disutilities which will probably be caused by the process of transition. If heads roll, that is contrary to the interests of their owners; and no doubt the economy will be disrupted at least temporarily, and the new rulers, whoever they are, may infringe liberty just as much as the old, and possibly in an even more arbitrary manner. Few revolutions are pleasant while they are going on. But if the revolution can be more or less smooth or even peaceful, it may well be that (given the arguments already adduced about the desirability of the future society thereby achieved) revolution can have a utilitarian justification, and therefore a justification on grounds of formal impartiality between people's interests. But it is likely to be better for all if the same changes can be achieved less abruptly by an evolutionary process, and those who try to persuade us that this is not so are often merely giving way to impatience and showing a curious indifference to the interests of those for whom they purport to be concerned.

The argument in favour of change from a slave-owning society to a wage-earning one has been extremely superficial, and has served only to illustrate the lines on which a utilitarian or a formalist might argue. If we considered instead the transition from a capitalist society to a socialist one, the same forms of argument would have to be employed, but might not yield the same result. Even if the introduction of a fully socialist economy would promote greater equality, or more equal liberties (and I can see no reason for supposing this, but rather the reverse; for socialism tends to produce very great inequalities of *power*), it needs to be argued what

the consequences would be, and then an assessment has to be made of the relative benefits and harms accruing from leaving matters alone and from having various sorts of bloody or bloodless change. Here again the rhetoric of rights will provide nothing but inflammatory material for agitators on both sides. It is designed to lead to, not to resolve, conflicts.

Remarks About Methods

But we must now leave this argument and attend to a methodological point which has become pressing. We have not, in the last few pages, been arguing about what state of society would be just, but about what state of society would best promote the interests of its members. All the arguments have been utilitarian. Where then does justice come in? It is likely to come into the propaganda of revolutionaries, as I have already hinted. But so far as I can see it has no direct bearing on the question of what would be the better society. It has, however, an important indirect bearing which I shall now try to explain. Our *prima facie* moral principles and intuitions are, as I have already said, the products of our upbringings; and it is a very important question *what* principles and intuitions it is best to bring up people to have. I have been arguing on the assumption that this question is to be decided by looking at the consequences for society, and the effects on the interests of people in society, of inculcating different principles. We are looking for the set of principles with the highest acceptance-utility.

Will these include principles of justice? The answer is obviously "Yes," if we think that society and the people in it are better off with *some* principles of justice than without any. A "land without justice" (to use the title of Milovan Djilas' book)[24] is almost bound to be an unhappy one. But what are the principles to be? Are we, for example, to inculcate the principle that it is just for people to perform the duties of their station and not envy those of higher social rank? Or the principle that all inequalities of any sort are unjust and ought to be removed? For my part, I would think that neither of these principles has a very high acceptance-utility. It may be that the principle with the highest acceptance-utility is one which makes just reward vary (but not immoderately) with desert, and assesses desert according to service to the interests of one's fellow-men. It would have to be supplemented by a principle securing equality of opportunity. But it is a partly empirical question what principles would have the highest acceptance-utility, and in any case beyond the scope of this paper. If some such principle is adopted and inculcated, people will *call* breaches of it unjust. Will they *be* unjust? Only in the sense that they will be contrary to a *prima facie* principle of distributive justice which we ought to adopt (not because it is itself a just principle, but because it is the best principle). The only sense that can be given to the question of whether it is a just principle (apart from the purely circular or tautological question of whether the principle obeys itself), is by asking whether the procedure by which we have selected the principle satisfies the logical requirements of critical moral thinking, i.e. is *formally* just. We might add that the adoption of such a formally just procedure and of the principles it selects is just in the *generic* sense mentioned at the beginning of this paper: it is the right thing to do; we morally ought to do it. The reason is that critical thinking, because it follows the requirements of formal justice based on the logical properties of the moral concepts, especially "ought" and "right," can therefore not fail, if pursued correctly in the light of the empirical facts, to lead to principles of justice which are in accord with morality. But because the requirements are all formal, they do not by themselves determine the content of the principles of justice. We have to do the thinking.

What principles of justice are best to try to inculcate will depend on the circumstances of particular societies, and especially on psychological facts about their members. One of these facts is their readiness to accept the principles themselves. There might be a principle of justice

which it would be highly desirable to inculcate, but which we have no chance of successfully inculcating. The best principles for a society to *have* are, as I said, those with the highest acceptance-utility. But the best principles to *try to inculcate* will not necessarily be these, if these are impossible to inculcate. Imagine that in our happy slave-society both slaves and slave-owners are obstinately conservative and know their places, and that the attempt to get the slaves to have revolutionary or egalitarian thoughts will result only in a very few of them becoming discontented, and probably going to the gallows as a result, and the vast majority merely becoming unsettled and therefore more unhappy. Then we ought not to try to inculcate such an egalitarian principle. On the other hand, if, as is much more likely, the principle stood a good chance of catching on, and the revolution was likely to be as advantageous as we have supposed, then we ought. The difference lies in the dispositions of the inhabitants. I am not saying that the probability of being accepted is the same thing as acceptance-utility; only that the rationality of trying to inculcate a principle (like the rationality of trying to do anything else) varies with the likelihood of success. In this sense the advisability of trying to inculcate principles of justice (though not their merit) is relative to these states of mind of those who, it is hoped, will hold them.

It is important to be clear about the extent to which what I am advocating is a kind of relativism. It is certainly not relativistic in any strong sense. Relativism is the doctrine that the truth of some moral statement depends on whether people accept it. A typical example would be the thesis that if in a certain society people think that they ought to get their male children circumcised, then they ought to get them circumcised, full stop. Needless to say, I am not supporting any such doctrine, which is usually the result of confusion, and against which there are well-known arguments. It is, however, nearly always the case that among the facts relevant to a moral decision are facts about people's thoughts or dispositions. For example, if I am wondering whether I ought to take my wife for a holiday in Acapulco, it is relevant to ask whether she would like it. What I have been saying is to be assimilated to this last example. If we take as given certain dispositions in the members of society (namely dispositions not to accept a certain principle of justice however hard we work at propagating it) then we have to decide whether, in the light of these facts, we ought to propagate it. What principles of justice we ought to propagate will vary with the probable effects of propagating them. The answer to this "ought"-question is not relative to what we, who are asking it, think about the matter; it is to be arrived at by moral thought on the basis of the facts of the situation. But among these facts are facts about the dispositions of people in the society in question.

The moral I wish to draw from the whole argument is that ethical reasoning *can* provide us with a way of conducting political arguments about justice and rights rationally and with hope of agreement; that such rational arguments have to rest on an understanding of the concepts being used, *and* of the facts of our actual situation. They key question is "What principles of justice, what attitudes towards the distribution of goods, what ascriptions of rights, are such that their acceptance is in the general interest?" I advocate the asking of this question as a substitute for one which is much more commonly asked, namely "What rights do I have?" For people who ask this latter question will, being human, nearly always answer that they have just those rights, whatever they are, which will promote a distribution of goods which is in the interest of their own social group. The rhetoric of rights, which is engendered by this question, is a recipe for class war, and civil war. In pursuit of these rights, people will, because they have convinced themselves that justice demands it, inflict almost any harms on the rest of society and on themselves. To live at peace, we need principles such as critical thinking can provide, based on

formal justice and on the facts of the actual world in which we have to live. It is possible for all to practise this critical thinking in cooperation, if only they would learn how; for all share the same moral concepts with the same logic, if they could understand them and follow it.

NOTES

1. See my "Ethical Theory and Utilitarianism" (*ETU*), in *Contemporary British Philosophy* 4, ed. H. D. Lewis (London, 1976).

2. See, e.g., my "Principles," *Ar. Soc.* 72 (1972/3), "Rules of War and Moral Reasoning," *Ph. and Pub. Aff.* 1 (1972) and *ETU*.

3. Rawls, J., *A Theory of Justice* (Cambridge, Mass., 1971), p. 130.

4. Richards, D. A. J., *A Theory of Reasons for Action* (Oxford, 1971).

5. See my *Freedom and Reason,* pt. II (Oxford, 1963) and *ETU*.

6. *Nicomachean Ethics,* bk. V.

7. ib. 1130 b 31, 1131 b 25.

8. ib. 1130 a 8.

9. Theognis 147; also attr. to Phocylides by Aristotle, ib. 1129 b 27.

10. The earliest version of this tag is attr. by the *Oxford Dictionary of Quotations* to the Emperor Ferdinand I (1503–64).

11. ib. 1137 b 8.

12. ib. 1130 a 14 ff.

13. *A Theory of Justice,* p. 136.

14. Pp. 115–7, 124.

15. *Ph Q.* 23 (1973), repr. in *Reading Rawls,* ed. N. Daniels (Oxford, 1975).

16. Nozick, R. D., *Anarchy, State and Utopia* (New York, 1974).

17. Pp. 106f.

18. "Relevance," in a volume in *Values and Morals,* eds. A Goldman and J. Kim (Reidel, 1978).

19. See note 2 above.

20. ib. 1131 a 25.

21. *Republic* 558 c.

22. ib. 414 b.

23. See, e.g., Anscombe, G. E. M., "Modern Moral Philosophy," *Philosophy* 33 (1958), and Williams, B. A. O., in Smart, J. J. C., and Williams, B. A. O., *Utilitarianism: For and Against* (Cambridge, Eng., 1973), p. 82.

24. Djilas, M., *Land without Justice* (London, 1958).

16 Utilitarianism and the Distinction Between Persons

JOHN RAWLS

THERE ARE MANY FORMS of utilitarianism, and the development of the theory has continued in recent years. I shall not survey these forms here, nor take account of the numerous refinements found in contemporary discussions. My aim is to work out a theory of justice that represents an alternative to utilitarian thought generally and so to all of these different versions of it. I believe that the contrast between the contract view and utilitarianism remains essentially the same in all these cases. Therefore I shall compare justice as fairness with familiar variants of intuitionism, perfectionism, and utilitarianism in order to bring out the underlying differences in the simplest way. With this end in mind, the kind of utilitarianism I shall describe here is the strict classical doctrine which receives perhaps its clearest and most accessible formulation in Sidgwick. The main idea is that society is rightly ordered, and therefore just, when its major institutions are arranged so as to achieve the greatest net balance of satisfaction summed over all the individuals belonging to it.[1]

We may note first that there is, indeed, a way of thinking of society which makes it easy to suppose that the most rational conception of justice is utilitarian. For consider: each man in realizing his own interests is certainly free to balance his own losses against his own gains. We may impose a sacrifice on ourselves now for the sake of a greater advantage later. A person quite properly acts, at least when others are not affected, to achieve his own greatest good, to advance his rational ends as far as possible. Now why should not a society act on precisely the same principle applied to the group and therefore regard that which is rational for one man as right for an association of men? Just as the well-being of a person is constructed from the series of satisfactions that are experienced at different moments in the course of his life, so in very much the same way the well-being of society is to be constructed from the fulfillment of the systems of desires of the many individuals who belong to it. Since the principle for an individual is to advance as far as possible his own welfare, his own system of desires, the principle for society is to advance as far as possible the welfare of the group, to realize to the greatest extent the comprehensive system of desire arrived at from the desires of its members. Just as an individual balances present and future gains against present and future losses, so a society may balance satisfactions and dissatisfactions among different individuals. And so by these reflections one reaches the principle of utility in a natural way: a society is properly arranged when its institutions maximize the net balance of satisfaction. The principle of choice for an association of men is interpreted as an extension of the principle of choice for one man. Social justice is the principle of rational prudence applied to an aggregative conception of the welfare of the group.[2] . . .

This idea is made all the more attractive by a further consideration. The two main concepts of ethics are those of the right and the good; the concept of a morally worthy person is, I believe, derived from them. The structure of an ethical theory is, then, largely determined by how it defines and connects these two basic notions. Now it seems that the simplest way of relating them is taken by teleological theories: the good is defined independently from the right, and then the right is defined as that which maximizes the good.[3] More precisely, those institutions and acts are right which, of the available alternatives, produce the most good, or at least as much good as any of the other institutions and acts open as real possibilities (a rider needed when the maximal class is not a singleton). Teleological theories have a deep intuitive appeal since they seem to embody the idea of rationality. It is natural to think that rationality is maximizing something and that in morals it must be maximizing the good. Indeed, it is tempting to suppose that it is self-evident that things should be arranged so as to lead to the most good.

It is essential to keep in mind that in a teleological theory the good is defined independently from the right. This means two things. First, the theory accounts for our considered judgments as to which things are good (our judgments of value) as a separate class of judgments intuitively distinguishable by common sense, and then proposes the hypothesis that the right is maximizing the good as already specified. Second, the theory enables one to judge the goodness of things without referring to what is right. For example, if pleasure is said to be the sole good, then presumably pleasures can be recognized and ranked in value by criteria that do not presuppose any standards of right, or what we would normally think of as such. Whereas if the distributions of goods is also counted as a good, perhaps a higher order one, and the theory

directs us to produce the most good (including the good of distribution among others), we no longer have a teleological view in the classical sense. The problem of distribution falls under the concept of right as one intuitively understands it, and so the theory lacks an independent definition of the good. The clarity and simplicity of classical teleological theories derive largely from the fact that they factor our moral judgments into two classes, the one being characterized separately while the other is then connected with it by a maximizing principle.

Teleological doctrines differ, pretty clearly, according to how the conception of the good is specified. If it is taken as the realization of human excellence in the various forms of culture, we have what may be called perfectionism. This notion is found in Aristotle and Nietzsche, among others. If the good is defined as pleasure, we have hedonism; if as happiness, eudaimonism, and so on. I shall understand the principle of utility in its classical form as defining the good as the satisfaction of desire, or perhaps better, as the satisfaction of rational desire. This accords with the view in all essentials and provides, I believe, a fair interpretation of it. The appropriate terms of social cooperation are settled by whatever in the circumstances will achieve the greatest sum of satisfaction of the rational desires of individuals. It is impossible to deny the initial plausibility and attractiveness of this conception.

The striking feature of the utilitarian view of justice is that it does not matter, except indirectly, how this sum of satisfactions is distributed among individuals any more than it matters, except indirectly, how one man distributes his satisfactions over time. The correct distribution in either case is that which yields the maximum fulfillment. Society must allocate its means of satisfaction whatever these are, rights and duties, opportunities and privileges, and various forms of wealth, so as to achieve this maximum if it can. But in itself no distribution of satisfaction is better than another except that the more equal distribution is to be preferred to break ties.[4] It is true that certain common sense precepts of justice, particularly those which concern the protection of liberties and rights, or which express the claims of desert, seem to contradict this contention. But from a utilitarian standpoint the explanation of these precepts and of their seemingly stringent character is that they are those precepts which experience shows should be strictly respected and departed from only under exceptional circumstances if the sum of advantages is to be maximized.[5] Yet, as with all other precepts, those of justice are derivative from the one end of attaining the greatest balance of satisfaction. Thus there is no reason in principle why the greater gains of some should not compensate for the lesser losses of others; or more importantly, why the violation of the liberty of a few might not be made right by the greater good shared by many. It simply happens that under most conditions, at least in a reasonably advanced stage of civilization, the greatest sum of advantages is not attained in this way. No doubt the strictness of common sense precepts of justice has a certain usefulness in limiting men's propensities to injustice and to socially injurious actions, but the utilitarian believes that to affirm this strictness as a first principle of morals is a mistake. For just as it is rational for one man to maximize the fulfillment of his system of desires, it is right for a society to maximize the net balance of satisfaction taken over all of its members.

The most natural way, then, of arriving at utilitarianism (although not, of course, the only way of doing so) is to adopt for society as a whole the principle of rational choice for one man. Once this is recognized, the place of the impartial spectator and the emphasis on sympathy in the history of utilitarian thought is readily understood. For it is by the conception of the impartial spectator and the use of sympathetic identification in guiding our imagination that the principle for one man is applied to society. It is this spectator who is conceived as carrying out the required organization of the desires of all persons into one coherent system of desire; it is

by this construction that many persons are fused into one. Endowed with ideal powers of sympathy and imagination, the impartial spectator is the perfectly rational individual who identifies with and experiences the desires of others as if these desires were his own. In this way, he ascertains the intensity of these desires and assigns them their appropriate weight in the one system of desire the satisfaction of which the ideal legislator then tries to maximize by adjusting the rules of the social system. On this conception of society separate individuals are thought of as so many different lines along which rights and duties are to be assigned and scarce means of satisfaction allocated in accordance with rules so as to give the greatest fulfillment of wants. The nature of the decision made by the ideal legislator is not, therefore, materially different from that of an entrepreneur deciding how to maximize his profit by producing this or that commodity, or that of a consumer deciding how to maximize his satisfaction by the purchase of this or that collection of goods. In each case there is a single person whose system of desires determines the best allocation of limited means. The correct decision is essentially a question of efficient administration. This view of social cooperation is the consequence of extending to society the principle of choice for one man, and then, to make this extension work, conflating all persons into one through the imaginative acts of the impartial sympathetic spectator. Utilitarianism does not take seriously the distinction between persons.

NOTES

1. I shall take Henry Sidgwick's *The Methods of Ethics,* 7th ed. (London, 1907), as summarizing the development of utilitarian moral theory. Book III of his *Principles of Political Economy* (London, 1883) applies this doctrine to questions of economic and social justice, and is a precursor of A. C. Pigou, *The Economics of Welfare* (London, Macmillan, 1920). Sidgwick's *Outlines of the History of Ethics,* 5th ed. (London, 1902), contains a brief history of the utilitarian tradition. We may follow him in assuming,

somewhat arbitrarily, that it begins with Shaftesbury's *An Inquiry Concerning Virtue and Merit* (1911) and Hutcheson's *An Inquiry Concerning Moral Good and Evil* (1725). Hutcheson seems to have been the first to state clearly the principle of utility. He says in *Inquiry*, sec. III, §8, that "that action is best, which procures the greatest happiness for the greatest numbers; and that, worst, which, in like manner, occasions misery." Other major eighteenth-century works are Hume's *A Treatise of Human Nature* (1739), and *An Enquiry Concerning the Principles of Morals* (1751); Adam Smith's *A Theory of the Moral Sentiments* (1759); and Bentham's *The Principles of Morals and Legislation* (1789). To these we must add the writings of J. S. Mill represented by *Utilitarianism* (1863) and F. Y. Edgeworth's *Mathematical Psychics* (London, 1888).

The discussion of utilitarianism has taken a different turn in recent years by focusing on what we may call the coordination problem and related questions of publicity. This development stems from the essays of R. F. Harrod, "Utilitarianism Revised," *Mind*, vol. 45 (1936); J. D. Mabbott, "Punishment," *Mind*, vol. 48 (1939); Jonathan Harrison, "Utilitarianism, Univeralisation, and Our Duty to be Just," *Proceedings of the Aristotelian Society*, vol. 53 (1952–53); and J. O. Urmson, "The Interpretation of the Philosophy of J. S. Mill," *Philosophical Quarterly*, vol. 3 (1953). See also J. J. C. Smart, "Extreme and Restricted Utilitarianism," *Philosophical Quarterly*, vol. 6 (1956), and his *An Outline of a System of Utilitarian Ethics* (Cambridge, The University Press, 1961). For an account of these matters, see David Lyons, *Forms and Limits of Utilitarianism* (Oxford, The Clarendon Press, 1965); and Allan Gibbard, "Utilitarianisms and Coordination" (dissertation, Harvard University, 1971). The problems raised by these works, as important as

they are, I shall leave aside as not bearing directly on the more elementary question of distribution which I wish to discuss.

Finally, we should note here the essay of J. C. Harsanyi, in particular, "Cardinal Utility in Welfare Economics and in the Theory of Risk-Taking," *Journal of Political Economy*, 1953, and "Cardinal Welfare, Individualistic Ethics, and Interpersonal Comparisons of Utility," *Journal of Political Economy*, 1955; and R. B. Brandt, "Some Merits of One Form of Rule—Utilitarianism," *University of Colorado Studies* (Boulder, Colorado, 1967). . . .

2. On this point see also D. P. Gauthier, *Practical Reasoning* (Oxford, Clarendon Press, 1963), pp. 126f. The text elaborates the suggestion found in "Constitutional Liberty and the Concept of Justice," *Nomos VI: Justice*, ed. C. J. Friedrich and J. W. Chapman (New York, Atherton Press, 1963), pp. 124f, which in turn is related to the idea of justice as a higher-order administrative decision. See "Justice as Fairness," *Philosophical Review*, 1958, pp. 185–187. . . . That the principle of social integration is distinct from the principle of personal integration is stated by R. B. Perry, *General Theory of Value* (New York, Longmans, Green, and Company, 1926), pp. 674–677. He attributes the error of overlooking this fact to Emile Durkheim and others with similar views. Perry's conception of social integration is that brought about by a shared and dominant benevolent purpose. . . .

3. Here I adopt W. K. Frankena's definition of teleological theories in *Ethics* (Englewood Cliffs, N.J., Prentice Hall, Inc., 1963), p. 13.

4. On this point see Sidgwick, *The Methods of Ethics*, pp. 416f.

5. See J. S. Mill, *Utilitarianism*, ch. V, last two parts.

17   The Rule of Law and Democracy

JÜRGEN HABERMAS

Iɴ ᴀᴄᴀᴅᴇᴍɪᴀ ᴡᴇ ᴏꜰᴛᴇɴ ᴍᴇɴᴛɪᴏɴ law and politics in the same breath, yet at the same time we are accustomed to consider law, including the rule of law, and democracy as subjects of different disciplines: jurisprudence deals with law, political science with democracy, and each deals with the constitutional state in its own way, one side in normative terms, the other from an empirical perspective. Even when legal scholars and social scientists refer from their different standpoints to the same objects, they treat law and the rule of law and, on the other hand, democracy as different matters. There are good reasons for this. Because political authority is, in whatever kind of regime, always exercised in forms of law, there exist legal orders where political force has not yet been domesticated by the rule of law. And there may again exist a rule of law, where the government has not yet been democratized. In short, there are legal systems without a rule of law, and a rule of law may exist without democratic forms of political will-formation. Both come together only within the frame of constitutional states. However, these *empirical* grounds for a division of labour in the analysis of the two subjects by no means implies that, from the *normative* standpoint of legal philosophy, the rule of law could be implemented without democracy. In this paper I want to treat several aspects of this internal relationship between the rule of law and democracy, which is essential for any constitutional state.

This relation results from the concept of modern law itself (section 1) as well as from the fact that positive law can no longer draw its legitimacy from a higher law (section 2). Modern law is legitimated by the autonomy guaranteed equally to each citizen, and legitimated in such a way that private and public autonomy reciprocally presuppose each other (section 3). This conceptual interrelation also makes itself felt in the dialectic of legal and factual equality. It was this dialectic that first elicited the social welfare paradigm of law as a response to the liberal understanding of law, and today this same dialectic necessitates a proceduralist self-understanding of constitutional democracy (section 4). In closing I will elucidate this proceduralist legal paradigm with the example provided by the feminist politics of equality (section 5).

1. Formal Properties of Modern Law

Since Locke, Rousseau, and Kant, a certain concept of law has gradually prevailed not only in philosophical thought but in the constitutional reality of Western societies. This concept is supposed to account simultaneously for both the positivity and the freedom-guaranteeing character of coercive law. The positivity of law, the fact that norms backed by the threat of state sanction stem from the changeable decisions of a political legislator, is bound up with the demand

From European Journal of Philosophy *3:1, pp. 12–20. Copyright © 1995 Basil Blackwell Ltd. Reprinted by permission.*

for legitimation. According to this demand, positively enacted law should equally guarantee the autonomy of all legal persons; and the democratic procedure of legislation should in turn satisfy this demand. In this way, an internal relation is established between, on the one hand, the coercibility and changeability of positive law and, on the other, a mode of law-making that engenders legitimacy. Hence, from a normative perspective there is a conceptual relation—and not simply an historically accidental relation—between law and democracy, between legal and democratic theory.

At first glance, this has the look of a philosophical trick. Yet, as a matter of fact, this internal relation is deeply rooted in the presuppositions of our everyday practice of law. For in the mode of validity that attaches to law, the facticity of the state's legal enforcement is intermeshed with the legitimating force of a legislative procedure that claims to be rational because it guarantees freedom. This is shown in the peculiar ambivalence with which the law presents itself to its addressees and expects their obedience: that is, it leaves its addressees free to approach the law in either of two ways. They can either consider norms merely as factual constraints on their freedom and take a strategic approach to the calculable consequences of possible rule-violations, or they can comply with legal statutes in a performative attitude, indeed comply out of respect for results of a common will-formation that claim legitimacy. Kant already expressed this point with his specific concept of 'legality', which highlighted the connection between these two moments without which legal obedience cannot reasonably be expected: legal norms must be so fashioned that they can be viewed simultaneously in two different ways, as coercive laws and as laws of freedom. These two aspects belong to our understanding of modern law; we consider the validity of a legal norm as equivalent to the explanation that the state can simultaneously guarantee factual enforcement and legitimate enactment—and thus

it can guarantee, on the one hand, the legality of behaviour in the sense of average compliance, which can if necessary be compelled by sanctions; and, on the other hand, the legitimacy of the rule itself, which should always make it possible to comply with the norm out of reasonable respect for the law.

Of course, this immediately raises the question of how the legitimacy of rules should be grounded when the rules in questions can be changed at any time by the political legislator. Constitutional norms too are changeable; and even the basic norms that the Constitution itself has declared non-amendable share, along with all positive law, the fate that they can be abrogated, say, after a change of regime. As long as one was able to fall back on a religiously or metaphysically grounded natural law, the whirlpool of temporality enveloping positive law could be held in check by morality. Situated in a hierarchy of law, temporalized positive law was supposed to remain *subordinate* to an eternally valid moral law and therefrom receive its lasting orientations. But even aside from the fact that in pluralistic societies such integrating worldviews and collectively binding comprehensive doctrines have disintegrated, modern law, simply by virtue of its formal properties, resists the direct control of a post-traditional morality of conscience, which is so to speak, all we have left.

2. The Complementary Relation between Positive Law and Autonomous Morality

Modern legal systems are built out of individual rights. Such rights have the character of releasing legal persons from moral obligations in a carefully circumscribed manner. By introducing rights that concede to agents the latitude to act according to personal preferences, modern law as a whole implements the principle that whatever is not explicitly prohibited is permitted. Whereas in morality an inherent symmetry exists between rights and duties, legal duties are a consequence of entitlements, that is, they result only from statutory constraints of individual liberties. This basic conceptual privileging of rights over duties is explained by the modern concepts of the 'legal person' and the 'legal community'. The moral universe, which is *unlimited* in social space and historical time, includes *all natural* persons in their life-historical complexity; morality itself extends protection to the integrity of fully individuated persons (*Einzelner*). By contrast, the legal community, which is always localized in space and time, protects the integrity of its members precisely insofar as they acquire the artificial status of *rights-bearers*. For this reason, the relation between law and morality is more one of complementarity than of subordination.

The same is true if one compares their relative scope. The matters that require legal regulation are at once narrower and broader in scope than morally relevant concerns: they are narrower in scope inasmuch as legal regulation has access only to external, that is, coercible, behavior; they are broader in scope inasmuch as law, as an organizational form of politics, pertains not only to the regulation of interpersonal conflicts but also to the pursuit of political goals and the implementation of policies. Hence, legal regulations touch not only on moral questions in the narrow sense, but also on pragmatic and ethical questions, and on compromise formation among conflicting interests. Moreover, unlike the clearly delimited normative validity claimed by moral norms, the *legitimacy* claimed by legal norms is based on various sorts of reasons. The legislative practice of justification depends on a complex network of discourses and bargaining, and not just on moral discourse.

The natural law idea of a hierarchy of laws (*Rechten*) at different levels of dignity is misleading. Law is better understood as a functional complement to morality. As positively valid, legitimately enacted and adjudicated, that is action-able, law can relieve the morally judging and acting person of the considerable cognitive, mo-

tivational, and organization demands of morality based entirely on individual conscience. Law can compensate for the weaknesses of a highly demanding morality that—if we judge from its empirical results—provides only cognitively indeterminate and motivationally unreliable results. Naturally, this does not absolve legislators and judges from a concern that the law be in harmony with morality. But legal regulations are too concrete to be legitimated *solely* through their compatibility with moral principles. From what, then, can positive law borrow its legitimacy, if not from a superior moral law?

Like morality, law too is supposed to protect the autonomy of all persons equally. Law too must prove its legitimacy under this aspect of securing freedom. Interestingly enough, though, the positive character of law forces autonomy to split up in a peculiar way, which has no parallel in morality. Moral self-determination in Kant's sense is a unified concept insofar as it demands of each person, *in propria persona,* that she obey just those norms that she herself posits according to her own impartial judgment, or according to judgment reached in common with all other persons. However, the binding quality of legal norms does not stem solely from processes or opinion- and will-formation, but arises also from the collectively binding decisions of authorities who make and apply law. This circumstance makes it conceptually necessary to distinguish the role of authors who make (and adjudicate) law from the that of addressees who are subject to established law. The autonomy that in the moral domain is all of a piece, so to speak, appears in the legal domain only in the dual form of private and public autonomy.

However, these two moments must then be mediated in such a way that the one form of autonomy does not detract from the other. Each form of autonomy, the individual liberties of the subject of private law and the public autonomy of the citizen, makes the other form possible. This reciprocal relation is expressed by the idea that legal persons can be autonomous only insofar as they can understand themselves, in the exercise of their civil rights, as authors of just those rights which they are supposed to obey as addressees.

3. *The Mediation of Popular Sovereignty and Human Rights*

It is therefore not surprising that modern natural law theories have answered the legitimation question by referring, on the one hand, to the principle of *popular sovereignty* and, on the other, to the *rule of law* as guaranteed by human rights. The principle of popular sovereignty is expressed in rights of communications and participation that secure the public autonomy of citizens; the rule of law is expressed in those classical basic rights that guarantee the private autonomy of members of society. Thus the law is legitimated as an instrument for the equal protection of private and public autonomy. To be sure, political philosophy has never really been able to strike a balance between popular sovereignty and human rights, or between the 'freedom of the ancients' and the 'freedom of the moderns'. The political autonomy of citizens is supposed to be embodied in the self-organization of a community that gives itself its laws through the sovereign will of the people. The private autonomy of citizens, on the other hand, is supposed to take the form of basic rights that guarantee the anonymous rule of law. Once the issue is set up in this way, the one idea can be upheld only at the expense of the other. The intuitively plausible co-originality of both ideas falls by the wayside.

Republicanism, which goes back to Aristotle and the political humanism of the Renaissance, has always given the public autonomy of citizens priority over the pre-political liberties of private persons. *Liberalism,* which goes back to John Locke, has invoked the danger of tyrannical majorities and postulated the priority of human rights. According to republicanism, human rights owed their legitimacy to the ethical self-understanding and self-determination achieved by a political community; in liberalism, such rights were supposed to provide, from the very start, legitimate barriers that prevented the sovereign will of the people from encroaching on inviolable spheres of individual freedom. In their concepts of the legal person's autonomy, Rousseau and Kant certainly aimed to conceive of sovereign will and practical reason as unified in such a way that popular sovereignty and human rights would reciprocally interpret one another. But even they failed to do justice to the co-originality of the two ideas; Rousseau suggests more of a republican reading, Kant more of a liberal one. They missed the intuition they wanted to articulate: the idea of human rights, which is expressed in the right to equal individual liberties, must neither be merely imposed on the sovereign legislator as an external barrier, nor be instrumentalist as a functional requisite for legislative goals.

To express this intuition properly it helps to view the democratic procedure—which alone provides legitimating force to the law-making process in the context of social and ideological pluralism—from a discourse-theoretical standpoint. Here I assume a principle that I cannot discuss in detail, namely, that a regulation may claim legitimacy only if all those possibly affected by it could consent to it after participating in rational discourses. Now, if discourses—and bargaining processes as well, whose fairness is based on discursively grounded procedures—represent the place where a reasonable political will can develop, then the presumption of reasonability, which the democratic procedure is supposed to ground, ultimately rests on an elaborate communicative arrangement: the presumption depends on the conditions under which one can legally institutionalize the forms of communication necessary for legitimate lawmaking. In that case, the desired internal relation between human rights and popular sovereignty consists in this: human rights themselves are what satisfy the requirement that a civic practice of the public use of communicative freedom be legally institutionalized.

Human rights, which make the exercise of popular sovereignty legally *possible*, cannot be imposed on this practice as an external constraint. Enabling conditions must not be confused with such constraints.

Naturally, this analysis is at first plausible only for those civil rights, specifically the rights of communication and participation, that safeguard the exercise of political autonomy. It is less plausible for the classical human rights that guarantee the citizen's private autonomy. Here we think of the fundamental right to the greatest possible degree of equal individual liberties, though we also think of basic rights that constitute membership status in a state and provide the individual with comprehensive legal protection. These rights, which are meant to guarantee to everyone an equal opportunity to pursue his or her private conceptions of the good, have an intrinsic value, or at least they are not reducible to their instrumental value for democratic will-formation. We will do justice to the intuition that the classical liberties are co-original with political rights only if we state more precisely the thesis that human rights legally enable the citizens' practice of self-determination. I turn now to this more precise statement.

4. The Relation between Private and Public Autonomy

However well-grounded human rights are, they may not be paternalistically foisted, as it were, on a sovereign. Indeed, the idea of citizens' legal autonomy demands that the addressees of law be able to understand themselves at the same time as its authors. It would contradict this idea if the democratic legislator were to discover human rights as though they were (pre-existing) moral facts that one merely needs to enact as positive law. At the same time, one must also not forget that when citizens occupy the role of co-legislators they are no longer free to choose the medium in which alone they can realize their autonomy. They participate in legislation only as legal subjects; it is no longer in their power to decide which language they will make use of. The democratic idea of self-legislation *must* acquire its validity in the medium of law itself.

However, when citizens judge in the light of the discourse principle whether the law they make is legitimate, they do so under communicative presuppositions that must themselves be legally institutionalized in the form of civil rights, and for such institutionalization to occur, the legal code as such must be available. But to establish this legal code it is necessary to create the status of legal persons who as bearers of individual rights belong to a voluntary association of citizens and when necessary effectively claim their rights. There is no law without the private autonomy of legal persons in general. As a result, without basic rights that secure the private autonomy of citizens there also would not be any medium in which to legally institutionalize the conditions under which these citizens, as citizens of a state, could make use of their public autonomy. Thus private and public autonomy mutually presuppose each other in such a way that neither human rights nor popular sovereignty can claim primacy over its counterpart.

This expresses the intuition that, on the one hand, citizens can make adequate use of their public autonomy only if, on the basis of their equally protected private autonomy, they are sufficiently independent; but that, on the other hand, they can arrive at a consensual regulation of their private autonomy only if they make adequate use of their political autonomy as enfranchised citizens.

This internal relation between the rule of law and democracy has been concealed long enough by the competition between the legal paradigms that have been dominant up to the present. The liberal legal paradigm reckons with an economic society that is institutionalized through private law—above all through property rights and contractual freedom—and left to the spontaneous workings of the market. This 'private law society' is tailored for the autonomy of legal subjects who as market participants more or less rationally pursue their personal life-plans. This model of society is associated with the normative expectation that social justice can be realized by guaranteeing such a negative legal status, and thus solely by delimiting spheres of individual freedom. The critique of this supposition gave rise to the social welfare model. The objection is obvious: if the free 'capacity to have and acquire' is supposed to guarantee social justice, then an equality in 'legal capacity' must exist. As a matter of fact, however, the growing inequalities in economic power, assets, and living conditions have increasingly destroyed the factual preconditions for an equal opportunity to make effective use of equally distributed legal powers. If the normative content of legal equality is not to be inverted into its opposite, then two correctives are necessary. On the one hand, existing norms of private law must be substantively specified and on the other hand, basic social rights must be introduced, rights that ground claims to a more just distribution of socially produced wealth and to more effective protection against socially produced dangers.

In the meantime, of course, this *materialization* of law has in turn created the unintended side effects of *welfare paternalism*. Clearly, efforts to compensate for actual living conditions and power positions must not lead to 'normalizing' interventions of a sort that once again restrict the presumptive beneficiaries' pursuit of an autonomous life-project. The further development of the dialectic of legal and factual equality has shown that both legal paradigms are equally committed to the productivist image of an economic society based on industrial capitalism. This society is supposed to function in such a way that the expectation of social justice can be satisfied by securing each individual's private pursuit of his or her conception of the good life. The only dispute between the two paradigms concerns whether private autonomy can be guaranteed straightaway by negative liberties (*Freiheitsrechte*), or whether (on the contrary) the conditions for private autonomy must be secured through the provisions

of welfare entitlements. In both cases, however, the internal relation between private and public autonomy drops out of the picture.

5. *The Example of the Feminist Politics of Equality*

In closing, I want to examine the feminist politics of equality to show that policies and legal strategies oscillate helplessly between the conventional paradigms as long as they remain limited to securing private autonomy and disregard how the individual rights of private persons are related to the public autonomy of citizens engaged in law-making. For, in the final analysis, private legal subjects cannot enjoy even equal individual liberties if they themselves do not exercise their civic autonomy in common in order to specify clearly which interests and standards are justified, and to agree on the relevant respects that determine when like cases should be treated alike and different cases differently.

Initially, the goal of liberal policies was to uncouple the acquisition of status from gender identity and to guarantee to women equal opportunities in the competition for jobs, social recognition, education, political power, etc., regardless of the outcome. However, the formal equality that was partially achieved merely made it more obvious how women were *in fact* treated unequally. Social welfare politics responded to this, especially in the areas of social labour, and family law, by passing special regulations relating, for example, to pregnancy and child care, or to social hardship in the case of divorce. In the meantime feminist critique has targeted not only the unredeemed demands, but also the ambivalent consequences of successfully implemented welfare programmes—for example, the higher risk of women losing their jobs as a result of compensatory regulations, the over-representation of women in lower wage brackets, the problematic issue of 'what is in the child's best interests', and in general the progressive feminization of poverty. From a legal standpoint, one reason for this reflexively generated discrimination is found in the over-generalized classifications used to label disadvantaged situations and disadvantaged groups of persons, because these 'false' classifications lead to 'normalizing' interventions into how people conduct their lives, interventions that transform what was intended as compensation for damages into new forms of discrimination. Thus instead of guaranteeing liberty, such over-protection takes it away. In areas of law that are of concern to feminism, welfare paternalism takes on literal meaning to the extent that legislation and adjudication are oriented by traditional patterns of interpretation and thus serve to buttress existing stereotypes of sexual identity.

The classification of gender-specific roles and differences touches on fundamental levels of a society's cultural self-understanding. Radical feminism has only now made us aware of the fallible character of this self-understanding, an understanding that is essentially contested and in need of revision. It rightly insists that the appropriate interpretation of needs and criteria be a matter of public debate *in the political public sphere*. It is here that citizens must clarify the aspects that determine which differences between the experiences and living situations of (specific groups of) men and women are relevant for an equal opportunity to exercise individual liberties. Thus, this struggle for the equal status of women is a particularly good example of the need for a change of the legal paradigm.

The dispute between the two received paradigms—whether the autonomy of legal persons is better secured through individual liberties for private competition or through publicly guaranteed entitlements for clients of welfare bureaucracies—this dispute is superseded by a *proceduralist conception of law*. According to this conception, the democratic process must secure private and public autonomy at the same time: the individual rights that are meant to guarantee to women the autonomy to pursue their lives in the private sphere cannot even be adequately formulated unless the affected persons themselves first articulate and justify in public debate those aspects which are relevant to equal or unequal treatment in typical cases. The private autonomy of equally entitled citizens can be secured only insofar as citizens actively exercise their civic autonomy.

Jürgen Habermas
Universität Frankfurt

18   The Foundations of Modern Democracy[1]

CHARLES LARMORE

J ÜRGEN HABERMAS IS ONE of the very few indisputably great moral and social thinkers of our time. We must situate our own thought with respect to his, in order to know what it is we truly think, even when we then find that we must disagree. Over a number of years, Habermas has been working out a new conception of moral philosophy which he calls 'discourse ethics' (*Diskursethik*). To some extent, this line of thought has developed at a very abstract level. Its most prominent feature perhaps has been the attempt to find the source of morality in a general principle of universalization which any agent must assume just by virtue of being a competent speaker with an understanding of the concept of reasons for action. It cannot be said that this attempt has met with evident success. Like all efforts to draw some fundamental set of moral obligations from the notion of practical rationality as such, Habermas' reflections at this level seem caught in a well-known, but inescapable dilemma: either the idea Habermas proposes of practical rationality (or 'communicative reason', as he terms it) proves too weak to deliver any moral principles, or it is made to yield the desired conclusions only by virtue of moral content having been built into it from the outset.

These exercises in 'first philosophy' have been however, only one part, and doubtlessly not the most deeply felt, of Habermas' project of a discourse ethics. Far more important has been the vision of a truly democratic politics which has

driven this project. That is why one of Habermas' most recent books, *Faktizität und Geltung*, represents so significant an event.[2] In it Habermas' political philosophy and his guiding conception of radical democracy have finally achieved the detailed articulation they deserve. This book allows us to take a more just measure of the contribution which Habermas' discourse ethics can make to an understanding of the nature and promise of political association.

1. Argument and Context

In the book, Habermas sets out to reply to the frequent objection that his discourse ethics promotes a sort of excessive moralizing which betrays a lack of contact with the reality of the modern liberal-democratic state. The general form of Habermas' response is to argue that reality (*Faktizität*) and validity (*Geltung*) form a relation of tension, which his political philosophy pursues in two opposing directions. On the one hand, he aims to show that social reality, even in the most elementary aspects of language use, rests on a normative dimension. Whenever we act or think reasonably, or believe we do, we make a 'validity claim' (*Geltungsanspruch*): we suppose that the reasons we have possess a certain objectivity and would command the rational assent of others in an appropriately conducted discussion (*Diskurs*). No satisfactory theory of the political

From European Journal of Philosophy 3:1, pp. 55–68. Copyright © 1995 Basil Blackwell Ltd. Reprinted by permission.

life of modern societies, however complex they may be, can therefore ignore or dismiss the normative claims of the modern liberal-democratic state. This conclusion is familiar from many of his earlier works, particularly from his *Theory of Communicative Action*.

But on the other hand, Habermas also acknowledges that the cultural and social realities of modern society impose certain tasks and constraints on our attempt to make sense of the proper nature of political association today. Modern societies are highly complex, he observes, in that they can no longer be understood as politically constituted. In functionally differentiated, or 'decentered' societies such as our own, where different social domains (or 'subsystems') such as law, the economy, political life, and religion take on specialized tasks in accord with their own criteria, the state may no longer serve, he claims, as the expression and guarantee of the goals and ideals of society as a whole (pp. 65, 365f.). For my part, I think one might better say that modern societies are so complex that such holistic conceptions are likely to have considerably less appeal, and not that they have only now become untrue. For probably they were never really adequate to their object. Be that as it may, Habermas is surely right to maintain (here principally in opposition to Niklas Luhmann's systems theory) that we need not think society to be politically constituted in order to suppose that the collectively binding decisions of the legal system and the underlying principles of our political life have a normative basis and can become an appropriate object of reflection for moral philosophy (pp. 70ff.). Sensitivity to the complexities of social reality cannot replace our need to reflect on the validity of the principles by which we live together. . . .

2. Politics and Modernity

In Habermas' view, the moral self-understanding of modern political association must today satisfy the requirements of 'post-metaphysical thought' (pp. 24, 127, 135, 492). One might well wonder just how 'post-metaphysically' Habermas himself is disposed to think, when he resorts so freely to his ideal of the Unconditioned. But let us begin by looking more closely at what he means by 'post-metaphysical'.

According to his earlier book, *Post-Metaphysical Thought* (*Nachmetaphysisches Denken*), our epoch requires that, in place of metaphysical modes of thought, we regard reason as finite, fallible, oriented toward achieving intersubjective agreement, and tied to procedural rationality.[3] Habermas' most recent book defends basically the same conception. Concepts of justice, and the legal systems corresponding to them, are constructed in a post-metaphysical fashion, he claims, when they aim to remain neutral with respect to religious and metaphysically conceived forms of life which have themselves become problematic and disputed. The normative foundations of the modern liberal-democratic state must consist in procedural principles of justice that do not presuppose the validity of controversial ideas of the good life (pp. 375f.). Here the right, as he says, must be prior to the good. Societies such as our own, which are functionally differentiated and culturally heterogeneous, have no common good other than a legal system that treats free citizens equally and deals with their conflicts according to standards of procedural justice. If patriotism is the virtue of loyalty to the common values constituting political life, then Habermas' position, succinctly put, is that only a 'constitutional patriotism' (*Verfassungspatriotismus*) is truly coherent today (p. 642).[4]

Consequently, Habermas turns a cold eye on some of the recent revivals of the 'civic republican' tradition. To the extent that these revivals have taken a 'communitarian' form (Habermas cites the work of Frank Michelman and Charles Taylor), and long for citizenship to express the substantial ethic (or *Sittlichkeit*) of a common vision of the meaning of life, they do not fit with the exigencies of modern political life (pp. 338f., 642). I agree. But I should point out that in reality the republican tradition is not essentially communitarian. The strand of republican thought represented paradigmatically by Machiavelli's *Discorsi* and recovered today in particular by Quentin Skinner appeals, not to the fusion of politics around a common ideal of the good life, and in particular not to the idea that political participation is itself the highest form of activity, but rather to the importance, limited but real, of the active virtues of citizenship and to the need to nurture the rule of law which is necessary for individual liberty.[5] As such, republicanism ought to be a central ingredient in the self-understanding of the modern liberal-democratic state and of Habermas' own political philosophy.

A principle of neutrality similar to that of Habermas, expressed as the demand that liberalism take the form of a 'political', not a 'comprehensive' doctrine, lies at the heart of the theory of justice John Rawls has made so famous. It is also a principle that I have defended, in some earlier writings of mine. Despite this common ground, which Habermas is kind enough to point out (pp. 376ff.), there are several respects in which I find myself in disagreement.

The first objection concerns an important matter, though it is one which does not affect, I believe, the basic contours of Habermas' position. It seems to me that, though he rightly rejects the communitarian longing to have politics express a common vision of the good life, Habermas rather underestimates the depth of the common life necessary, even today, for the fundamental principles of political association to command allegiance. This common life must run deeper than just constitutional patriotism. If the political identity of a people did not extend beyond that level, if it consisted therefore only in the affirmation of procedural principles of equal freedom and respect, which clearly purport to govern political life everywhere, then such a people would have to espouse as its ultimate goal the construction of a world political order. Its fundamental political aspiration would have to be cosmopolitan. Whether or not this goal is really desirable, it seems to me wrong to regard it as inscribed in the very logic of the modern liberal-democratic state. Political allegiance today, even when its object is liberal democracy, remains essentially shaped by the conviction that a people can rightly enjoy a form of political association that sets it off from other peoples, even from those sharing the same fundamental political values.

How then should we understand this further, necessary dimension of the common life underlying political association? The mistake of communitarians, but apparently of Habermas as well, is to suppose that it can consist only in a shared allegiance to additional values. That is not so. It can instead be a matter of being shaped by common circumstances. For example, a people can think of itself as a distinct people in terms of a shared language and geographical situation. Neither of these is either necessary or sufficient for the sense of belonging to a people, though each can certainly play a significant role. The most important factor, however, is that a people can be bound together by a common historical experience, including the memory of past conflicts, even bloody ones, which were ignited by political programmes attempting to impose contrary ideals of the good life (different religious confessions, for instance), but which have been superseded by a practice of equal respect. The political identity of a people may be forged by a shared memory of the violent struggles they have been through and the quarrels they have left behind, in addition to the principles of a 'constitutional patriotism' they have put in their place.

This was the idea Ernest Renan sought to express when he observed (in his *Qu'est-ce qu'une nation?* of 1882) that 'every French citizen must have forgotten the St Bartholomew's Day massacre.'[6] This famous statement is paradoxical, not just because many Frenchmen had not forgotten that fateful day when Catholics slaughtered Protestants by the thousands, but also because Renan addressed the statement to his French readers. In fact, what Renan meant to highlight is not a shared amnesia, but rather a shared memory. A common sense of French citizenship has been forged precisely by people forsaking together, though not forgetting, the passions that once drove their ancestors to make political authority an instrument of religious confession. Similarly formative memories play a role in the self-understanding of other Western liberal democracies.

Only by keeping in mind this aspect of its underlying common life, can we make sense of an important fact about liberal democracy. Not just as a matter of historical record, but in its very character, it presents itself as a *latecomer* amongst the forms of political life. Liberal democracy builds upon the memory of past conflict and the hard-won knowledge that many of the ideals that used to shape political life now form the object of reasonable disagreement. For this reason, individuals may rightly see themselves as sharing a political destiny that goes beyond the values they can affirm in patriotic declarations. They may feel united in what they have learned together from the things that came to divide them. This shared memory is itself sustained, of course, by a common allegiance to the constitutional principles of equal freedom and respect. It is indeed, the historical colouring these principles have for a specific people, the expression of how they came to accept them. That is why a recognition of this further dimension of common life is compatible with the principle of neutrality mentioned above. And why it can be fitted into the basic structure of Habermas's thought as well.

There are, however, two fundamental and consequential points where it seems to me Habermas goes wrong in his reconstruction of the normative basis of modern liberal democracy. The first of them concerns the very designation of 'post-metaphysical'. In Habermas' view, reason should proceed 'post-metaphysically' in the political realm, not simply in order to solve the problem of the principles of political association, but rather in order to apply to this realm the

general philosophical perspective which alone, he believes, fits our contemporary intellectual situation. Again and again he insists that certain political principles (the primacy of procedural justice or the priority of the right over the good, the idea of popular sovereignty as the source of individual rights) recommend themselves because the age of metaphysical and religious worldviews is over and practical reason must thus abandon the frameworks of natural law and of the individual subject in favour of his own model of communicative interaction (pp. 17, 24, 51f., 127).

This argumentative strategy seems to me a mistake. It is not that I want to assert that the ambitions of metaphysics retain their plausibility or that some particular religious worldview has not really lost its authority. My own considered views on these matters are, in fact, somewhat more complex than those of Habermas. But the present question properly involves not all that we might reasonably believe to be true of the world, but rather what we ought to consider as relevant to the establishment of principles of political association. These two perspectives are not, I continue to believe, the same.[7] So the important point here is that in modern culture such assertions about the vitality or obsolescence of metaphysics and religion are something about which reasonable people—aiming, that is, to think and converse in good faith and apply, as best they can, the general capacities of reason—can disagree. Even today, reasonable people can come to believe that the naturalistic worldview should be replaced by a broader, metaphysical or 'platonistic', vision that recognizes the existence of ideal entitles, neither physical nor psychological in character. Thus, I myself think that we must believe there to exist such things as reasons, which we discover by reflection, if we are to suppose that there can be normative knowledge, that is, knowledge of how we ought to think and act.[8] Similarly, reasonable people can also find a basis for believing that the world is guided by divine providence; just as other people equally reasonable—and this includes Habermas himself—can conclude, to the contrary, that mind and knowledge must be understood without platonistic assumptions and that religion can belong (at best) to the realm of subjective conviction. Indeed, people can also find themselves in reasonable disagreement, as we have seen, about what should count as metaphysical and what should not.

As a political principle, the priority of the right over the good should therefore not be thought dependent on the supposed obsolescence of metaphysical and religious worldviews. This principle is not 'post-metaphysical', if that means that it gives expression to a new, general vision of thought and world. Instead, the priority of the right should be seen as stemming from the recognition that such worldviews, like the philosophical attempts to overcome them, are and will remain the object of controversy among reasonable people. Again, it may well be the case, on general philosophical grounds, that our best understanding of reason today would be along the lines of the 'post-metaphysical' characterization Habermas gives: finite, fallible, oriented toward achieving agreement, and tied to procedural rationality. Such a conception of reason is indeed one I am inclined to share, though I think Habermas wrongly supposes that it escapes the need to assume the existence of ideal entities. But the point here is that such a conception, however ultimately correct, remains the object of reasonable disagreement. To that extent, it shows itself to be unfit to play a foundational role in what ought to be the moral self-understanding of the modern liberal-democratic state. For the priority of the right, as a political principle, expresses the conviction that in the wake of ongoing ethical, religious, and philosophical controversy political association today must rest on a core morality, which reasonable people despite their deep differences can all accept. At the heart of this core morality lies, as I shall explain in the next section, a principle of equal respect. This political doctrine of liberalism is 'post-metaphysical' only in a trivial sense: metaphysical and religious assumptions are too controversial to have a place at its basis. But the same is equally true for general philosophical conceptions of so-called 'post-metaphysical thought'.

Habermas' aim is to bring out the fundamental dimension of modern experience that finds expression in the liberal-democratic state. This project is a very sensible one. But to me it seems that Habermas has missed the feature of modern experience which is relevant. It does not lie in the demise of metaphysical and religious worldviews, though the widespread abandonment of such views is certainly a significant aspect of modernity. It consists instead in the growing recognition that reasonable disagreement about the nature of the good life and even about the philosophical foundations of morality is not a passing phenomenon, but rather is the situation we should expect. The more we discuss with one another, and in a thoughtful and informed way, the meaning of life, the more likely it is that we will find that we differ and disagree. The expectation of reasonable disagreement is the phenomenon that ought to guide our political thought today.

Though I have discussed in detail elsewhere this fundamental experience of modern life,[9] let me point out here again that it is very far from recommending a general moral scepticism. First, there is the fact that the expectation of irresolvable controversy has been aroused most of all by questions of the speculative sort. However much such controversies may engage our deepest aspirations, they still leave generally untouched the moral commitments of everyday life. Controversy about ultimate and fundamental matters can go hand in hand with the conviction that we can nonetheless agree upon a core morality that is adequate for the purposes of political association. Indeed, it is only such a core morality that can tell us that we ought to give reasonable disagreement about the meaning of life a decisive role in the establishment of political principles.

Secondly, the fact that our vision of the good life is the object of reasonable disagreement does not entail that we should withdraw our allegiance to it or regard it as henceforth a mere article of faith. On the contrary, we may still have good reasons to affirm it, based on our experience and reflection. We should remember only that such reasons are not likely to be acceptable to other people, who are equally reasonable, but have a different history of experience and reflection. Just as the basis they have for their different conceptions of life will not be such as to win our assent. The good reasons which move reasonable people, disposed as they are to think and converse in good faith and to exercise, to the best of their abilities, the general capacities of reason, need not be reasons they all must share. Their grounds for belief and action draw upon their different background convictions. As their starting points differ, so do the positions at which they may legitimately arrive. Reasonable people may thus have good reason to believe in the visions which divide them. But they would be foolish not to expect that a careful and informed discussion would lead them into disagreement.

I could sum up this criticism of Habermas, therefore, by saying that he has presented a concept of modernity which is not sufficiently broad. Modern experience is characterized, not just by a new, 'post-metaphysical' understanding of the true and the right, but also by the expectation that metaphysics and post-metaphysics will remain an enduring object of reasonable disagreement.

3. Liberalism and Democracy

My second major criticism is directed toward the way in which Habermas proposes to conceive the relation between basic individual rights (the right to freedom of conscience, freedom of speech, assembly and private property) and the democratic ideal of popular sovereignty. As I have noted, he does not share the communitarian assumption that individual rights need to be nurtured and shaped by an antecedent, substantial vision of the good life (*Sittlichkeit*). But equally significantly, he rejects the contrary standpoint of liberalism. As Habermas rightly observes, liberalism has usually assigned to individual rights—at least those of a fundamental kind—the function of delimiting the proper scope of popular sovereignty (pp. 130, 329, 610). That is, liberal thinkers have generally seen fundamental individual rights as a distinct value from democratic self-rule and as taking precedence over it. This outlook finds expression indeed in the very term 'liberal democracy', but it is nonetheless one Habermas refuses. His explicit aim is to cut a middle way between the opposing camps of liberalism and communitarianism, which divide between them so much of contemporary Anglo-American political philosophy.

This *via media* is announced in the thesis that fundamental individual rights and democratic self-rule are 'co-original' (*gleichursprünglich*) values. At one level this co-originality is for Habermas a relation of mutual presupposition. Just as self-government can serve to protect individual rights, so rights are best understood as providing the necessary conditions for the exercise of popular sovereignty (pp. 133f., 161, 610). But at bottom Habermas unmistakably privileges the second of these values. Individual rights in his view draw their rationale from their supposed ability to make democratic self-rule possible. Their basic purpose cannot be, as liberals generally believe, to limit the authority of popular sovereignty.

A clear sign of the priority Habermas assigns to democracy is the basic value he sees as underlying the co-originality of rights and self-government. It is what he calls 'autonomy' (pp. 52f.). In a post-metaphysical age, he argues, where the appeal of metaphysical and religious world-pictures is on the wane, we can have reason to consider ourselves subject to practical norms only if we are able at the same time to see ourselves as the source of these norms. Democratic self-rule is but the application of this idea of autonomy to the political realm (pp. 52, 153f., 160). Citizens can regard themselves as legitimately bound by the rules of political association, only to the extent that these rules spring from no higher source than the citizens themselves. Again, because of widespread and deeply rooted controversies about the nature of the good life, however, citizens must locate their role as the source of law, not in a given substantial form of life they might already share, but instead in their own common will, which they mobilize for this political purpose alone. This is why communitarianism is unacceptable. Citizens can form and express this collective will only in public discussion (*Diskurs*) with one another about the principles of the common life which they are to affirm.

This line of Habermas' thought contains an important element which other liberal-democratic thinkers have embraced before him: legitimate principles of political association must be rationally acceptable to all citizens whom they are meant to bind. This is why in the face of reasonable disagreement about the good life, political association must rely on the priority of the right. But the distinctive feature of Habermas' position is the further claim which he believes to underlie this and which breaks with the usual conception of liberal democracy. It is his claim that fundamental individual rights have their proper basis only in the ideal of popular sovereignty, so that citizens will understand their collective will as the source of all the norms which bind them. In Habermas' eyes, the essentially protective function of such rights does not lie primarily in restricting the power of the state, but instead at the deeper level of empowering individuals to participate in this democratic self-rule. The right to freedom of speech, for example, is held to recommend itself as a means to the formation of a common political will. Individual rights serve, not to protect us against the collective will, but

rather to protect the means necessary for creating a collective will.

In essence, Habermas thus wants to see democratic self-rule as the sole normative foundation of the modern liberal-democratic state. Liberal democracy ought best to be understood, he believes, not as that term itself suggests (the subordination of democracy to liberal principles), but rather as *radical democracy*. Political association must be understood as truly and thoroughly self-governing. It cannot subordinate itself to any pre-given norms. It can acknowledge only those moral norms to which it has itself given rise (pp. 123, 154). This ideal of popular sovereignty forms the heart of Habermas' political philosophy. It is why he thinks, for example, that instead of regarding fundamental legal, i.e. constitutional, principles as the application of moral principles already held to be valid, we should understand law and morality as equally basic, though often overlapping, specifications of an even more general normative principle D, which gives expression to the fundamental value of autonomy (pp. 135–138): 'Only those action norms are valid to which all those who might be affected by their establishment could assent as the result of a rational discussion.'

At first glance, Habermas' vision of radical democracy seems to lack the defining features of the liberal point of view. Liberal thinkers have always argued that political association must rest ultimately on moral principles that serve to protect certain basic individual freedoms. Typically, such principles have consisted in the affirmation of fundamental rights, with the result that democratic self-rule is subordinated to the protection of individual freedoms. Habermas' unqualified fondness for the ideal of popular sovereignty seems to make him something very different from a liberal.

But the appearance is misleading. In reality, Habermas' description of his theory as involving the primacy of popular sovereignty fails to capture its actual structure. Democratic self-rule, at least as Habermas understands it, depends on an unacknowledged premise, a premise expressing an antecedent moral commitment and affirming the existence of a fundamental individual right. Other conceptions of popular sovereignty would have, no doubt, a different character. But Habermas' conception is so constituted as to imply that political principles ought to be rationally acceptable to all those whom they are to bind. And that is the feature which brings his idea of democracy back within the liberal fold, as generally understood.

For let us ask why indeed we should believe that political principles ought to be rationally acceptable to all. It will not do to reply, as Habermas suggests, that the authority of traditional views of the world, in which being subject to law and being the source of the law do not coincide, has simply vanished. For that is first of all false. As I have pointed out, the authority of such worldviews remains for many the object of a living conviction. Indeed, we cannot in particular understand how there can be such a thing as moral knowledge, I have suggested, unless we suppose 'metaphysically' that there exist such things as reasons that we do not create, but rather discover by reflection. It is too narrow a conception of modernity, or at least of that aspect of it which is relevant to the problem of political association, that fails to recognize the existence of reasonable disagreement on this point. Secondly, the waning of these worldviews, where it has occurred, cannot suffice to justify the idea that the principles of political association must be rationally acceptable to all. It would, for example, be just as possible under these circumstances for political principles to be geared instead to the maximization of the general welfare.

The crucial fact about the idea that the rules of political association must be rationally acceptable to all those whom they are to bind is that it takes into account the respect in which political principles differ from other moral principles. In general, political principles are precisely those principles which we believe may be enforced by coercion, if need be. The idea that such principles must be rationally acceptable to those who are to be subject to them rests on a moral view about the conditions under which norms may be backed up by force. This underlying moral commitment is that no one should be made by force to comply with a norm of action when it is not possible for him to recognize through reason the validity of that norm. Moral principles with which we do not intend to bring about compliance by force if necessary need not meet this condition: we may judge others in their light, without having to suppose they would agree to their validity. There is nothing *per se* wrong with doing so: we do it all the time when we judge others in terms of our religious convictions or ideals of the good life, which they do not and cannot share given their own settled convictions. (Consequently, I cannot accept Habermas' view that his Principle D concerns all moral norms, and not just politically instituted ones.) But the matter is different with moral principles we mean to back up with coercive force. Such principles, which are precisely political in nature, are ones we should accept only if they could command the rational assent of those whom they are to bind. It is, as I have said, a fundamental moral commitment that makes this so.

This moral conviction amounts, in fact, to the Kantian formula that every person is always to be treated as an end in himself. No-one should be made to do, for the sake of some ulterior end, what cannot also win his rational assent. This is, at root, a norm of equal respect, according to which individuals are to be treated as beings whose exercise of their capacity of rational agency cannot be sacrificed for the sake of achieving some social goal. It lies at the heart of the core morality which can be affirmed by people who otherwise differ about the merits of metaphysical and post-metaphysical views of the world, and which sustains the political principle of the priority of the right. Most importantly of all in the present context, this moral principle gives expression to an individual right, though certainly one more fundamental than the political rights which tend to be the object of explicit constitutional guarantees. Habermas is probably right that the familiar individual rights serve to make possible democratic self-rule. But that cannot be their entire rationale. They also give concrete expression to the deepest individual right which is that of equal respect and which itself underlies the ideal of democratic self-rule. Popular sovereignty cannot form therefore the ultimate layer of our political self-understanding. It draws instead on a fundamentally liberal conception of the political world.

This result also means that, contrary to Habermas, the concept of discussion (*Diskurs*)—be it the actual public discussion in which democratic self-rule is exercised or even the hypothetical discussion we might imagine to be carried out under ideal conditions—cannot play the fundamental role in our moral and political self-understanding. At a deeper level still must lie the moral principle of respect for persons. The 'ideal conditions of justification' which political argument in a liberal democracy must aim to heed have to embody at their heart this moral principle. For equal respect is precisely what makes democratic self-rule the proper form of political association. Citizens can therefore understand themselves as the source of law only insofar as they have already accepted this principle and judge the validity of their collective decisions from this standpoint. The moral principle of equal respect belongs to the innermost core of our moral consciousness. It forms the historically situated point of departure for our moral reflection, the framework within which we can conceive of moral argument.

Charles Larmore
Columbia University

NOTES

1. This article draws on material originally published as a review of Jürgen Habermas' book, *Faktizität und Geltung*, in the *Deutsche Zeitschrift für Philosophie*, 41 (1993), pp. 321–327.

2. J. Habermas (1992). All page references in the text are to this book.

3. J. Habermas (1988), pp. 41 ff.

4. This formulation appears in a celebrated essay, 'Staatsbürgerschaft und nationale Identität' (1990), reprinted at the end of Habermas (1992).

5. See Skinner (1991).

6. See Renan (1992), p. 42.

7. See Larmore (1987), chapter 4.

8. See the chapter 'De la connaissance morale' in Larmore (1993a) and the chapter 'Moral Knowledge' in Larmore (forthcoming).

9. See Larmore (1994).

REFERENCES

Habermas, J. (1988), *Nachmetaphysisches, Denken*. Frankfurt: Suhrkamp.

Habermas, J. (1992), *Faktizität und Geltung*. Frankfurt: Suhrkamp.

Larmore, C. (1987), *Patterns of Moral Complexity*. Cambridge: Cambridge University Press.

Larmore, C. (1993a), *Modernité et morale*. Paris: Presses Universitaires de France.

Larmore, C. (1993b), 'Beyond Religion and Enlightenment', in *San Diego Law Review*, vol. 30, no. 4, pp. 799–815.

Larmore, C. (1994), 'Pluralism and Reasonable Disagreement', in E. F. Paul *et al.* (eds.), *Cultural Pluralism and Moral Knowledge*. Cambridge: Cambridge University Press.

Larmore, C. (forthcoming), *The Morals of Modernity*. Cambridge: Cambridge University Press.

Renan, E. (1992), *Qu'est-ce qu'une nation? et autres essais politiques*, ed. by J. Roman. Paris: Presses Pocket.

Skinner, Q. (1991), 'Two Views on the Maintenance of Liberty', in P. Pettit (ed.), *Contemporary Political Theory*. New York: Macmillan.

19 Toward a Deliberative Model of Democratic Legitimacy

SEYLA BENHABIB

Democratic Legitimacy and Public Goods

COMPLEX MODERN DEMOCRATIC societies since the Second World War face the task of securing three public goods. These are legitimacy, economic welfare, and a viable sense of collective identity. These are "goods" in the sense that their attainment is considered worthy and desirable by most members of such societies; furthermore, not attaining one or a combination thereof would cause problems in the functioning of these societies such as to throw them into crises.

These goods stand in a complex relation to one another: excessive realization of one such good may be in conflict with and may jeopardize the realization of others. For example, economic welfare may be attained at the cost of sacrificing legitimacy by curtailing union rights, by limiting a more rigorous examination of business accounting practices, or by encouraging the unfair use of protectionist state measures. Too great an emphasis on collective identity may come at the cost of minorities and dissidents whose civil and political rights may be impinged upon by a revival of a sense of collective identity. Thus legitimacy claims and collective identity demands, particularly if they take a nationalist tone, may come into conflict. There can also be conflicts between the claims of economic welfare and the demands of collective identity, as when excessive forms of protectionism and nationalism isolate countries in the world economic context, possibly leading to declining standards of living. Conversely, too great an emphasis on economic welfare may undermine a sense of collective identity by increasing competition among social groups and by weakening the claims of political sovereignty vis-à-vis other states. In a well-functioning democratic society the demands of legitimacy, economic welfare, and collective identity ideally exist in some form of equilibrium.

The present essay is concerned with one good among others which democratic societies must

This essay is a much-revised version of an article that originally appeared in Constellations 1, no. 1 (April 1994), under the title "Deliberative Rationality and Models of Democratic Legitimacy." It is part of a manuscript in progress tentatively entitled In Search of the Civic Polity: Democracy, Legitimacy, and Citizenship at Century's End.

I would like to acknowledge my thanks to members of the New York University "Law and Social Theory" symposium and the Yale University "Legal Theory Workshop" for comments and criticisms on earlier drafts. In particular, I am thankful to Professors Ronald Dworkin and Thomas Nagel for their rigorous criticisms on the question of the status of basic rights and liberties within the framework of a theory of deliberative democracy. I would also like to thank Stephen Macedo, whose comments on an earlier version of this paper delivered at the Political Theory Colloquium of the Harvard University Department of Government in the spring of 1994 have greatly contributed to my thoughts.

attain: the good of legitimacy. I am concerned to examine the philosophical foundations of democratic legitimacy. I will argue that legitimacy in complex democratic societies must be thought to result from the free and unconstrained public deliberation of all about matters of common concern. Thus a public sphere of deliberation about matters of mutual concern is essential to the legitimacy of democratic institutions.

Democracy, in my view, is best understood as a model for organizing the collective and public exercise of power in the major institutions of a society on the basis of the principle that decisions affecting the well-being of a collectivity can be viewed as the outcome of a procedure of free and reasoned deliberation among individuals considered as moral and political equals. Certainly any definition of essentially contested concepts like democracy, freedom, and justice is never a mere definition; the definition itself already articulates the normative theory that justifies the term. Such is the case with the preceding definition. My understanding of democracy privileges a deliberative model over other kinds of normative considerations. This is not to imply that economic welfare, institutional efficiency, and cultural stability would not be relevant in judging the adequacy of a normative definition of democracy. Economic welfare claims and collective identity needs must also be satisfied for democracies to function over time. However, the normative basis of democracy as a form of organizing our collective life is neither the fulfillment of economic welfare nor the realization of a stable sense of collective identity. For just as the attainment of certain levels of economic welfare may be compatible with authoritarian political rule, so too antidemocratic regimes may be more successful in assuring a sense of collective identity than democratic ones.

My goal in the first half of this article will be to examine the relationship between the normative presuppositions of democratic deliberation and the idealized content of practical rationality. The approach I follow is consonant with what John Rawls has called "Kantian constructivism," and what Jürgen Habermas refers to as "reconstruction."[1] In this context, the differences in their methodologies are less significant than their shared assumption that the institutions of liberal democracies embody the idealized content of a form of practical reason. This idealized content can be elucidated and philosophically articulated; in fact, the task of a philosophical theory of democracy would consist in the clarification and articulation of the form of practical rationality represented by democratic rule.[2]

The methodology of "philosophical reconstruction" differs from "ethnocentric liberalism" (Richard Rorty) as well as from more a prioristic forms of Kantianism.[3] As distinguished from certain kinds of Kantianism, I would like to acknowledge the historical and sociological specificity of the project of democracy while, against ethnocentric liberalism, I would like to insist that the practical rationality embodied in democratic institutions has a culture-transcending validity claim. This form of practical reason has become the collective and anonymous property of cultures, institutions, and traditions as a result of the experiments and experiences, both ancient and modern, with democratic rule over the course of human history.[4] The insights and perhaps illusions resulting from these experiments and experiences are sedimented in diverse constitutions, institutional arrangements, and procedural specifics. When one thinks through the form of practical rationality at the core of democratic rule, Hegel's concept of "objective Spirit" (*objektiver Geist*) appears to me particularly appropriate.[5] To make this concept useful today we have to think of it without recourse to the metaphorical presence of a supersubject; we have to desubstantialize the model of a thinking and acting supersubject that still governs Hegelian philosophy. Without this metaphor of the subject implicitly governing it, the term "objective spirit" would refer to those *anonymous yet intelligible* collective rules, procedures, and practices that form a way of life. It is the rationality intrinsic to these anonymous yet intelligible rules, procedures and practices that any attempt aiming at the reconstruction of the logic of democracies must focus upon.

A Deliberative Model of Democracy

According to the deliberative model of democracy, it is a necessary condition for attaining legitimacy and rationality with regard to collective decision-making processes in a polity, that the institutions of this polity are so arranged that what is considered in the common interest of all results from processes of collective deliberation conducted rationally and fairly among free and equal individuals.[6] The more collective decision-making processes approximate this model the more increases the presumption of their legitimacy and rationality. Why?

The basis of legitimacy in democratic institutions is to be traced back to the presumption that the instances which claim obligatory power for themselves do so because their decisions represent an impartial standpoint said to be equally in the interests of all. This presumption can be fulfilled only if such decisions are in principle open to appropriate public processes of deliberation by free and equal citizens.

The discourse model of ethics formulates the most *general principles* and *moral intuitions* behind the validity claims of a deliberative model of democracy.[7] The basic idea behind this model is that only those norms (i.e., general rules of action and institutional arrangements) can be said to be valid (i.e., morally binding), which would be agreed to by all those affected by their consequences, if such agreement were reached as a consequence of a process of deliberation that had the following features: 1) participation in such deliberation is governed by the norms of equality and symmetry; all have the same chances to initiate speech acts, to question, to interrogate, and to open debate; 2) all have the right to question the assigned topics of conversation; and 3) all have the right to initiate reflexive arguments about the very rules of the discourse procedure and the way in which they are applied or carried out. There are no prima facie rules limiting the agenda of the conversation, or the identity of the participants, as long as each excluded person or group can justifiably show that they are relevantly affected by the proposed norm under question. In certain circumstances this would mean that citizens of a democratic community would have to enter into a practical discourse with noncitizens who may be residing in their countries, at their borders, or in neighboring communities if there are matters that affect them all. Ecology and environmental issues in general are a perfect example of such instances when the boundaries of discourses keep expanding because the consequences of our actions expand and affect increasingly more people.

The procedural specifics of those special argumentation situations called "practical discourses" are not automatically transferable to a macro-institutional level, nor is it necessary that they should be so transferable. A theory of democracy, as opposed to a general moral theory, would have to be concerned with the question of institutional specifications and practical feasibility. Nonetheless, the procedural constraints of the discourse model can act as test cases for critically evaluating the criteria of membership and the rules for agenda setting, and for the structuring of public discussions within and among institutions. . . .

According to the deliberative model, procedures of deliberation generate legitimacy as well as assure some degree of practical rationality.[8] But what are the claims to practical rationality of such deliberative democratic processes? Deliberative processes are essential to the rationality of collective decision-making processes for three reasons. First, as Bernard Manin has observed in an excellent article "On Legitimacy and Deliberation," deliberative processes are also processes that impart information.[9] New information is imparted because 1) no single individual can anticipate and foresee all the variety of perspectives through which matters of ethics and politics would be perceived by different individuals; and 2) no single individual can possess all the information deemed relevant to a certain decision affecting all.[10] Deliberation is a procedure for being informed.

Furthermore, much political theory under the influence of economic models of reasoning in particular proceeds from a methodological fiction: this is the methodological fiction of an individual with an ordered set of coherent preferences. This fiction does not have much relevance in the political world. On complex social and political issues, more often than not, individuals may have views and wishes but no ordered set of preferences, since the latter would imply that they would be enlightened not only about the preferences but about the consequences and relative merits of each of their preferred choices in advance. It is actually the deliberative process itself that is likely to produce such an outcome by leading the individual to further critical reflection on his already held views and opinions; it is incoherent to assume that individuals can start a process of public deliberation with a level of conceptual clarity about their choices and preferences that can actually result only from a successful process of deliberation. Likewise, the formation of coherent preferences cannot precede deliberation; it can only succeed it. Very often individuals' wishes as well as views and opinions conflict with one another. In the course of deliberation and the exchange of views with others, individuals become more aware of such conflicts and feel compelled to undertake a coherent ordering.

More significantly, the very procedure of articulating a view in public imposes a certain reflexivity on individual preferences and opinions. When presenting their point of view and position to others, individuals must support them by articulating good reasons in a public context to their co-deliberators. This process of *articulating good reasons in public* forces the individual to think of what would count as a good reason for all others involved. One is thus forced to think from the standpoint of all involved for whose agreement one is "wooing." Nobody can convince others in public of her point of view without being able to state why what appears good, plausible, just, and expedient to her can also be considered so from the standpoint of all

involved. Reasoning from the standpoint of all involved not only forces a certain coherence upon one's own views but also forces one to adopt a standpoint that Hannah Arendt, following Kant, had called the "enlarged mentality."[11]

A deliberative model of democracy suggests a necessary but not sufficient condition of practical rationality, because, as with any procedure, it can be misinterpreted, misapplied, and abused. Procedures can neither dictate outcomes nor define the quality of the reasons advanced in argumentation nor control the quality of the reasoning and rules of logic and inference used by participants. Procedural models of rationality are underdetermined. Nonetheless, the discourse model makes some provisions against its own misuses and abuses in that the reflexivity condition built into the model allows abuses and misapplications at the first level to be challenged at a second, metalevel of discourse. Likewise, the equal chance of all affected to initiate such discourse of deliberation suggests that no outcome is prima facie fixed but can be revised and subjected to reexamination. Such would be the normative justification of majority rule as a decision procedure following from this model: in many instances the majority rule is a fair and rational decision procedure, not because legitimacy resides in numbers but because if a majority of people are convinced at one point on the basis of reasons formulated as closely as possible as a result of a process of discursive deliberation that conclusion A is the right thing to do, then this conclusion can remain valid until challenged by good reasons by some other group. It is not the sheer numbers that support the rationality of the conclusion, but the presumption that if a large number of people see certain matters a certain way as a result of following certain kinds of rational procedures of deliberation and decision-making, then such a conclusion has a presumptive claim to being rational until shown to be otherwise. The simple practice of having a ruling and an opposition party in democracies in fact incorporates this principle: we accept the will of the majority at the end of an electoral process that has been fairly and correctly carried out, but even when we accept the legitimacy of the process we may have grave doubts about the rationality of the outcome. The practice of there being parliamentary opposition says that the grounds on which the majority party claims to govern can be examined, challenged, tested, criticized, and rearticulated. Parliamentary procedures of opposition, debate, questioning, and even impeachment proceedings, and investigatory commissions incorporate this rule of deliberative rationality that majoritarian decisions are temporarily agreed-upon conclusions, the claim to rationality and validity of which can be publicly reexamined.

This deliberative model of democracy is proceduralist in that it emphasizes first and foremost certain institutional procedures and practices for attaining decisions on matters that would be binding on all. Three additional points are worthy of note with respect to such a conception of democracy: first, I proceed from the assumption of value pluralism. Disagreement about the highest goods of human existence and the proper conduct of a morally righteous life are a fundamental feature of our modern value-universe since the end of natural law cosmologies in the sixteenth and seventeenth centuries, and the eventual separation of church and state.[12] The challenge to democratic rationality is to arrive at acceptable formulations of the common good despite this inevitable value-pluralism. We cannot resolve conflicts among value systems and visions of the good by reestablishing a strong unified moral and religious code without forsaking fundamental liberties. Agreements in societies living with value-pluralism are to be sought for not at the level of substantive beliefs but at that of procedures, processes, and practices for attaining and revising beliefs. Proceduralism is a rational answer to persisting value conflicts at the substantive level.[13]

Second, the deliberative model of democracy proceeds not only from a conflict of values but also from a conflict of interests in social life. Social life necessitates both conflict of interests and cooperation. Democratic procedures have to convince, even under conditions when one's interests as an individual or as a group are negatively affected, that the conditions of mutual cooperation are still legitimate. Procedures can be regarded as methods for articulating, sifting through, and weighing conflicting interests. The more conflicts of interests there are the more it is important to have procedural solutions of conflict adjudication through which parties whose interests are negatively affected can find recourse to other methods of the articulation and representation of their grievances. Proceduralist models of democracy allow the articulation of conflicts of interests under conditions of social cooperation mutually acceptable to all.[14]

Finally, any proceduralist and deliberative model of democracy is prima facie open to the argument that no modern society can organize its affairs along the fiction of a mass assembly carrying out its deliberations in public and collectively. Here more than an issue of size is at stake. The argument that there may be an invisible limit to the size of a deliberative body that, when crossed, affects the nature of the reasoning process is undoubtedly true. Nonetheless the reason why a deliberative and proceduralist model of democracy does not need to operate with the fiction of a general deliberative assembly is that the procedural specifications of this model privilege a *plurality of modes of association* in which all affected can have the right to articulate their point of view. These can range from political parties, to citizens' initiatives, to social movements, to voluntary associations, to consciousness-raising groups, and the like. *It is through the interlocking net of these multiple forms of associations, networks, and organizations that an anonymous "public conversation" results. It is central to the model of deliberative democracy that it privileges such a public sphere of mutually interlocking and overlapping networks and associations of deliberation, contestation, and argumentation.* The fiction of a general deliberative assembly in which the united people expressed their will belongs to the early history of democratic theory; today our guiding model has to be that of a medium of loosely associated, multiple foci of opinion formation and dissemination which affect one another in free and spontaneous processes of communication.[15]

Such a strong model of deliberative democracy is subject to three different kinds of criticism: first, liberal theorists will express concern that such a strong model would lead to the corrosion of individual liberties and may in fact destabilize the rule of law. In his earlier work, Bruce Ackerman had formulated a theory of "conversational neutrality" to voice some of these concerns.[16] Stephen Holmes has defended the plausibility of certain "gag rules" on public conversation.[17] Second, feminist theorists are skeptical about this model, because they see it as privileging a certain mode of discourse at the cost of silencing others: this is the rationalist, male, univocal, hegemonic discourse of a transparent polity that disregards the emotions, polyvocity, multiplicity, and differences in the articulation of the voice of the public. . . .

Basic Rights and Deliberative Democracy

Deliberative democracy models often seem subject to the argument that they do not protect individuals' basic rights and liberties sufficiently.[18] This objection is rooted in two assumptions: first, insofar as deliberative models appear to make a high degree of consensus or unanimity of public issues a value, it is fair to suspect that such unanimity could only be attained at the cost of silencing dissent and curtailing minority viewpoints. Second, what protection does a deliberative model allow against the tyranny of democratic majorities from imposing its choices and norms upon the minority?

I believe that these objections are fair when raised against most versions of radical participatory democratic theories that also prioritize political deliberation. I think it is fair to ask whether the radical democratic theories of Hannah Arendt, Benjamin Barber, or Mouffe and Laclau allow for a coherent theory of rights such as would protect both basic rights and liberties for all, and defend minority rights against the tyranny of the majority. But such objections are not applicable to the model of deliberative democracy developed here.

Precisely because I share with the Kantian liberal tradition the assumption that moral respect for the autonomous personality is a fundamental norm of morality and democracy, the deliberative model of democracy presupposes a discourse theory of ethics to supply it with the most general moral principles upon which rights claims would be based.[19] Insofar as a discourse theory of ethics considers participants to be equal and free beings, equally entitled to take part in those discourses which determine the norms that are to affect their lives, it proceeds from a view of persons as beings entitled to certain "moral rights." I have named this moral right the entitlement to *universal moral respect,* and have attempted in *Situating the Self* to give a nonfoundationalist but principled justification for the recognition of this norm.[20] I further maintain that within a discourse theory each individual has the same symmetrical rights to various speech acts, to initiate new topics, to ask for reflection about the presuppositions of the conversations, and so on. I call this the principle of *egalitarian reciprocity.* In my view the norms of universal moral respect and egalitarian reciprocity are moral rights in that they are entitlements that accrue to individuals insofar as we view them as moral persons.

The step that would lead from a recognition of these two moral rights to the formulation of a principle of basic rights and liberties is certainly not very wide.[21] Basically it would involve a hypothetical answer to the question, If it is plausible for individuals to view one another as beings entitled to universal moral respect and egalitarian reciprocity, which most general principles of basic rights and liberties would such individuals also be likely to accept as determining the conditions of their collective existence?[22]

Although the discourse theory shares this kind of hypothetical and counter-factual moral reasoning procedure with Kant and Rawls, it would be different from a Kantian deduction of the concept of right and from a Rawlsian construction of the "original position," in that it would privilege a discourse model of practical debate as being the appropriate forum for determining rights claims. But are we not thereby landing in a vicious circle, that is, discourses, even to get started, presuppose the recognition of one another's moral rights among discourse participants; on the other hand, such rights are said to be specified as a result of the discursive situation.

I have indicated elsewhere that this is not a vicious circle but rather the hermeneutic circle that characterizes all reasoning about morals and politics.[23] We never begin our deliberations concerning these matters at a "moral ground zero." Rather, in moral theory as in everyday morality, in political theory as in everyday political discourse, we are always situated within a horizon of presuppositions, assumptions, and power relations, the totality of which can never become wholly transparent to us. This much we must have learned from all the criticisms of rationalism in the last three centuries. Discourse ethics in this sense presupposes the reciprocal moral recognition of one another's claims to be participants in the moral-political dialogue. I am still enough of a Hegelian to maintain, however, that such reciprocal recognition of one another's rights to moral personality is a result of a world-historical process that involves struggle, battle and resistance, as well as defeat, carried out by social classes, genders, groups, and nations.

What is distinctive about the discourse model is that although it presupposes that participants must recognize one another's entitlement to moral respect and reciprocity in some sense, the determination of the precise content and extent of these principles would be a consequence of discourses themselves.[24] Insofar as the precise meaning and entailment of the norms of universal moral respect and egalitarian reciprocity would be subject to discursive validation, we can speak here of a procedure of "recursive validation."[25] The methodological procedure of recursive validation rules out the two consequences most feared by liberals vis-à-vis the model of deliberative democracy—namely, too strong a formulation of the conditions of consent, and the tyranny of the majority. The norms of universal moral respect and egalitarian reciprocity allow minorities and dissenters both the right to withhold their assent and the right to challenge the rules as well as the agenda of public debate. For what distinguishes discourses from compromises and other agreements reached under conditions of coercion is that only the *freely given assent of all concerned* can count as a condition of having reached agreement in the discourse situation.[26]

Deliberative Democracy and Constitutionalism

Upon reflection, we can see that institutionally as well, complex constitutional democracies, and particularly those in which a *public sphere* of opinion formation and deliberation has been developed, engage in such recursive validation continually. Basic human civil and political rights, as guaranteed by the Bill of Rights to the U.S. Constitution and as embodied in the constitution of most democratic governments, are never really "off the agenda" of public discussion and debate. They are simply constitutive and regulative institutional norms of debate in democratic societies that cannot be transformed and abrogated by simple majority decisions. The language of keeping these rights off the agenda mischaracterizes the nature of democratic debate in our kinds of societies: although we cannot change these rights without extremely elaborate political and juridical procedures, we are always disputing their meaning, their extent, and their jurisdiction. Democratic debate is like a ball game where there is no umpire to interpret the rules of the game and their application definitively. Rather, in the game of democracy the rules of the game no less than their interpretation and even the position of the umpire are essentially contestable. Contestation means neither the complete abrogation of these rules nor silence about them. When basic rights and liberties are violated the game of democracy is suspended and becomes either martial rule, civil war, or dictatorship; when democratic politics is in full session, the debate about the meaning of these rights, what they do or do not entitle us to, their scope and enforcement, is what politics is all about. One cannot challenge the specific interpretation of basic rights and liberties in a democracy without taking these absolutely seriously.

The deliberative theory of democracy transcends the traditional opposition of majoritarian politics vs. liberal guarantees of basic rights and liberties to the extent that the normative conditions of discourses, like basic rights and liberties, are to be viewed as rules of the game that can be contested within the game but only insofar as one first accepts to abide by them and play the game at all. This formulation seems to me to correspond to the reality of democratic debate and public speech in real democracies much more accurately than the liberal model of deliberation upon constitutional essentials or the reasoning of the Supreme Court. Crucial to the deliberative model of democracy is the idea of a "public sphere" of opinion-formation, debate, deliberation, and contestation among citizens, groups, movements, and organizations in a polity. When this concept of a public sphere is introduced as the concrete embodiment of discursive democracy in practice, it also becomes possible to think of the issue of conversational constraints in a more nuanced way. While the deliberative model of democracy shares with liberalism a concern for the protection of the rights to autonomy of equal citizens, the conceptual method of discursive validation and the institutional reality of a differentiated public sphere of deliberation and contestation provide plausible beginning points for a mediation of the stark opposition between liberalism and deliberative democracy.

Bruce Ackerman's conception of dualist democracy is based upon a similar strategy of overcoming the opposition between the standpoint of foundationalist rights-liberals on the one hand and monist majoritarian democrats on the other: "The basic mediating device is the dualist's two-track system of democratic lawmaking. It allows an important place for the foundationalist's view of 'rights as trumps' without violating the monist's deeper commitment to the primacy of democracy."[27] In a constitutional democracy the question as to which aspects of the higher law are entrenched against revision by the people as opposed to which aspects may be repealed is itself always open and contestable. Conceptually as well as sociologically, models of deliberative and dualistic democracy focus on this process of "recursive" and "hermeneutic" interdependence between constitution-making and democratic politics.[28]

Feminist Suspicions toward Deliberative Democracy

While liberals criticize the model of deliberative democracy for possibly overextending itself and corroding the sphere of individual privacy, feminist theorists criticize this model for not extending itself broadly enough to be truly inclusive. In an illuminating article entitled "Impartiality and the Civic Public," Iris Young, for example, has argued:

> The distinction between public and private as it appears in modern political theory expresses a will for homogeneity that necessitates the exclusion of many persons and groups, particularly women and radicalized groups culturally identified with the body, wildness and rationality. In conformity with the modern idea of normative reason, the idea of the public in modern political theory and practice designates a sphere of human existence in which citizens express their

rationality and universality, abstracted from their particular situations and need, and opposed to feeling. . . . Examination of the exclusionary and homogeneous ideal in modern political theory, however, shows that we cannot envision such renewal of public life as a recovery of Enlightenment ideals. Instead, we need to transform the distinction between public and private that does not correlate with an opposition between reason and affectivity and desire, or universal and particular.[29]

Iris Young's cogent and penetrating feminist critique of the ideal of the impartial public applies to the model of deliberative democracy suggested in the preceding only in certain respects. Certainly, the model of a general deliberative assembly that governed our conceptions of the public sphere well into the twentieth century was historically, socially, and culturally a space for male bodies. I mean this not only in the sense that only men were active citizens entitled to hold office and appear in public, but also in the sense that the institutional iconography of early democratic theory privileged the male mode of self-representation.[30]

Yet here we must distinguish between the *institutional* and the *conceptual* critiques. There is a certain ambivalence in the feminist critique of such models of the public sphere and deliberative democracy. On the one hand, the critique appears to take democratic institutions at their principled best and to criticize their biased and restrictive implementations in practice; on the other hand, the feminist critique appears to aim at a rejection of the ideals of free public reason and impartiality altogether. As Joan Landes puts it, the democratic public sphere appears to be essentially and not just accidentally "masculinist."[31] A normative theory of deliberative democracy requires a strong concept of the public sphere as its institutional correlate. The public sphere replaces the model of the general deliberative assembly found in early democratic theory. In this context, it is important for feminist theorists to specify the level of their concep-

tual objection, and to differentiate among institutional and normative presuppositions.[32]

Iris Young does not reject the ideal of a public sphere, only its Enlightenment variety. She proposes to replace the ideal of the "civil public" with that of a heterogeneous public. In her recent work she has advocated a number of institutional measures that would guarantee and solidify group representation in such a public sphere.[33] Yet wanting to retain the public sphere and according it a place in democratic theory is not compatible with the more radical critique of the ideal of impartial reason that Young also develops in some of her essays.

In her essay "Communication and the Other: Beyond Deliberative Democracy" Iris Young distinguishes between "deliberative" and "communicative" democracy on the grounds that most theories of deliberative democracy offer too narrow a conception of the democratic process because they continue to privilege an ideal of "a common good in which [the discussion participants] are all supposed to leave behind their particular experience and interests"(126).

By contrast, Young advocates a theory of communicative democracy according to which individuals would attend to one another's differences in class, gender, race, religion, and so on. Each social position has a partial perspective on the public that it does not abandon; but through the communicative process participants transcend and transform their initial situated knowledges (127). Instead of critical argumentation, such processes of communicative confrontation privilege modalities of communication like "greeting, rhetoric, and storytelling"(120).

I think this distinction between deliberative and communicative democracy is more apparent than real. To sustain her critique of the ideals of impartiality and objectivity, which she associates with the deliberative model, Young must be able to distinguish the kind of *transformation* and *transcendence* of partial perspectives that occurs in communicative democracy from the *mutual agreement* to be reached in processes of deliberative democracy. Yet how can we distinguish between the emergence of common opinion among members of one group, if we do not apply to such processes of communication or deliberation some standards of fairness and impartiality in order to judge the manner in which opinions were allowed to be brought forth, groups were given chances to express their points of view, and the like? The model of communicative democracy, far from dispensing with the need for standards of impartiality and fairness, requires them to make sense of its own formulations. Without some such standards, Young could not differentiate the genuine transformation of partial and situated perspectives from mere agreements of convenience or apparent unanimity reached under conditions of duress.

With respect to modes of communication like "greeting, rhetoric, and storytelling," I would say that each of these modes may have their place within the *informally structured process of everyday communication among individuals who share a cultural and historical life world*. However, it is neither necessary for the democratic theorist to try to formalize and institutionalize these aspects of communicative everyday competence, nor is it plausible—and this is the more important objection—to build an opposition between them and critical argumentation. Greeting, storytelling, and rhetoric, although they may be aspects of informal communication in our everyday life, cannot become the public language of institutions and legislatures in a democracy for the following reason: to attain legitimacy, democratic institutions require the articulation of the bases of their actions and policies in discursive language that appeals to commonly shared and accepted public reasons. In constitutional democracies such public reasons take the form of general statements consonant with the rule of law. The rule of law has a certain rhetorical structure of its own: it is general, applies to all members of a specified reference group on the basis of legitimate reasons. Young's attempt to transform the language of

the rule of law into a more partial, affective, and situated mode of communication would have the consequence of inducing arbitrariness, for who can tell how far the power of a greeting can reach? It would further create capriciousness— what about those who simply cannot understand my story? It would limit rather than enhance social justice because rhetoric moves people and achieves results without having to render an account of the bases upon which it induces people to engage in certain courses of action rather than others. In short, some moral ideal of impartiality is a regulative principle that should govern not only our *deliberations* in public but also the *articulation* of reasons by public institutions. What is considered impartial has to be "in the best interests of all equally." Without such a normative principle, neither the ideal of the rule of law can be sustained nor deliberative reasoning toward a common good occur. Some Enlightenment ideals are part of any conception of democratic legitimacy and the public sphere. The point therefore is not a rejection of the Enlightenment in toto but a critical renegotiation of its legacy.

Expanding on the model of a heterogeneous, dispersed network of many publics, Nancy Fraser has suggested how, in fact, once the unitary model of the public sphere is abandoned, women's concerns, as well as those of other excluded groups, can be accommodated. Such a nonunitary and dispersed network of publics can accommodate women's desires for their own spaces, in their own terms. In such "subaltern counterpublics," to use Fraser's term,[34] the lines between the public and the private, for example, can be renegotiated, rethought, challenged, and reformulated. It is nonetheless a long step from the cultural and social rethinking and reformulation of such distinctions as between the public and the private to their implementation in legislation and governmental regulation. While sharing the concern of liberal theorists that the precipitous reformulation of such a divide may corrode individual liberties, Fraser rightly points out that there is a distinction between "opinion-making" and "policy-making" public bodies, and that the same kinds of constraints may not apply to each alike.[35] Opinion-making publics, as found in social movements, for example, can lead us to reconsider and rethink very controversial issues about privacy, sexuality, and intimacy; but this does not imply that the only or even most desirable consequence of such processes of public deliberation should be general legislation. Thus when conceived as an anonymous, plural, and multiple medium of communication and deliberation, the public sphere need not homogenize and repress difference. Heterogeneity, otherness, and difference can find expression in the multiple associations, networks, and citizens' forums, all of which constitute public life under late capitalism.[36]

Institutionalist Distrust of Deliberative Democracy

. . . My goal in this essay has been to outline a deliberative model of democracy that incorporates features of practical rationality. Central to practical rationality is the possibility of free public deliberation about matters of mutual concern to all. The discourse model of ethics and politics suggests a procedure for such free public deliberation among all concerned. Such processes of public deliberation have a claim to rationality because they increase and make available necessary information, because they allow the expression of arguments in the light of which opinions and beliefs need to be revised, and because they lead to the formation of conclusions that can be challenged publicly for good reasons. Furthermore, such procedures allow self-referential critique of their own uses and abuses. The chief institutional correlate of such a model of deliberative democracy is a multiple, anonymous, heterogeneous network of many publics and public conversations. In other domains of social life as well, the model of deliberative democracy based on the centrality of public deliberation can inspire the proliferation of many institutional designs.

NOTES

1. See John Rawls, "Kantian Constructivism in Moral Theory," *Journal of Philosophy* 77, no 9 (1980): 515–72, a revised and enlarged version of which is included in *Political Liberalism* (New York: Columbia University Press, 1993), 89–131; Jürgen Habermas, *Moral Consciousness and Communicative Action*, trans. Christian Lenhardt and Shierry Weber Nicholsen (Cambridge, Mass.: MIT Press, 1990), and in particular the essay "Discourse Ethics: Notes on a Program of Philosophical Justification," 76ff.

2. In a helpful survey article entitled "Freedom, Consensus, and Equality in Collective Decision Making," *Ethics* 101, no. 1 (October 1990): 151ff., Thomas Christiano examines different approaches to the philosophical foundations of democracy.

3. It is well known that nearly a decade ago now, John Rawls retracted the Kantian strategy of normative justification followed in his *Theory of Justice* in favor of a more historicist, and social and politically situated concept of an "overlapping consensus." The two principles of justice were valid, he claimed, not sub specie aeternitatis but because they articulated some deeply shared convictions in liberal democracies of the West about the foundations of their forms of government. These deeply held convictions would constitute, when properly sifted through, clarified, and articulated, the bases of an "overlapping consensus" in such societies. See John Rawls, "Justice as Fairness: Political Not Metaphysical," *Philosophy and Public Affairs* 14 (1985): 223–51; and "The Idea of an Overlapping Consensus," *Oxford Journal of Legal Studies* 7 (1987): 1–25. This shift from a Kantian strategy of justification to a more historicist mode has been celebrated by some. Richard Rorty has seen in these recent developments of Rawls's work a confirmation for his own brand of "ethnocentric liberalism." See Richard Rorty, "The Priority of Democracy to Philosophy," in *Objectivism, Relativism, and Truth* (New York: Cambridge University Press, 1991), 175–96. For a lucid account of these developments in Rawls's position and a critical examination of the idea of an "overlapping consensus," see Kenneth Baynes, "Constructivism and Practical Reason in Rawls," in *Analyse und Kritik. Zeitschrift für Sozialwissenschaften* 14 (June 1992): 18–32.

4. See M. I. Finley's still-classic essays in *Democracy: Ancient and Modern* (New Brunswick, N.J.: Rutgers University Press, 1985).

5. The most brilliant example of Hegels methodology remains the 1821 *Philosophy of Right*, trans. T. M. Knox (New York: Oxford University Press, 1973). The kind of anonymous collective rationality

I have in mind has been developed by Karl Popper in the domain of epistemology. See Karl R. Popper, *Objective Knowledge: An Evolutionary Approach* (Oxford: Clarendon, 1972).

6. My formulation is wholly akin to that proposed by Joshua Cohen, "Deliberation and Democratic Legitimacy," in *The Good Polity: Normative Analysis of the State*, ed. Alan Hamlin and Philip Pettit (London: Blackwell, 1989), 17–34; see also Joshua Cohen, "Procedure and Substance in Deliberative Democracy."

7. I have outlined my understanding of this project as well as indicating the manner in which my interpretation of the general program of discourse ethics differs from that of Habermas and Apel in *Situating the Self* (New York: Routledge, 1992). This article presupposes the general argument set forth in that book in chapters 1, 2, and 3 in particular, and documents my effort to apply the principles of discourse ethics to political-institutional life. Independently of the project of discourse ethics but in fascinating affinity to it, in recent years there has also been a revival of deliberative models of democracy among political theorists and legal philosophers. See in particular Frank I. Michelman, "Law's Republic," *Yale Law Journal* 93 (1984): 1013ff.; and Cass R. Sunstein, "Beyond the Republican Revival," *Yale Law Journal* 97 (1988): 1539.

8. In some contemporary models of deliberative democracy, a distinction between "constitutional" (high) politics and "ordinary" (low) politics dominates. The claim is that deliberative politics more properly characterizes constitution-making processes, whereas mundane, day-to-day politics may be governed by nondeliberative and narrowly instrumental, self-regarding pursuits. See David Gauthier, "Constituting Democracy," in *The Idea of Democracy*, ed. David Copp et al. (Cambridge: Cambridge University Press, 1993), 314–15; and David M. Estlund's very instructive discussion, "Who's Afraid of Deliberative Democracy? On the Strategic/Deliberative Dichotomy in Recent Constitutional Jurisprudence." *Texas Law Review* 71, no. 7 (June 1993): 1437–77. Although I believe that a distinction between "constitution-making" and "ordinary" politics is extremely useful and unavoidable for democratic theory, I think that it can be and has been overdrawn. The main motivation for overdrawing this distinction seems to be traditional liberal fears about unbridled majoritarian decisions and distrust in the rationality of political judgment as exercised by ordinary people. The deliberative model of democracy that I am advocating seeks to bridge the gap between high and low politics by raising the quality of ordinary people's everyday deliberations. This does not mean that constitutional issues are always and at all times open for reconsideration. Not at all; but it does suggests that ordinary politics cannot but be informed by such constitutional issues and principles—as examples take debates ranging from prayer in public schools to violence in the media to pornography and abortion. My assumption is that the more such ordinary political deliberation approximates the model suggested above, the more the likelihood increases that it will be informed by constitutional principles in the "right way." For further discussion see also the "Deliberative Democracy and Constitutionalism" section that follows.

9. Bernard Manin, "On Legitimacy and Political Deliberation." *Political Theory* 15, no. 3 (August 1987): 338–68.

10. In a recent article, "The Voice of the People," Sidney Verba discusses citizens' communications to their representatives and other governmental offices via letters, calls, and increasingly faxes and e-mail. (677ff.) Reflecting upon the phenomenal increase of such direct communication (about a fifth to a quarter of the public in the U.S.A. report contacting an official—"depending on the way the question is framed" [679]), Verba expresses the hope that "perhaps citizen-initiated messages, especially when enhanced by new technology, can become part of a public discourse" (685). See Sidney Verba, "The Voice of the People," 1993 James Madison Award Lecture, *PS: Political Science and Politics* 26, no 4 (December 1993): 677–86.

11. Hannah Arendt, "The Crisis in Culture," in *Between Past and Future: Six Exercises in Political Thought* (New York: Meridian, 1961), 220–21.

12. Charles Larmore has provided an eloquent statement of this view in recent years. See *Patterns of Moral Complexity* (Cambridge: Cambridge University Press, 1987), 119ff.; and "Political Liberalism," *Political Theory* 18, no. 3 (August 1990): 342ff.

13. I would like to attempt to answer here a very important objection raised by Donald Moon. How plausible is it to distinguish value disagreements concerning *substantive* moral, religious, or philosophical doctrines from *procedural* agreement about processes for adjudicating and revising beliefs in a public context? Very often, such substantive beliefs will not permit one to distinguish so sharply between content and form, substance and procedure. As examples of cases when value systems do not permit a sharp distinction between substance and procedure we can think of religious sects living within the boundaries of the liberal-democratic constitutional state such as certain Orthodox Jewish sects in Israel who refuse to recognize the secular authority of the State of Israel;

Orthodox Moslems living in some European states, like Germany and France for example, who experience conflict between their views of the proper education and place of women and the views of the liberal-democratic state; or Christian Scientists in the United States who want to provide medical treatment to their children consonant with their own beliefs and who come into conflict with local and federal authorities. In each of these cases clashes can and do arise that prima facie cannot be solved by resorting to a simple substance/form distinction. To deal properly with the issues raised by such examples and in particular to explore the ways in which a deliberative model of democracy based upon discourse ethics may or may not presuppose too strong a model of agreement clearly goes beyond the scope of this article. However, I do think that in the face of all these cases as well a form of deliberative proceduralism is the most viable normative answer.

Insofar as these groups live within the jurisdiction of the liberal-constitutional and democratic state they have accepted certain "constitutional minimums." Debates usually arise not around these constitutional minimal rights, which are guaranteed to all citizens and residents (in varying degrees) under the rule of law, but around whether certain cultural and religious practices do or do not contradict these constitutional minimums or whether they can be considered matters of the religious and cultural autonomy of a group. Is the duty to serve in the Israeli army a constitutional obligation to which there can be no exceptions on religious grounds? Can Orthodox Muslim families choose not to send their daughters to public schools? And when they do send them to public schools, should these children be allowed to wear head scarves or should they be obliged to wear school uniforms? Can a Christian Scientist family refuse medical treatment to a child suffering from an infectious disease that requires standard medication? Should the state protect the rights of the child against the judgment of the family in this case? I am inclined to think that vis-à-vis such issues there is no single answer applicable to each case but more or less a gradation of moral and political principles and intuitions. The possibility not to serve in the army on the basis of religious beliefs is a right of conscientious objection recognized by many modern states, which can be made consonant with the principle of the separation of church and state. On the other hand, to deny a child the fundamentals of a secular education in our world or the best treatment that medical science can offer violate the respect and equality we owe that child as a future citizen of our polity. Yet whether Muslim girls

can wear their head scarves (the chador) to French schools or whether Sikh soldiers can wear their turbans in the Canadian Royal Police strikes me as being a qualitatively different matter from the provision of either education or health care. A more pluralistic conception of the public sphere and of civic identity than that displayed by the French public and authorities in the debate around the chador is perfectly compatible with, and in fact required by, the model of deliberative democracy and public dialogue developed in this essay.

14. See Jane Mansbridge's article "Using Power/Fighting Power: The Polity" for an exploration of the dilemmas of deliberative democracy models in the face of persistent and ineliminable conflicts of interests and wills in public life, and the problems involved in the use of coercion.

15. For a recent statement of the transformation of the concept of the public sphere from a centralized to a decentered model, see Jürgen Habermas, "Ist der Herzschlag der Revolution zum Stillstand gekommen? Volkssouveränität als Verfahren. Ein normativer Begriff der Öffentlichkeit?" in *Die Iden von* 1789, ed. Forum für Philosophie Bad Homburg (Frankfurt: Suhrkamp, 1989), 7ff.

16. Bruce Ackerman, *Social Justice in the Liberal State* (New Haven: Yale University Press, 1980) and "Why Dialogue?" *Journal of Philosophy* 86 (January 1989). I have dealt with Bruce Ackerman's model of liberal conversation in several articles. See Benhabib, "Liberal Dialogue vs. a Critical Model of Discursive Legitimacy" and "Models of Public Space: Hannah Arendt, the Liberal Tradition and Jürgen Habermas," in *Situating the Self*.

17. Cf. Stephen Holmes, "Gag Rules or the Politics of Omission," in *Constitutionalism and Democracy*, ed. Jon Elster and R. Slagstad (Cambridge: Cambridge University Press, 1988), 19–58; and John Rawls, "The Idea of an Overlapping Consensus."

18. For a further exploration of these themes see the article by Josh Cohen, "Procedure and Substance in Deliberative Democracy," in this volume.

19. This issue has been recently well formulated by Kenneth Baynes in "The Liberal/Communitarian Controversy and Communicative Ethics," *Philosophy and Social Criticism* 14, nos. 3–4 (1988): 305 (my emphasis).

20. See *Situating the Self*, 29ff.

21. Jürgen Habermas has embarked on this task in his new book, *Faktizität und Geltung* (Frankfurt: Suhrkamp, 1992), chap. 3.

22. In her contribution to this volume, "Diversity and Democracy: Representing Differences," Carol

Gould objects that discourse-ethical theory cannot justify fundamental human rights. I would counter her criticisms by further exploring the implications of the counterfactual suggested above for a theory of rights.

23. In *Situating the Self*, 30ff.

24. Perhaps an example may clarify this procedure further: let us take the cases of Great Britain, the United States of America, and Israel as three models of liberal-democratic societies whose political and legal order is based upon some form of recognition of the norm of moral respect for persons. Certainly all three societies enjoy a system of parliamentary democracy in which, through legislatively or constitutionally determined periodic elections, public officials are brought to and removed from office. In all three societies individuals enjoy certain rights and liberties that are upheld by the political system and protected by the courts. However, these societies have radically divergent and at times incompatible views of what constitutes the legitimate exercise of the right of free speech. Whereas in the United States considerations of public propriety, fair trial, or national security would hardly serve as routine grounds on the basis of which to curtail First Amendment rights, in Great Britain and Israel they are commonly invoked. In Great Britain the media's access to court hearings and trials is restricted, while in Israel even the publication of certain scholarly articles can be subjected to the prohibition of the military censor if they are deemed to contain "security-sensitive information."

The relevance of this example to the theoretical principle of discursive validation is the following: just as differences in the extent and application of the fundamental right of free speech would not lead us to deny that Great Britain and Israel are democratic societies just as the United States is, so too a number of more specific interpretations of the norms of universal moral respect and egalitarian reciprocity are compatible with democratic political dialogue. What results from a deliberative theory of democracy based upon the discourse model is not a catalog of unabridgeable basic rights and liberties but two most general moral norms that are compatible, within certain well-defined limits, with a variety of legal and political arrangements.

25. See Kenneth Baynes, *The Normative Grounds of Political Criticism: Kant, Rawls, Habermas* (Albany: SUNY Press, 1992). 1ff.

26. In his interesting criticism of some of my earlier formulations concerning discourse ethics in *Critique, Norm, and Utopia* (New York: Columbia University Press, 1986), Donald Moon charges that practical discourse could be potentially "coercive, leading to institutional forms that involve domination or imposition. It is hard to see how any form of 'discourse' could achieve a consensus that is genuinely free and uncoerced unless participants enjoy some rights of privacy and personal integrity, unless they can resist the demand for self-disclosure." Donald Moon, *Constructing Community: Moral Pluralism and Tragic Conflicts* (Princeton: Princeton University Press, 1993), 95. Given the norms of universal moral respect and egalitarian reciprocity presupposed by discourses, and given the strong emphasis on voluntarily given assent, based upon one's evaluation of certain kinds of validity claims, I fail to see how discourses could violate individual privacy or force self-disclosure. I maintain, however, that discourses can challenge the line between the public and the private spheres, in the sense that citizens in a polity may make into a public issue some areas of concern that were hitherto considered private matters, such as domestic violence, or, conversely, may plead for the privacy of certain kinds of information, such as buying and consumption patterns or other kinds of personal facts contained in data banks, for example. What moral and political theory should not do is freeze the historical and essentially contestable outcomes of democratic discourses into some immutable catalog of rights; rather moral and political theory should provide us with general principles to guide our moral intuitions and concrete deliberations when we are confronted with such controversial cases as domestic violence, child abuse, and marital rape, or using the sex of an unborn baby as a basis for aborting that fetus.

27. Bruce Ackerman, *We the People*, vol. 1: *Foundations* (Cambridge, Mass.: Harvard University Press, 1991), 12.

28. Some questions of democratic legitimacy and antifoundationalism as they apply to the Supreme Court's dilemma in a democracy have been most fruitfully explored by Morton J. Horwitz in "The Constitution of Change: Legal Fundamentality without Fundamentalism," *Harvard Law Review* 107 (1993): 32–117.

29. Iris Young, "Impartiality and the Civic Public," in *Feminism as Critique*, ed. Seyla Benhabib and Drucilla Cornell (London: Polity Press).73.

30. For historical analyses, see Joan B. Landes, *Women and the Public Sphere in the Age of the French Revolution* (Ithaca: Cornell University Press, 1988); and Linda Kerber, *Women of the Republic: Intellect and Ideology in Revolutionary America* (New York: Norton, 1986).

31. Landes's illuminating early work *Women and the Public Sphere in the Age of the French Revolution* was marred by one conceptual issue. Particularly in her critique of Habermas's work on the public sphere, Landes conflated the Habermasian model of the public sphere that was part of civil society with the Rousseauian-republican model based upon an opposition to civil society. Much of criticism of the "masculinism" of the public sphere applies only to this republican, civic-virtue version that has little to do with the Enlightenment conception of the public sphere, which Habermas defines as "private individuals using their reason about public matters." Clearly the concept of the public sphere developed in this essay emerges out of this second tradition. See Keith Baker's illuminating discussion of this issue in "Defining the Public Sphere in Eighteenth-Century France: Variations on a Theme by Habermas," in *Habermas and the Public Sphere*, ed. Craig Calhoun (Cambridge, Mass.: MIT Press, 1992), 181–212.

32. A provocative but inadequate critique of the public sphere concept has been given by Dana Villa who minimizes the role and significance of this concept in securing legitimation in democratic theory while focusing on its agonistic and performative dimensions. See "Postmodernism and the Public Sphere," *American Political Science Review* 86, no. 3 (September 1992): 712–25.

33. Iris Marion Young, *Justice and the Politics of Difference* (Princeton: Princeton University Press, 1990).

34. Nancy Fraser, "Rethinking the Public Sphere: A Contribution to the Critique of Actually Existing Democracy," in Calhoun, ed. *Habermas and the Public Sphere*, 123.

35. Ibid., 132ff.

36. Ibid., 108ff.

Part V

Communitarian Justice

20 The Nature of Justice

ARISTOTLE

With regard to justice[1] and injustice, the points we have to consider are—with what class of actions are they connected, in what sense is justice a middle state, and between what extremes is that which is just intermediate? Our enquiry shall follow the same procedure as our previous investigations.

We observe that by the term justice everybody means that state of character which renders men disposed to act justly, and which causes them to do and to wish what is just; and similarly by injustice they mean the disposition that makes men do and wish what is unjust. Let us then accept these definitions to go upon as broadly correct.

The fact is that it is not the same with a state of character as with the sciences and faculties. It appears that the same science or faculty deals with opposite objects,[2] but a state that produces one result does not also produce the opposite result—for instance, health does not cause us to do actions that are the reverse of healthy, but only those that are healthy: A sound gait in walking means walking like a man in good health, not walking lame.

Hence it is often possible to infer one of two opposite states from the other, and often states can be identified from the subjects that exhibit them. Thus if we find out what constitutes good bodily condition we learn what bad condition is as well; but we can also learn what good bodily condition is from actual persons that are in good condition, while from knowing what good condition is we can recognize things that produce good condition. If good condition is firmness of flesh, bad condition must necessarily be flabbiness of flesh, and also 'wholesome' must mean productive of firmness of flesh. Also if one of two opposite terms has more than one meaning, it follows as a rule that the other also has more than one meaning—for instance, the terms "just" and "unjust." And "justice" and "injustice" appear to have more than one meaning, but owing to their two meanings not being widely separate, the ambiguity escapes notice and is not rather obvious, as it is in the case of two meanings that are widely separate. Let us then take the different senses in which the word "unjust" is used. A man who breaks the law is unjust, and so also is a man who is grasping and unfair; so that obviously a law-abiding man and a man who is fair in business are both of them just. "Just" therefore denotes both what is lawful and what is fair, and "unjust" denotes both what is unlawful and what is unfair.

As the unjust man is grasping, his injustice will be exercised in regard to things that are good—not all of them but those with which good and bad fortune are concerned, which though always good in the absolute sense are not always good for a particular person. These are the goods that men pray for and seek after, although they ought

From Chapter V of Aristotle's Ethics for English Readers, *rendered from the Greek of the* Nicomachean Ethics *by H. Rackham (1943). Reprinted by permission of Basil Blackwell, Publisher.*

not to do so; they ought to pray that the things which are good in the absolute sense may also be good for themselves, though choosing the things that are good for themselves. The unjust man does not always choose the larger share—in the case of things that are bad absolutely he chooses the smaller share; but because the smaller quantity of a bad thing seems to be good in a sense, and a grasping nature means that one grasps something good, this makes him appear to be grasping. Let us call him "unfair," as that term includes taking too much of good things and taking too little of bad ones, and covers both.

We saw that the man who breaks the law is unjust and the law-abiding man just. This shows that all that is lawful is just in a sense, since it is the business of legislature to define what is lawful, and the various decisions of the legislature are what we term the principles of justice. Now all the edicts of the laws are aimed either at the common advantage of everybody or at the interest of a ruling class selected by merit or in some other similar way. Consequently in one sense we apply the word "just" to things which produce and preserve happiness, and the things that form part of happiness for the community. And the law prescribes certain conduct: the conduct of a brave man (for instance, not to desert one's post, not to run away in battle, not to throw down one's arms); that of a self-controlled man (for instance, not to commit adultery or violent assault); that of a good-tempered man (for instance, not to strike a person or to use abusive language), and similarly as to all the other forms of virtue—some acts the law enjoins and others it forbids, rightly if the law has been rightly framed and not so well if it has been drafted carelessly.

Justice in this sense then is perfect virtue, though with the qualification that it is virtue in relation to our neighbors. Because of this the view is often held that in the list of virtues justice occupies the top place, and that

Neither the evening nor the morning star[3]

is so sublime; and we have the proverb:

The whole of virtue is comprised in justice.[4]

Justice is perfect because it is our mode of practicing perfect virtue; and it is supremely perfect because its possessor can use it in his relations with others and not only by himself. There are plenty of people who can practice virtue in their personal affairs but who are incapable of displaying it in their relations with others. This shows the truth of the saying of Bias,[5] "Office will show a real man"; when somebody obtains a position of authority he is brought into contact with other people, and is a member of a partnership. For this same reason, justice alone among the virtues is thought to be "another person's good,"[6] because it is exercised in relation to one's neighbors; it does what is in the interest of somebody else, a superior or a partner. The wickedest man therefore is he who exercises his wickedness in his relations with his friends and not merely in his personal affairs; and the best man is the one who practices his virtue not in regard to himself but in relation to someone else, as that is a difficult thing to do.

Justice thus understood therefore is not a part of virtue, but the whole of it; and its opposite, injustice, is not a part of vice, but the whole. The distinction between justice in this sense and virtue is clear from what has been said; they are the same quality of character but differently viewed: what as exercised in relation to others is justice, considered simply as a disposition of a certain sort is virtue.

Justice as a Part of Virtue

But it is justice as a particular part of virtue that we are investigating, that being as we say one sort of justice; and similarly we are considering injustice as a particular vice, not in the sense of wickedness in general.

That there is such a vice is indicated by the following considerations: When a man practices one of the other vices (for instance, when owing to cowardice he throws away his shield,[7] or owing to ill-temper uses abusive language, or owing to meanness refuses to help a friend out of a difficulty with money), he is committing an injustice but he is not taking an unfair share of something. But when he takes an unfair share, he is not displaying one of the vices of the kind specified, and certainly not all of them, but clearly he does display a vice of some sort, as we blame his conduct—in fact he displays injustice. Therefore there is another sort of injustice which is a part of injustice as a whole, and there is a form of unjust action which is a subdivision of unjust and illegal conduct in general. Again, suppose that A commits adultery for gain and gets something by it, whereas B does it out of inclination and loses by his indulgence. B would appear to be self-indulgent rather than avaricious, whereas A would seem unjust but not self-indulgent at all. It is clear then that A's motive would be profit. And yet another reason—whereas all other offenses are always attributed to some particular vice; for instance, adultery is ascribed to self-indulgence, desertion of a comrade in battle to cowardice, assault to anger—an offense out of which a man has made a profit is not put down to any other vice but injustice.

Hence it is clear that beside injustice in the wide sense there is another kind of injustice which is a particular form of vice. It bears the same name because it comes under the same general definition—both forms of injustice being exercised in our relations with other people; but injustice in the special sense is concerned with honor or money or security, or perhaps all of these things included under some general term, and its motive is the pleasure derived from gain, whereas injustice in the wide sense is concerned with the whole of things in relation to which virtue is displayed.

The next step is to ascertain the nature and the attributes of justice in this special sense of the term, as distinct from justice denoting the whole of virtue.

Now we have distinguished two meanings of the term "unjust"—namely, unlawful and unequal or unfair; and we have shown that "just" means both lawful and equal or fair. Injustice of the kind mentioned above corresponds with "unlawful." But the unfair is not the same thing as the unlawful, but is related to it as part to whole—everything unfair is unlawful, but not everything unlawful is unfair. Consequently the unjust and injustice in the special sense are not the same as the unjust and injustice in the wide sense; although they also are related to each other as part to whole—injustice in this sense is a part of injustice in the wide sense, and likewise justice in this sense is a part of justice in the wide sense. We must consequently discuss justice and injustice, and what is just and unjust, in the special sense also. We may therefore leave on one side that form of justice which is coextensive with virtue as a whole, and the corresponding form of injustice–namely, the exercise of the whole of virtue and of vice in our relations with another person.

It is also clear how we should define what is just and what unjust in the corresponding senses; for almost a majority of the actions ordained by law are those which are prescribed on the basis of virtue taken as a whole, since the law specifies the particular virtues which we are to practice and the particular vices which we are to avoid; and the means for producing virtue as a whole are the regulations laid down by law for education in the duties of a citizen. But in regard to our education as individuals, which renders us simply good *men,* the question whether this is the concern of politics or of another art will have to be decided later,[8] for perhaps to be a good man is not the same thing as to be a good citizen of some particular state.

Special justice, on the other hand, and that which is just in the sense corresponding to it, is of two kinds. One kind is the principle that regulates distributions of honor or money or the other divisible assets of the community, which may be divided among its members in equal or unequal shares. The other kind is that which regulates private transactions. The latter form of justice has two divisions, inasmuch as some transactions are voluntary and others nonvoluntary.[9] Instances of voluntary transactions are selling, buying, lending at interest, lending free of interest, pledging, depositing, letting for hire: these are called voluntary because they are voluntarily entered upon. Of nonvoluntary transactions some are clandestine, such as theft, adultery, poisoning, procuring, enticing slaves to leave their owners, assassination, giving false witness; and some are violent, such as assault, imprisonment, murder, rape, mutilation, abusive language, contumelious treatment.

Distributive and Corrective Justice

Now as an unjust man is unfair and an unjust thing unequal, it is clear that corresponding to the unequal there is a middle point or mean; namely, that which is equal; for any kind of action admitting of more or less also admits what is equal. If then what is unjust is unequal, what is just is equal, as everyone will agree without argument; and since the equal is a mean, the just will be a sort of mean too. Now equality involves at least two terms; it follows therefore not only that the just is a mean and equal, but also that (1) as a mean it implies two extremes, the more and the less, (2) as equal it implies two equal shares, and (3) as just it implies certain persons for whom it is just. Consequently justice involves at least four terms, two persons for whom it is just and two shares which are just. And there will be the same equality between the shares as between the persons, that is, the ratio between the shares will be the same as the ratio between the persons. If the persons are not equal, they will not have equal shares; it is when equals possess or are assigned unequal shares, or persons who are not equal equal shares, that quarrels and complaints arise.

Moreover the same point also clearly follows from the principle of assignment by merit. Everybody agrees that just distribution must be in accordance with merit of some sort, though everybody does not mean the same sort of merit. Democrats take merit to mean free status, adherents of oligarchy take it to mean wealth or noble birth, supporters of aristocracy excellence.

The just then is that which is proportionate and the unjust is that which runs counter to proportion; the man who acts unjustly has too much, and the man who is unjustly treated too little, of the good. In the case of evil, it is the other way about, as the lesser evil is accounted as good in comparison with the greater evil, because the lesser evil is more desirable than the greater, and what is desirable is a good, and what is more desirable a greater good. This then is one species of justice.

The species of justice that remains is the justice of redress, which operates in the case of voluntary and involuntary transactions. This form of justice has a different specific character from the preceding one. The justice that distributes common property always follows the kind of proportion mentioned above (because in the case of distribution from the common funds of a partnership it will follow the same ratio as that existing between the sums put into the business by the partners); and the unjust that is opposed to this form of the just is that which violates that proportion. But justice in transactions between individuals, although it is equality of a sort and injustice inequality, does not go by the kind of proportion mentioned, but by arithmetical proportion.[10] It makes no difference[11] whether a good man has defrauded a bad one or a bad man a good one, nor whether a good man or a bad man has committed adultery; the law only looks at the nature of the injury, and treats the parties as equal if one has done and the other suffered a wrong or if one has inflicted and the other sustained damage. Consequently, in such cases the judge tries to equalize this injustice, which consists in inequality—for even in a case where one person has received and the other has inflicted a blow, or where one has killed and the other been killed, the suffering and the action have been distributed in unequal shares, while the judge's endeavor is to make them equal by means of the penalty he inflicts, taking something away from the gain of the assailant. The term "gain" is applied to such cases in a general sense, even though to some, for instance a person who has inflicted a wound, it is not specially appropriate, and the term "loss" is applied to the sufferer; at all events the terms "gain" and "loss" are employed when the amount of the suffering inflicted has been assessed. Consequently, while equal is intermediate between more and less, gain and loss are at once both more and less in contrary ways—more of what is good and less of what is bad are gain, and more of what is bad and less of what is good are loss, intermediate between them being, as we said, the equal, which we pronounce to be just. Consequently the justice of redress will be what is intermediate between loss and gain. This is why when a dispute arises the parties have recourse to a judge; to go to a judge is to appeal to the just, inasmuch as a judge is virtually justice personified;[12] and they have recourse to a judge as intermediary—indeed, in some countries judges are called "mediators"—on the ground that if the litigants get the medium amount they will get what is just. Thus justice is a sort of medium, as the judge is a medium between the litigants. What he does is to restore equality: it is as if there were a line divided into two unequal parts, and he took away the amount by which the larger segment exceeded half the line and added it to the smaller segment. When the whole has been divided into two equal parts, people say that they "have got their own," having got an equal share. This is the arithmetic mean between the greater amount and the less.

Therefore the just is intermediate between gain and loss due to breach of contract; it consists in having an equal amount both before and after the transaction.

Justice in Exchange

Some people hold the view that mere reciprocity is justice. But reciprocity does not coincide with either distributive justice or with corrective justice; it often conflicts with them—for example, if an officer strikes a man it is wrong for the man to hit back, but if a man strikes an officer, not only should the officer hit him but he must be punished as well. Further, there is a wide distinction between an act done with the consent of the other party and one done without consent. But in association for exchange this sort of justice, reciprocity, is the bond uniting the parties; but it must be reciprocity on a basis of proportion and not of equality. It is proportionate requital that keeps the state together. Men seek to return either evil for evil, failing which they feel themselves mere slaves, or good for good, in default of which no exchange of goods and services takes place; but it is exchange which holds society together. This is why men build a shrine of the Graces in their cities, as a reminder that favors should be returned, since to return favors received is a characteristic of grace. When somebody has done one a service, it behoves one not only to do him a service in return but also on the next occasion to take the initiative in doing him a service oneself.

Proportional requital is achieved by diagonal conjunction. Let A be a builder, B a shoemaker, C a house, and D a pair of shoes. Then the builder has to take from the shoemaker a part of the produce of his labor and give him in return a part of his own product. If proportionate equality between the products be first established, and then reciprocation takes place, the condition indicated will have been satisfied. But if this is not done, the bargain is not equal, and does not hold, since it may happen that the work of one party is worth more than that of the other, so that they have to be equalized. For two doctors do not combine to exchange their services, but a doctor and a farmer, and in general persons who are different and who may be unequal, but in that case they need to be equated. Consequently exchange of commodities requires that the commodities must be in some way commensurable; and it was to achieve this that money was invented. Money serves as a sort of middle term, as it measures all things, and so indicates their superior or inferior value—just how many shoes are the equivalent of a house or a certain quantity of food. The number of shoes exchanged for a house must correspond to the ratio between a builder and a shoemaker. Failing this, there will be no exchange, and no business will be done. And this cannot be secured unless the goods are equated in some way.

It is therefore necessary to have some one standard of measurement for all commodities, as was said before. And this standard is in reality demand; it is demand which keeps commerce together, since if people were to cease to have wants or if their wants were to alter, exchange will not go on, or it will be on different lines. But it has been agreed to accept money as representing demand. Money is a convention, and we can alter the currency if we choose, rendering the old coinage useless. Thus reciprocity will be achieved when the factors have been equated, bringing it about that as farmer is to shoemaker so the amount of shoemaker's work is to the amount of farmer's work exchanged for it.

That demand serves as a single factor holding commerce together is shown by the fact that when there is no demand for mutual service in the case of both parties or at least of one of the two, exchange of services does not take place. And money serves us as a security for future exchange, if we do not need a thing now; money guarantees that we shall have it if we do need it, as we shall be able to get it by producing the money. Now money fluctuates in value, just like goods; but it tends to be steadier. Consequently all goods must have a price given to them, as then exchange of goods will always be possible, and consequently association between men. Currency therefore is a sort of measure, which equates goods by making them commensurable. In fact there would be no association between man and man if there were no exchange, and no exchange if there were no equalization of values, and no equalization of values if there were no commensurability. No doubt it is not really possible for articles that are so different to be made exactly commensurable in value, but they can be made sufficiently commensurable for the practical purpose of exchange. That is why there has to be a single standard fixed by agreement, making all commodities commensurable; for everything can be measured by money. Let A be a house, B 20 minae and C a bedstead. Then A = B/2 (supposing a house to be worth—that is, equal to—5 minae) and C (the bedstead) = B/10. We can now say how many bedsteads are equal to one house; namely, five. Obviously before money existed this is how the rate of exchange was quoted—five beds for a house; there is no real difference between bartering five bedsteads for a house and buying the house for the price of five bedsteads.

We have now defined "just" and "unjust"; and our definitions show that just action is intermediate between doing injustice and suffering injustice, since the former is to get too much and the latter is to get too little. Justice is a sort of middle state, but not in the same manner as the other virtues are middle states; it is middle because it attaches to a middle amount, injustice being the quality of extremes. Also justice is the virtue which disposes the just man to resolve to act justly, and which leads him, when distributing things between himself and another, not to give himself a larger portion and his neighbor a smaller one of what is desirable, and the other way about in regard to what is detrimental, but to allot shares that are proportionately equal; and similarly when making a distribution between two other persons. Injustice on the contrary stands in the same relation to what is unjust, this being disproportionate excess or deficiency of something useful or harmful. Thus injustice is excess and deficiency in the sense of being productive of excess and deficiency, in one's own case excess of what is simply useful and deficiency of what is harmful, and in the case of others taken as a whole it is the same as in one's own case, but the disproportion may be in either direction.[13] In an unjust distribution to get too little is to suffer injustice and to get too much is to do injustice.

Political Justice and Analogous Kinds of Justice

But it must be borne in mind that what we are investigating is not only justice in the abstract but also political justice. This exists between men living in a community for the purpose of satisfying their needs, men who are free and who enjoy either absolute or proportional equality. Between men who do not fulfill these conditions no political justice exists, but only justice in a special sense and so called by analogy. Justice exists between those whose mutual relations are regulated by law; and law exists for those between whom there is a possibility of injustice, the administration of the law being the discrimination of what is just and what is unjust. Persons therefore between whom may be injustice may act unjustly toward each other (although unjust action does not necessarily imply injustice); and unjust action means appropriating too large a share of things essentially good and taking too small a share of things essentially bad. On this account we do not allow a man to govern, but only the law, because a human ruler governs in his own interest and becomes a tyrant; whereas the true function of a ruler is to be the guardian of justice, and therefore of equality. A just ruler, we think, gets no profit out of his office, as he does not assign to himself the larger share of what is essentially good unless such a share is proportionate to his merits. So he labors for the sake of others: this explains the saying "Justice is other men's good." Consequently it is necessary to give him some recompense in the form of honor and privilege. Rulers not content with such rewards become tyrants.

The justice of a master or a father is not the same thing as absolute justice or political justice, but only analogous to them; for there is no such thing as injustice in the absolute sense toward things that belong to one. Slaves, who are a man's chattels, and also children till they reach a certain age and start an independent life, are in a manner part of oneself, and nobody deliberately does harm to himself, so that there is no such thing as being unjust to oneself. Therefore justice and injustice in the political sense are not exercised in these relations, because they are regulated by law, as we saw, and exist between persons naturally governed by law, who, as we saw, are people who have an equal share in governing and being governed. Consequently justice exists in a fuller degree between a man and his wife than between a man and his children and chattels; it is in fact domestic justice. But this also is different from political justice.

Natural and Conventional Justice

Civil justice is partly natural and partly conventional.[14] A natural rule of justice is one which has the same validity everywhere, independently of whether people accept it or not. A conventional rule is a practice that at the outset may equally well be settled one way or the other, but which when once enacted becomes a regulation—for instance, the rule that the ransom for a prisoner of war shall be a mina, or that a certain sacrifice shall consist of one goat or two sheep; as well as enactments dealing with particular cases; for instance, the sacrifice celebrated in honor of Brasidas;[15] and special regulations promulgated by decree. Some people hold that all justice is a matter of fixed regulations, because a law of nature never alters and has the same validity everywhere—for instance, fire burns both here and in Persia—but they see men's conceptions of justice changing. This is not absolutely true, but only with qualifications—among the gods indeed it is perhaps not true at all. But among us, although there is such a thing as natural justice, nevertheless all rules can be altered. For instance, the right hand is naturally stronger than the left, but anybody can train himself to be ambidextrous. And in all other matters the same distinction will apply. But among things which admit of variation, it is not clear what kind is natural and what is not natural but due to convention and based on agreements, as both kinds alike are equally susceptible of change. But nevertheless it is the case that one thing is natural and another not natural. Rules of justice fixed by agreement and for the sake of expediency are like weights and measures. Wine and corn measures are not the same everywhere, but are larger in wholesale and smaller in retail markets. Similarly those rules of justice which are not due to nature but are enacted by man are not the same everywhere, since the constitution of the state is not the same everywhere; yet there is only one form of constitution which is everywhere in accordance with nature, namely the best form. . . .

Justice and Equity

The next subject to discuss is equity and its relation to justice. They appear on examination to be neither absolutely identical nor yet different in kind. Sometimes, it is true, we praise equity and the equitable man, and virtually employ the word as a term of general approval, using "more equitable" to mean merely "better."[16] But sometimes, when we think the matter out, it seems curious that the equitable should be praiseworthy if it is something different from what is just. If they are different, either the just or the equitable is not good, or if both are good, they are the same thing.

These then more or less are the considerations that make the meaning of "equity" a difficult problem. In one way, however, all the different uses of the term are correct, and there is no real inconsistency between them. Although equity is superior to one kind of justice, it is not better than justice as being generically different from it. Justice and equity are the same thing, and both are good, although equity is the better of the two.

The problem arises from the fact that equity, although just, is not justice as enacted by law, but a rectification of legal justice. The reason of this is that all law is universal, but there are some things about which it is not possible to make a universal statement which will be correct. In matters therefore in which a universal statement is necessary but it is not possible for it to be absolutely correct, the law follows the line that is valid as a general rule—though with full recognition of the error involved. Nevertheless this does not make it bad law, for the error does not lie in the law nor in the lawgiver, but in the nature of the case: the material of practical affairs is essentially irregular. When therefore the law lays down a general rule and afterwards a case arises that is not covered by the rule, the proper course is to rectify the omission in the law where it is defective and where it errs by oversimplification, and to insert the provision which the author of the law would himself suggest if he were present, and would have inserted if he had been cognizant of the case in question. Therefore while equity is just, and is better than one kind of justice, it is not superior to absolute justice, but only to the error that is caused by the absolute statement of what is just. This is the essential nature of equity—it is a rectification of the law where it is defective owing to its universality. Indeed this is the reason why law does not cover everything: there are some things for which it is impossible to provide by legislation, and consequently they require a special decree. When a thing is indefinite the rule dealing with it is also indefinite, like the mason's rule made of lead that is used by builders in Lesbos. This is not rigid but can be bent to fit the shape of the stone; and similarly a special decree can be adapted to suit the circumstances of the case.

The nature of equity has now been explained, and it has been shown to be just, and to be superior to one kind of justice. And from this it is clear what the equitable man is: he is a man who is of set purpose and habitually does what is equitable, and does not stand on his rights unduly but is ready to accept less than his share although he has the law on his side. This quality of character is equity; it is a special kind of justice, not an entirely distinct quality.

Can a Man Treat Himself Unjustly?

The foregoing remarks supply an answer to the question, is it possible for a man to do an injustice to himself? One class of just acts consists of those acts, in conformity with one of the virtues, which are ordained by law. For instance, the law does not sanction suicide, and any form of homicide which it does not expressly permit it must be understood to forbid. Further, when a man in violation of the law voluntarily injures another man (not in retaliation), he acts unjustly ("voluntarily" meaning with a knowledge of the person affected and the instrument employed). Now a man who in a fit of anger stabs himself commits voluntarily an injury that is not a legitimate act of retaliation, and this the law does not permit. He is therefore committing an unjust offense. But against whom? Presumably against the state, not himself, for he suffers the act voluntarily, and no one is voluntarily treated unjustly. Moreover it is for this that the state inflicts a penalty: suicide is punished by certain marks of dishonor, as an offense against the state.[17]

Secondly, in one sense a man who "acts unjustly" is merely unjust, and not wicked in every way; and in this sense it is not possible to act unjustly toward oneself (this is a different sense of the term from the one above; in one sense injustice is a particular evil quality, and does not imply complete wickedness, so that the unjust act specified does not display general wickedness). For, (1) that would imply that a quality was both present and absent in the same person

at the same time, which is impossible. Justice and injustice must always belong to different people. Moreover, (2) to be unjust an act must be voluntary and deliberate, and also unprovoked: a man who retaliates and does to another what that other has done to him is not thought to commit an injustice. But one who does harm to himself is both doing and suffering the same thing at the same time. Again, (3) if it were possible for a man to inflict an injustice on himself, it would be possible voluntarily to suffer injustice. And in addition, (4) acting unjustly means committing a particular act of injustice; for instance, adultery, burglary, theft; but a man cannot commit adultery with his own wife or steal his own property. And broadly speaking, the question "Can a man act unjustly toward himself?" is solved by our answer to the question about suffering injustice voluntarily.

(It is also clear that although both doing and receiving injustice are bad things, the former meaning to have more and the latter to have less than the medium amount, which corresponds to health in the art of medicine and to good bodily condition in the art of athletic training, yet to act unjustly is the worse of the two. For it involves wickedness and deserves reprehension, and its wickedness is complete or nearly complete; but to suffer injustice does not involve wickedness, viz., injustice, in the victim. In itself therefore to suffer injustice is the lesser evil, although it may well be the greater evil incidentally. But with this science is not concerned: it pronounces pleurisy to be a more serious malady than a sprain, in spite of the fact that a sprain might on occasion be a more serious mishap, if owing to it you stumbled in a battle and were taken prisoner and killed by the enemy.)

But in a metaphorical and analogical sense there is such a thing as justice not toward oneself but between the different parts of one's nature, not indeed justice in the full sense of the term but such as exists between master and servant or the head of a household and the members of his family. For in the discourses on these questions[18]

[handwritten marginalia: But you can't own a person; so there is no such thing as justice to one's property. H that prop. is another person.]

distinction is made between the rational and irrational parts of the soul; and this has suggested the view that there is such a thing as injustice toward oneself, because these parts of the self may thwart each other in their respective desires, and consequently there is a sort of mutual justice between them as there is between ruler and subject.

NOTES

1. The Greek term normally thus rendered is stated in what follows to have two senses, the wider sense of righteousness in general, any right conduct in relation to others, and the narrower sense of right conduct in matters involving gain or loss to the agent or to others. It is justice in the latter sense that this chapter deals with; in some places we should rather term it honesty.

2. For instance, medicine studies both health and disease.

3. A quotation from a play of Euripides that has not come down to us.

4. From the poet Theognis.

5. One of the Seven Sages.

6. Plato, *Republic* 343 c.—the definition given by the sophist Thrasymachus.

7. I.e., so as to be able to run away quickly.

8. It is discussed in Aristotle's *Politics,* Book III.

9. Viz., lacking the consent of one of the parties.

10. I.e., two pairs of terms (e.g., 1, 3, 7, 9) the second of which exceeds the first by the same amount as the fourth exceeds the third. We do not call this proportion, but if the third term also exceeds the second by the same amount (e.g., 1, 3, 5, 7), an arithmetical progression.

11. For corrective justice the merits of the parties are immaterial.

12. Cf. our expressions "Mr. Justice So-and-so," "Justice of the Peace."

13. When A makes an unjust distribution not between himself and B but between B and C, the result for either B or C may be either too large or too small a share of something beneficial and either too small or too large a share of something detrimental.

14. The word thus rendered also means "legal."

15. This Spartan general won the city of Amphipolis from the Athenian Empire, 424 B.C., and fell in defending it two years later. He was consecrated as a local hero, and an annual celebration was held in his honor, with sacrifices and races (for the Greeks races had religious associations).

16. In English "reasonable" is similarly used as a term of general approval.

17. At Athens a suicide's hand, as the guilty instrument, was cut off and buried separately from the body.

18. Plato's *Republic* and the writings of Plato's pupils in the Academy.

21 The Public Philosophy of Contemporary Liberalism

MICHAEL SANDEL

Liberal and Republican Freedom

THE POLITICAL PHILOSOPHY by which we live is a certain version of liberal political theory. Its central idea is that government should be neutral toward the moral and religious views its citizens espouse. Since people disagree about the best way to live, government should not affirm in law any particular vision of the good life. Instead, it should provide a framework of rights that respects persons as free and independent selves, capable of choosing their own values and ends.[1] Since this liberalism asserts the priority of fair procedures over particular ends, the public life it informs might be called the procedural republic.[2]

In describing the prevailing political philosophy as a version of liberal political theory, it is important to distinguish two different meanings of liberalism. In the common parlance of American politics, liberalism is the opposite of conservatism; it is the outlook of those who favor a more generous welfare state and a greater measure of social and economic equality.[3] In the history of political theory, however, liberalism has a different, broader meaning. In this historical sense, liberalism describes a tradition of thought that emphasizes toleration and respect for individual rights and that runs from John Locke, Immanuel Kant, and John Stuart Mill to John Rawls. The public philosophy of contemporary American politics is a version of

this liberal tradition of thought, and most of our debates proceed within its terms.

The idea that freedom consists in our capacity to choose our ends finds prominent expression in our politics and law. Its province is not limited to those known as liberals rather than conservatives in American politics; it can be found across the political spectrum. Republicans sometimes argue, for example, that taxing the rich to pay for welfare programs is a form of coerced charity that violates people's freedom to choose what to do with their own money. Democrats sometimes argue that government should assure all citizens a decent level of income, housing, and health, on the grounds that those who are crushed by economic necessity are not truly free to exercise choice in other domains. Although the two sides disagree about how government should act to respect individual choice, both assume that freedom consists in the capacity of persons to choose their values and ends.

So familiar is this vision of freedom that it seems a permanent feature of the American political and constitutional tradition. But Americans have not always understood freedom in this way. As a reigning public philosophy, the version of liberalism that informs our present debates is a recent arrival, a development of the last forty or fifty years. Its distinctive character can best be seen by contrast with a rival public philosophy that it gradually displaced. This rival public philosophy is a version of republican political theory.

Central to republican theory is the idea that liberty depends on sharing in self-government. This idea is not by itself inconsistent with liberal freedom. Participating in politics can be one among the ways in which people choose to pursue their ends. According to republican political theory, however, sharing in self-rule involves something more. It means deliberating with fellow citizens about the common good and helping to shape the destiny of the political community. But to deliberate well about the common good requires more than the capacity to choose one's ends and to respect others' rights to do the same. It requires a knowledge of public affairs and also a sense of belonging, a concern for the whole, a moral bond with the community whose fate is at stake. To share in self-rule therefore requires that citizens possess, or come to acquire, certain qualities of character, or civic virtues. But this means that republican politics cannot be neutral toward the values and ends its citizens espouse. The republican conception of freedom, unlike the liberal conception, requires a formative politics, a politics that cultivates in citizens the qualities of character self-government requires.

Both the liberal and republican conceptions of freedom have been present throughout our political experience, but in shifting measure and relative importance. Broadly speaking, republicanism predominated earlier in American history, liberalism later. In recent decades, the civic or formative aspect of our politics has largely given way to the liberalism that conceives persons as free and independent selves, unencumbered by moral or civic ties they have not chosen.

This shift sheds light on our present political predicament. For despite its appeal, the liberal vision of freedom lacks the civic resources to sustain self-government. This defect ill-equips it to address the sense of disempowerment that afflicts our public life. The public philosophy by which we live cannot secure the liberty it promises, because it cannot inspire the sense of community and civic engagement that liberty requires.

How the liberal conception of citizenship and freedom gradually crowded out the republican conception involves two intersecting tales. One traces the advent of the procedural republic from the first stirrings of American constitutionalism to recent debates about religious liberty, free speech, and privacy rights. Another traces the decline of the civic strand of American political discourse from Thomas Jefferson's day to the present.[4]

These stories, taken together, bring to clarity the self-image that animates—and sometimes debilitates—our public life. They do not reveal a golden age when all was right with American democracy. The republican tradition coexisted with slavery, with the exclusion of women from the public realm, with property qualifications for voting, with nativist hostility to immigrants; indeed it sometimes provided the terms within which these practices were defended.

And yet, for all its episodes of darkness, the republican tradition with its emphasis on community and self-government, may offer a corrective to our impoverished civic life. Recalling the republican conception of freedom as self-rule may prompt us to pose questions we have forgotten how to ask: What economic arrangements are hospitable to self-government? How might our political discourse engage rather than avoid the moral and religious convictions people bring to the public realm? And how might the public life of a pluralist society cultivate in citizens the expansive self-understandings that civic engagement requires? If the public philosophy of our day leaves little room for civic considerations, it may help to recall how earlier generations of Americans debated such questions, before the procedural republic took hold. But in order to identify the relevant strands of the story, we need to specify more fully the version of liberalism that informs our present politics.

The Aspiration to Neutrality

The idea that government should be neutral on the question of the good life is distinctive to modern political thought. Ancient political theory held that the purpose of politics was to cultivate the virtue, or moral excellence, of citizens. All associations aim at some good, Aristotle wrote, and the polis, or political association, aims at the highest, most comprehensive good: "any polis which is truly so called, and is not merely one in name, must devote itself to the end of encouraging goodness. Otherwise, a political association sinks into a mere alliance, which only differs in space from other forms of alliance where the members live at a distance from one another. Otherwise, too, law becomes a mere covenant—or (in the phrase of the Sophist Lycophron) 'a guarantor of men's rights against one another'—instead of being, as it should be, a rule of life such as will make the members of a polis good and just."[5]

According to Aristotle, political community is more than "an association for residence on a common site, or for the sake of preventing mutual injustice and easing exchange." Although these are necessary conditions for political community, they are not its purpose of ultimate justification. "The end and purpose of a polis is the good life, and the institutions of social life are means to that end." It is only as participants in political association that we can realize our nature and fulfill our highest ends.[6]

Unlike the ancient conception, liberal political theory does not see political life as concerned with the highest human ends or with the moral excellence of its citizens. Rather than promote a particular conception of the good life, liberal political theory insists on toleration, fair procedures, and respect for individual rights—values that respect people's freedom to choose their own values. But this raises a difficult question. If liberal ideals cannot be defended in the name of the highest human good, then in what does their moral basis consist?

It is sometimes thought that liberal principles can be justified by a simple version of moral relativism. Government should not "legislate morality," because all morality is merely subjective, a matter of personal preference not open to argument or rational debate. "Who is to say what is literature and what is filth? That is a value judgment, and whose values should decide?" Relativism usually appears less as a claim than as a question: "Who is to judge?" But the same question can be asked of the values that liberals defend. Toleration and freedom and fairness are values too, and they can hardly be defended by the claim that no values can be defended. So it is a mistake to affirm liberal values by arguing that all values are merely subjective. The relativist defense of liberalism is no defense at all.

Utilitarianism versus Kantian Liberalism

What, then, is the case for the neutrality the liberal invokes? Recent political philosophy has offered two main alternatives—one utilitarian, the other Kantian.[7] The utilitarian view, following John Stuart Mill, defends liberal principles in the name of maximizing the general welfare. The state should not impose on its citizens a preferred way of life, even for their own good, because doing so will reduce the sum of human happiness, at least in the long run. It is better that people choose for themselves, even if, on occasion, they get it wrong.

"The only freedom which deserves the name," writes Mill in On Liberty, "is that of pursuing our own good in our own way, so long as we do not attempt to deprive others of theirs, or impede their efforts to obtain it." He adds that his argument does not depend on any notion of abstract right, only on the principle of the greatest good for the greatest number. "I regard utility as the ultimate appeal on all ethical questions; but it must be utility in the largest sense, grounded on the permanent interests of man as a progressive being."[8]

Many objections have been raised against utilitarianism as a general doctrine of moral philosophy. Some have questioned the concept of utility and the assumption that all human goods are in principle commensurable. Others have objected that by reducing all values to preferences and desires, utilitarians are unable to admit qualitative distinctions of worth, unable to distinguish noble desires from base ones. But most recent debate has focused on whether utilitarianism offers a convincing basis for liberal principles, including respect for individual rights.[9]

At first glance, utilitarianism seems well suited to liberal purposes. Seeking to maximize overall happiness does not require judging people's values, only aggregating them. And the willingness to aggregate preferences without judging them suggests a tolerant spirit, even a democratic one. When people go to the polls we count their votes, whatever they are.

But the utilitarian calculus is not always as liberal as it first appears. If enough cheering Romans pack the Coliseum to watch the lion devour the Christian, the collective pleasure of the Romans will surely outweigh the pain of the Christian, intense though it be. Or if a big majority abhors a small religion and wants it banned, the balances of preferences will favor suppression, not toleration. Utilitarians sometimes defend individual rights on the grounds that respecting them now will serve utility in the long run. But this calculation is precarious and contingent. It hardly secures the liberal promise not to impose on some the values of others.

The case against utilitarianism was made most powerfully by Immanuel Kant. He argued that empirical principles such as utility were unfit to serve as a basis for morality. A wholly instrumental defense of freedom and rights not only leaves rights vulnerable but fails to respect the inherent dignity of persons. The utilitarian calculus treats people as means to the happiness of others, not as ends in themselves, worthy of respect.[10]

Contemporary liberals extend Kant's argument with the claim that utilitarianism fails to take seriously the distinction between persons. In seeking above all to maximize the general welfare, the utilitarian treats society as a whole as if it were a single person; it conflates our many, diverse desires into a single system of desires. It is indifferent to the distribution of satisfactions among persons, except insofar as this may affect the overall sum. But this fails to respect our plurality and distinctness. It uses some as means to the happiness of all, and so fails to respect each as an end in himself or herself.

In the view of modern-day Kantians, certain rights are so fundamental that even the general welfare cannot override them. As John Rawls writes in *A Theory of Justice*, "Each person possesses an inviolability founded on justice that even the welfare of society as a whole cannot override. . . . The rights secured by justice are not subject to political bargaining or to the calculus of social interests."[11]

So Kantian liberals need an account of rights that does not depend on utilitarian considerations. More than this, they need an account that does not depend on any particular conception of the good, that does not presuppose the superiority of one way of life over others. Only a justification neutral among ends could preserve the liberal resolve not to favor any particular ends or to impose on its citizens a preferred way of life. But what sort of justification could this be? How is it possible to affirm certain liberties and rights as fundamental without embracing some vision of the good life, without endorsing some ends over others?

The solution proposed by Kantian liberals is to draw a distinction between the "right" and the "good"—between a framework of basic rights and liberties, and the conceptions of the good that people may choose to pursue within the framework. It is one thing for the state to support a fair framework, they argue, something else to affirm some particular ends. For example, it is one thing to defend the right to free speech so that people may be free to form their own opinions and choose their own ends, but something else to support it on grounds that a life of political discussion is inherently worthier than a life unconcerned with public affairs, or on the grounds that free speech will increase the general welfare. Only the first defense is available on the Kantian view, resting as it does on the ideal of a neutral framework.

Now the commitment to a framework neutral with respect to ends can be seen as a kind of value—in this sense the Kantian liberal is no relativist—but its value consists precisely in its refusal to affirm a preferred way of life or conception of the good. For Kantian liberals, then, the right is prior to the good, and in two senses. First, individual rights cannot be sacrificed for the sake of the general good; and second, the principles of justice that specify these rights cannot be premised on any particular vision of the good life. What justifies the rights is not that they maximize the general welfare or otherwise promote the good, but rather that they constitute a fair framework within which individuals and groups can choose their own values and ends, consistent with a similar liberty for others.

The claim for the priority of the right over the good connects the ideal of neutrality with the primacy of individual rights. For Kantian liberals, rights "function as trump cards held by individuals." They protect individuals from policies, even democratically enacted ones, that would impose a preferred conception of the good and so fail to respect people's freedom to choose their own conceptions.[12]

Of course, proponents of the liberal ethic notoriously disagree about what rights are fundamental and what political arrangements the ideal of the neutral framework requires. Egalitarian liberals support the welfare state and favor a scheme of civil liberties together with certain social and economic rights—rights to welfare, education, health care, and so on. They argue that respecting the capacity of persons to pursue their own ends requires government to assure the minimal prerequisites of a dignified life. Libertarian liberals (usually called conservatives in contempo-

rary politics) defend the market economy and claim that redistributive policies violate people's rights. They argue that respect for persons requires assuring to each the fruits of his or her own labor, and so favor a scheme of civil liberties combined with a strict regime of private property rights. Whether egalitarian or libertarian, Kantian liberalism begins with the claim that we are separate, individual persons, each with our own aims, interests, and conceptions of the good life. It seeks a framework of rights that will enable us to realize our capacity as free moral agents, consistent with a similar liberty for others.

The Liberal Self

The Kantian case against utilitarianism derives much of its force from its contrasting conception of the person, its view of what it means to be a moral agent. Where utilitarians conflate our many desires into a single system of desire, Kantian liberals insist on the separateness of persons. Where the utilitarian self is simply defined as the sum of its desires, the Kantian self is a choosing self, independent of the desires and ends it may have at any moment. Kant expressed this idea by attributing to human beings the capacity to act with an autonomous will. Contemporary liberals rely on the similar notion of a self given prior to and independent of its purposes and ends.

The claim for the priority of the right over the good, and the conception of the person that attends it, oppose Kantian liberalism not only to utilitarianism but also to any view that regards us as obligated to fulfill ends we have not chosen—ends given by nature or God, for example, or by our identities as members of families, peoples, cultures, or traditions. Encumbered identities such as these are at odds with the liberal conception of the person as free and independent selves, unbound by prior moral ties, capable of choosing our ends for ourselves. This is the conception that finds expression in the ideal of the state as a neutral framework. For Kantian liberals, it is precisely because we are freely choosing, independent selves that we need a neutral framework, a framework of rights that refuses to choose among competing values and ends. For the liberal self, what matters above all, what is most essential to our personhood, is not the ends we choose but our capacity to choose them. "It is not our aims that primarily reveal our nature," but rather the framework of rights we would agree to if we could abstract from our aims. "For the self is prior to the ends which are affirmed by it; even a dominant end must be chosen from among numerous possibilities."[13]

The liberal ethic derives much of its moral force from the appeal of the self-image that animates it. This appeal has at least two sources. First, the image of the self as free and independent, unencumbered by aims and attachments it does not choose for itself, offers a powerful liberating vision. Freed from the sanctions of custom and tradition and inherited status, unbound by moral ties antecedent to choice, the liberal self is installed as sovereign, cast as the author of the only obligations that constrain. More than the simple sum of circumstance, we become capable of the dignity that consists in being persons of our "own creating, making, choosing."[14] We are agents and not just instruments of the purposes we pursue. We are "self-originating sources of valid claims."[15]

A second appeal of the liberal self-image consists in the case it implies for equal respect. The idea that there is more to a person than the roles he plays or the customs she keeps or the faith he affirms suggests a basis for respect independent of life's contingencies. Liberal justice is blind to such differences between persons as race, religion, ethnicity, and gender, for in the liberal self-image, these features do not really define our identity in the first place. They are not constituents but merely attributes of the self, the sort of things the state should look beyond. "Our social position and class, our sex and race should not influence deliberations made from a moral point of view."[16] Once these contingencies are seen as products of our situation rather than as aspects of our person, they cease to supply the familiar grounds for prejudice and discrimination.

Nor does it matter, from the standpoint of liberal justice, what virtues we display or what values we espouse. "That we have one conception of the good rather than another is not relevant from a moral standpoint. In acquiring it we are influenced by the same sort of contingencies that lead us to rule out a knowledge of our sex and class."[17] Despite their many differences, libertarian and egalitarian liberals agree that people's entitlements should not be based on their merit or virtue or moral desert, for the qualities that make people virtuous or morally deserving depend on factors "arbitrary from a moral point of view."[18] The liberal state therefore does not discriminate; none of its policies or laws may presuppose that any person or way of life is intrinsically more virtuous than any other. It respects persons as persons, and secures their equal right to live the lives they choose.

Critique of Kantian Liberalism

Kantian liberals thus avoid affirming a conception of the good by affirming instead the priority of the right, which depends in turn on a picture of the self given prior to its ends. But how plausible is this self-conception? Despite its powerful appeal, the image of the unencumbered self is flawed. It cannot make sense of our moral experience, because it cannot account for certain moral and political obligations that we commonly recognize, even prize. These include obligations of solidarity, religious duties, and other moral ties that may claim us for reasons unrelated to a choice. Such obligations are difficult to account for if we understand ourselves as free and independent selves, unbound by moral ties we have not chosen. Unless we think of ourselves as encumbered selves, already claimed by certain projects and commitments, we cannot make sense of these indispensable aspects of our moral and political experience.

Consider the limited scope of obligation on the liberal view. According to Rawls, obligations can arise in only one of two ways, as "natural duties" we owe to human beings as such or as voluntary obligations we incur by consent. The natural duties are those we owe persons *qua* persons—to do justice, to avoid cruelty, and so on. All other obligations, the ones we owe to particular others, are founded in consent and arise only in virtue of agreements we make, be they tacit or explicit.[19]

Conceived as unencumbered selves, we must respect the dignity of all persons, but beyond this, we owe only what we agree to owe. Liberal justice requires that we respect people's rights (as defined by the neutral framework), not that we advance their good. Whether we must concern ourselves with other people's good depends on whether, and with whom, and on what terms, we have agreed to do so.

One striking consequence of this view is that "there is no political obligation, strictly speaking, for citizens generally." Although those who run for office voluntarily incur a political obligation (that is, to serve their country if elected), the ordinary citizen does not. "It is not clear what is the requisite binding action or who has performed it."[20] The average citizen is therefore without any special obligations to his or her fellow citizens, apart from the universal, natural duty not to commit injustice.

The liberal attempt to construe all obligation in terms of duties universally owed or obligations voluntarily incurred makes it difficult to account for civic obligations and other moral and political ties that we commonly recognize. It fails to capture those loyalties and responsibilities whose moral force consists partly in the fact that living by them is inseparable from understanding ourselves as the particular persons we are—as members of this family or city or nation or people, as bearers of that history, as citizens of this republic. Loyalties such as these can be more than values I happen to have, and to hold, at a certain distance. The moral responsibilities they entail may go beyond the obligations I voluntarily incur and the "natural duties" I owe to human beings as such.[21]

Some of the special responsibilities that flow from the particular communities I inhabit I may owe to fellow members, such as obligations of solidarity. Others I may owe to members of those communities with which my own community has some morally relevant history, such as the morally burdened relations of Germans to Jews, of American whites to American blacks, or of England and France to their former colonies.[22] Whether they look inward or outward, obligations of membership presuppose that we are capable of moral ties antecedent to choice. To the extent that we are, the meaning of our membership resists redescription in contractarian terms.

It is sometimes argued, in defense of the liberal view, that loyalties and allegiances not grounded in consent, however psychologically compelling, are matters of sentiment, not of morality, and so do not suggest an obligation unavailable to unencumbered selves. But it is difficult to make sense of certain familiar moral and political dilemmas without acknowledging obligations of solidarity and the thickly constituted, encumbered selves that they imply.

Consider the case of Robert E. Lee on the eve of the Civil War. Lee, then an officer in the Union army, opposed secession, in fact regarded it as treason. And yet when war loomed, Lee concluded that his obligation to Virginia outweighed his obligation to the Union and also his reported opposition to slavery. "With all my devotion to the Union," he wrote, "I have not been able to make up my mind to raise my hand against my relatives, my children, my home. . . . If the Union is dissolved, and the Government disrupted, I shall return to my native State and share the miseries of my people. Save in her defense, I will draw my sword no more."[23]

One can appreciate the poignance of Lee's predicament without necessarily approving of the choice he made. But one cannot make sense of his dilemma as a *moral* dilemma without acknowledging that the call to stand with his people, even to lead them in a cause he opposed, was a claim of moral and not merely sentimental import, capable at least of weighing in the balance against other duties and obligations. Otherwise, Lee's predicament was not really a moral dilemma at all, but simply a conflict between morality on the one hand and mere sentiment or prejudice on the other.

A merely psychological reading of Lee's predicament misses the fact that we not only sympathize with people such as Lee but often admire them, not necessarily for the choices they make but for the quality of character their deliberation reflects. The quality at stake is the disposition to see and bear one's life circumstances as a reflectively situated being—claimed by the history that implicates me in a particular life, but self-conscious of its particularity, and so alive to other ways, wider horizons. But this is precisely the quality that is lacking in those who would think of themselves as unencumbered selves, bound only by the obligations they choose to incur.

As the Lee example illustrates, the liberal conception of the person is too thin to account for the full range of moral and political obligations we commonly recognize, such as obligations of solidarity. This counts against its plausibility generally. But it may even be too weak to support the less strenuous communal obligations expected of citizens in the modern welfare state. Some stronger conception of community may be required, not only to make sense of tragic-heroic dilemmas such as Lee's, but even to sustain the rights that many liberals defend.

While libertarian liberals ask little of citizens, more generous expressions of the liberal ethic support various policies of public provision and redistribution. Egalitarian liberals defend social and economic rights as well as civil and political rights, and so demand of their fellow citizens a high measure of mutual engagement. They insist on the "plurality and distinctness" of individuals but also require that we "share one another's fate" and regard the distribution of natural talents as "a common asset."[24]

Liberalism as an ethic of sharing emphasizes the arbitrariness of fortune and the importance of certain material prerequisites for the meaningful exercise of equal liberties. Since "necessitous men are not free men," and since in any case the distribution of assets and endowments that make for success is "arbitrary from a moral point of view," egalitarian liberals would tax the rich to help the poor secure the prerequisites of a dignified life. Thus the liberal case for the welfare state depends not on a theory of the common good or on some strong notion of communal obligation, but instead on the rights we would agree to respect if we could abstract from our interests and ends.

The liberal case for public provision seems well suited to conditions in which strong communal ties cannot be relied on, and this is one source of its appeal. But it lies vulnerable nonetheless to the libertarian objection that redistributive policies use some people as means to others's ends, and so offend the "plurality and distinctness" of individuals that liberalism seeks above all to secure.[25] In the contractual vision of community alone, it is unclear how the libertarian objection can be met. If those whose fate I am required to share really are, morally speaking, *others,* rather than fellow participants in a way of life with which my identity is bound, then liberalism as an ethic of sharing seems open to the same objections as utilitarianism. Its claim on me is not the claim of a community with which I identify, but rather the claim of an arbitrarily defined collectivity whose aims I may or may not share.

If the egalitarian replies that social and economic rights are required as a matter of equal respect for persons, the question remains why *these* persons, the ones who happen to live in my country, have a claim on my concern that others do not. Tying the mutual responsibilities of citizenship to the idea of respect for persons *qua* persons puts the moral case for welfare on a par with the case for foreign aid—a duty we owe strangers with whom we share a common humanity but possibly little else. Given its conception of the person, it is unclear how liberalism can defend the particular boundaries of concern its own ethic of sharing must presuppose.

What egalitarian liberalism requires, but cannot within its own terms provide, is some way of defining the relevant community of sharing, some way of seeing the participants as mutually indebted and morally engaged to begin with. It needs a way of answering Emerson's challenge to the man who solicited his contribution to the poor—"Are they *my* poor?"[26] Since liberal social and economic rights cannot be justified as expressing or advancing a common life of shared pursuits, the basis and bounds of communal concern become difficult to defend. For as we have seen, the strong notion of community or membership that would save and situate the sharing is precisely the one denied to the liberal self. The moral encumbrances and antecedent obligations it implies would undercut the priority of right.

Minimalist Liberalism

If we are not the freely choosing, unencumbered selves that Kantian liberals imagine us to be, does it follow that government need not be neutral, that politics should cultivate the virtue of its citizens after all? Some political philosophers argue that the case for neutrality can be detached from the Kantian conception of the person. The case for liberalism, they argue, is political, not philosophical or metaphysical, and so does not depend on controversial claims about the nature of the self. The priority of the right over the good is not the application to politics of Kantian moral philosophy, but a practical response to the familiar fact that people in modern democratic societies typically disagree about the good. Since this defense of neutrality does not depend on a Kantian conception of the

person but instead "stays on the surface, philosophically speaking," it might be described as minimalist liberalism.[27]

Minimalist liberals acknowledge that we may sometimes be claimed by moral or religious obligations unrelated to a choice. But they insist that we set these obligations aside when we enter the public realm, that we bracket our moral and religious convictions when deliberating about politics and law. In our personal lives, we may regard it as unthinkable to view ourselves "apart from certain religious, philosophical, and moral convictions, or from certain enduring attachments and loyalties." But we should draw a distinction between our personal and our political identities. However encumbered we may be in private, however claimed by moral or religious convictions, we should bracket our encumbrances in public and regard ourselves, *qua* public selves, as independent of any particular loyalties or conceptions of the good.[28]

The insistence that we separate our identity as citizens from our identity as persons gives rise to an obvious challenge. Why should our political identities not express the moral and religious convictions we affirm in our personal lives? Why, in deliberating about justice and rights, must we set aside the moral judgments that inform the rest of our lives? Minimalist liberals reply that separating our identity as citizens from our identity as persons honors an important fact about modern democratic life. In traditional societies, people sought to shape political life in the image of their own moral and religious ideals. But modern democratic societies are marked by a plurality of moral and religious ideals. Moreover, this pluralism is reasonable; it reflects the fact that, even after reasoned reflection, decent, intelligent people will come to different conceptions about the nature of the good life. Given the fact of reasonable pluralism, we should try to decide questions of justice and rights without affirming one conception of the good over others. Only in this way can we affirm the political value of social cooperation based on mutual respect.[29]

Minimalist liberalism seeks to detach liberal principles from political controversy, including debates about the nature of the self. It presents itself "not as a conception of justice that is true," but as one that can serve as a basis for political agreement in a democratic society. It asserts "the priority of democracy over philosophy." It offers a political conception of justice, not a metaphysical or philosophical one.[30]

The minimalist case for liberalism depends on the plausibility of separating politics from philosophy, of bracketing moral and religious questions where politics is concerned. But this raises the question why the practical interest in securing social cooperation and mutual respect is always so compelling as to defeat any competing moral interest that could arise from within a substantive moral or religious view. One way of assuring the priority of the practical is to deny that any of the moral or religious conceptions it brackets could be true. But this is precisely the sort of controversial metaphysical claim the minimalist liberal wants to avoid. If the liberal must therefore allow that some such conceptions might be true, then the question remains: What guarantees that no moral or religious doctrine can generate interests sufficiently compelling to burst the brackets, so to speak, and morally outweigh the practical interest in social cooperation?

Critique of Minimalist Liberalism

Minimalist liberalism lacks a convincing answer to this question. For notwithstanding the importance of political values such as toleration, social cooperation, and mutual respect, it is not always reasonable to set aside competing values that may arise from substantive moral and religious doctrines. At least where grave moral questions are concerned, whether it is reasonable to bracket moral and religious controversies for the sake of political agreement partly depends on which of the contending moral or religious doctrines is true. Minimalist liberalism wants to separate the case for toleration from any judgment about the moral worth of the practices being tolerated. But this separation is not always defensible. We cannot determine whether toleration is justified in any given case without passing moral judgment on the practice in question.

This difficulty is illustrated by two political controversies that bear on grave moral and religious questions. One is the contemporary debate about abortion rights. The other is the famous debate in 1858 between Abraham Lincoln and Stephen Douglas over popular sovereignty and slavery.[31]

THE ABORTION DEBATE

Given the intense disagreement over the moral permissibility of abortion, the case for seeking a political solution that brackets the moral and religious issues—that is neutral with respect to them—would seem especially strong. But whether it is reasonable to bracket, for political purposes, the moral and religious doctrines at stake depends largely on which of those doctrines is true. If the doctrine of the Catholic church is true, if human life in the relevant moral sense really does begin at conception, then bracketing the moral-theological question of when human life begins is far less reasonable than it would be on rival moral and religious assumptions. The more confident we are that fetuses are, in the relevant moral sense, *different* from babies, the more confident we can be in affirming a political conception of justice that sets aside the controversy about the moral status of fetuses.

As the contemporary debate over abortion reflects, even a political conception of justice presupposes a certain view of the controversies it would bracket. For the debate about abortion is not only a debate about when human life begins, but also a debate about how reasonable it is to abstract from that question for political purposes. Opponents of abortion resist the translation from moral to political terms because they know that more of their view will be lost in the translation; the neutral territory offered by minimalist liberalism is likely to be less hospitable to their religious convictions than to those of their opponents. For defenders of abortion, little comparable is at stake; there is little difference between believing that abortion is morally permissible and agreeing that, as a political matter, women should be free to decide the moral question for themselves. The moral price of political agreement is far higher if abortion is wrong than if it is permissible. How reasonable it is to bracket the contending moral and religious views depends partly on which of those views is more plausible.

The minimalist liberal might reply that the political values of toleration and equal citizenship for women are sufficient grounds for concluding that women should be free to choose for themselves whether to have an abortion; government should not take sides on the moral and religious controversy over when human life begins. But if the Catholic church is right about the moral status of the fetus, if abortion is morally tantamount to murder, then it is not clear why the political values of toleration and women's equality, important though they are, should prevail. If the Catholic doctrine is true, then the minimalist liberal's case for the priority of political values must become an instance of just-war theory; he or she would have to show why these values should prevail even at the cost of some 1.5 million civilian deaths each year.

Of course, to suggest the impossibility of bracketing the moral-theological question of when human life begins is not to argue against a right to abortion. It is simply to show that the case for abortion rights cannot be neutral with respect to the underlying moral and religious controversy. It must engage rather than avoid the substantive moral and religious doctrines at stake. Liberals often resist this engagement because it violates the priority of the right over the good. But the abortion debate shows that this priority cannot be sustained. The case for respecting a woman's right to decide for herself whether to have an abortion depends on showing that there is a relevant moral difference between aborting a fetus at a relatively early stage of development and killing a child.

THE LINCOLN-DOUGLAS DEBATES

Perhaps the most famous case for bracketing a controversial moral question for the sake of political agreement was made by Stephen Douglas in his debates with Abraham Lincoln. Since people were bound to disagree about the morality of slavery, Douglas argued, national policy should be neutral on that question. The doctrine of popular sovereignty he defended did not judge slavery right or wrong but left the people of the territories free to make their own judgments. "To throw the weight of federal power into the scale, either in favor of the free or the slave states," would violate the fundamental principles of the constitution and run the risk of civil war. The only hope of holding the country together, he argued, was to agree to disagree, to bracket the moral controversy over slavery and respect "the right of each state and each territory to decide these questions for themselves."[32]

Lincoln argued against Douglas' case for a political conception of justice. Policy should express rather than avoid a substantive moral judgment about slavery, he maintained. Although Lincoln was not an abolitionist, he believed that government should treat slavery as the moral wrong it was and prohibit its extension to the territories. "The real issue in this controversy—pressing upon every mind—is the sentiment on the part of one class that looks upon the institution of slavery as a wrong, and of another class that does not look upon it as a wrong." Lincoln and the Republican party viewed slavery as a wrong and insisted that it "be treated as a wrong, and one of the methods of treating it as a wrong is to make provision that it shall grow no larger."[33]

Whatever his personal moral views, Douglas claimed that, for political purposes at least, he was agnostic on the question of slavery; he did not care whether slavery was "voted up or voted down." Lincoln replied that it was reasonable to bracket the question of the morality of slavery only on the assumption that it was not the moral evil he regarded it to be. Any man can advocate political neutrality "who does not see anything wrong in slavery, but no man can logically say it who does see a wrong in it; because no man can logically say he don't care whether a wrong is voted up or voted down."[34]

The debate between Lincoln and Douglas was not primarily about the morality of slavery, but about whether to bracket a moral controversy for the sake of political agreement. In this respect, their debate over popular sovereignty is analogous to the contemporary debate over abortion rights. As some contemporary liberals argue that government should not take a stand one way or another on the morality of abortion, but let each woman decide the question for herself, so Douglas argued that national policy should not take a stand one way or the other on the morality of slavery, but let each territory decide the question for itself. There is of course the difference that in the case of abortion rights, those who would bracket the substantive moral question typically leave the choice to the individual, while in the case of slavery, Douglas' way of bracketing was to leave the choice to the territories.

But Lincoln's argument against Douglas was an argument about bracketing as such, at least where grave moral questions are at stake. Lincoln's point was that the political conception of justice defended by Douglas depended for its plausibility on a particular answer to the substantive moral question it sought to bracket. Even in the face of so dire a threat to social cooperation as the prospect of civil war, it made neither moral nor political sense to aspire to political neutrality. As Lincoln concluded in his final debate with Douglas, "Is it not a false statesmanship that undertakes to build up a system of policy upon the basis of caring nothing about the very thing that every body does care the most about?"[35]

Present-day liberals will surely resist the company of Douglas and want national policy to oppose slavery, presumably on the grounds that slavery violates people's rights. But it is doubtful that liberalism conceived as a political conception of justice can make this claim without violating its own strictures against appeals to comprehensive moral ideals. For example, a Kantian liberal can oppose slavery as a failure to treat persons as ends in themselves, worthy of respect. But this argument, resting as it does on a Kantian conception of the person, is unavailable to minimalist liberalism. So too are the antislavery arguments of many American abolitionists in the 1830s and 1840s, who emphasized the sin of slavery and made their case in religious terms.

The debates over abortion and slavery show that a political conception of justice must sometimes presuppose an answer to the moral and religious questions it purports to bracket. At least where grave moral questions are at stake, it is not possible to detach politics and law from substantive moral judgment. But even in cases where it is possible to conduct political debate without reference to our moral and religious convictions, it may not always be desirable. The effort to banish moral and religious argument from the public realm for the sake of political agreement may end up impoverishing political discourse and eroding the moral and civic resources necessary to self-government.

This tendency can be seen in our present public life. With a few notable exceptions, such as the civil rights movement of the 1950s and 1960s, our political discourse in recent decades has come to reflect the liberal resolve that government be neutral on moral and religious questions,that matters of policy and law be debated and decided without reference to any particular conception of the good life. But we are beginning to find that a politics that brackets morality and religion too completely soon generates its own disenchantment. A procedural republic cannot contain the moral energies of a vital democratic life. It creates a moral void that opens the way for narrow, intolerant moralisms. And it fails to cultivate the qualities of character that equip citizens to share in self-rule.

In the chapters that follow, I try to show that the liberalism of the procedural republic provides the public philosophy by which we live. Despite its philosophical failings, it is the theory most thoroughly embodied in our practices and institutions. Now it might be thought that the very existence of the procedural republic as a sustained practice puts to rest the philosophical objections raised against it. If the neutral state succeeds in securing a scheme of rights without appealing to a sense of community beyond the social contract, if its members can exercise their agency as free citizens without seeing themselves as claimed by civic obligations beyond consent, then abstract worries about community and self-government, toleration and moral judgment, would seem at best beside the point. Either those objections are mistaken, or liberal politics is sufficiently autonomous of theory to proceed unimpaired by philosophical infirmity.

But its prevalence as practice is no proof against its poverty as theory. To the contrary, what goes wrong with the philosophy shows up in the practice. The predicament of liberal democracy in contemporary America recapitulates the tensions that inhabit its ideals. Far from proving the autonomy of liberal politics, its practice confirms what its philosophy foretells: The procedural republic cannot secure the liberty it promises, because it cannot sustain the kind of political community and civic engagement that liberty requires.

NOTES

1. See John Rawls, *A Theory of Justice* (Cambridge, Mass.: Harvard University Press, 1971); Ronald Dworkin, "Liberalism," in Stuart Hampshire, ed., *Public and Private Morality* (Cambridge: Cambridge University Press, 1978), pp. 114–143; idem, *Taking Rights Seriously* (Cambridge, Mass.: Harvard University Press, 1977); Robert Nozick, *Anarchy, State, and Utopia* (New York: Basic Books, 1977); Bruce Ackerman, *Social Justice in the Liberal State* (New Haven: Yale University Press, 1980).

2. The term "procedural republic" was suggested to me by Judith N. Shklar.

3. On the meaning of "liberal" as used in contemporary American politics, see Ronald D. Rotunda, *The Politics of Language* (Iowa City: Iowa University Press, 1986).

4. Chapters 2–4 tell the first story; Chapters 5–9 tell the second.

5. Aristotle, *The Politics*, trans. Ernest Barker, book 3, chap. 9 (London: Oxford University Press, 1946), p. 119.

6. Ibid., pp. 119–120.

7. In this section I draw on my introduction to Michael Sandel, ed., *Liberalism and Its Critics* (Oxford: Basil Blackwell, 1984), pp. 1–11.

8. John Stuart Mill, *On Liberty* (1859), chap. 1.

9. For a sampling of arguments for and against utilitarianism, see Amartya Sen and Bernard Williams, eds., *Utilitarianism and Beyond* (Cambridge: Cambridge University Press, 1982).

10. See Immanuel Kant, *Groundwork of the Metaphysics of Morals* (1785), trans. H. J. Paton (New York: Harper and Row, 1956); idem, *Critique of Practical Reason* (1788), trans. L. W. Beck (Indianapolis: Bobbs-Merrill, 1956); idem, "On the Common Saying: 'This May Be True in Theory, But It Does Not Apply in Practice,'" in *Kant's Political Writings*, ed. Hans Reiss (Cambridge: Cambridge University Press, 1970), pp. 61–92.

11. Rawls, *A Theory of Justice*, pp. 3–4.

12. Dworkin, "Liberalism," p. 136.

13. Rawls, *A Theory of Justice*, p. 560.

14. George Kateb, "Democratic Individuality and the Claims of Politics," *Political Theory*, 12 (August 1984), 343.

15. John Rawls, "Kantian Constructivism in Moral Theory," *Journal of Philosophy*, 77 (Summer 1980), 543.

16. John Rawls, "Fairness to Goodness," *Philosophical Review*, 84 (October 1985), 537.

17. Ibid.

18. Rawls, *A Theory of Justice*, p. 312, and, generally, pp. 310–315. See also Friedrich A. Hayek, *The Constitution of Liberty* (Chicago: University of Chicago Press, 1960), chap. 7; and Nozick, *Anarchy, State, and Utopia*, pp. 155–160.

19. Rawls, *A Theory of Justice*, pp. 108–117.

20. Ibid., p. 114.

21. See Michael J. Sandel, *Liberalism and the Limits of Justice* (Cambridge: Cambridge University Press, 1982), pp. 179–183.

22. Alasdair MacIntyre, *After Virtue* (Notre Dame: University of Notre Dame Press, 1981), pp. 204–206.

23. Lee quoted in Douglas Southall Freeman, *R. E. Lee* (New York: Charles Scribner's Sons, 1934), pp. 443, 421. See also the discussions of Lee in Morton Grodzins, *The Loyal and the Disloyal* (Chicago: University of Chicago Press, 1965), pp. 142–143; and Judith Shklar, *Ordinary Vices* (Cambridge, Mass.: Harvard University Press, 1984), p. 160.

24. Rawls, *A Theory of Justice,* pp. 101–102.

25. See Nozick, *Anarchy, State, and Utopia,* p. 228.

26. Ralph Waldo Emerson, "Self Reliance," in Emerson, *Essays and Lectures* (New York: Library of America, 1983), p. 262.

27. The view I describe here as minimalist liberalism is represented by John Rawls's recent book, *Political Liberalism* (New York: Columbia University Press, 1993), and his article "Justice as Fairness: Political Not Metaphysical," *Philosophy & Public Affairs,* 14 (1985), 223–251. It is also presented in a somewhat different version, in Richard Rorty, "The Priority of Democracy to Philosophy," in *The Virginia Statute for Religious Freedom,* ed. Merrill D. Peterson and Robert C. Vaughan (Cambridge: Cambridge University Press, 1988). The quotation is from Rawls, "Justice as Fairness," p. 230.

28. Rawls, *Political Liberalism,* p. 31; see generally pp. 29–35.

29. Ibid., pp. xvi–xviii.

30. Rawls, "Justice as Fairness," p. 230; Rorty, "Priority of Democracy," p. 257.

31. I draw in this discussion from Michael J. Sandel, "Political Liberalism," *Harvard Law Review,* 107 (1994), 1765–94.

32. Paul M. Angle, ed., *Created Equal? The Complete Lincoln-Douglas Debates of 1858* (Chicago: University of Chicago Press, 1958), pp. 369, 374.

33. Ibid., p. 390.

34. Ibid., p. 392.

35. Ibid., p. 389.

22 The Privatization of Good

ALASDAIR MACINTYRE

W HEN IN 1879 in the encyclical *Aeterni Patris* Leo XIII contrasted the moral and political philosophy of Aquinas with that of the secular liberalism of the late nineteenth century, he directed our attention to an area of conflict whose importance has not diminished in the succeeding century. Nowhere is this conflict more evident or persistent than in the radical disagreement between Aquinas and the moral philosophy of modern liberalism over the question of the relationship between how the human good is to be conceived and achieved and how those rules, obedience to which is required for morally right action, are to be formulated, understood and justified.

For Aquinas, as for Aristotle, we can only understand the right in the light afforded by the good. The good for the members of each species is that end to which, *qua* members of that species, those members move in achieving their specific perfection. The rules for right action for rational animals are those rules intentional conformity to which is required if their specific perfection is to be achieved. The content of those rules, their exceptionless character and their authority all derive from the end which obedience to them serves. But they are not to be understood as specifying types of actions the performance of which as a matter of merely contingent fact will bring about some particular type of end-state. They are not specifications of means *externally* related to an end. They are rather rules partially constitutive of a form of life, the living out of which is the peculiar function of human beings as rational animals, and the completion of which lies in that activity which is itself supreme happiness and which makes of the life of which it is the completion of a happy life. So to disobey such rules in any way and to any degree is in that way and to that degree to separate oneself from one's good. And, insofar as anyone lacks knowledge of his or her true good, such a person is also deprived of the only sound reasons for right action.

This is not of course to imply that, either for Aristotle or for Aquinas, human beings do or are able to begin with a fully-fledged knowledge of the good and from it deduce the rules of right action. Each of us learns how to articulate his or her own initial inner capacity for comprehending what the good is in the course of also learning from others about rules and about virtues, so that, through a dialectical process of questioning the ways in which rules, virtues, goods and *the* good are interrelated, we gradually come to understand the unity of the deductive structures of practical reasoning. But what we thus come to understand is in part that, to the extent that what we take to be the case about the human good is false or confused, to that extent our understanding of the rules defining right action will also be apt to be false and confused and that, to the

From Alasdair MacIntyre, "The Privatization of Good," Review of Politics 52 (Summer 1990), p. 3. Reprinted by permission of the publisher.

extent to which we ignore or put out of mind or otherwise fail to take account of the distinctive character of the human good, to that extent we shall be unable to provide an adequately determinate or authoritative formulation of those same rules. Adequate knowledge of moral rules is inseparable from and cannot be had without genuine knowledge of human good.

It follows that on any substantively Aristotelian or Thomistic view rational agreement on moral rules always presupposes rational agreement on the nature of the human good. Any political society therefore, which possesses a shared stock of adequately determinate and rationally defensible moral rules, publicly recognized to be the rules to which characteristically and generally unproblematic appeals may be made, will therefore, implicitly or explicitly, be committed to an adequately determinate and rationally justifiable conception of the human good. And insofar as the rational justification of particular moral stances is a feature of its public life, that conception will have had to be made explicit in a way and to a degree which will render general allegiance to that particular conception itself a matter of public concern.

This is not of course how things are in the contemporary advanced societies of Western modernity. What shared moral rules there are—and later I shall need to enquire how far there are in fact shared moral rules in such societies—are and cannot but be invoked and upheld independently of any corresponding shared conception of *the* human good. For as to the nature of the human good, as to whether there is indeed any such thing as the human good, disagreements are numerous and fundamental. This socially embodied divorce between rules defining right action on the one hand and conceptions of the human good on the other is one of those aspects of such societies in virtue of which they are entitled to be called liberal. For it is a central tenet of recent liberal moral and political theory that public institutions and more especially the institutions of government should be systematically neutral as between rival conceptions of what the human good is. Allegiance to any particular conception of human good ought, on this liberal view, to be a matter of private individual preference and choice, and it is contrary to rationality to require of anyone that he or she should agree with anyone else in giving his or her allegiance to some particular view.

In this respect the status of conceptions of the human good is very different from that of moral rules. Moral rules, on this modern liberal view, prescribe those actions and those refrainings from action which any rational person may require of any other. About them, about their content, about their binding force, and presumably about the appropriate ways of responding to their breach, agreement among rational persons is therefore required. The type of agreement required about moral rules by liberals and the type of disagreement permitted and expected by those same liberals about conceptions of the good can both be characterized in terms of one and the same understanding of the relationship of freedom to reason. The autonomy of a free and rational individual, according to liberalism, is not infringed by, but requires that individual to assent to the deliverances of reason, where these are unequivocal; and so it is with assent to moral rules. But where the state of the argument is such that there are alternative and incompatible views on some matter, and rational argument currently does not, and provides no prospect of being able to provide unequivocal support for only one set of conclusions out of those which are in contention, the autonomy of a free and rational individual can be exercised in embracing any one of the contending views. It is in the light of this contrast that concerns about elaborating, defending and living out particular conceptions of the good are, on this type of liberal view, to be assigned to and restricted to the sphere of the private life of individuals, while concerns about obedience to what are taken to be the moral rules required of every rational person can be legitimately pursued in the public realm. So appeals to particular moral rules always provide *relevant,* although not necessarily *sufficient* grounds for advocating legislation of various kinds, while appeals to particular conceptions of the human good never do. Insofar as it is this liberal view which has been embodied in social practice in contemporary advanced societies, the good has been privatized.

There are of course important differences between liberal theorists in the ways in which they articulate their positions, but there is also a remarkable degree of concurrence. So Virginia Held, who expresses the contrast between the right and the good in terms of principles defining rights asserts that "We can agree that persons' conceptions of the good will diverge and that, although not all such conceptions will be equally admirable, persons can legitimately pursue a pluralism of admirable goals. But their recognition of principles of freedom, justice, and equality yielding a system of rights for human beings is not a matter of preference, or choice between goods. . . . That all persons ought as moral beings to adhere to principles assuring respect for rights can be asserted and defended" (*Rights and Goals* [Chicago: University of Chicago Press, 1984], p. 19).

Ronald Dworkin had earlier identified a distinctively liberal theory of equality as one which "supposes that political decisions must be, so far as is possible, independent of any particular conception of the good life, or of what gives value to life. Since the citizens of a society differ in their conceptions, the government does not treat them as equals if it prefers one conception to another, either because the officials believe that one is intrinsically superior, or because one is held by the more numerous or more powerful group" ("Liberalism," in *Public and Private Morality,* ed. S. Hampshire [Cambridge: Cambridge University Press, 1978], p. 127). And John Rawls had already gone further than either Held or Dworkin in contending not only that

"agreement upon the principles of rational choice" is presupposed in arriving at principles of justice, while in the case of planning one's life in the light of some conception of the good, "unanimity concerning the standards of rationality is not required," since "each person is free to plan his life as he pleases (so long as his intentions are consistent with the principles of justice)," but also that "variety in conceptions of the good is itself a good thing" (*A Theory of Justice* [Cambridge, MA: Harvard University Press, 1971], pp. 447–48).

Notice that for liberalism understood in this way everything turns on two contentions: first, that in the debate between particular rival and alternative conceptions of the human good, not only has none established a claim to decisive rational superiority over its rivals, but that it should not even be a matter of public, as against private interest how we ought to proceed in evaluating the rational merits of rival claims in this area; and secondly that rational agreement on moral rules can be—and indeed, given the liberal case, must already have been—somehow or other secured in a way which deserves to secure the consent and compliance of all rational persons, and that this agreement is available or can be made available as a key point of reference in public debate and decision-making. It is with this last claim that I am going to be first of all concerned in this lecture. For it is a claim that we have the strongest of reasons to doubt.

It is not that we do not have a variety of recommended methods for arriving at rational agreement of the kind required. It is rather that we have all too many such methods, each of them incompatible in important ways with some of the others, not only in the type of argument proposed as appropriate for settling disputes about the nature and content of moral rules, but also in the substantive conclusions arrived at about the nature and content of such rules. So we have a range of types of Kantianism, a similar range of types of utilitarianism, and of intuitionism, contractarianism and various blends of these. And since each of these rival and competing views claims to supply the *ultimate* principles by which disputed questions in this area are to be adjudicated, we lack any further rational court of appeal, whose verdicts might settle such questions. Radical and *de facto* ineliminable disagreement confronts us.

Moreover what these various types of philosophical theory mirror are just the types of reasoning upon which ordinary nonphilosophical reflective persons in our culture rely in their moral reasoning. Universalizabilty arguments, utilitarian attention to consequences, intuitionist appeals to not further to be argued for principles of duty and invocations of contractarian thoughts are as much part of the common currency of everyday practical argument as they are of the academic study of moral philosophy. So that we should expect to find the same range of disagreements at the level of everyday morality. But recently Jeffrey Stout has argued that this is in fact not the case, that disagreements do of course occur on some major issues, but that we have a stock of agreements embodied in what Stout calls "moral platitudes," learned as children in the nursery (*Ethics After Babel* [Boston: Beacon Press, 1988], p. 211). Disagreements presuppose a background of agreement, for "we are initiated into a moral consensus as very young children" (p. 43). Such differences as there may be in modes of reasoning do not at least on many fundamental topics issue in significant differences in moral conclusions.

Against Stout I want to suggest that he is indeed right in thinking that there is a consensus of platitudes in our moral culture, but that this belongs to the rhetorical surface of that culture, and not to its substance. The rhetoric of shared values is of great ideological importance, but it disguises the truth about how action is guided and directed. For what we genuinely share in the way of moral maxims, precepts and principles is insufficiently determinate to guide action and what is sufficiently determinate to guide action is not shared. And this after all is what we

might expect, if it were the case *both* that the variety and heterogeneity of the types of moral reasoning recognized among us issued in as wide a range of disparate normative conclusions in everyday practical life as it does in the realm of moral theory *and* that a refusal, or perhaps a failure, to allow that this is so was a prerequisite for the effective function of our central political, legal and educational institutions. I take as a test case for deciding the issue between Stout and myself, not those much debated issues such as the wrongness of abortion or the nature of a just war by focussing on which, so Stout claims, I have in the past exaggerated the degree of conflict in our culture, but the subject matter of one of the maxims—platitudes in Stout's idiom—which constitute the moral consensus into which children are initiated, the matter of truth-telling and lying.

What is the shared maxim, so far as there is one, by which children are instructed in this area by parents, teachers and other authoritative adults? It runs as follows: "Never tell a lie" (this first part is uttered loudly and firmly) "except when" (and here the adult voice tends to drop) and there then follows a list of exceptions of varying types ending with an "etc." We all agree on the maxim; where we disagree is first of all upon which types of exception are to be included in the appended list. Is it permissible to lie when the utterance of the truth will be discourteous? Is it permissible or perhaps obligatory to lie when an innocent human life is immediately at stake? Is it permissible to lie when a lie just *might* contribute to the future saving of such a life? Is it permissible to lie to save face? Is it permissible or even obligatory to lie to help a friend out of a difficulty? If I am in fact the best candidate for a job, but I will only get it if I lie, may I lie? If it will serve the national interest or if some highly placed official says that it will serve the national interest, ought I to lie? If it furthers the cause of the National Rifle Association, the ACLU or the girl scouts, should I lie? If doing my job as journalist, a private detective, or an investigator of insurance claims involves lying, should I change my employment?

There is no socially established agreement on the answers to these questions. And both between and within different influential moral and religious traditions, Catholic, Protestant, Jewish and secular, rival and conflicting answers are defended. But our disagreements are not confined to the question of which types of lie, if any, are permissible. For even when it is agreed by some large number of persons that a particular type of lie is impermissible, there will still be extensive disagreements as to how serious an offence it is to tell that type of lie. We disagree as to how to rank order offenses against truth-telling in terms of their gravity. But even this is not all. For we also disagree about how lies, when exposed as such, ought to be responded to by the exposed liar, by those who have been lied to and by members of the society at large. Is it guilt or shame that the offender should feel if exposed in various types of lie, and to what degree, and what kind of subsequent conduct is to be required of the guilty or the ashamed? When, if ever, is the liar to be punished or, if not punished, reproached or shunned and by whom and for how long? From membership in what bodies should proven liars be excluded? Once again we have a range of questions to which different and incompatible answers are given.

Nor is it the case that different individuals each give one clear and consistent set of answers to each of these questions, albeit disagreeing with the other individuals. To some significant, even if unmeasured extent these disagreements seem to occur within individuals, one and the same individual hovering between two or more rival opinions, inclining to one on some occasions and in some contexts, to another on others. Only thus can the inconsistency and instability of our shared public responses to lying be made fully intelligible. For what is apparently one and the same type of lie will among the same groups of people or in the same political institution be treated as a grave offence on some occasions, as a minor offence upon others and upon yet others

be simply ignored. In our public and political life there are strange oscillations between wild outbursts of self-righteous indignation on the one hand and complacent silences on the other. We do know from empirical psychological research that lying is endemic in the population at large: Bella de Paulo, a psychologist at the University of Virginia, who studies lying by having her experimental subjects keep a diary of the lies which they tell, has concluded that "People tell about two lies a day, or at least that is how many they will admit to" (*New York Times*, 12 February 1985, p. 17). And the indeterminacy of our shared public maxims and the unpredictability of our public responses about truth-telling point to widespread uncertainties about both our own behavior and that of others.

There have been in the past and there are now rival and contending moral traditions about what a strict determinate rule about truth-telling and lying should in fact be. But these disagreements were and are rooted in more fundamental disagreements about the place and purpose of speech and writing within that kind of life which it is best for human beings to lead. The determinate character of such rules in each case arises from their relationship to and their implementation of some particular determinate conception of the good and the best. And whatever rational authority each may possess, that in virtue of which rational persons ought to treat it as binding is derived from whatever rational authority that particular conception of human good may possess.

As against Stout, therefore, and indeed against contemporary liberal theory in general I initially conclude that a necessary precondition for a political community's possession of adequately determinate shared rationally founded moral rules is the shared possession of a rationally justifiable conception of human good. And that insofar as appeals to moral rules are to play a part in the public life of such a community, respect for and allegiance to that shared conception of the human good will have had to be institutionalized in the life of that community.

On this issue then a Thomistic Aristotelianism is so far vindicated. Notice that it is in an important way a specifically Thomistic Aristotelianism which is thus vindicated. In what way becomes clear when we consider a rival attempt to render Aristotle's ethics of virtue relevant to the debates of contemporary moral philosophy, one undertaken in different versions by a number of thinkers who agree in recognizing the superiority of Aristotelianism to Kantianism and utilitarianism, but who aspire to do this in a way compatible with a modern liberal allegiance. It is this latter which leads them to substitute for the single and unitary, if complex, final good conceived by Aristotle a multiplicity of goods, each *qua* good worthy of being pursued, and each, at least in certain circumstances and perhaps as such, incommensurable with the others. Which good or set of goods any particular individual pursues is to be determined by the particular individual's preferences. And the choice of any one such good or set of goods will characteristically exclude the choice of certain others.

When Aristotle is thus emended however, practical reasoning, as understood by Aristotle, ceases to yield unambiguous directives for action. For the first premise of such reasoning—often of course left tacit—is, as Aristotle remarks, of the form "Since the *telos* and the best is such and such" (*Nicomachean Ethics* vi, 1144a32–33), and where there are alternative and competing goods, each of which may equally be treated as the *telos* and the best, there will also in particular situations be alternative and competing practical syllogisms with alternative and competing courses of action as their conclusions. So it will be equally rational to act in any one out of a number of different and incompatible ways and nonrational preference will have become sovereign in decision-making.

It is not then surprising that, while Aristotle found no need to discuss practical dilemmas, this kind of would-be-Aristotelian characteristically finds them of notable importance in the moral life, for practical rationality thus reconceived renders systematically indeterminate what is re-

quired of us in just too many types of situation. So that if this were indeed a faithful rendering of Aristotle, Aristotelianism would afford us no resources with which to challenge the indeterminacy of public shared moral rules in contemporary culture. It is only Aristotelianism understood as specifying in adequate outline a single and unitary, albeit complex, conception of the human good, Aristotelianism, that is, understood very much as Thomists have understood it, which is capable of challenging effectively the privatization of conceptions of the good, their exclusion from the public realm, that privatization which precludes the possession of an adequately determinate, rationally justifiable morality. But this is not all that it precludes.

For there are certain issues of the moral life which cannot get raised at all in any adequately systematic way in the public realm, if appeal to conceptions of the overall human good is excluded from that realm. Consider two areas of concern often considered separately in our society: on the one hand, the horrifying infant mortality rate in the United States, one which comes close in some parts of the country to ranking it with Third World rather than other advanced countries, and on the other the condemnation of the old in our society to boredom, nursing homes, and Alzheimer's disease. What these together represent is a distribution of resources, such that more and more has been directed to the mindless extension of the length of human life by medical science into a more and more mindless old age, while the unborn and the very young have continued to be radically deprived. And this maldistribution of resources represents an answer to a set of questions which have not yet been systematically asked, let alone answered.

Aristotle makes it clear that what the living out of the best life for human beings requires of us is not the same at every period of life; and in specifying what participation in which activities is required at each stage in the movement from early childhood to old age; on an Aristotelian view each age has its tasks and functions, including old age; no period of life is functionless—and in what the relationship between older and younger is at each stage, one would have had to have made considerable progress in specifying what the best life for human beings is. Conversely, without some determinate conception of the good and the best it would be impossible to provide adequate answers to these questions. So answering questions in any systematic way, which could be implemented in practice, concerning the overall relationships of the very young, the adolescent, the working adult and the old within families, parishes, schools, clinics, work places and local neighborhood communities, so that we can agree in recognizing what the old owe to the young and the young to the old, is a task inseparable from that of formulating a conception of the good and the best. And when that task is one excluded from the public realm, then it will become impossible to ask and answer such questions, let alone questions about a just distribution of resources between the young and the old. The privatization of the good thus ensures not only that we are deprived of adequately determinate shared moral rules, but that central areas of moral concern cannot become the subject of anything like adequate public shared systematic discourse or enquiry.

Morality is thereby diminished in scope. And hence in part the sterility of much public debate, on issues which *are* admitted to the public realm, such as that of abortion. For what one holds rationally about abortion is inseparable from what one holds about the point and purpose of family life, about the place of the conception and upbringing of children in that life and about the relationship of family ties to other social ties. To abstract the issue of abortion from these contexts is necessarily to obscure what is at issue. Moral questions treated one by one piecemeal in isolation from larger contexts of argument and of practice always begin to appear rationally unanswerable; and since, when morality is defined independently of the good, the relationships between different moral rules disappears from view, one result is that moral questions tend to

be presented as a grab bag of separable, isolable and so insoluble problems.

So we confront a situation in which there is great danger and great difficulty. The danger arises from our inhabiting a political and economic system in which a rhetoric of moral consensus masks fundamental dissensus and moral impoverishment. The difficulty arises from the fact that a standard liberal retort to the arguments which I have advanced is at first inspection highly plausible. It runs as follows.

Even if it were the case that the absence of a shared conception of the human good both rendered our shared moral rules indeterminate and impoverished the definition of our moral concerns, we could not find a remedy in the adoption of such a shared conception, for in our culture radical disagreement about the nature of the good does seem to be ineliminable among rational persons. We need do no more than point to the range and diversity and incompatibility of widely held rival and conflicting conceptions of the good for this to be evident. But what ought we to conclude from this range and diversity and incompatibility? Is it the case that there has been somewhere or other in our past history a prolonged and systematic rational debate, whose procedures were fair and impartial, between such conceptions, whose outcome was a failure on the part of each contending party to defeat its rivals, so that by the best test which the resources of rationality can afford radical disagreement and conflict has indeed proved ineliminable? The answer to this question is "No." It is a piece of false mythology to suppose that our fundamental disagreements have either emerged from or been tested by prolonged rational debate. Even such debate as has occurred has been defective in at least three ways.

First what have in fact taken place over the past two hundred years have been at best a series of particular and intermittent engagements of relatively sporadic and unsustained kinds on particular, local issues and problems practical or theoretical. There have been few occasions, perhaps none, in which one point of view, presenting itself systematically and as a whole, has been able to engage with its major rivals, also presented systematically and as a whole. And it is easy to understand why this should be so. The genres of debate, the institutionalizations of the expressions of disagreement, either restrict it to the piecemeal treatment of isolable issues in the more serious academic journals or to relatively brief and rhetorically insinuating treatments in other media.

Secondly liberalism has played two roles in the modern world. It has been and is one of the contending parties with respect to theories of the good. But it has also by and large controlled the terms of both public and academic debate. Other points of view have generally been invited to debate with liberalism only within a framework of procedures whose presuppositions were already liberal. But, important as these two points are, they are much less crucial than a third.

Fundamental disagreement over the nature of the good is not only a matter of theoretical contention, but also and essentially of practice. It is rival conceptions of practical rationality, of the relationship of human beings to the good in their actions, of the practically embodied rules and virtues which are specific to each rival conception of the good, which are in contention. And practical claims cannot be made in exclusively theoretical ways. Certainly the theory of practice is important, but only as in key part arising reflectively from, throwing light upon and being vindicated or failing to be vindicated by the practice of which it is the theory. Hence there can be no genuine abstract, merely theoretical debate between rival conceptions of the good. Such conceptions only confront one another in any decisive way, when presented with the embodied life of particular communities which exemplify each specific conception. It is in key part in the lives of families, parishes, schools, clinics, work places and local neighborhood communities that any particular conception of the good achieves recognizable form.

So just as we only know what a particular conception of the good and the corresponding conceptions of virtues, intellectual and moral, and of rules really amount to when we encounter them to some significant degree embodied in the particularities of social life, so also genuine debate between rival conceptions only occurs when the actualities of one mode of social life, embodying one such conception, are matched against the actualities of its rivals. It is as it is concretely lived out that one fundamental standpoint is or is not vindicated against its rivals. And my earlier criticism of liberalism was expressed in a way that was designed to recognize this. My accusation was not or not only that liberal theory involves a fundamental indeterminateness in respect of moral rules and of impoverishment in respect of moral concerns; it was that as such theory is lived out in practice, this indeterminateness and this impoverishment are exemplified in social reality. And correlatively if it is, as it is, a Thomistic contention that the Thomistic conception of human good can supply a more adequate determinateness in respect of rules and a more adequate specification of moral concerns, that contention too can be vindicated only insofar as it can be translated into the actualities of social life.

To say this is not of course to deny that any particular social embodiment of any particular standpoint about the goods, virtues and rules is always a more or less imperfect embodiment. But it is crucial to note that a central aspect of any such social embodiment is the institutionalization of standard responses to rule-breaking, whether mild or flagrant, and to what are taken to be vices and errors about the good; indeed without such responses there can be no adequate institutionalization of rule-observance or of the recognition of virtues or goods. So what would it be for us here now to give particularized social form to a Thomistic conception of the good and of those virtues the cultivation of which and those rules the observance of which are integral to the achievement of the good thus conceived? And how would that conception, when thus socially embodied, contrast with the actualities of recent liberalism? These are large questions and here I can only gesture toward them. But even such a gesture may be worthwhile. So let me focus attention on the same two issues which I identified as relevant to the critique of liberalism: truth-telling and lying, and the relationship of the young to the old.

Aquinas, like Augustine before him and Kant after him, but unlike John Chrysostom, Benjamin Constant and John Stuart Mill, held that lying is unconditionally and exceptionlessly prohibited. Not all lies are equally grave offenses, but all lying defects from what is required of us by the virtue of justice. If I lie to someone else, I fail to give to him or to her what is his or her due as a rational being. And since rational beings can only achieve their good and the good in and through a variety of social relationships, familial and political, informed by friendship, it follows that I both injure those relationships and put in crucial danger my relationship to the good whenever I lie. The virtue of justice and the rules of truth-telling, which partly specify that virtue, are not of course means external to the end toward which rational beings move; they are partially constitutive of that end. So that, if and when I lie, it is not that I have been inefficient in my choice of means to achieve my good; it is rather that I have temporarily at least put my good and the good out of mind and renounced them. And if someone lies to me, they have thereby affronted me by denying my status as a rational being, and ought to be responded to accordingly. There is no room for indeterminateness here, either in action or in response.

It is not of course possible to observe justice in speech merely by refraining from lying. No moral rule, no particular precept of the natural law, can be adequately understood in isolation from other such precepts or from that good, movement toward the achievement of which gives to obedience to such rules their point and purpose. Hence we always need to supply a good deal more than the statement of some particular rule itself supplies in order to understand that rule. What else is it then that we need to understand, if we are to make adequately intelligible the rule which prohibits lying, and to do so in such a way as to know how to institutionalize it in our practices?

Someone would certainly not have understood that rule adequately who supposed that, while we are required to speak and write truthfully, utterance in other respects can be allowed to be whatever we want it to be. It is to the place and purpose of utterance in human life as a whole that this rule is addressed. The ethics of conversation, as understood by Aquinas, is a complex matter and there are some important aspects of it with which I shall not be concerned here. Aquinas, for example, devotes no less than eight questions of the IIa-IIae of the *Summa* to types of use of language which sin against charity and justice, characteristically uses informed by either malice or negligence. And it is of course, on Aquinas's view, the adding of malice to lying which makes of lying a mortal sin. Nonetheless it is lying as such that is prohibited.

Moreover, Aquinas holds that the human good cannot be achieved without games, jokes and dramatic entertainment—even inaugural lectures perhaps—and failure either to engage in these, or to be responsive to and appreciative of others so engaging, is both vicious and sinful. So an institutionalization of any Thomistic conception of the moral and political life will have to be one which provides both for negative responses to malice and for positive responses to wit and to laughter. And once again such wit and laughter and the responses to them will, as Aquinas notes explicitly, have to be truthful. But what gives to this continuous insistence upon truthfulness its point?

A care for truth as a standard of rectitude in life, says Aquinas, following Jerome, is a constitutive part of all the virtues. And although truthfulness is a special virtue and an aspect of the virtue of justice (*Summa Theologiae* IIa-IIae 109, 2, 3) the detail of Aquinas's discussions makes it clear that all the virtues involve truthfulness as part of their exercise. For all the virtues, moral as well as intellectual, have to be developed throughout one's entire life, and this development requires a lifelong process of learning and imparting truths, learning in which reflection upon experience needs initially to be guided by teachers who enable one to learn from experience and so, later on in one's interactions with others, to contribute to their learning as well as to one's own, and in so doing to learn from them.

So mutual relationships of teaching and learning inform all well-ordered relationships and consistent truthfulness is therefore an essential ingredient of all such relationships. There is an informative analogy between the high value which the modern scientific community sets on truthfulness within the community of scientific enquirers, a value expressed in the penalties imposed upon those who falsify data, and the value which, on a Thomistic view, is to be set on truthfulness within any human community. For, on a Thomistic view, every human community is a community of practical enquiry, the subject-matter of whose enquiry consists of everything actually and potentially relevant to the relationship of the individuals who compose it and of the community itself to its and their good. Hence it is precisely as enquirers, as rational beings, that the truth is part of what we owe to one another. And this enquiry is lifelong, having at each particular stage of life its own peculiar tasks, tasks which involve the contribution which those at each such stage have to make both to each other and to those at other stages of life.

To spell out in full what this view of the relationships of those of different ages to each other involves would of course by an immense task, one in which Aristotle's brief, but illuminating remarks on this matter would have to be developed in a way appropriate to our own very different circumstances. But for the purposes of my present argument I need only consider two related implications of this standpoint. One is that we have to think of the old, those approaching and at retirement from earning their living, as both learners and teachers, as people who owe it

to the young in a variety of ways to transmit what they have learned and are still learning. The grandparent and the great aunt and the elderly neighbor have to be once again thought of as teachers, so reconstituting one older type of family. How *are* they to do this? In part it will be through telling stories, in part through instructing in the performance of tasks, through making the past present and restoring those various links to the past which modern social mobility and the increasing brevity of the modern attention span all too often break.

Another implication is that we have to stop thinking of teaching and learning as activities restricted to specialized, compartmentalized areas of life within schools, colleges and universities. Of course schools, colleges and universities have their own highly specific tasks, but these tasks need to be defined in terms of their contribution to lifelong learning and teaching, most of it carried out in nonscholastic and nonacademic contexts. We need, that is, to think of formal academic education not primarily as a preparation for something else, a life of work, which terminates when that life of work begins, but rather as itself the beginning of, and the providing of skills, virtues and resources for, a lifelong education directed toward and informed by the achievement of the good.

We need, for example, to teach our students to read, so that they go on reading throughout their lives. We need to make such reading a way of illuminating their social relationships, so that their familial and communal lives continue to be enriched by a stock of common reading. We need to rethink the time-scale of education so that we make one of the tests of the adequacy of what we teach now the answer to the question: "What will our students be reading when they are forty, sixty, seventy-five?" and to accept that if they are not then returning to the *Republic* and the *Confessions*, to *Don Quixote* and Dostoievski and Borges, we will have failed as teachers.

It is within this kind of overall perspective that moral questions about truthfulness and moral questions about the relationship of the old to the young can be seen to be rationally answerable together or not at all. And this exemplifies what I have already suggested is true of moral questions in general, that we cannot expect anything but frustration from a problem by problem or issue by issue approach. To do so will be sterile just because adequately determinate moral rules can only be identified and characterized as parts of the specification of some particular overall conception of the human good and how it is to be achieved. Hence rational debate about what our shared moral rules are to be will always inescapably be also debate about the competing claims of rival conceptions of that good.

To this claim I have added another. It is that even such debate can still be sterile, if it is restricted to competing statements and arguments at the level of a theory which isolates itself from practice. The central weaknesses of recent liberalism are, on the view which I have advanced, only to be understood in the light of those institutionalized practices of contemporary American society which give concrete and particularized expression to the present condition of liberalism. And correspondingly the strengths of an Aristotelian and Thomistic position will only become clear insofar as it too is seen to be embodied in particularized forms of practice in a variety of local modes of communal activity, in teaching and learning, in farming, in craftsmanship of various kinds. Debate and conflict as to the best forms of practice have to be debate and conflict between rival institutions and not merely between rival theories.

Not everyone who contributes to the making and sustaining of the type of practices and institutions which Aristotelianism and Thomism require will of course think of themselves as Aristotelian or Thomist. What, for example, Andrew Lytle and Wendell Berry, neither of whom thinks of himself as such, have written and done for the practices of farming and writing

provide as good examples of what I am saying as any available. And to a Thomist this should not be in the least surprising. For it is Aquinas's view that rational persons, who are able to develop their practical rationality in undistorted ways, become natural Thomists without having had to read Aquinas. But in our culture—indeed in any culture—how relatively few of such persons there are!

The argument of this lecture began from reflections on the consequences for contemporary society of the modern liberal attempt to render our public shared morality independent of conceptions of the human good. I have tried to explain why this attempt is bound to fail, but indicating what kinds of argument would have to be developed and sustained in detail, both in theory and practice, to make an alternative view, one drawing upon Aristotle and Aquinas, rather than upon Hume and Kant and Mill, compelling. Notice however that the remaking and the sustaining of our own local institutions and practices, which, on the view which I have been developing, is a necessary first step in the transformation of public debate, let alone of public moral practice, are primarily activities worthwhile in themselves and immensely so, and only secondarily a means to further outcomes. As to whether we can even contrive a reopening of genuine public debate about rival conceptions of the good in contemporary America, let alone bring such a debate to an effective conclusion, the evidence, as I understand it, suggests that we ought to be as deeply pessimistic as is compatible with a belief in Divine Providence. But as to that remaking of ourselves and our own local practices and institutions through a better understanding of what it is that, in an Aristotelian and Thomistic perspective, the unit of moral theory and practice now require of us, we have as much to hope for as we have to do, and not least within the community of this university.

23   The Liberals Strike Back

JEAN HAMPTON

Communitarianism

SINCE THE 1980s some political theorists have criticized not just particular liberal views but the entire liberal family of theories, claiming they are too focused on the individual, too focused on the importance of individual liberty, and insufficiently appreciative of the way in which human beings require a place in a well-functioning community in order to flourish. One might say that whereas liberals encourage each person to define and seek her own "good" within a political structure that defines and enforces what is "right," communitarians believe that a political structure has an important role to play in defining both the right and the good and in helping those people in that political structure to seek the good. This is because like Plato, communitarians believe human beings can achieve a good life only if they live within a well-functioning society that government must help to create (although, as I noted, communitarians, are unlike Plato, generally committed to democratic forms of government).

As their name suggests, communitarians are first and foremost concerned with *community:* They insist that each of us, as an individual, develops an identity, talents, and pursuits in life only in the context of a community. Political life, then, must start with a concern for the community (not the individual), since the community is what determines and shapes individuals' natures. One communitarian, Alasdair MacIntyre, ridicules the liberals' "autonomous moral agent" operating disconnected from any social context and argues that individuals flourish only within the context of what he calls "practices," through which individuals develop and perfect virtues. For MacIntyre, a practice is

> any coherent and complex form of socially established cooperative human activity through which goods internal to that form of activity are realized in the course of trying to achieve those standards of excellence which are appropriate to, and partially definitive of, that form of activity, with the result that human powers to achieve excellence, and human conceptions of the ends and goods involved, are systematically extended.[1]

So on this view the state's role is to help develop and protect practices that encourage the development of human excellence. Were the state to let individuals loose to realize their "autonomy" (as liberals seem to wish), treating them as if they were socially disconnected beings who are concerned with their "rights," MacIntyre and other communitarians believe that the result would be social disintegration and moral disaster. Indeed, they argue that such disintegration and degeneration have already started to occur in modern liberal states, given the prevalence of crime and

249

violence, the breakdown of the family and drug abuse in these societies.[2]

MacIntyre's criticisms have been echoed by Charles Taylor, who attacks the plausibility of the liberals' "atomistic" conception of human beings as autonomous choosers, arguing that it treats the human being as primarily a "will" and does not acknowledge the complexities of the human personality and the fact that it is (and must be) situated in a society in order to develop.[3] These same themes have been echoed by some feminists: As Jean Bethke Elshtain has put it, "There is no way to create real communities out of an aggregate of 'freely choosing' adults."[4] Such sentiments are usually attended by dissatisfaction with the morality of rights upon which many (albeit not all) liberal theories are based.[5] Finally, certain religious thinkers have argued that liberals' reliance on individualism and reason are in reality hostile to religious belief and religious community life.[6]

Another communitarian critic of liberalism is Michael Sandel, whose work focuses on the form of liberalism exemplified by Rawls in *A Theory of Justice*. Sandel is struck by the disconnected, disembodied nature of the people in Rawls's original position. That Rawls could even conceive of people in this way shows, according to Sandel, the extent to which he and many other liberals in the past few hundred years try to understand human beings independently of all activities, desires, ideas, roles, and pursuits that characterize human lives in an actual society. But why should we think there is anything left of the person when we subtract all of this? Isn't the Rawlsian (and for that matter any liberal) view of the person woefully impoverished? Writes Sandel:

> We cannot regard ourselves as independent in this way without great cost to those loyalties and convictions whose moral force consists partly in the fact that living by them is inseparable from understanding ourselves as the particular persons we are—as members of this family or community or nation or people, as bearers of

this history, as sons and daughters of that revolution, as citizens of this republic. Allegiances such as these are more than values I happen to have or aims I "espouse at any given time." They go beyond the obligations I voluntarily incur and the "natural duties" I owe to human beings as such. They allow that to some I owe more than justice requires or even permits, not by reason of agreements I have made but instead in virtue of those more or less enduring attachments and commitments which taken together partly define the person that I am.[7]

So Sandel is saying that liberal theories fail to come to grips with the nature of our "embeddedness" in a particular time, place, and culture. Not only is this embeddedness a fact, it is also a fact that a political theory must recognize if it is going to generate laws, institutions, and practices that are genuinely good for us and constitutive of an ideal and fully just society. He calls for us to pursue justice not by working out ways that independent and separately conceived selves might profitably relate to one another (e.g., in markets or in political institutions) but by thinking about how people with attachments that partially constitute their identities can come to know and relate to one another as friends.[8] Only in this way, says Sandel, can we create a "deeper commonality" than benevolence allows, one of "shared self-understanding" as well as affection.[9]

Communitarians have also taken issue with the liberal penchant for freedom and autonomy. Communitarians insist that many adult human beings (because of illness, personality, mental impairment, or immaturity) are simply not capable of the kind of autonomous choice of life plan that liberals believe a state must respect, and they point out that even highly mature and intelligent people frequently use their freedom to make bad (sometimes dreadfully bad) choices. Does a state respect its citizen if it tries to pretend that the residual "childishness" in all of our natures simply isn't there? Does it respect people when it permits them to make choices that will clearly preclude their own future happiness (and indirectly affect the happiness of those who are connected to them)? And finally, why think that autonomy is one of the most important political values that a society must respect? (Wouldn't Plato be profoundly puzzled by the liberal penchant for liberty as a primary political value?) Aren't there other values a government must implement that are at least as important as—and maybe more important than—autonomy, such as stability, the preservation of social bonds, the preservation of culture, and the safety of its citizens?[10] . . .

Whereas liberals believe that the most important political values are freedom and equality . . . , communitarians regard other values to be as important, and perhaps more important—in particular, what might be called the "values of community life," as I have just articulated them above. Moreover, whereas liberals are committed to the idea that the state's role must be defined such that it enhances the freedom and equality of the people, meaning that it should be democratically organized, pursue policies that implement toleration and freedom of conscience for all citizens, and stay out of the individual's construction of his own life plans and "conception of the good" . . . , communitarians believe the state's primary role is to ensure the health and well-being of the community life that makes possible all human flourishing and all human good. They are particularly adamant in rejecting the idea that in order to ensure human liberty the state must refrain from articulating a conception of the good to which all people must conform. Communitarians regard as a ridiculous illusion the liberal idea that we can autonomously pursue the good as individuals independent of cultural traditions and social roles; instead, they believe, in order to ensure that its citizens flourish, the ideal state must use its power and authority to encourage the continuation and health of the cultural traditions and roles through which each person must find her good life. . . .

Finally, communitarians dismiss the liberal acceptance of . . . reason as the tool by which the liberal state governs. The problem with the liberals' reliance on reason, say the communitarians, is that their conception of reason is disconnected from social traditions, operating in a vacuum (think of the reasoning in Rawls's original position) and hence unconnected to the real concerns, assumptions, goals, aspirations, and belief systems that real, socially embedded people actually have. In contrast, communitarians insist that the way to social harmony and health is through discourse that is informed by the culture of the community. We can achieve the ideal state only by engaging in discourse that is tied to the social practices that constitute and define the goals of the culture of the community.

The communitarian challenge has generated considerable response by liberals, the outlines of which I review and evaluate here. The first response liberals have made to the communitarians is: We care about communities, too! Whereas Hobbes (as we saw) was inclined to think that people were radically asocial, other liberals, including Locke, Rousseau, Kant, and, in modern times, Rawls, Gauthier, and Feinberg, have insisted on the social nature of human beings.[11] To quote Feinberg:

> Whatever else a human being is "by nature", he is essentially a social product. He is born into a family, itself part of a tribe or clan and a larger political community, each with its ongoing record or history, his first concepts shaped by a language provided for him by the larger group of which he is a member, his roles and status assigned by social custom and practice, his membership and sense of belonging imprinted from the start. He finds himself, as Alasdair MacIntyre puts it, "embedded" in a human culture not of his own original design or "contractual agreement," but one that is simply given.[12]

Such remarks endorse all sorts of communitarian ideas, yet they are made by a liberal who obviously feels that an enthusiastic endorsement of human sociality in no way threatens liberal political theory. Indeed, much of the liberal interest in allowing individuals to pursue their own conception of the good comes from their view that individuals should be able (and need to be able) to develop or pursue social connections— especially of a religious nature—that they take to be vital to their well-being and identity without being in any way impeded by government.

So both groups care about communities and acknowledge the sociality of human nature. What really differentiates them is their different views of state power: Whereas communitarians want the state to use its power to protect and encourage the development of communities and community values, liberals want the state to stay out of community life, so as not to harm, threaten, or limit those who are participating in it. This way of putting their disagreement shows that liberals and communitarians have very different views of the dangers, advantages, and consequences of state power. Whereas communitarians "seem to assume that whatever is properly social must become the province of the political,"[13] liberals want to limit the state's role in this province since they distrust it, fear its effects, and have faith in the ability of social groups to flourish without its help.

There are at least two reasons for the liberals' concern to limit the state's responsiveness to and interference in community life. The first reason has to do with the liberal commitment to the value of human autonomy. It is really this value that is driving the liberals' concern for the individual, and not some sort of implausible theory of the person as a socially naked atom. Again, to quote Feinberg: "The liberal can give up the excesses of individualism, acknowledge the social nature of man, and still hold on to what is essential in his normative theory, the doctrine of the human right of autonomous self-government within the private sphere."[14] The liberal is convinced that the best way to ensure that an individual can flourish within the community is to give her the freedom she needs to live (what will surely be) a highly social life in the way that she chooses.

The second reason arises from the liberals' deep distrust of state power and authority. Judith Shklar has argued that this distrust was born in the early modern period, in the midst of Calvinist proclamations of the innate sinfulness of the human soul, misanthropic writings of men of letters such as Michel de Montaigne, and grim experiences with the abusiveness and cruelty of state power and authority.[15] The lesson learned by the early moderns, whose thinking provides . . . the foundation for modern liberals, is that no human being can be counted upon to be "good enough" not to abuse extensive state power and authority. (As the saying goes, power corrupts and absolute power corrupts absolutely. . . . Hence in order to ensure that individuals will not be harmed in their pursuits—pursuits that (particularly when they concern religion) are generally highly social— liberals have insisted on constraining state power and authority in order to protect those subject to it from being abused by it.

Communitarians, in contrast, have been influenced by different thinkers and different historical experiences in ways that have given them a far more benign view of state power. They tend to agree, for example, with the nineteenth-century German philosopher G. W. F. Hegel, who considered the state "the actuality of the ethical idea"[16]—that is, that aspect of society which articulates and maintains the conditions for moral life in a society, drawing from the social traditions that compose it. They are also influenced by the way in which many modern states appear to have successfully taken on all sorts of moral roles, including the provision of education, health care, and art (supporting dramatic arts, fine arts, literature, music); the responsibility for caring for the poor; even the moral improvement of the citizenry (through programs designed to improve their mental health and social functioning). Those liberals who reject these Hegelian sentiments are either hostile to many of the moral roles Hegelians would have the state play or are concerned to limit them, lest the state's power and authority get out of control and compromise the liberty of the people.

Liberals and communitarians, however, disagree not only about the benignity of state authority and power but also about the benignity of culture. Consider that the communitarian sees the state as playing a moral role that is responsive to and at least partly defined by the traditions and moral views of the cultural traditions of the society it governs. But in many ways liberals have been just as suspicious of cultures as they have been of governments—and with good reason. For example, the American cultural experience has been sexist, racist, and antihomosexual. It has also been strongly influenced by a variety of philosophical traditions, ethnic groups, and religions. Were a U.S. government to rule in a way that was responsive to any one of these elements in American cultural life, many other groups would be subject to state power that enforced ideas they would regard as discordant with or antithetical to their beliefs and interests. So if communitarians would have the state respond to "social roles" and community values," how can they ensure that when it does so, it will not, say, compromise religious liberty or enact laws that reflect the prejudices of a majority against a minority? Why couldn't either use of state power and authority endanger not only the liberty and equality of certain people but also their very well-being? As one liberal critic of communitarianism puts it:

> The communitarian critics [of liberalism] want us to live in Salem, but not to believe in witches. Or human rights. Perhaps the Moral Majority would cease to be a threat were the United States a communitarian society; benevolence and fraternity might take the place of justice. Almost anything is possible, but it does not make moral sense to leave liberal politics behind on the strength of such speculation.[17]

Such worries show that to persuade the liberal opposition, communitarians can't simply hope for the best. They need to develop their theory so that it can show us how we can take a morally critical attitude toward community, even while recognizing the importance of community. Otherwise, their theory gives them no critical moral distance from existing social practices, which means that it could be used to license any abuse, injustice, and cruelty implicit in the community's culture.

Liberals influenced by those early modern thinkers who were impressed by the human capacity for cruelty have been very willing to recognize the way in which human beings and human social institutions can be morally corrupted and abusive. It is, I believe, for this reason that in their argumentation liberals start from the individual. By insisting that the individual is the focus of moral concern, the liberal gets the critical moral distance from community and the government that the communitarian lacks. In particular, by requiring that social arrangements are to work to the benefit of each person, the liberal has a way of recommending political policies that are not indebted to potentially cruel or unjust cultural practices of that community. This means liberal arguments start from the individual, not because they deny the sociality of human beings, but because they require that *all* social arrangements, to be morally acceptable, must be morally acceptable from the individual standpoint.

Hence liberalism has implicit within it a kind of critical facility for judging cultures that communitarianism appears to be lacking. Perhaps the best example of this is Rawls's original position procedure: That procedure, contra some communitarians, doesn't deny human sociality. Instead, quite the opposite is true—it affirms the extent to which our lives are influenced by a variety of social structures. The point of the original position procedure is to give us a way of *morally evaluating those social structures* or, in other words, a moral vantage point from which to reliably assess and evaluate social structures (what Rawls calls an "Archimedian point").[18]

The original position is a moral standpoint from which we attempt to assess the effects of a social practice on *every* member of society by freeing ourselves of beliefs, biases, and traditions that can prejudice that assessment. A social practice is easy to affirm if one uses the ideas generated by that practice to do so; the trick is to figure out a way of freeing oneself of the effects of a practice (which might be racist or sexist or in some other way unjust) so that one can come up with an effective moral assessment of it.

Indeed, this sort of "freeing" is what Rawls's original position procedure aims to do. Communitarians have attacked that procedure, . . . contending that it implicitly denies our thoroughly social natures. But is each of us *entirely* a product of the confluence of social forces on her biological nature? Can none of us critically assess the social forces to which we have been subject, because each of us is so completely a product of those forces that anything we would use to assess those forces would itself be generated by them? To say yes to this question is to raise an interesting (and chilling) possibility: If such complete social definition of human beings were possible, could not a government learn to control these social forces so effectively that it could design a society in which some individuals were socially constructed so as to be contented subordinates (happy "socialized" slaves), while other individuals were socially constructed to be fully comfortable in their role as superiors (happy "socialized" masters)?

If one answers no to this last question, one is postulating that there is something in individuals that will inevitably object to and fight social "definition" that attempts to oppress and subordinate them. It is this "something" that Rawls attempts to isolate in his original position procedure: The veil of ignorance, he says, tries to isolate each individual's "moral conception"— that is, that aspect of our personhood that is the source of our moral evaluations not only of individuals (including ourselves) but also of societies, cultures, and governments. Whether or not

Rawls succeeds in defining this moral component of individuals is arguable, but it would seem that communitarians must recognize such a component if they are to construct a way of morally assessing cultures. And doing so would seem to require them to take individuals, rather than social groups, as the foundational moral concern of all well-ordered societies, because social groups can be as much the source of the abuse of individuals as they are the source of roles that contribute to their happiness.

Still, communitarians can insist that even if they have trouble formulating a critical stance toward the community, liberalism has trouble formulating a way to respect and use (what might be called) the "moral wisdom" implicit in that community. If one's political theorizing is too individualistic and fails to focus on the community, it can fail to acknowledge that all sorts of social structures in our society, including our legal institutions, family structures, and systems of educating the young, have been worked out by generations of people responding to a variety of problems in ways that are complicated, nuanced, and often highly successful. One argument in favor of communitariansim . . . is that it encourages us to respect the moral wisdom implicit in these social structures and not to adopt the hubristic attitude that any one of us could do better by reasoning about these social structures by ourselves. This argument for communitarianism therefore links it with philosophical conservatism, a position associated with the writings of Edmund Burke (1729–1797).[19] An important political figure and member of the British Parliament, Burke argued that a society is ill advised to try to govern itself by relying on abstract reasoning, because such reasoning cannot compete with the accumulated wisdom of generations of people struggling with highly complicated issues in various areas. How can a single individual, for example, generate an adequate code of criminal conduct simply by using her reason? Moreover, Burke argued that custom, human sentiments, and the lessons we learn from experience are as important as reason in giving us the tools to construct a well-functioning political society. (These themes are also present in the novels of George Eliot, who criticized certain zealous attempts at reform in the nineteenth century by people who had no respect for the moral life of the community.[20])

As we have seen, liberals such as Feinberg have also been persuaded of the importance of respect for custom and community life and have sought to incorporate such respect in their theories. Still, these liberals are committed to assessing these commitments by reference to a reason-based theory of what is good for, or owed to, individuals. Such liberals will surely want to know how communitarians can assess and criticize the status quo in their society unless they rely upon some such reason-based individualistic theory. Thus far, communitarians have not yet developed a way of supplementing their respect for custom and culture with a fully worked out theory of how we are to critically assess custom and culture.

Liberals have other arguments against the communitarian position. For example, they can object to the way such a position seems to license a paternalistic attitude toward the citizenry. That is, rather than respecting individual pursuits of the good, the communitarian state seems to be licensed to dismiss them as "wrong" in the way that a parent may dismiss a child's pursuits as wrong. They can also contend that communitarianism rests on the wildly implausible idea that governmental officials know better than those whom they rule what counts as the good in life. Unless a group of Platonic guardians turns up among us, liberals would insist that state officials as a group are no wiser about what ought to be pursued in life than any other group of human beings and thus should not be allowed to use the state's power to insist that *their* view of the good be accepted. Such sentiments may also be related to the liberals' commitment to the Jeffersonian idea that truth is something each individual must seek for herself if she is to be rightly related to it

and effectively incorporate it into her own life, so that it cannot be foisted upon her by culture or society.[21]

These liberal responses to communitarianism, while compelling, do not refute the communitarian view completely, but they do show that communitarians have more work to do in order to develop their theory effectively: In particular, they must defend their trust of government power to pursue the good, and they must develop a way of achieving critical moral distance from the communities they would have the government respect so that this "respect" does not end up encouraging any oppression, subordination, and abuse that has been part of that culture's traditions.

NOTES

1. See Alasdair MacIntyre, *After Virtue* (Notre Dame: University of Notre Dame Press, 1981), p. 187; see also chaps. 5 and 6, where MacIntyre argues for the failure of moral theories of the sort that undergird liberalism.

2. For an argument that uses communitarian ideas to attack the effect of current liberal ideas on university education, see Allan Bloom, *The Closing of the American Mind* (New York: Simon and Schuster, 1987).

3. These views are put forward in a series of essays assembled in Taylor's *Philosophical Papers* (Cambridge; Cambridge University Press, 1985). Note that communitarians such as Taylor and Michael Sandel also object to liberalism because of what they take to be its advocacy of the neutral state; for example, see Sandel's "Morality and the Liberal Ideal," *New Republic*, May 7, 1984, and Taylor's "Alternative Futures: Legitimacy, Identity and Alienation in Late Twentieth Century Canada," in Alan Cairns and Cynthia Williams, eds., *Constitutionalism, Citizenship and Society in Canada* (Toronto Press, 1986). However, that is to object to only one *form* of liberalism. As my discussion in the previous section shows, there are nonneutral forms of liberalism that advocate a moral role for the liberal state, such as rights-based liberalism and perfectionist liberalism, and neither Sandel's nor Taylor's attack on neutrality refutes these forms of liberal theory.

4. Jean Bethke Elshtain, "Family, Feminism and Community," *Dissent* 29 (Fall 1982): 442. See also

Elshtain's *Public Man, Private Woman* (Princeton University Press, 1981.)

5. See MacIntyre, *After Virtue,* p. 67.

6. For a discussion of whether or not religious life and liberalism are in conflict, see William Galston, *Liberal Purposes: Goods, Virtues and Diversity in the Liberal State* (Cambridge: Cambridge University Press, 1991), chap. 12.

7. Michael J. Sandel, *Liberalism and the Limits of Justice* (Cambridge: Cambridge University Press, 1982), p. 179.

8. Ibid., p. 181.

9. Ibid., p. 182.

10. For a discussion of some of these objections, see Will Kymlicka, *Contemporary Political Philosophy: An Introduction* (Oxford: Clarendon Press, 1990), pp. 199–207. Kymlicka also discusses some communitarians' objections to some liberals' view of the autonomous self as "empty"; see ibid., pp. 208–209.

11. I have already discussed Rawls's insistence on the social construction of human beings as a motivation for constructing the original position procedure, which tries to give us a vantage point from which we can assess that social construction. See the section on Rawls in Chapter 4. Gauthier's commitment to our sociality comes out not only in his book *Morals by Agreement* (Oxford: Oxford University Press, 1986) but also in a very interesting essay, "The Social Contract as ideology," *Philosophy and Public Affairs* 6, 2 (1977): 130–164. For a discussion of the way in which liberals are able to accommodate the sociality of persons, see Kymlicka, *Contemporary Political Philosophy,* pp. 216–230.

12. Feinberg, *Harmless Wrongdoing,* p. 83.

13. Kymlicka, *Contemporary Political Philosophy,* p. 222.

14. Feinberg, *Harmless Wrongdoing,* p. 84.

15. See Judith Shklar, *Ordinary Vices* (Cambridge: Harvard University Press, 1984).

16. G. W. F. Hegel, *The Philosophy of Right,* trans. T. M. Knox (London: Oxford University Press, 1976), sec. 257, p. 155.

17. Amy Gutmann, "Communitarian Critics of Liberalism," *Philosophy and Public Affairs* 14, 3 (Summer 1985): 319.

18. Rawls, *A Theory of Justice,* pp. 260–263.

19. Burke's most famous political works include *Reflections on the Revolution in France* (1790) and *A Philosophical Enquiry into the Origin of Our Ideas of the Sublime and the Beautiful.* These and other political works are available in Edmund Burke, *Reflections on the Revolution in France* (Harmondsworth: Penguin, 1969).

20. But Eliot did believe that her society needed reform, and she had respect for those reformers who were not contemptuous of custom. Both respect for and Burkian concern about reformist zeal are present in her masterpiece, *Middlemarch.*

21. Jefferson maintains that one reason there must be freedom of religion in an ideal political society is that coercion is useless in bringing a person to religious truth "Constraint may make him worse by making him a hypocrite, but it will never make him a truer man." See Jefferson, "Query XVII:Religion," p. 159. Later in the same essay Jefferson makes the very Millian argument that a diversity of opinion in religious matters is good for society and for each individual in it. See ibid., pp. 160 f.

Part VI

Feminist Justice

24   The Subjection of Women

JOHN STUART MILL

THE OBJECT OF THIS ESSAY is to explain as clearly as I am able, the grounds of an opinion which I have held from the very earliest period when I had formed any opinions at all on social or political matters, and which, instead of being weakened or modified, has been constantly growing stronger by the progress of reflection and the experience of life: That the principle which regulates the existing social relations between the two sexes—the legal subordination of one sex to the other—is wrong in itself, and now one of the chief hindrances to human improvements; and that it ought to be replaced by a principle of perfect equality, admitting no power or privilege on the one side, nor disability on the other.

The very words necessary to express the task I have undertaken, show how arduous it is. But is would be a mistake to suppose that the difficulty of the case must lie in the insufficiency or obscurity of the grounds of reason on which my conviction rests. The difficulty is that which exists in all cases in which there is a mass of feeling to be contended against. So long as an opinion is strongly rooted in the feelings, it gains rather than loses in stability by having a preponderating weight of argument against it. For if it were accepted as a result of argument, the refutation of the argument might shake the solidity of the conviction; but when it rests solely on feeling, the worse it fares in argumentative contest, the more persuaded its adherents are that their feeling must have some deeper grounds, which the

arguments do not reach; and while the feeling remains, it is always throwing up fresh intrenchments of argument to repair any breach made in the old. And there are so many causes tending to make the feelings connected with this subject the most intense and most deeply-rooted of all those which gather round and protect old institutions and customs, that we need not wonder to find them as yet less undermined and loosened than any of the rest by the progress of the great modern spiritual and social transition; nor suppose that the barbarisms to which men cling longest must be less barbarisms than those which they earlier shake off. . . .

In the first place, the opinion in favour of the present system, which entirely subordinates the weaker sex to the stronger, rests upon theory only; for there never has been trial made of any other; so that experience, in the sense in which it is vulgarly opposed to theory, cannot be pretended to have pronounced any verdict. And in the second place, the adoption of this system of inequality never was the result of deliberation, or forethought, or any social ideas, or any notion whatever of what conduced to the benefit of humanity or the good order of society. It arose simply from the fact that from the very earliest twilight of human society, every woman (owing to the value attached to her by men, combined with her inferiority in muscular strength) was found in a state of bondage to some man. Laws and systems of polity always begin by recognising

From The Subjection of Women, *Chap. 1. First published in 1869.*

the relations they find already existing between individuals. They convert what was a mere physical fact into a legal right, give it the sanction of society, and principally aim at the substitution of public and organized means of asserting and protecting these rights, instead of the irregular and lawless conflict of physical strength. Those who had already been compelled to obedience became in this manner legally bound to it. Slavery, from being a mere affair of force between the master and the slave, became regularized and a matter of compact among the masters, who, binding themselves to one another for common protection, guaranteed by their collective strength the private possessions of each, including his slaves. In early times, the great majority of the male sex were slaves, as well as the whole of the female. And many ages elapsed, some of them ages of high cultivation, before any thinker was bold enough to question the rightfulness and absolute social necessity, either of the one slavery or of the other. . . .

If people are mostly so little aware how completely, during the greater part of the duration of our species, the law of force was the avowed rule of general conduct—any other being only a special and exceptional consequence of peculiar ties—and from how very recent a date it is that the affairs of society in general have been even pretended to be regulated according to any moral law, as little do people remember or consider how institutions and customs, which never had any ground but the law of force, last on into ages and states of general opinion which never would have permitted their first establishment. Less than forty years ago, Englishmen might still by law hold human beings in bondage as saleable property; within the present century they might kidnap them and carry them off, and work them literally to death. This absolutely extreme case of the law of force, condemned by those who can tolerate almost every other form of arbitrary power, and which, of all others, presents features the most revolting to the feelings of all who look

at it from an impartial position, was the law of civilized and Christian England within the memory of persons now living: and in one half of Anglo-Saxon America three or four years ago, not only did slavery exist, but the slave trade, and the breeding of slaves expressly for it, was a general practice between slave states. Yet not only was there a greater strength of sentiment against it, but, in England at least a less amount either of feeling or of interest in favour of it, than of any other of the customary abuses of force: for its motive was the love of gain, unmixed and undisguised; and those who profited by it were a very small numerical fraction of the country, while the natural feeling of all who were not personally interested in it, was unmitigated abhorrence. So extreme an instance makes it almost superfluous to refer to any other; but consider the long duration of absolute monarchy. In England at present it is the almost universal conviction that military despotism is a case of the law of force, having no other origin or justification. Yet in all the great nations of Europe except England it either still exists, or has only just ceased to exist, and has even now a strong party favourable to it in all ranks of the people, especially among persons of station and consequence. Such is the power of an established system, even when far from universal, when not only in almost every period of history there have been great and well-known examples of the contrary system, but these have almost invariably been afforded by the most illustrious and most prosperous communities. In this case, too, the possessor of the undue power, the person directly interested in it, is only one person, while those who are subject to it and suffer from it are literally all the rest. The yoke is naturally and necessarily humiliating to all persons, except the one who is on the throne, together with, at most, the one who expects to succeed to it. How different are these cases from that of the power of men over women! I am not now prejudging the question of its justifiableness. I am showing how vastly more permanent it could not but be, even if not justifiable, than these other dominations which have nevertheless lasted down to our own time. Whatever gratification of pride there is in the possession of power, and whatever personal interest in its exercise, is in this case not confined to a limited class, but common to the whole male sex. Instead of being, to most of its supporters, a thing desirable chiefly in the abstract, or, like the political ends usually contended for by factions, of little private importance to any but the leaders, it comes home to the person and hearth of every male head of a family, and of every one who looks forward to being so. The clodhopper exercises, or is to exercise, his share of the power equally with the highest nobleman. And the case is that in which the desire of power is the strongest: for every one who desires power, desires it most over those who are nearest to him with whom his life is passed, with whom he has most concerns in common, and in whom any independence of his authority is oftenest likely to interfere with his individual preferences. If, in the other cases specified, power manifestly grounded only on force, and having so much less to support them, are so slowly and with so much difficulty got rid of, much more must it be so with this, even if it rests on no better foundation than those. We must consider, too, that the possessors of the power have facilities in this case, greater than in any other, to prevent any uprising against it. Every one of the subjects lives under the very eye, and almost, it may be said, in the hands, of some of the masters—in closer intimacy with him than with any of her fellow-subjects—with no means of combining against him, no power of even locally overmastering him, and, on the other hand, with the strongest motives for seeking his favour and avoiding to give him offence. In struggles for political emancipation, everybody knows how often its champions are bought off by bribes, or daunted by terrors. In the case of women, each individual of the subject-class is in a chronic state of bribery and intimidation combined. In setting up the standard of resistance, a large number of the leaders, and still more of the followers, must make an almost complete sacrifice of the pleasures or the alleviations of their own individual lot. If ever any system of privilege and enforced subjection had its yoke tightly riveted on the necks of those who are kept down by it, this has. . . .

All causes, social and natural, combine to make it unlikely that women should be collectively rebellious to the power of men. They are so far in a position different from all other subject classes, that their masters require something more from them than actual service. Men do not want solely the obedience of women, they want their sentiments. All men, except the most brutish, desire to have in the woman most nearly connected with them, not a forced slave but a willing one, not a slave merely, but a favourite. They have therefore put everything in practice to enslave their minds. The masters of all other slaves rely, for maintaining obedience, on fear; either fear of themselves, or religious fears. The masters of women wanted more than simple obedience, and they turned the whole force of education to effect their purpose. All women are bought up from the very earliest years in the belief that their ideal of character is the very opposite to that of men; not self-will, and government by self-control, but submission, and yielding to the control of others. All the moralities tell them that it is the duty of women, and all the current sentimentalities that it is their nature, to live for others; to make complete abnegation of themselves, and to have no life but in their affections. And by their affections are meant the only ones they are allowed to have—those to the men with whom they are connected, or to the children who constitute an additional and indefeasible tie between them and a man. When we put together three things—first, the natural attraction between opposite sexes; secondly, the wife's entire dependence on the husband, every privilege or pleasure she has being either his gift, or depending entirely on his will;

and lastly, that the principal object of human pursuit, consideration, and all objects of social ambition, can in general be sought or obtained by her only through him, it would be a miracle if the object of being attractive to men had not become the polar star of feminine education and formation of character. And, this great means of influence over the minds of women having been acquired, an instinct of selfishness made men avail themselves of it to the utmost as a means of holding women in subjection, by representing to them meekness, submissiveness, and resignation of all individual will into the hands of a man, as an essential part of sexual attractiveness. Can it be doubted that any other yokes which mankind have succeeded in breaking, would have subsisted till now if the same means had existed, and had been as sedulously used, to bow down their minds to it? If it had been made the object of the life of every young plebeian to find personal favour in the eyes of some patrician, of every young serf with some seigneur; if domestication with him, and a share of his personal affections, had been held out as the prize which they all should look out for, the most gifted and aspiring being able to reckon on the most desirable prizes; and if, when this prize had been obtained, they had been shut out by a wall of brass from all interests not centering in him, all feelings and desires but those which he shared or inculcated; would not serfs and seigneurs, plebeians and patricians, have been as broadly distinguished at this day as men and women are? and would not all but a thinker here and there, have believed the distinction to be a fundamental and unalterable fact in human nature?

The preceding considerations are amply sufficient to show that custom, however universal it may be, affords in this case no presumption, and ought not to create any prejudice, in favour of the arrangements which place women in social and political subjection to men. But I may go farther, and maintain that the course of history, and the tendencies of progressive human society, afford not only no presumption in favour of this system of inequality of rights, but a strong one against it; and that, so far as the whole course of human improvement up to this time, the whole stream of modern tendencies, warrants any inference on the subject, it is, that this relic of the past is discordant with the future, and must necessarily disappear.

For, what is the peculiar character of the modern world—the difference which chiefly distinguishes modern institutions, modern social ideas, modern life itself, from those of times long past? It is, that human beings are no longer born to their place in life, and chained down by an inexorable bond to the place they are born to, but are free to employ their faculties, and such favourable chances as offer, to achieve the lot which may appear to them most desirable. Human society of old was constituted on a very different principle. All were born to a fixed social position, were mostly kept in it by law, or interdicted from any means by which they could emerge from it. As some men are born white and others black, so some were born slaves and others freemen and citizens; some were born patricians, others plebeians; some were born feudal nobles, others commoners and *roturiers*. A slave or serf could never make himself free, nor, except by the will of his master, become so. In most European countries it was not till towards the close of the middle ages, and as a consequence of the growth of regal power, that commoners could be ennobled. Even among nobles, the eldest son was born the exclusive heir to the paternal possessions, and a long time elapsed before it was fully established that the father could disinherit him. Among the industrious classes, only those who were born members of a guild, or were admitted into it by its members, could lawfully practise their calling within its local limits; and nobody could practise any calling deemed important, in any but the legal manner—by processes authoritatively prescribed. Manufacturers have stood in the pillory for presuming to carry on their business by new and improved methods. In modern Europe, and most in those parts of it which have participated most largely in all other modern improvements, diametrically opposite doctrines now prevail. Law and government do not undertake to prescribe by whom any social or industrial operation shall or shall not be conducted, or what modes of conducting them shall be lawful. These things are left to the unfettered choice of individuals. Even the laws which required that workmen should serve an apprenticeship, have in this country been repealed: there being ample assurance that in all cases in which an apprenticeship is necessary, its necessity will suffice to enforce it. The old theory was, that the least possible should be left to the choice of the individual agent; that all he had to do should, as far as practicable, be laid down for him by superior wisdom. Left to himself he was sure to go wrong. The modern conviction, the fruit of a thousand years of experience is, that things in which the individual is the person directly interested, never go right but as they are left to his own discretion; and that any regulation of them by authority, except to protect the rights of others, is sure to be mischievous. This conclusion, slowly arrived at, and not adopted until almost every possible application of the contrary theory had been made with disastrous result, now (in the industrial department) prevails universally in the most advanced countries, almost universally in all that have pretensions to any sort of advancement. It is not that all processes are supposed to be equally good, or all persons to be equally qualified for everything; but that freedom of individual choice is now known to be the only thing which procures the adoption of the best processes, and throws each operation into the hands of those who are best qualified for it. Nobody thinks it necessary to make a law that only a strong-armed man shall be a blacksmith. Freedom and competition suffice to make blacksmiths strong-armed men, because the weak-armed can earn more by engaging in occupations for which they are more fit. In consonance with this doctrine, it is felt to be an overstepping of the proper bounds of authority to fit beforehand, on some general presumption, that certain persons are not fit to do certain things. It is now thoroughly known and admitted that if some such presumptions exist, no such presumption is infallible. Even if it be well grounded in a majority of cases, which it is very likely not to be, there will be a minority of exceptional cases in which it does not hold; and in those it is both an injustice to the individuals, and a detriment to society, to place barriers in the way of their using their faculties for their own benefit and for that of others. In the cases, on the other hand, in which the unfitness is real, the ordinary motives of human conduct will on the whole suffice to prevent the incompetent person from making, or from persisting in, the attempt.

If this general principle of social and economical science is not true; if individuals, with such help as they can derive from the opinion of those who know them, are not better judges than the law and the government, of their own capacities and vocation; the world cannot too soon abandon this principle, and return to the old system of regulations and disabilities. But if the principle is true, we ought to act as if we believed it, and not to ordain that to be born a girl instead of a boy, and more than to be born black instead of white, or a commoner instead of a nobleman, shall decide the person's position through all life—shall interdict people from all the more elevated social positions, and from all, except a few, respectable occupations. Even were we to admit the utmost that is ever pretended as to the superior fitness of men for all the functions now reserved to them, the same argument applies which forbids a legal qualification for members of Parliament. If only once in a dozen years the conditions of eligibility exclude a fit person, there is a real loss, while the exclusion of thousands of unfit persons is no gain; for if the constitution of the electoral body disposes them to choose unfit persons, there are always plenty of such persons to choose from. In all things of any difficulty and importance, those who can do them well are fewer than the need, even with the most unrestricted latitude of choice; and any limitation of the field of selection deprives society of some chances of being served by the competent, without ever saving it from the incompetent.

At present, in the more improved countries, the disabilities of women are the only case, save one, in which laws and institutions take persons at their birth, and ordain that they shall never in all their lives be allowed to compete for certain things. . . .

The social subordination of women thus stands out an isolated fact in modern social institutions; a solitary breach of what has become their fundamental law; a single relic of an old world of thought and practice exploded in everything else, but retained in the one thing of most universal interest. . . .

The least that can be demanded is, that the question should not be considered as prejudged by existing fact and existing opinion, but open to discussion on its merits, as a question of justice and expediency; the decision on this, as on any of the other social arrangements of mankind, depending on what an enlightened estimate of tendencies and consequences may show to be most advantageous to humanity in general, without distinction of sex. And the discussion must be a real discussion descending to foundations, and not resting satisfied with vague and general assertions. It will not do, for instance, to assert in general terms, that the experience of mankind has pronounced in favour of the existing system. Experience cannot possibly have decided between two courses, so long as there has only been experience of one. If it be said that the doctrine of the equality of the sexes rests only on theory, it must be remembered that the contrary doctrine also has only theory to rest upon. All that is proved in its favour by direct experience, is that mankind have been able to exist under it, and to attain the degree of improvement and prosperity which we now see; but whether that prosperity has been attained sooner, or is now greater, than it would have been under the other system, experience does not say. On the other hand, experience does say, that every step in improvement has been so invariably accompanied by a step made in raising the social position of women, that historians and philosophers have been led to adopt their elevation or debasement as on the whole the surest test and most correct measure of the civilization of a people or an age. Through all the progressive period of human history, the condition of women has been approaching nearer to equality with men. This does not of itself prove that the assimilation must go on to complete equality; but it assuredly affords some presumption that such is the case.

Neither does it avail anything to say that the *nature* of the two sexes adapts them to their present functions and position, and renders these appropriate to them. Standing on the ground of common sense and the constitutions of the human mind, I deny that any one knows, or can know, the nature of the two sexes, as long as they have only been seen in their present relation to one another. If men had ever been found in society without women, or women without men, or if there had been a society of men and women in which the women were not under the control of the men, something might have been positively known about the mental and moral differences which may be inherent in the nature of each. What is now called the nature of women is an eminently artificial thing—the result of forced repression in some directions, unnatural stimulation in others. It may be asserted without scruple, that no other class of dependents have had their character so entirely distorted from its natural proportions by their relation with their masters; for, if conquered and slave races have been, in some respects, more forcibly repressed, whatever in them has not been crushed down by an iron heel has generally been let alone, and if left with any liberty of development, it has developed itself according to its own laws; but in the case of women, a hot-house and stove cultivation has always been carried on of some of the capabilities of their nature, for the benefit and pleasure of their masters. . . .

Hence, in regard to that most difficult question, what are the natural differences between the two sexes—a subject on which it is impossible in the present state of society to obtain complete and correct knowledge—while almost everybody dogmatizes upon it, almost all neglect and make light of the only means by which any partial insight can be obtained into it. This is, an analytic study of the most important department of psychology, the laws of the influence of circumstances on character. For, however great and apparently ineradicable the moral and intellectual differences between men and women might be, the evidence of their being natural differences could only be negative. Those only could be inferred to be natural which could not possibly be artificial—the residuum, after deducting every characteristic of either sex which can admit of being explained from education or external circumstances. The profoundest knowledge of the laws of the formation of character is indispensable to entitle any one to affirm even that there is any difference, much more what the difference is, between the two sexes considered as moral and rational beings; and since no one, as yet, has the knowledge, (for there is hardly any subject which, in proportion to its importance, has been so little studied), no one is thus far entitled to any positive opinion on the subject. Conjectures are all that can at present be made; conjectures more or less probable, according as more or less authorized by such knowledge as we yet have of the laws of psychology, as applied to the formation of character.

Even the preliminary knowledge, what the differences between the sexes now are, apart from all questions as to how they are made what they are, is still in the crudest and most incomplete state. . . .

One thing we may be certain of—that what is contrary to women's nature to do, they never will be made to do by simply giving their nature free play. The anxiety of mankind to interfere in behalf of nature, for fear lest nature should not succeed in effecting its purpose, is an altogether necessary solicitude. What women by nature cannot do, it is quite superfluous to forbid them from doing. What they can do, but not so well as the men who are their competitors, competition suffices to exclude them from, since nobody asks for protective duties and bounties in favour of women; it is only asked that the present bounties and protective duties in favour of men should be recalled. If women have a greater natural inclination for some things than for others, there is no need of laws or social inculcation to make the majority of them do the former in preference to the latter. Whatever women's services are most wanted for, the free play of competition will hold out the strongest inducements to them to undertake. And, as the words imply, they are most wanted for the things for which they are most fit; by the apportionment of which to them, the collective faculties of the two sexes can be applied on the whole with greatest sum of valuable result.

The general opinion of men is supposed to be, that the natural vocation of a woman is that of a wife and mother. I say, is supposed to be, because, judging from acts—from the whole of the present constitution of society—one might infer that their opinion was the direct contrary. They might be supposed to think that the alleged natural vocation of women was of all things the most repugnant to their nature; insomuch that if they are free to do anything else—if any other means of living, or occupation of their time and faculties, is open, which has any chance of appearing desirable to them—there will not be enough of them who will be willing to accept the condition said to be natural to them. If this is the real opinion of men in general, it would be well that it should be spoken out. I should like to hear somebody openly enunciating the doctrine (it is already implied in much that is written on the subject)—"It is necessary to society that women should marry and produce children. They will not do so unless they are compelled. Therefore it is necessary to compel them." The merits of the case would then be clearly defined. It would be exactly that of the slaveholders of

South Carolina and Louisiana. "It is necessary that cotton and sugar should be grown. White men cannot produce them. Negroes will not, for any wages which we choose to give. *Ergo* they must be compelled." An illustration still closer to the point is that of impressment. Sailors must absolutely be had to defend the country. It often happens that they will not voluntarily enlist. Therefore there must be the power of forcing them. How often has this logic been used! and, but for one flaw in it, without doubt it would have been successful up to this day. But it is open to the retort—First pay the sailors the honest value of their labour. When you have made it as well worth their while to serve you, as to work for other employers, you will have no more difficulty than others have in obtaining their services. To this there is no logical answer except "I will not": and as people are now not only ashamed, but are not desirous, to rob the labourer of his hire, impressment is no longer advocated. Those who attempt to force women into marriage by closing all other doors against them, lay themselves open to a similar retort. If they mean what they say, their opinion must evidently be, that men do not render the married condition so desirable to women, as to induce them to accept it for its own recommendations. It is not a sign of one's thinking the boon one offers very attractive, when one allows only Hobson's choice, "that or none." And here, I believe, is the clue to the feelings of those men, who have a real antipathy to the equal freedom of women. I believe they are afraid, not lest women should be unwilling to marry, for I do not think that any one in reality has that apprehension; but lest they should insist that marriage should be on equal conditions; lest all women of spirit and capacity should prefer doing almost anything else, not in their own eyes degrading, rather than marry, when marrying is giving themselves a master, and a master too of all their earthly possessions. And truly, if this consequence were necessarily incident to marriage, I think that the apprehension would be very well founded. I agree in thinking it probable that few women, capable of anything else, would, unless under an irresistible *entrainement*, rendering them for the time insensible to anything but itself, choose such a lot, when any other means were open to them of filling a conventionally honourable place in life: and if men are determined that the law of marriage shall be a law of despotism, they are quite right, in point of mere policy, in leaving to women only Hobson's choice. But, in that case, all that has been done in the modern world to relax the chain on the minds of women, has been a mistake. They never should have been allowed to receive a literary education. Women who read, much more women who write, are, in the existing constitution of things, a contradiction and a disturbing element: and it was wrong to bring women up with any acquirements but those of an odalisque, or of a domestic servant.

25 Justice and Gender

SUSAN OKIN

W E AS A SOCIETY PRIDE ourselves on our democratic values. We don't believe people should be constrained by innate differences from being able to achieve desired positions of influence to improve their well-being; equality of opportunity is our professed aim. The Preamble to our Constitution stresses the importance of justice, as well as the general welfare and the blessings of liberty. The Pledge of Allegiance asserts that our republic preserves "liberty and justice for all."

Yet substantial inequalities between the sexes still exist in our society. In economic terms, full-time working women (after some very recent improvement) earn on average 71 percent of the earnings of full-time working men. One-half of poor and three-fifths of chronically poor households with dependent children are maintained by a single female parent. The poverty rate for elderly women is nearly twice that for elderly men.[1] On the political front, two out of a hundred U.S. senators are women, one out of nine justices seems to be considered sufficient female representation on the Supreme Court, and the number of men chosen in each congressional election far exceeds the number of women elected in the entire history of the country. Underlying and intertwined with all these inequalities is the unequal distribution of the unpaid labor of the family.

An equal sharing between the sexes of family responsibilities, especially child care, is "the great revolution that has not happened."[2] Women, including mothers of young children, are, of course, working outside the household far more than their mothers did. And the small proportion of women who reach high-level positions in politics, business, and the professions command vastly disproportionate amount of space in the media, compared with the millions of women who work at low-paying, dead-end jobs, the millions who do part-time work with its lack of benefits, and the millions of others who stay home performing for no pay what is frequently not even acknowledged as work. Certainly, the fact that women are doing more paid work does not imply that they are more equal. It is often said that we are living in a postfeminist era. This claim, due in part to the distorted emphasis on women who have "made it," is false, no matter which of its meanings is intended. It is certainly not true that feminism has been vanquished, and equally untrue that it is no longer needed because its aims have been fulfilled. Until there is justice within the family, women will not be able to gain equality in politics, at work, or in any other sphere.

. . . The typical current practices of family life, structured to a large extent by gender, are not just. Both the expectation and the experience of the division of labor by sex make women vulnerable. As I shall show, a cycle of power relations and decisions pervades both family and workplace, each reinforcing the inequalities between the sexes that already exist within the other. Not only women, but children of both sexes, too, are often made vulnerable by gender-structured marriage. One-quarter of children in the United States now live in families with only one parent—in almost 90 percent of cases, the mother. Contrary to common perceptions—in which the situation of never-married mothers looms largest—65 percent of single-parent families are a result of marital separation or divorce.[3] Recent research in a number of states has shown that, in the average case, the standard of living of divorced women and the children who live with them plummets after divorce, whereas the economic situation of divorced men tends to be better than when they were married.

A central source of injustice for women these days is that the law, most noticeably in the event of divorce, treats more or less as equals those whom custom, workplace discrimination, and the still conventional division of labor within the family have made very unequal. Central to this socially created inequality are two commonly made but inconsistent presumptions: that women are primarily responsible for the rearing of children; and that serious and committed members of the work force (regardless of class) do not have primary responsibility, or even shared responsibility, for the rearing of children. The old assumption of the workplace, still implicit, is that workers have wives at home. It is built not only into the structure and expectations of the workplace but into other crucial social institutions, such as schools, which make no attempt to take account, in their scheduled hours or vacations, of the fact that parents are likely to hold jobs.

Now, of course, many wage workers do not have wives at home. Often, they *are* wives and mothers, or single, separated, or divorced mothers of small children. But neither the family nor the workplace has taken much account of this fact. Employed wives still do by far the greatest proportion of unpaid family work, such as child care and housework. Women are far more likely to take time out of the workplace or to work part-time because of family responsibilities than are their husbands or male partners. And they are much more likely to move because of their husbands' employment needs or opportunities that their own. All these tendencies, which are due to a number of factors, including the sex segregation and discrimination of the workplace itself, tend to be cyclical in their effects: wives advance more slowly than their husbands at work and thus gain less seniority, and the discrepancy between their wages increases over time. Then, because both the power structure of the family and what is regarded as consensual "rational" family decision-making reflect the fact that the husband usually earns more, it will become even less likely as time goes on that the unpaid work of the family will be shared between the spouses. Thus the cycle of inequality is perpetuated. Often hidden from view within a marriage, it is in the increasingly likely event of marital breakdown that the socially constructed inequality of married women is at its most visible.

This is what I mean when I say that gender-structured marriage *makes* women vulnerable. These are not matters of natural necessity, as some people would believe. Surely nothing in our natures dictates that men should not be equal participants in the rearing of their children. Nothing in the nature of work makes it impossible to adjust it to the fact that people are parents as well as workers. That these things have not happened is part of the historically, socially constructed differentiation between the sexes that feminists have come to call *gender*. We live in a society that has over the years regarded the innate characteristic of sex as one of the clearest legitimizers of different rights and restrictions, both formal and informal. While the legal sanctions that uphold male dominance have begun to be eroded in the past century, and more rapidly in the last twenty years, the heavy weight of tradition, combined with the effects of socialization, still works powerfully to reinforce sex roles that are commonly regarded as of unequal prestige and worth. The sexual division of labor has not only been a fundamental part of the marriage contract, but so deeply influences us in our formative years that feminists of both sexes who try to reject it can find themselves, struggling against it with varying degrees of ambivalence. Based on the linchpin, "gender"—by which I mean *the deeply entrenched institutionalization of sexual difference*—still permeates our society.

The Construction of Gender

Due to feminism and feminist theory, gender is coming to be recognized as a social factor of major importance. Indeed, the new meaning of the word reflects the fact that so much of what has traditionally been thought of a sexual difference is now considered by many to be largely socially produced.[4] Feminist scholars from many disciplines and with radically different points of view have contributed to the enterprise of making gender fully visible and comprehensible. At one end of the spectrum are those whose explanations of the subordination of women focus primarily on biological difference as causal in the construction of gender,[5] and at the other end are those who argue that biological difference may not even lie at the core of the social construction that is gender;[6] the views of the vast majority of feminists fall between these extremes. The rejection of biological determinism and the corresponding emphasis on gender as a social construction characterize most current feminist scholarship. Of particular relevance is work in psychology, where scholars have investigated the importance of female primary parenting in the formation of our gendered identities,[7] and in history and anthropology,[8] where emphasis has been placed on the historical and cultural variability of gender. Some feminists have been criticized for developing theories of gender that do not take sufficient account of differences

among women, especially race, class, religion, and ethnicity.[9] While such critiques should always inform our research and improve our arguments, it would be a mistake to allow them to detract our attention from gender itself as a factor of significance. Many injustices are experienced by women *as women*, whatever the differences among them and whatever other injustices they also suffer from. The past and present gendered nature of the family, and the ideology that surround it, affects virtually all women, whether or not they live or ever lived in traditional families. Recognizing this is not to deny or de-emphasize the fact that gender may affect different subgroups of women to a different extent and in different ways.

The potential significance of feminist discoveries and conclusions about gender for issues of social justice cannot be overemphasized. They undermine centuries of argument that started with the notion that not only the distinct differentiation of women and men but the domination of women by men, being natural, was therefore inevitable and not even to be considered in discussions of justice. As I shall make clear in later chapters, despite the fact that such notions cannot stand up to rational scrutiny, they not only still survive but flourish in influential places.

During the same two decades in which feminists have been intensely thinking, researching, analyzing, disagreeing about, and rethinking the subject of gender, our political and legal institutions have been increasingly faced with issues concerning the injustices of gender and their effects. These issues are being decided within a fundamentally patriarchal system, founded in a tradition in which "individuals" were assumed to be male heads of households. Not surprisingly, the system has demonstrated a limited capacity for determining what is just, in many cases involving gender. Sex discrimination, sexual harassment, abortion, pregnancy in the workplace, parental leave, child care, and surrogate mothering have all become major and well-publicized issues of public policy, engaging both courts and legislatures. Issues of family justice, in particular—from child custody and terms of divorce to physical and sexual abuse of wives and children—have become increasingly visible and pressing, and are commanding increasing attention from the police and court systems. There is clearly a major "justice crisis" in contemporary society arising from issues of gender.

Theories of Justice and the Neglect of Gender

During these same two decades, there has been a great resurgence of theories of social justice. Political theory, which had been sparse for a period before the late 1960s except as an important branch of intellectual history, has become a flourishing field, with social justice as its central concern. Yet, remarkably, major contemporary theorists of justice have almost without exception ignored the situation I have just described. They have displayed little interest in or knowledge of the findings of feminism. They have largely bypassed the fact that the society to which their theories are supposed to pertain is heavily and deeply affected by gender, and faces difficult issues of justice stemming from its gendered past and present assumptions. Since theories of justice are centrally concerned with whether, how, and why persons should be treated differently from one another, this neglect seems inexplicable. These theories are *about* which initial or acquired characteristics or positions in society legitimize differential treatment of persons by social institutions, laws, and customs. They are *about* how and whether and to what extent beginnings should affect outcomes. The division of humanity into two sexes seems to provide an obvious subject for such inquires. But, as we shall see, this does not strike most contemporary theorists of justice, and their theories suffer in both coherence and relevance because of it. This book is about this remarkable case of neglect. It is also an attempt to rectify it, to point the way toward a more fully humanist

theory of justice by confronting the question, "How just is gender?"

Why is that when we turn to contemporary theories of justice, we do not find illuminating and positive contributions to this question? How can theories of justice that are ostensibly about people in general neglect women, gender, and all the inequalities between the sexes? One reason is that most theorists *assume*, though they do not discuss, the traditional, gender-structured family. Another is that they often employ gender-neutral language in a false, hollow way. Let us examine these two points.

THE HIDDEN GENDER-STRUCTURED FAMILY

In the past, political theorists often used to distinguish clearly between "private" domestic life and the "public" life of politics and the marketplace, claiming explicitly that the two spheres operated in accordance with different principles. They separated out the family from what they deemed the subject matter of politics, and they made closely related, explicit claims about the nature of women and the appropriateness of excluding them from civil and political life. Men, the subjects of the theories, were able to make the transition back and forth from domestic to public life with ease, largely because of the functions performed by women in the family.[10] When we turn to contemporary theories of justice, superficial appearances can easily lead to the impression that they are inclusive of women. In fact, they continue the same "separate spheres" tradition, by ignoring the family, its division of labor, and the related economic dependency and restricted opportunities of most women. The judgment that the family is "nonpolitical" is implicit in the fact that it is simply not discussed in most works of political theory today. In one way or another, as will become clear in the chapters that follow, almost all current theorists continue to assume that the "individual" who is the basic subject of their theories is the male head of a fairly traditional household. Thus the application of principles of justice to relations between the sexes, or within the household, is frequently, though tacitly ruled out from the start. In the most influential of all twentieth-century theories of justice, that of John Rawls, family life is not only assumed, but is assumed to be just—and yet the prevalent gendered division of labor within the family is neglected, along with the associated distribution of power, responsibility, and privilege. . . .

Moreover, this stance is typical of contemporary theories of justice. They persist, despite the wealth of feminist challenges to their assumptions, in their refusal even to discuss the family and its gender structure, much less to recognize the family as a political institution of primary importance. Recent theories that pay even less attention to issues of family justice than Rawls's include Bruce Ackerman's *Social Justice in the Liberal State,* Ronald Dworkin's *Taking Rights Seriously,* William Galston's *Justice and the Human Good,* Alasdair MacIntyre's *After Virtue* and *Whose Justice? Whose Rationality?,* Robert Nozick's *Anarchy, State, and Utopia,* and Robert Unger's *Knowledge and Politics* and *The Critical Legal Studies Movement.*[11] Philip Green's *Retrieving Democracy* is a welcome exception.[12] Michael Walzer's *Spheres of Justice,* too, is exceptional in this regard, but . . . the conclusion that can be inferred from his discussion of the family—that its gender structure is unjust—does not sit at all easily with his emphasis on the shared understandings of a culture as the foundation of justice.[13] For gender is one aspect of social life about which clearly, in the United States in the latter part of the twentieth century, there are no shared understandings.

What is the basis of my claim that the family, while neglected, is *assumed* by theorists of justice? One obvious indication is that they take mature, independent human beings as the subjects of their theories without any mention of how they got to be that way. We know, of course, that human beings develop and mature only as a result of a great deal of attention and hard work, by far the greater part of it done by women. But when theorists of justice talk about "work," they mean paid work performed in the marketplace. They must be assuming that women, in the gender-structured family, continue to do their unpaid work of nurturing and socializing the young and providing a haven of intimate relations—otherwise there would be no moral subjects for them to theorize about. But these activities apparently take place outside the scope of their theories. Typically, the family itself is not examined in the light of whatever standard of justice the theorist arrives at.[14]

The continued neglect of the family by theorists of justice flies in the face of a great deal of persuasive feminist argument . . . Scholars have clearly revealed the interconnections between the gender structure inside and outside the family and the extent to which the personal is political. They have shown that the assignment of primary parenting to women is crucial, both in forming the gendered identities of men and women and in influencing their respective choices and opportunities in life. Yet, so far, the simultaneous assumption and neglect of the family has allowed the impact of these arguments to go unnoticed in major theories of justice.

FALSE GENDER NEUTRALITY

Many academics in recent years have become aware of the objectionable nature of using the supposedly generic male forms of nouns and pronouns. As feminist scholars have demonstrated, these words have most often *not* been used, throughout history and the history of philosophy in particular, with the intent to include women. *Man, mankind,* and *he* are going out of style as universal representations, though they have by no means disappeared. But the gender-neutral alternatives that most contemporary theorists employ are often even more misleading than the blatantly sexist use of male terms of reference. For they serve to disguise the real and continuing failure of theorists to confront the fact that the human race consists of persons of two sexes. They are by this means able to ignore the fact that there are *some* socially relevant physical differences between women and men, and the even more important fact that the sexes have had very different histories, very different assigned social roles and "nature," and very different degrees of access to power and opportunity in all human societies up to and including the present.

False gender neutrality is not a new phenomenon. Aristotle, for example, used *anthropos*—"human being"—in discussions of "the human good" that turn out not only to exclude women but to depend on their subordination. Kant even wrote of "all rational beings as such" in making arguments that he did not mean to apply to women. But it was more readily apparent that such arguments or conceptions of the good were not about all of us, but only about male heads of families. For their authors usually gave at some point an explanation, no matter how inadequate, of why what they were saying did not apply to women and of the different characteristics and virtues, rights, and responsibilities they thought women ought to have. Nevertheless, their theories have often been read as though they pertain (or can easily be applied) to all of us. Feminist interpretations of the last fifteen years or so have revealed the falsity of this "add women and stir" method of reading the history of political thought.[15]

The falseness of the gender-neutral language of contemporary political theorists is less readily apparent. Most, though not all, contemporary moral and political philosophers use "men and women," "he or she," "persons," or the increasingly ubiquitous "self." Sometimes they even get their computers to distribute masculine and feminine terms of reference randomly.[16] Since they do not explicitly exclude or differentiate women, as most theorists in the past did, we may be tempted to read their theories as inclusive of all of us. But we cannot. Their merely terminological responses to feminist challenges, in spite of giving a superficial impression of tolerance and inclusiveness, often strain credulity and sometimes result in nonsense. They do this in two ways: by ignoring the irreducible biological differences between the sexes, and/or by ignoring their different assigned social roles and consequent power differentials, and the ideologies that have supported them. Thus gender-neutral terms frequently obscure the fact that so much of the real experience of "persons," so long as they live in gender-structured societies, *does* in fact depend on what sex they are.

False gender neutrality is by no means confined to the realm of theory. Its harmful effects can be seen in public policies that have directly affected large numbers of women adversely. It was used, for example, in the Supreme Court's 1976 decision that the exclusion of pregnancy-related disabilities from employers' disability insurance plans was "not a gender-based discrimination at all." In a now infamous phrase of its majority opinion, the Court explained that such plans did not discriminate against women because the distinction drawn by such plans was between pregnant women and "non-pregnant *persons*."[17]

Examples of false gender neutrality in contemporary political theory will appear throughout this book; I will illustrate the concept here by citing just two examples. Ackermans' *Social Justice in the Liberal State* is a book containing scrupulously gender-neutral language. He breaks with this neutrality only, it seems, to *defy* existing sex roles; he refers to the "Commander," who plays the lead role in the theory, as "she." However, the argument of the book does not address the existing inequality or role differentiation between the sexes, though it has the potential for doing so.* The full impact of Ackerman's gender-neutral language without attention to gender is revealed in his section on abortion: a two-page discussion written, with the exception of a single "she," in the completely gender-neutral language of fetuses and their "parents."[18] The impression given is that there is no relevant respect in which the relationship of the two

---

* Ackerman's argument about how we arrive at social justice is in most essentials similar to Rawls's. . . . I think such methods can be useful in challenging gender and achieving a humanist theory of justice.

parents to the fetus differs. Now it is, of course, possible to imagine (and in the view of many feminists, would be desirable to achieve) a society in which differences in the relation of women and men to fetuses would be so slight as to reasonably play only a minor role in the discussion of abortion. But this would have to be a society without gender—one in which sexual difference carried no social significance, the sexes were equal in power and interdependence, and "mothering" and "fathering" a child meant the same thing, so that parenting and earning responsibilities were equally shared. We certainly do not live in such a society. Neither is there any discussion of one in Ackerman's theory, in which the division of labor between the sexes is not considered a matter of social (in)justice. In such a context, a "gender-neutral" discussion of abortion is almost as misleading as the Supreme Court's "gender-neutral" discussion of pregnancy.

A second illustration of false gender neutrality comes from Derek Phillips's *Toward a Just Social Order.* Largely because of the extent of his concern—rare among theorists of justice—with how we are to *achieve and maintain* a just social order, Phillips pays an usual amount of attention to the family. He writes about the family as the locus for the development of a sense of justice and self-esteem, of an appreciation of the meaning of reciprocity, of the ability to exercise unforced choice, and of an awareness of alternative ways of life.[19] The problem with this otherwise admirable discussion is that, apart from a couple of brief exceptions, the family itself is presented in gender-neutral terms that bear little resemblance to actual, gender-structured life.[20]* It is because of "parental affection," "parental nurturance,"

and "child rearing" that children in Phillips's families become the autonomous moral agents that his just society requires its citizens to be. The child's development of a sense of identity is very much dependent upon being raised by "parental figures who themselves have coherent and well-integrated personal identities," and we are told that such a coherent identity is "ideally one built around commitments to work and love." This all sounds very plausible. But it does not take into account the multiple inequalities of gender. In gender-structured societies—in which the child rearers are women, "parental nurturance" is largely mothering, and those who do what society regards as "meaningful work" are assumed *not* to be primary parents—women in even the best of circumstances face considerable conflicts between love (a fulfilling family life) and "meaningful work." Women in less fortunate circumstances face even greater conflicts between love (even basic care of their children) and any kind of paid work at all.

It follows from Phillips's own premises that these conflicts are very likely to affect the strength and coherence in women of that sense of identity and self-esteem, coming from love and meaningful work, that he regards as essential for being an autonomous moral agent. In turn, if they are mothers, it is also likely to affect their daughters' and sons' developing senses of their identity. Gender is clearly a major obstacle to attainment of a social order remotely comparable to the just one Phillips aspires to—but his false gender-neutral language allows him to ignore this fact. Although he is clearly aware of how distant in some other respects this vision of a just social order is from contemporary societies,[21] his use of falsely gender-neutral language leaves him quite unaware of the distance between the type of family that might be able to socialize just citizens and typical families today.

The combined effect of the omission of the family and the falsely gender-neutral language in recent political thought is that most theorists are

---

*He points out the shortcomings of the "earlier ethic of sacrifice," especially for women. He also welcomes the recent lessening of women's dependence on their husbands, but at the same time blames it for tending to weaken family stability. The falseness of Phillips's gender neutrality in discussing parenting is clearly confirmed later in the book (chaps 8 and 9), where paid work is "men's" and it is "fathers" who bequeath wealth or poverty on their children.

continuing to ignore the highly political issue of gender. The language they use makes little difference to what they actually do, which is to write about men and about only those women who manage, in spite of the gendered structures and practices of the society in which they live, to adopt patterns of life that have been developed to suit the needs of men. The fact that human beings are born as helpless infants—not as the purportedly autonomous actors who populate political theories—is obscured by the implicit assumption of gendered families, operating outside the range of the theories. To a large extent, contemporary theories of justice, like those of the past, are about men with wives at home.

Gender as a Issue of Justice

For three major reasons, this state of affairs is unacceptable. The first is the obvious point that women must be fully included in any satisfactory theory of justice. The second is that equality of opportunity, not only for women but for children of both sexes, is seriously undermined by the current gender injustices of our society. And the third reason is that, as has already been suggested, the family—currently the linchpin of the gender structure—must be just if we are to have a just society, since it is within the family that we first come to have that sense of ourselves and our relations with others that is at the root of moral development.

COUNTING WOMEN IN

When we turn to the great tradition of Western political thought with questions about the justice of the treatment of the sexes in mind, it is to little avail. Bold feminists like Mary Astell, Mary Wollstonecraft, William Thompson, Harriet Taylor, and George Bernard Shaw have occasionally challenged the tradition, often using its own premises and arguments to overturn its explicit or implicit justification of the inequality of women. But John Stuart Mill is a rare exception to the rule that those who hold central positions in the tradition almost never question the justice of the subordination of women.[22] This phenomenon is undoubtedly due in part to the fact that Aristotle, whose theory of justice has been so influential, relegated women to a sphere of "household justice"—populated by persons who are not fundamentally equal to the free men who participate in political justice, but inferiors whose natural function is to serve those who are more fully human. The liberal tradition, despite its supposed foundation of individual rights and human equality, is more Aristotelian in this respect than is generally acknowledged.[23] In one way or another, almost all liberal theorists have assumed that the "individual" who is the basic subject of the theories is the male head of a patriarchal household.[24] Thus they have not usually considered applying the principles of justice to women or to relations between the sexes.

When we turn to contemporary theories of justice, however, we expect to find more illuminating and positive contributions to the subject of gender and justice. As the mission of the family and the falseness of their gender-neutral language suggest, however, mainstream contemporary theories of justice do not address the subject any better than those of the past. Theories of justice that apply to only half of us simply won't do; the inclusiveness falsely implied by the current use of gender-neutral terms must become real. Theories of justice must apply to all of us, and to all of human life, instead of *assuming* silently that half of us take care of whole areas of life that are considered outside the scope of social justice. In a just society, the structure and practices of families must afford women the same opportunities as men to develop their capacities, to participate in political power, to influence social choices, and to be economically as well as physically secure.

Unfortunately, much feminist intellectual energy in the 1980s has gone into the claim that "justice" and "rights" are masculinist ways of thinking about morality that feminists should eschew or radically revise, advocating a morality of care.[25] The emphasis is misplaced, I think, for several reasons. First, what is by now a vast literature on the subject shows that the evidence for differences in women's and men's ways of thinking about moral issues is not (at least yet) very clear; neither is the evidence about the source of whatever differences there might be.[26] It may well turn out that any differences can be readily explained in terms of roles, including female primary parenting, that are socially determined and therefore alterable. There is certainly no evidence—nor could there be, in such a gender-structured society— for concluding that women are somehow naturally more inclined toward contextuality and away from universalism in their moral thinking, a false concept that unfortunately reinforces the old stereotypes that justify separate spheres. The capacity of reactionary forces to capitalize on the "different moralities" strain in feminism is particularly evident in Pope John Paul II's recent Apostolic Letter, "On the Dignity of Women," in which he refers to women's special capacity to care for others in arguing for confining them to motherhood or celibacy.[27]

Second, . . . I think the distinction between an ethic of justice and an ethic of care has been overdrawn. The best theorizing about justice, I argue, has integral to it the notions of care and empathy, of thinking of the interests and well-being of others who may be very different from ourselves. It is, therefore, misleading to draw a dichotomy as though they were two contrasting ethics. The best theorizing about justice is not some abstract "view from nowhere," but results from the carefully attentive consideration of everyone's point of view. This means, of course, that the best theorizing about justice is not good enough if it does not, or cannot readily be adapted to, include women and their points of view as fully as men and their points of view.

GENDER AND EQUALITY OF OPPORTUNITY

The family is a crucial determinant of our opportunities in life, of what we "become." It has frequently been acknowledged by those concerned with real equality of opportunity that the family presents a problem.[28] But though they have discerned a serious problem, these theorists have underestimated it because they have seen only half of it. They have seen that the disparity among families in terms of the physical and emotional environment, motivation, and material advantages they can give their children has a tremendous effect upon children's opportunities in life. We are not born as isolated, equal individuals in our society, but into family situations: some in the social middle, some poor and homeless, and some superaffluent; some to a single or soon-to-be-separated parent, some to parents whose marriage is fraught with conflict, some to parents who will stay together in love and happiness. Any claims that equal opportunity exists are therefore completely unfounded. Decades of neglect of the poor, especially of poor black and Hispanic households, accentuated by the policies of the Reagan years, have brought us farther from the principles of equal opportunity. To come close to them would require, for example, a high and uniform standard of public education and the provision of equal social services— including health care, employment training, job opportunities, drug rehabilitation, and decent housing—for all who need them. In addition to redistributive taxation, only massive reallocations of resources from the military to social services could make these things possible.

But even if all these disparities were somehow eliminated, we would still not attain equal opportunity for all. This is because what has not been recognized as an equal opportunity problem, except in feminist literature and circles, is the disparity *within* the family, the fact that its gender structure is itself a major obstacle to equality of opportunity. This is very important in itself, since one of the factors with most influence on our opportunities in life is the social significance attributed to our sex. The opportunities of girls and women are centrally affected by the structure and practices of family life, particularly by the fact that women are almost invariably primary parents. What nonfeminists who see in the family an obstacle to equal opportunity have *not* seen is that the extent to which a family is gender-structured can make the sex we belong to a relatively insignificant aspect of our identity and our life prospects or an all-pervading one. This is because so much of the social construction of gender takes place in the family, and particularly in the institution of female parenting.

Moreover, especially in recent years, with the increased rates of single motherhood, separation, and divorce, the inequalities between the sexes have *compounded* the first part of the problem. This disparity among families has grown largely because of the impoverishment of many women and children after separation or divorce. The division of labor in the typical family leaves most women far less capable than men of supporting themselves, and this disparity is accentuated by the fact that children of separated or divorced parents usually live with their mothers. The inadequacy—and frequent nonpayment—of child support has become recognized as a major social problem. Thus the inequalities of gender are now directly harming many children of both sexes as well as women themselves. Enhancing equal opportunity for women, important as it is in itself, is also a crucial way of improving the opportunities of many of the most disadvantaged children.

As there is a connection among the parts of this problem, so is there a connection among some of the solutions: much of what needs to be done to end the inequalities of gender, and to work in the direction of ending gender itself, will also help to equalize opportunity from one family to another. Subsidized, high-quality day care is obviously one such thing; another is the adaptation of the workplace to the needs of parents. . . .

THE FAMILY AS A SCHOOL OF JUSTICE

One of the things that theorists who have argued that families need not or cannot be just, or who have simply neglected them, have failed to explain is how, within a formative social environment that is *not* founded upon principles of justice, children can learn to develop that sense of justice they will require as citizens of a just society. Rather than being one among many co-equal institutions of a just society, a family is its essential foundation.

It may seem uncontroversial, even obvious, that families must be just because of the vast influence they have on the moral development of children. But this is clearly not the case. I shall argue that unless the first and most formative example of adult interaction usually experienced by children is one of justice and reciprocity, rather than one of domination and manipulation or of unequal altruism and one-sided self-sacrifice, and unless they themselves are treated with concern and respect, they are likely to be considerably hindered in becoming people who are guided by principles of justice. Moreover, I claim, the sharing of roles by men and women, rather than the division of roles between them, would have a further positive impact because the experience of *being* a physical and psychological nurturer—whether of a child or of another adult—would increase that capacity to identify with and fully comprehend the viewpoints of others that is important to a sense of justice. In a society that minimized gender this would be more likely to be the experience of all of us.

Almost every person in our society starts life in a family of some sort or other. Fewer of these families now fit the usual, though by no means universal, standard of previous generations, that is, wage-working father, homemaking mother, and children. More families these days are headed by a single parent; lesbian and gay parenting is no longer so rare; many children have two wage-working parents, and receive at least some of their early care outside the home. While its forms are varied, the family in which a child is raised, especially in the earliest years, is clearly a crucial place for early moral development and for the formation of our basic attitudes to others. It is, potentially, a place where we can *learn to be just*. It is especially important for the development of a sense of justice that grows from sharing the experiences of others and becoming aware of the points of view of others who are different in some respects from ourselves, but with whom we clearly have some interests in common.

The importance of the family for the moral development of individuals was far more often recognized by political theorists of the past than it is by those of the present. Hegel, Rousseau, Tocqueville, Mill, and Dewey are obvious examples that come to mind. Rousseau, for example, shocked by Plato's proposal to abolish the family, says that it is

> as though there were no need for a natural base on which to form conventional ties; as though the love of one's nearest were not the principle of the love one owes the state; as though it were not by means of the small fatherland which is the family that the heart attaches itself to the large one.[29]

Defenders of both autocratic and democratic regimes have recognized the political importance of different family forms for the formation of citizens. On the one hand, the nineteenth-century monarchist Louis de Bonald argued against the divorce reforms of the French Revolution, which he claimed had weakened the patriarchal family, on the grounds that "in order to keep the state out of the hands of the people, it is necessary to keep the family out of the hands of women and children."[30] Taking this same line of thought in the opposite direction, the U.S. Supreme Court decided in 1879 in *Reynolds v. Nebraska* that familial patriarchy fostered despotism and was therefore intolerable. Denying Mormon men the freedom to practice polygamy, the Court asserted that it was an offense "subversive of good order" that "leads to the patriarchal principle, . . . [and] when applied to large communities, fetters the people in stationary despotism, while that principle cannot long exist in connection with monogamy."[31]

However, while de Bonald was consistent in his adherence to an hierarchical family structure

as necessary for an undemocratic political system, the Supreme Court was by no means consistent in promoting an egalitarian family as an essential underpinning for political democracy. For in other decisions of the same period—such as *Bradwell v. Illinois,* the famous 1872 case that upheld the exclusion of women from the practice of law—the Court rejected women's claims to legal equality, in the name of a thoroughly patriarchal, though monogamous, family that was held to require the dependence of women and their exclusion from civil and political life.[32] While bigamy was considered patriarchal, and as such a threat to republican, democratic government, the refusal to allow a married woman to employ her talents and to make use of her qualifications to earn an independent living was not considered patriarchal. It was so far from being a threat to the civil order, in fact, that it was deemed necessary for it, and as such was ordained by both God and nature. Clearly in both *Reynolds* and *Bradwell,* "state authorities enforced family forms preferred by those in power and justified as necessary to stability and order."[33] The Court noticed the despotic potential of polygamy, but was blind to the despotic potential of patriarchal monogamy. This was perfectly acceptable to them as a training ground for citizens.

Most theorists of the past who stressed the importance of the family and its practices for the wider world of moral and political life by no means insisted on congruence between the structures or practices of the family and those of the outside world. Though concerned with moral development, they bifurcated public from private life to such an extent that they had no trouble reconciling inegalitarian, sometimes admittedly unjust, relations founded upon sentiment within the family with a more just, even egalitarian, social structure outside the family. Rousseau, Hegel, Tocqueville—all thought the family was centrally important for the development of morality in citizens, but all defended the hierarchy of the marital structure while spurning such a degree of hierarchy in institutions and practices outside the household. Preferring instead to rely on love, altruism, and generosity as the basis for family relations, none of these theorists argued for *just* family structures as necessary for socializing children into citizenship in a just society.

The position that justice within the family is irrelevant to the development of just citizens was not plausible even when only men were citizens. John Stuart Mill, in *The Subjection of Women*, takes an impassioned stand against it. He argues that the inequality of women within the family is deeply subversive of justice in general in the wider social world, because it subverts the moral potential of men. Mill's first answer to the question, "For whose good are all these changes in women's rights to be undertaken?" is: "the advantage of having the most universal and pervading of all human relations regulated by justice instead of injustice." Making marriage a relationship of equals, he argues, would transform this central part of daily life from "a school of despotism" into a "a school of moral cultivation."[34] He goes on to discuss, in the strongest of terms, the noxious effect of growing up in a family not regulated by justice. Consider, he says, "the self-worship, the unjust self-preference," nourished in a boy growing up in a household in which "by the mere fact of being born a male he is by right the superior of all and every one of an entire half of the human race." Mill concludes that the example set by perpetuating a marital structure "contradictory to the first principles of social justice" must have such "a perverting influence" that it is hard even to imagine the good effects of changing it. All other attempts to educate people to respect and practice justice, Mill claims, will be superficial "as long as the citadel of the enemy is not attacked." Mill felt as much hope for what the family might be as he felt despair at what it was not. "The family, justly constituted, would be the real school of the virtues of freedom," primary among which was "justice, . . . grounded as before on equal, but now also on sympathetic association."[35] Mill both saw clearly and had the courage to address what so many other political philosophers either could not see, or saw and turned away from.

Despite the strength and fervor of his advocacy of women's rights, however, Mill's idea of a just family structure falls far short of that of many feminists even of his own time, including his wife, Harriet Taylor. In spite of the fact that Mill recognized both the empowering effect of earnings on one's position in the family and the limiting effect of domestic responsibility on women's opportunities, he balked at questioning the traditional division of labor between the sexes. For him, a woman's choice of marriage was parallel to a man's choice of a profession: unless and until she had fulfilled her obligations to her husband and children, she should not undertake anything else. But clearly, however equal the legal rights of husbands and wives, this position largely undermines Mill's own insistence upon the importance of marital equality for a just society. His acceptance of the traditional division of labor, without making any provision for wives who were thereby made economically dependent upon their husbands, largely undermines his insistence upon family justice as the necessary foundation for social justice.

Thus even those political theorists of the past who have perceived the family as an important school of moral development have rarely acknowledged the need for congruence between the family and the wider social order, which suggests that families themselves need to be just. Even when they have, as with Mill, they have been unwilling to push hard on the traditional division of labor within the family in the name of justice or equality.

Contemporary theorists of justice, with few exceptions, have paid little or no attention to the question of moral development—of how we are to *become* just. Most of them seem to think, to adapt slightly Hobbes's notable phrase, that just men spring like mushrooms from the earth.[36] Not surprisingly, then, it is far less often acknowledged in recent than in past theories that the family is important for moral development, and especially for instilling a sense of justice. As I have already noted, many theorists pay no attention at all to either the family or gender. In the rare case that the issue of justice within the family is given any sustained attention, the family is not viewed as potential school of social justice.[37] In the rare case that a theorist pays any sustained attention to the development of a sense of justice or morality, little if any attention is likely to be paid to the family.[38] Even in the rare event that theorists pay considerable attention to the family *as* the first major locus of moral socialization, they do not refer to the fact that families are almost all still thoroughly gender-structured institutions.[39]

Among major contemporary theorists of justice, John Rawls alone treats the family seriously as the earliest school of moral development. He argues that a just, well-ordered society will be stable only if its members continue to develop a sense of justice. And he argues that families play a fundamental role in the stages by which this sense of justice is acquired. From the parents' love for their child, which comes to be reciprocated, comes the child's "sense of his own value and the desire to become the sort of person that they are."[40] The family, too, is the first of that series of "associations" in which we participate, from which we acquired the capacity, crucial for a sense of justice, to see things from the perspectives of others. . . . This capacity—the capacity for empathy—is essential for maintaining a sense of justice of the Rawlsian kind. For the perspective that is necessary for maintaining a sense of justice is not that of the egoistic or disembodied self, or of the dominant few who overdetermine "our" traditions or "shared understandings," or (to use Nagel's term) of "the view from nowhere," but rather the perspective of every person in the society for whom the principles of justice are being arrived at. . . . The problem with Rawls's rare and interesting discussion of moral development is that it rests on the unexplained *assumption* that family institutions are just. If gendered family

institutions are *not* just, but are, rather, a relic of caste or feudal societies in which responsibilities, roles, and resources are distributed, not in accordance with the principles of justice he arrives at or with any other commonly respected values, but in accordance with innate differences that are imbued with enormous social significance, then Rawls's theory of moral development would seem to be built on uncertain ground. This problem is exacerbated by suggestions in some of Rawls's most recent work that families are "private institutions," to which it is not appropriate to apply standards of justice. But if families are to help form just individuals and citizens, surely they must be *just families*.

In a just society, the structure and practices of families must give women the same opportunities as men to develop their capacities, to participate in political power and influence social choices, and to be economically secure. But in addition to this, families must be just because of the vast influence that they have on the moral development of children. The family is the primary institution of formative moral development. And the structure and practices of the family must parallel those of the larger society if the sense of justice is to be fostered and maintained. While many theorists of justice, both past and present, appear to have denied the importance of at least one of these factors, my own view is that both are absolutely crucial. A society that is committed to equal respect for all of its members, and to justice in social distributions of benefits and responsibilities, can neither neglect the family nor accept family structures and practices that violate these norms, as do current gender-based structures and practices. It is essential that children who are to develop into adults with a strong sense of justice and commitment to just institutions spend their earliest and most formative years in an environment in which they are loved and nurtured, *and* in which principles of justice are abided by and respected. What is a child of either sex to learn about fairness in the average household with two full-time working parents, where the mother does, at the very least, twice as much family work as the father? What is a child to learn about the value of nurturing and domestic work in a home with a traditional division of labor in which the father either subtly or not so subtly uses the fact that he is the wage earner to "pull rank" on or to abuse his wife? What is a child to learn about responsibility for others in a family in which, after many years of arranging her life around the needs of her husband and children, a woman is faced with having to provide for herself and her children but is totally ill-equipped for the task by the life she agreed to lead, has led, and expected to go on leading?

NOTES

1. U.S. Department of Labor, *Employment and Earnings: July 1987* (Washington, D.C.; Government Printing Office, 1987); Ruth Sidel, *Women and Children Last: The Plight of Poor Women in Affluent America* (New York: Viking, 1986), pp. xvi, 158. See also David T. Ellwood, *Poor Support: Poverty in the American Family* (New York: Basic Books, 1988), pp. 84–85, on the chronicity of poverty in single-parent households.

2. Shirley Williams, in Williams and Elizabeth Holtzman, "Women in the Political World: Observations," *Daedalus* 116, no. 4 (Fall 1987): 30.

3. Twenty-three percent of single parents have never been married and 12 percent are widowed. (U.S. Bureau of the Census, Current Population Reports, *Household and Family Characteristics: March 1987* [Washington, D.C.: Government Printing Office, 1987], p. 79). In 1987, 6.8 percent of children under eighteen were living with a never-married parent. ("Study Shows Growing Gap Between Rich and Poor," *New York Times,* March 23, 1989, p. A24). The proportions for the total population are very different from those for black families, of whom in 1984 half of those with adult members under thirty-five years of age were maintained by single, female parents, three-quarters of whom were never married. (Frank Levy, *Dollars and Dreams: The Changing American Income Distribution* [New York: Russel Sage, 1987], p. 156).

4. As Joan Scott has pointed out, *gender* was until recently used only as a grammatical term. See "Gender: A Useful Category of Historical Analysis," in Joan Wallach Scott, *Gender and the Politics of History* (New York: Columbia University Press, 1988), p. 28, citing Fowler's *Dictionary of Modern English Usage.*

5. Among Anglo-American feminists see, for example, Mary Daly, *Gyn/Ecology: The Metaethics of Radical Feminism* (Boston: Beacon Press, 1978); Susan Griffin, *Woman and Nature: The Roaring Inside Her* (New York: Harper & Row, 1978). For a good succinct discussion of radical feminist biological determinism, see Alison Jaggar, *Feminist Politics and Human Nature* (Totowa, N.J.: Rowman and Allanheld, 1983).

6. See, for example, Sylvia Yanagisako and Jane Collier, "The Mode of Reproduction in Anthropology," in *Theoretical Perspectives on Sexual Difference,* ed. Deborah Rhode (New Haven: Yale University Press, in press).

7. Nancy Chodorow, *The Reproduction of Mothering: Psychoanalysis and the Sociology of Gender* (Berkeley: University of California Press, 1978); Dorothy Dinnerstein, *The Mermaid and the Minotaur: Sexual Arrangements and Human Malaise* (New York: Harper & Row, 1976). For further discussion of this issue and further references to the literature, see chapter 6, note 58, and accompanying text.

8. Linda Nicholson, *Gender and History* (New York: Columbia University Press, 1986); Michelle Z. Rosaldo, "The Use and Abuse of Anthropology," *Signs* 5, no. 3 (1980); Joan Wallach Scott, *Gender and the Politics of History* (New York: Columbia University Press, 1986).

9. For such critiques, see Bell Hooks, *Ain't I a Woman: Black Women and Feminism* (Boston: South End Press, 1981), and *Feminist Theory: From Margin to Center* (Boston: South End Press, 1984); Elizabeth V. Spelman, *Inessential Woman: Problems of Exclusion in Feminist Thought* (Boston: Beacon Press, 1989).

10. There is now an abundant literature on the subject of women, their exclusion from nondomestic life, and the reasons given to justify it, in Western political theory. See, for example, Lorenne J. Clark and Lynda Lange, eds., *The Sexism of Social and Political Thought* (Toronto: University of Toronto Press, 1979); Jean Bethke Elshtain, *Public Man, Private Woman: Women in Social and Political Thought* (Princeton: Princeton University Press, 1981); Genevieve Lloyd, *The Man of Reason: "Male" and "Female" in Western Philosophy* (Minneapolis: University of Minnesota Press, 1984); Mary O'Brien, *The Politics of Reproduction* (London: Routledge & Kegan Paul, 1981); Susan Moller Okin, *Women in Western Political Thought* (Princeton: Princeton University Press, 1979); Carole Pateman, "Feminist Critiques of the Public/Private Dichotomy," in *Public and Private in Social Life,* ed. S. Benn

and G. Gaus (London: Croom Helm, 1983); Carole Pateman and Elizabeth Gross, eds., *Feminist Challenges: Social and Political Theory* (Boston: Northeastern University Press, 1987); Carole Pateman, *The Sexual Contract* (Stanford: Stanford University Press, 1988); Carole Pateman and Mary L. Shanley, eds. *Feminist Critiques of Political Theory* (Oxford: Polity Press, in press).

11. Bruce Ackerman, *Social Justice in the Liberal State* (New Haven: Yale University Press, 1980); Ronald Dworkin, *Taking Rights Seriously* (Cambridge: Harvard University Press, 1977); William Galston, *Justice and the Human Good* (Chicago: University of Chicago Press, 1980); Alasdair MacIntyre, *After Virtue* (Notre Dame: University of Notre Dame Press, 1981), and *Whose Justice? Which Rationality?* (Notre Dame: University of Notre Dame Press, 1988); Robert Nozick, *Anarchy, State, and Utopia* New York: Basic Books, 1974); Roberto Unger, *Knowledge and Politics* (New York: The Free Press, 1975), and *The Critical Legal Studies Movement* (Cambridge: Harvard University Press, 1986).

12. Philip Green, in *Retrieving Democracy: In Search of Civic Equality* (Totowa, N.J.: Rowman and Allanheld, 1985), argues that the social equality that is prerequisite to real democracy is incompatible with the current division of labor between the sexes. See pp. 96–108.

13. Michael Walzer, *Spheres of Justice* (New York: Basic Books, 1983).

14. This is commented on and questioned by Francis Schrag, "Justice and the Family," *Inquiry* 19 (1976): 200, and Walzer, *Spheres of Justice,* chap. 9.

15. See note 10 of this chapter. The phrase is Dale Spender's.

16. See, for example, David Gauthier, *Morals by Agreement* (Oxford: Oxford University Press, 1986), passim and p. vi. Fortunately, Gauthier's computer was able to control its zeal for randomization enough to avoid referring to Plato and Rawls as "she" and Queen Gertrude and Mary Gibson as "he."

17. *General Electric v. Gilbert,* 429 U.S. 125 (1976), 135–36; second phrase quoted from *Geduldig v. Aiello,* 417 U.S. 484 (1974), 496–97, emphasis added.

18. Ackerman, *Social Justice,* pp. 127–28. He takes gender neutrality to the point of suggesting a hypothetical case in which "a couple simply *enjoy* abortions so much that they conceive embryos simply to kill them a few months later."

19. Derek L. Phillips, *Toward a Just Social Order* (Princeton: Princeton University Press, 1986), esp. pp. 187–96.

20. Ibid., pp. 224–26.

21. Ibid., esp. chap. 9.

22. I have analyzed some of the ways in which theorists in the tradition avoided considering the justice of gender in "Are Our Theories of Justice Gender-Neutral?" in *The Moral Foundations of Civil Rights,* ed. Robert Fullinwider and Claudia Mills (Totowa, N.J.: Rowman and Littlefield, 1986).

23. See Judith Hicks Stiehm, "The Unit of Political Analysis: Our Aristotelian Hangover," in *Discovering Reality: Feminist Perspectives on Epistemology, Metaphysics, Methodology, and Philosophy of Science,* ed. Sandra Harding and Merrill B. Hintikka (Dordrecht, Holland: Reidel, 1983).

24. See Carole Pateman and Theresa Brennan, "'Mere Auxiliaries to the Commonwealth': Women and the Origins of Liberalism," *Political Studies* 27, no. 2 (June 1979); also Susan Moller Okin, "Women and the Making of the Sentimental Family," *Philosophy and Public Affairs* 11, no. 1 (Winter 1982). This issue is treated at much greater length in Pateman, *The Sexual Contract.*

25. This claim, originating in the moral development literature, has significantly influenced recent feminist moral and political theory. Two central books are Carol Gilligan, *In a Different Voice* (Cambridge: Harvard University Press, 1982); and Nel Noddings, *Caring: A Feminine Approach to Ethics and Moral Education* (Berkeley: University of California Press, 1984). For the influence of Gilligan's work on feminist theory, see, for example, Seyla Benhabib, "The Generalized and the Concrete Other: The Kohlberg-Gilligan controversy and Feminist Theory," in *Feminism as Critique,* ed. Benhabib and Drucilla Cornell (Minneapolis: University of Minnesota Press, 1987); Lawrence Blum, "Gilligan and Kohlberg: Implications for Moral Theory," *Ethics* 98, no. 3 (1988); and Eva Kittay and Diana Meyers, eds., *Women and Moral Theory* (Totowa N.J.:Rowman and Allenheld, 1986). For a valuable alternative approach to the issues, and an excellent selective list of references to what has now become a vast literature, see Owen Flanagan and Kathryn Jackson, "Justice, Care and Gender: The Kohlberg-Gilligan Debate Revisited," *Ethics* 97, no. 3 (1987).

26. See, for example, John M. Broughton, "Women's Rationality and Men's Virtues: A Critique of Gender Dualism in Gilligan's Theory of Moral Development," *Social Research* 50, no. 3 (1983); Owen Flanagan, *Varieties of Moral Personality: Ethics and Psychological Realism* (Cambridge: Harvard University Press, forthcoming), ch. 8; Catherine G. Greeno and Eleanor E. Maccoby, "How Different Is the 'Different Voice'?" and Gilligan's reply, *Signs* 11, no. 2 (1986);

Debra Nails "Social-Scientific Sexism: Gilligan's Mismeasure of Man," *Social Research* 50, no. 3 (1983); Joan Tronto, "'Women's Morality': Beyond Gender Difference to a Theory of Care," *Signs* 12, no. 2 (1987); Lawrence J. Walker, "Sex Differences in the Development of Moral Reasoning: A Critical Review," *Child Development* 55 (1984).

27. See extracts from the Apostolic Letter in *New York Times*, October 1, 1988, pp. A1 and 6. On the reinforcement of the old stereotypes in general, see Susan Moller Okin, "Thinking Like a Woman," in Rhode, ed., *Theoretical Perspectives*.

28. See esp. James Fishkin, *Justice, Equal Opportunity and the Family* (New Haven: Yale University Press, 1983); Phillips, *Just Social Order*, esp. pp. 346–49; Rawls, *Theory*, pp. 74, 300–301, 511–12.

29. Jean-Jacques Rousseau, *Emile: or On Education*, trans. Allan Bloom (New York: Basic Books, 1979), p. 363.

30. Louis de Bonald, in *Archives Parlementaires*, 2e série (Paris, 1869), vol. 15, p. 612; cited and translated by Roderick Phillips, "Women and Family Breakdown in Eighteenth-Century France: Rouen 1780–1800," *Social History* 2, (1976): 217.

31. *Reynolds v. Nebraska*, 98 U.S. 145 (1879), 164, 166.

32. *Bradwell v. Illinois*, 83 U.S. 130 (1872).

33. Martha Minow, "We, the Family: Constitutional Rights and American Families," *The American Journal of History* 74, no. 3 (1987); 969, discussing *Reynolds* and other nineteenth-century cases.

34. John Stuart Mill, *The Subjection of Women* (1869), in *Collected Works*, ed. J. M. Robson (Toronto: University of Toronto Press, 1984), vol. 21, pp. 324, 293–95. At the time Mill wrote, women had no political rights and coverture deprived married women of most legal rights, too. He challenges all this in his essay.

35. Mill, *Subjection of Women*, pp. 324–25, 294–95.

36. Hobbes writes of "men . . . as if but even now sprung out of the earth . . . like mushrooms." "Philosophical rudiments Concerning Government and Society," in *The English Works of Thomas Hobbes*, ed. Sir William Molesworth (London: John Bohn, 1966), vol. 2, p. 109.

37. For example, Walzer, *Spheres of Justice*, chap. 9, "Kinship and Love."

38. See Alan Gewirth, *Reason and Morality* (Chicago: University of Chicago Press, 1978). He discusses moral development from time to time, but places families within the broad category of "voluntary associations" and does not discuss gender roles within them.

39. This is the case with both Rawls's *A Theory of Justice* (Cambridge: Harvard University Press, 1971), . . . and Phillips's sociologically oriented *Toward a Just Social Order*, as discussed above.

40. Rawls, *Theory*, p. 465.

26   Feminist Justice and the Family

JAMES P. STERBA

CONTEMPORARY FEMINISTS almost by definition seek to put an end to male domination and to secure women's liberation. To achieve these goals, many feminists support the political ideal of a gender-free or androgynous society.[1] According to these feminists, all assignments of rights and duties are ultimately to accord with the ideal of a gender-free or androgynous society. Since a conception of justice is usually thought to provide the ultimate grounds for the assignment of rights and duties, I refer to this ideal of a gender-free or androgynous society as "feminist justice."

The Ideal of a Gender-Free or Androgynous Society

But how is this ideal of a gender-free or androgynous society to be interpreted? It is a society where basic rights and duties are not assigned on the basis of a person's biological sex. Being male or female is not the grounds for determining what basic rights and duties a person has in a gender-free society. But this is to characterize the feminist ideal only negatively. It tells us what we need to get rid of, not what we need to put in its place. A more positive characterization is provided by the ideal of androgyny. Putting the ideal of feminist justice more positively in terms of the ideal of androgyny also helps to bring out why men should be attracted to feminist justice.

In a well-known article, Joyce Trebilcot distinguishes two forms of androgyny.[2] The first postulates the same ideal for everyone. According to this form of androgyny, the ideal person "combines characteristics usually attributed to men with characteristics usually attributed to women." Thus, we should expect both nurturance and mastery, openness and objectivity, compassion and competitiveness from each and every person who has the capacities for these traits.

By contrast, the second form of androgyny does not advocate the same ideal for everyone but rather a variety of options from "pure" femininity to "pure" masculinity. As Trebilcot points out, this form of androgyny shares with the first the view that biological sex should not be the basis for determining the appropriateness of gender characterization. It differs in that it holds that "all alternatives with respect to gender should be equally available to and equally approved for everyone, regardless of sex."

It would be a mistake, however, to distinguish sharply between these two forms of androgyny. Properly understood, they are simply two different facets of a single ideal. For, as Mary Ann Warren has argued, the second form of androgyny is appropriate *only* "with respect to feminine and masculine traits which are largely matters of personal style and preference and which have little direct moral significance."[3] However, when we consider so-called feminine and masculine *virtues,*

Adapted from Perspectives on the Family *(1990) edited by Robert Moffat, Joseph Grcic, and Michael Bayles. Reprinted with revisions by permission.*

it is the first form of androgyny that is required, because then, other things being equal, the same virtues are appropriate for everyone.

We can even formulate the ideal of androgyny more abstractly so that it is no longer specified in terms of so-called feminine and masculine traits. We can specify the ideal as requiring no more than that the traits that are truly desirable in society be equally open to both women and men or, in the case of virtues, equally expected of both women and men, other things being equal.

There is a problem, of course, in determining which traits of character are virtues and which are largely matters of personal style and preference. To make this determination, Trebilcot has suggested that we seek to bring about the second form of androgyny, where people have the option of acquiring the full range of so-called feminine and masculine traits.[4] But surely when we already have good grounds for thinking that such traits as courage and compassion, fairness and openness are virtues, there is no reason to adopt a laissez-faire approach to moral education. Although, as Trebilcot rightly points out, proscribing certain options would involve a loss of freedom, nevertheless we should be able to determine, at least with respect to some character traits, when a gain in virtue is worth the loss of freedom. It may even be the case that the loss of freedom suffered by an individual now will be compensated for by a gain of freedom to that same individual in the future once the relevant virtues have been acquired.

So understood, the class of virtues will turn out to be those desirable traits which can be reasonably expected of both women and men. Admittedly, this is a restrictive use of the term "virtue." In normal usage, "virtue" is almost synonymous with "desirable trait."[5] But there is good reason to focus on those desirable traits that can be reasonably expected of both women and men, and for present purposes I will refer to this class of desirable traits as virtues.[6]

Unfortunately, many of the challenges to the ideal of androgyny fail to appreciate how the ideal can be interpreted to combine a required set of virtues with equal choice from among other desirable traits. For example, some challenges interpret the ideal as attempting to achieve "a proper balance of moderation" among opposing feminine and masculine traits and then question whether traits such as feminine gullibility or masculine brutality could ever be combined with opposing gender traits to achieve such a balance.[7] Other challenges interpret the ideal as permitting unrestricted choice of personal traits and then regard the possibility of Total Women and Hells Angels androgynes as a *reductio ad absurdum* of the idea.[8] But once it is recognized that the ideal of androgyny cannot only be interpreted to require of everyone a set of virtues (which need not be a mean between opposing extreme traits) but can also be interpreted to limit everyone's choice to desirable traits, then such challenges to the ideal clearly lose their force because they only work against objectionable interpretations of androgyny.

Actually, the main challenge raised by feminists to the ideal of androgyny is that the ideal is self-defeating in that it seeks to eliminate sexual stereotyping of human beings at the same time that it is formulated in terms of the very same stereotypical concepts it seeks to eliminate.[9] Or, as Warren puts it, "Is it not at least mildly paradoxical to urge people to cultivate both 'feminine' and 'masculine' virtues, while at the same time holding that virtues ought not to be sexually stereotyped?"

One response to this challenge contends that to build a better society we must begin where we are now, and where we are now people still speak of feminine and masculine character traits. Consequently, if we want to refer easily to such traits and to formulate an ideal with respect to how these traits should be distributed in society, it is plausible to refer to them in the way that people presently refer to them, that is, as feminine or masculine traits.

Another response, which attempts to avoid misunderstanding altogether, is to formulate the ideal in the more abstract way I suggested earlier, so that it no longer specifically refers to so-called feminine or masculine traits. So formulated, the ideal requires that the traits that are truly desirable in society be equally open to both women and men or, in the case of virtues, be equally expected of both women and men. So characterized, the ideal of androgyny represents neither a revolt against so-called feminine virtues and traits nor their exaltation over so-called masculine virtues and traits.[10] Accordingly, the ideal of androgyny does not view women's liberation as *simply* the freeing of women from the confines of traditional roles, which makes it possible for them to develop in ways heretofore reserved for men. Nor does the ideal view women's liberation as *simply* the reevaluation and glorification of so-called feminine activities such as housekeeping or mothering or so-called feminine modes of thinking as reflected in an ethic of caring. The first perspective ignores or devalues genuine virtues and desirable traits traditionally associated with women while the second ignores or devalues genuine virtues and desirable traits traditionally associated with men. In contrast, the ideal of androgyny seeks a broader-based ideal for both women and men that combines virtues and desirable traits traditionally associated with women with virtues and desirable traits traditionally associated with men. Nevertheless, the ideal of androgyny will clearly reject any so-called virtues or desirable traits traditionally associated with women or men that have been supportive of discrimination or oppression against women or men. In general, the ideal of androgyny substitutes a socialization based on natural ability, reasonable expectation, and choice for socialization based on sexual difference.

It also seems that those who claim that we cannot escape a gendered society are simply confused about what a gender-free society would be like;[11] for they seem to agree with those who favor a gender-free or androgynous society that

the assignments of roles in society should be based on (natural) ability, rational expectation, and choice. But what they also maintain is that some of these assignments will be based on sex as well, because some of the natural abilities that people possess will be determined by their sex. But even assuming this is the case, it wouldn't show that society was gendered in the sense that its roles in society are based on sex rather than on (natural) ability, rational expectation, and choice. And this is the only sense of gendered society to which defenders of feminist justice would be objecting.[12] So once the notion of a gender-free society is clarified, there should be widespread agreement that the assignments of roles in society should be based on (natural) ability, rational expectation, and choice. The ideal of androgyny simply specifies this notion of a gender-free society a bit further by requiring that the traits that are truly desirable in society be equally open to (equally qualified) women and men or, in the case of virtues, equally expected of (equally capable) women and men.

Of course, insofar as natural abilities are a function of sexual difference, there will be differences in the desirable traits and virtues that women and men acquire, even in a gender-free or androgynous society. And some contend that these differences will be substantial.[13] But given that we have been slow to implement the degree of equal opportunity required by the ideal of a gender-free or androgynous society, it is difficult to know what differences in desirable traits and virtues, if any, will emerge that are both sex-based and natural-ability-based. What we can be sure of is that given the variety and types of discrimination employed against women in existing societies, a gender-free or androgynous society will look quite different from the societies that we know.

Defenses of Androgyny

Now there are various contemporary defenses of the ideal of androgyny. Some feminists have attempted to derive the ideal from a Liberal

Democratic Conception of Justice. Others have attempted to derive the ideal from a Socialist Conception of Justice. Let us briefly consider each of these defenses in turn.

In attempting to derive the ideal of androgyny from a Democratic Liberal Conception of Justice, feminists have tended to focus on the right to equal opportunity which is a central requirement of a Liberal Democratic Conception of Justice.[14] Of course, equal opportunity could be interpreted minimally as providing people only with the same legal rights of access to all advantaged positions in society for which they are qualified. But this is not the interpretation given the right by liberal democrats. In a Liberal Democratic Conception of Justice, equal opportunity is interpreted to require in addition the same prospects for success for all those who are relevantly similar, where the relevant similarity involves more than simply present qualifications. For example, Rawls claims that persons in his original position would favor a right to "fair equality of opportunity," which means that persons who have the same natural assets and the same willingness to use them would have the necessary resources to achieve similar life prospects.[15] The point feminists have been making is simply that failure to achieve the ideal of androgyny translates into a failure to guarantee equal opportunity to both women and men. The present evidence for this failure to provide equal opportunity is the discrimination that exists against women in education, employment and personal relations. Discrimination in education begins early in a child's formal educational experience as teachers and school books support different and less desirable roles for girls than for boys.[16] Discrimination in employment has been well documented.[17] Women continue to earn only a fraction of what men earn for the same or comparable jobs and although women make up almost half of the paid labor force in the U.S., 70% of them are concentrated in just 20 different job categories, only 5 more than in 1905.[18] Finally, discrimination in personal relations is the

most entrenched of all forms of discrimination against women.[19] It primarily manifests itself in traditional family structures in which the woman is responsible for domestic work and childcare and the man's task is "to protect against the outside world and to show how to meet this world successfully."[20] In none of these areas, therefore, do women have the same prospects for success as compared with men with similar natural talents and similar desires to succeed.

Now the support for the ideal of androgyny provided by a Socialist Conception of Justice appears to be much more direct than that provided by a Liberal Democratic Conception of Justice.[21] This is because the Socialist Conception of Justice and the ideal of androgyny can be interpreted as requiring the very same equal right of self-development. What a Socialist Conception of Justice purports to add to this interpretation of the ideal of androgyny is an understanding of how the ideal is best to be realized in contemporary capitalist societies. For according to advocates of this defense of androgyny, the ideal is best achieved by socializing the means of production and satisfying people's nonbasic as well as their basic needs. Thus, the general idea behind this approach to realizing the ideal of androgyny is that a cure for capitalist exploitation will also be a cure for women's oppression.

Yet despite attempts to identify the feminist ideal of androgyny with a right to equal opportunity endorsed by a Liberal Democratic Conception of Justice or an equal right of self-development endorsed by a Socialist Conception of Justice, the ideal still transcends both of these rights by requiring not only that desirable traits be equally available to both women and men but also that the same virtues be reasonably expected of both women and men. Of course, part of the rationale for reasonably expecting the same virtues in both women and men is to support such rights. And if support for such rights is to be fairly allocated, the virtues needed to support such rights must be reasonably expected of both women and men. Nevertheless, to hold that the virtues required to support a right to equal opportunity or an equal right to self-development must be reasonably expected of both women and men is different from claiming, as the ideal of androgyny does, that human virtues, sans phrase, should be reasonably expected of both women and men. Thus, the ideal of androgyny clearly requires an inculcation of virtues beyond what is necessary to support a right to equal opportunity or an equal right to self-development. What additional virtues are required by the ideal obviously depends upon what other rights should be recognized. In this regard, the ideal of androgyny is somewhat open-ended. Feminists who endorse the ideal would simply have to go along with the best arguments for additional rights and corresponding virtues. In particular, I would claim that they would have to support a right to welfare that is necessary for meeting the basic needs of all legitimate claimants given the strong case that can be made for such a right from liberal democrat, socialist, and even libertarian perspectives.[22]

Now, in order to provide all legitimate claimants with the resources necessary for meeting their basic needs, there obviously has to be a limit on the resources that will be available for each individual's self-development, and this limit will definitely have an effect upon the implementation of the ideal of androgyny. Of course, some feminists would want to pursue various possible technological transformations of human biology in order to implement their ideal. For example, they would like to make it possible for women to inseminate other women and for men to lactate and even to bring fertilized ova to term. But bringing about such possibilities would be very costly indeed.[23] Consequently, since the means selected for meeting basic needs must be provided to all legitimate claimants including distant peoples and future generations, it is unlikely that such costly means could ever be morally justified. Rather it seems preferable radically to equalize the opportunities that are conventionally provided to women and men and wait for such changes to ultimately have their effect on human

biology as well. Of course, if any "technological fixes" for achieving androgyny should prove to be cost efficient as a means for meeting people's basic needs, then obviously there would be every reason to utilize them.

Unfortunately, the commitment of a Feminist Conception of Justice to a right of equal opportunity raises still another problem for the view. For some philosophers have contended that equal opportunity is ultimately an incoherent goal. As Lloyd Thomas has put the charge, "We have a problem for those who advocate competitive equality of opportunity: the prizes won in the competitions of the first generation will tend to defeat the requirements of equality of opportunity for the next."[24] The only way to avoid this result, Thomas claims, "is by not permitting persons to be dependent for their self-development on others at all," which obviously is a completely unacceptable solution.

But this is a problem, as Thomas points out, that exists for competitive opportunities. They are opportunities for which, even when each person does her best, there are considerably more losers than winners. With respect to such opportunities, the winners may well be able to place themselves and their children in an advantageous position with respect to subsequent competitions. But under a Liberal Democratic Conception of Justice, and presumably a Feminist Conception of Justice as well, most of the opportunities people have are not competitive opportunities at all, but rather noncompetitive opportunities to acquire the resources necessary for meeting their basic needs. These are opportunities with respect to which virtually everyone who does her best can be a winner. Of course, some people who do not do their best may fail to satisfy their basic needs, and this failure may have negative consequences for their children's prospects. But under a Liberal Democratic Conception of Justice, and presumably a Feminist Conception of Justice as well, every effort is required to ensure that each generation has the same opportunities to meet their basic needs, and as long as most of the opportunities that are available are of the noncompetitive sort, this goal should not be that difficult to achieve.

Now it might be objected that if all that will be accomplished under the proposed system of equal opportunity is, for the most part, the satisfaction of people's basic needs, then that would not bring about the revolutionary change in the relationship between women and men that feminists are demanding. For don't most women in technologically advanced societies already have their basic needs satisfied, despite the fact that they are not yet fully liberated?

In response, it should be emphasized that the concern of defenders of the ideal of androgyny is not just with women in technologically advanced societies. The ideal of androgyny is also applicable to women in Third World and developing societies, and in such societies it is clear that the basic needs of many women are not being met. Furthermore, it is just not the case that all the basic needs of most women in technologically advanced societies are being met. Most obviously, their basic needs for self-development are still not being met. This is because they are being denied an equal right to education, training, jobs and a variety of social roles for which they have the native capabilities. In effect, women in technologically advanced societies are still being treated as second-class persons, no matter how well-fed, well-clothed, well-housed they happen to be. This is why there must be a radical restructuring of social institutions even in technologically advanced societies if women's basic needs for self-development are to be met.

Androgyny and the Family

Now the primary locus for the radical restructuring required by the ideal of androgyny is the family. Here two fundamental changes are needed. First, all children irrespective of their sex must be given the same type of upbringing consistent with their native capabilities. Second, mothers and fathers must also have the same opportunities for education and employment consistent with their native capabilities.

Surprisingly, however, some liberal democrats have viewed the existence of the family as imposing an acceptable limit on the right to equal opportunity. Rawls, for example, claims the principle of fair opportunity can be only imperfectly carried out, at least as long as the institution of the family exists. The extent to which natural capacities develop and reach fruition is affected by all kinds of social conditions and class attitudes. Even the willingness to make an effort, to try, and so to be deserving in the ordinary sense is itself dependent upon happy family and social circumstances. It is impossible in practice to secure equal chances of achievement and culture for those similarly endowed, and therefore we may want to adopt a principle which recognizes this fact and also mitigates the arbitrary effects of the natural lottery itself.[25]

Thus, according to Rawls, since different families will provide different opportunities for their children, the only way to fully achieve "fair equality of opportunity" would require us to go too far and abolish or radically modify traditional family structures.

Yet others have argued that the full attainment of equal opportunity requires that we go even further and equalize people's native as well as their social assets.[26] For only when everyone's natural and social assets have been equalized would everyone have exactly the same chance as everyone else to attain the desirable social positions in society. Of course, feminists have no difficulty recognizing that there are moral limits to the pursuit of equal opportunity. Accordingly, feminists could grant that other than the possibility of special cases, such as sharing a surplus organ like a second kidney, it would be too much to ask people to sacrifice their native assets to achieve equal opportunity.

Rawls, however, proposes to limit the pursuit of equal opportunity still further by accepting the inequalities generated by families in any given sector of society, provided that there is still equal opportunity between the sectors or that the existing inequality of opportunity can be justified in terms of its benefit to those in the least-advantaged position.[27] Nevertheless, what Rawls is concerned with here is simply the inequality of opportunity that exists between individuals owing to the fact that they come from different families. He fails to consider the inequality of opportunity that exists in traditional family structures, especially between adult members, in virtue of the different roles expected of women and men. When viewed from the original position, it seems clear that this latter inequality of opportunity is sufficient to require a radical modification of traditional family structures, even if the former inequality, for the reasons Rawls suggests, does not require any such modifications.

Yet at least in the United States this need radically to modify traditional family structures to guarantee equal opportunity confronts a serious problem. Given that a significant proportion of the available jobs are at least 9 to 5, families with pre-school children require day care facilities if their adult members are to pursue their careers. Unfortunately, for many families such facilities are simply unavailable. In New York City, for example, more than 144,000 children under the age of six are competing for 46,000 full-time slots in day care centers. In Seattle, there is licensed day care space for 8,800 of the 23,000 children who need it. In Miami, two children, 3 and 4 years old, were left unattended at home while their mother worked. They climbed into a clothes dryer while the timer was on, closed the door and burned to death.[28]

Moreover, even the available day care facilities are frequently inadequate either because their staffs are poorly trained or because the child/adult ratio in such facilities is too high. At best, such facilities provide little more than custodial care; at worst, they actually retard the development of those under their care. What this suggests is that at least under present conditions if pre-school children are to be adequately cared

for, frequently, one of the adult members of the family will have to remain at home to provide that care. But since most jobs are at least 9 to 5, this will require that the adult members who stay at home temporarily give up pursuing a career. However, such sacrifice appears to conflict with the equal opportunity requirement of Feminist Justice.

Families might try to meet this equal opportunity requirement by having one parent give up pursuing a career for a certain period of time and the other give up pursuing a career for a subsequent (equal) period of time. But there are problems here too. Some careers are difficult to interrupt for any significant period of time, while others never adequately reward latecomers. In addition, given the high rate of divorce and the inadequacies of most legally mandated child support, those who first sacrifice their careers may find themselves later faced with the impossible task of beginning or reviving their careers while continuing to be the primary caretaker of their children.[29] Furthermore, there is considerable evidence that children will benefit more from equal rearing from both parents.[30] So the option of having just one parent doing the child-rearing for any length of time is, other things being equal, not optimal.

It would seem, therefore, that to truly share child-rearing within the family what is needed is flexible (typically part-time) work schedules that also allow both parents to be together with their children for a significant period every day. Now some flexible job schedules have already been tried by various corporations.[31] But if equal opportunity is to be a reality in our society, the option of flexible job schedules must be guaranteed to all those with pre-school children. Of course, to require employers to guarantee flexible job schedules to all those with pre-school children would place a significant restriction upon the rights of employers, and it may appear to move the practical requirements of Feminist Justice closer to those of Socialist Justice. But if the case for flexible job schedules is grounded on a right to equal opportunity then at least defenders of Liberal Democratic Justice will have no reason to object. This is clearly one place where Feminist Justice with its focus on equal opportunity within the family tends to drive Liberal Democratic Justice and Socialist Justice closer together in their practical requirements.

Recently, however, Christina Hoff Sommers has criticized feminist philosophers for being "against the family."[32] Sommer's main objection is that feminist philosophers have criticized traditional family structures without adequately justifying what they would put in its place. In this paper, I have tried to avoid any criticism of this sort by first articulating a defensible version of the feminist ideal of androgyny which can draw upon support from both Liberal Democratic and Socialist Conceptions of Justice and then by showing what demands this ideal would impose upon family structures. Since Sommers and other critics of the feminist ideal of androgyny also support a strong requirement of equal opportunity, it is difficult to see how they can consistently do so while denying the radical implications of that requirement (and the ideal of androgyny that underlies it) for traditional family structures.[33]

NOTES

1. See, for example, Ann Ferguson, "Androgyny as an Ideal for Human Development," in *Feminism and Philosophy*, Mary Vetterling-Braggin *et al.*, eds. (Totowa: Rowman and Littlefield, 1977), pp. 45–69; Mary Ann Warren, "Is Androgyny the Answer to Sexual Stereotyping?" in *"Femininity," "Masculinity," and "Androgyny,"* Mary Vetterling-Braggin, ed. (Totowa: Rowman and Littlefield, 1982), pp. 170–186; A. G. Kaplan and J. Bean, Eds. *Beyond Sex-Role Stereotypes: Reading Toward a Psychology of Androgyny* (Totowa: Rowman and Littlefield, 1976); Andrea Dworkin, *Women Hating* (New York: Dutton, 1974), Part IV; Carol Gould, "Privacy Rights and Public Virtues: Women, the Family and Democracy," in Carol Gould, *Beyond Domination* (Totowa: Rowman and Littlefield, 1983), pp. 3–18; Carol Gould, "Women and Freedom," *The Journal of Social Philosophy* Vol. 15 (1984), 20–34; Linda Lindsey, *Gender Roles* (Englewood Cliffs, NJ: Prentice Hall, 1990);

Marilyn Friedman, "Does Sommers like Women?" *Journal of Social Philosophy* Vol. 22 (1991), 75–90. For some feminists who oppose the ideal of androgyny, see Mary Daly *Gyn-Ecology: The Meta-Ethics of Radical Feminism* (Boston: Beacon Press, 1978); Kathryn Pauly Morgan, "Androgyny: A Conceptual Critique," *Social Theory and Practice*, Vol. 8 (1982); Jean Bethke Elshtain, "Against Androgyny," *Telos*, Vol. 47 (1981), 5–21; Kari Weil, *Androgyny and the Denial of Difference* (Charlottesville: University of Virginia, 1992), especially Part III.

2. Joyce Trebilcot, "Two Forms of Androgynism" reprinted in *Feminism and Philosophy*, Mary Vetterling-Braggin, *et al.*, eds. (Totowa: Rowman and Littlefield, 1977), pp. 70–78.

3. Mary Ann Warren, "Is Androgyny the Answer to Sexual Stereotyping?" pp. 178–179.

4. Trebilcot, "Two Forms of Androgynism," pp. 74–77.

5. On this point, see Edmund Pincoffs, *Quandaries and Virtues* (Lawrence: University of Kansas, 1986), Chapter 5.

6. Of course, I cannot provide a full account of how these virtues are to be justifiably inculcated, although I will make some specific recommendations later in this chapter.

7. See, for example, Morgan, "Androgyny: A Conceptual Critique," pp. 256–257.

8. See, for example, Mary Daly, *Gyn-Ecology: The Meta-Ethics of Radical Feminism*, p. xi.

9. Margrit Eichler, *The Double Standard* (New York: St. Martin's Press, 1980), pp. 69–71; Elizabeth Lane Beardsley, "On Curing Conceptual Confusion" in *"Feminity," "Masculinity," and "Androgyny,"* Mary Vetterling-Braggin, *et al.*, eds. (Totowa: Littlefield and Adams, 1982), pp. 197–202; Mary Daly, "The Qualitative Leap Beyond Patriarchal Religion," *Quest* Vol. 1 (1975), 20–40; Janice Raymond, "The Illusion of Androgyny," *Quest* Vol. 2 (1975), 57–66.

10. For a valuable discussion and critique of these two viewpoints, see Iris Young, "Humanism, Gynocentrism and Feminist Politics," *Women's Studies International Forum* (1985) Vol. 8, pp. 173–183.

11. Elizabeth Wolgast, *Equality and the Rights of Women* (Ithaca: Cornell University Press, 1980).

12. Moreover, given that the basic rights that we have in society, such as a right to equal opportunity and a right to welfare, are equal for all citizens and are not based on our differing natural abilities, these rights are not even in this derivative sense based on one's sex.

13. Anne Moir and David Jessel, *Brain Sex* (New York: Dell Publishing Co., 1991).

14. See, for example, Virginia Held, *Rights and Goods* (New York: Free Press, 1984), especially chap. 11; and

Gloria Steinem "What It Would Be Like if Women Win," *Time,* 31 August 1979, pp. 22–23; Mary Jeanne Larrabee, "Feminism and Parental Roles: Possibilities for Changes," *Journal of Social Philosophy* 14 (1983): 18. See also National Organization for Women (NOW) Bill of Rights, and United States Commission on Civil Rights, *Statement on the Equal Rights Amendment* (1978).

15. John Rawls, *A Theory of Justice* (Cambridge: Harvard University Press, 1971), p. 73.

16. See, for example, Elizabeth Allgeier and Naomi McCormick, eds. *Changing Boundaries* (Palo Alto, Calif.: Mayfield Publishing Co., 1983), Part I.

17. See, for example, *Toward Economic Justice for Women,* prepared by Women's Economic Agenda Working Group (Institute for Policy Studies, Washington, D.C., 1985); Jo Freeman, ed., *Women: A Feminist Perspective* (Palo Alto, Calif.: Mayfield Publishing Co. 1984), Part 4; *The Women's Movement: Agenda for the '80s,* an Editorial Research Report (Washington, D.C.: Congressional Quarterly Inc., 1981).

18. Alison M. Jagger and Paula Rothenberg, *Feminist Frameworks,* 2nd ed. (New York: McGraw-Hill, 1984), p. 216.

19. See, for example, Joyce Trebilcot, *Mothering* (Totowa, N.J.: Rowman & Allanheld, 1984); Irene Diamond, *Families, Politics and Public Policy* (New York: Longman Inc., 1983).

20. Bruno Bettelheim, "Fathers Shouldn't Try to Be Mothers," *Parents Magazine,* October 1956, pp. 40 and 126–29.

21. See, for example, Ann Ferguson, "Androgyny as an Ideal for Human Development," in *Feminism and Philosophy,* ed. Vetterling-Braggin et al.; and Evelyn Reed, "Women: Caste, Class or Oppressed Sex?", in *Morality in Practice,* ed. James P. Sterba (Belmont, Calif.: Wadsworth Publishing Co., 1983), pp. 222–28.

22. See James P. Sterba, *How to Make People Just* (Totowa, N.J.: Rowman & Allanheld, 1988), especially chaps. 7–9.

23. See Barbara Katz Rothman, "How Science Is Redefining Parenthood." *Ms.,* August 1982, pp. 154–58.

24. D. A. Lloyd Thomas, "Competitive Equality of Opportunity," *Mind* (1977): 398.

25. Rawls, *Theory of Justice,* p. 74.

26. See Bernard Williams, "The Idea of Equality," in *Philosophy, Politics and Society,* 2nd series, ed. Peter Laslett and W. G. Runciman (Oxford: Oxford University Press, 1969), pp. 110–31. For a literary treatment, see Kurt Vonnegut, Jr., "Harrison Bergeron," in *Welcome to the Monkey House* (New York: Dell, 1968), pp. 7–13.

27. Rawls, *Theory of Justice,* pp. 300–01.

28. *New York Times,* 25 November 1987.

29. See Lenore Weitzman, *The Divorce Revolution: The Unexpected Social and Economic Consequences for Women and Children in America* (New York: Free Press, 1985).

30. Dorothy Dinnerstein, *The Mermaid and the Minotaur* (New York: 1977); Nancy Chodorow, *Mothering: Psychoanalysis and the Sociology of Gender* (Berkeley: 1978); Vivian Gornick, "Here's News: Fathers Matter as Much as Mothers," *Village Voice,* 13 October 1975.

31. *New York Times,* 27 November 1987.

32. Christina Hoff Sommers, "Philosophers Against the Family," in *Person to Person,* ed. Hugh LaFollette and George Graham (Philadelphia: Temple University Press, 1988).

33. In "The Equal Obligation of Mothers and Fathers," in *Having Children,* ed. Onora O'Neill and William Ruddick (New York: Oxford University Press, 1979), pp. 227–40, Virginia Held approaches the problem of what should be the relationship of parents to child-rearing by first assuming that both parents have an equal obligation to contribute to the rearing of their children and then seeking to determine what that equal obligation requires. She determines that parents have an obligation to exert an equal effort in contributing what their children need. As far as I can tell, Held's results about what parents owe their children complement my results about what parents ought to have coming to them in rearing their children, namely, day care facilities and/or flexible job schedules sufficient to maintain equal opportunity.

27   Philosophers against the Family

CHRISTINA SOMMERS

MUCH OF WHAT COMMONLY counts as personal morality is measured by how well we behave within family relationships. We live our moral lives as son or daughter to this mother and that father, as brother or sister to that sister or brother, as father or mother, grandfather, grand-daughter to that boy or girl or that man or woman. These relationships and the moral duties defined by them were once popular topics of moral casuistry; but when we turn to the literature of recent moral philosophy, we find little discussion on what it means to be a good son or daughter, a good mother or father, a good husband or wife, a good brother or sister.

Modern ethical theory concentrates on more general topics. Perhaps the majority of us who do ethics accept some version of Kantianism or utilitarianism, and these mainstream doctrines are better designed for telling us about what we should do as persons in general than about our special duties as parents or children or siblings. We believe, perhaps, that these universal theories can fully account for the morality of special relations. In any case, modern ethics is singularly silent on the bread and butter issues of personal morality in daily life. But silence is only part of it. With the exception of marriage itself, the relationships in the family are biologically given. The contemporary philosopher is, on the whole, actively unsympathetic to the idea that we have *any* duties defined by relationships that we have not voluntarily entered into. We do not, after all,

choose our parents or siblings, and even if we do choose to have children, this is not the same as choosing, say, our friends. Because the special relationships that constitute the family as a social arrangement are, in this sense, not voluntarily assumed, many moralists feel bound in principle to dismiss them altogether. The practical result is that philosophers are to be found among those who are contributing to an ongoing disintegration of the traditional family. In what follows I expose some of the philosophical roots of the current hostility to family morality. My own view that the ethical theses underlying this hostility are bad philosophy is made evident throughout the discussion.

The Moral Vantage

Social criticism is a heady pastime to which philosophers are professionally addicted. One approach is Aristotelian in method and temperament. It is antiradical, though it may be liberal, and it approaches the task of needed reform with a prima facie respect for the norms of established morality. It is conservationist and cautious in its recommendations for change. It is therefore not given to such proposals as abolishing the family or abolishing private property and, indeed, does not look kindly on such proposals from other philosophers. The antiradicals I am concerned about are not those who would be called Burkean. I call them liberal but this use of the term is somewhat perverse since, in my stimulative use, a liberal is a philosopher who advocates social reform but always in a conservative spirit. My liberals share with Aristotle the conviction that the traditional arrangements have great moral weight and that common opinion is a primary source of moral truth. A good modern example is Henry Sidgwick with his constant appeal to common sense. But philosophers like John Stuart Mill, William James, and Bertrand Russell can also be cited. On the other hand, since no radical can be called a liberal in my sense, many so-called liberals could be perversely excluded. Thus when John Rawls toys with the possibility of abolishing the family because kinship bias is a force inimical to equality of opportunity, he is no liberal.

The more exciting genre of social criticism is not liberal-Aristotelian but radical and Platonist in spirit. Its vantage is external or even supernal to the social institutions it has placed under moral scrutiny. Plato was as aware as anyone could be that what he called the cave was social reality. One reason for calling it a cave was to emphasize the need, as he saw it, for an external, objective perspective on established morality: Another point in so calling it was his conviction that common opinion was benighted, and that reform could not be accomplished except by a great deal of consciousness raising and enlightened social engineering. Plato's supernal vantage made it possible for him to look on social reality in somewhat the way the Army Corps of Engineers looks upon a river that needs to have its course changed and its waywardness tamed. In our own day much social criticism of a Marxist variety has taken this radical approach to social change. And of course much of contemporary feminist philosophy is radical. . . .

Feminism and the Family

I have said that the morality of the family has been relatively neglected. The glaring exception to this is, of course, the feminist movement.

This movement is complex, but I am primarily confined to its moral philosophers, of whom the most influential is Simone de Beauvoir. For de Beauvoir, a social arrangement that does not allow all its participants the scope and liberty of a human subjectivity is to be condemned. De Beauvoir criticizes the family as an unacceptable arrangement since, for women, marriage and childbearing are essentially incompatible with their subjectivity and freedom:

> The tragedy of marriage is not that it fails to assure woman the promised happiness . . . but that it mutilates her: It dooms her to repetition and routine. . . . At twenty or thereabouts mistress of a home, bound permanently to a man, a child in her arms, she stands with her life virtually finished forever (1952, 534).

For de Beauvoir the tragedy goes deeper than marriage. The loss of subjectivity is unavoidable as long as human reproduction requires the woman's womb. De Beauvoir starkly describes the pregnant woman who ought to be a "free individual" as a "stockpile of colloids, an incubator of an egg." And as recently as 1977 she compared childbearing and nurturing to slavery.

It would be a mistake to say that de Beauvoir's criticism of the family is outside the mainstream of Anglo-American philosophy. Her criterion of moral adequacy may be formulated in continental existentialist terms, but its central contention is generally accepted: Who would deny that an arrangement that systematically thwarts the freedom and autonomy of the individual is *eo ipso* defective? What is perhaps a bit odd to Anglo-American ears is that de Beauvoir makes so little appeal to ideals of fairness and equality. For her, it is the loss of autonomy that is decisive.

De Beauvoir is more pessimistic than most feminists she has influenced about the prospects for technological and social solutions. But implicit in her critique is the ideal of a society in which sexual differences are minimal or nonexistent. This ideal is shared by many contemporary feminist philosophers: . . . Richard Wasserstrom

(1980), Ann Ferguson (1977), and Alison Jaggar (1977; 1983; 1986) are representative.

Wasserstrom's approach to social criticism is Platonist in its use of a hypothetical good society. The ideal society is nonsexist and "assimilationist": "In the assimilationist society in respect to sex, persons would not be socialized so as to see or understand themselves or others as essentially or significantly who they were or what their lives would be like because they were either male or female" (1980, 26). Social reality is scrutinized for its approximation to this ideal, and criticism is directed against all existing norms. Take the custom of having sexually segregated bathrooms: Whether this is right or wrong "depends on what the good society would look like in respect to sexual differentiation." The key question in evaluating any law or arrangement in which sex difference figures is: "What would the good or just society make of [it]?"

Thus the supernal light shines on the cave revealing its moral defects. *There*, in the ideal society; gender in the choice of lover or spouse would be of no more significance than eye color. *There* the family would consist of adults but not necessarily of different sexes and not necessarily in pairs. *There* we find equality ensured by a kind of affirmative action which compensates for disabilities. If women are somewhat weaker than men, or if they are subject to lunar disabilities, then this must be compensated for. (Wasserstrom compares women to persons with congenital defects for whom the good society makes special arrangements.) Male-dominated sports such as wrestling and football will . . . be eliminated, and marriage as we know it will not exist.

Other feminist philosophers are equally confident about the need for sweeping change. Ann Ferguson (1977) wants a "radical reorganization of child rearing." She recommends communal living and a deemphasis on biological parenting. In the ideal society "love relationships would be based on the meshing together of androgynous human beings." Carol Gould (1983) argues for androgyny and for abolishing legal marriage. She favors single parenting, co-parenting, and communal parenting. The only arrangement she emphatically opposes is the traditional one where the mother provides primary care for the children. Janice Raymond (1975) is an assimilationist who objects to the ideal of androgyny, preferring instead to speak of a genderless ideal free of male or female stereotypes. Alison Jaggar's ideal is described in a science-fiction story depicting a society in which "neither sex bears children, but both sexes, through hormone treatments, suckle them . . . thus [the author] envisions a society where every baby has three social 'mothers,' who may be male or female, and at least two of whom agree to breast-feed it" (1983). To those of us who find this bizarre, Jaggar replies that this shows the depth of our prejudice in favor of the natural family.

Though they differ in detail, these feminists hold to a common social ideal that is broadly assimilationist in character and inimical to the traditional family. Sometimes it seems as if the radical feminist simply takes the classical Marxist eschatology of the *Communist Manifesto* and substitutes "gender" for "class." Indeed, the feminist and the old-fashioned Marxist do have much in common. Both see their caves as politically divided into two warring factions: one oppressing, the other oppressed. Both see the need of raising the consciousness of the oppressed group to its predicament and to the possibility of removing its shackles. Both look forward to the day of a classless or genderless society. And both are zealots, paying little attention to the tragic personal costs to be paid for the revolution they wish to bring about. The feminists tell us little about that side of things. To begin with, how can the benighted myriads in the cave who do not wish to mesh together with other androgynous beings be reeducated? And how are children to be brought up in the genderless society? Plato took great pains to explain his methods. Would the new methods be as thoroughgoing? Unless these questions can be given plausible answers, the supernal attack on the family must always be irresponsible. The appeal to the just society justifies nothing until it can be shown that the radical proposals do not have monstrous consequences. That has not been shown. Indeed, given the perennially dubious state of the social sciences, it is precisely what *cannot* be shown.

Any social arrangement that falls short of the assimilationist ideal is labeled sexist. It should be noted that this characteristically feminist use of the term differs significantly from the popular or literal sense. Literally, and popularly, sexism connotes unfair discrimination. But in its extended philosophical use it connotes discrimination, period. Wasserstrom and many feminists trade on the popular pejorative connotations of sexism when they invite us to be antisexist. Most liberals are antisexist in the popular sense. But to be antisexist in the technical, radical philosophical sense is not merely to be opposed to discrimination against women; it is to be *for* what Wasserstrom calls the assimilationist ideal. The philosopher antisexist opposes any social policy that is nonandrogynous, objecting, for example, to legislation that allows for maternity leave. As Alison Jaggar remarks: "We do not, after all, elevate 'prostate leave' into a special right of men" (1977). From being liberally opposed to sexism, one may in this way insensibly be led to a radical critique of the family whose ideal is assimilationist and androgynous. For it is very clear that the realization of the androgynous ideal is incompatible with the survival of the family as we know it.

The neological extension of labels such as "sexism," "slavery," and "prostitution" is a feature of radical discourse. The liberal too will sometimes call for radical solutions to social problems. Some institutions are essentially unjust. To reform slavery or totalitarian systems of government is to eliminate them. The radical trades on these extreme practices in characterizing other practices—for example, characterizing low wages as "slave" wages and the worker who is paid them as a "slave" laborer. Taking these descriptions seriously may put one on the way to treating a system of a free labor market as a "slave system," which, in simple justice, must be overthrown and replaced by an alternative system of production.

Comparing mothers and wives to slaves is a common radical criticism of the family: Presumably most slaves do not want to be slaves. In fact, the majority of wives and mothers want to be wives and mothers. Calling these women slaves is therefore a pejorative extension of the term. To be slaves in the literal sense these women would have to be too dispirited and oppressed or too corrupt even to want freedom from slavery. Yet that is how some feminist philosophers look upon women who opt for the traditional family. It does seem fanciful and not a little condescending to see them so, but let us suppose that it is in fact a correct and profound description of the plight of married women and mothers. Would it now follow that the term "slave" literally applies to them? Not quite yet. Before we could call these women slaves, we should have to have made a further assumption. Even timorous slaves too fearful of taking any step to freedom are under no illusion that they are not slaves. Yet it is a fact that most women and mothers do not *think* of themselves as slaves, so we must assume that the majority of women have been systematically deluded into thinking they are free. And that assumption, too, is often explicitly made. Here the radical feminist will typically explain that, existentially, women, being treated by men as sex objects, are especially prone to bad faith and false consciousness. Marxist feminists will see them as part of an unawakened and oppressed economic class. Clearly we cannot call on a deluded woman to cast off her bonds before we have made her *aware* of her bondage. So the first task of freeing the slave woman is dispelling the thrall of a false and deceptive consciousness. One must raise her consciousness to the reality of her situation. (Some feminists acknowledge that it may in fact be too late for many of the women who have fallen too far into the delusions of marriage and motherhood. But the educative process can save many from falling into the marriage and baby trap.)

In this sort of rhetorical climate nothing is what it seems. Prostitution is another term that has been subjected to a radical enlargement. Alison Jaggar believes that a feminist interpretation of the term "prostitution" is badly needed and asks for a "philosophical theory of prostitution" (1986). Observing that the average woman dresses for men, marries a man for protection, and so on, she says: "For contemporary radical feminists, prostitution is the archetypal relationship of women to men" (1986, 115).

Of course, the housewife Jaggar has in mind might be offended at the suggestion that she herself is a prostitute, albeit less well paid and less aware of it than the professional street prostitute. To this the radical feminist reply is, to quote Jaggar:

> Individuals' intentions do not necessarily indicate the true nature of what is going on. Both man and woman might be outraged at the description of their candlelit dinner as prostitution, but the radical feminist argues this outrage is due simply to the participants' failure or refusal to perceive the social context in which the dinner occurs (1986, 117).

Apparently, this failure or refusal to perceive affects most women. Thus we may even suppose that the majority of women who have been treated by a man to a candlelit dinner prefer it to other dining alternatives they have experienced. To say that these preferences are misguided is a hard and condescending doctrine. It would appear that most feminist philosophers are not overly impressed with Mill's principle that there can be no appeal from a majority verdict of those who have experienced two alternatives.

The dismissive feminist attitude to the widespread preferences of women takes its human toll. Most women, for example, prefer to have children, and few of those who have them regret having them. It is no more than sensible, from a utilitarian standpoint, to take note of the widespread preference and to take it seriously in planning one's own life. But a significant number of women discount this general verdict as benighted, taking more seriously the idea that the reported joys of motherhood are exaggerated and fleeting, if not altogether illusory. These women tell themselves and others that having babies is a trap to be avoided. But for many women childlessness has become a trap of its own, somewhat lonelier than the more conventional traps of marriage and babies. Some come to find their childlessness regrettable; this sort of regret is common to those who flout Mill's reasonable maxim by putting the verdict of ideology over the verdict of human experience.

It is a serious defect of American feminism that it concentrates its zeal on impugning femininity and feminine culture at the expense of the grassroot fight against economic and social injustices to which women are subjected. As we have seen, the radical feminist attitude to the woman who enjoys her femininity is condescending or even contemptuous. Indeed, the contempt for femininity reminds one of misogynist biases in philosophers such as Kant, Rousseau, and Schopenhauer, who believed that femininity was charming but incompatible with full personhood and reasonableness. The feminists deny the charm, but they too accept the verdict that femininity is weakness. It goes without saying that an essential connection between femininity and powerlessness has not been established by *either* party.

By denigrating conventional feminine roles and holding to an assimilationist ideal in social policy, the feminist movement has lost its natural constituency. The actual concerns, beliefs, and aspirations of the majority of women are not taken seriously *except* as illustrations of bad faith, false consciousness, and successful brainwashing. What women actually want is discounted and reinterpreted as to what they have been led to *think* they want (a man, children). What most women *enjoy* (male gallantry; candlelit dinners, sexy clothes, makeup) is treated as an obscenity (prostitution).

As the British feminist Jennifer Radcliffe Richards says:

> Most women still dream about beauty, dress, weddings, dashing lovers, domesticity, and babies . . . but if feminists seem (as they do) to want to eliminate nearly all of these things—beauty, sex conventions, families, and all—for most people that simply means the removal of everything in life which is worth living for (1980, 341–342).

Radical feminism creates a false dichotomy between sexism and assimilation, as if there were nothing in between. This is to ignore completely the middle ground in which it could be recognized that a woman can be free of oppression and nevertheless feminine in the sense abhorred by many feminists. For women are simply not waiting to be freed from the particular chains the radical feminists are trying to sunder. The average woman enjoys her femininity. She wants a man, not a roommate. She wants fair economic opportunities, and she wants children and the time to care for them. These are the goals that women actually have, and they are not easily attainable. But they will never be furthered by an elitist radical movement that views the actual aspirations of women as the product of a false consciousness. There is room for a liberal feminism that would work for reforms that would give women equal opportunity in the workplace and in politics, but would leave untouched and unimpugned the basic institutions that women want and support: marriage and motherhood. Such a feminism is already in operation in some European countries. But it has been obstructed in the United States by the ideologues who now hold the seat of power in the feminist movement (Hewlett, 1986).

In characterizing and criticizing American feminism, I have not taken into account the latest revisions and qualifications of a lively and variegated movement. There is a kind of feminism-of-the-week that one cannot hope to keep abreast of, short of giving up all other concerns. The best one can do for the present purposes is attend to central theses and arguments that bear on the feminist treatment of the family. Nevertheless, even for this limited purpose, it would be wrong to omit discussion of an important turn taken by feminism in the past few years. I have in mind the recent literature on the idea that there is a specific female ethic that is more concrete, less rule-oriented, more empathetic and caring, and more attentive to the demands of a particular context. The kind of feminism that accepts the idea that women differ from men in approaching ethical dilemmas and social problems from a care perspective is not oriented to androgyny as an ideal. Rather it seeks to develop this special female ethic and give it greater practical scope.

The stress on context might lead one think these feminists are more sympathetic to the family as the social arrangement that shapes the moral development of women and is the context for many of the moral dilemmas that women actually face. However, one sees as yet no attention being paid to the fact that feminism itself is a force working against the preservation of the family. Psychologists like Carol Gilligan and philosophers like Lawrence Blum concentrate their attention on the moral quality of the caring relationships, but these relationships are themselves not viewed in their concrete embeddedness in any formal social arrangement.

It should also be said that some feminists are moving away from earlier hostility to motherhood (Trebilcot, 1984). Here, too, one sees the weakening of the assimilationist ideal in the acknowledgment of a primary gender role. However, childrearing is not primarily seen within the context of the family but as a special relationship between mother and daughter or—more awkwardly—between mother and son, a relationship that effectively excludes the male parent. And the often cultist celebration of motherhood remains largely hostile to traditional familial arrangements.

It is too early to say whether a new style of nonassimilationist feminism will lead to a mitigation of the assault on the family or even on femininity. In any case, the recognition of a female ethic of care and responsibility is hardly inconsistent with a social ethic that values the family as a vital, perhaps indispensable, institution. And the recognition that women have their own moral style may well be followed by a more accepting attitude to the kind of femininity that the more assimilationist feminists reject.

REFERENCES

De Beauvoir, Simone. 1952. *The Second Sex.* H. M. Parshley, trans. New York: Random House.

———. 1977. "Talking to De Beauvoir." In *Spare Rib.*

Ferguson, Ann. 1977. "Androgyny as an Ideal for Human Development." In M. Vetterling-Braggin, F. Elliston, and J. English, eds. *Feminism and Philosophy,* pp. 45–69. Totowa: N.J.: Rowman and Littlefield.

Gould, Carol. 1983. "Private Rights and Public Virtues: Woman, the Family and Democracy." In Carol Gould, ed. *Beyond Domination,* pp. 3–18. Totowa, N.J.: Rowman and Allanheld.

Hewlett, Sylvia Ann. 1986 *A Lesser Life: The Myth of Woman's Liberation in America.* New York: Morrow.

Jaggar, Alison. 1977. "On Sex Equality." In Jane English, ed. *Sex Equality,* Englewood Cliffs, N.J.: Prentice-Hall.

———. 1983. "Human Biology in Feminist Theory: Sexual Equality Reconsidered." In Gould, ed. *Beyond Domination.*

———. 1986. "Prostitution." In Marilyn Pearsell, ed. *Women and Values: Readings in Recent Feminist Philosophy,* pp. 108–121. Belmont, Calif.: Wadsworth.

Raymond, Janice. 1975. "The Illusion of Androgyny." *Quest: A Feminist Quarterly.* 2.

Richards, Jennifer Radcliffe. 1980. *The Skeptical Feminist.* Hardmondsworth: Penguin.

Trebilcot, Joyce, ed. 1984. *Mothering: Essays in Feminist Theory.* Totowa, N.J.: Rowman and Allanheld.

Wasserstrom, Richard. 1980. *Philosophy and Social Issues.* Notre Dame, Ind.: University of Notre Dame Press.

28 Sommers and the Family

MARILYN FRIEDMAN

1. IN A SERIES OF PAPERS which has recently appeared in several philosophical and general academic publications,[1] Christina Sommers mounts a campaign against feminist philosophers (1989a, 85; 1989b, B2) and "American feminism" in general (1989a, 90–91). Sommers blames feminists for contributing to the current divorce rate and the breakdown of the traditional family, and she repudiates feminist critiques of traditional forms of marriage, family, and femininity. In this paper, I explore Sommers's views in some detail. My aim is not primarily to defend her feminist targets, but to ferret out Sommers's own views of traditional marriage, family, and femininity, and to see whether or not they have any philosophical merit.

2. In her writings, Sommers generally defends what she claims that feminists have challenged. Whether or not she is actually discussing the same things is often open to question since she fails to define the key terms behind which she rallies. Sommers, for examples, endorses "the family," the "traditional family," and "the family as we know it" (1989a, 87–88). These are not equivalent expressions. The so-called traditional family—a nuclear family consisting of a legally married heterosexual couple and their children, in which the man is the sole breadwinner and "head" of the household, and the woman does the domestic work and childcare—comprised only 16% of all U.S. households in 1977, accord-

ing to the U.S. Census Bureau.[2] Hence, the "traditional family" is no longer "*the family*" or "*the* family as we know it" (italics mine) but is only one sort of family that we know.

Sommers also rallies behind "femininity," "feminine culture," "conventional feminine roles," and "a primary gender role" (1989a, 90, 92). These expressions, as well, call for clarification; they do not necessarily refer to the same practices. In recent years, many feminists have defended various aspects of what might also be called "feminine culture." Sommers notes a few of these authors and works (Carol Gilligan, for example), but finds one reason or another for repudiating each one that she cites.[3]

3. To see what Sommers is promoting under the banner of "feminine culture," we should look to Sommers's claims about what women value, want, and enjoy.[4] First, there are wants, values, and enjoyments pertaining to men.[5] Sommers claims that women want "a man," "marriage," and "to marry good providers."[6] She asserts that "most women" enjoy "male gallantry," that the "majority of women" enjoy being "treated by a man to a candlelit dinner," and that "many women . . . swoon at the sight of Rhett Butler carrying Scarlett O'Hara up the stairs to a fate undreamt of in feminist philosophy."[7]

Second, there are wants, values, and enjoyments having to do with children. Women, Sommers tells us, want children, motherhood,

From "*They Lived Happily Ever After: Sommers on Women and Marriage,*" Journal of Social Philosophy Vol. XXI (1990). *Reprinted by permission.*

"*conventional* motherhood," "family," and "the time to care for children."[8] In a revealing turn of phrase, Sommers also asserts that women are "willing to pay the price" for family and motherhood (1989b, B2). Sommers does not say, however, what she thinks the price is.

Third, there are wants, values, and enjoyments having to do with femininity: Women are said to enjoy their "femininity," makeup, "sexy clothes," and, even more specifically, "clothes that render them 'sex objects.'"[9] On the topic of femininity, Sommers also quotes approvingly (1989a, 90–91) the words of Janet Radcliffe Richards who wrote that, "Most women still dream about beauty, dress, weddings, dashing lovers," and "domesticity," and that, for "most people," "beauty, sex conventions, families, and all" comprise "everything in life which is worth living for."[10]

4. A very few of the wants which Sommers attributes to women do not fit into my three-part classification scheme (men, children, femininity.) Sommers claims that women want "fair economic opportunities" (1989a, 91), and that they are "generally receptive to liberal feminist reforms that enhance their political and economic powers" (1989b, B2). Sommers ironically, does not recognize that the enhanced economic and political power of women makes them less needful of traditional marriage to a "good provider," and when they are married, makes them less afraid to resort to divorce to solve marital and family problems. The economic concerns of liberal feminism directly threaten one colossal support for the "traditional family," namely, the extreme economic vulnerability of the non-income-earning woman and her concomitant material dependence on a "good provider."

Under traditional arrangements, most women not only *wanted* marriage, they *needed* it. It was by far a woman's most socially legitimate option for economic survival. Take away the need, as liberal feminism seeks to do, and at least some of the want also disappears. One otherwise very traditional aunt of mine became a wealthy widow in her late fifties when my rich uncle died. She never remarried. Now a dynamic woman of 82 who travels widely and lives well, she confesses that no man has interested her enough to make it worthwhile to give up her freedom a second time. "I'm lucky," she confides, "I don't need a meal-ticket." Even a nonfeminist can understand what she is getting at.

5. Before assessing Sommers's overall views, let us rescue Scarlett O'Hara. Sommers's remark that Scarlett O'Hara's rape by Rhett Butler is a fate undreamt of in feminist philosophy is . . . simply stunning. (Note that Sommers does not use the word *rape* here—one of many omissions in her writings.) Even a passing knowledge of feminist philosophy reveals that rape is hardly undreamt of in it.[11] Rape, of course, is not a dream; it is a nightmare. Any form of sexual aggression can involve coercion, intimidation, degradation, physical abuse, battering, and, in extreme cases, death.

The reality of rape is rendered invisible by the many novels and films, such as *Gone With the Wind,* which romanticize and mystify it. They portray the rapist as a handsome man whose domination is pleasurable in bed, and portray women as happy to have their own sexual choices and refusals crushed by such men. In a culture in which these sorts of portrayals are routine, it is no surprise that this scene arouses the sexual desire of some women. However, the name of Richard Speck,[12] to take one example, can remind us that real rape is not the pleasurable fantasy intimated in *Gone With the Wind.* To put the point graphically: Would "many women" still swoon over Butler's rape of O'Hara if they knew that he urinated on her? When you're the victim of rape, you don't have much choice over what goes on.

6. Let us move on to femininity. Sommers never spells out exactly what she means by femininity. For guidance on this topic, we could turn to literature in social psychology which identifies

the important traits of femininity and which explores the social devaluation of the feminine (Eagly, 1987). However, it might be more revealing to turn to a different sort of "expert." By a lucky coincidence, I recently acquired a gem of a cultural artifact, a 1965 book entitled, *Always Ask a Man: Arlene Dahl's Key to Femininity,* written by a rather well-known actress and model of the 1960s, Arlene Dahl. I have learned a great deal from this femininity manifesto.

As you might guess from the title, one guiding theme of the book, and of the femininity it aims to promote, is utter deference to the opinions of men. Dahl instructs the female reader: "Look at Yourself Objectively (try to see yourself through a man's eyes)" (p. 2). In Dahl's view, the "truly feminine" woman works "instinctively" at pleasing men and making men feel important. "When [a man] speaks to her, she listens with rapt attention to every word" (p. 5). Dahl believes that every woman has the capacity to measure up to men's ideals of femininity. This is because "Every woman is an actress. (Admit it!) Her first role is that of a coquette. (If you have any doubts just watch a baby girl with her father)" (p. 6).

Dahl's book is laced with quotations from male celebrities who are treated as incontrovertible authorities on what women should be like. Yul Brynner, for example, wants women to be good listeners who are not particularly logical (p. 3). Richard Burton likes women who are "faintly giggly" (p. 3). Tony Perkins thinks that a "girl should act like a girl and not like the head of a corporation—even if she is" (p. 8). The most revealing observation comes from George Hamilton: "A woman is often like a strip of film—obliterated, insignificant—until a man puts a light behind her" (pp. 5–6).

Surprisingly, some of the traits advocated for women by these male celebrities are actually valuable traits; honesty, straightforwardness, maturity, ingenuity, understanding, dignity, generosity, and humor. These traits are not distinctively feminine, however, and that may be the reason why they quickly disappear from Dahl's discussion. The twin themes that resound throughout this femininity manual are that of cultivating one's physical attractiveness and slavishly deferring to men. Instead of a chapter on honesty; a chapter on dignity, and so on, the book features chapters on every aspect of bodily grooming and adornment, including a separate chapter on each of the four basic categories of Caucasian hair color: blonde, redhead, "brownette," and brunette.

The slavish deference to men is crucial, since the whole point of the enterprise is to get a man. Thus, Dahl explains in the introduction that this book is written to counteract a tendency for women to dress to please other women, and it is also not for "women who want to be beautiful for beauty's sake. Such beauty serves no purpose, other than self-satisfaction, if that can be considered a purpose" (pp. x–xi).

The quintessential prohibition involved in femininity seems to be this: "NEVER upstage a man. Don't try to top his joke, even if you have to bite your tongue to keep from doing it. Never launch loudly into your own opinion on a subject—whether it's petunias or politics. Instead, draw out his ideas to which you can gracefully add your footnotes from time to time" (p. 12). Dahl is less sanguine than Sommers that the role of motherhood fits comfortably into a feminine life; she advises, ". . . don't get so involved with your role of MOTHER that you forget to play WIFE" (p. 9). Once married, your own interests should never override your husband's interests, job, and even hobbies, and, "There should be nothing that takes precedence in your day's schedule over making yourself attractive and appealing for the man in your life," not even your "children's activities" (p. 175)!

Voila, femininity. Such servility shows the dubiousness of Sommers's claim that "a woman can be free of oppression and nevertheless feminine in the sense abhorred by many feminists" (1989a, 91).

7. Let us turn now to Sommer's overall philosophical defense of traditional marriage, family,

and femininity. Having asserted that most women value or want all of these traditions, Sommers charges feminist views with a serious defect: They either dismiss or disparage these popular feminine wants and values.[13] Sommers herself defers to these alleged views of most women as if they were as such authoritative: Because "most women" (as she alleges) want traditional marriage and family, therefore these practices must be better than any alternatives. It is important to note that Sommers does not argue that traditional marriage and so on, on balance, promote important moral values better than any feminist alternatives.[14] No comprehensive moral comparisons appear in her writings. Her argument begins (and ends, as I will argue) with an appeal to popular opinion.

8. Is Sommers right about what "most women" think? She refers to no studies, no representative samples whatsoever to support her generalizations. Whole categories of women are patently excluded from her reference group and are invisible in her writings. This is a fitting moment to mention the "L" word—and I don't mean "liberal." Obviously, no lesbians, unless seriously closeted, are among Sommers's alleged majority of women who want "a man," conventional marriage, or a traditional family.

Even among nonlesbians, [many] women these days do not want a *traditional* marriage or a *traditional* family. Some heterosexual women simply do not want to marry or to have children at all, and many others want *nontraditional* marriages and *nontraditional* families. Surveys show that this attitude, and not the preference for tradition alleged by Sommers, is actually in the majority. In one 1983 study, 63 percent of women surveyed expressed preferences for nontraditional family arrangements (Sapiro, 1990, 355). Sommers's factual claims are, thus, debatable.

Even apart from questions of popularity, the wants, values, and enjoyments which Sommers attributes to "most women" are frankly suspicious as an ensemble. Candlelit dinners do not combine easily with babies. Dashing lovers (extramarital) can be disastrous for a marriage. This list of wants and values seems to show a failure to separate what is idealized and mythic from what is (to put it very advisedly) authentic and genuinely possible in the daily reality of marital and family relationships over the long haul. To hear Sommers tell it, women are blandly unconcerned about wife-battering, incest, marital rape, or the profound economic vulnerability of the traditional non-incoming-earning wife. This is hard to believe. What is more likely is that, for many women, ". . . they got married and lived happily ever after," is only a fairy tale—especially for those who have been married for awhile. Even the most traditional of women, I am convinced, has some sense of the risks involved in traditional heterosexual relationships. As an old saying goes, "When two hearts beat as one, someone is dead."[15]

Sommers's list of women's wants and values is also woefully short. It suggests that this is *all* that "most women" want, that women's aspirations extend no farther than to being "feminine," getting a man—any man—and having babies. On the contrary, many women want meaningful and fulfilling work apart from childcare and domestic labor. Many women aspire to making a social contribution, or they have artistic impulses seeking expression, spiritual callings, deep friendships with other women, and abiding concerns for moral value and their own integrity.[16] One foundational motivation for feminism has always been the aim to overcome the *constraints* on women's genuinely wide-ranging aspirations posed by traditional marital and family arrangements.

9. What philosophical difference would it make if Sommers were right about women's wants and values in general? The popularity of an opinion is hardly an infallible measure of its empirical or moral credibility. Even popular opinions may be based on misinformation, unfounded rumor, and so on. Sommers ignores these possibilities and recommends that we defer to popular opinion on the basis of ". . . Mill's principle that there can be no appeal from a

majority verdict of those who have experienced two alternatives" (1989a, 89–90). Sommers is evidently suggesting that feminist critiques of traditional family, marriage, and femininity should be judged by whether or not they conform to the "majority verdict of those who have experienced" the relevant alternatives. Now, carefully understood, this is actually not such a bad idea. However, rather than supporting Sommers's deference to popular opinion, this principle repudiates it.

First, there are more than just "two" feminist alternatives to any of the traditions in question. Consider, for example, the traditionally married, heterosexual couple comprised of dominant, breadwinning male and domestic, childrearing female. Feminists have recommended various alternative family arrangements, including egalitarian heterosexual marriage, communal living, lesbian relationships, and single parenting when economic circumstances are favorable.[17] To decide the value of traditional marriage and family, one would have to try all the relevant alternatives—or at least *some* of them. And on Mill's view, merely experiencing alternatives is not enough; one must also be capable of "appreciating and enjoying" them (Mill, 1979, 9). If Sommers is right, however, most women want and choose traditional family, traditional marriage, and traditional femininity, and thus, do not either experience or enjoy living according to any feminist alternatives. Women such as they are not what Mill calls "competent judges" of the value of those traditions since "they know only their own side of the question" (p. 10). And it is only from the verdict of *competent judges* that Mill believes that "there can be no appeal" (p. 11).

Second, of the "competent judges," in Mill's sense that is, of the women who *have* experienced and enjoyed feminist alternatives to traditional marriage and family, most (I would wager) *prefer the feminist alternatives*. I am referring, among others, to women in lesbian relationships, and women in genuinely egalitarian heterosexual relationships. If I am right

about this, then by Mill's principle, we must reject "popular opinion" along with traditional marriage and the rest.

10. The truth of the matter is that in the end, Sommers does not rest her case on Mill's principle. Apparently without realizing that she changes her argument, she ends by appealing to something less vaunted than the majority verdict of those who have experienced and enjoyed *both* traditional family, etc., and various feminist alternatives. Her final court of appeal is simply to "what most people think," "common sense," and "tradition" itself (1989a, 95, 97). Sommers urges that "A moral philosophy that does not give proper weight to the customs and opinions of the community is presumptuous in its attitude and pernicious in its consequences" (1989a, 103). She speaks warmly of the Aristotelian conviction that "traditional arrangements have great moral weight and that common opinion is a primary source of moral truth" (1989a, 83). When it comes to tradition, Sommers would do well to consider Mill again. Mill often deferred to tradition, but it was not a deference from which he thought there was "no appeal," as he amply demonstrated in the important *indictment* of nineteenth century marital traditions on which he collaborated with Harriet Taylor (Mill & Taylor, 1970). (It would be interesting to know what "pernicious . . . consequences," to use Sommers' phrase, flowed from Mill's and Taylor's critique.)

Tradition is a fickle husband. He is constantly changing his mind. On the grounds of tradition, eighty years ago, Sommers would have opposed women's suffrage. One hundred and fifty years ago, she would have opposed women speaking in public (She would have had to do so in private!), opposed the rights of married women to property in their own names, opposed the abolition of slavery, and so on. She would have supported wife-battering since it was permitted by legal tradition—so long as the rod was no bigger around than the size of the husband's thumb.

Not only is tradition ever-changing, it is also plural, both within our own society and globally.

Which tradition shall we follow when there is more than one from which to choose? Islam is the world's most widely practiced religion. Shall we non-Islamic women heed the most globally numerous of our sisters' voices and don the veil, retire from public life, and allow husbands to marry up to four wives? Within our own society, marital traditions also vary. Shall we follow the traditions of orthodox Jewish and orthodox Catholic women and avoid all contraceptives? My maternal grandmother did so; she had fourteen births. At nine months per gestation, she spent ten and a half years of her life being pregnant. Although she lingered to the age of eighty-seven, she seemed even older than her age for the final sixteen, worn-out years in which I knew her. Doubtless, that too was part of her tradition.

Why suppose that there is special merit to any of the alternative traditions that we happen to have at this historical moment in this particular geopolitical location? Why suppose that any of our current traditions are better or more deserving of loyalty and support than the traditions toward which we are evolving? And how will we ever evolve if we remain deadlocked in loyalty to all of the traditions we happen to have today?

11. Sommers allows that our traditions may need reform and even recommends "piecemeal social engineering" to deal with "imperfections" in the family (1989a, 97)—although it is noteworthy that she never specifies what these imperfections are, and, in a different passage, she inconsistently calls upon American feminism to leave marriage and motherhood simply "untouched and unimpugned" (1989a, 91).[18] Nevertheless, she insists that her arguments are directed only against those radical feminists who seek the abolition of the family and the "radical reform of preferences, values, aspirations, and prejudices" (1990, 151, 148).

A serious concern to reform imperfections in the family should lead someone to consider the views of nonradical feminist reformers who also criticize marital and family traditions. Many feminists would be content with piecemeal family reform—so long as it was genuine reform (Thorne & Yalom, 1982; Okin, 1987, 1989). Anyway, this issue is a red herring. A dispute over the pace of reform does not show that radical feminist critiques of family traditions are wrong in substance. Most important, by allowing that change is *needed* in family traditions, Sommers effectively concedes that we should not automatically defer to tradition. To admit that reform of tradition is morally permissible is to reject tradition *per se* as an incontestable moral authority. The controversy can only be decided by directly evaluating the conditions of life established by marital and family traditions—and their alternatives.

12. Sommers has one final twist to her argument which we should consider. She notes briefly—all too briefly—that traditions "have *prima facie* moral force" so long as they are not "essentially unjust" (1989a, 97). Sommers does not explain what she means by "essential injustice." Just how much injustice makes a traditional practice "essentially unjust?"

Despite its vagueness, this concession to injustice is critically important. It makes the merit of Sommers's own appeal to tradition contingent on the essential noninjustice of the particular traditions in question. Sommers, however, provides no argument to establish that traditional marriage practices and so forth are not essentially unjust. Nor does she respond substantively to those feminist arguments which claim to locate important injustices in these traditional practices. She rejects all feminist criticisms of the traditional family because they do not coincide with "popular opinion," "common sense," or tradition. Traditional marriage and family are not essentially unjust, in Sommers's view, simply because most people allegedly do not *think* they are.

We seem to have come full circle. Sommers rejects feminist critiques of traditional marriage and so on because they are inconsistent with popular opinion, common sense, and tradition. Tradition is to be relied on, in turn, so long as it is not essentially unjust. But Sommers rejects feminist arguments to show injustices in marital and family traditions simply on the grounds that those arguments are inconsistent with popular opinion, common sense, and tradition itself. Sommers's defense of traditional marriage and family is, in the final analysis, circular and amounts to nothing more than simple *deference to tradition*—indeed, to particular traditions which are no longer so pervasive or popular as Sommers thinks.

13. One final concern: Sommers blames feminists for contributing to the growing divorce rate and the "disintegration of the traditional family."[19] However, feminism could only contribute to the divorce rate if married women ended their marriages as a result of adopting feminist ideas. If Sommers is right, however, in thinking that "most women" reject nonliberal feminist values, then nonliberal feminists could not be having a significant impact on the divorce rate. Sommers cannot have it both ways. Either feminism *is* significantly contributing to the growing divorce rate, in which case it must be in virtue of the wide appeal of feminist ideas about marriage and family, or feminist ideas do *not* have wide appeal, in which case they cannot be significantly contributing to the growing divorce rate.

14. To conclude: My overall assessment of Sommers's views on marriage, family, and femininity is grim.[20] Most important, Sommers rejects feminist views of marriage, family, and femininity ultimately on the basis of her own simple deference to (allegedly) popular opinion, common sense, and tradition. This deference is defensible only if feminist views about injustices in those traditions can be shown, on *independent* grounds, to be misguided—and Sommers never provides this independent argument.

NOTES

1. Sommers, 1988, 1989a, 1989b, and 1990.
2. Cited in Thorne & Yalom, 1982, 5.
3. Sommers repudiates the feminist literature which explores the value of mothering (e.g., Trebilcot, 1984) on the grounds that it "remains largely hostile to tra-

ditional familial arrangements." She also claims that this literature focuses only on an abstracted mother-child relationship, especially the mother-daughter relationship—a focus that "effectively excludes the male parent" (1989a, 92). Aside from inaccurately summarizing a body of literature, this latter comment, ironically, ignores the fact that under "traditional familial arrangements," the male parent plays a *negligible role* in day-to-day primary childcare, especially in a child's early years.

The comment also ignores the work of Dorothy Dinnerstein (1977) and, especially, of Nancy Chodorow (1978), which precisely urges *shared parenting* and a prominent role for the male parent. This work has been extremely influential and widely cited among feminists. I suspect, however, that shared parenting is not the way in which Sommers wants to include the male parent, since this arrangement is not "traditional" and it challenges the idea of a "primary gender role" that Sommers appears to support (1989a, 92). Sommers, herself, thus fails to clarify the role of the male parent in her account.

4. Sommers complains that feminist philosophers have not been entrusted by ordinary women with a mission of speaking on behalf of those ordinary women (1989b, B3). Sommers, however, appears to think that she is thus entrusted, since she does not hesitate to make claims about what "most women . . . prefer," what "women actually want," and what "most women *enjoy*" (1989a, 90).

5. The following classification scheme is my own. The categories are not meant to be mutually exclusive.

6. Quotations are, respectively, from: 1989a, 90; 1989a, 91; and 1990, 150.

7. Quotations are, respectively, from: 1989a, 90; 1989a, 89; and 1989b, B3.

8. Quotations are, respectively, from: 1989a, 90; 1989a, 91; 1990, 150, italics mine; 1989b, B2; and 1989a, 91.

9. Quotations are, respectively, from: 1989a, 90; 1989a, 90; 1989a, 90; and 1990, 150.

10. Richards, 1980, 341–342. Quoted in Sommers, 1989a, 90–91.

11. Some important early papers are anthologized in: Vetterling-Braggin et al., 1977, Part VI. Another important, relatively early study is Brownmiller, 1976.

12. In 1966, Richard Speck stunned the city of Chicago and the nation by raping, killing, and, in some cases, mutilating the bodies of eight out of nine nursing students who shared a house together on Chicago's South Side. The nurse who survived did so by hiding under a bed until Speck left the house after

having apparently lost count. That woman might well swoon over Scarlett O'Hara's rape, but it would not be a swoon of ecstasy.

13. 1989a, 88–91. Sommers writes: "It is a serious defect of American feminism that it concentrates its zeal on impugning femininity and feminine culture at the expense of the grass root fight against economic and social injustices to which women are subjected" (p. 90). American feminism has hardly neglected the fight against economic or social injustice against women. Apart from that, the *Philosopher's Index* back to 1970 contains no citations of writings by Sommers herself on "the economic and social injustices to which women are subjected." In the essays reviewed here, she does not even identify the injustices she has in mind.

14. Sommers does warn that "many women" who avoid motherhood find themselves lonely (1989a, 90), and she suggests that those who avoid or divorce themselves from the patriarchal family "often" suffer harm and "might" feel "betrayed by the ideology" which led them to this state (1989b, B3). These faintly threatening suggestions are left unexplained and unsupported.

15. I was reminded of this old saying by an article by Janyce Katz (1990, 88) in which Dagmar Celeste, then the "First Lady of Ohio," is quoted as mentioning it.

16. Raising children involves awesome moral responsibilities, as Sommers herself emphasizes when lamenting the increasing divorce rate. These profound moral responsibilities entail that we should not casually reinforce the cultural ideology which declares that the only hope of women's fulfillment in life depends on their *having* children. Sommers complains about divorce because of the harm it inflicts on children (1989a, 98–102), but she never cautions women to consider these moral obligations before marrying or having children in the first place.

17. Cf. Hunter College Women's Studies Collective, 1983, Ch. 9.

18. My worry is that Sommers's occasional, reasonable call for piecemeal family reform disguises a hidden agenda that aims to deadlock us in certain family traditions as we know them now (or knew them three decades ago). This appearance might be dispelled if she were to identify the imperfections she recognizes in the family.

19. 1989a, 82–83, 99–102. Sommers admits that "no reliable study has yet been made comparing children of divorced parents to children from intact families who [sic] parents do not get on well together." She claims cavalierly that "any such study would be compromised by some arbitrary measures of parental incompatibility and one could probably place little reliance on them" (1989a, 101). However, she ignores her own claims of limited evidence on this issue and argues as if it were fact that children of divorced parents are invariably worse off than if their parents had remained married.

When Sommers discusses the problem of divorce, she tends to assimilate the philosophical culprits onto one model: They are all wrong for disregarding "special duties" to family members, especially to children. This latter accusation is simply irrelevant in regard to feminists; no serious feminist literature suggests that responsibilities toward children should be disregarded.

20. Overall, her presentations are marred by ambiguities, inconsistencies, dubious factual claims, misrepresentations of feminist literature, and faulty arguments.

REFERENCES

Brownmiller, Susan. 1976. *Against Our Will: Men, Women and Rape*. New York: Bantam.

Chodorow, Nancy: 1978. *The Reproduction of Mothering*. Berkeley: University of California Press.

Dahl, Arlene. 1965. *Always Ask a Man: Arlene Dahl's Key to Femininity*. Englewood Cliffs, N.J.: Prentice-Hall.

Dinnerstein, Dorothy: 1977. *The Mermaid and the Minotaur: Sexual Arrangements and Human Malaise*. New York: Harper & Row.

Eagly, Alice. 1987. *Sex Differences in Social Behavior*. Hillsdale, N.J.: Erlbaum.

Hunter College Women's Studies Collective. 1983. *Women's Realities, Women's Choices*. New York: Oxford University Press.

Katz, Janyce. 1990. "Celestial Reasoning: Ohio's First Lady Talks About Love and Feminism." *Ms: The World of Women*, 1, 2 (September/October), p. 88.

Mill, John Stuart, 1979. *Utilitarianism*. George Sher, ed. Indianapolis: Hackett.

Mill, John Stuart and Harriet Taylor. 1970. *Essays on Sex Equality*. Alice S. Rossi, ed. Chicago: University of Chicago Press.

Okin, Susan Moller. 1987. "Justice and Gender." *Philosophy & Public Affairs*, 16 (Winter), pp. 42–72.

———. 1989. *Justice, Gender, and the Family*. New York: Basic Books.

Richards, Janet Radcliffe, 1980. *The Sceptical Feminist*. Harmondsworth: Penguin.

Sapiro, Virginia, 1990. *Women in American Society*. Mountain View, Calif.: Mayfield Publishing Co.

Sommers, Christina. 1988. "Should the Academy Support Academic Feminism?" *Public Affairs Quarterly*, 2, 3 (July), 97–120.

———. 1989a. "Philosophers Against the Family." In: George Graham and Hugh LaFollette, eds. *Person to Person*. Philadelphia: Temple University Press, 82–105.

———. 1989b. "Feminist Philosophers Are Oddly Unsympathetic to the Women They Claim to Rep-resent." *Chronicle of Higher Education*, October 11, pp. B2–B3.

———. 1990. "The Feminist Revelation," *Social Philosophy and Policy Center*, 8, 1 (Autumn), 141–158.

Thorne, Barrie, with Marilyn Yalom, eds. 1982. *Rethinking the Family*. New York: Longman.

Trebilcot, Joyce, ed. 1984. *Mothering: Essays In Feminist Theory*. Totowa, N.J.: Rowman and Allanheld.

Vetterling-Braggin, Mary, Frederick A. Elliston, and Jane English, eds. 1977. *Feminism and Philosophy*. Totowa, N.J.: Littlefield, Adams & Co.

Part VII

Postmodern Justice

29 The Postmodern Condition

JEAN-FRANÇOIS LYOTARD

THE OBJECT OF THIS STUDY is the condition of knowledge in the most highly developed societies. I have decided to use the word *postmodern* to describe that condition. The word is in current use on the American continent among sociologists and critics: it designates the state of our culture following the transformations which, since the end of the nineteenth century, have altered the game rules for science, literature, and the arts. The present study will place these transformations in the context of the crisis of narratives.

Science has always been in conflict with narratives. Judged by the yardstick of science, the majority of them prove to be fables. But to the extent that science does not restrict itself to stating useful regularities and seeks the truth, it is obliged to legitimate the rules of its own game. It then produces a discourse of legitimation with respect to its own status, a discourse called philosophy. I will use the term modern to designate any science that legitimates itself with reference to a metadiscourse of this kind making an explicit appeal to some grand narrative, such as the dialectics of Spirit, the hermeneutics of meaning, the emancipation of the rational or working subject, or the creation of wealth.[1] For example, the rule of consensus between the sender and addresse of a statement with truth-value is deemed acceptable if it is cast in terms of a possible unanimity between rational minds: this is the Enlightenment narrative, in which the hero of knowledge works toward a good ethico-political end—universal peace. As can be seen from this example, if a metanarrative implying a philosophy of history is used to legitimate knowledge, questions are raised concerning the validity of the institutions governing the social bond: these must be legitimated as well. Thus justice is consigned to the grand narrative in the same way as truth.

Simplifying to the extreme, I define *postmodern* as incredulity toward metanarratives. This incredulity is undoubtedly a product of progress in the sciences: but that progress in turn presupposes it. To the obsolescence of the metanarrative apparatus of legitimation corresponds, most notably the crisis of metaphysical philosophy and of the university institutions which in the past relied on it. The narrative function is losing its functors, its great hero, its great dangers, its great voyages, its great goal. It is being dispersed in clouds of narrative language elements—narrative, but also denotative, prescriptive, descriptive, and so on. Conveyed within each cloud are pragmatic valencies specific to its kind. Each of us lives at the intersection of many of these. However, we do not necessarily establish stable language

Jean-François Lyotard, The Postmodern Condition: A Report on Knowledge, *trans. Geoff Bennington and Brian Massumi (Minneapolis: University of Minnesota Press. 1984). Introduction and Sections 9 to 11, and 14, pp. xxiii–xxv. 31–47, 64–67. Originally published in France as* Le condition postmoderne: rapport sur le savoir, *copyright 1979 by Les Éditions de Minuit. English translation and Foreward copyright 1984 by the University of Minnesota. Reprinted by permission.*

combinations, and the properties of the ones we do establish are not necessarily communicable.

Thus the society of the future falls less within the province of a Newtonian anthropology (such as structuralism or systems theory) than a pragmatics of language particles. There are many different language games—a heterogeneity of elements. They only give rise to institutions in patches—local determinism.

The decision makers, however, attempt to manage these clouds of sociality according to input/output matrices, following a logic which implies that their elements are commensurable and that the whole is determinable. They allocate our lives for the growth of power. In matters of social justice and of scientific truth alike, the legitimation of that power is based on its optimizing the system's performance—efficiency. The application of this criterion to all of our games necessarily entails a certain level of terror, whether soft or hard: be operational (that is, commensurable) or disappear.

The logic of maximum performance is no doubt inconsistent in many ways, particularly with respect to contradiction in the socio-economic field: it demands both less work (to lower production costs) and more (to lessen the social burden of the idle population). But our incredulity is now such that we no longer expect salvation to rise from these inconsistencies, as did Marx.

Still, the postmodern condition is as much a stranger to disenchantment as it is the blind positivity of delegitimation. Where, after the metanarratives, can legitimacy reside? The operativity criterion is technological; it has no relevance for judging what is true or just. Is legitimacy to be found in consensus obtained through discussion, as Jürgen Habermas thinks? Such consensus does violence to the heterogeneity of language games. And invention is always born of dissension. Postmodern knowledge is not simply a tool of the authorities; it refines our sensitivity to differences and reinforces our ability to tolerate the incommensurable. . . .

In contemporary society and culture—post-industrial society, postmodern culture[2]—the question of the legitimation of knowledge is formulated in different terms. The grand narrative has lost its credibility, regardless of what mode of unification it uses, regardless of whether it is a speculative narrative or a narrative of emancipation.

The decline of narrative can be seen as an effect of the blossoming of techniques and technologies since the Second World War, which has shifted emphasis from the ends of action to its means; it can also be seen as an effect of the redeployment of advanced liberal capitalism after its retreat under the protection of Keynesianism during the period 1930–60, a renewal that has eliminated the communist alternative and valorized the individual enjoyment of goods and services.

Anytime we go searching for causes in this way we are bound to be disappointed. Even if we adopted one or the other of these hypotheses, we would still have to detail the correlation between the tendencies mentioned and the decline of the unifying and legitimating power of the grand narratives of speculation and emancipation.

It is, of course, understandable that both capitalist renewal and prosperity and the disorienting upsurge of technology would have an impact on the status of knowledge. But in order to understand how contemporary science could have been susceptible to those effects long before they took place, we must first locate the seeds of "delegitimation"[3] and nihilism that were inherent in the grand narratives of the nineteenth century.

First of all, the speculative apparatus maintains an ambiguous relation to knowledge. It shows that knowledge is only worthy of that name to the extent that it reduplicates itself ("lifts itself up," *hebt sich auf:* is sublated) by citing its own statements in a second-level discourse (autonymy) that functions to legitimate them. This is as much as to say that, in its immediacy, denotative discourse bearing on a certain referent (a living organism, a chemical property, a physical phenomenon, etc.) does not really know what it thinks it knows. Positive science is not a form of knowledge. And speculation feeds on its suppression. The Hegelian speculative narrative thus harbors a certain skepticism toward positive learning, as Hegel himself admits.[4]

A science that has not legitimated itself is not a true science; if the discourse that was meant to legitimate it seems to belong to a prescientific form of knowledge, like a "vulgar" narrative, it is demoted to the lowest rank, that of an ideology or instrument of power. And this always happens if the rules of the science game that discourse denounces as empirical are applied to science itself.

Take for example the speculative statement: "A scientific statement is knowledge if and only if it can take its place in a universal process of engendering." The question is: Is this statement knowledge as it itself defines it? Only if it can take its place in a universal process of engendering. Which it can. All it has to do is to presuppose that such a process exists (the Life of spirit) and that it is itself an expression of that process. This presupposition, in fact, is indispensable to the speculative language game. Without it, the language of legitimation would not be legitimate; it would accompany science in a nosedive into nonsense, at least if we take idealism's word for it.

But this presupposition can also be understood in a totally different sense, one which takes us in the direction of postmodern culture: we could say, in keeping with the perspective we adopted earlier, that this presupposition defines the set of rules one must accept in order to play the speculative game.[5] Such an appraisal assumes first that we accept that the "positive" sciences represent the general mode of knowledge and second, that we understand this language to imply certain formal and axiomatic presuppositions that it must always make explicit. This is exactly what Nietzsche is doing, though with a different terminology, when he shows that "European nihilism" resulted from the truth requirement of science being turned back against itself.[6]

There thus arises an idea of perspective that is not far removed, at least in this respect, from the idea of language games. What we have here is a process of delegitimation fueled by the demand for legitimation itself. The "crisis" of scientific knowledge, signs of which have been accumulating since the end of the nineteenth century, is not born of a chance proliferation of sciences, itself an effect of progress in technology and the expansion of capitalism. It represents, rather, an internal erosion of the legitimacy principle of knowledge. There is erosion at work inside the speculative game, and by loosening the weave of the encyclopedic net in which each science was to find its place, it eventually sets them free.

The classical dividing lines between the various fields of science are thus called into question—disciplines disappear, overlappings occur at the borders between sciences, and from these new territories are born. The speculative hierarchy of learning gives way to an immanent and, as it were, "flat" network of areas of inquiry, the respective frontiers of which are in constant flux. The old "faculties" splinter into institutes and foundations of all kinds, and the universities lose their function of speculative legitimation. Stripped of the responsibility for research (which was stifled by the speculative narrative), they limit themselves to the transmission of what is judged to be established knowledge, and through didactics they guarantee the replication of teachers rather than the production of researchers. This is the state in which Nietzsche finds and condemns them.[7]

The potential for erosion intrinsic to the other legitimation procedure, the emancipation apparatus flowing from the *Aufklärung* [Enlightenment], is no less extensive than the one at work within speculative discourse. But it touches a different aspect. Its distinguishing characteristic is that it grounds the legitimation of science and truth in the autonomy of interlocutors involved in ethical, social, and political praxis. As we have seen, there are immediate problems with this form of legitimation: the difference between a denotative statement with cognitive value and a prescriptive statement with practical value is one of relevance therefore of competence. There is nothing to prove that if a statement describing a real situation is true, it follows that a prescriptive statement based upon it (the effect of which will necessarily be a modification of that reality) will be just.

Take, for example, a closed door. Between "The door is closed" and "Open the door" there is no relation of consequence as defined in propositional logic. The two statements belong to two autonomous sets of rules defining different kinds of relevance, and therefore of competence. Here, the effect of dividing reason into cognitive or theoretical reason on the one hand, and practical reason on the other, is to attack the legitimacy of the discourse of science. Not directly, but indirectly, by revealing that it is a language game with its own rules (of which the a priori conditions of knowledge in Kant provide a first glimpse) and that it has no special calling to supervise the game of praxis (nor the game of aesthetics, for that matter). The game of science is thus put on a par with the others.

If this "delegitimation" is pursued in the slightest and if its scope is widened (as Wittgenstein does in his own way, and thinkers such as Martin Buber and Emmanuel Lévinas in theirs)[8] the road is then open for an important current of postmodernity: science plays its own game; it is incapable of legitimating the other language games. The game of prescription, for example, escapes it. But above all, it is incapable of legitimating itself, as speculation assumed it could.

The social subject itself seems to dissolve in this dissemination of language games. The social bond is linguistic, but is not woven with a single thread. It is a fabric formed by the intersection of at least two (and in reality an indeterminate number) of language games, obeying different rules. Wittgenstein writes: "Our language can be seen as an ancient city: a maze of little streets and squares, of old and new houses, and of houses with additions from various periods; and this surrounded by a multitude of new boroughs with straight regular streets and uniform houses."[9] And to

drive home that the principle of unitotality—or synthesis under the authority of a metadiscourse of knowledge—is inapplicable, he subjects the "town" of language to the old sorites paradox by asking" "how many houses or streets does it take before a town begins to be a town?"[10]

New languages are added to the old ones, forming suburbs of the old town: "the symbolism of chemistry and the notation of the infinitesimal calculus."[11] Thirty-five years later we can add to the list: machine languages, the matrices of game theory, new systems of musical notation, systems of notation for nondenotative forms of logic (temporal logics, deontic logics, modal logics), the language of the genetic code, graphs of phonological structures, and so on.

We may form a pessimistic impression of this splintering: nobody speaks all of those languages, they have no universal metalanguage, the project of the system-subject is a failure, the goal of emancipation has nothing to do with science, we are all stuck in the positivism of this or that discipline of learning, the learned scholars have turned into scientists, the diminished tasks of research have become compartmentalized and no one can master them all.[12] Speculative or humanistic philosophy is forced to relinquish its legitimation duties,[13] which explains why philosophy is facing a crisis wherever it persists in arrogating such functions and is reduced to the study of systems of logic or the history of ideas where it has been realistic enough to surrender them.[14]

Turn-of-the-century Vienna was weaned on this pessimism: not just artists such as Musil, Kraus, Hofmannsthal, Loos, Schönberg, and Broch, but also the philosophers Mach and Wittgenstein.[15] They carried awareness of and theoretical and artistic responsibility for delegitimation as far as it could be taken. We can say today that the mourning process has been completed. There is no need to start all over again. Wittgenstein's strength is that he did not opt for the positivism that was being developed by the Vienna Circle,[16] but outlined in his investigation of language games a kind of legitimation not based on performativity. That is what the postmodern world is all about. Most people have lost the nostalgia for the lost narrative. It in no way follows that they are reduced to barbarity. What saves them from it is their knowledge that legitimation can only spring from their own linguistic practice and communicational interaction. Science "smiling into its beard" at every other belief has taught them the harsh austerity of realism. . . .[17]

. . . Let us say at this point that the facts we have presented concerning the problem of the legitimation of knowledge today are sufficient for our purposes. We no longer have recourse to the grand narratives—we can resort neither to the dialectic of Spirit nor even to the emancipation of humanity as a validation for postmodern scientific discourse. But as we have just seen, the little narrative remains the quintessential form of imaginative invention, most particularly in science.[18] In addition, the principle of consensus as a criterion of validation seems to be inadequate. It has two formulations. In the first, consensus is an agreement between men, defined as knowing intellects and free wills, and is obtained through dialogue. This is the form elaborated by Habermas, but his conception is based on the validity of the narrative of emancipation. In the second, consensus is a component of the system, which manipulates it in order to maintain and improve its performance.[19] It is the object of administrative procedures, in Luhmann's sense. In this case, its only validity is as an instrument to be used toward achieving the real goal, which is what legitimates the system—power. . . .

From the beginning of this study, I have emphasized the differences (not only formal, but also pragmatic) between the various language games, especially between denotative, or knowledge, games and prescriptive, or action, games. The pragmatics of science is centered on denotative utterances, which are the foundation upon which it builds institutions of learning (institutes, centers, universities, etc.). But its postmodern development brings a decisive "fact" to

the fore: even discussions of denotative statements need to have rules. Rules are not denotative but prescriptive utterances, which we are better off calling metaprescriptive utterances to avoid confusion (they prescribe what the moves of language games must be in order to be admissible). The function of the differential or imaginative or paralogical activity of the current pragmatics of science is to point out these metaprescriptives (science's "presuppositions")[20] to petition the players to accept different ones. The only legitimation that can make this kind of request admissible is that it will generate ideas, in other words, new statements.

Social pragmatics does not have the "simplicity" of scientific pragmatics. It is a monster formed by the interweaving of various networks of heteromorphous classes of utterances (denotative, prescriptive, performative, technical, evaluative, etc.). There is no reason to think that it would be possible to determine metaprescriptives common to all of these language games or that a revisable consensus like the one in force at a given moment in the scientific community could embrace the totality of metaprescriptions regulating the totality of statements circulating in the social collectivity. As a matter of fact, the contemporary decline of narratives of legitimation—be they traditional or "modern" (the emancipation of humanity, the realization of the Idea)—is tied to the abandonment of this belief. It is its absence for which the ideology of the "system," with its pretensions to totality, tries to compensate and which it expresses in the cynicism of its criterion of performance.

For this reason, it seems neither possible, nor even prudent, to follow Habermas in orienting our treatment of the problem of legitimation in the direction of a search for universal consensus[21] through what he calls *Diskurs,* in other words, a dialogue of argumentation.[22]

This would be to make two assumptions. The first is that it is possible for all speakers to come to agreement on which rules or metaprescriptions are universally valid for language games, when it is clear that language games are heteromorphous, subject to heterogeneous sets of pragmatic rules.

The second assumption is that the goal of dialogue is consensus. But as I have shown in the analysis of the pragmatics of science, consensus is only a particular state of discussion, not its end.

This double observation (the heterogeneity of the rules and the search for dissent) destroys a belief that still underlies Habermas's research, namely, that humanity as a collective (universal) subject seeks its common emancipation through the regularization of the "moves" permitted in all language games and that the legitimacy of any statement resides in contributing to that emancipation.[23]

It is easy to see what function this recourse plays in Habermas's argument against Luhmann. *Diskurs* is his ultimate weapon against the theory of the stable system. The cause is good, but the argument is not.[24] Consensus has become an outmoded and suspect value. But justice as a value is neither outmoded nor suspect. We must thus arrive at an idea and practice of justice that is not linked to that of consensus.

A recognition of the heteromorphous nature of language games is a first step in that direction. This obviously implies a renunciation of terror, which assumes that they are isomorphic and tries to make them so. The second step is the principle that any consensus on the rules defining a game and the "moves" playable within it *must* be local, in other words, agreed on by its present players and subject to eventual cancellation. The orientation then favors a multiplicity of finite meta-arguments, by which I mean argumentation that concerns metaprescriptives and is limited in space and time.

This orientation corresponds to the course that the evolution of social interaction is currently taking; the temporary contract is in practice supplanting permanent institutions in the professional, emotional, sexual, cultural, family, and international domains, as well as in political affairs. This evolution is of course ambiguous: the temporary contract is favored by the system due to its greater flexibility, lower cost, and the creative turmoil of its accompanying motivations—all of these factors contribute to increased operativity. In any case, there is no question here of proposing a "pure" alternative to the system: we all now know, that an attempt at an alternative of that kind would end up resembling the system it was meant to replace. We should be happy that the tendency toward the temporary contract is ambiguous: it is not totally subordinated to the goal of the system, yet the system tolerates it. This bears witness to the existence of another goal within the system: knowledge of language games as such and the decision to assume responsibility for their rules and effects.

We are finally in a position to understand how the computerization of society affects this problematic. It could become the "dream" instrument for controlling and regulating the market system, extended to include knowledge itself and governed exclusively by the performativity principle. In that case, it would inevitably involve, the use of terror. But it could also aid groups discussing metaprescriptives by supplying them with the information they usually lack for making knowledgeable decisions. The line to follow for computerization to take the second of these two paths is, in principle, quite simple: give the public free access to the memory and data banks.[25] Language games would then be games of perfect information at any given moment. But they would also be non-zero-sum games, and by virtue of that fact discussion would never risk fixating in a position of minimax equilibrium because it had exhausted its stakes. For the stakes would be knowledge (or information, if you will) and the reserve of knowledge—language's reserve of possible utterances—is inexhaustible. This sketches the outline of a politics that would respect both the desire for justice and the desire for the unknown.

NOTES

1. These grand narratives are what Lyotard calls "metanarratives," philosophical stories which legitimate all other discourse.

2. Certain scientific aspects of postmodernism are inventoried by Ihab Hassan in "Culture, Indeterminacy, and Immanence: Margins of the (Postmodern) Age," *Humanitites in Society,* 1 (1978): 51–85.

3. Claus Mueller uses the expression "a process of delegitimation" in *The Politics of Communication* (New York: Oxford University Press, 1973), p. 164.

4. "Road of doubt . . . road of despair . . . skepticism," writes Hegel in the preface to the *Phenomenology of Spirit* to describe the effect of the speculative drive on natural knowledge.

5. For fear of encumbering this account, I have postponed until a later study the exposition of this group of rules.

6. Nietzsche, "Der europäische Nihilismus" (MS. N VII 3): "der Nihilism, ein normaler Zustand" (MS. W II 1): "Kritik der Nihilism" (MS. W VII 3): "Zum Plane" (MS. W II 1), in *Nietzshes Werke kritische Gesamtausgabe,* vol. 7, pts. 1 and 2 (1887–89) (Berlin: De Gruyter, 1970). These texts have been the object of a commentary by K. Ryjik, *Nietzsche, le manuscrit de Lenzer Heide* (typescript, Départment de philosophie, Université de Paris VIII [Vincennes]).

7. "On the future of our educational institutions," in *Complete Works,* vol. 3.

8. Martin Buber, *Ich und Du* (Berlin: Schocken Verlag, 1922) [Eng. trans. Ronald G. Smith, *I and Thou* (New York: Charles Scribner's Sons, 1937)], and *Dialogisches Leben* (Zürich: Müller, 1947); Emmanuel Lévinas, *Totalité et Infinité* (Lay Haye: Nijhoff, 1961) [Eng. trans. Alphonso Lingis, *Totality and Infinity: An Essay on Exteriority* (Pittsburgh: Duquesne University Press, 1969)], and "Martin Buber und die Erkenntnish theorie" (1958), in *Philosophen des 20. Jahrhunderts* (Stuttgart: Kohlhammer, 1963).

9. *Philosophical Investigations,* sec. 18, p. 8 [by Ludwig Wittgenstein, trans. G. E. M. Anscombe (New York: Macmillan, 1958)].

10. Ibid.

11. Ibid.

12. See for example, "La taylorisation de la recherche," in *(Auto) critique de la science,* pp. 291–3. And especially D. J. de Solla Price. *Little Science, Big Science* (New York: Columbia University Press, 1963), who emphasizes the split between a small number of highly productive researchers (evaluated in terms of publication) and a large mass of researchers with low productivity. The number of the latter grows as the square of the former, so that the number of high productivity researchers only really increases every twenty years. Price concludes that science considered as a social entity is "undemocratic" (p. 59) and that "the eminent scientist" is a hundred years ahead of "the minimal one" (p. 56).

13. See J. T. Desanti, "Sur le rapport traditional des sciences et de la philosophie," in *La Philosophie silencieuse, ou critique des philosophies de la science* (Paris: Seuil, 1975).

14. The reclassification of academic philosophy as one of the human sciences in this respect has a significance far beyond simply professional concerns. I do not think that philosophy as legitimation is condemned to disappear, but it is possible that it will not be able to carry out this work, or at least advance it, without revising its ties to the university institution. See on this matter the preamble to the *Projet d'un institut polytechnique de philosophie* (typescript, Départment de philosophie, Université de Paris VIII, 1979).

15. See Allan Janik and Stephan Toulmin, *Wittgenstein's Vienna* (New York: Simon & Schuster, 1973), and J. Piel (ed.) "Vienne début d'un siècle," *Critique,* 330–40 (1975).

16. See Jürgen Habermas, "Dogmatismus, Vernunft unt Entscheidung—Zu Theorie und Praxis in der verwissenschaftlichen Zivilisation" (1963), in *Theorie und Praxis [Theory and Practice,* abr. edn of 4th German edn. trans. John Viertel (Boston: Beacon Press, 1971)].

17. "Science Smiling into its Beard" is the title of chap. 72, vol. 1 of Musil's *The Man Without Qualities.* Cited and discussed by J. Bouveresse, "La Problématique du sujet".

18. It has not been possible within the limits of this study to analyze the form assumed by the return of narrative in discourses of legitimation. Examples are: the study of open systems, local determinism, antimethod—in general, everything that I group under the name *paralogy.*

19. Nora and Minc, for example, attribute Japan's success in the field of computers to an "intensity of social consensus" that they judge to be specific to Japanese society (*L'Informatisation de la Société,* p. 4). They write in their conclusion, "The dynamics of extended social computerization leads to a fragile society: such a society is constructed with a view to facilitating consensus, but already presupposes its existence, and comes to a standstill if that consensus cannot be realized" (p. 125). Y. Stourdzé, "Les Etats-Unis", emphasizes the fact that the current tendency to deregulate, destabilize, and weaken administration is encouraged by society's loss of confidence in the State's performance capability.

20. This is at least one way of understanding this term, which comes from Ducrot's problematic, *Dire*.

21. *Legitimationsprobleme*, passim, especially pp. 21–2: "Language functions in the manner of a transformer . . . changing cognitions into propositions needs and feelings into normative expectations (commands, values). This transformation produces the far-reaching distinction between the subjectivity of intention and willing, of pleasure and unpleasure on the one hand, and expressions and norms with a *pretension to universality* on the other. Universality signifies the objectivity of knowledge and the legitimacy of prevailing norms: both assume the community constitutive of lived social experience." We see that by formulating the problematic in this way, the question of legitimacy is fixated on one type of reply, universality. This on the one hand presupposes that the legitimation of the subject of knowledge is identical to that of the subject of action (in opposition to Kant's critique, which dissociates conceptual universality, appropriate to the former, and ideal universality, or "supersensible nature," which forms the horizon of the latter, on the other hand), and maintains that consensus (*Gemeinschaft*) is the only possible horizon for the life of humanity.

22. Ibid., p. 20. The subordination of the meta-prescriptives of prescription (i.e. the normalization of laws) to *Diskurs* [Discourse] is explicit, for example, on p. 144: "The normative pretension to validity is itself cognitive in the sense that it always assumes it could be accepted in a rational discussion."

23. Garbis Kortian, *Métacritique* (Paris: Editions de Minuit, 1979) [Eng. trans. John Raffan, *Metacritique: The Philosophical Argument of Jürgen Habermas* (Cambridge: Cambridge University Press, 1980)], pt. 5, examines this enlightenment aspect of Habermas's thought. See by the same author, "Le Discours philosophique et son objet," *Critique*, 384 (1979): 407–19.

24. See J. Poulain ("Vers une pragmatique nucléaire"), and for a more general discussion of the pragmatics of Searle and Gehlen, see J. Poulain, "Pragmatique de la parole et pragmatique de la vie," *Phi zéro* 7, no. 1 (Université de Montréal, September 1978): 5–50.

25. See Tricot et al., *Informatique et libertés*, government report (La Documentation française, 1975); L. Joinet, "Les 'pièges liberaticides' de l'informatique," *Le Monde dipolomatique*, 300 (March 1979): these traps (pièges) are "the application of the technique of 'social profiles' to the management of the mass of the population; the logic of security produced by the automatization of society." See too the documents and analysis in *Interférences*, 1 and 2 (Winter 1974–Spring 1975), the theme of which is the establishment of popular networks of multimedia communication. Topics treated include: amateur radios (especially their role in Quebec during the FLQ affair of October 1970 and that of the "Front commun" in May 1972); community radios in the United States and Canada; the impact of computers on editorial work in the press; pirate radios (before their development in Italy); administrative files, the IBM monopoly, computer sabotage. The municipality of Yverdon (Canton of Vaud), having voted to buy a computer (operational in 1981), enacted a certain number of rules: exclusive authority of the municipal council to decide which data are collected, to whom and under what conditions they are communicated; access for all citizens to all data (on payment); the right of every citizen to see the entries on his file (about 50), to correct them and address a complaint about them to the municipal council and if need be to the Council of State; the right of all citizens to know (on request) which data concerning them is communicated and to whom (*La Semaine media* 18, 1 March 1979, 9).

Postmodern Argumentation and Post-postmodern Liberalism

JEFFREY REIMAN

The Paradox of Postmodernism

MODERNISM IS, ROUGHLY SPEAKING, the Enlightenment belief in a single unified rational perspective, founded on some indubitable evidence given in human experience—either innate concepts à la Descartes and the rationalists or sensations à la Locke and the empiricists—and elaborated according to reliable logical rules. This view was first attacked for its "foundationalism." Philosophers such as Nietzsche, Dewey, Heidegger, and the later Wittgenstein denied that there is any indubitable given upon which truth can be founded. There is no experience, no testimony of the senses or of reason, that blazons forth the undeniable truth. Rather, the "given" is, so to speak, constructed—which is to say, not given to us, but made by us. Some experience or other evidence is interpreted as this or that with this or that epistemological status, on the basis of beliefs that one already has about, say, space or mathematics or sense perception or the nature of what is ultimately real. Postmodernism is an intensification of this attack, with a distinctive political spin.

The intensification takes the following form. If there is no given, interpretation is "fundamental" (not, of course, in the sense of a new foundational given, rather quite the reverse, in the sense of something beneath or behind which we cannot get, something that stands eternally between us and any foundational given). Interpretation is fundamental in the sense that it is the furthest down we can ever get.[1] If interpretation is as far as we can ever get, then every experience is part of a tapestry (textile, text) of beliefs against which it gets its interpretation. And the beliefs themselves are only what they are for us as a result of interpretation of their meaning in light of other beliefs, and other interpretations, and so on.

Accordingly, there can never be just one interpretation of anything. This is sometimes exaggerated into the claim that there are unlimited valid interpretations of everything, a claim that would make it impossible to write a single sentence, since one would have no reason for choosing one string of words rather than another to express one's thoughts! The more modest claim is enough, however, to ground the distinctive postmodern strategy of *deconstruction*. Any supposedly canonical interpretation can be shown to have been purchased by the arbitrary exclusion of other possible ones. There can only be a canonical interpretation if some meaning in a text has been taken as if it were an unquestioned given from which the canonical interpretation then follows. The deconstructer finds the meaning that has been taken as if simply given and shows that it is in fact only one interpretation among other possible ones in view of the "textily" way in which it is woven together with other beliefs.

From Critical Moral Liberalism *by Jeffrey Reiman (1997), pp. 53–56, 67–69. Reprinted by permission of the publisher, Rowman & Littlefield.*

Then, taking a different meaning than the supposedly given one as her starting point, the deconstructer shows that other interpretation of the whole text can be spun. Such alternative interpretations must still meet the normal standards for successful interpretation, namely, plausibility, fit with the text, and so on. This is not the "anything goes" that is sometimes associated with deconstructive technique. Rather, the canonical interpretation is deconstructed by means of showing its illicit appeal to sheer given meanings, and the way in which it has been promoted by excluding other possible plausible interpretations.

Related to this technique is the political dimension of postmodernism. Much as any canonical interpretation is necessarily based on excluding alternative possible interpretations, any universal vision is based on excluding what doesn't fit by defining it as "other," "lesser," "lower," "bad," "crazy," "primitive," and so forth. Consequently, Enlightenment universalism based on, say, the shared rationality of human beings reflects (in various versions of the critique) the definition of rationality by exclusion of deviants, or women, or third-world people. Or, at the very least, the establishment of the universal standard becomes a tool or weapon by means of which some can be defined as second rate because they are held not to share the prevailing trait, or not to embody it completely, or the like. Thus, for example, Zygmunt Bauman, in his *Postmodern Ethics*, describes the moral universalism of the modern era "as but a thinly disguised declaration of intent to embark on *Gleichschaltung,* on an arduous campaign to smother the differences."[2] With this, deconstruction becomes a political weapon in defense of the people who have been oppressed because their natures or ways have been excluded from the universal standard—as the means to define that very standard.

Here enters the paradox: The critique of universal standards because they exclude certain individuals or groups of individuals is a critique of

those standards for not being universal enough! Consequently, rather than abandoning or opposing universalism, the critique is itself based on an implicit universal valuation, albeit one that aims to be more inclusive than the ones critiqued.

In short, what postmodernism needs, what virtually every postmodern writer writes as if he or she had, but in fact does not have, is a universal standard for valuing human beings that is compatible with the postmodern critique of universals. I will argue that such a universal can be found and can be defined while keeping to postmodernism's own critical requirements of argumentation.

The Requirements of Postmodern Argumentation

If postmodernism understands itself as (*a*) a form of antifoundationalism and (*b*) a protest against the exclusion of certain human individuals and/or groups from the universal measure of full moral standing, then certain things follow about the way arguments must be made if they are to be acceptable to postmodernists. First of all, arguments must be explicitly based on assumptions actually held by those to whom they are addressed (rather than appealing to foundational givens). Second, arguments must be addressed to all human beings. Putting the two together, arguments must start from assumptions that are shared by all human beings. Arguments must be *universal* in their aim and *ad hominem* in their logical structure.

Actually, the second condition is already suggested by antifoundationalism. If there is no indubitable given, if all starting points are, so to speak, created by interpretation in light of other beliefs, then there is no Archimedean point from which all of a person's beliefs can be shown true or false. Consequently, all arguments must proceed from beliefs that people already hold, which is to say, they must be ad hominem.

Two examples from different contemporary philosophical directions will show the prevalence of ad hominem argumentation in present-day thought. Consider, for example, Rawls's political liberalism, which starts openly by appeal to beliefs held by participants in liberal democratic cultures, assumes explicitly that even within this framework there will be irreconcilable disagreements among reasonable people on fundamental metaphysical and moral beliefs, and proceeds to argue for its very modest liberalism from the hopefully actual overlapping consensus among those fundamental views that presumably permit allegiance to liberal ideals.[3] Consider, for a quite different example, the approach of Habermas's "discourse ethics," which starts from the presuppositions of rational argument aimed at justifying moral norms. Since the implicit aim of such argument is rational persuasion, and since rational persuasion is uncoerced assent in the face of open argumentation and full information, those who engage in justification can be taken as implicitly committed to seeking uncoerced and fully informed assent to their proposals.[4] Accordingly, one can justify only moral norms to which all can freely and informedly consent—the result being not very far from contractarianism of the Rawlsian sort.

There can be postmodern universals if there are ad hominem arguments that can appeal to assumptions necessarily made by all human beings. However, the demand that arguments must appeal to assumptions that all human beings can be taken to share surely seems impossible in the condition of postmodernism, with its objections to universalism and its emphasis on irreducible differences. But the situation is more hopeful than it appears at first, for postmodernists do assume that human beings are rational insofar as postmodernists speak of and to human beings as users of language, interpreters of texts, bearers of culture, and so on—all of which require rational operations. I shall argue that the assumption that human beings are rational leads to other beliefs, which form the basis for a universal moral principle. . . .

Habermas maintains that anyone who engages in rational justification to others implicitly accepts rational argument's commitment to uncoerced and informed assent from its audience. On these grounds, Habermas contends that the arguer is committed to treating the other according to norms to which the other can uncoercedly and informedly assent.[5] The problem, however, is that, even if the arguer presupposes commitment to persuasion by uncoerced consent, *nothing requires him to shape his actions by the conditions of interpersonal argument.* Put otherwise, even if there are morally laden commitments built into justification to others, these commitments do not require people (*a*) to engage in justification in the first place or (*b*) to conform their actions to their justifications if they do so engage. Requirements (*a*) and (*b*) are separate substantive moral requirements, not provided for by the conditions of justification themselves. Thus Habermas's theory can have no moral claim on anyone who does not believe that he must justify his actions to others before acting or that he must act only in ways that he can justify to others.

The needed substantive moral requirements are provided by . . . the notion that wholehearted recognition of people as rational authority-claiming subjects requires that we allow them to form their own judgments and that we refrain from treating them according to judgments they do not themselves make—except where necessary to assure that no one is so treated. Here, then, we derive the obligation to conform to the conditions of argument, regarding both beliefs and actions, from recognition of, and respect for, the nature of human beings as rational subjects.

In *Political Liberalism*,[6] Rawls defends a version of liberalism that is political both in its subject and in its justification. Its subject is the basic structure of society (the main political, economic, and social institutions), thus leaving large areas of "private" or "civil" life subject to citizens' personally held ideals. As for justification, Rawls's liberalism is put forth as a "freestanding view."[7] By this Rawls means that it is not based on a comprehensive philosophical, religious, or moral doctrine that aims to determine all or most of what is valuable in life. Thus it is unlike Mill's liberalism, which was founded on the comprehensive doctrine of utilitarianism, and unlike Kant's, which was founded on his comprehensive doctrine of pure reason. To establish his liberalism as a freestanding view, Rawls hopes to avoid taking a position on any metaphysical issues by starting instead from an idea he finds embedded in our democratic culture: the idea "of society as a fair system of social cooperation between free and equal persons."[8] This way, Rawls's political liberalism is meant to appeal to the holders of a wide range of irreconcilable though reasonable comprehensive doctrines—religious, philosophical, and moral—as long as they can find within their particular doctrines some reasons to join an "overlapping consensus" on the ideas distinctive to liberal democratic culture. As he has recently summarized it in replying to Habermas,

> The central idea is that political liberalism moves within the category of the political and leaves philosophy as it is. It leaves untouched all kinds of doctrines religious, metaphysical, and moral, with their long traditions of development and interpretation. Political philosophy proceeds apart from all such doctrines, and presents itself in its own terms as freestanding. Hence, it cannot argue its case by invoking any comprehensive doctrines, or by criticizing or rejecting them, so long of course as those doctrines are reasonable, politically speaking. When attributed to persons, the two basic elements of the conception of the reasonable are, first, a willingness to propose fair terms of social cooperation that others as free and equal also might endorse, and to act on these terms, provided others do, even contrary to one's own interest; and, second, a recognition of the burdens of judgment [grounds for expecting that reasonable people will differ irreconcilably in their comprehensive doctrines] and accepting their consequences for one's attitude (including toleration) toward other comprehensive doctrines.[9]

As for the notion of "citizens as reasonable," it is drawn "from the public political culture of a democratic society."[10]

The problem here is that if the concept of the reasonable only holds for those who share a democratic culture, then those who do not share that culture—though they live within its midst as say, Ku Klux Klanners or other extremists—cannot be said to be unreasonable, only different. Then, the upholders of democratic liberal politics cannot say that the dissenters are wrong, only different. And that means that the relation between the democratic liberal state and the dissenters, particularly when the state uses force to repress the dissenters' "principled" violence, is strictly a power relation rather than a moral one. The dissenters cannot be said to have failed in an obligation owed to the democratic liberal citizens, since the claim for that obligation goes no further than the shared beliefs of those citizens.

Put more generally, a liberal political theory that aims to be "political not metaphysical"[11] cannot generate a moral obligation for those who do not share its liberal political culture. Indeed, even those who do share that political culture only *believe* they are obligated. They are *truly* obligated only if liberal political values are truly worthy of allegiance independent of any comprehensive doctrine and/or if the comprehensive doctrines that teach them that liberal values are worthy are true. However, as a political doctrine, Rawls's theory eschews appeal to, or even judgment about, its own truth (Rawls will only call it reasonable)[12] or the truth of the comprehensive doctrines held by citizens. Thus, political liberalism cannot generate a moral obligation to its own liberal values. It must rest content with the hope that the citizens will fill this in for themselves.

The needed moral obligation is provided by . . . the notion that it is most appropriate to the nature of rational beings to treat them only according to the judgments they are prepared to make. Then, it is wrong not to be reasonable in just the way that Rawls and democratic culture have defined it. And there is a moral obligation to be reasonable that goes beyond subscribing to reasonable comprehensive doctrines supportive of reasonable liberal political values. It is an obligation on all rational beings, including the extremists in, but not of, "the public political culture of a democratic society." Of course, this would make Rawls's theory, not just political, but ever so slightly metaphysical.[13]

NOTES

This chapter is a revised version of an article originally published in the *Canadian Journal of Philosophy*, supplementary volume 21: *On the Relevance of Metaethics: New Essays on Metaethics*, ed. J. Couture and K. Nielsen (1996): 251–72. I am indebted to Joseph Flay, emeritus professor of philosophy at Pennsylvania State University, and Jonathan Loesberg, professor of literature at American University, for numerous helpful comments, many of which I have incorporated into this chapter.

1. In *Speech and Phenomena*, Jacques Derrida gives an argument for nongivenness of meaning and thus for the fundamentality of interpretation from within phenomenology itself. He does so by playing Husserl's *Phenomenology of Internal Time-Consciousness* (trans. James Churchill [Bloomington, Ind.: Indiana University Press, 1964; originally published 1928]) off against Husserl's own theory of the intuitive givenness of linguistic meaning. The latter requires there to be an instantaneous grasp of the meaning of a term, while the former shows that there is nothing in consciousness that is instantaneous. Everything in consciousness is elapsing in time, and that implies that the appearance of an instantaneous grasp of meaning is really the product of a gathering up of flowing elements of experience into some meaningful totality, which is to say, interpretation. Nor should the term "elements" here be taken as implying yet other instantaneous givens, since that too is denied by the elapsing nature of consciousness. As far down as we go, all we get are interpretations. See Jacques Derrida, *Speech and Phenomena, and Other Essays on Husserl's Theory of Signs* (Evanston, Ill.: Northwestern University Press, 1973).

2. Zygmunt Bauman, *Postmodern Ethics* (Oxford: Blackwell, 1993), p. 13.

3. John Rawls, *Political Liberalism* (New York: Columbia University Press, 1993).

4. See Jürgen Habermas, "Discourse Ethics," in his *Moral Consciousness and Communicative Action* (Cambridge, Mass.: Massachusetts Institute of Technology Press, 1990), pp. 43–115.

5. See Habermas, "Discourse Ethics."

6. See Rawls, *Political Liberalism*.

7. Ibid., pp. 12–13, inter alia.

8. Ibid., p. 9, inter alia.

9. John Rawls, "Reply to Habermas," *Journal of Philosophy* 92, no. 3 (March 1995): 134 (I have omitted Rawls's references).

10. Ibid., 135.

11. Rawls, *Political Liberalism*, p. 10; see also Rawls, "Justice as Fairness: Political Not Metaphysical," *Philosophy and Public Affairs* 14 (Summer 1985): 223–51.

12. "[P]olitical liberalism, rather than referring to its political conception of justice as true, refers to it as reasonable instead." Rawls, *Political Liberalism*, p. xx.

13. Actually, I think that this would vastly improve Rawls's theory and that it is in any event necessary at other points in the theory as well. Consider the fact that the abortion controversy needs a solution within the nonmetaphysical framework of political liberalism. Rawls is quite sure this is possible, as he points out in a lengthy footnote:

> As an illustration, consider the troubled question of abortion. Suppose . . . that we consider the question in terms of three important political values: the due respect for human life, the ordered reproduction of political society over time, including the family in some form, and finally the equality of women as equal citizens. (There are, of course, other important political values besides these.) Now I believe *any reasonable balance of these three political values will give a woman a duly qualified right to decide whether or not to end her pregnancy during the first trimester.* The reason for this is that at this early stage of pregnancy the political value of the equality of women is overriding, and this right is required to give it substance and force. (Rawls, *Political Liberalism*, p. 243, n. 32 [emphasis mine])

But note right away that Rawls's conclusion about abortion only follows on the assumption that a first-trimester fetus is not among those equal persons who are to be protected by the laws of a liberal state (otherwise, the political value of women's equality would not be overriding). This is clearly a metaphysical, not merely a political, claim.

31 An Encounter between Feminism and Postmodernism

NANCY FRASER AND LINDA J. NICHOLSON

Feminism and postmodernism have emerged as two of the most important political-cultural currents of the last decade. So far, however, they have kept an uneasy distance from one another. Indeed, so great has been their mutual wariness that there have been remarkably few extended discussions of the relations between them.[1]

Initial reticences aside, there are good reasons for exploring the relations between feminism and postmodernism. Both have offered deep and far-reaching criticisms of the institution of philosophy. Both have elaborated critical perspectives on the relation of philosophy to the larger culture. And, most central to the concerns of this essay, both have sought to develop new paradigms of social criticism which do not rely on traditional philosophical underpinnings. Other differences notwithstanding, one could say that during the last decade feminists and postmodernists have worked independently on a common nexus of problems: They have tried to rethink the relation between philosophy and social criticism so as to develop paradigms of criticism without philosophy.

The two tendencies have proceeded from opposite directions. On the one hand, postmodernists have focused primarily on the philosophy side of the problem. They have begun by elaborating antifoundational metaphilosophical perspectives and from there have drawn conclusions about the shape and character of social criticism. For feminists, on the other hand, the question of philosophy has always been subordinate to an interest in social criticism. Consequently, they have begun by developing critical political perspectives and from there have drawn conclusions about the status of philosophy. As a result of this difference in emphasis and direction, the two tendencies have ended up with complementary strengths and weaknesses. Postmodernists offer sophisticated and persuasive criticisms of foundationalism and essentialism, but their conceptions of social criticism tend to be anemic. Feminists offer robust conceptions of social criticism, but they tend at times to lapse into foundationalism and essentialism.

Thus, each of the two perspectives suggests some important criticisms of the other. A postmodernist reflection on feminist theory

This essay has previously appeared in Communication, *Vol. 10, Nos. 3 and 4, 1988, pp. 345–366;* Theory, Culture and Society, *Vol. 5, Nos. 2 and 3, June 1988, pp. 373–394;* Universal Abandon? The Politics of Postmodernism, *ed. Andrew Ross (Minneapolis: University of Minnesota Press, 1988) pp. 83–104;* The Institution of Philosophy; A Discipline in Crisis? *ed. Avner Cohen and Marcelo Dascal (Peru, Illinois: Open Court Press, 1989). We are grateful for the helpful suggestions of many people, especially Jonathan Arac, Ann Ferguson, Marilyn Frye, Nancy Hartsock. Alison Jaggar, Berel Lang, Thomas McCarthy, Karsten Struhl, Iris Young, Thomas Wartenburg, and the members of SOFPHIA. We are also grateful for word-processing help from Marina Rosiene. Reprinted by permission.*

reveals disabling vestiges of essentialism while a feminist reflection on postmodernism reveals androcentrism and political naivete.

It follows that an encounter between feminism and postmodernism will initially be a trading of criticism. But there is no reason to suppose that this is where matters must end. In fact, each of these tendencies has much to learn from the other; each is in possession of valuable resources which can help remedy the deficiencies of the other. Thus, the ultimate stake of an encounter between feminism and postmodernism is the prospect of a perspective which integrates their respective strengths while eliminating their respective weaknesses. It is the prospect of a postmodernist feminism.

In what follows, we aim to contribute to the development of such a perspective by staging the initial, critical phase of the encounter. In the first section, we examine the ways in which one exemplary postmodernist, Jean-François Lyotard, has sought to derive new paradigms of social criticism from a critique of the institution of philosophy. We argue that the conception of social criticism so derived is too restricted to permit an adequate critical grasp of gender dominance and subordination. We identify some internal tensions in Lyotard's arguments, and we suggest some alternative formulations which could allow for more robust forms of criticism without sacrificing the commitment to antifoundationalism. In the second section, we examine some representative genres of feminist social criticism. We argue that in many cases feminist critics continue tacitly to rely on the sorts of philosophical underpinnings which their own commitments, like those of the postmodernists, ought in principle to rule out. We identify some points at which such underpinnings could be abandoned without any sacrifice of social-critical force. Finally, in a brief conclusion, we consider the prospects for a postmodernist feminism. We discuss some requirements which constrain the development of such a perspective, and we identify some pertinent conceptual resources and critical strategies.

Postmodernism

Postmodernists seek, *inter alia*, to develop conceptions of social criticism which do not rely on traditional philosophical underpinnings. The typical starting point for their efforts is a reflection on the condition of philosophy today. Writers like Richard Rorty and Jean-François Lyotard begin by arguing that Philosophy with a capital *P* is no longer a viable or credible enterprise. They go on to claim that philosophy and, by extension, theory in general, can no longer function to *ground* politics and social criticism. With the demise of foundationalism comes the demise of the view that casts philosophy in the role of *founding* discourse vis-à-vis social criticism. That "modern" conception must give way to a new "postmodern" one in which criticism floats free of any universalist theoretical ground. No longer anchored philosophically, the very shape or character of social criticism changes; it becomes more pragmatic, *ad hoc*, contextual, and local. With this change comes a corresponding change in the social role and political function of intellectuals.

Thus, in the postmodern reflection of the relationship between philosophy and social criticism, the term 'philosophy' undergoes an explicit devaluation; it is cut dow to size, if not eliminated altogether. Yet, even as this devaluation is argued explicitly, the term 'philosophy' retains an implicit structural privilege. It is the changed condition of philosophy which determines the changed character of social criticism and of engaged intellectual practice. In the new postmodern equation, then, philosophy is the independent variable while social criticism and political practice are dependent variables. The view of theory which emerges is not determined by considering the needs of contemporary criticism and engagement. It is determined, rather, by considering the contemporary status of philosophy. This way of proceeding has important consequences, not all of which are positive. Among the results is a certain underestimation and premature foreclosing of possibilities for social criticism and engaged intellectual practice. This limitation of postmodern thought will be apparent when we consider its results in the light of the needs of contemporary feminist theory and practice.

Let us consider as an example the postmodernism of Jean-François Lyotard, since it is genuinely exemplary of the larger tendency. Lyotard is one of the few social thinkers widely considered postmodern who actually uses the term; indeed, it was he himself who introduced it into current discussions of philosophy, politics, society, and social theory. His book *The Postmodern Condition* has become the *locus classicus* for contemporary debates, and it reflects in an especially acute form the characteristic concerns and tensions of the movement.[2]

For Lyotard, postmodernism designates a general condition of contemporary Western civilization. The postmodern condition is one in which "grand narratives of legitimation" are no longer credible. By grand narratives he means overarching philosophies of history like the Enlightenment story of the gradual but steady progress of reason and freedom, Hegel's dialectic of Spirit coming to know itself, and most importantly, Marx's drama of the forward march of human productive capacities via class conflict culminating in proletarian revolution. For Lyotard, these metanarratives instantiate a specifically modern approach to the problem of legitimation. Each situates first-order discursive practices of inquiry and politics within a broader totalizing metadiscourse which legitimates them. The metadiscourse narrates a story about the whole of human history which purports to guarantee that the pragmatics of the modern sciences and of modern political processes—the norms and rules which govern these practices, determining what counts as a warranted move within them—are themselves legitimate. The story guarantees that some sciences and some politics have the *right* pragmatics, and so, are the *right* practices.

We should not be misled by Lyotard's focus on narrative philosophies of history. In his conception of legitimating metanarrative, the stress properly belongs on the *meta* and not on the *narrative*. For what most interests him about the Enlightenment, Hegelian, and Marxist stories is what they share with other nonnarrative forms of philosophy. Like ahistorical epistemologies and moral theories, they aim to show that specific first-order discursive practices are well formed and capable of yielding true and just results. *True* and *just* here mean something more than results reached by adhering scrupulously to the constitutive rules of some given scientific and political games. They mean, rather, results which correspond to Truth and Justice as they really are in themselves independently of contingent, historical social practices. Thus, in Lyotard's view, a metanarrative is *meta* in a very strong sense. It purports to be a privileged discourse capable of situating, characterizing, and evaluating all other discourses but not itself to be infected by the historicity and contingency which render first-order discourses potentially distorted and in need of legitimation.

In *The Postmodern Condition*, Lyotard argues that metanarratives, whether philosophies of history or nonnarrative foundational philosophies, are merely modern and dépassé. We can no longer believe, he claims, in the availability of a privileged metadiscourse capable of capturing once and for all the truth of every first-order discourse. The claim to *meta* status does not stand up. A so-called metadiscourse is in fact simply one more discourse among others. It follows for Lyotard that legitimation, both epistemic and political, can no longer reside in philosophical metanarratives. Where, then, he asks, does legitimation reside in the postmodern era?

Much of *The Postmodern Condition* is devoted to sketching an answer to that question. The answer, in brief, is that in the postmodern era legitimation becomes plural, local, and immanent. In this era, there will necessarily be many discourses of legitimation dispersed among the plurality of first-order discursive practices. For example, scientists no longer look to prescriptive philosophies of science to warrant their procedures of inquiry. Rather, they themselves problematize, modify, and warrant the constitutive norms of their own practice even as they engage in it. Instead of hovering above, legitimation descends to the level of practice and becomes immanent in it. There are no special tribunals set apart from the sites where inquiry is practiced. Rather, practitioners assume responsibility for legitimizing their own practice.

Lyotard intimates that something similar is or should be happening with respect to political legitimation. We cannot have and do not need a single, overarching theory of justice. What is required, rather, is a "justice of multiplicities."[3] What Lyotard means by this is not wholly clear. On one level, he can be read as offering a normative vision in which the good society consists in a decentralized plurality of democratic, self-managing groups and institutions whose members problematize the norms of their practice and take responsibility for modifying them as situations require. But paradoxically, on another level, he can be read as ruling out the sort of larger-scale, normative political theorizing which, from a modern perspective at least, would be required to legitimate such a vision. In any case, his justice of multiplicities conception precludes one familiar, and arguably essential, genre of political theory: identification and critique of macro-structures of inequality and injustice which cut across the boundaries separating relatively discrete practices and institutions. There is no place in Lyotard's universe for critique of pervasive axes of stratification, for critique of broad-based relations of dominance and subordination along lines like gender, race, and class.

Lyotard's suspicion of the large extends to historical narrative and social theory as well. Here, his chief target is Marxism, the one meta-narrative in France with enough lingering credibility to be worth arguing against. The problem with Marxism, in his view, is twofold. On the one hand, the Marxian story is too big, since it spans virtually the whole of human history. On the other hand, the Marxian story is too theoretical, since it relies on a *theory* of social practice and social relations which claims to *explain* historical change. At one level, Lyotard simply rejects the specifics of this theory. He claims that the Marxian conception of practice as production occludes the diversity and plurality of human practices; and that the Marxian conception of capitalist society as a totality traversed by one major division and contradiction occludes the diversity and plurality of contemporary societal differences and oppositions. But Lyotard does not conclude that such deficiencies can and should be remedied by a better social theory. Rather, he rejects the project of social theory *tout court*.

Once again, Lyotard's position is ambiguous, since his rejection of social theory depends on a theoretical perspective of sorts of its own. He offers a postmodern conception of sociality and social identity, a conception of what he calls "the social bond." What holds a society together, he claims, is not a common consciousness or institutional substructure. Rather, the social bond is a weave of crisscrossing threads of discursive practices, no single one of which runs continuously throughout the whole. Individuals are the nodes or posts where such practices intersect, and so, they participate in many practices simultaneously. It follows that social identities are complex and heterogeneous. They cannot be mapped onto one another nor onto the social totality. Indeed, strictly speaking, there is no social totality and *a fortiori* no possibility of a totalizing social theory.

Thus, Lyotard insists that the field of the social is heterogeneous and nontotalizable. As a result, he rules out the sort of critical social theory which employs general categories like gender, race, and class. From his perspective, such categories are too reductive of the complexity of social identities to be useful. There is apparently nothing to be gained, in his view, by situating an account of the fluidity and diversity of discursive practices in the context of a critical analysis of large-scale institutions and social structures.

Thus, Lyotard's postmodern conception of criticism without philosophy rules out several recognizable genres of social criticism. From the premise that criticism cannot be grounded by a foundationalist philosophical metanarrative, he infers the illegitimacy of large historical stories, normative theories of justice, and social-theoretical accounts of macrostructures which institutionalize inequality. What, then, *does* postmodern social criticism look like?

Lyotard tries to fashion some new genres of social criticism from the discursive resources that remain. Chief among these is smallish, localized narrative. He seeks to vindicate such narrative against both modern totalizing metanarrative and the scientism that is hostile to all narrative. One genre of postmodern social criticism, then, consists in relatively discrete, local stories about the emergence, transformation, and disappearance of various discursive practices treated in isolation from one another. Such stories might resemble those told by Michel Foucault, although without the attempts to discern larger synchronic patterns and connections that Foucault sometimes made.[4] Like Michael Walzer, Lyotard evidently assumes that practitioners would narrate such stories when seeking to persuade one another to modify the pragmatics or constitutive norms of their practice.[5]

This genre of social criticism is not the whole postmodern story, however. For it casts critique as strictly local, *ad hoc*, and ameliorative, thus supposing a political diagnosis according to which there are not large-scale, systemic problems which resist local, *ad hoc*, ameliorative initiatives. Yet, Lyotard recognizes that postmodern society does contain at least one unfavorable structural tendency which requires a more coordinated response. This is the tendency to universalize instrumental reason, to subject *all* discursive practices indiscriminately to the single criterion of efficiency, or "performativity." In Lyotard's view, this threatens the autonomy and integrity of science and politics, since these prac-

tices are not properly subordinated to performative standards. It would pervert and distort them, thereby destroying the diversity of discursive forms.

Thus, even as he argues explicitly against it, Lyotard posits the need for a genre of social criticism which transcends local mininarrative. Despite his strictures against large, totalizing stories, he narrates a fairly tall tale about a large-scale social trend. Moreover, the logic of this story, and of the genre of criticism to which it belongs, calls for judgments which are not strictly practice-immanent. Lyotard's story presupposes the legitimacy and integrity of the scientific and political practices allegedly threatened by performativity. It supposes that one can distinguish changes or developments which are *internal* to these practices from externally induced distortions. But this drives Lyotard to make normative judgments about the value and character of the threatened practices. These judgments are not strictly immanent in the practices judged. Rather, they are metapractical.

Thus, Lyotard's view of postmodern social criticism is neither entirely self-consistent nor entirely persuasive. He goes too quickly from the premise that Philosophy cannot ground social criticism to the conclusion that criticism itself must be local, *ad hoc*, and nontheoretical. As a result, he throws out the baby of large historical narrative with the bathwater of philosophical metanarrative and the baby of social-theoretical analysis of large-scale inequalities with the bathwater of reductive Marxian class theory. Moreover, these allegedly illegitimate babies do not in fact remain excluded. They return like the repressed within the very genres of postmodern social criticism with which Lyotard intends to replace them.

We began this discussion by noting that postmodernists orient their reflections on the character of postmodern social criticism by the falling star of foundationalist philosophy. They posit that, with philosophy no longer able credibly to ground social criticism, criticism itself must be local, *ad hoc*, and untheoretical. Thus, from the critique of foundationalism, they infer the illegitimacy of several genres of social criticism. For Lyotard, the illegitimate genres include large-scale historical narrative and social-theoretical analyses of pervasive relations of dominance and subordination.[6]

Suppose, however, one were to choose another starting point for reflecting on postfoundational social criticism. Suppose one began, not with the condition of Philosophy, but with the nature of the social object one wished to criticize. Suppose, further, that one defined that object as the subordination of women to and by men. Then, we submit, it would be apparent that many of the genres rejected by postmodernists are necessary for social criticism. For a phenomenon as pervasive and multifaceted as male dominance simply cannot be adequately grasped with the meager critical resources to which they would limit us. On the contrary, effective criticism of this phenomenon requires an array of different methods and genres. It requires at minimum large narratives about changes in social organization and ideology, empirical and social-theoretical analyses of macrostructures and institutions, interactionist analyses of the micropolitics of everyday life, critical-hermeneutical and institutional analyses of cultural production, historically and culturally specific sociologies of gender, and so on. The list could go on.

Clearly, not all of these approaches are local and untheoretical. But all are nonetheless essential to feminist social criticism. Moreover, all can in principle be conceived in ways that do not take us back to foundationalism, even though, as we argue in the next section, many feminists have not wholly succeeded in avoiding that trap.

Feminism

Feminists, like postmodernists, have sought to develop new paradigms of social criticism which do not rely on traditional philosophical underpinnings. They have criticized modern foundationalist epistemologies and moral and political theories, exposing the contingent, partial, and historically situated character of what has passed in the mainstream for necessary, universal, and ahistorical truths. They have called into question the dominant philosophical project of seeking objectivity in the guise of a "God's eye view" which transcends any situation or perspective.[7]

However, if postmodernists have been drawn to such views by a concern with the status of philosophy, feminists have been led to them by the demands of political practice. This practical interest has saved feminist theory from many of the mistakes of postmodernism: Women whose theorizing was to serve the struggle against sexism were not about to abandon powerful political tools merely as a result of intramural debates in professional philosophy.

Yet, even as the imperatives of political practice have saved feminist theory from one set of difficulties, they have tended at times to incline it toward another. Practical imperatives have led some feminists to adopt modes of theorizing which resemble the sorts of philosophical metanarrative rightly criticized by postmodernists. To be sure, the feminist theories we have in mind here are not pure metanarratives; they are not ahistorical normative theories about the transcultural nature of rationality or justice. Rather, they are very large social theories—theories of history, society, culture, and psychology—which claim, for example, to identify causes and constitutive features of sexism that operate cross-culturally. Thus, these social theories purport to be empirical rather than philosophical. But, as we hope to show, they are actually quasi-metanarratives. They tacitly presuppose some commonly held but unwarranted and essentialist assumptions about the nature of human beings and the conditions for social life. In addition, they assume methods and concepts which are uninflected by temporality or historicity and which therefore function *de facto* as permanent, neutral matrices for inquiry. Such theories then, share some of the essentialist and ahistorical features of metanarratives: They are insufficiently attentive to historical and cultural diversity, and they falsely universalize features of the theorist's own era, society, culture, class, sexual orientation and ethnic, or racial group.

On the other hand, the practical exigencies inclining feminists to produce quasi-metanarratives have by no means held undisputed sway. Rather, they have had to coexist, often uneasily, with counterexigencies which have worked to opposite effect, for example, political pressures to acknowledge differences among women. In general, then, the recent history of feminist social theory reflects a tug of war between forces which have encouraged and forces which have discouraged metanarrative-like modes of theorizing. We can illustrate this dynamic by looking at a few important turning points in this history.

When in the 1960s, women in the New Left began to extend prior talk about women's rights into the more encompassing discussion of women's liberation, they encountered the fear and hostility of their male comrades and the use of Marxist political theory as a support for these reactions. Many men of the New Left argued that gender issues were secondary because they were subsumable under more basic modes of oppression, namely, class and race.

In response to this practical-political problem, radical feminists such as Shulamith Firestone resorted to an ingenious tactical maneuver: Firestone invoked biological differences between women and men to explain sexism. This enabled her to turn the tables on her Marxist comrades by claiming that gender conflict was the most basic form of human conflict and the source of all other forms, including class conflict.[8] Firestone drew on the pervasive tendency within modern culture to locate the roots of gender differences in biology. Her coup was to use biologism to establish the primacy of the struggle against male domination rather than to justify acquiescence to it.

The trick, of course, is problematic from a postmodernist perspective in that appeals to biology to explain social phenomena are essentialist and monocausal. They are essentialist insofar as they project onto all women and men qualities which develop under historically specific social conditions. They are monocausal insofar as they look to one set of characteristics, such as women's physiology or men's hormones, to explain women's oppression in all cultures. These problems are only compounded when appeals to biology are used in conjunction with the dubious claim that women's oppression is the cause of all other forms of oppression.

Moreover, as Marxists and feminist anthropologists began insisting in the early 1970s, appeals to biology do not allow us to understand the enormous diversity of forms which both gender and sexism assume in different cultures. In fact, it was not long before most feminist social theorists came to appreciate that accounting for the diversity of the forms of sexism was as important as accounting for its depth and autonomy. Gayle Rubin aptly described this dual requirement as the need to formulate theory which could account for the oppression of women in its "endless variety and monotonous similarity."[9] How were feminists to develop a social theory adequate to both demands?

One approach which seemed promising was suggested by Michelle Zimbalist Rosaldo and other contributors in the influential 1974 anthropology collection, *Woman, Culture, and Society.* They argued that common to all known societies was some type of separation between a domestic sphere and a public sphere, the former associated with women and the latter with men. Because in most societies to date, women have spent a good part of their lives bearing and raising children, their lives have been more bound to the domestic sphere. Men, on the other hand, have had both the time and mobility to engage in those out of the home activities which generate political structures. Thus, as Rosaldo argued, while in many societies women possess some or even a great deal of power, women's power is always viewed as illegitimate, disruptive, and without authority.[10]

This approach seemed to allow for both diversity and ubiquity in the manifestations of sexism. A very general identification of women with the domestic and of men with the extra-domestic could accommodate a great deal of cultural variation both in social structures and in gender roles. At the same time, it could make comprehensible the apparent ubiquity of the assumption of women's inferiority above and beyond such variation. This hypothesis was also compatible with the idea that the extent of women's oppression differed in different societies. It could explain such differences by correlating the extent of gender inequality in a society with the extent and rigidity of the separation between its domestic and public spheres. In short, the domestic/public theorists seemed to have generated an explanation capable of satisfying a variety of conflicting demands.

However, this explanation turned out to be problematic in ways reminiscent of Firestone's account. Although the theory focused on differences between men's and women's spheres of activity rather than on differences between men's and women's biology, it was essentialist and monocausal nonetheless. It posited the existence of a domestic sphere in all societies and thereby assumed that women's activities were basically similar in content and significance across cultures. (An analogous assumption about men's activities lay behind the postulation of a universal public sphere.) In effect, the theory falsely generalized to all societies an historically specific conjunction of properties: women's responsibility for early child rearing, women's tendency to spend more time in the geographical space of the home, women's lesser participation in the affairs of the community, a cultural ascription of triviality to domestic work, and a cultural ascription of inferiority to women. The theory thus failed to appreciate that, while each individual property may be true of many societies, the conjunction is not true of most.[11]

One source of difficulty in these early feminist social theories was the presumption of an overly grandiose and totalizing conception of theory. Theory was understood as the search for the one key factor which would explain sexism cross-culturally and illuminate all of social life. In this sense, to theorize was by definition to produce a quasi-metanarrative.

Since the late 1970s, feminist social theorists have largely ceased speaking of biological determinants or a cross-cultural domestic/public separation. Many, moreover, have given up the assumption of monocausality. Nevertheless, some feminist social theorists have continued implicitly to suppose a quasi-metanarrative conception of theory. They have continued to theorize in terms of a putatively unitary, primary, culturally universal type of activity associated with women, generally an activity conceived as domestic and located in the family.

One influential example is the analysis of mothering developed by Nancy Chodorow. Setting herself to explain the internal, psychological dynamics which have led many women willingly to reproduce social divisions associated with female inferiority, Chodorow posited a cross-cultural activity, mothering, as the relevant object of investigation. Her question thus became: How is mothering as a female-associated activity reproduced over time? How does mothering produce a new generation of women with the psychological inclination to mother and a new generation of men not so inclined? The answer she offered was in terms of gender identity: Female mothering produces women whose deep sense of self is relational and men whose deep sense of self is not.[12]

Chodorow's theory has struck many feminists as a persuasive account of some apparently observable psychic differences between men and women. Yet, the theory has clear metanarrative overtones. It posits the existence of a single activity, mothering, which while differing in specifics in different societies, nevertheless constitutes enough of a natural kind to warrant one label. It stipulates that this basically unitary activity gives rise to two distinct sorts of deep selves, one relatively common across cultures to women, the other relatively common across cultures to men. It claims that the difference thus generated between feminine and masculine gender identity causes a variety of supposedly cross-cultural social phenomena, including the continuation of female mothering, male contempt for women, and problems in heterosexual relationships.

From a postmodern perspective, all of these assumptions are problematic because they are essentialist. But the second one, concerning gender identity, warrants special scrutiny, given its political implications. Consider that Chodorow's use of the notion of gender identity presupposes three major premises. One is the psychoanalytic premise that everyone has a deep sense of self which is constituted in early childhood through one's interactions with one's primary parent and which remains relatively constant thereafter. Another is the premise that this deep self differs significantly for men and for women but is roughly similar among women, on the one hand, and among men, on the other hand, both across cultures and within cultures across lines of class, race, and ethnicity. The third premise is that this deep self colors everything one does; there are no actions, however trivial, which do not bear traces of one's masculine or feminine gender identity.

One can appreciate the political exigencies which made this conjunction of premises attractive. It gave scholarly substance to the idea of the pervasiveness of sexism. If masculinity and femininity constitute our basic and ever present sense of self, then it is not surprising that the manifestations of sexism are systemic. Moreover, many feminists had already sensed that the concept of sex-role socialization, an idea Chodorow explicitly criticized, ignored the depth and intractability of male dominance. By implying that measures such as changing images in school textbooks or allowing boys to play with dolls would be sufficient to bring about equality between the sexes, this concept seemed to trivialize and coopt the message of feminism. Finally, Chodorow's depth-psychological approach gave a scholarly sanction to the idea of sisterhood. It seemed to legitimate the claim that the ties which bind women are deep and substantively based.

Needless to say, we have no wish to quarrel with the claim of the depth and pervasiveness of sexism nor with the idea of sisterhood. But we do wish to challenge Chodorow's way of legitimating them. The idea of a cross-cultural, deep sense of self, specified differently for women and men, becomes problematic when given any specific content. Chodorow states that women everywhere differ from men in their greater concern with "relational interaction." But what does she mean by this term? Certainly not any and every kind of human interaction, since men have often been more concerned than women with some kinds of interactions, for example, those which have to do with the aggrandizement of power and wealth. Of course, it is true that many women in modern Western societies have been expected to exhibit strong concern with those types of interactions associated with intimacy, friendship, and love, interactions which dominate one meaning of the late twentieth-century concept of relationship. But surely this meaning presupposes a notion of private life specific to modern Western societies of the last two centuries. Is it possible that Chodorow's theory rests on an equivocation on the term *relationship*?[13]

Equally troubling are the aporias this theory generates for political practice. While gender identity gives substance to the idea of sisterhood, it does so at the cost of repressing differences among sisters. Although the theory allows for some differences among women of different classes, races, sexual orientations, and ethnic groups, it construes these as subsidiary to more basic similarities. But it is precisely as a consequence of the request to understand such differences as secondary that many women have denied an allegiance to feminism.

We have dwelt at length on Chodorow because of the great influence her work has enjoyed. But she is not the only recent feminist social theorist who has constructed a quasi-metanarrative around a putatively cross-cultural female-associated activity. On the contrary, theorists like Ann Ferguson and Nancy Folbre, Nancy Hartsock, and Catharine MacKinnon have built similar theories around notions of sex-affective production, reproduction, and sexuality, respectively.[14] Each claims to have identified a basic kind of human practice found in all societies which has cross-cultural explanatory power. In each case, the practice in question is associated with a biological or quasi-biological need and is construed as functionally necessary to the reproduction of society. It is not the sort of thing, then, whose historical origins need be investigated.

The difficulty here is that categories like sexuality, mothering, reproduction, and sex-affective production group together phenomena which are not necessarily conjoined in all societies while separating off from one another phenomena which are not necessarily separated. As a matter of fact, it is doubtful whether these categories have any determinate cross-cultural content. Thus, for a theorist to use such categories to construct a universalistic social theory is to risk projecting the socially dominant conjunctions and dispersions of her own society onto others, thereby distorting important features of both. Social theorists would do better first to construct genealogies of the *categories* of sexuality, reproduction, and mothering before assuming their universal significance.

Since around 1980, many feminist scholars have come to abandon the project of grand social theory. They have stopped looking for *the* causes of sexism and have turned to more concrete inquiry with more limited aims. One reason for this shift is the growing legitimacy of feminist scholarship. The institutionalization of women's studies in the United States has meant a dramatic increase in the size of the community of feminist inquirers, a much greater division of scholarly labor, and a large and growing fund of concrete information. As a result, feminist scholars have come to regard their enterprise more collectively, more like a puzzle whose various pieces are being filled in by many different people than like a construction to be completed by a single grand theoretical stroke. In short, feminist scholarship has attained its maturity.

Even in this phase, however, traces of youthful quasi-metanarratives remain. Some theorists who have ceased looking for *the* causes of sexism still rely on essentialist categories such as gender identity. This is especially true of those scholars who have sought to develop gynocentric alternatives to mainstream androcentric perspectives but who have not fully abandoned the universalist pretensions of the latter.

Consider, as an example, the work of Carol Gilligan. Unlike most of the theorists we have considered so far, Gilligan has not sought to explain the origins or nature of cross-cultural sexism. Rather, she set herself the more limited task of exposing and redressing androcentric bias in the model of moral development of psychologist Lawrence Kohlberg. Thus, she argued that it is illegitimate to evaluate the moral development of women and girls by reference to a standard drawn exclusively from the experience of men and boys. She proposed to examine women's moral discourse on its own terms in order to uncover its immanent standards of adequacy.[15]

Gilligan's work has been rightly regarded as important and innovative. It challenged mainstream psychology's persistent occlusion of women's lives and experiences and its insistent but false claims to universality. Yet insofar as Gilligan's challenge involved the construction of an alternative feminine model of moral development, her position was ambiguous. On the one hand, by providing a counterexample to Kohlberg's model, she cast doubt on the possibility of any single, universalist development schema. On the other hand, by constructing a female countermodel, she invited the same charge of false generalization she had herself raised against Kohlberg, although now from other perspectives such as class, sexual orientation, race, and ethnicity. Gilligan's disclaimers notwithstanding,[16] to the extent that she described women's moral development in terms of *a* different voice; to the extent that she did not specify which women, under which specific historical circumstances have spoken with the voice in question; and to the extent that she grounded her analysis in the explicitly cross-cultural framework of Nancy Chodorow, her model remained essentialist. It perpetuated in a newer, more localized fashion traces of previous more grandiose quasi-metanarratives.

Thus, vestiges of essentialism have continued to plague feminist scholarship, even despite the decline of grand theorizing. In many cases, including Gilligan's, this represents the continuing subterranean influence of those very mainstream modes of thought and inquiry with which feminists have wished to break.

On the other hand, the practice of feminist politics in the 1980s has generated a new set of pressures which have worked against metanarratives. In recent years, poor and working-class women, women of color, and lesbians have finally won a wider hearing for their objections to feminist theories which fail to illuminate their lives and address their problems. They have exposed the earlier quasi-metanarratives, with their assumptions of universal female dependence and confinement to the domestic sphere, as false extrapolations from the experience of the white, middle-class, heterosexual women who dominated the beginnings of the second wave. For example, writers like Bell Hooks, Gloria Joseph, Audre Lord, Maria Lugones, and Elizabeth Spelman have unmasked the implicit reference to white Anglo women in many classic feminist texts. Likewise, Adrienne Rich and Marilyn Frye have exposed the heterosexist bias of much mainstream feminist theory.[17] Thus, as the class, sexual, racial, and ethnic awareness of the movement has altered, so has the preferred conception of theory. It has become clear that quasi-metanarratives hamper rather than promote sisterhood, since they elide differences among women and among the forms of sexism to which different women are differentially subject. Likewise, it is increasingly apparent that such theories hinder alliances with other progressive movements, since they tend to occlude axes of domination other than gender. In sum, there is growing interest among feminists in modes of theorizing which are attentive to differences and to cultural and historical specificity.

In general, then, feminist scholarship of the 1980s evinces some conflicting tendencies. On the one hand, there is decreasing interest in grand social theories as scholarship has become more localized, issue-oriented, and explicitly fallibilistic. On the other hand, essentialist vestiges persist in the continued use of ahistorical categories like gender identity without reflection as to how, when, and why such categories originated and were modified over time. This tension is symptomatically expressed in the current fascination, on the part of U.S. feminists, with French psychoanalytic feminisms: The latter propositionally decry essentialism even as they performatively enact it.[18] More generally, feminist scholarship has remained insufficiently attentive to the *theoretical* prerequisites of dealing with diversity, despite widespread commitment to accepting it politically.

By criticizing lingering essentialism in contemporary feminist theory, we hope to encourage such theory to become more consistently postmodern. This is not, however, to recommend merely any form of postmodernism. On the contrary, as we have shown, the version developed by Jean-François Lyotard offers a weak and inadequate conception of social criticism without philosophy. It rules out genres of criticism, such as large historical narrative and historically situated social theory, which feminists rightly regard as indispensable. But it does not follow from Lyotard's shortcomings that criticism without philosophy is in principle incompatible with criticism with social force. Rather, as we argue next, a robust postmodern-feminist paradigm of social criticism without philosophy is possible.

Toward a Postmodern Feminism

How can we combine a postmodernist incredulity toward metanarratives with the social-critical power of feminism? How can we conceive a version of criticism without philosophy which is robust enough to handle the tough job of analyzing sexism in all its endless variety and monotonous similarity?

A first step is to recognize, *contra* Lyotard, that postmodern critique need forswear neither large historical narratives nor analyses of societal macrostructures. This point is important for feminists, since sexism has a long history and is deeply and pervasively embedded in contemporary societies. Thus, postmodern feminists need not abandon the large theoretical tools needed to address large political problems. There is nothing self-contradictory in the idea of a postmodern theory.

However, if postmodern-feminist critique must remain theoretical, not just any kind of theory will do. Rather, theory here would be explicitly historical, attuned to the cultural specificity of different societies and periods and to that of different groups within societies and periods. Thus, the categories of postmodern-feminist theory would be inflected by temporality, with historically specific institutional categories like the modern, restricted, male-headed, nuclear family taking precedence over ahistorical, functionalist categories like reproduction and mothering. Where categories of the latter sort were not eschewed altogether, they would be genealogized, that is, framed by a historical narrative and rendered temporally and culturally specific.

Moreover, postmodern-feminist theory would be nonuniversalist. When its focus became cross-cultural or transepochal, its mode of attention would be comparativist rather than universalizing, attuned to changes and contrasts instead of to covering laws. Finally, postmodern-feminist theory would dispense with the idea of a subject of history. It would replace unitary notions of woman and feminine gender identity with plural and complexly constructed conceptions of social identity, treating gender as one relevant strand among others, attending also to class, race, ethnicity, age, and sexual orientation.

In general, postmodern-feminist theory would be pragmatic and fallibilistic. It would tailor its methods and categories to the specific task at hand, using multiple categories when appropriate and forswearing the metaphysical comfort of a single feminist method or feminist epistemology. In short, this theory would look more like a tapestry composed of threads of many different hues than one woven in a single color.

The most important advantage of this sort of theory would be its usefulness for contemporary feminist political practice. Such practice is increasingly a matter of alliances rather than one of unity around a universally shared interest or identity. It recognizes that the diversity of women's needs and experiences means that no single solution, on issues like child care, social security, and housing, can be adequate for all. Thus, the underlying premise of this practice is that, while some women share some common interests and face some common enemies, such commonalities are by no means universal; rather, they are interlaced with differences, even with conflicts. This, then, is a practice made up of a patchwork of overlapping alliances, not one circumscribable by an essential definition. One might best speak of it in the plural as the practice of feminisms. In a sense, this practice is in advance of much contemporary feminist theory. It is already implicitly postmodern. It would find its most appropriate and useful theoretical expression in a postmodern-feminist form of critical inquiry. Such inquiry would be the theoretical counterpart of a broader, richer, more complex, and multilayered feminist solidarity, the sort of solidarity which is essential for overcoming the oppression of women in its "endless variety and monotonous similarity."

NOTES

1. Exceptions are Jane Flax, "Gender as a Social Problem: In and For Feminist Theory," *American Studies/Amerika Studien*, June 1986, (an earlier version of the paper in this book); Sandra Harding, *The Science Question in Feminism* (Ithaca, NY: Cornell University Press, 1986) and "The Instability of the Analytical Categories of Feminist Theory," *Signs: Journal of Women in Culture and Society*, Vol. 11, No. 4, 1986, pp. 645–664; Donna Haraway, "A Manifesto for Cyborgs: Science, Technology, and Socialist Feminism in the 1980s," *Socialist Review*, No. 80, 1983, pp. 65–107; Alice A. Jardine, *Gynesis: Configurations of Women and Modernity* (Ithaca, NY: Cornell University Press, 1985); Jean-François Lyotard, "Some of the Things at Stake in Women's Struggles," trans. Deborah J. Clarke, Winifred Woodhull, and John Mowitt, *Sub-Stance*, No. 20, 1978; Craig Owens, "The Discourse of Others: Feminists and Postmodernism," *The Anti-Aesthetic: Essays on Postmodern Culture*, ed. Hal Foster (Port Townsend, WA: Bay Press, 1983).

2. Jean-François Lyotard, *The Postmodern Condition: A Report on Knowledge*, trans. G. Bennington and B. Massumi (Minneapolis: University of Minnesota Press, 1984).

3. Ibid. Cf. Jean-François Lyotard and Jean-Loup Thebaud, *Just Gaming* (Minneapolis: University of Minnesota Press, 1987); also Jean-François Lyotard, "The Differend," *Diacritics*, Fall 1984, trans. Georges Van Den Abbeele, pp. 4–14.

4. See, for example Michel Foucault, *Discipline and Punish: The Birth of the Prison*, trans. Alan Sheridan (New York: Vintage Books, 1979).

5. Michael Walzer, *Spheres of Justice: A Defense of Pluralism and Equality* (New York: Basic Books, 1983).

6. It should be noted that, for Lyotard, the choice of philosophy as a starting point is itself determined by a metapolitical commitment, namely, to antitotalitarianism. He assumes erroneously, in our view, that totalizing social and political theory necessarily eventuates in totalitarian societies. Thus, the "practical intent" that subtends Lyotard's privileging of philosophy (and which is in turn attenuated by the latter) is anti-Marxism. Whether it should also be characterized as neoliberalism is a question too complicated to be explored here.

7. See, for example, the essays in *Discovering Reality: Feminist Perspectives on Epistemology, Metaphysics, Methodology, and Philosophy of Science*, ed. Sandra Harding and Merrill B. Hintikka (Dordrecht, Holland: D. Reidel, 1983).

8. Shulamith Firestone, *The Dialectic of Sex* (New York: Bantam, 1970).

9. Gayle Rubin, "The Traffic in Women," *Toward an Anthropology of Women*, ed. Rayna R. Reiter, (New York: Monthly Review Press, 1975), p. 160.

10. Michelle Zimbalist Rosaldo, "Woman, Culture, and Society: A Theoretical Overview," *Woman, Culture, and Society*, ed. Michelle Zimbalist Rosaldo and Louise Lamphere (Stanford: Stanford University Press, 1974), pp. 17–42.

11. These and related problems were soon apparent to many of the domestic/public theorists themselves. See Rosaldo's self-criticism, "The Use and Abuse of Anthropology: Reflections on Feminism and Cross-cultural Understanding," *Signs: Journal of Women in Culture and Society*, Vol. 5, No. 3, 1980, pp. 389–417. A more recent discussion, which points out the circularity of the theory, appears in Sylvia J. Yanagisako and Jane F. Collier, "Toward a Unified Analysis of Gender and Kinship," *Gender and Kinship: Essays Toward a Unified Analysis*, ed. Jane Fishburne Collier and Sylvia Junko Yanagisako, (Stanford: Stanford University Press, 1987).

12. Nancy Chodorow, *The Reproduction of Mothering: Psychoanalysis and the Sociology of Gender* (Berkeley: University of California Press, 1978).

13. A similar ambiguity attends Chodorow's discussion of the family. In response to critics who object that her psychoanalytic emphasis ignores social structures, Chodorow has rightly insisted that the family is itself a social structure, one frequently slighted in social explanations. Yet, she generally does not discuss families as historically specific social institutions whose specific relations with other institutions can be analyzed. Rather, she tends to invoke the family in a very abstract and general sense defined only as the locus of female mothering.

14. Ann Ferguson and Nancy Folbre, "The Unhappy Marriage of Patriarchy and Capitalism" *Women and Revolution*, ed. Lydia Sargent (Boston: South End Press, 1981), pp. 313–338; Nancy Hartsock, *Money, Sex, and Power: Toward a Feminist Historical Materialism* (New York: Longman, 1983); Catharine A. MacKinnon, "Feminism, Marxism, Method, and the State: An Agenda for Theory," *Signs: Journal of Women in Culture and Society*, Vol. 7, No. 3, Spring 1982, pp. 515–544.

15. Carol Gilligan, *In a Different Voice: Psychological Theory and Women's Development* (Cambridge, MA: Harvard University Press, 1983).

16. Cf. Ibid., p. 2.

17. Marilyn Frye, *The Politics of Reality: Essays in Feminist Theory* (Trumansburg, NY: The Crossing

Press, 1983); Bell Hooks, *Feminist Theory from Margin to Center* (Boston: South End Press, 1984); Gloria Joseph, "The Incompatible Menage à Trois: Marxism, Feminism and Racism," *Women and Revolution,* ed. Lydia Sargent (Boston: South End Press, 1981), pp. 91–107; Audre Lord, "An Open Letter to Mary Daly," *This Bridge Called My Back: Writings by Radical Women of Color,* ed. Cherríe Moraga and Gloria Anzaldúa (Watertown, MA: Persephone Press, 1981), pp. 94–97; Maria C. Lugones and Elizabeth V. Spelman, "Have We Got a Theory for You! Feminist Theory, Cultural Imperialism and the Demand for the Woman's Voice," *Hypatia, Women's Studies International Forum,* Vol. 6, No. 6, 1983, pp. 578–581; Adrienne Rich, "Compulsory Heterosexuality and Lesbian Existence," *Signs: Journal of Women in Culture and Society,* Vol. 5, No. 4, Summer 1980, pp. 631–660; Elizabeth Spelman, "Theories of Race and Gender: The Erasure of Black Women," *Quest,* Vol. 5, No. 4, 1980/81, pp. 36–62.

18. See, for example, Hélène Cixous, "The Laugh of the Medusa," trans. Keith Cohen and Paula Cohen, *New French Feminisms,* ed. Elaine Marks and Isabelle de Courtivron (New York: Schocken Books, 1981), pp. 245–261; Hélène Cixous and Catherine Clément, *The Newly Born Woman,* trans. Betsy Wing (Minneapolis: University of Minnesota Press, 1986); Luce Irigaray, *Speculum of the Other Woman* (Ithaca, NY: Cornell University Press, 1985) and *This Sex Which Is Not One* (Ithaca, NY: Cornell University Press, 1985); Julia Kristeva, *Desire in Language: A Semiotic Approach to Literature and Art,* ed. Leon S. Roudiez (New York: Columbia University Press, 1980) and "Women's Time," trans. Alice Jardine and Harry Blake, *Signs: Journal of Women in Culture and Society* Vol. 7, No. 1, Autumn 1981, pp. 13–35. See also the critical discussions by Ann Rosalind Jones, "Writing the Body: Toward an Understanding of l'Ecriture Féminine," *The New Feminist Criticism: Essays on Women, Literature and Theory,* ed. Elaine Showalter (New York: Pantheon Books, 1985), and Toril Moi, *Sexual/Textual Politics: Feminist Literary Theory* (London: Methuen, 1985).

Suggestions for Further Reading

Anthologies

Garner, Richard T., and Andrew Oldenquist, *Society and the Individual: Readings in Political and Social Philosophy*. Belmont, CA: Wadsworth, 1990.

Solomon, Robert, and Mark Murphy, *What is Justice?* New York: Oxford University Press, 1990.

Sterba, James P., *Social and Political Philosophy: Classical Western Texts in Feminist and Multicultural Perspectives*. 2nd edition. Belmont: Wadsworth. 1998.

Basic Concepts

Plato, *The Republic*. Trans. Francis Cornford. New York: Oxford University Press, 1945.

Sterba, James P., *Contemporary Social and Political Philosophy*. Belmont: Wadsworth, 1995.

Libertarian Justice

Hospers, John, *Libertarianism*. Los Angeles: Nash, 1971.

Machan, Tibor, *Individuals and Their Rights*. LaSalle, IL: Open Court, 1989.

————, and Rasmussen, Douglas, *Liberty for the 21st Century*. Lanham, MD: Rowman and Littlefield, 1995.

Narveson, Jan, *The Libertarian Idea*. Philadelphia: Temple University Press, 1989.

Nozick, Robert, *Anarchy, State and Utopia*. New York: Basic Books, 1974.

Rasmussen, Douglas, and Douglas Den Uyl, *Liberty and Nature*. LaSalle, IL: Open Court, 1990.

Socialist Justice

Buchanan, A., *Marx and Justice: The Radical Critique of Liberalism*. Totowa, NJ: Rowman and Allanheld, 1982.

Cauthen, Kenneth, *The Passion for Equality*. Totowa, NJ: Rowman and Littlefield, 1987.

Engels, Friedrich, "Socialism: Utopian and Scientific," in Arthur Mendel, Ed., *Essential Works of Marxism*, pp. 45–82. New York: Bantam Books, 1961.

Fisk, Milton, *Ethics and Society: A Marxist Interpretation of Value*. New York: New York University Press, 1980.

Harrington, Michael, *Socialism Past and Future*. New York: Arcade, 1989.

Peffer, R. G., *Marxism, Morality, and Social Justice*. Princeton, NJ: Princeton University Press, 1990.

Liberal Democratic Justice: The Contractarian Perspective

Barry, Brian, *Justice as Impartiality*. Oxford: Oxford University Press, 1995.
Kekes, John, *Against Liberalism*. Ithaca: Cornell University Press, 1997.
Rawls, John, *A Theory of Justice*. Cambridge, MA: Harvard University Press, 1971.
————, *Political Liberalism*. New York: Columbia University Press, 1993.
Raz, J. *The Morality of Freedom*. Oxford: Oxford University Press, 1986.
Sterba, James P., *Justice for Here and Now*. New York: Cambridge University Press, 1998.

Liberal Democratic Justice: The Utilitarian Perspective

Glover, Jonathan, *Utilitarianism and its Critics*. New York: Macmillan, 1990.
Goodin, Robert, *Utilitarianism as a Public Philosophy*. New York: Cambridge University Press, 1995.
Sidgwick, Henry, *The Methods of Ethics*. New York: Dover, 1966.
Singer, Peter, *Practical Ethics*. Cambridge, England: Cambridge University Press, 1979.
Smart, J. J. C., and Bernard Williams, *Utilitarianism For and Against*. Cambridge, England: Cambridge University Press, 1973.

Liberal Democratic Justice: The Discourse Ethics Perspective

Baynes, Kenneth, *Normative Grounds of Social Criticism*. New York: SUNY Press, 1992.
Benhabib, Seyla, *Situating the Self*. New York: Routledge, 1992.
————, and Dallmayr, Fred, *The Communicative Ethics Controversy*. Cambridge: MIT, 1990.
Fraser, N., "What's Critical about Critical Theory?, The Case of Habermas and Gender," in *Feminism as Critique: On the Politics of Gender*, edited by S. Benhabib and D. Cornell. Minneapolis, MN: University of Minnesota Press, 1987.
Habermas, Jürgen, *Between Facts and Norms*. Cambridge: MIT, 1996.
White, Stephen, *The Cambridge Companion to Habermas*. Cambridge: Cambridge University Press, 1995.

Communitarian Justice

Daly, Markate, *Communitarianism*. Belmont: Wadsworth, 1994.
Hegel, G. W. F., *Philosophy of Right*. Trans. T.M. Knox. New York: Oxford University Press, 1962. (Originally published 1921.)
Horton, John, and Mendus, Susan, Eds., *After MacIntyre*. Notre Dame, IN: University of Notre Dame Press, 1994.
Kymlika, W., *Liberalism, Community and Culture*. Oxford: Oxford University Press, 1989.
MacIntyre, Alasdair, *After Virtue*. Notre Dame, IN: University of Notre Dame Press, 1981.
Sandel, Michael, *Democracy's Discontent*. Cambridge: Harvard University Press, 1996.

Feminist Justice

Held, Virginia, *Justice and Care*, Boulder, CO: Westview Press, 1995.
Kourany, Janet, James Sterba, and Rosemarie Tong, *Feminist Philosophies*. 2nd edition, Upper Saddle River, NJ: Prentice Hall, 1998.
Sommers, Christina, *Who Stole Feminism?* New York: Simon and Schuster, 1994.

Tong, Rosemarie, *Feminist Thought*. 2nd edition. Boulder, CO: Westview Press, 1998.

Wollstonecraft, Mary, *A Vindication of the Rights of Women*. New York: Norton, 1967. (Originally published 1792.)

Young, Iris, *Justice and the Politics of Difference*. Princeton: Princeton University Press, 1990.

Postmodern Justice

Best, Steven, and Douglas Kellner, *Postmodern Theory*. New York: The Guilford Press, 1991.

Cahoone, Lawrence, *From Modernism to Postmodernism*. Cambridge: Blackwell, 1996.

Foucault, Michel, *The Archaeology of Knowledge*. New York: Pantheon, 1972.

Lyotard, Jean-François, *The Postmodern Condition*. Minneapolis: University of Minnesota Press, 1984.

Nicholson, Linda, *Feminism/Postmodernism*. New York: Routledge, 1990.

Rabinow, Paul, Ed., *Foucault Reader*. New York: Pantheon Books, 1984.

negative right — freedom from

positive right — freedom to